ENTREPRENEURIAL DEVELOPMENT

Potential Beyond Boundaries

- The Concept
- Theories
- Development
- Promotion
- Motivation
- Behaviour
- Ideas
- Search

VASANT DESAI

Director
Visveswaraya Institute of
Socio-economic Research, Mumbai.

Himalaya Publishing House

ISO 9001:2015 CERTIFIED

First Edition : 2010
Edition : 2011, 2015
Edition : 2017, 2018, 2020
Edition : 2025
Edition : 2026

Published by : Mrs. Meena Pandey
for **HIMALAYA PUBLISHING HOUSE PVT. LTD.,**
Vishal Industrial Estate, 1st Floor, Office No. 63/64,
Bhandup Village Road, Subhash Nagar (Opp. CEAT Tyres),
Nahur (W), Mumbai - 400 078. **Phone:** 022-35131464/65/66/67
E-mail: himpub@bharatmail.co.in; **Website:** www.himpub.com

Branch Offices :

New Delhi : "Pooja Apartments", 4-B, Murari Lal Street, Ansari Road, Darya Ganj, New Delhi - 110 002. Phone: 011-23270392, 23278631; Fax: 011-23256286

Nagpur : Kundanlal Chandak Industrial Estate, Ghat Road, Nagpur - 440 018. Mobile: 09325409992, 09325908881

Bengaluru : Plot No. 91-33, 2nd Main Road, Seshadripuram, Behind Nataraja Theatre, Bengaluru - 560 020. Phone: 080-41138821; Mobile: 09379847017, 09379847005

Hyderabad : No. 3-4-184, Lingampally, Besides Raghavendra Swamy Matham, Kachiguda, Hyderabad - 500 027. Phone: 040-27560041, 27550139

Chennai : No. 34/44, Motilal Street, T. Nagar, Chennai - 600 017. Mobile: 09380460419

Pune : "Laksha" Apartment, First Floor, No. 527, Mehunpura, Shaniwarpeth (Near Prabhat Theatre), Pune - 411 030. Phone: 020-24496323, 24496333; Mobile: 09370579333

Cuttack : Plot No. 5F-755/4, Sector-9, CDA Markat Nagar, Cuttack - 753 014, Odisha. Mobile: 09338746007

Kolkata : 3, S.M. Bose Road, Near Gate No. 5, Agarpara Railway Station, North 24 Parganas, West Bengal - 700 109. Mobile: 09674536325

DTP by : **Sudhakar Shetty**

Printed at : Geetanjali Press Pvt. Ltd., Nagpur. On behalf of HPH (P).

The Human Face of Industry

Jamsetji N. Tata
(March 3, 1839 - May 19, 1904)

J.R.D. Tata
(July 29, 1904 - November 29, 1993)

These are the leaders who left an indelible mark on the Tata Group, on industry, on the community and on the country. Much of their enterprise was an expression of self-belief that the country could manufacture steel, generate power and use modern technologies. From building India's first luxury hotel, to pioneering civil aviation, to taking the lead in the development of harmonious industrial relations in the country. Paying back to the community is a cherished article of faith and enshrined the Tata way of business. The Tata Group has been driven by the vision of its leaders.

This vision also emphasized the importance of returning to society the wealth that was generated. Over the years, the Tata Group has funded and established schools, hospitals, community centres and institutions of higher learning. It has also extended support towards management of natural resources, livelihood and other welfare projects across India.

Built on the cornerstones of integrity and honesty, for over 100 years, Tata stands for trust in any language or dialect spoken in this vast land. This philosophy has been carried through the generational change in the group.

This study is humbly dedicated to cherish the memory of the giants who touched tomorrow.

I believe that nothing can be greater than a business, however small it may be, that is governed by conscience; and that nothing can be meaner or more petty than a business, however large, governed without honesty and without brotherhood.

— The First Viscount Leverhulme

THE MISSION

Our deep roots in local cultures and markets give us our strong relationship with consumers and are the foundation for our future growth. We will bring our wealth of knowledge and international expertise to the service of local consumers — a truly multi-local multinational.

Our long-term success requires a total commitment to exceptional standards of performance and productivity, to working together effectively, and to willingness to embrace new ideas and learn continuously.

To succeed also requires, we believe, the highest standards of corporate behaviour towards everyone we work with, the communities we touch, and the environment on which we have an impact.

This is our road to sustainable, profitable growth, creating long-term value for our shareholders, our people, and our business partners.

PREFACE

Entrepreneurship has come of age in India. While passionate entrepreneurs have always created successes, the enablers now available in the forms of capital, ready talent, and fast-growing markets, are making entrepreneurship the aspiration of a wide variety of people. Hence, entrepreneurial development is in the forefront of discussion and learning.

The success of India's liberalization and opening up has been built by individual entrepreneurs and companies, which have grown at a dazzling pace. Of course Government's role in huge infrastructure investments cannot be underestimated either. From this heady churn, a number of new entrepreneurs have emerged to join the big boys. And this is not confined to only the big cities.

Entrepreneurship is an important aspect of the business and industrial growth of a modern nation. The spirit of entrepreneurship is marked by enthusiasm, persistence and ability to seek opportunities. It is at the core of all commercial and industrial activities.

One need not have a business and financial background in order to be a successful entrepreneur. But an entrepreneur must have the ability to assume risk and take opportunities for profit and advantage. The best way to minimize the risk is to prepare oneself for the road that lies ahead.

Although everyone may not be an entrepreneur at heart, it is possible to acquire most of the skills and abilities which are necessary for success in business. The business climate of our country is fast improving and many individuals and families are venturing into enterprises, small and big. Knowledge and understanding of entrepreneurship are a necessary part of today's business education.

Entrepreneurial Development has come to be recognised globally as the key to rapid and sustained economic growth. Indeed, the entrepreneurs with their vision, passion, ability and innovative qualities lay down a strong foundation for sustainable economic development.

Successful new business ventures and economic development do not just happen. They are the result of the combination of right environment, planning, effort, and innovation. And this right mix can only be achieved by the entrepreneurs. They provide a clear blueprint for stimulating research, technology, finance to help promote matured enterprises. At the same time, they enrich the eco-system and give a boost to economic growth. Economic growth refers to an increase in a country's production or income per capita, with economy's total output of goods and services being measured by Gross National Product (GNP). At the present juncture, the country needs much more than growth. Economic development, on the other hand, goes beyond economic growth to include changes in output, distribution and economic structure, which may affect such things as improvement in material well-being of the poor, technical breakthrough, increase in economic activities, increase in the educational level and improvement in health.

Contributing Factors

The factors contributing to economic development are labour, technology, natural resources, capital and entrepreneurship. New business formation is the result of harnessing human skills with the developed technology, added by available capital as well as other infrastructure to set in a development process. The key factor in this development process is the entrepreneur. This is the forte of the entrepreneur whose policies and strategies cover such broad areas as production, marketing, financing, pricing and personnel relations. The growth of entrepreneurship largely depends upon effective policies and their efficient implementation.

Whose contributions as an innovator and coordinator will go towards the economic development of the country. Thus entrepreneurship is the coordination of the production elements.

Entrepreneurship management is basically concerned with the development, and coordination of entrepreneurial functions. An effective organisation, sound planning, proper coordination of business activities and rational decision-making are the important aspects of entrepreneurship management. The foundation of effective management needs both policy and strategy to be determined and made known.

Literature on entrepreneur development and management has been growing in recent years. Though there have been numerous articles in various journals on entrepreneurial development, especially in India and quite a few edited books containing articles on different aspects of the subject by different authors, there remains an imbalance in the coverage of topics. It is, therefore, no exaggeration to say that there has not been a single comprehensive book on the subject, explaining, analysing and assessing the various aspects of the subject. This book is intended to help evolve a perspective of development of the vital sectors of the national economy and furnish the much needed information on this subject.

The purpose of the book is to describe the essential features of an entrepreneur and entrepreneurship to provide a sense of direction for planners and policymakers, on the one end, and the emerging crop of young entrepreneurs, both men and women, educated, uneducated, professional and non-professional, to reap immense benefits and decide the future course of action, on the other. In fact, this book is not a fresh beginning. Nor is it the last word. Subsequent studies will elaborate on many of the issues raised here.

The study can be read by any one interested in economic revitalisation, rapid industrialisation, growth and development of an area, economic planners, big and small entrepreneurs, bankers, industrialists, members of chamber of commerce and industry and every concerned citizen, who is an entrepreneur at heart. It is hoped that the book will stimulate entrepreneurs to actively participate in the economic growth of the country. It serves as a tool kit to all entrepreneurs with a new vision and a new insight.

A Creative Study

The present study is not only a creative, but also cohesive and integrated. In fact, the study will assist in accelerating and steering the process of economic growth in the right direction. Indeed entrepreneurs are partners in growth.

Outline of the Book

The study consists of Thirty Two chapters grouped into four units:

Unit I discusses the concept of entrepreneur, entrepreneurship, characteristics of entrepreneurial types, qualities and functions, traits, types, role and importance of entrepreneurs in economic growth.

Unit II dwells on theories of entrepreneurship, entrepreneurial development programmes, objectives and the Government policies.

Unit III examines in-depth the entrepreneurial bahaviour, motivation, management process and success. This apart, it also discusses innovation and systems.

Unit IV assesses business ideas, their source and process, finance, working capital, seed capital, technical assistance, marketing, feasibility report, legal formalities, sickness and remedial measures. It also includes success stories of importance.

I do not make any claim to originality or comprehensiveness. Rather I have sincerely attempted to bring together the scattered literature on the subject. However, the presentation of the subject is my own creation.

In the preparation of this book, I have drawn heavily from the published works in the sphere of entrepreneurial development and management.

I hope that the students, teachers, the policy makers, entrepreneurs, and others interested in the subject will find the study useful.

I look forward to receiving suggestions from all quarters for improving the contents and presentation of this study.

Acknowledgement

I am grateful to those who have helped me in compiling the matter for this book. While I take this opportunity to thank all of them – they are too numerous to be mentioned in this brief preface – I would like to acknowledge my deep sense of gratitude to Dr. Narendra Kumar for his ungrudging help at all stages, and to the many veteran professional entrepreneurs and consultant economists for their precise guidance. Thanks are also due to Shri K.N. Pandey, Anuj Pandey, Neeraj Pandey, Phalguni Ravi and M.V. Desai for their suggestions for affecting a number of stylistic improvements.

I take this opportunity to express my sincere appreciation and gratitude to Ms. Pratibha Choudhary for reading the book carefully and suggesting changes to make it more crisp, lucid and informative. If the book spontaneously arouses the attention of the students, entrepreneurs, faculty members of entrepreneurial studies, policy makers and researchers, the credit naturally goes to Pratibha for her studied help in presenting this volume in a new look and newer format.

I am extremely grateful and wish to thank Mr. Sudhakar Shetty for bringing out this study in a neat, compact and presentable form. I would also like to thank Shri Harish Paralkar for presenting this study in its unique form and newer format.

Lastly, no words can adequately express my debt of gratitude to my late father, Shri Ranganath Balwant Mutalik Desai (1909-2006), and my late mother, Smt. Laxmidevi (1914-2000), for generating in me a perennial interest in higher studies. I will be failing in my duty if I do not mention here the tremendous co-operation I received from my wife and my daughter in the completion of this voluminous work, in particular, whose patience, support, encouragement, understanding and love helped to bring this effort to fruition.

Mumbai VASANT DESAI
March 24, 2010

A BEEHIVE OF ENTREPRENEURIAL GROWTH

A rewarding feature of economic development in India has been the impressive growth of entrepreneurs, particularly in modern small-scale industries. In fact, modern small sector has emerged as a potential sector enhancing the growth of highly skilled entrepreneurs who not only make profits, but also contribute to a better quality of life for the millions who make the profit possible. The small enterprises have by now established their competence to manufacture a wide variety of sophisticated goods in different product-lines requiring a high degree of skill and precision. They have made a notable contribution in realising the principal objectives of expanded employment opportunities, adoption of modern techniques and dispersal of industries in small towns and rural areas. This has been possible as a result of the successful implementation of the programme for assistance to small-scale industries. The diversified, rapid growth of small-scale industries is a significant feature of India's economic development in recent years.

The small-scale industry has emerged as the most dynamic sector of Indian industrial economy, accounting for over 60-65 per cent of the total value of industrial production, for over 42-45 per cent of the country's aggregate export and over 65-75 per cent of exports of manufactured goods in 2009-10. More importantly, it provides direct employment opportunities to over 196 lakh people, accounting for 75 per cent of employment in the country. Indirectly, this sector provides employment to 360 lakh persons. All along, it has shown a growing spirit of entrepreneurship. 27 lakh entrepreneurs is just a fraction who give filling to entrepreneurship in business and service sector in a big way.

It is estimated that the small-scale sector has opened up new avenues to over 210 lakh entrepreneurs creating employment opportunities to over 550 lakh people. These entrepreneurs have harnessed the natural resources with little capital and Indian technology, for the betterment of the society. Small businesses have, potentially, a crucial role to play in a country's growth and development. They generally employ workers with limited formal training, who then learn skills on the job. More importantly small enterprises act as an incubator to breed new entrepreneurs on an ongoing basis. Cultivating entrepreneurship often involves changing and sustaining a new set of social values. A big part of cultivating entrepreneurship involves establishing an environment where business can flourish.

Truly, small-scale sector is a beehive of entrepreneurial growth. A brief panoramic macro-view of the contribution of small entrepreneurs to industrial growth *inter alia* economic growth, exports and employment is covered in the contents.

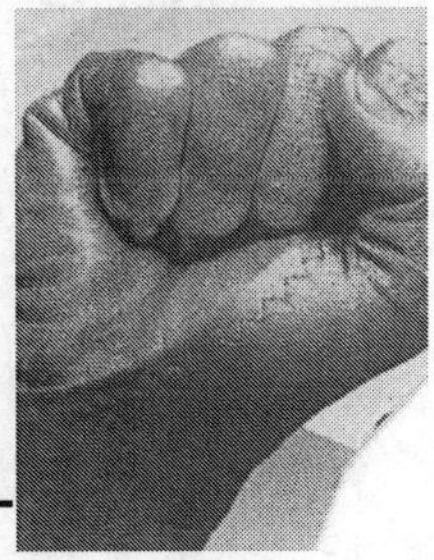

CONTENTS

Unit III: Motivation and Behaviour

Unit IV: Search for Ideas

Kris GOPALKISHNAN | **R** GOPALKRISHNAN | **Subroto** BAGCHI | **Sanjiv** BAJAJ | **Ashwani** WINDLASS | **Jason** JENNINGS

THE WILL TO WIN, THE DESIRE TO SUCCEED, THE URGE TO REACH YOUR FULL POTENTIAL... THESE ARE THE KEYS THAT WILL UNLOCK THE DOOR TO PERSONAL EXCELLENCE

— Eddie Robinson

CODE OF CONDUCT

(As evolved by the Industry)

The Company has adopted a Code of Conduct specifically for the members of the Board of Directors and/or members of the Senior Management of the Company, which sets out as follows:

- To act in the best interests of, and fulfill fiduciary obligations to the Company; act honestly, fairly, ethically and with integrity, conduct themselves in professional, courteous and respectful manner and not take improper advantage of the position of Director;
- To comply with all applicable laws, rules and regulations;
- To act in good faith, responsibly, with due care, competence and diligence, without allowing their independent judgement to be subordinated;
- To act in a manner to enhance and maintain the reputation of the Company;
- To disclose any personal interest that they may have regarding any matters that may come before the Board and abstain from discussion, voting or otherwise influencing decision on any matter in which the concerned Director has or may have such interest;
- To respect the confidentiality of information relating to the affairs of the Company acquired in the course of their service as Directors, while continuing as such a Director and even after ceasing to be such a Director, for a reasonable period of say two years, except when authorised or legally required to disclose such information;
- Restrain from using the Company's property or position for personal gain;
- Avoid using any information or opportunity received in the capacity as Directors for personal gain or in a manner that would be detrimental to the Company's interests;
- Abstain from discussion, voting or otherwise influencing decision on any matters that may come before the Board in which they may have a conflict or potential conflict of interest;
- Not to use confidential information acquired in the course of their service as Directors for their personal advantage or for the advantage of any other entity in which they have a direct or indirect interest, or where they occupy a position of board or executive responsibility with influence over their decisions;
- Help create and maintain a culture of high ethical standards and commitment to compliance.

Code of Business Principles

The code of business principles describes the operational standards that everyone at Unilever follows, wherever they are in the world. It also supports our approach to governance and corporate responsibility.

Standard of Conduct

We conduct our operations with honesty, integrity and openness, and with respect for the human rights and interests of our employees. We shall similarly respect the legitimate interests of those with whom we have relationships.

Obeying the Law

The entrepreneurs and our employees are required to comply with the laws and regulations of the countries in which we operate.

Employees

The entrepreneur is committed to diversity in a working environment where there is mutual trust and respect and where everyone feels responsible for the performance and reputation of the enterprise. We will recruit, employ and promote employees on the sole basis of the qualifications and abilities needed for the work to be performed. We are committed to safe and healthy working conditions for all employees. We will not use any form of forced, compulsory or child labour. We are committed to working with employees to develop and enhance each individual's skills and capabilities. We respect the dignity of the individual and the right of employees to freedom of association. We will maintain good communication with employees through company based information and consultation procedures.

Consumers

The entrepreneur is committed to providing branded products and services which consistently offer value in terms of price and quality, and which are safe for their intended use. Products and services will be accurately and properly labelled, advertised and communicated.

Stakeholders

The entrepreneur will conduct its operations in accordance with internationally accepted principles of good corporate governance. We will provide timely, regular and reliable information on our activities, structure, financial situation and performance to all shareholders.

Business Partners

The entrepreneur is committed to establishing mutually beneficial relations with our suppliers, customers and business partners. In our business dealings we expect our partners to adhere to business principles consistent with our own.

Community Involvement

The entrepreneur strives to be a trusted corporate citizen and, as an integral part of society, to fulfill our responsibilities to the societies and communities in which we operate.

A SENSE OF PURPOSE

Entrepreneurs must aim for ideas that impact the lives of others, and are accessible to all

Prathap C. Reddy
Chairman, Apollo Hospitals

Fortune favours the brave and all our efforts should be aimed at realising the goal we want to accomplish. Giving your best will ensure that you learn what is necessary to handle larger; more meaningful things in the future.

"Industrialisation is an ongoing process which accelerates economic growth and induces social change."

1

Introduction

In Perspective

The success of India's economic progress is closely linked to its capabilities to manufacture and export quality products in a highly competitive global market. In fact, the changing business scenario in India is influenced by three driving forces – customer, competition and change. The objective of the economic reforms that were initiated in India was to move the economy into a higher growth plane by relying more on market-oriented process to stand-up firmly in a global and highly competitive business environment.

Jamsetji N. Tata
(March 3, 1839 - May 19, 1904)

New Opportunities

The liberalisation process has created enormous new opportunities for Indian industry. At the same time, it has created new threats. Managers unfamiliar with the dynamics of open and competitive markets recognise that their profit sanctuaries and safe havens cannot be defended. This has led to a wide array of responses.

Use the new freedoms in Indian industry to move into new growth areas such as power, telecom, financial services, software, and agri-business. The goal here is to rethink and reconfigure the corporate portfolio and position the firm for the future. The approach is similar to what South Korean firms did so well over the last 20 years, using MNCs to move into new areas such as shipbuilding, consumer electronics, semiconductors and automotive industries. And, focus on traditional businesses in particular knowledge based and build world class capabilities.

If the goal is to build world-class Indian MNCs, managers have no choice but to focus on competencies. In a complex transformation process such as the one India is going through, no single answer is appropriate or possible. The patterns of investment and diversification represent a mix of different strategies. Top managers are often experimenting, but the few who hope to usher their firms to the ranks of global companies have no choice but to focus on building competencies that support their business portfolios.

Core Competence

Core competency provides a competitive advantage. A core competence represents a bundle of skills that are not widely available in an industry. It is not easily copied, is capable of being applied across several existing and new businesses, and provides clear benefits to customers. Assets (large factories) infrastructure (distribution systems), privileged access to resources (low-cost energy sources), and protected markets (government-sanctioned monopolies) are not core competencies even though they may lead to higher than average profits under some circumstances.

Four Ways of Going Global

There are four entry level options for Indian players seeking a global market. The first route which is the most basic, and followed by the majority of Indian players, entails a local manufacturer serving as a *sourcing agent* for local distributors in that country. However, this is at best a short-term strategy susceptible to the whims of distributors.

The second entry option is a collaborative effort wherein local agents provide the distribution and marketing input to the Indian company. This is route followed by many Indian players including Titan, Balsara, Maruti Udyog and Bajaj Auto.

The Indian company retains control over key marketing and branding issues. Clearly a long-term entry option, the arrangement gives the marketer a controlling interest and an assurance of commonality of product messaging and packaging, irrespective of the country the brand is being sold in. In such an arrangement, the Indian marketer provides development material and business promotion options to local distributors, and media costs are shared jointly by the two parties involved.

Marketers opting to follow the third route make a solo entry through independent distributors, in a manner similar to the route followed in India. However, this route is usually followed only in countries that offer a consumer profile closest to India, since it is a highly expensive route and open to failure.

The fourth more convenient and easily accessible alternative is to start as a private label supplier at the lower price and through the mass merchandising outlets of foreign buyers. Balsara is probably the best example of an Indian company taking the private label route articulately in the North American and European tooth paste markets. Of late, however, market analysts claim that this route is no longer as viable as it once was with private label marketing wars rampant in the US. Moreover, private label manufacturers can at best be called global suppliers.

Socio-Economic Change

The process of socio-economic change is an intrinsic part of human civilization. Man has been striving ceaselessly to discover the secrets of nature and thereby benefit immensely in creating a peaceful, rich life for himself and his fellow-beings. Man has benefited by agricultural, industrial and information activities. According to J. K. Galbraith, there are three types of economic development that are currently in vogue. These are symbolic modernisation, maximised economic growth and selective growth. Economic growth is the *sine qua non* of change and better living standards. Over the years, a middle-of-the road social democratic thinking is becoming consolidated.

Global Competitiveness

Globalisation is praised for bringing new opportunities for expanded markets and the spread of technology and management expertise, which in turn hold out the promise of greater productivity and a higher standard of living. Conversely, globalisation is feared and condemned because of the instability and undesired changes it *can* bring; to workers who fear losing jobs to competition from imports; to banks financial systems and even the entire economics that can be overwhelmed and driven into recession by flows of foreign capital.

The vital need for attaining global competitiveness has resulted in widespread restructuring across corporate India. Increasing consolidation – in search of globally scaled capacities, technology of upgradation and focus on core competencies are the cornerstones of this restructuring process. The Government too has recognised the significance of corporate restructuring in a competitive environment and accordingly, several fiscal and legal changes are envisaged to facilitate the process of mergers and de-mergers.

Globalization has been a two-way process and in the context, globally competitive players have been actively seeking opportunities for wealth creation. The shift from industrial revolution to the information revolution and now the knowledge revolution has ensured that knowledge intensive industries are poised for tremendous growth. The information technology and pharmaceutical industries are two clear examples. Companies in these sunrise industries have created a sustainable and difficult-to-replicate "intangible" advantage based on their human capital. As Indian industry matures, many of these companies will act as pathbreakers and trendsetters.

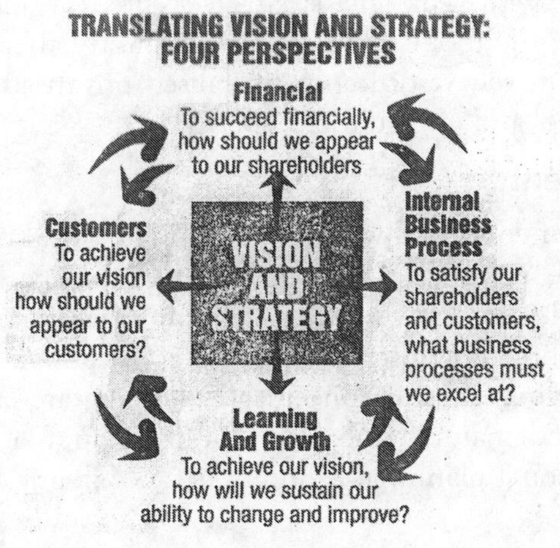

Fig. 1 Strategy Perspective

As business becomes more global and competition for capital increases, greater emphasis is being laid on corporate governance as a mechanism for effective control and enhancement of stakeholder value.

The globalisation of production has created tremendous economic opportunities, but major efforts will be needed to make the India's economy flexible enough to reap the benefits, while minimising the associated dislocations. Adjustment costs are already evident in growing income disparities in the varied spheres.

With India's growing importance in the world economy, India has a unique role. Reforms are needed to balance manufacturing and service sectors, to rebalance growth away from self-reliance towards exports. Such efforts would not only be in India's interest but would also have positive spillovers to the rest of the world.

Following reforms in the early 1990s, India has become a global leader in service exports, eventhough its impact on the regional and global economies has so far been more limited.

Economic Reforms

The economic reforms initiated in 1991 have had an invigorating effect on various sectors of the economy which is now poised for accelerated growth in the years to come. Industrial production has picked to an impressive rate and in fact is a major contributor to the high growth rates of GDP. Progress have to be made slowly and steadily, but we must continue to move towards transparency, quality awareness and Total Quality Management. If Indian industry is to be globally competitive, then the liberalisation process has to be sustained over the next decade.

Sustained Economic Growth

The primary objective of developing countries like India is to achieve rapid, balanced and sustained rate of economic growth. Hence, efforts are directed towards the creation of conditions in which a fast development of productive resources can take place. This inevitable necessitates the transformation of social and economic structures which will not restrain the potential productive forces and inhibit the development of resources. The state has, therefore, to devise efficient and effective political, economic, social, technological and cultural strategies so as to ensure a desirable co-ordination of all sectors of the economy and assure deliberate and requisite interest and involvement of the people. With this approach social change can be achieved. This is largely secured by adopting politically the technique of planning and, economically, the tool of management. Country after country in the underdeveloped world is progressively and intensively resorting to liberalised privatised globalised and market-oriented economy and to a restructured and neo-cultured society.

Economic Development

Economic development, if conceived without appropriate social changes, soon becomes stultified and stagnated. Comprehensive national planning is increasingly becoming an instrument of socio-economic transformation in developing countries. Planning delineates strategies. It also determines policies consistent with the political philosophy of the party in power. There seems, however, nothing like universal precepts of planning, though concepts of planning are emerging with experience gained all over the world. One does not naturally observe a uniform approach to planning. There is bound to be as much diversity in national planning, as multiplicity of political philosophies and dissimilarity in the state of economies.

Objectives of Planning

There would, however, be no two opinions on the basic objective of planning. Planning must impart dynamism to the process of development. In different developing countries, diverse economic systems exist. Despite the apparent similarities between the different economies, they are at various stages of development. Furthermore, different regions and sub-regions in the same country are also not at the same levels, economically, socially, technologically and culturally. Dissimilarities are wide. The process of planning in one and the same country, therefore, tends to be very complex and, at times, beset with formidable problems obstructing the process of rapid, balanced and sustained economic development. It is, thus, becoming patently evident that planning to become a potent tool and an effective technique of economic development must descend from the Olympian altitudes of the national level to the low lands of the regions. Formulation of development plans can be all-inclusive and well-integrated only at the regional and the sub-regional level. Every region and sub-region, due to its distinctive character, demands a special treatment. It is relatively easy and simple to accelerate production, stimulate consumption and motivate transformation of economic and social structure at the regional and sub-regional level, particularly in a vast and diverse country like India. Some of our states and regions are as big as nations. If the creation of conditions facilitating rapid growth of physical and human productive resources is the aim of planning, the peculiarities of the region and sub-regions have to be taken into account – perhaps more than the points of similarity. Rapid and balanced economic development pre-supposes co-originated and deliberate activity in all sectors of the country.

People's Participation

In a country like India, economic development must be consistent with the principles of democracy, ensuring that the economic tasks will be in full accord with the interests of humanity, ground for ages in chronic and abysmal poverty. Poverty has killed interest, initiative and enterprise. The greatest social tragedy in a poor country is the loss of will. There is an urgent need to overcome economic backwardness and cultural weakness and to promote their social and intellectual advance. The challenge to developmental planning in countries like India lies in laying down firm material foundations for a more equitable, equal and egalitarian society. This is possible when backwardness of regions and sub-regions is clinically examined and correctly diagnosed. Prescriptions need be written on the basis of social psychology and economic pathology of the regions and sub-regions and medication, nursing as well as nourishment be provided to gain economic strength and infuse 'development will.' The success of planning is closely linked with the readiness with which the people respond to the demand of economic progress. Rapid economic development is largely dependent on the degree of popular response, and the intensity of this response indicates the extent of development which will be generated in the community or the region concerned. The first task, therefore, is to stimulate and arouse the people to action aimed at improving their lot by undertaking productive, economic activity. Such an awakening will facilitate numerous changes in the social and economic fabric of the region concerned and will also catalyse structural transformation. The process of regional and sub-regional development is triggered off by combining all aspects of economic development into meaningful policies, quantified targets and viable programmes. It must be appreciated that planning goes beyond purely economic factors.

Laws of Dynamics of Economic Development

(i) 'Economic development is organically related to the impulse of change, reflecting the developmental urge of the society for self-reliance and willingness to observe rigorous discipline.'

This is a social law. This explains why there is no economic development in a particular society – regional, national or continental. The impulse to change must lead to action aimed at becoming self-reliant as quickly as possible. Self-reliance demands observance of a rigorous discipline. An urge for development, efforts towards self-reliance and a sense of discipline are the three important elements in the social law of dynamics of economic development.

(ii) Economic Development is quickened with the degree of appropriate and intimate relationship established between and/or among competing claims, of various apparently conflicting objectives.

This is a political law. With the growing consciousness, undeveloped and underdeveloped sectors clamour for and claim priority in development plans. Fixing of sectoral priorities and deciding the rate of progress at a given time are political decisions. The conflicting claims are to be resolved by the political leadership of the country by weaving them into supplementary and complementary relationships so as to minimise, if not entirely neutralise, their dissipating influence. The economic statesmanship of a national political leadership is displayed in harmonising the conflicting claims for economic development sectorwise, section-wise and region-wise.

(iii) Economic development depends upon the ability to restructure the economy with the identification of and the insistence on the economies of scale and the operational choices of technologies, resolving to the highest degree possible, the seeming or real conflict of capital versus labour.

This is a technological law. Economy must be restructured, if it is to be balanced and self-sustained. There are economies of scale. It is the economies of scale which should determine the scale of economy. The relationship between large and small-scale industry sectors should progressively settle down on this teleological basis. Technologies change constantly in modern scientific age and consequently, even the economies of scale undergo corresponding changes. This re-adjustment in the large and small-scale industries should be painlessly brought about. So also, the capital-intensive and labour-intensive operations ought to be carefully sorted out, categorised and communicated to the entrepreneurs and managers for compliance. For instance, capital-intensive techniques should give way to labour-intensive techniques in economies where labour is abundant; but this may not apply rigidly to all spheres of the economy.

(iv) Economic development takes place in proportion to the administrative calibre and motivation and in the direction of the comprehensive infrastructural facilities – social, educational, fiscal, financial, technical, distributional, medical, logistical and others.

This is an administrative law. Developmental plans founder due to administrative inadequacies and procedures. Demands of development planning outstrip the administrative capabilities – not so much in terms of talent but of skills. For economic development, the administration needs to know and be in tune with developmental processes, techniques and will. The administration must be fully involved and committed to development. It must be motivated so as to feel that it has the highest stake in the participation and execution of the programmes of development. Furthermore, the administration should not forget that economic development is something like a living being. It tends to move in the direction of and relishes to thrive in the location, where comprehensive infrastructure exists or is shortly expected to exist. Again, economic infrastructure and fiscal/financial benefits are not enough. Man brings about development. Economic developmental facilities, without doubt, need be provided. But, many more amenities expected by the modern man are also required to be created. This naturally leads to identification of the growth centres, which when furnished with a comprehensive infrastructure, would initiate industrial and productive activities in ever-widening circles round the potential epicentre.

(v) Economic development originates and fosters in relation to the strength and health of the local entrepreneurship and depends on the rate of its generation and equally to the intensity of its sense of social responsibility, its innovation quotient and its index of managemental capabilities.

This is an entrepreneurial law. It is the entrepreneur who powers the process of economic development. The strength of an economy is in one way the strength of the entrepreneur class in the society. Mere mercantile entrepreneurship has different attributes and thrives in an entirely different atmosphere. It has to be cultured systematically in the underdeveloped regions and sub-regions. The higher the rate of genuine industrial and innovative entrepreneurship, faster will be the rate of economic growth. Entrepreneurship must also acquire new managemental skills. Entrepreneurial density, innovative propensity and managemental capability in the society in a particular period determine the character and future of economic development.

(vi) Economic development is decisively dependent on the state of the balance of trade.

This is a commercial law. Adverse balance of trade position restricts the development process, particularly in underdeveloped countries importing machinery, raw materials, know-how and even experts. Favourable balance of trade provides considerable latitude in the choice of imports and in the source of imports. International trade brings economic strength and techno-economic self-reliance. Again, mere exports outgrowing imports is not necessarily a sign of commercial strength. Composition of imports and exports is of great importance in this context. Commodities and unprocessed minerals may earn a fairly good amount of foreign exchange for the country; but the share of manufactured goods in the total exports of the country will indicate the degree of industrial progress and strength achieved by that country. While attempting to balance exports with imports, effort should be made to constantly expand the contribution of the manufacturing sector to national exports.

(vii) Economic development is directly related to the rate of national savings and of national investment in conformity with national priorities and real needs, based on social justice, economic stability and national security.

This is a financial law. The countries and communities in which the rate of savings is high and where savings are institutionalised and thus made available for investment in productive activities according to the national priorities, are without doubt advancing faster.

Economic stability leads to increased savings. Stability cannot be ensured without growth. In fact, growth and stability can be said to be synonymous terms. National investment must also ensure national security. This is possible if ample investable funds would be available at reasonable rates of interest for desirable productive purposes. It is, therefore, necessary to ensure an adequate rate of savings and institutional investment for productive activities. Mobilisation of public savings is possible when adequate incentives are provided.

The techniques of planning may have to be based on these laws of dynamics of economic development. Their ignorance or non-compliance is likely to retard and restrict the process and pace of economic development, which all the developing communities and countries cherish. Development is essentially a matter of social and economic management. In India the emphasis was and still is largely on the economic aspect rather than on the social. If the social motivation is taken care of, economic development will begin to take care of itself. Perhaps our planners need this advice. But will they heed?

Trends in Economic Development

There are twelve major trends affecting the direction of economic development:

1. Technology as a resource
2. Competition in domestic and international markets
3. The role of invention
4. Government as stimulator
5. Entrepreneurial and Intrapreneurial development
6. Innovative capital formation
7. Active financial sector
8. Innovative entrepreneurship

9. Progressive management
10. Quality as a goal
11. Supremacy of the customer
12. Collaborative relationships

Technology is more than a thing, stratagem or even a process. It is a self-generating resource that is not consumed in the process of use. Consequently, it is an important form of economic wealth.

Competition is forcing a reassessment of our individual and collective responses to the marketplace. Fierce domestic and international competition for scientific, technological, and economic pre-eminence, forcing communities and regions to leverage all their resources – human, technological and financial – to compete effectively for vibrant and diversified economies.

The countries are experiencing an unprecedented burst of invention. Myriad technological advances are occurring with incredible speed and frequency. The ability to commercialize these inventions will have direct and immediate economic consequences.

The governments are trying to find positive non-interventionist approaches to encouraging entrepreneurship and technological diversification. They seek to create jobs, provide benefits to the small business sector, and forward technology. The creation of an environment that promotes entrepreneurial activity has become a more important focal point in the government's policy on development.

People with raw energy and a proclivity for risk-taking built and sustained the countries. They are continuing to build it today – in new ways and with new approaches. These entrepreneurs and intrapreneurs are breaking tradition and providing a dynamic source of creative and innovative enterprises.

Innovative capital formation is providing the catalyst for the entrepreneurial process. Mechanisms for providing seed capital and venture capital as well as an expanding venture capital industry are helping to build new ventures. If the entrepreneurial process is to succeed, it is essential to continue to support and expand the formation of capital and its innovative utilisation in new business development.

Finally, creative collaborative relationships being formed between business, government, and academic are forging opening new opportunities for commercialisation and thus accelerating the technology transfer process.

⏩ Man – A Crucial Factor in Development

The absence of universal precepts of planning should not worry any planner unduly, because it is still possible to enunciate the basic laws that motivate economic development, drawing on the experiences of planning under different political systems. These should hold good in all economies and for all countries at any time. There is something which can be described as the laws of dynamics of economic development. If they are respected while planning and complied with while implementing, the process of economic development may not prove to be unfruitful and wasteful. Like the laws of nature, these laws of dynamics of economic development are inexorable and the degree of alienation with them will render planning unsuccessful. These laws embrace various aspects of the process of planning. As has been emphasised above, economic development is a multilateral and multidirectional movement. In fact, economic developmental potential remains a dormant asset due to the undeveloped or underdeveloped economic man. Man is much more crucial to development than other economic factors. As such, when man plans to initiate change, economic development rolls on. Other factors are ancillary, though quite necessary. Sufficiency of other resources, without the necessary human "development will" does not lead us anywhere. Resources to be developed may exist in plenty but if development-linked human minds are absent, hardly any economic development will take place. So, the creation of the development will is the key factor which engines the economic progress. Once such a will emerges, it is necessary to see that the laws are corrected and co-ordinated action is planned, and whatever is planned is well executed. A humble attempt has been made below to present the seven laws of dynamics of economic development, as they are quite relevant to the regional and sub-regional planning contemplated in India at present.

Human Resources

While the availability of industrial resources is an important advantage for development through industrialisation, responsive human resources are the major conduit for the development and upgrading of technology. After all, the human factor is the greatest factor in the process of its own development.

Among the inputs that go into industrial development, such as capital, industrial resources, scientific research and human resources, social scientists emphasize the last-named factor as the most significant for achieving rapid industrialisation. The human factor consists broadly of individuals with a reasonable level of general education and skills in specific areas. While human skills include manufacturing, technical, supervisory, managerial, administrative and entrepreneurial competence, it is the entrepreneurial quality which is a key ingredient. It often sets the limit to the degree of industrial development and the speed with which it can be achieved in a particular country or region.

In the knowledge economy, Indian entrepreneurs have spread all over the world and are playing a unique role in fostering economic development of a country at an accelerated space. Of late, Indian entrepreneurs have earned their laurels in China too.

Top Entrepreneurial Personalities

N.R. Narayan Murthy
INFOSYS TECHNOLOGIES

N. Nilekani
INFOSYS TECHNOLOGIES

L.N. Mittal
MITTAL STEEL

Bill Gates
MICROSOFT

Ratan Tata
TATA GROUP

Indra Nooyi
PEPSI

Azim Premji
WIPRO

Lack of Entrepreneurship

Lack of entrepreneurship inhibits the process of industrialisation in the newly-developed countries. Although there is not such thing as a zero level of entrepreneurship, it is well recognised that entrepreneurs can be developed through appropriately-designed Entrepreneurship Development Programmes (EDP). These programmes broadly consist of three distinct stages: firstly, that of developing achievement motivation, and sharpening entrepreneurial trait and behaviour; second, that of project planning and development; and at the third stage, guidance is provided on industrial opportunities, incentives and facilities, rules and regulations and the development of managerial and operational capabilities. With the growth of technical manpower, it is necessary to organise entrepreneurship development programmes on a wider canvas to attract potential entrepreneurs to small business. While doing so, the characteristics of an entrepreneur have to be kept in the view.

Broadly, they are as follows:

- Development in any walk of life has always depended on individual qualities of entrepreneurship. A study of human history shows ample evidence of the role of individuals in the process of development.
- Industrial development in almost all countries has always started with individual enterprises.
- Even huge multinational and national corporations have mostly received their inspiration from one or a few individuals.
- In the case of small industries, the project is usually centred around a single individual.
- Small enterprises are mostly initiated, managed and developed by one or a few individuals.
- Qualities of entrepreneurship constitute one of the major resources in the promotion of an enterprise.
- An entrepreneur is someone who ventures out; prefers change as a means of growth; and is prepared to take calculated risks.
- While taking a risk, the entrepreneur is aware of the possibilities of success as well as the consequences of failure.
- He analyses the pros and cons carefully before making decisions.
- He is involved in the planning activities, both before and after the decision to start the enterprise.
- He is motivated by an urge to make a success of the project.
- He proceeds to accept the situation as a challenge.
- He equips himself with all the necessary tools.
- He is persistent and is full of perseverance for making a success of himself.
- Entrepreneurship is a product of interaction among a number of factors. Some of the these factors are in the individual (psychological) and the rest are in the social, cultural and economic milieu.

In brief the ingredients for a successful entrepreneur are:

- He is confident in facing challenges and is eager to achieve.
- He identifies the product.
- He plans for a venture.

– He selects the technology commensurate with the means available and tuned to the social and economic environment.
– He is eager to improve quality.
– He is able to manage men and material.
– He finds markets.
– He is innovative.
– He is progressive.
– He always strives to climb up.
– He always imbibes new technology for improvement.
– He always strives for modernisation, diversification.
– He is well-informed.
– He strives to meet the changing needs of the customer or hold customer as king.

In India, a large number of institutions and organisations are engaged in the development of entrepreneurship, resulting in the speedy growth of industrial ventures.

The example of India is fascinating. During its First Five Year Plan, technical education was given importance. Industrial training institutes for low-level semi-skilled workers, polytechnics and prototype development and training centres for skilled workers and supervisors, engineering colleges for managers and institutes of technology for the higher managerial group were established all over the country. This resulted in India becoming the third largest technical power.

CHANGE STRATEGY: CHARACTERISTICS

Evolutionary Institution Building
↓
- Focus on contextual, Indirect changes
- Values
- Structure
- Performance measures
↓
- Long-term performance impact
↓
- More emphasis on enabling moves to shape behaviour and future performance than on short-term results
↓
- Driven by line

Jolt & Refocus
↓
- Top-down initiation
- Initial focus on contextual and indirect change
- Power at the team and top levels
- Business unit structure, Strategy
- Vertical process
↓
- Delayed, then accelerated, performance improvement
↓
- Driven by new leadership or external agents

Follow The Leader
↓
- Very top-down
↓
- Leader's aspirations & preferences dominate
↓
- Emphasis on direct change with decisive debottlenecking of indirect barriers
↓
- Rapid performance improvement
↓
- Driven by leader with agents
↓
- Ultimately sustained or stalled by leader

Multi-front Direct
↓
- Top-down design
↓
- Focus on direct levers; emphasis on financial impact
↓
- Evolving to indirect and contextual levers later
↓
- Extremely rapid performance improvement
↓
- Driven by change agents; huge resources

Synthetic Redesign
↓
- Top-down
↓
- Simultaneous direct and indirect levers
↓
- Designed in advance
↓
- Rapid performance improvement
↓
- Driven by change agents; huge resources

Unit-Level Mobilising
↓
- Initiated by top: Improvements from bottom
↓
- Focus on direct unit-based levers
↓
- Mobilisation not design
↓
- Rapid performance improvement
↓
- Driven by temporary power structure
↓
- More complex indirect levers follow

Sustaining Momentum of Change

The dynamics of change have wider implications. It is a continuous process. And, changes inside and outside the enterprise/organisation can move the goal posts.

Transforming an enterprise is not a science: there are no formulae for success. The enterprises studied were not following some masterplan; indeed, much of what the entrepreneur did was intuitive, almost an art form. Examining their experience yields valuable insights into creating a strategy that will realise the promise of transformation. By viewing an enterprise from three perspectives – how performance needs to change and how fast; a leader's aspirations and preference; and the sources of energy available to drive the change – we can gain insight into what strategy will work.

A successful strategy demands effective execution. Choose initiatives that link the sources of energy to the right performance levers. Grouping initiatives into four basic types – executive de-bottlenecking decisions, direction-setting or redesign task teams, mobilising and communicating and coaching – helps simplify the choice. Then, be sure to exploit the interdependent dynamics of the initiatives to keep the change moving ahead.

Conclusion

Industrialisation is one of the important means to usher in economic and social transformation in the developing countries. More so when agriculture cannot sustain the burden of the population growth, it is the industry and service sectors which have shouldered the responsibility to sustain as well as, accelerate the pace of growth. So industrialisation is indispensable for survival and growth.

Industrialisation results from the interaction of technological change, innovation, entrepreneurial growth, specialisation and trade. Good transportation and efficient communication system and an educated labour force help promote the rapid development of industries. Well-defined rules reduce the costs of transactions as specialisation increases and economies become more complex.

Large industrial units and business houses also play an important role in developing and sustaining new entrepreneurship. For, it should be noted that while the growth of entrepreneurship in India in the last 25-30 years have been remarkable, entrepreneurship is still a comparatively scarce factor in India, as indeed in all developing countries. In spite of our fairly good economic progress, India is one of the poorest countries in the world. On the other hand, our natural and human resources are such that we can be a fairly prosperous country. So, what we require is more entrepreneurship on the part of the government and the private sector.

Entrepreneurship is a core sector which can be developed in a big way. What with so many technological and management institutes in India, it should not be difficult to develop thousands of entrepreneurs every year. In this connection, economic policies of the government leave an important impact on the growth of entrepreneurship. Sometimes, the government gives the impression that the private sector will only be tolerated. This impression should be removed and there must be a formal recognition of the fact that in a country like India, we require entrepreneurship at various levels and of various sizes – Central Government, State Government, large, medium and small private sector units and also foreign entrepreneurship.

The entrepreneurship development movement in India has received significant attention; this is borne out by the fact that the small manufacturing enterprises have made phenomenal progress during the last three decades and today occupy an important position in the industrial economy of India.

Rely on your own strength of body and soul. Take for your star self-reliance, faith, honesty and industry. Energy, invincible determination with the right motive, are the levers that move the world. ***— Noah Porter***

Effective leadership is not about making speeches or being liked; leadership is defined by results not attributes. ***— Peter Drucker***

UNIT – I

The Concept

- The Concept
- Characteristics
- Qualities
- Functions
- Traits
- Types
- Role
- Importance

John D. Rockefeller Once controlled 90 per cent of the nation's **oil** business.

Cornelius Vanderbilt Undercut competitors' **steamboat** prices; bought **railroad** lines in his late 60s.

John Jacob Astor Sold his **fur** business to invest in New York City real estate.

Stephen Girard Used his shipping fortune to enter **banking**; helped finance the War of 1812.

Bill Gates Co-founder of **Microsoft.**

Andrew Carnegie Built a **steel** empire, then gave most of his money away.

A.T. Stewart Founded the first **department store** in New York, on lower Broadway.

The words *entrepreneur, intrapreneur and entrepreneurship* have acquired special significance in the context of economic growth in a rapidly changing socio-economic and socio-cultural climates, particularly in industry, both in developed and developing countries. The experience in the industrialised countries like the United States of America, Germany, Japan and the United Kingdom are authoritatively cited in support of this claim. An in-depth study of the subject thus becomes not only relevant but also necessary.

Entrepreneurial development is a complex phenomenon. Productive activity undertaken by him and constant endeavour to sustain and improve it are the outward expression of this process of development of his personality. Such process is crystallisation of social milieu from which he comes, family imbibes, make-up of his mind, personal attitudes, caste system, educational level, parental occupation, and so on.

An entrepreneur is one of the important segments of economic growth. Basically he is a person responsible for setting up a business or an enterprise. In fact, he is one who has the initiative, skill for innovation and who looks for high achievements. He is a catalytic agent of change and works for the good of people. He puts up new green-field projects that create wealth, open up many employment opportunities and leads to the growth of other sectors.

▸▸ Who is an Entrepreneur?

The entrepreneur as a person brings in overall change through innovation for the maximum social good. Human values remain sacred and inspire him to serve society. He has firm belief in social betterment and he carries out this responsibility with conviction. In this process, he accelerates personal, economic as well as human development. The entrepreneur is a visionary and an integrated man with outstanding leadership qualities. With a desire to excel, he gives top priority to Research and Development. He always works for the well-being of the society. More importantly, entrepreneurial activities encompass all fields/sectors and fosters a spirit of enterprise for the welfare of mankind.

▸▸ Urges of an Entrepreneur

An urge to exercise power over things and objects persists among all human beings. The urge may vary in degree from person to person. This urge is an intrinsic quality of an entrepreneur. Sociologists consider him as a sensitive *energiser* – in the modernisation of societies. The psychologists look upon him as an "*entrepreneurial man*", his motivations and aspirations as conducive to development. Political scientists regard him as a leader of the system. To economists, he is a harbinger of economic growth. In all he combines entrepreneurial drive with leadership and innovativeness.

The entrepreneur is a critical factor in the socio-economic change. He is the key person who envisages new opportunities, new techniques, new lines of production, new products and co-ordinates all other activities.

▸▸ Importance of an Entrepreneur

The Entrepreneur is one of the most important inputs in the economic development of a country or of regions within the country. Entrepreneurial competence makes all the difference in the rate of economic growth. In India, state and private entrepreneurship co-exist. The small-scale industrial sector and business are left completely to private entrepreneurs. It is in this context that an increasingly important role has been assigned to the identification and promotion of entrepreneurs for this sector.

The need for a broad-based entrepreneurial class in India arises from the need to speed up the process of activating the factors of production, leading to a higher rate of economic growth, dispersal of economic activities, development of backward and tribal areas, creation of employment opportunities, improvement in the standard of living of the weaker sections of the society and involvement of all sections of the society in the process of growth.

Several factors go into the making of an entrepreneur. Individuals who initiate, establish, maintain and expand new enterprises constitute the entrepreneurial class. The socio-political and economic conditions, the availability of industrial technology and know-how, state of art and culture of business and trading, existence of markets for products and services and the incentives and facilities available for starting an industry or business, all have a bearing on the growth of entrepreneurship. A conducive environment is created through the policies and interest of the government in economic and industrial development.

Want to be an Entrepreneur?

Do you have what it takes to succeed as an entrepreneur? Take this qui.

1. When it comes to developing relationships with new people:
   (*a*) I enjoy it, meeting new people energises me.
   (*b*) I do when I have to, but i find meeting new people intimidating.
2. When I make decisions:
   (*a*) I always consider how my decisions will affect the bottom line.
   (*b*) I think more about how my decision will affect those involved.
3. My talent lies in:
   (*a*) Analyzing the current situation.
   (*b*) Looking at the possibilities.
4. When it comes to selling my products, myself:
   (*a*) I enjoy the challenge.
   (*b*) I feel uncomfortable with the whole process.
5. What really gets my juices going is:
   (*a*) Planning and competing a project.
   (*b*) Conceiving the idea for a project.
6. When it comes to day-to-day administrative duties:
   (*a*) I am detail-oriented and organized.
   (*b*) I have trouble staying focused.
7. I feel most comfortable.
   (*a*) After I make a decision I like to know that things are settled
   (*b*) Before I make a decision, i prefer to stay open to possibilities.
8. When things don't go as planned;
   (*a*) I get thrown off-balance.
   (*b*) I go with the flow.
9. I prefer a work environment that is:
   (*a*) Lively, where I am able to interact with others throughout the day.
   (*b*) Quiet, where I am able to focus on my work.
10. When I think about writing a business plan:
    (*a*) I start planning how and where to begin.
    (*b*) I shudder.

Mostly 'a': Your natural talent for developing relationships will make it easier to build a customer/ client base. Your ability to be detail-oriented and organised will help you stay focused. And, an objective decision-making style often helps when it's time to make decisions.

The Entrepreneurship Audit

Do you measure upto the tough task of being your own boss? Assess yourself impartially and objectively your positive and negative points in becoming your own boss. If need be, negative points might be corrected by training and education. Take this test to find out:

	Yes	No
1. Do you enjoy taking big, even unwarranted, risks?	☐	☐
2. Do you plan ahead on most things you do?	☐	☐
3. Do you have a head for numbers and finances?	☐	☐
4. Do you make it a point to complete what you start?	☐	☐
5. Can you survive a drop in your standard of living?	☐	☐
6. Are you able to take decisions without dithering?	☐	☐
7. Are you free of major financial commitments?	☐	☐
8. Can you get along with different kinds of people?	☐	☐
9. Is your career path in your company flattening out?	☐	☐
10. Do you enjoy travelling on work?	☐	☐
11. Are you capable of leading people?	☐	☐
12. Do you have a clear vision about your dreams?	☐	☐
13. Do you have innovative ideas about projects and services?	☐	☐
14. Have you acquired specific skills to run the new venture?	☐	☐
15. Do you plan your work methodically?	☐	☐
16. Are you adaptable and flexible?	☐	☐
17. Do you prefer working alone to teams?	☐	☐
18. Do you find yourself envying entrepreneurs?	☐	☐
19. Can you cope with punishing work schedules?	☐	☐
20. Does your spouse support your plans?	☐	☐

The Scoring

Give yourself 5 points for every YES, and 0 for every NO.

TOTAL

The Rating

0-35	You won't get for with I Inc. Be satisfied with what you already have in hand
40-60	The passion a sa self-starter is weak. You seek the status quo rather than a crisis.
65-100	All systems go. Greener pastures and challenges await you.

"A good entrepreneur is one who is capable of inspiring confidence in people, and has the ability to motivate them to work with him in fulfilling the economic goals set by him."

2

The Concept

Introduction

J.R.D. Tata
(July 29, 1904 - November 29, 1993)

The entrepreneur is an important input of economic development. He is a catalyst of development; with him we prosper, without him we are poor. The journey of India Inc. is, above all, the journey of its men and women – those who lead the charge into the new era of competition and globalisation. We have accordingly divided these entrepreneurs into four sections: The Recreators, The Pathbreakers, The Pioneers, and The Gamblers.

The first is a generation of entrepreneurs who had the foresight to adapt their old family-run businesses for the modern era. The next group laid the foundation for new business opportunities during the final years of the command economy and saw the fruition of their unrelenting efforts during the 1990s. They were followed by another generation of nimble entrepreneurs who quickly used the social and economic changes of the 1990s to make their fortunes. The final category consists of a brash, new breed of entrepreneurs who overwhelmingly see opportunities in new life-styles and global marketplaces. They might make it big – or they might burn.

The entrepreneurs of the world are the wisest minds who leave an indelible mark in the history of mankind. They make it possible through their action, and not through words. They do things in a completely new way. They think beyond the obvious. They go deeper. They think from different perspectives and angles.

You give them any job, they do it with perfection. Nothing is impossible for them. They respond positively to the situation and tell, "Certainly I can do this." Then they get busy and find out how to do it.

The entrepreneur of the world do have a larger quest quotient than the intelligence quotient. They have always something to learn. They keep learning because they enjoy challenges. They believe, "who so neglects learning in his youth, loses the past and is dead for the future." They know, "Learning is not compulsory ... neither the survival." Agreeably, the whole world is a laboratory to the inquiring mind of entrepreneurs of the world.

In this chapter, we discuss the definitions and structure of entrepreneur.

➧ Definition of an Entrepreneur

The term "entrepreneur" is defined in a variety of ways. Yet no consensus has been arrived at on the precise skills and abilities that make a person a successful entrepreneur.

The concept of entrepreneur varies from country to country as well as from period to period and the level of economic development thoughts and perceptions. A review of research done in different disciplines over the years would improve our understanding of the concept of entrepreneur.

The word 'entrepreneur' is derived from the French verb *enterprendre.* It means "to undertake." In the early 16th century, the Frenchmen who organised and led military expeditions were referred to as "entrepreneurs." Around 1700 A.D., the term was used for architects and contractors of public works.

Bernard Belidor applied it to the function of buying labour and material and uncertain prices and selling the resultant product at contracted price.

Quesnay regarded the rich farmer as an entrepreneur who manages and makes his business profitable by his intelligence, skill and wealth.

In many countries, the entrepreneur is often associated with a person who starts his own new and small business. Business encompasses manufacturing, transport, trade and all other self-employed vocations in the service sector. But not every new small business is entrepreneurial or represents entrepreneurship.

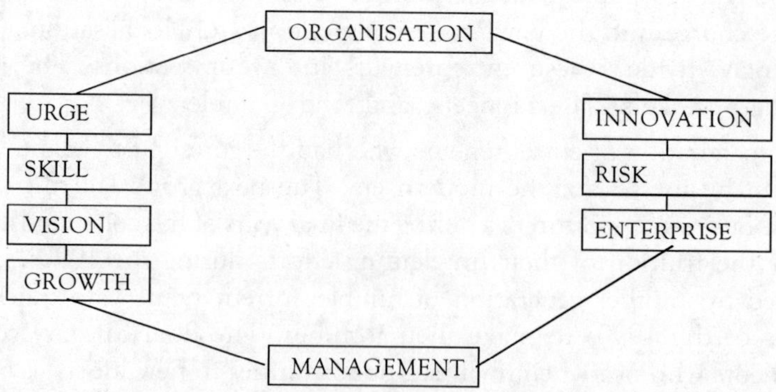

Fig. 1 Basics of an Entrepreneur

The term "entrepreneur" was applied to business initially by the French economist, Cantillon, in the 18th century, to designate a dealer who purchases the means of production for combining them into marketable products. Another Frenchman, J.B. Say, expanded Cantillon's ideas and conceptualised the entrepreneur as an organiser of a business firm, central to its distributive and production functions. Beyond stressing the entrepreneur's importance to the business, Say did little with his entrepreneurial analysis.

According to Jean Baptiste Say, an entrepreneur is the economic agent who unties all means of production, the labour force of the one and the capital or land of the others and who finds in the value of the products his results from their employment, the reconstitution of the entire capital that he utilises and the value of the wages, the interest and the rent which he pays as well as profit belonging to himself. He emphasised the functions of co-ordination, organisation and supervision. Further, it can be said that the entrepreneur is an organiser and speculator of a business enterprise. The entrepreneur lifts economic resources out of an area of lower into an area of higher productivity and greater yield.

The New Encyclopaedia Britannica considers an entrepreneur as "an individual who bears the risk of operating a business in the face of uncertainty about the future conditions." Leading economists of all schools, including Karl Marx have emphasised the contribution of the entrepreneurs to the development of economies, but Joseph Schumpeter who argues that the rate of growth in an economy depends to a great extent on the activities of entrepreneurs, has probably put greater emphasis on the entrepreneurial function than any other economist.

As Professor Jan Tinbergen points out: "The best entrepreneur in any developing country is not necessarily the man who uses much capital, but rather the man who knows how to organise the employment and training of his employees. Whoever concentrates on this is rendering a much more important service to his country than the man who uses huge capital."

Adam Smith, the father of classical economics, did not use the term *entrepreneur* anywhere. Instead, he used the words like *employer*, the *merchant*, the *undertaker* and the *master*.

Alfred Marshall wrote about the capitalists and management but he was silent about their difference. As such, the classical economists ignored the term *entrepreneur* entirely.

According to **A.P. Usher**: "Specialization or division of labour necessitates an entrepreneurial function the crux of which is to coordinate different economic activities. This view on entrepreneurship was very narrow and it reduced the entrepreneurship activities to no more than a managerial function."

F.H. Knight, in his article on *Risk, Uncertainty and Profit* propounded the maxim that "entrepreneur are a specialized group of persons who bear risks and deal with uncertainty." He also identified social, psychological and economic factors which govern the supply of entrepreneurship.

According to **David Ricardo**, a contemporary of **J.B. Say**: "The foremost motive of a risk taker is to mass capital and capital accumulation is the *sine qua non* of economic development."

J.S. Mill viewed the word *entrepreneur* as organizer who was paid for his non-manual type of work. According to him: "Extraordinary skills acted as the bedrock in production process that ought to be possessed by the entrepreneur.'

Leon Walrus, in his papers, *The Theory of Social Wealth* (Allen and Unwin, London, 1954) pointed out that entrepreneur is the coordinator of basic factors of production. He treated *'entrepreneur'* as the fourth factor of production who combines other factors such as land, labour and capital.

In 1882, **F.B. Hawley** contemplated *risk taking* as the prime characteristic feature of the entrepreneur which was comparable to the elementary agents of production like land, labour and capital. All classical and neoclassical economists believed in the significance of entrepreneurial action but did not incorporate the term 'entrepreneur' into their theories and thus entrepreneurship remained as a clandestine factor.

With **J.A. Schumpeter**, the term *entrepreneur* had received a wide acclaim. He defined the entrepreneur as an *innovator* who carries out new combinations to initiate the process of economic development through introduction of new products, new markets, conquests of new source of raw materials and establishment of a new organization of industry. He said, "The carrying out of a new combination we call *enterprise*, the individuals whose function is to carry them out we call *entrepreneurs*. He has put emphasis on *profit*, which is the product of innovation and the prime mover of economic development. According to **Schumpeter**, "The process of development is a deliberate and continuous phenomenon which is actively promoted by the escort services of a change agent who provides economic leadership. This change agent is what is called *entrepreneur*."

Core described entrepreneur as an individual who unertakes "to initiate, maintain or aggrandize a profit-oriented busines unit for production or distribution of economic goods and services."

▸▸ Schumpeter's Definition of Entrepreneur

Joseph A. Schumpeter thus writes: "The entrepreneur in an advanced economy is an individual who introduces something new in the economy – a method of production not yet tested by experience in the branch of manufacture concerned, a product with which consumers are not yet familiar, a new source of raw material or of new markets and the like." He further states the entrepreneur's function is to "reform or revolutionise the pattern of production by exploiting an invention or more generally, an untried technological possibility for producing a new commodity...."

Briefly, an entrepreneur is one who innovates, raises money, assembles inputs, chooses managers and sets the organisation going with his ability to identify them. Innovation occurs through (1) the introduction of a new quality in a product, (2) a new product, (3) a discovery of a fresh demand and a fresh source of supply and (4) by changes in the organisation and management.

In the case of a developing economy like India, the concept is being understood differently. An entrepreneur in a developing economy is one who starts an industry (old or new), undertakes risk, bears uncertainties and also performs the managerial functions of decision-making and co-ordination. He also puts the new process based on technological research into operation. Even if he imitates any technique of production from a developed economy, he is called an entrepreneur. In point of fact, entrepreneurship in developing economies is one form of labour that tells the rest of labour what to do and sees to it that it gets things done. Unlike in the developed industrial world, emphasis is not put (nor is there any need for it) only on "Schumpeterian innovations" in the case of developing countries.

Schumpter's entrepreneur only exists if the factors of production are combined for the first time. To him, maintenance of a combination is not entrepreneurial activity. As such, he differs from the theory of Rent enunciated by Ricardo. Ricardo included the term "entrepreneurial ability" as an independent factor of production. To Ricardo, profit is the reward for entrepreneurial ability.

▸▸ Drucker's Views on Entrepreneur

Peter Drucker has aptly observed that, "Innovation is the specific tool of entrepreneurs, the means by which they exploit changes as an opportunity for a different business or a different service. It is capable of being presented as a discipline, capable of being learned and practised. Entrepreneurs need to search purposefully for the sources of innovation, the changes and their symptoms that indicate opportunities for successful innovation. And they need to know and to apply the principles of successful innovation."

Box 1

PROLOGUE: WHO HE WAS AND WHAT HE DID

If capitalism was the most influential single economic and social force of the 20th century (and continuing today), there is no better guide to understanding its power and complexity than famed economist Joseph schumpeter, for the first time put the human agent at the centre of the process of economic development. According to Schumpeter, 'The Entrepreneurship is essentially a creative activity or it is an innovative sanction." — *Joseph Alois Schumpeter*

"Without innovations, no entrepreneurs; without entrepreneurial achievement, no capitalist returns and no capitalist propulsion." Schumpeter wrote this during the Great Depression of the 1930s. Many smart people of that time believed that technology had reached its limits and capitalism had passed its peak. Schumpeter believed the exact opposite, and of course he was right.

Economist Joseph Schumpeter was perhaps the most powerful thinker ever on innovation, entrepreneurship, and capitalism. He was also one of the most unusual personalities of the 20th century, schumpeter, who assessed capitalism as an expression of innovation, human drama, and sheer havoc – all going on it once. He told of capitalism in the way most people experience it as consumer desires aroused by endless advertising; as forcible jolts up and down the social peaking order; as goals reached, shattered, altered then reached once more as people try, try again. For capitalism, and for Schumpeter personally, nothing was ever stable. Uproar was their only music.

Joseph Alois Schumpeter

Like nearly everyone who has thought deeply about capitalism, Schumpeter came away with mixed feelings .... Schumpeter abhorred some of the benalities of business culture and reversed the artistic attainments of the Old World. He knew that creative destruction fosters economic growth but also that it undercuts cherished human values. He saw that poverty brings misery but also that prosperity cannot assure peace of mind....

He applied his immense energy to analysing and explaining capitalist innovation not only for other experts but sometimes for the non-specialist. From the compelling story of his life and work, a reader can grasp the basic mechanism of the capitalist engine about as well as from a whole shelf of textbooks. The subject is momentous, and its full social mechanism quite intricate. But its economic essence is not very complicated. As Schumpeter himself wrote in 1946, at the beginning of his long article of capitalism for the Encyclopaedia Britannica, "A society is called capitalist if it entrusts its economic process to the guidance of the private businessman. This may be said to imply, first, private ownership of non-personal means of production... second, production for private account, *i.e.*, production by private initiative or private profit." He went on to say that a third element is "so essential to the functioning of the capitalist system" that it must be added to the other two.

This third element is the creation of credit. The core ethos of capitalism looks constantly ahead and relies on credit and launching new ventures.

Excerpts from 'Prophet of Innovation: Joseph Schumpeter and Creative Destruction.'

Systematic innovation, according to him, consists in the purposeful and organised search for changes and in the systematic analysis of the opportunities such changes might offer scope for economic and social innovation.

According to Drucker, three conditions have to be fulfilled:

1. Innovation at work. It requires knowledge and ingenuity. It makes great demands on diligence, persistence and commitment.
2. To succeed, innovation must build on their strengths.
3. Innovation always has to be close to the market focused on the market, indeed market-driven.

Specially, systematic innovation means monitoring six sources for innovative opportunity.

The first three sources lie within the enterprise, whether it be a business or a public service institution or within an industry or service sector. They are therefore, visible primarily to people within that industry or service sector. They are basically symptoms. But they are highly reliable indicators of changes that have already occurred or can be made to occur with little effort. These four source areas are:

1. The unexpected – the unexpected success, the unexpected failure, the unexpected outside event.
2. The incongruity – between reality as it actually is and reality as it is assumed to be or as it "ought to be."
3. Innovation in industry structure or market structure that catches everyone unawares.
4. The second set of sources for innovative opportunity, a set of three, involves changes outside the enterprise or industry:
   - Demographics (population changes).
   - Changes in perception, mood and meaning.
   - New knowledge, both scientific and non-scientific.

Walker's Views on Entrepreneur

According to Francis A. Walker, the true entrepreneur is one who is endowed with more than average capacities in the task of organising and coordinating the various other factors of production. He should be a pioneer, a captain of industry. The supply of such entrepreneurship is however quite limited and enterprise in general consists of several grades of organisational skill and capability. The more efficient entrepreneurs receive a surplus reward over and above the managerial wages and this sum constitutes true profit ascribable to superior talent.

New Concept of Entrepreneur

The term "entrepreneur" has been defined as one who detects and evaluates a new situation in his environment and directs the making of such adjustments in the economic systems as he deems necessary. He conceives of an industrial enterprise for the purpose, displays considerable initiative, grit and determination in bringing his project to fruition, and in this process, performs one or more of the following:

(i) perceives opportunities for profitable investments;

(ii) explores the prospects of starting such a manufacturing enterprise;

(iii) obtains necessary industrial licences;

(iv) arranges initial capital;

(v) provides personal guarantees to the financial institutions;

(vi) promises to meet the shortfalls in the capital; and

(vii) supplies technical know-how.

Box 2

THE ERA OF ENTREPRENEURS

It's heartening to see young students, fresh from college, say "I want to be an entrepreneur." For a country of aspiring doctors, engineers and civil servants, this is quite a transformation. This is a new resurgent India, sure of itself and confident of challenging the best.

Not too many of us would have anticipated the profound impact that liberalisation would have on our economy. Today, the country is witnessing a revolution in telecom, IT, retail, exports, banking, real estate and other related sectors. India is one of the first investment destination. It's the second fastest growing GDP in the world after China. Our forex reserves are healthy and many Indian companies are competing with or complementing the best in the world. Economic reforms and the process of liberalisation has been the key to unlocking the potential of various sectors in the country.

In fact, liberalisation has pushed forward the need for a more open and market oriented economy. Measures like scrapping of the industrial licensing regime, reduction in the number of areas reserved for public sector, amendment of the Monopolies and Restrictive Trade Practices Act, reduction in tariff rates and a change over to market determined exchange rate, propelled the growth process.

More than anything else, it's the impact of all this change on the mindset of average Indians that signals the triumph of the process. The current generation of business leaders no longer belong to the metros alone. They come from everywhere – Ludhiana, Meerut and Mangalore. Twenty years ago, nobody would have believed that places like these would produce national business leaders. To me, this age is the second golden age of Indian business. The first golden age was between 1947 and 1960. A lot of young entrepreneurs are being motivated to try and establish an enterprise that creates employment, catalyses growth and transforms lives. Entrepreneurship is fast becoming a mass movement.

Bharti itself is a product of economic reform. And after a decade of being a part of the telecom revolution in the country; we feel elated to have been able to connect India across the length and breadth of the country.

Economic reforms have set the foundation for building enduring, profitable relationships with customers because it rewards entrepreneurs for continuously creating new propositions and innovating on existing ones.

India is poised to emerge as one of the most developed nations by 2020, which will be more literate, knowledgeable and economically at the forefront. The massive growth in telecom is yet to come. By the turn of the century; India is expected to rank amongst the top five countries in wireless subscription. The economy is expected to grow between 6% and 8% over the next one year with an increased focus on the rural sector.

⏩ Some Observations

The term "entrepreneur" has now been attributed to all small industrialists, small business, traders and industrialists. All people who are gainfully engaged in work – manufacturing, distribution or service and other sectors are called entrepreneurs. Again, even the founder creator and risk-taker are called entrepreneurs. Each of these terms focus on some aspect of entrepreneurs. They have some attributes, but they are not entrepreneurs in the strict sense. Many successful people have been good at copying and/or imitating others. For example, the first commercial manufacture of two-wheelers is to be called an entrepreneur, who has visualised the importance of two wheelers in modern times for the benefit of the maximum users and all subsequent scores of people engaged in are just imitators. Likewise, a brothel-keeper or a call-girl business organiser cannot be an entrepreneur, though he takes risks, creates a market and gets a reward more than visualised. So also a bootlegger, drug peddler, black-marketer etc. These occupations are not for the social good. They violate business ethics. The term "entrepreneur" is to be understood in its totality and not in a fabricated manner. The term "entrepreneur" can only be understood with a bearing on economic, psychological, sociological, and cultural bearings. The social responsibility is essentially a part of entrepreneurial outlook on life.

W. Robert Maclaurin divides the elements of technical advances into:

(i) development of pure science,

(ii) invention,

(iii) innovation,

(iv) financing of innovation, and

(v) acceptance of the innovation.

In the less developed economies first three elements of technical advancement can be skipped, and the emphasis should be on the adoption of business practice of discoveries already made. In such countries, the role of the Schumpetarian entrepreneur is somewhat limited. A large number of indigenous Schumpetarian entrepreneurs are trading entrepreneurs whose innovations are the opening of new markets. In the light of the possibilities of technical transfers from advanced economies, no undue emphasis should be put on the development of entirely new combinations. Hoselitz also remarks that in an underdeveloped economy, not to speak of Schumpetarian innovators, even imitator entrepreneurs have a distinct role to play. Such entrepreneurs provide a fillip to the process of economic growth, sometimes having as strong or perhaps even stronger impact on economic growth as real or alleged innovations.

Finding no clues to the meaning of the term 'entrepreneur', **Peter Kilby** likened entrepreneur with 'Heffalump'– a large and very important animal which was hunted by many individuals, but no one succeeded in capturing him. All those persons who claim to have seen him describe differently about his particularities and thus no agreement exists in their description about the animal. Hence a detailed note on the entrepreneur's functions in a developing economy was given by Kilby, which included some of the managerial functions also. These functions can be delegated to subordinates for efficient performance, which are as follows:

A. Exchange Relationship

1. Perception of market opportunities (novel or Imitative),
2. Gaining command over scarce resources,
3. Purchasing inputs,
4. Marketing of the products and responding to competition.

B. Political Administration

1. Dealing with the public bureaucracy (concessions, licences, and taxes),
2. Management of human relations within the firm,
3. Management of customer and supplier relations,
4. Financial management,

5. Production management (control by written records, supervision, co-ordinating input flows with orders, maintenance).

C. Technology

1. Acquiring and overseeing assembly of the factory,
2. Industrial engineering (minimising inputs with a given production process),
3. Upgrading process and product quality, and
4. Introduction of new production techniques and products.

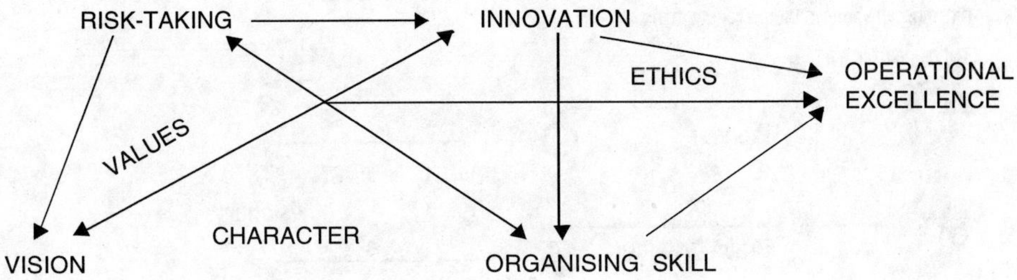

Fig. 2 Key Eements of Entrepreneur

Entrepreneurship may be defined in various ways, but the four key elements involved in it are: *(i)* Innovation, *(ii)* Risk-taking, *(iii)* Vision and *(iv)* Organising skill. All the four elements are inter-related and form a continuous process in business. Entrepreneurial vision encompasses the relentless pursuit for operational excellence, innovative technology and being responsive to the needs of the market place.

⏩ A Classic Example

Since the dawn of civilisation, there have appeared at periodic intervals men who have led mankind shaping the future out of the lessons of the past and the experiences of the present. Visionaries, builders, thinkers, scientists were those who saw ahead of their times and whose presence benefited not only the country, but all mankind. In this illustrious company of uncommon people a special place is occupied by an Indian who was born 155 years ago – Jamesetji Nusserwanji Tata. His inspired vision of modern industrialised India was to sustain economic growth to support freedom.

To breathe life into his dream, he set about to create steel, electric power and scientific-cum-technical education as the vital ingredients of economic growth. Today, the Tata organisation covers a bright landscape in Indian economy. To this day, Jamsetji Tata's industrial philosophy, including his firm belief in the principle of trusteeship, his insistence on absolute standards of integrity and the realisation that to survive and prosper, free enterprise must serve the needs of society, were all remarkably in tune with modern thinking and the ethical and social standards of the most advanced societies of today.

Jamsetji Tata, Jamnalal Bajaj, Laxmanrao Kirloskar, Ghanshyamdas Birla are some of the entrepreneurs in their truest sense.

A WAY OF VAST BUSINESS

⏩ Family Businesses

In India, family businesses account for about 70 per cent of the total sales and net profits of the biggest 250 private sector companies. Big families have carved up the big industries. In vehicles, for example, the Tatas make lorries, the Birlas make Ambassador cars, the Bajaj family makes two wheelers and the Mahindras make jeeps. They diversified into any business where they could get a permit to operate. Borrowing, mainly from public sector institutions, was easy, and company law make it simple to control subsidiaries through very small shareholdings. The Tata empire, for example, embraces some 70 companies, making everything from tea to watches, in which the parent company's average stake is rarely above 15 per cent.

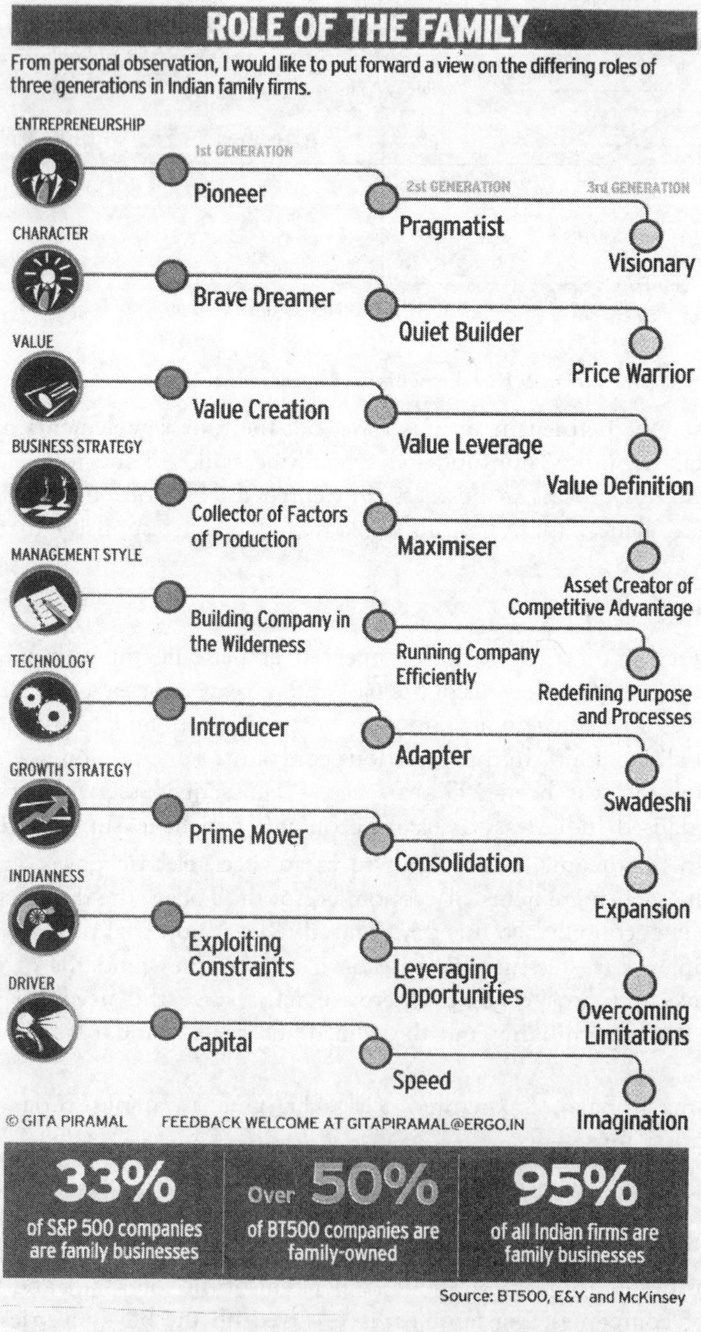

TOP 25 FAMILY BUSINESSES IN INDIA RANKED BY ASSETS

Circa 1939			Circa 1969			Circa 1997			Circa 2009		
Rank	*Group*	*Assets*	*Rank*	*Group*	*Assets*	*Rank*	*Group*	*Assets*	*Rank*	*Group*	*Assets*
1.	Tata	62.42	1.	Tata	505.36	1.	Tata	37,510,80	1.	Mukesh Ambani	2,00,469.13
2.	Martin Burn	18.02	2.	Birla	456.40	2.	BK.-K.M. birla	19,497.94	2.	Tata	1,44,183.63
3.	Bird	12.40	3.	Martin burn	153.06	3	Ambani	19,345.59	3.	ADAG	1,41,304.36
4.	Andrew yule	12.38	4.	bangur	104.31	4.	R.p. Goenka	9,664.12	4.	Birla Aditya	78,943.79
5.	Inchcape	10.70	5.	Thapar	98.80	5.	Ruia	9,593.78	5.	Om Prakash Jindal	37,545.16
6.	E.D. Sassoon	9.56	6.	Surajmull Nagarmull	95.61	6.	O.P. Jindal	5,456.10	6.	Essar	36,837.49
7.	ACC	8.68	7.	Mafatlal	92.70	7.	M.A. Chidambaram	4,782.10	7.	Sunil Mittal	35,357.61
8.	BEGG	5.75	8.	ACC	89.80	8.	L.M. Thapar	4,434.09	8.	Hinduja	35,138.37
9.	Oriental Te. & Elec.	5.60	9.	Walchand	81.11	9	M.L. Mittal	4,425.35	9.	Shriram Transport	28,126.00
10.	Dalmia	5.51	10.	Shriram	74.13	10	Rai	4,210.87	10	Vedanta	22,204.41
11.	Jardine	5.33	11	bird Heilgers	68.62	11	Lalbhai	4,112.44	11	DLF	21,989.79
12.	Wallace Bros	5.33	12	J.K. Singhania	66.84	12	Dhoot	3,737.87	12	Jaiprakash	21,620.50
13.	Birla	4.85	13	Goenka	65.34	13	Gupta	3,705.80	13	Mahindra & Mahindra	21,251.67
14	Wadia	4.70	14	Sahu Jain	58.75	14	Bajaj	3,415.87	14	Krishna	20,187.74
15	Duncan	4.54	15	Macneill & Barry	57.28	15	B.K. Khgaitan	3,351.62	15	Adani	10,837.68
16	Finlay	3.84	16	Sarabhai	56.72	16	H.S. Singhania	3,275.80	16	Indiabulls	17,583.37
17	Scindia	3.66	17	Scindia	55.99	17	K.K. Birla	3,094.90	17	Wipro	17,528.80
18	Killick	3.51	18	lalbhai	51.20	18	Mehta	3,088.23	18	Bajaj	14,853.68
19	Kilburn	3.23	19	Killick	51.08	19	hinduja	2,967.20	19	Suzlon	13,927.44
20	Sarabhai	3.00	20	ICI	50.06	20	Mafatlal	2,862.94	20	Murugappa Chettiar	12,844.82
21.	Brady	2.82	21	Andrew Yule	46.75	21	Murugappa	2,840.62	21	TVS Iyengar	12,523.39
22	Rajputana Textiles	2.80	22	TVS	43.33	22	nanda	2,642.22	22	RPG Enterprises	12,232.33
23	Steel Bros	2.77	23	kirloskar	43.02	23	mahindra	2,633.70	23	UB	10,111.20
24	Macleod	2.67	24	Parry	41.93	24	G.P. Goenka	2,630.43	24	ISPAT	10,010.32
25	Walchand	2.61	25	Jardine Henderson	40.19	25	G.P. Birla	2,530.32	25	birla BK	9,293.25

Exclusions: BAT, Thomas Duff, J. Taylor, Assam Company, Burmah Oil, F. Peek & Hukamchand
Source: Indian business & Nationalist Policies, 1939

Source: Report of The Industrial Licensing Policy Inquiry Committee, 1969.

Source: Business Today, August 22, 1997 issue.

Source: Accord Fintech

Note: Whilst it is true that many yester year's families have faded away, a cursory glance of India's top business houses will reveal that most are family run, with the Tatas, the ambanis and Kumar mangalam Birla hogging much space of the top 50 in the 2009 edition of the BT 500, some 70 per cent are family owned.

FAMILY BUSINESS READY RECKONER

Every year, business school IMD awards one family business from around the world. BT picked the award's selection parameters and asked three experts in family business to rank each parameter's relevance in the Indian context

A. VELLAYAN
Chairman
Murugappa Group

KAVIL RAMACHANDRAN
Professor, ISB

NABANKUR GUPTA
Chairman
Blue Ocean Capital

	A. VELLAYAN, Chairman, Murugappa Group		KAVIL RAMACHANDRAN, Professor, ISB		NABANKUR GUPTA, Chairman, Blue Ocean Capital	
	Importance of the factor	Adherence to the factor by Indian families	Importance of the factor	Adherence to the factor by Indian families	Importance of the factor	Adherence to the factor by Indian families
FAMILY VALUES						
Adherence to mission across generations	HIGH	MEDIUM	HIGH	LOW	HIGH	MEDIUM
Active collaboration across generations	MEDIUM	LOW	HIGH	MEDIUM	HIGH	MEDIUM
True to background/values/heritage	HIGH	MEDIUM	HIGH	HIGH	MEDIUM	HIGH
Faithful reinforcing of core family values/business values/srengthening the soul of the company	HIGH	LOW	HIGH	MEDIUM	HIGH	MEDIUM
Loyalty to employees, shareholders, clients, suppliers and the commuity	MEDIUM	MEDIUM	MEDIUM	MEDIUM	HIGH	MEDIUM
Must have reached at least the third generation of family ownership and management	MEDIUM	LOW	LOW	LOW	MEDIUM	LOW
Contribution to the society	MEDIUM	LOW	MEDIUM	MEDIUM	MEDIUM	LOW
BUSINESS VALUES						
Excellence in performance standards	MEDIUM	LOW	HIGH	MEDIUM	HIGH	MEDIUM
Family values-driven	HIGH	MEDIUM	MEDIUM	MEDIUM	MEDIUM	LOW
Growing and profitable company	HIGH	MEDIUM	HIGH	MEDIUM	HIGH	HIGH
Credibility of the communicated strategy	MEDIUM	MEDIUM	HIGH	MEDIUM	HIGH	LOW
Global in business scope	MEDIUM	LOW	LOW	LOW	MEDIUM	LOW
Clarity of the communication strategy → corporate sponsorship (marketing), corporate reputation (identity/branding)	MEDIUM	LOW	MEDIUM	LOW	HIGH	MEDIUM
Personal, hands-on, engagement of much of the family	MEDIUM	LOW	MEDIUM	HIGH	MEDIUM	MEDIUM
Brand (reputation) building	MEDIUM	LOW	HIGH	MEDIUM	HIGH	MEDIUM
SUCCESSION						
Excellence in governance – selection, development, independence, unifying the family	MEDIUM	MEDIUM	HIGH	LOW	HIGH	LOW
Sharing learning within the family	MEDIUM	MEDIUM	HIGH	LOW	HIGH	MEDIUM
Strategically adaptive over time and generations	HIGH	LOW	HIGH	MEDIUM	HIGH	MEDIUM

Clarification: These ratings are indicative as generalisations across family businesses cannot be made.
Use this grid to benchmark and self-appraise rather than for direct comparison with another business family.
Full IMD methodology at www.imd.ch/research/centers/lodh/Family-Business-Award.cfm

Entrepreneurship is not just a way to increase the level of innovation and productivity of organisations, although it will do that. More importantly, it is a way of initiating vast business so that work becomes a joyful expression of one's contribution to society. The Indian entrepreneur, intrapreneur and/or manager of the 90s have to be moulded in psycho-philosophy rooted in the Indian context and values.

"The crisis in business is spiritual," says Prof. Sitangshu Kumar Chakraborty, "All management ideas till now have been external-directed paradigms, developing behaviour and skills, not character and values. But meaning and richness must flow from mind to work, not the other way. We need a fundamental shift from the current reductionist, fragmentist, materialistic paradigm to one which recognises relationships, consciousness and spirit as the right approach."

The concept of entrepreneur and entrepreneurship incorporates basic qualities of leadership, innovation, enterprise, hard work, vision and maximisation of profits. All his socio-economic, organisational and managerial qualities are always directed towards the well-being of the society and the community. He is committed to progress. He is a catalytic agent of development and change. Personal satisfaction and monetary rewards are blended with social betterment and welfare of mankind.

THE FIVE ATTRIBUTES OF ENDURING FAMILY BUSINESSES

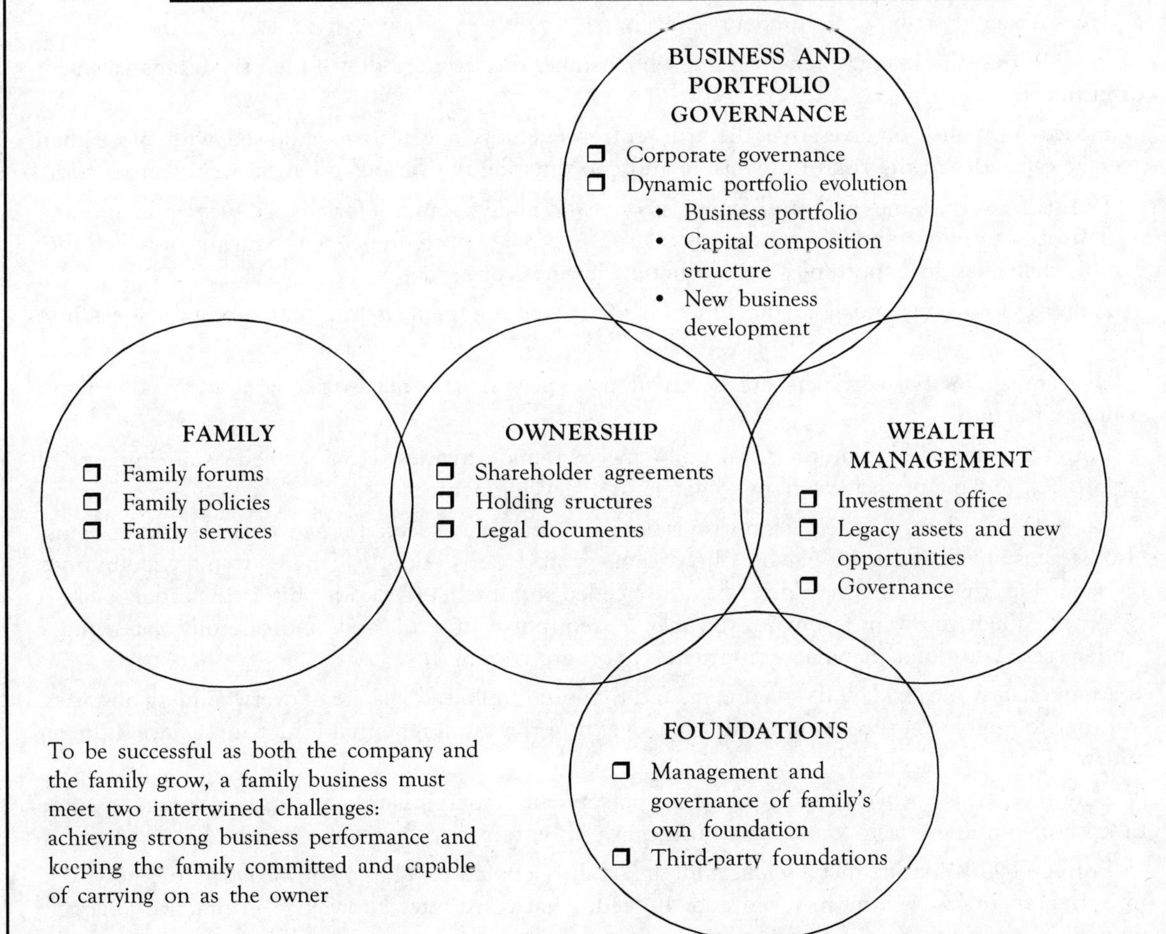

THE ENTREPRENEUR: OTHER DEFINITIONS

Quesnay recognised a rich farmer as an entrepreneur who manages and makes his business profitable by his intelligence and wealth.

Adam Smith described entrepreneur as a person who only provides capital without taking active part in the leading role in enterprise.

Richard Cantillon considered all persons engaged in economic activity as entrepreneurs.

Jean Baptiste Say opined that the entrepreneur was a person endowed with the qualities of judgement, perseverance and a knowledge of the world as well as of business. The entrepreneur shifts economic resources out of an area of lower and into an area of higher productivity and greater yield. The definition included the concept of bringing together the factors of production.

French tradition regard an entrepreneur as a person translating a profitable idea into a productive activity.

Marx regarded entrepreneur as a social parasite.

Joseph A. Schumpeter recognised person who introduces innovation changes is an entrepreneur. He treated entrepreneur as an integral part of economic growth. The fundamental source of equilibrium was the entrepreneur.

Frank Young describes entrepreneur as a change agent.

Noah Webster thinks entrepreneur is one who assumes the responsibility of the risk and management of business.

Francis A. Walter observes that the true entrepreneur is one who is endowed with more than average capacities in the risk of organising and coordinating the various other factors of production.

Peter F. Drucker defines an entrepreneur as one who always searches for change, responds to it and exploits it as an opportunity. Innovation is the specific tool of entrepreneurs, the means by which they exploit change as an opportunity for a different business or service.

Arthur Dewing conceptualised the function of the entrepreneur as one that promotes ideas into business.

Clarence H. Dantrof considers entrepreneur as a person who makes decision under alternative courses of action.

Entrepreneur has become the focal point in economic activities. He is viewed as an initiator of action, a stimulant of socio-economic change and development.

Robert D. Hisrich says, "The person who is going to establish a successful new business venture must also be a visionary leader – a person who dreams great dreams. Although there are many definitions of leadership, the one that best describes the needed intrapreneurial leadership is: A leader is like a gardener. When you want a tomato, you take a seed, put it in fertile soil, and carefully water under tender care. You don't manufacture tomatoes, you grow them."

Martin Luther King said, "I have a dream, and thousands followed in spite of overwhelming obstacles. In order to establish a successful new business venture the intrapreneurial leader must have a dream and work against all obstacles to achieve it."

Entrepreneur is one who distinguishes as a person who undertakes to organise, manage and assume the risk of running a factory and/or a business or an enterprise.

Entrepreneurship is neither a science nor an art. It is a practice. It has a knowledge base. Knowledge in entrepreneurship is a mean to an end. Indeed, what constitutes knowledge in practice is largely defined by the ends, that is by practice.

According to *Mark Casson*: "An entrepreneur is a person who specialises in taking judgemental decision about the coordination of scarce resources."

According to *Max Weber*: "Entrepreneurs are a product of particular social condition in which they are brought up and it is the society which shapes individuals as entrepreneurs."

International Labour Organisation (ILO) defines entrepreneurs as those people who have the ability to see and evaluate business opportunities, together with the necessary resources to take advantage of them and to initiate appropriate action to ensure success.

According to *E.E. Haggen*, an entrepreneur is an economic man who tries to maximise his profits by innovations. Innovations involve problem-solving and the entrepreneur gets satisfaction from using his capabilities in attacking problems.

The New Encyclopaedia Britannica considers an entrepreneur as "an individual who bears the risk of operating a business in the face of uncertainty about the future conditions." Leading economists of all schools, including Karl Marx, have emphasised the contribution of the entrepreneurs to the development of economies, but Joseph Schumpeter, who argues that the rate of growth in an economy depends to a great extent on the activities of entrepreneurs, has probably put greater emphasis on the entrepreneurial function than any other economist.

Robert E. Nelson defined entrepreneur as a person who is able to look at the environment.

According to ***David McClelland***: "An entrepreneur is someone who exercises some control over the means of production and produces more than what he can consume in order to sell (or exchange) it for individual (or household) income."

An entrepreneur, as defined by *Robert E. Nelson*, is a person who is able to look at environment, identify opportunities to improve the environment, marshall resources and implement action to maximize those opportunities.

According to *J.K. Galbraith*: "An entrepreneur must accept the challenge and should be willing hard to achieve something."

Akhouri, M.M.P. describes entrepreneur as a character who contributes innovativeness, readiness to take risk, sensing opportunities, identifying and mobilising potential resources concern for excellence, and who is persistent in achieving the goal. The term entrepreneur contain notions of newness, innovation, vision, organising, creating wealth, mobilising resources, risk taking and achievement. A driving force of economic development.

Not every new small business is entrepreneurial or represents entrepreneurship. To be entrepreneurial, an enterprise has to have special characteristics over and above being new and small. Indeed, entrepreneurs create something new, something different, they change or transmute value.

Laura Parkin: Entrepreneurs are both born and made. While some people are born with natural talent and risk tolerance. Entrepreneurship is a discipline and entrepreneurship skills can be learned by everyone.

Albert Shapero observes that the entrepreneur takes initiative, organises some social and economic mechanisms, and accepts risks of failure.

Karl Vesper affirms that the entrepreneur is seen differently by economists, psychologists, business persons and politicians.

Robert C. Ronstadt considers that the wealth is created by individuals who assume the major risks in terms of equity, time, commitment, and value for some product or service.

According to ***David Ricardo***, the foremost motive of a risk taker is to a mass capital and capital accumulation is the *sine qua non* of economic development.

John Stuart Mill viewed the world entrepreneur as organiser who is paid for his non-manual type of work.

Leon Walrus pointed out that entrepreneur is the coordinator of basic factors of production. He treated 'entrepreneur' as the fourth factor of production who combines other factors such as land, labour and capital.

Carl Menger (1840-1921) considers the entrepreneur as the change agent who transforms resources into useful goods and services, often creating the circumstances that lead to industrial growth.

Frank H. Knight points out that entrepreneurs are a specialised group of persons who bear risk and deals with uncertainty.

Mark Cassons opines that an entrepreneur is a person who specialises in taking judgemental decision about the coordination of scarce resources.

Max Weber states that the entrepreneurs are a product of particular social condition in which they are brought up and it is the society which shapes individuals as entrepreneurs.

A. David Silver described the entrepreneur as 'energetic, single minded, and having "a mission and clear vision; he or she intends to create out of this vision a product or service in a field many have determined is important to improve the lives of millions."

Henry Ford who created the manufacturing miracle that launched a modern era in industry, said that, Entrepreneur can do anything with passion and enthusiasm. Enthusiasm is the yeast that makes his hopes rise to the stars. Enthusiasm is the spark in his eye, the swing in his gait, the grip of his hand, the irresistible surge of his will and his energy to execute his ideas. Enthusiasts are fighters, they have fortitude, they have strong qualities. Enthusiasm is at the bottom of all progress. With it there is accomplishment. Without it there are only alibis.

FACT FILE OF ENTREPRENEURS

NO KIDSTUFF

Name	: Anupam Joshi
Age	: 32 years
Education	: B.A. Kumano Univ., U.P., 1985
Work Experience	: Marketing Executive, Blowplast, 1985-86; assistant manager (production), Stallion Industries, 1986-88; manager (marketing), Indus Craft Export House, 1988-89; manager (export marketing), Inertia Industries, 1989-92; set up Premier Clothing in August 1992
No. of Employees	: 350 direct, 400 on contract
Initial Investment	: Rs. 25,000 + Rs. 5 lakh loan
Track Record	: Turnover has grown from Rs. 26 lakh in 1992-93 to Rs. 10 crore in 1994-95
Management Philosophy	: Always strive for total quality
Work Style	: Hands-off, but always in the know
Hobbies	: Photography; playing golf, billiards

In August 1992, with their combined savings of Rs. 25,000, Alka and Anupam Joshi Launched Premier clothing as an export-oriented unit.

The premier clothing has been licensed to market, for the first time, the Disney Babies range of products in India.

Having several international mail-order companies, not to mention store chains, in the bag isn't enough for Joshi. Now, he's planning a move into the booming readymade shirts business. As always, Joshi plans to hedge his bets: he's talking to some foreign companies about starting off by producing shirts for them. That's clearly part of his philosophy of manufacturing for a ready-made market. And, as in the case of the Disney Babies line, to a ready-made mindset, either ways, it's a premier strategy.

KENT CARS

Name	: Chandan Sumaya
Age	: 34 years
Education	: B. Com., H.R. College, Mumbai, 1981
Work Experience	: Helped his uncle operate a car-rental service
Initial Investment	: Rs. 30,000
Track Record	: Turnover has grown from zero in 1985 to Rs. 4.50 crore in 1994-95
No. of Employees	: 252
Work Style	: Hands-on
Management Philosophy	: Never say no to a client
Hobbies	: Working out, swimming, watching Amitabh Bachchan movies

Chandan Sumaya look plunge in 1985 armed with only "a passion for cars," borrowing Rs. 30,000 from his mother to float Kent – a name he chose because it rhymed with rent and had an international ring-Cars. Apparently, he fell in love with the business while helping his uncle run one. Working out of his home on Mumbai's Napean Sea Road, Sumaya installed a desk and a telephone in the front half of his garage; the car took up the rest. Only by the end of the second year could he afford to invest in two more Ambassadors.

He has invested in a fleet of 136 cars and concentrates on the corporate sector, where they are market leaders.

Kent Cars is now poised to drive into the national market-place through the franchising route. Whether or not he does as well in these cities as he has in Mumbai, Chandan Sumaya has driven a long way from the home garage he started from. And that's the spirit of Kent.

➧ What is the best age to become an Entrepreneur?

There is still a widespread idea that entrepreneurs are, by and large, people who drop out of school, go and invent something in the shed and ride on this to fame and fortune. Entrepreneurs with this profile do exist, but despite popular entrepreneur folklore, they are very much in the minority.

The Global Entrepreneurship Monitor report for 2005 found that those with post-secondary or graduate education are more than twice as likely to be involved in an entrepreneurial firm as those with a lesser education level. This figure is identical with the findings of a 1998 study of the fastest growing entrepreneurial companies in Europe, which found that 67% of the CEOs of the 500 companies studied held a university degree, and nearly half of these also had some form of post-graduate degree. The world's youngest entrepreneur is Suhas Gopinath the Bangalore based wizkid started Globals Inc. when he was barely 15.

So if people with post-secondary level education are twice as likely to become entrepreneurs, then logically, most will do so after their studies, in other words, at age 22-23 or older.

Working in exactly the same direction is the fact that virtually all entrepreneurial ventures require the founder to at least partially finance the start-up. Generally speaking, it takes some time for a young would-be entrepreneur to accumulate some capital to enable him to invest in his own start-up. This too is mostly beyond the reach of people in their early 20s.

Thus, it is that the majority of entrepreneurs are in their 30s when they launch themselves into their entrepreneurial career, and this fact has been borne out by various studies. For example, in a 1984 study, Robert Ronstadt found that the average age of entrepreneurs at start-up was 32 years. In similar vein, a suvey of INSEAD MBA graduates carried out in 2001, showed that the average age of entrepreneur graduates when they started their first business was 36.

Box 3

SENIORS WHO STILL ROCK BUSINESS

It often seems that since the dotcom boom young people rule when it comes to business. Just ask the guys from Google (GOOG) and Facebook. What might surprise you, though, is just how many senior citizens – from media moguls to casino kings to Chinese tycoons – are cutting deals, starting new busineses, and generally kicking boomer and Gen Y. butt. If 60 is the new 40, then 80 is the new 60. Here are eight of them, ranked from oldest to youngest. Take a look and you decide how much value should be placed on experience.

Run Run Shaw
Chairman,
Television Broadcasts
Age: 100

The legendary TV tycoon is slowing down, going into the office just a few days a week. But TVB, which he founded 31 years ago and still controls through Shaw Brothers, remains Hong Kong's preeminent broadcaster. His wife, Mona Fong, is continuing the Shaw family's hands-on style of management. The one major cloud on the horizon: a real estate developer from mainland China is looking to take over the entertainment empire that Shaw built.

The highly spiritual Basant Kumar Birla, patriarch of the Birla Group of companies, with interests ranging fom cement and textiles to education and commodities, still maintains his 9-to-5 office routine. his father, GD Birla, was an industrialist and friend of Mahatma Gandhi. although many of the businesses are run by the younger generation, the octogenarian is still very much in control of several companies, which he runs from his hometown of Kolkata. Birla officially willed his businesses to his two daughters, Jayashree and Manjushree, and the largest chunk to grandson Kumar Mangalam Birla. Birla still pursues his passion for music, playing the harmonium (an indian keyboard insrument) and singing with his wife Sarla Devi every evening in his majestic birla mansion.

Basant Kumar Birla
Chairman, Birla Group
Age: 87

⏩ Educational Quotient of Entrepreneurs

Empirical studies have shown that there is less co-relation between education and an entrepreneur. Many a successful entrepreneur are not qualified, yet they built entrepreneurial empires. But, of late in the IT industry education plays a crucial role in bringing efficiency to the fore. In fact, Gujarat boasts of undergraduate entrepreneurs. Education helps but not a criterion.

Entrepreneurial Process

Entrepreneurial Process is a leadership function which centres round the dynamics of entrepreneurial growth and change. It is a process comprising several distinct stages.

The *first* stage in the entrepreneurial process is some change in the socio-economic environment leading to changes in the every aspect of life in the country. *Inter alia*, the change creates needs for new goods and services.

The *second* stage is by starting a new venture.

The *third* process is intrapreneurship. It is the process of extending the enterprises domain of competence by exploiting new opportunities through new combinations of its available resources.

The *fourth* process is to coordinating the varied activities to achieve the entrepreneurial goal.

Entrepreneurial Structure

Structure represents the formal, official task relationships of people in entrepreneurial activities. In other words, structure is the logical culmination of authority and responsibility at different levels. It implies a system.

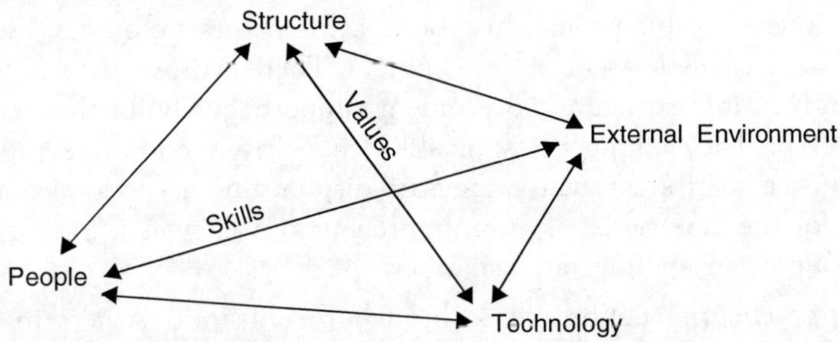

Fig. 4. Entrepreneurial Structural Relationship

Basic Source: Davis & Newstrom, Human Behaviour at Work Organisation Behaviour, 7th Eds. p. 5.

In entrepreneurial activity, policies, programmes, practices and measurement make possible for innovation and growth. They create the proper attitudes and provide the proper tools.

Entrepreneurial activity confines to the tasks of planning, directing, controlling, marketing, leading, motivating and channelising the activities of individuals and the groups towards entrepreneurial goal. The structure and relationships should be such that they allow people to be entrepreneurial.

The main requirements of such a structure are as follows:

1. The new enterprise should be organised separately from the existing.
2. There should be a special law for the new venture.
3. The new enterprise should be the specific responsibility of entrepreneur/intrapreneur in top management.
4. The new innovative project requires different policies, rules and evaluation criteria.
5. The entrapreneur is accountable for the success or failure of the enterprise.
6. The returns on innovation are distinctively different from existing business.
7. An entrepreneurial project requires right relationship, right rewards and right working culture.

A business that wants to be able to innovate wants to have a chance to succeed and prosper in a time frame of rapid change, has to build entrepreneurial management into its own system. It has to adopt policies, principles and practices that create through the entire organisation the desire to innovate and the habits of entrepreneurship and innovation. To be a successful entrepreneur, the existing business, large or small has to be managed as an entrepreneurial business. Entrepreneurial structure is thus the corner stone of success in business, whether it is in production or marketing or service. The empirical studies have shown that the solid structure determines the growth potential of entrepreneurial activities.

⏩ An Ideal Entrepreneur

History has shown that societies which are more open have advanced technologically more rapidly. Political controls and free markets cannot co-exist. And the example of Eastern Europe bears testimony to this. Since we have committed ourselves already to the democratic system, we must take steps to encourage the entrepreneurial drive and create an environment conducive to its growth.

An ideal entrepreneur is one who combines values in the market economy; that profits do not somehow preclude ethical behaviour; that growth is possible even if political patronage is not used to vend rules and cut corners, and quite simply that pursuit of wealth can be grateful and mannerly one. He takes with him the interest of his people, his country, his natural resources, the ecology and sees that his enterprise becomes a catalytic agent of development. There is thus a need of true entrepreneurs, who do not need incentives, infrastructure, government support; but build their enterprises, harness the resources and develop. They adopt a responsible value-driven corporate philosophy for their enterprises and/or business activities. As such, there is no dispute among economists and social thinkers about the urgent need for the emergence of an entrepreneurial society as a forerunner of accelerated development of the economy in an integrated manner.

The ethos of entrepreneurial culture runs through the business society in the 21st century. Indeed entrepreneurial culture lays a strong foundation for a well regulated, sustainable and environmentally friendly society.

⏩ Conclusion

To an economist, an entrepreneur is one who brings resources, labour, materials, and other assets into combinations that make their value greater than before, and also one who introduces changes, innovations, and a new order. To a psychologist, such a person is typically driven by certain forces – the need to obtain or attain something, to experiment, to accomplish, or perhaps to escape the authority of others. To one businessman, an entrepreneur appears as a threat, an aggressive competitor, whereas to another businessman the same entrepreneur may be an ally, a source of supply, a customer, or someone who creates wealth for others, as well as finds better ways to utilize resources, reduce waste, and produce jobs others are glad to get.

A number of entrepreneurial managers have attempted to identify the true nature of entrepreneur, intrapreneur entrepreneurship in the post industrial revolution. The definition as well as entrepreneurial process and structure have, therefore, undergone changes with the changes in the socio-economic environment and will continue to undergo changes with the changing times. However, some basic concepts of innovation, risk-taking, vision and organising skill continue to be the four pillars on which the edifice of entrepreneurial concept has to be perceived from time to time.

The eight-step transformation process for entrepreneur begins with creating a sense of urgency and then moves to building a guiding team. The third and fourth steps involve a clear vision of the future and how it will be different from the past and then communicating it to everybody in the organisation in order to get there buy-in. As progress is made, it is important to celebrate short-term wins, without letting up the pressure to achieve long-term wins, without letting up the pressure to achieve long-term change. Finally, transformation that has been achieved has to be institutionalised and the connections between behaviours and who have wrought the change then have to develop the next generation of entrepreneurs for succession. Thus, entrepreneur is a continuous source of change, economic development and an engine of growth.

The rapid growth of intrapreneurs owes basically to rapid and diversified growth of enterprise. The main objective is to grow far faster than it is possible, to unleash the core strength – its entrepreneurial spirit – in full force, to face new global competition and to exploit huge new opportunities profitably. Intrapreneurs are generated by totally decentralising the decision-making process, bank-rolling powerful business ideas, working with new generation of entrepreneurs. In the process, entrepreneurial talents are spotted and new ventures are set up on an ongoing basis. By spinning off each individual business as a separate enterprise the intrapreneurial culture is developed for the benefit of industrial growth in the country.

I raise a toast to all the entrepreneurs in our country – past, present and most of all, the future, who have built economic value the world over. The young achievers (entrepreneurs) pursue in building their business to greater heights.

Their pursuits are diverse: from Nirav Mehta, a geek who started a software company magnet-I because he was inspired by Bill Gates, to Simran Kohli who is building training centres to address needs of the broadcasting sector.

Perhaps one of the most outstanding entrepreneurs of our times is Bharti's Sunil Mittal who embodies the experimental entrepreneur who never gave up his efforts in building his business. The entrepreneurs will build an Incredibly Entrepreneurial India that will make our country truly incredible. They have set the tone for a new economic mission.

GOVINDBHAI KAKADIA
A 'gem' of a Cowherd

Govindbhai Kakadia, owner of the Rs. 800 crore Sheetal Manufacturing Co., is a typical rags to riches story. He is now famous as the world's largest volume manufacturer of polished diamonds and branded jewellery.

Govind in Sanskrit means a cowherd. At age 10, Govindbhai Kakadia used to graze cows in his native village of Patana in Bhavnagar district of Gujarat. Oblivious of the world outside the village, the young cowherd wore nothing on his body barring a soiled loincloth, and walked barefoot all over the dusty, muddy pathways of the sprawling village expanse. He was born in a poor family and his farmer father could hardly afford two square meals for his children. There was grinding poverty and Govindbhai and his two siblings could never even go to a village-level primary school. "We hadn't even touched a book," recalls Govindbhai.

"And we knew nothing but poverty."

Then one day a cousin came home wearing a shirt and slippers and informed Govindbhai and his family that his luck had changed ever since he had left the village to work in Bhavnagar. "What do you do there?" Govindbhai asked him. "I polish diamonds and make Rs. 70 per month," his cousin told him and added, "I eat well, clothe well and also go to see the movies."

Progress Chart
PROMOTER Govindbhai Kakadia
COMPANY Sheetal Manufacturing Company
ESTABLISHED 1991
TURNOVER Rs. 800 crore
LOCATION Mumbai
Skill Aquired June 1969
Skilled Worker Till 1992
Job Work and Trading 1976

Govindbhai Kakadia: "Growth will come from jewellery and not so much from loose diamonds."

"I would like to polish diamonds too," said Govindbhai, without even a clue as to what diamonds looked like. "And wear clothes and watch films." But diamond polishing required special skills and one had to undergo training to learn that, his cousin told him. "Moreover," he warned him, "you have to pay Rs. 600 up front to undergo training. Where will you raise that kind of money from?" He'll ask his father for the money, said Govindbhai, and went to his father to arrange the money for the training. His father was stunned. "Where am I to get that kind of money from," he told his eldest son and tried to dissuade him further, by saying, "You are still very young. Wait for two more years before you enter the big bad world."

"No, I can't wait for another two years," insisted Govindbhai. "I must start the training now itself." His father tried to dilly-dally for some more time but, when Govindbhai became persistent, his mother gave in. His father pawned her jewellery for Rs. 600 and sent him along with his cousin to Bhavnagar. The next six months were gruelling but Govindbhai had learnt the art of polishing to perfection by June 1969. "As if he was born to a diamond trader's family," recalls Vallabhbhai, an old associate.

Govindbhai was now making Rs. 70 per month. Out of this earning, he used to send Rs. 40 to his family and manage his boarding, lodging and even watching movies with the Rs. 30 he was left with. He had developed a great passion for movies, which has remained intact till date. "Food or no food," he remembers, "I had to watch movies – at any cost. They had become my main source of inspiration."

RECESSION 1979
Shifted to Mumbai 1984
Full Time Trader 1986
COMPANY Sheetal Manufacturing Company
ESTABLISHED 1991
TURNOVER Rs. 800 crore
LOCATION Mumbai
Branded Jewellery 2004 Sheetal Brand
Exclusive Outlets 2005

Three years down the line, with savings of Rs. 200, he sent a message to his younger brother to come and join him in the city. "Having learnt the trade," recalls Govindbhai, "I did not want to be a paid worker for others. I wanted to branch out on my own and take up job work in diamond polishing on a freelance basis." He started looking out for opportunities. A co-worker had some contacts in the trade from where he could get job work. In 1976, he and a partner rented two diamond-polishing machines for Rs. 240. But being new to the trade, he could not inspire other workers to join him. Finally, he asked his younger brother to work with him. But the kid was reluctant and wanted to continue as a job worker. "Don't forget," Govindbhai egged him on. "This is going to be our own business, with none to boss over us."

That did the trick and both the brothers started working on their own venture. The first three years proved to be good, but a recession in 1979 wiped off the entire business and left Govindbhai with a debt of Rs. 50,000 which he had borrowed for trading in diamonds. Govindbhai, his younger brother and some other workers once again embarked on diamond polishing and worked through the wee hours. By 1981, he was able to wipe off the entire debt burden. As luck would have it, a Mumbai-based jeweller liked his work and gave him a reasonably lucrative assignment.

But shuttling between Bhavnagar and Mumbai was proving too much, as it was both costly and meant loss of job work during his absence in Mumbai. In 1984, Govindbhai shifted to Mumbai for good, even though he had to move from under one roof to another and constantly change eateries. Recall Rajubhai Shah, managing director of Next Diamond, "Despite all the hardships, Govindbhai presented a calm and well-poised exterior and did fantastic work. And he had stars in his eyes – talking big, thinking big."

Recalls another well-known diamond merchant Anoopbhai, "Govindbhai always looked relaxed. After work hours, he'll either rush to the movies or stroll along Marine Drive. Sitting on the parapet, he would say: The Malabar Hill area looks beautiful. I must have a house there – not at Borivli or Ghatkopar. That was the time when most strugglers in the diamond trade used to dream about a small house in the far-off western or central suburbs. But, Govindbhai was a quintessential dreamer, dreaming big dreams all the time."

"His sincerity, perseverance, hard work and the will to achieve excellence in anything he did, paid off," says Sanjay Kothari, former Chairman of the Gems and Jewellery Promotion Council, who has known Govindbhai for a long time. "He has realised all his dreams," adds Rajubhai Shah. Including the dream house in Malabar Hill area, his friends say. "There came a time when he made his house in one of the most beautiful buildings in Malabar Hill," says another friend.

⏩ The Beginning

In 1986, when he decided to quit job work to become a full-time trader in diamonds, very few realised that, within the next few years, he was going to become an icon among the diamond fraternity. "He had very little money to invest, but he had very well invested himself in building up relationships to raise any amount for a start-up. Moreover, he was one of the few Kathiawadis," says an eminent Palanpuri diamond merchant "who had started making inroads into the bastion of the Palanpuri diamond merchants in an area which was perceived as traditionally theirs."

In the past 10 years, Govindbhai's enterprise has grown to become one of the foremost diamond houses in the country, and a major exporter in the international market. While his diamond export clocked sales of Rs. 770 crore in 2004-05, the business has seen a 25-30 per cent growth year-on-year in the past five years.

"But commodity is not what I want to grow in," says Govindbhai. "My ambitions are greater – to become number one company in the branded jewellery segment." While his more than 120 cousins and family members work with him to grow the Sheetal brand, both Govindbhai and his son Ajay are now focusing on brand building. Sheetal launched two major jewellery brands – Kiah and Bulaire for women and men, respectively.

The company has already invested around Rs. 100 crore to develop the two brands. With eight manufacturing facilities already existing in Mumbai and Surat, the company has two more large factories underway in Mumbai's SEEPZ and MIDC, to roll out large volumes of jewellery production. "Eventually," says Govindbhai, "it will be the branded jewellery that would take care of the diamond industry's growth in this country."

Govindbhai has already invested Rs. 12 crore in advertising, promotion and marketing of the two brands. "I'll invest more, if need be," he says, "Because, in our business, growth will come from jewellery and not so much from loose diamonds." This is his major mental preoccupation.

He has another obsession: promoting the English language school in his native village. "I had to start this school as I wanted all youngsters there to learn some English to make some progress in life. I can't read or write. And that hurts me." But what hurts him even more is that he couldn't get his son Ajay admitted in an English medium school in Bhavnagar because he couldn't write his name in that language. "My son's admission was turned down on that score, and that memory hurts. That is why I want all youngsters to learn English," he concludes.

Salient Traits of Govindbhai Kakadia

- Sincerity
- Ambitious
- Commitment
- Dreamer
- Visionary
- Hardowork
- Perseverance
- Will to excel promoter
- Family support
- Zealous
- Learning skills
- Simplicity
- Calm
- Well-poised
- Relaxed
- Building up relationships
- Innovator
- Promoter
- Social commitment
- Strategist

- Obsession
- Other Traits
- Stars in his eyes
- Talking big
- Thinking big
- Dreaming big
- Dreaming all the time
- Learning the art & business.

Box 4

ENTREPRENEURS FOR THE AGES

They are early colonial traders and 19th century industrialists. Throughout history, there have been a handful of people who had the vision to successfully exploit untapped markets. They changed the world in the process. See who they are, what they did, and why they matter today.

Admiral Zheng He (b. around 1371, d. 1433)

Zheng He, a Muslim from southwestern China's Yunnan province, was captured by the emperor's troops as a boy and pressed into Prince Zhu Di's corps of eunuch servants in the 14th century. When the prince became emperor, he charged Zheng He with building a trading fleet to make China an imperial economic power.

The servant-turned-admiral built the vaunted Treasure Fleets, comprising dozens of ships and tens of thousands of sailors, and led them in trade missions across south Asia and as far west as Africa and the Strait of Hormuz in the Persian Gulf. In seven voyages from 1405 to 1433, Zheng He spread China's goods across the world and returned with treasures for the Ming Dynasty. Along the way, Zheng He battled pirates and established trading centers in cities like Calicut, India, during a brief era of Chinese naval dominance.

Key takeaway: Zheng He's journeys matched the risks taken by the boldest entrepreneurs – and the payoff set a high bar for six centuries of risk takers to follow.

John D. Rockefeller (b. 1839, d. 1937)

Rockefeller started his first business selling grain and other goods before he was 20. He turned to oil a few years after it was discovered in western Pennsylvania in 1859. By buying out refineries around Cleveland and New York after the Civil War, Rockefeller soon dominated the market. Vertical integration was key. His company made its own oil barrels and owned storage and shipping facilities.

Although Standard Oil was later broken up under antitrust laws, Rockefeller had created a modern industry. He stepped back from the business in 1896 to devote himself to philanthropy, endowing the University of Chicago and the Rockefeller Foundation.

Key takeaway: Rockefeller used economies of scale and vertical integration to modernize an industry.

Andrew Carnegie (b. 1835, d. 1919)

The Scottish immigrant and weaver's son built a steel empire whose mills churned out the railroads, ships, and structures of post-Civil War America and created a fortune for himself in the process. Carnegie's quick adoption of the Bessemer process and other techniques to efficiently refine steel enabled him to lower costs and undercut his competitors.

After he sold his steel business to J.P. Morgan for $480 million at the start of the 20th century, Carnegie devoted his life and his wealth to endowing institutions that would let other poor sons of weavers better themselves. His "Gospel of Wealth" became a model for future entrepreneurs-turned-philanthropists like Bill Gates.

Key takeaway: Recognizing the innovations that will catalyze an industry means the difference between shutting down the competition and getting shut down.

Benjamin Franklin (b. 1706, d. 1790)

Franklin was a prime example of America's entrepreneurial spirit. He started as an apprentice in his brother's print shop and went on to publish the Pennsylvania Gazette newspaper and Poor Richard's Almanacki, one of the most widely read books in early America, which was filled with Franklin's aphorisms and proverbs.

Even before the colonies broke with England, Franklin helped create the infrastructure that would allow enterprise to thrive in an independent America: universities (he founded what would become the University of Pennsylvania), libraries, and the postal system. A writer, publisher, inventor, politician and diplomat, he always considered himself a businessman.

Key takeaway: Franklin's idea that people can improve their lives through their own hard work and enterprise, as he did, continues to encourage the American Dream.

Mayer Amschel Rothschild (b. 1744, d. 1812)

Born in Frankfurt's Jewish ghetto, Rothschild's banking empire would stretch across Europe, essentially becoming the world's first international bank. He sent his five sons to cities across the continent – to London, Paris, Vienna, Naples, and Frankfurt – where they established banks. The network banked merchants and, more importantly, governments, financing the British war against Napoleon.

Rothschild made control of information paramount within the business, even to the point of discouraging his children from marrying outside the family. He created communication channels across Europe, including carrier pigeons, to gather and relay information from one branch of the dynasty to another.

Key takeaway: In an era of nation-states that were just beginning to industrialize, Rothschild created the world's first multinational. Because his company crossed borders, it was not beholden to any one ruler.

W.K. Kellogg (b. 1860, d.1951)

Kellogg changed the notion of breakfast for a century of Americans when he and his older brother, John Harvey Kellogg, stumbled on a way to make dry cereal while preparing food for patients at the world-famous Battle Creek (Mich.) Sanitarium. The company he formed in 1906 quickly became successful: corn flakes and other ready-to-eat cereals filled bowls on breakfast tables across America.

Kellogg grasped the idea that kids influence buying decisions – galvanizing the brand's success. As early as 1931, the company sponsored children's radio programs, tried other forms of national advertising and expanded its operations overseas. In 1930, Kellogg used his wealth to endow the Kellogg Foundation.

Key takeaway: Kellogg's accidental discovery, promoted with savvy marketing, transformed the way Americans ate breakfast.

Estee Lauder (b. 1907, d. 2004)

Young Estee Lauder, born Josephine Esther Mentzer to immigrant parents in the Corona, Queens section of New York City, began experimenting as a child with skin treatments her uncle cooked up. In 1946, she founded the company that bears her name to sell makeup and perfume in high-end department stores around the world.

Lauder's business philosophy centered on selling products she considered to be of the highest quality, and she used her products themselves as advertisements. Lauder pioneered giving free samples at stores like Saks Fifth Avenue to hook customers. Although Lauder died in 2004, her grandson William still runs the company, with more than 9,000 products and $6.5 billion in sales in 2006.

Key takeaway: Lauder became a giant in the nascent beauty industry by making sure the quality of her products exceeded the expectations of her target market, namely, wealthy society women.

Madam C.J. Walker (b. 1867, d. 1919)

Born the daughter of former Louisiana slaves and orphaned at age 7, Walker developed a homemade scalp lotion to stop her hair loss. She then turned her remedy into a business and a movement.

Walker's line of hair-and-beauty products geared toward blacks tapped into a market ignored by other businesses because of racism. She also used her clout and fortune to advocate for change, pushing for anti-lynching laws and contributing to civil rights causes. She set an example for generations of entrepreneurs in a time when women were still struggling for voting rights and Brown v. Board of Education was a half-century away.

Key takeaway: The era's ingrained racism left a huge part of the population underserved by the market. Walker profited by making them her customers.

Thomas Edison (b. 1847, d. 1931)

Edison's relentless innovation made him the most prolific inventor of his time. He got his start as a telegraph operator but soon moved on to refining that technology and creating others that would turn the world on its head: a device to turn power into light, a machine to record and playback sound. Edison's labs were always working on new consumer products – a model familiar to today's crop of innovators like Google and Apple.

But only Edison's business sense allowed him to transform his ideas into enterprises that turned a profit. The Wizard of Menlo Park understood the importance of owning his ideas – he registered 1,093 patents – so he could retain profits on his products and discourage competitors.

Key takeaway: Innovation is crucial, but new ideas alone will not make a business successful. Ideas need to be focused into products that customers will value.

Box 5

INSPIRING AND INNOVATIVE ENTREPRENEURS

Adding Value to Merchandise

Samuel Moore Walton, founder and former chairperson of Wal-Mart, started his career as a supervisor in the US Army Intelligence Corps. In 1945, after leaving the military, Walton purchased a Ben Franklin variety store with a loan of $20,000. With the concept of discount merchandising, Walton drove up the volume of sales in this variety store. This helped him to open a chain of Ben Franklin stores.

He set up the first Wal-Mart store in 1962 and this was a beginning of a great success story. Within five years of opening, Wal-Mart opened 24 stores across the state of Arkansas in US. And as of July 31, 2007, Wal-Mart had a total of 4,091 retail units in the US alone. The company also operates more than 2500 units internationally.

Dusting-off Old Practices

James Dyson was an innovator who used his inventions to start his entrepreneurial journey. He started his career with the invention of industrial appliances and went on to open a manufacturing unit for developing dual cyclone cleaners. The Sea Truck, Dyson's first product, was launched in 1970 whilst he was at the Royal College of Art. His next product, the Ballbarrow, was a modified version of a wheelbarrow using a ball to replace the wheel. In the late 1970s, Dyson came up with an idea of using cyclonic separation to create a vacuum cleaner that would not clog and lose suction as it picked up dirt. He picked up the idea of cyclones from the spray-finishing room's air filter in his Ballbarrow factory. Finally, Dyson launched the world's first bagless vacuum cleaner, 'G·Force' cleaner, in 1983. Unfortunately, no manufacturer or related distributor was ready to pick his product in the UK, as it would have edged the cleaner-bag market. So Dyson launched it in Japan through catalogue sales where it won the 1991 International Design Fair prize. He finally obtained his first US patent on the idea in 1986.

Stall to Fast-food Chain

Ray Kroc started as a multi-mixer salesperson, and this business led him to his largest customers, the McDonald brothers. Dubbed as 'Hamburger King', he was the man behind the making of McDonalds. He was the first businessman to introduce the principles of mass production in a service industry.

Kroc had the competency to recognise popular trends in the form of customer preferences. He identified the market for convenient and cheap dining, and balanced this trend with traditional American foods, Kroc was successful in transforming a highly ritualistic, structured and code-oriented restaurant delivery system into a friendly, fast and reasonable dining service. He also took the entire menu range through a very effective product development process in order to revive the 'nine-item menu' earlier offered by the McDonald brothers. Kroc's ability to master the fast food concept helped him to expand McDonald globally, turning it into a multi-million dollar business.

Driven by Trends

Dhirubhai Ambani, founder of Reliance Industries Ltd. started his entrepreneurial career by selling fried snacks to pilgrims at Mount Girnar. On completing matriculation, Mr. Ambani moved to Aden

in Yemen where he worked as a gas station attendant. He simultaneously also worked as a clerk in an oil company. In 1960, he returned to India and started his first textile mill in 1966 with Rs. 50,000, under the brand name Vimal.

In the late seventies, Mr. Ambani started the equity cult, with more than 58,000 retail investors from rural and urban parts of India, who subscribed to Reliance's IPO. In 1992, Reliance became the first Indian company to raise money in global markets, its high credit-taking in international markets reserved only by India's autonomous rating. His vision and efforts pushed Reliance to feature in the Forbes 500 list and led to the company's expansion into other sectors like petrochemicals, telecom, IT, energy, power, retail, infrastructure services, capital markets and logistics.

Vision Build on Values

Azim Hashim Premji, Chairman, Wipro Technologies, is rated as one of the richest persons in India. Mr. Premji's wealth is estimated at US $17.1 billion. His vision to build an organisation based on values led Wipro to great heights.

Wipro initially dealt with moong oils and consumer products but gradually expanded as a provider of IT and SPO services. Mr. Premji's passion for delivering value to consumers gave birth to world class quality processes. This craving for quality made Wipro the first Indian Company to embrace Six Sigma solutions, becoming the first software services Company in the world to achieve SEI CMM Levels.

Mr. Premji's success is based on strong beliefs, which include favour for excellence building collective self-confidence, team building, creating efficient processes and being patient towards change.

Illustrious but Humble

Pallonji Shapoorji Mistry, Chairman, Shapoorji Pallonji Group, is considered to be one of the construction tycoons in India. Over the past years, his determination has earned many firsts for his company, Shapoorji Pallonji Co. & Ltd. It has been the first Indian construction company to enter the Middle East in the 1970s, to earn the ISO 9001 Certification and construct two, 60-storey residential towers in the heart of Mumbai. Mr. Mistry firmly believes in modern management skills, state-of-the-art technology, innovation and customer satisfaction.

Mr. Mistry's passion for quality and commitment has resulted in the diversification of his company. Today, Shapoorji Pallonji Co. & Ltd. is one of the biggest players in the construction of roads and textile & IT parks. The company is credited with many civil and structural engineering tour de forces like industrial units, hotels, hospitals, residential quarters, townships, water treatment plants, roads, power plants and biotech facilities.

An Apple a Day

Steve Paul Jobs' vision in the world of personal computers led the entire industry to restructure itself. When he was just twenty-one, with the help of a friend, he built a personal computer called the Apple. Apple was an underdog that took on the big player called IBM. Steve revolutionised personal computing with the launch of the Apple Macintosh computer. This technology was a giant step ahead in the marketability of PCs. PC was once believed to be a government and large corporation's equipment. But, with a graphical user interface that made it easier to use, Steve brought computers to every household across North America.

In 1982, Apple went public and this made him a very rich man. However, instead of retiring, he strived further in making Apple a great company. While doing so, he also helped make his other company Pixar into an animation powerhouse that made animated movies like Toy Story and A Bug's Life.

He Did It!

Perhaps the biggest inspirational lesson that entrepreneurs can learn from Philip Knight is in brand building. Phil, as he is popularly known, revolutionised the sports goods industry and in the process created one of the best known global brands – Nike. As a young man who was passionate about track and field, Phil was smart enough to see the opportunity in creation of sports goods that could enhance performance. He started with a small company and transformed it into a multi-billion dollar giant.

Of course, the growth has not been an accident. As an entrepreneur, Phil ensured that he delivered great quality to his customers. He regularly brought innovations in his products, expanded the product offerings and backed it all with great management skills. He also made excellent use of advertising and brand building exercises. Today, he continues to inspire his employees and many budding entrepreneurs. Whenever a list of all time great entrepreneurs is created, Phil's name will certainly fear on in it as the man who just did it!

Grit Amidst Gross Circumstances

Christopher Paul Gardner, CEO of stockbrokerage firm, Gardner Rich & Co. has achieved 'big' amidst extreme poverty. Gardner started his career as a hospital corpsman in Navy, but later shifted his career and went on to become a stockbroker. The learning Gardner received from stock brokerage training programs equipped him enough to start a brokerage firm of his own. In 1987, Gardner started Gardner Rich & Co. with a paltry amount. In 2006, Gardner sold a small stake in Gardner Rich in a multi-million dollar deal, which led to expansion of Gardner Rich into Christopher Gardner International Holdings.

His brokerage firm specialises in the execution of debt, equity and derivative products transactions for some of the largest institutions, public pension plans and unions in US. Gardner is an enthusiastic and motivational speaker, addressing survival strategies. He is also an avid humanitarian committed to many noble causes. Briefly, Gardner's is a remarkable story of struggle with homelessness and also about his personal struggle of establishing himself as a stock broker while managing fatherhood.

COUNTING ON CHARISMA

"Charisma still counts. Charistimatic leadership is important both for substance and for the intangible confidence it represents to people. Approximately, 10-15% of the performance comes from the degree of charisma of the CEO."

— Jeffrey Sonnenfeld, President, Yale Leadership Institute

3

Characteristics of Entrepreneurial Types

Introduction

An entrepreneur who has a high level of administrative capability, flair and ability for decision-making, computational skill, delegation skill, organisational skill, good at communication and has a sound technical knowledge stands a much better chance of success than his counterpart who possesses none or a low level of these basic qualities. It is the possession of these scarce qualities which confers an advantage on some people in becoming an entrepreneur. Besides these qualities, however, the entrepreneur also needs either to be himself a generalist so that he can discharge his function without delegation, or to possess delegation and organisational skills.

Box 1

PERSONALITY IN BUSINESS (EDWARD MULLER)

Every enterprise, great or small, is characterised by the personalities of those who direct it and participate in its affairs. Its development, progress and reputation are in their hands. Therefore, if I were asked what I consider to be the most important individual attribute in business, I think I should put Personality at the head of my list.

> We are inclined to forget occasionally that personalities in every organisation can be, and are, judged from several viewpoints. The "Boss" has to judge those under him from his position as head of affairs. On the other hand, his collaborators may have quite a different perspective, especially where they themselves are concerned.
>
> Moreover, they usually have some very definite views about the chief himself and others senior in rank. It behoves all executives therefore, in every capacity, to see to it that these judgements or opinions – provided they are unbiased – mainly reflect their own good qualities and, to that end, the example they set day-by-day is worth far more than an occasional lecture.
>
> There are two sides to every business, the human and the material: both need to be interwoven into one harmonious whole.
>
> Obviously no section or division of any business can operate independently. At the same time we should never regard organisation as an end in itself, only a means to an end.

The entrepreneurial qualities are to some extent innate. But not all of them are entirely innate. Some can be enhanced by training, or simply by experience. For example, analytical ability and computational skill can be enhanced by education at school and university, while practical knowledge and foresight skills can be enhanced by the general experience of everyday life. Entrepreneurial careers will be strongly influenced by the desire to enhance qualities which are scarce, yet difficult to obtain through delegation because of the problems involved in screening for them. Of the two indispensable qualities of the entrepreneur, imagination is almost entirely innate, while foresight, though to some extent innate, can be enhanced by a varied experience. Imagination and foresight are the scarce qualities which are difficult to analyse and quantify. Delegation skill and organisation skill, though to some extent innate, can be enhanced by a varied experience. Imagination and foresight are the scarce qualities which are difficult to analyse and quantify. Delegation skill and organisation skill, though not essential, are highly desirable whenever large-scale decision-making is contemplated. These too are qualities which can be enhanced through experience.

➤➤ Characteristics of Entrepreneurs

The characteristics of an entrepreneur that contribute to success are the result of his achievement motivation. The characteristics of achievement motivated persons as identified by McClelland have been discussed in the chapter on "Future of Entrepreneurship in India." A successful entrepreneur must be a person with technical competence, initiative, good judgement, intelligence, leadership qualities, self-confidence, energy, attitude, creativeness, fairness, honesty, tactfulness and emotional stability.

1. Mental ability: Mental ability consists of intelligence and creative thinking. An entrepreneur must be reasonably intelligent, and should have creative thinking and must be able to engage in the analysis of various problems and situations in order to deal with them. The entrepreneur should anticipate changes and must be able to study the various situations under which decisions have to be made.

2. Clear objectives: An entrepreneur should have a clear objective as to the exact nature of the business, the nature of the goods to be produced and subsidiary activities to be undertaken. A successful entrepreneur may have the objective to establish the product, to make profit or to render social service.

3. Business secrecy: An entrepreneur must be able to guard business secrets. Leakage of business secrets to trade competitions is a serious matter which should be carefully guarded against by an entrepreneur. An entrepreneur should be able to make a proper selection of his assistants.

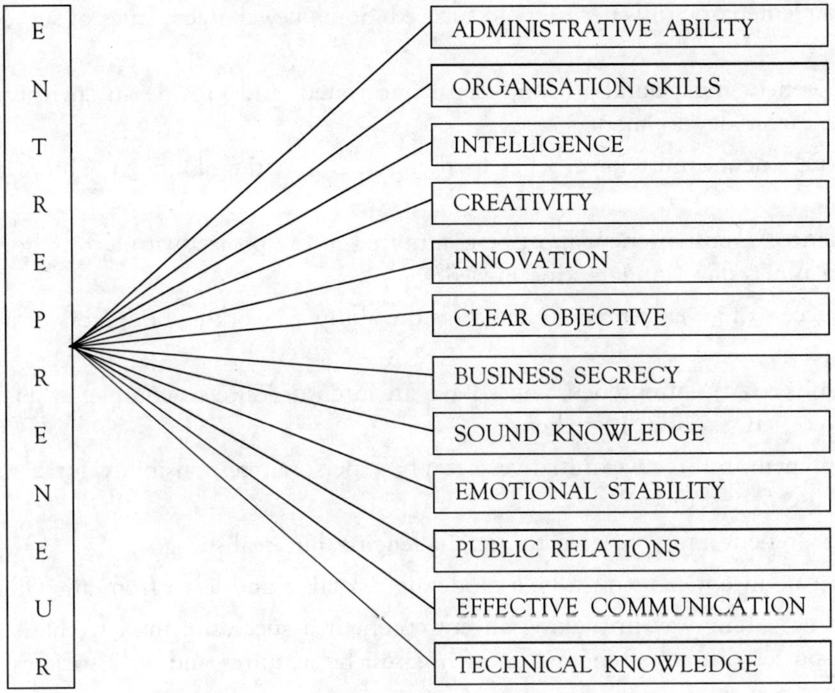

Fig. 1 Characteristics of an Entrepreneur

4. Human relation ability: The most important personality factors contributing to the success of an entrepreneur are emotional stability, personal relations, consideration and tactfulness. An entrepreneur must maintain good relation with his customers if he is to establish relations that will encourage them to continue to patronise his business. He must also maintain good relations with his employees if he is to motivate them to perform their jobs at a high level of efficiency. An entrepreneur who maintains good human relation with customers, employees, suppliers, creditors and the community is much more likely to succeed in his business than the individual who does not practice good human relations.

5. Communication ability: Communication ability is the ability to communicate effectively. Good communication also means that both the sender and the receiver understand each other and are being understood. An entrepreneur who can effectively communicate with customers, employees, suppliers and creditors will be more likely to succeed than the entrepreneur who does not.

6. Technical knowledge: An entrepreneur must have a reasonable level of technical knowledge. Technical knowledge is the one ability that most people are able to acquire if they try hard enough.

An entrepreneur who has a high level of administrative ability, mental ability, human relations ability, communication ability, and technical knowledge stands a much better chance of success than his counterpart who possesses low levels of these basic qualities. Brilliant men with first class degrees from university shy away from becoming entrepreneurs because the one thing they cannot be taught is coping with human emotions.

Robert D. Hisrich has identified a few more capabilities or personal characteristics that an entrepreneur should possess. According to him, the entrepreneur must have an adequate commitment, motivation, and skills to start and build a business. The entrepreneur must determine if the management team has the necessary complementary skills necessary to succeed. Some key characteristics of successful entrepreneur are:

Motivator: An entrepreneur must build a team, keep it motivated, and provide an environment for individual growth and career development.

Self-confidence: Entrepreneurs must have belief in themselves and the ability to achieve their goals.

Long-term involvement: An entrepreneur must be committed to the project with a time horizon of five to seven years. No ninety-day wonders are allowed.

High energy level: Success of an entrepreneur demands the ability to working hours for sustained periods of time.

Persistent problem-solver: An entrepreneur must have an intense desire to complete a task or solve a problem. Creativity is an essential ingredient.

Initiative: An entrepreneur must have initiative, accepting personal responsibility for actions, and above all make good use of resources.

Goal setter: An entrepreneur must be able to set challenging but realistic goals.

Moderate risk-taker: An entrepreneur must be a moderate risk-taker and learn from any failures.

These personal traits go a long way in making an entrepreneur a successful man/woman. But, however, no entrepreneur possesses total strengths. In such cases, he acquires and/or associates and thus strengthens his enterprise.

Success Depends on ...

Buildiing value propositions for customer groups

Dealing with competitors as business partners

Tracking and analysing customer database for trends

Setting up strong front-end solutions units

Potential Pitfalls are ...

The absence of product specific sales teams

Managing culturally diverse alliance partners

Focusing on volumes rather than profits

Keeping up the pace of new product launches.

Table 1

CHARACTERISTICS OF ENTREPRENEURS

Small-Scale Entrepreneurs	*Large-Scale Entrepreneurs*
1. Young men	1. Middle aged Professionals
2. Ambitious	2. Professional Specialists
3. Intelligent	3. Shareholders contribute venture Capital
4. Energetic	4. Energetic
5. Enthusiastic	5. Outsourcing
6. Minimum education	6. Net-workers
7. Hard-working	7. Ability to get along with people
8. Confident	8. Tolerant

9. Passionate	9. Risk Takers
10. Dedicated	10. Large Assets controlled
11. Practical	11. Engaged in Diversified Activities
12. Goal-oriented	12. Diversified products
13. Mobile	13. Multiple activities
14. Adaptable	14. Easy access to institutional finance
15. Able	15. Leverages
16. Aggressive	16. Well connected with Politics Bureacrats
17. Innovative	17. Trend setters
18. Well-mannered	18. Demand creators
19. Self-made person	19. Value-driven
20. Disciplined	20. Corporate Philosophy
21. Zealous	21. Ambitious
22. Flexible	22. Drive to go ahead
23. Courageous	23. Self-confident
24. Skilful	24. Innovative/immitative
25. Creative	25. Adaptable
26. Experienced	26. Trained
27. Meager capital	27. Large capital
28. Small operation	28. Large operation
29. Employ few people	29. Skilled manpower
30. Small turnover	30. Large turnover/sales/profit
31. Honest	31. Honest
32. Progressive	32. Progressive
33. Patient	33. Pragmatic
34. Perseverance	34. Perseverance
35. Self-reliant	35. Self-Reliant
36. Common sense	36. Abundant common sense
37. Adaptive	37. Competitive
38. Ability to strive	38. Versatile
39. Compassionate	39. Quality conscious
40. Dreamer	40. Visionaries
41. Conscious	41. Focussed
42. Intuitive	42. Singleness of purpose
43. Practical	43. Ability to change
44. Imaginative	44. Educated
45. Achiever	45. A strong need to achieve
46. Hopeful	46. Passionate
47. Independent	47. Analytical
48. Self-starter	48. Optimistic
49. Individualist	49. Organisation man
50. Sensitive	50. Loyal
51. Perceptive	51. Pleasing personality
52. Quality conscious	52. Dynamic
53. Desire to share experience	53. Tolerant
54. Ability to change	54. Active
55. Money oriented	55. Contributor
56. Driven by values	56. Knowledgeable
57. Intrapreneurial	57. Motivator
58. Facilitator	58. Strategist
59. Learner	59. Goal conscious
60. Opportunist	60. Compassionate
61. Ability to strive	61. Leader
62. Task master	62. Scanner – Looking for opportunities
63. Striving Richness	63. Planner
64. Gut-Feeler	64. Thinker
65. Dictator	65. People Manager

Entrepreneurial Initiative

Recent data on entrepreneurial initiative and self-employment reveal a few problems. To overcome these problems it is essential to develop entrepreneurial skills for which the entrepreneur has to initiate the process of development. This is a challenging task. This unprecedented, perpetual change with unlimited barriers makes entrepreneurial initiative in the future more significant and more dynamic.

This means that entrepreneurial initiative is a strategic process which embodies calculated strategic choices. There are strategies open to the entrepreneur himself in terms of industry choice and individual and resource-task fit, and there are strategies open to the regulators and support agencies in terms of industrial policy tools, incentive and explicit stimulation of industrial sector or branches. A conceptual framework that contains both dimensions will provide a convenient base for analysis and possible policy action.

Encouraging entrepreneurial initiative is an issue applicable to both developed and developing countries and the search for effective means is proceeding in earnest. The analysis has dealt with a way of viewing the constraints embodied in the process of creating a new business or manufacturing operation.

The slow pace of the propensity to enterprise is mainly due to the existence of a tangible set of barriers prohibiting the process of entry into, continuity in, and an eventual exit from a business venture of a would-be entrepreneur if it is a function of forces that one may view as barriers limiting full-fledged business performance. There may be *entry barriers and exit barriers.*

Entry barriers are those forces limiting access to identified business opportunities and capitalisation on these opportunities. Survival barriers are constraints on the conditions essential for the small business entity. Exit barriers are constraints limiting the termination of small industrial ventures that have outlived their business viability or the growth of such ventures to a different size category.

The existing entry barriers are:

1. A cultural bias in identifying and managing the entrepreneurial development process.
2. Limited industry-specific data and insufficient market information.
3. Limited effectiveness of the infrastructural base.
4. Existence of visible and invisible obstacles to entry of a specific societal group (e.g., women) into business.
5. Unorganised capital market and traditional feasibility assessment processes.
6. Unsympathetic and cumbersome government attitude.
7. Hostile environment.
8. Limited access to technology.

Observed Survival barriers include the following:

1. A behavioural pattern that could impair basic managerial practices.
2. Constraining practices within the capital market.
3. The threatening shadow of changing technology.
4. Limited learning.
5. The cultural management of resources.
6. Failure of guidance agencies to guide.
7. Scarce information and limited dissemination of that information.

Identified exit barriers include:

1. The emotional commitment of the entrepreneur to his venture.
2. Specialised assets, sunk funds.
3. The increasing demand for managerial skills.
4. Fear of failure.

Barriers, single or combined are said to have an impact on to strategic and long-term planning perspective of the small entrepreneur and could, equally, have an impact on the government's promotional policies within the sector. Low entry and low survival industries (or industrial branches) could provide policymakers with an area for quick and intensive intervention. At the other extreme, industries with high entry barriers and high survival barriers, can probably be regarded as low priority areas that deserve a different kind of attention, i.e., barrier adjustment instead of enterprise development. The relationship between entry and exit barriers could lead to a similar set of conclusions. One of those conclusions is the advisability of the management of enterprise flow and the early identification of the potential for switching (a form of exit), or planned divestment. Again this can prove valuable for government policies for small industry promotion at the national and regional levels.

Progress in economic development and technological diversification does not happen accidentally or haphazardly. In a hyper competitive environment, the economic renaissance of an area depends on a city's or region's ability to address critical needs. To sustain the momentum of positive economic growth, communities must establish programmes for investment in a viable public/private infrastructure. This includes not only meeting the other essential infrastructure needs such as roads, water, and services but also providing for educational needs and diversified cultural amenities.

A vibrant financial environment is essential for continued economic development. This includes sophisticated banking community that understands the unique problems and needs of emerging companies, especially technologically based companies, and an expanding venture capital industry that can address the requirements of high-risk ventures. Only in this way can an area ensure diversified opportunities for entrepreneurs.

A pool of capable people hold the responsibility for economic development. A community, therefore, has to find ways to ensure a locally-trained workforce with a minimum reliance on imported services. As needs are supplied locally there are more opportunities for entrepreneurs. By responding to a rapidly changing environment, it engenders a dynamic entrepreneurial spirit.

What Makes an Entrepreneur?

What makes an entrepreneur is the combination of various factors that have enabled the personality formation right from the childhood as also the psychological urge that exists intensively in the person. These psychological processes which lead men to set up on their own a successful business enterprise beginning the very early life and have cumulative effect. The influence of early childhood and other social roles are determinate factors for the formation of that personality which motivates an individual towards becoming an independent businessman or entrepreneur.

In the case of persons who take up jobs, it has always been found that they have secured success in the established organisations. These people do not have a rejection towards the established institutions and neither do they attempt to rebel against the traditional path to success. On the other hand, an entrepreneur fails to achieve educational success through the established organisations and this is because of the general rejection of the established organisations at all levels. People who tend to like security and not uncertainty gets more satisfied by taking up jobs which are less risk-oriented and hence are not motivated towards building up their own industrial enterprise.

Men who establish new business are men who have right from the childhood faced a different set of environment in their family, school and other social situations. Research studies have indicated that successful entrepreneurs identify a crisis before they venture into new entrepreneurial activities. Even in their childhood most of them had threatening non-supportive and disgusting adult figures who had much say in their social and economic life. Most of these have a childhood of impoverishment and stress. Economic deprivation also works as a motivational factor towards creating something on their own and free oneself from the clutches of oppressing forces which attempt to kill their spirit of individualism. Thus it has been found that creating a successful new business is not due to an isolated incidence in the life of an individual but it has been as a result of learned response to their total social, emotional and economic environment.

The family background plays an important role in building up personality necessary for turning into an entrepreneur later in life. In family situations where security and non-risk bearing activities are encouraged right from childhood, the individual likes to be more security-oriented rather than attempt on his own in areas where adventures and uncertainty conditions prevail. Also in families where deep attachments and emotional relationships are encouraged, it has been found that the child growing under such situations tends to take up activities which are more security-oriented than risk-oriented. Since in most of the middle-class families, attachment and security-oriented activities are encouraged despite seeking academic excellence, it itself does not help the person to develop a deep urge to be independent and create a framework required for enjoying autonomy.

As a result of this attitude building, many bright graduates shy away from placing themselves in open positions but instead choose to stay in the established organisations because they have developed a favourable attitude towards the establishment. On the other hand, the entrepreneurial personality would rather face the impersonal forces of the economy than cope with inter-personal relations of the established organisations. Due to this characteristic of an entrepreneur, they tend to shift from job to job till they have finally found a field of activity in which they will ultimately have a say and also enjoy the happenings of events by their sheer will, determination and efforts.

While people who take up jobs prefer to see success in the traditional and highly structured roles in the established undertakings, entrepreneurs, on the other hand, prefer to have a different approach toward success and be unique in their own way. They find more satisfaction in their creative faculties getting an opportunity to express themselves fully rather than submitting themselves to forces which are already structured and rigid. The bright graduates may very often lack creativity and are not in a position to break through the undifferentiated mask of circumstances and make something of their own.

The entrepreneurs, on the other hand, find such situations extraordinarily challenging and attempt with determination and persistence to come out of this web of oppressing factors, which tend to keep them in the rigid framework. Thus we find entrepreneurial characteristics are formed through a combination of various social, economic and psychological factors to which the person becomes subjected right from childhood. These factors reinforce in him the urge to excel others and seek satisfaction in creating on his own a new enterprise instead of seeking a security-oriented job, in the absence of these reinforcing elements which go into the formation of the entrepreneurial personality, however bright a person may be in the academic life, it is not a guarantee that he would also become a successful entrepreneur. Something more than mere academic excellence is a pre-requisite for becoming an entrepreneur of success and repute. These requisites are embodied in the various qualities that the entrepreneur must have basically within himself in order to establish himself as a successful entrepreneur. But many graduates do lack in these qualities.

Conclusion

A number of entrepreneurial managers have attempted to identify the true nature of entrepreneurs and entrepreneurship in the post-industrial revaluation. The definition has, therefore, undergone changes with the changes in the socio-economic environment and will continue to undergo changes with the changing times. However, some basic concepts of innovation, risk-taking, vision and organising skills continue to be the four pillars on which the edifice of entrepreneurial concept has to be perceived from time to time.

An ideal entrepreneur is one who confines values in the market economy, that profits do not somehow preclude ethical behaviour, that growth is possible even if political patronage is not used to bend rules and cut corners, and quite simply that pursuit of wealth can be grateful and mannerly one. He takes with him the interest of his people, his country, his natural resources, the ecology and see that his enterprise becomes a catalytic agent of development. There is thus a need of true entrepreneurs, who do not opt for incentives, infrastructure, government support: but build his enterprises, harness the available resources and develop. They adopt a responsible value-driven corporate philosophy for their enterprises and/or business activities. As such, there is no dispute among economists and social thinkers about the urgent need for the emergence of an entrepreneurial society as a forerunner of accelerated development of the economy in an integrated manner.

CHARACTERISTICS OF A SUCCESSFUL ENTREPRENEUR

A successful entrepreneur is a person who has started the business where there was none before. A successful entrepreneur is essentially an enterprising individual who is able to recognise the potential profitable opportunity and who initiates to produce marketable products by combining the various technologies and through bringing together the people, finance, material resources, marketing tools, in order to ultimately translate the idea in the minds to physical realities. In short entrepreneur is a person who initiates, establishes, maintains and expands a new enterprise. He is basically an innovator, creator and accomplisher.

According to research studies, there are more than 50 personality traits and all these traits and attitudes constitute the characteristic of a successful entrepreneur. Though all the characteristics cannot be found in a single entrepreneur yet the presence of greater number of these characteristics in an individual makes him an entrepreneur and only then it is possible for him to be a successful to achieve the goals of entrepreneurship. Some of the characteristics or qualities of such a person or such entrepreneur are discussed below:

(1) Need for achievement, (2) Risk taking, (3) Need for Independence, (4) Sense of effectiveness, (5) Social consciousness, (6) Need for extension, (7) Optimistic, (8) Open minded, (9) Non-fatalist, (10) Low Affiliation, (11) Pragmatist, (12) Aggressive, (13) Persistent, (14) Commitment and conviction, (15) Capacity to analyse, (16) Initiative, (17) Hopeful and (18) Efficiency.

(1) Need for achievement: The urge to achieve or the urge to excel others is the forceful psychological factor which is an essential characteristics found in almost all the individuals with enterprising qualities. McCelland Winter have through their research studies indicated that this is the single critical factor present in the entrepreneurs. Entrepreneurs belong to that category of people who are willing to work hard and to achieve something excellent despite the challenges and threats in the environment. Under such challenging and threatening forces many people would loss or give up and would not care at all for achieving something better. But the high need of achievement present in the entrepreneurs drive them to excel others. This trait also indicates the urge to be different from others and strive to achieve the goal which are difficult to be achieved by other ordinary people. At the same time these people do not aim at practically impossible goals. Their goals set are achievable in reality. The high need of achievement urge results in a high drive in individuals and as a result a high activity level is present in these persons. As a consequence of this driving force thought processes are always linked with the problems of doing things better than the others. Unless the person possesses this urge to accomplish, excel or achieve through a balanced sense autonomy and tolerance it is difficult to be a successful entrepreneur.

(2) Risk taking: Risk taking is another attribute of entrepreneurs. Entrepreneurs like to take risks which are calculated and not extreme ones. They undertake challenging risks which are difficult to overcome but are not impossible. They do not have the attitude of depending upon chance factors to get the expected results instead they would like their own efforts to give the desired results. By this way of influencing the results by their own efforts they like to enjoy the sense of having accomplished the tasks by their own efforts. In this process the risks involved are calculated risks. To ensure success in the accomplishment of the goals. Entrepreneurs see to it that they spend lot of time in planning their enterprises and ensure success before actually launching the project. This is done by studying in detail the various interfering forces and obstacles and keeping ready the solutions to overcome these interferences. Moderate risk taking and safeguarding against anticipated difficulties are the qualities that can be found in successful entrepreneurs.

(3) Need for Independence and Autonomy: The strong need to be an independent or autonomous individual is another driving force working within the entrepreneurs. The entrepreneurs dislike controls from outsiders as a result conformations to set ideas and standards are not, their forte to appreciate. This non-conformative attitude is also responsible for their starting a new enterprise based on new ideas of their own. Autonomy coupled with a sense of determination is an essential characteristics of entrepreneurs.

(4) Sense of Effectiveness: Entrepreneurs like to see the problem solved through their involved efforts. They do not like to avoid the problems but like to be effective or be instrumental in solving problems rather than avoiding them. Their attitudes towards a problem is always one of directing the efforts and finding ways and means to give solution to such problems. Since they are full of confidence in their own capacities they tend to be action oriented, rather than being passive conformists.

(5) Social Consciousness: Rightful entrepreneurs tend not to take undue advantage of social and economic conditions of society in general. Instead there is a universal urge among the entrepreneurs for social change and economic development. As a result entrepreneurs are always in the look out for new methods of producing or developing new products that would create jobs for many. Hence the pursuit of such business activities are directed to achieve social goals on larger interest than personal goals of individual interest.

Entrepreneurs in the real sense do not patronage or indulge in anti-social activities like black-marketing, hoarding, profiteering and such other malpractices which causes considerable damages to interest of the consumer as a whole. They dislike economic backwardness of the society which is the result of such anti-social and unfair business practice. Instead they direct their energies in the eradication of the undesired implications by finding new suitable opportunities of business and by providing the services at the prices that the community can afford. An entrepreneur since is socially concerned respects labour. They spread the message of dignity of manual labour through their own example. They have very low resistance towards doing a work manually. They are ever ready to get the work done through their own hands if the situation demands without any hesitation. This kind of respecting labour enables them to work in co-operation with the people by generating high morale among the people with whom they work. Persons who hesitate to do the work with their own hands feel why to do such work manually, and will find it difficult to succeed as an entrepreneur. Hence this quality of respecting labour is also a driving force which enables them to be successful by setting example of doing the work manually. The examples set by them enables others to learn and follow suit. Cooperation therefore becomes easy and effective under such situation.

(6) Need for Extension: An entrepreneur though likely to be self-centered in the pursuit of his goals so that his urge for achievement are satisfied, yet in the true sense he is not so. Many entrepreneurs understand the importance of industrialisation and faster economic development through rapid growth and expansion of the industries, hence they tend to share their experiences with others who have similar attributes and accomplish the task through joining hands with the suitable persons. But the degree of such participations by entrepreneurs in developing economy is very low, hence by giving appropriate training the entrepreneurs should be motivated towards this goal of expansion through joint ventures. In a country like India the need of the entrepreneurs for the rapid development in every field for the economy is more a necessity and therefore Government efforts should be directed towards this end.

(7) Optimistic: The entrepreneurs have the quality of being optimistic and hoping to succeed than to fail. This hope to succeed would enable a sense of determination which boosts their confidence in carrying out the task successfully. Hence this quality of being optimistic is of none the less important. As a consequence of their self confidence they are more successful in their efforts than those with pessimistic attributes.

Thus pessimistic approach or fear of failure does not find the place in their mind and they undertake all the tasks after careful planning and with the hope of succeeding towards their efforts.

(8) Non-fatalist: Entrepreneurs though they have faith in God or in the power of nature yet they disapprove the belief that outside forces will change the environment towards the desired needs. They would like to be instrumental through their own efforts rather than to be dependent upon chance factors or luck or those forces which are beyond their control, for attaining desired goals. Man's destiny can be changed by man himself by his own efforts is their strong belief. Psychologically this type of an attribute is called internal locus of control. This drives them to do things with extra vigour and help them to change the happenings by their own efforts and enjoy the feeling of making things to happen. This nature helps them to accept the mistaken efforts in case any and to attempt to with improvements in their approaches in future actions.

(9) Open Minded: Entrepreneurs develop the habit of learning from experience the limitations of achievements. They modify the goal according to the environmental challenges and threats. This modification does not mean avoiding the problems or the tasks instead they like to face it. The modification is done in order to make it possible to achieve the goal within the given environmental conditions. They always like to get the feedback of their efforts and effectiveness of the programmes modified so that chances or modifications if needed can be effected as and when required. Entrepreneurs in a sense, therefore, always test their capabilities and for the purpose they tend to keep their mind open to receive information on their abilities or otherwise to achieve the desired goals.

(10) Low affiliation: Entrepreneurs do not get attached emotionally with the people with whom they work. They know that if they do get into emotional involvement with the people, they would be working more for the people with whom they are working rather than for the institutions which they intend to build. But even with this attribute they can show concern for their employees by checking, or restraining the behaviour that tends to show obviously their true reactions.

(11) Need for power and influencing: Entrepreneurs always feel the need to influence people and implement the ideas so that the organisation takes the shape in actuality. Excellence is no doubt a criteria for the entrepreneurs but leading others and influencing them to a great extent through the effective dealing is not secondary to an entrepreneur. Since they have a strong belief in their own capacity they tend to a very high sense of morale which ultimately helps to influence others to their own way of thinking and action. Here the entrepreneur takes the role of successful manager and influencing others in the accomplishment of the goals.

(12) Aggressive and persistent: These are also the characteristics which help the entrepreneurs to continue with drive till the goals are achieved. Aggressiveness indicates the presence of driving force which enables the efforts to come out with full vigour through persistent attempts. This quality, therefore, indicates that entrepreneurs are not problem avoiders. They pursue the goals till they are achieved by modifying the same as and when required as also by removing the obstacles in the way so that the goals are finally achieved. With every failure the entrepreneur learns to improve the method of approach rather than being passive in the face of frustrating experiences.

(13) Pragmatists: Another attribute of an entrepreneur is to be concerned with the present than the past or future. Though he learns from the past and intends to change the future through his visions and dreams yet he is down right a practical person living in the present. He is a pragmatist who lives in the present effectively. He is not a man of mere day dreams or one who is overwhelmed by the past achievements or failures. Though entrepreneurs may at time give the impression of past oriented personalities by narrating their pasts profusely yet really speaking they are pragmatists who cannot easily be overwhelmed by either the past or the future orientations.

Other characteristics of a successful entrepreneur are high expectations from their employees, pleasing personality, dynamic opportunity seeker, self starter, individualise sensitive and perceptive of environment, high tolerance towards ambiguities and uncertain happenings, materialist tendencies, always hoping and believing in the existence of better ways of doing things, many interests, mentally very active, courageous, etc.

(14) Commitment and conviction:

- Fully commits himself to the project and rests only when achieved.
- Leaves no effort to complete the task in time.

(15) Capacity to analyse:

- Knows the need for information, its relevance, where and how to find it.
- Has a thought process for diagnosing problems, conceiving and comparing alternative courses of actions and approaches in the direction to solve rather than to avoid.

(16) Initiative:

- Takes initiative and does not wait for others to do first.
- Likes to lead rather than being led.
- Likes to act on his own rather than follow others' directions.

(17) Hopeful about future and search for environment:

– Reasonably optimistic and tends to look at future with hope.

– Tends to search the environment in order to seek answers to questions.

– Sets goal and plan his line of operations.

– Perceives opportunities.

(18) High personal efficiency:

– Has a sense of effectiveness.

– Presents himself with ability to do things with higher degree of efficiency.

There could be a long series of characteristics, but, in my opinion, these are some of the very important and essential ones which should fit into the profile of a successful entrepreneur, it is actually not necessary that he may have high degree of all these traits but a fairly good combination of these is required to be reasonably available. The level of degrees could, however, be increased by motivation and proper training through entrepreneurship development programmes.

Conclusion

A number of entrepreneurial managers have attempted to identify the true nature of entrepreneur, entrepreneurship in the post industrial revaluation. The definition has, therefore, undergone changes with the changes in the socio-economic environment and will continue to undergo changes with the changing times. However, some basic concept of innovation, risk-taking, vision and organising skill continue to be the four pillars on which the edifice of entrepreneurial concept has to be perceived from time to time.

An ideal entrepreneur is one who combines values in the market economy; that profits do not somehow preclude ethical behaviour: that growth is possible even if political patronage is not used to bend rules and cut corners, and quite simply that pursuit of wealth can be grateful and mannerly one. He takes with him the interest of his people, his country, his natural resources, the ecology and sees that his enterprise becomes a catalytic agent of development. There is thus a need of true entrepreneurs, who do not beg for incentives, infrastructure, government support: but build their enterprises, harness the resources and develop. They adopt a responsible value-driven corporate philosophy for their enterprises and/or business activities. As such, there is no dispute among economists and social thinkers about the urgent need for the emergence of an entrepreneurial society as a forerunner of accelerated development of the economy in an integrated manner.

ANNEXURE-I

BUSINESS SKILLS INVENTORY

The following inventory will help you to assess your strengths and weaknesses as a future small business owner. In this exercise, you need to identify how much knowledge and/or experience you have in relation to each of the skills listed in the inventory. These are the most important skills that you will need to start and run your future contracting business. They have been grouped under various management functions representing the key roles that you will have to play as a business owner.

It is important that you realistically examine your background knowledge and your experience in these key roles. The success of your business depends on how well you are prepared to assume these roles.

Rate yourself on a tour-point scale and circle the figure that you feel most accurately represents your explanation of each category:

1. No knowledge, no experience
2. Some knowledge, but no experience
3. Some experience
4. Much experience

Question: How much knowledge or experience do you have in relation lo each skill listed in the inventory?

I. Marketing the Construction Firm	Your Rating			
I. Identify the Construction Firm				
• Determine the territory within which you will operate.	1	2	3	4
• Determine the types of customers you will serve.	1	2	3	4
• Use Statistics of India as information to assess the size of the target market.	1	2	3	4
• Design a questionnaire to identify potential customers and their needs.	1	2	3	4
• Choose a location for the business.	1	2	3	4
Give yourself an overall rating reflecting low level of competency in identifying your target market.	1	2	3	4
II. Competing with Others				
• Find out how best your competitors are doing.	1	2	3	4
• Analyse how the competitors obtain their contracts.	1	2	3	4
• Determine how your firm will be different from the competition.	1	2	3	4
Give yourself an overall rating reflecting your level of competency in competing with others.	1	2	3	4
Pricing Your Services				
• Set a competitive hourly labour rate.	1	2	3	4
• Prepare an estimate of the costs for providing your services.	1	2	3	4
• Submit bids with/without cost-escalating clauses.	1	2	3	4
• Negotiate contracts with other parties.	1	2	3	4
Give yourself an overall rating reflecting your level of competency in properly pricing your services.	1	2	3	4

Promoting Your Business

• Develop a promotional strategy.	1	2	3	4
• Design promotional materials.	1	2	3	4
• Prepare a budget for advertising.	1	2	3	4
• Use quality of workmanship and customer service as a promotional tool.	1	2	3	4
Give yourself an overall rating reflecting your level of competency in promoting your future construction firm.	1	2	3	4

III. Managing Finances

1. Borrowing Money

• Determine how much money is needed to start and run your business.	1	2	3	4
• Forecast the need for additional capital or cash.	1	2	3	4
• Identify appropriate sources for short-term/ long-term financing.	1	2	3	4
• Negotiate loans.	1	2	3	4
Give yourself an overall rating reflecting your level of competency in borrowing money.	1	2	3	4

2. Managing Money

• Do book-keeping.	1	2	3	4
• Establish and use financial controls.	1	2	3	4
• Set up a cost control system for separate jobs or contracts	1	2	3	4
• Analyse overhead costs.	1	2	3	4
• Prepare profit and loss statements, and balance sheets.	1	2	3	4
• Prepare budgets.	1	2	3	4
Give yourself an overall rating reflecting your level of competency in managing money.	1	2	3	4

3. Analysing Financial Statements

• Prepare a cash flow analysis.	1	2	3	4
• Prepare a break-even analysis.	1	2	3	4
• Understand profit and loss statements, and balance sheets.	1	2	3	4
Give yourself an overall rating reflecting your level of competency in analyzing financial statements.	1	2	3	4

4. Handling Credit and Collection

• Understand current credit policies in the construction industry set by sub-contractor, general contractors and developers.	1	2	3	4
• Design accounts payable and receivable ageing systems.	1	2	3	4
• Use various collection techniques.	1	2	3	4
• Know-how and when to commence legal action, file a lien, go to Small Claim Court.	1	2	3	4
Give yourself an overall rating reflecting your level of competency in handling credit and collection.	1	2	3	4

IV. Organising the Business

1. Handling Legal Issues

• Choose the appropriate: proprietorship, partnership, incorporation.	1	2	3	4
• Write a partnership agreement.	1	2	3	4
• Write a valid contract with general contractors, subcontractors and/or clients.	1	2	3	4
• Determine appropriate terms for a leasing agreement.	1	2	3	4
• Use the litigation process or other alternatives to resolve construction disputes.	1	2	3	4
• Choose a lawyer who can understand your legal problems.	1	2	3	4
Give yourself an overall rating reflecting your level of competency in handling legal issues.	1	2	3	4

2. Complying with Government Regulations

• Obtain appropriate business licences and permits.	1	2	3	4
• Comply with federal, provincial and municipal tax laws.	1	2	3	4
• Comply with the Labour Code: minimum wage, payment of wages, holidays, hours of work. Human Rights code. Worker's Compensation Board.	1	2	3	4
Give yourself an overall rating reflecting your level of competency in complying with government regulations.	1	2	3	4

3. Insuring Your Business

• Purchase proper insurance coverage for important business risks.	1	2	3	4
• Select an insurance broker or company.	1	2	3	4
• Obtain performance bonds.	1	2	3	4
Give yourself an overall rating reflecting your level of competency in insuring your business.	1	2	3	4

V. Managing Business Operations

• Buy supplies from the best sources at the best price possible (including discount).	1	2	3	4
• Buy reliable equipment with adequate warranties.	1	2	3	4
• Negotiate contracts with suppliers.	1	2	3	4
• Use techniques for controlling material inventories.	1	2	3	4
• Set up quality control procedures to ensure quality of workmanship.	1	2	3	4
• Coordinate own work schedule with the schedule of other trades people on the same project.	1	2	3	4
• Set up a system for recording work orders.	1	2	3	4
Give yourself an overall rating reflecting your level of competency in managing your business operations.	1	2	3	4

VI. Managing People

• Develop a job description.	1	2	3	4
• Interview applicants for job available.	1	2	3	4
• Provide employees with feedback on their performance.	1	2	3	4

• Supervise and motivate employees.	1	2	3	4
• Train employees.	1	2	3	4
• Schedule workers on a daily or weekly basis.	1	2	3	4
• Work effectively with other trades on a construction job.	1	2	3	4
Give yourself an overall rating reflecting your level of competency in managing people.	1	2	3	4

The skills for which you have rated yourself as 1 or 2 represent your weaknesses. Before you start your business you should plan on acquiring these skills or find a partner who has such an expertise. You must also plan to improve those skills which are rated 3.

In any case, attempting to develop or improve your skills as you run your business may be very costly and lead to bankruptcy. There will be numerous tasks to accomplish and they will put high demands on your ability to make your business profitable. If you are not sufficiently prepared and organised to have them done, you will soon fall behind and the problems will rapidly pile up with no relief in sight.

The skills which you rated as 4 represent the strengths that will contribute to the success of your future contracting business.

You should not expect to be equally strong in all the functions necessary for operating a business. However, knowing your weaknesses will allow you to see assistance for solving problems requiring those skills.

Consult the overall rates you have assigned to the main functions listed in the inventory (there are 13 overall rates). List your four strongest management functions and your four weakest management functions.

Strongest management functions:

....

....

Weakest management functions:

....

....

"Excellence doesn't happen miraculously but springs from pace setting levels of personal effectiveness and efficiency. Great business, government and non-profit organisations owe their greatness to a few individuals who mastered leadership skills and passed those skills on to others."

4

Qualities and Functions of Entrepreneurs

Introduction

The world is rapidly changing and unless we are also able to change our attitudes and approaches, there is a real danger that a country of India's size and potential will become peripheral in the context of world economy. The process of development includes creation of infrastructure and setting up and management of public utilities. Non-conventional energy sources have to be developed on a commercial scale. Similarly, application of modern scientific techniques in agriculture and horticulture is essential for providing a sound base for a more rapid growth of employment and incomes. There is also a need for rapid growth of industries well distributed and in a multi-directional way. Apart from land, labour and capital, there is greater need for entrepreneurs to strive for growth on an ongoing basis. In this context an attempt has been made in this chapter to analyse the nature and importance of entrepreneurs.

Ratan Tata
(December 28-1937)

Entrepreneurial Qualities

The entrepreneurial qualities are to some extent innate. But not all of them are entirely innate. Some can be enhanced by training, or simply by experience. For example, analytical ability and computational skill can be enhanced by education at school and university, while practical knowledge and foresight skills can be enhanced by the general experience of everyday life. Entrepreneurial careers will be strongly influenced by the desire to enhance qualities which are scarce, yet difficult to obtain through delegation because of the problems involved in screening for them. Of the two indispensable qualities of the entrepreneur, imagination is almost entirely innate, while foresight, though to some extent innate, can be enhanced by a varied experience. Imagination and foresight are the scarce qualities which are difficult to analyse and quantify. Delegation skill and organisation skill, though not essential, are highly desirable whenever large-scale decision-making is contemplated. These too are qualities which can be enhanced through experience.

Entrepreneurial Functions

A successful entrepreneur recognises the commercial potential of a product or service, designs operating policies in marketing, production, product development and the organisational structure. He carries out the whole set of activities of the business. He has a high capacity for taking calculated risks and has faith in his own capabilities.

According to some writers, the functions of an entrepreneur are co-ordination of the business management of the enterprise, risk-taking, controlling the enterprise, innovation for change, motivation and other related activities. In reality, an entrepreneur has to carry out a combination of these in keeping with time and environment. Truly, the entrepreneur has to react to new ideas, demands and exploit the opportunities, and thereby contribute to technical progress. He is thus a nucleus of high growth of the enterprise.

An entrepreneur is expected to perform the following functions:

1. Assumption of Risk: The entrepreneur assumes all possible risks of business. A business risk also involves the risk due to the possibility of changes in the tastes of consumers, techniques of production and new inventions. Such risks are not insurable. If they materialise, the entrepreneur has to bear the loss himself. Thus, risk-bearing or uncertainty bearing still remains the most important function of an entrepreneur. An entrepreneur tries to reduce the uncertainties by his initiative, skill and good judgment.

2. Business Decisions: The entrepreneur has to decide the nature and type of goods to be produced. He enters the particular industry which offers him the best prospects and produces whatever commodities he thinks will pay him the most and employs those methods of production which seem to him the most profitable. He effects suitable changes in the size of the business, its location, techniques of production and does everything that is needed for the development of his business.

3. Managerial Functions: The entrepreneur performs the managerial functions though the managerial functions are different from entrepreneurial functions. He formulates production plans, arranges finance, purchases raw materials, provides production facilities, organises sales and assumes the task of personal management. In a large establishment, these management functions are delegated to the paid managerial personnel.

4. Function of Innovation: An important function of an entrepreneur is "innovation." He conceives the idea for the improvement in the quality of production line. He considers the economic viability and technological feasibility in bringing about improved quality. The introduction of different kinds of electronic gadgets is an example of such an innovation of new products. Innovation is an ongoing function rather than once for all, or possibly intermittent activity.

The entrepreneurial functions can be performed by very different kinds of people under different economic systems. In principle, the entrepreneur could be a planner in a socialist economy, or even a priest or king in a traditional society. In practice, entrepreneurship is closely identified with private enterprise in a market economy.

An entrepreneur performs many useful functions. He undertakes a venture, assumes risk and earns profit. He is the man having a strong motivation to achieve success. He is self-confident in his entrepreneurial abilities. He exploits opportunities wherever and whenever they arise.

The entrepreneur can identify opportunities to start a business either as a manufacturer or as a distributor, for entrepreneurship exists in every field of economic endeavour. Manufacturing activities required a relatively high capital investment and a greater degree of entrepreneurial abilities than distribution activities. Entrepreneurship has also been developed in the trading sector. Britain, for example, has developed trading entrepreneurship while Germany and Japan have developed industrial entrepreneurship. A manufacturing entrepreneur demonstrates his entrepreneurial talents by bringing out new products while a trading entrepreneur performs his entrepreneurial functions in creating demand for the business in which he deals.

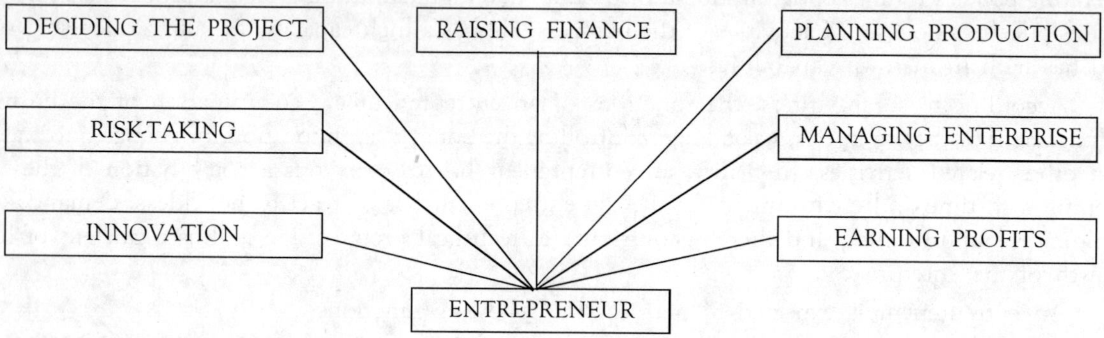

Fig. 1 Entrepreneurial Functions

▸▸ Qualities of an Entrepreneur

A true entrepreneur besides possessing functional qualities, must also possess the broad personality which help in developing initiative and drive to accomplish great tasks and face challenges squarely.

James J. Berne has stressed the following qualities of a good entrepreneur:

1. He is an enterprising individual. He is energetic, hard working, resourceful aware of new opportunities, able to adjust himself to changing conditions with ease and willing to assume risks involved in change.
2. He is interested in advancing technologically and in improving the quality of his product or service.
3. He is interested in expanding the scale of his operations by reinvesting his earnings.
4. He visualises changes and adapts.
5. He is a firm believer in planning and systematic work.
6. He works for the society at large and for the good of his fellow-beings.

These qualities sum up, what is usually implied from the phrase, the "spirit of enterprise." It is difficult to conceivers of a first-rate industrial entrepreneur who is not adaptable to change, anxious to grow larger and improve technologically.

Entrepreneurship appears as a personal quality which enables certain individuals to make decisions with far-reaching consequences. The personal qualities that contribute to the success of an entrepreneur are as follows:

1. Motivation Towards Achievement: A successful entrepreneur should be a good administrator. He should know the art of getting things done by other people without hurting their feelings or self-respect. He should have a strong motivation towards the achievement of a task and must be able to exert considerable efforts in getting things done by others.

2. Creativity: Mental ability consists of intelligence, an analytical approach and creative things. An entrepreneur should have creative thinking and be able to engage in the analysis of various problems and situations in order to deal with them. The entrepreneur should anticipate changes and must be able to study various situations in which decisions may have to be made.

3. Clarity: An entrepreneur should have clear objectives as to the exact nature of the business, the nature of the goods to be produced and the subsidiary activities to be undertaken.

The qualities of an entrepreneur are given in Fig. 2.

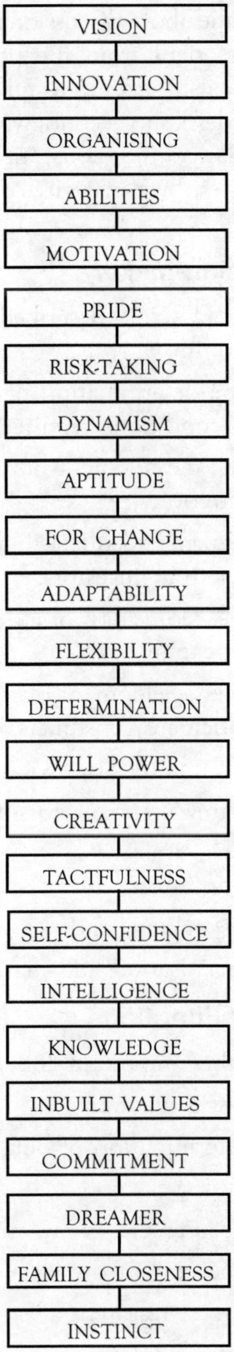

Fig. 2 Qualities of a Successful Entrepreneur

Kilby has rightly enumerated the following activities for a successful entrepreneur in an underdeveloped economy:

1. Perception of market opportunities (novel or imitative).
2. Gaining command over scarce resources.
3. Purchasing of inputs.
4. Marketing of the product and responding effectively to competition.
5. Dealing with public bureaucracy as regards concessions, licences, taxes, etc. provided through the various fiscal policies of the government.
6. Management of the human relations within the enterprise.
7. Management of customer and supplier relations.
8. Financial Management.
9. Production management, including control through written records, supervision, coordinating input flows with orders, maintenance.
10. Acquiring and overseeing assembly of the plant.
11. Taking care for minimising inputs for a given production process.
12. Maintaining the production process and improving the quality of the product.
13. Introduction of new production techniques and product lines.

From the above discussion and definitions, it can be stated that entrepreneurial activities encompass those factors right from the perception of the profitable opportunity to its translation into reality through establishing a successful enterprise and further leading to its growth and development. Especially in an underdeveloped economy, the expectations from entrepreneurial units are much more varied and related to many dimensions, including socio-economic objectives. This is because this type of economy is characterised by a majority of low income strata than the developed economy characterised by high income.

⏩ Decision-maker

Arther H. Cole described an entrepreneur as a decision-maker and attributed the following functions to him:

1. The determination of those objectives of the enterprise and the change of those objectives as conditions required or made advantageous;
2. The development of an organisation, including efficient relations with subordinates and all employees;
3. Securing adequate financial resources, and maintaining good relations with the existing and potential investors;
4. The requisition of efficient technological equipment and the revision of it as new machinery appeared;
5. The development of a market for the products and the devising of new products to meet or anticipate consumers' demand; and
6. The maintenance of good relations with public authorities and with the society at large.

Modern writers on this subject have outlined the following three broad functions of an entrepreneur:

1. Innovation,
2. Risk-taking, and
3. Organisation and management of business so as to have leadership and control over it.

⏩ Other Functions

The other important functions of the entrepreneurs are:

1. Idea generation
2. Determination of objectives
3. Raising of funds
4. Procurement of raw materials, machinery
5. Procuring of the necessary licences and clearance from the respective authorities
6. Market research
7. Determination of the form of enterprise
8. Recruitment of manpower
9. Implementation of the project
10. Organising production
11. Ensuring quality

12. Branding products
13. Promoting brands/products
14. Innovating technology
15. Improving working conditions
16. Controlling costs, quality etc.

▸▸ Entrepreneur vs. Entrepreneurship

The term "entrepreneur" is often used interchangeably with "entrepreneurship." But, conceptually, they are different, yet they are just like the two sides of a coin. Their differences are as follows:

Entrepreneur	*Entrepreneurship*
Refers to a Person:	Refers to a Process:
Visualiser	Vision
Creator	Creation
Organiser	Organisation
Innovator	Innovation
Technician	Technology
Initiator	Initiative
Decision-maker	Decision
Planner	Planning
Leader	Leadership
Motivator	Motivation
Programmer	Action
Risk-taker	Risk-taking
Communicator	Communication
Administrator	Administration

Entrepreneurship management is basically concerned with the development and co-ordination of entrepreneurial functions. In a way, entrepreneur precedes entrepreneurship.

Experience shows that entrepreneurship as an economic function is not a single point but rather a range of behaviour. There are six critical dimensions that distinguish entrepreneurial behaviour from more administratively-oriented behaviour: (1) strategic orientation (2) commitment to opportunity (3) the resource commitment process (4) the concept of control over resources (5) the concept of management and (6) compensation policy.

		Desired future state involves growth or change	
		Yes	No
Self-perceived power to achieve goals	Yes	Entrepreneur	Satisfied manager
	No	Frustrated potential entrepreneur	Bureaucratic functionary

Fig. 3 Manager's Opportunity Matrix

A matrix defining entrepreneurship is shown in Fig. 3, one can see how the present position influences whether one is entrepreneurial or not. It is also clear that particular skills, talents, and attitudes toward risk influence the perception as to whether an outcome is feasible. Training, knowledge, and self-confidence contribute to such perceptions.

The importance of this figure cannot be overemphasized since individuals place themselves in their particular box for rational reasons relating to their own lives; however, for the firms desiring to build the entrepreneurial spirit, action is required.

Creation of a Dream

Creating a dream gives entrepreneurs the energy and desire to become involved in its implementation and to be willing to change. During the formulation of the dream, everyone participates (including the leaders), and this allows people to start seeing each other in a different light. How long they will maintain their commitment depends upon (*a*) how well the organisation's leaders function in their new role of facilitating resolution of the needs or issues that are at variance with the dream, (*b*) how clearly the leaders articulate and share information about the business needs, and (*c*) how well the leaders openly acknowledge their willingness to change in whatever fashion to attain the dream.

The process of creating the dream should be tailored to the situation with the objective of having the entire organisation ultimately own the dream. In a large organisation, there will be many dreams formulated by interdependent parts of the organisation. At some point, these should be integrated into a total organisational dream. We have found that creating a dream in a bottoms-up manner where all organisational levels participate in some fashion is better than a tiered, top-down approach.

To illustrate the content of a typical dream, let us look at the leadership portion of one from a Honeywell factory, which evolved as follows:

Leadership should be the ability of those leading work units (managers, supervisors, engineers, technical support, and group leaders) to create an atmosphere of acceptance, openness, and trust that will properly motivate members of the work units.

Interpersonal competence should be the ability to relate to people in a considerate and effective way.

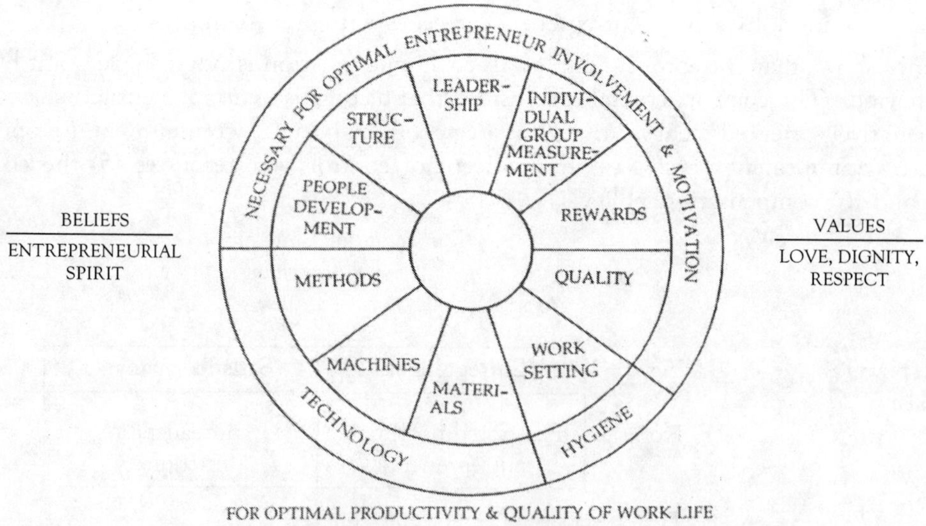

For Optimal Productivity & Quality of Work Life

Fig. 4 Basic Elements — Entrepreneurial Involvement

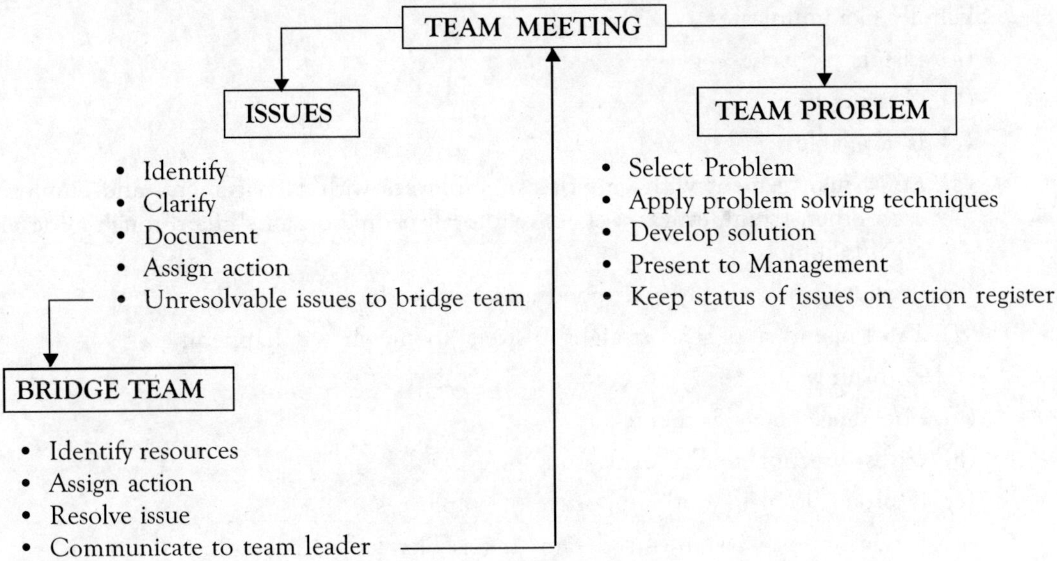

Fig. 5 Team Process

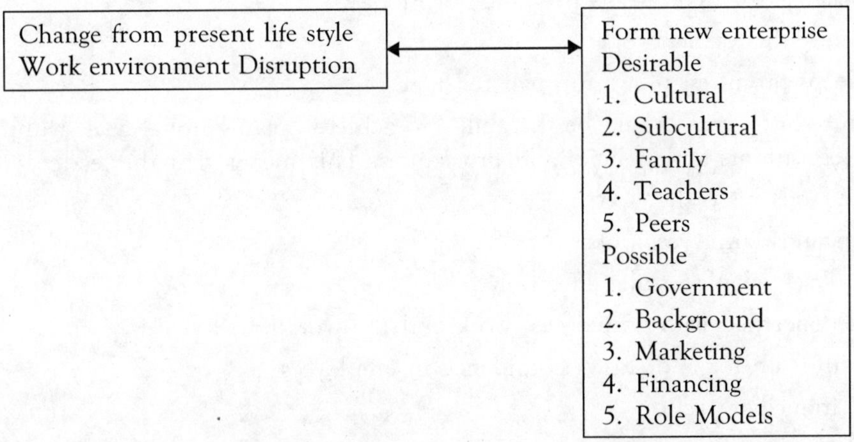

Fig. 5 Decision for a Potential Entrepreneur

This means that the leader:

1. Cares
   - (*a*) Gives positive feedback for a good job.
   - (*b*) Shows confidence in employees.
   - (*c*) Is fair and objective, not vindictive.
   - (*d*) Practises what is preached; does not ask for something that he or she would not be willing to do.
   - (*e*) Has a down-to-earth, person-to-person approach acts as part of a team.
   - (*f*) Is compassionate and understanding; creates an atmosphere of acceptance and trust.

2. Skillfully Communicates
   (*a*) Listens actively.
   (*b*) Clarifies priorities.
   (*c*) Is available.
   (*d*) Links management with employees, employees with management, and employees with each other. Communicates effectively to all people on all shifts through all levels of the organisation.
   (*e*) Provides feedback for both good and bad work.
   (*f*) Talks openly and gives straight answers about what is happening.
3. Guides, Inspires
   (*a*) Encourages advancement.
   (*b*) Gives direction to the work unit.
   (*c*) Is proud, loyal to, and supportive of employees.
   (*d*) Has a sense of vision – a dream that is blended with employees' dream.
   (*e*) Projects a positive attitude.
   (*f*) Is courageous.
   (*g*) Sets a good example; is friendly, not moody.
   (*h*) Enjoys his or her work.
   (*i*) Keeps promises; plows through red tape.

Administrative competence should be the ability to achieve organisational goals within the bounds of the business constraints and policies and procedures. This means that the leader:

1. Understands his or her job.
2. Understands employees' jobs:
   (*a*) Utilises people's skills effectively.
   (*b*) Is concerned with employees' work and the workflow.
   (*c*) Stands up for and shows confidence in employees.
3. Takes immediate action:
   (*a*) Does not ignore problems.
   (*b*) Follows up on promises.
   (*c*) Gets tough when necessary.
   (*d*) Takes action to remove poor performers.
   (*e*) Assures that the next in command knows his role and has authority to act.
   (*f*) Provides proper human resources for all shifts and all levels of organisation.

▸▸ Entrepreneurial Decision

Entrepreneurial decisions occur despite recession, inflation, high interest rates, lack of infrastructure, economic uncertainty etc. Each of these decisions is a personal human process that, although unique, has some common characteristics. The impulsive motive to change his/her life style and create something new and an inner urge to do something worthy, are the forces behind these decisions. At times, perhaps seven more stimulation for change comes from a negative force – disruption. At times, the available opportunities force a decision on individuals to take up entrepreneurial work. Like all processes, it entails movement from something to something new as indicated in Fig. 6.

What causes this change due to the work environment or disruption to result in a new company being formed instead of something else? The decision to start a new company occurs when an individual perceives that it is both desirable and possible.

⏩ Conclusion

The perception that starting a new company is desirable results from an individual's culture, subculture, teachers, family, and peers. A culture that values an individual who successfully creates a new business will spawn more company formations than one that does not. For example, India places a high value on being your own boss, individual opportunity, being a success, and making money – all aspects of entrepreneurship. What is more, many different sub-cultures that shape value, systems are operating within a cultural framework. More importantly, these subcultures support and even promote entrepreneurship. Thus, entrepreneurial decision has more bearing on sociological, cultural, subcultural, psychological and political environment, while, satisfaction and adequate reward are the optimistic goals.

Thus emerges the notion of the "genius entrepreneur" whose success is in a large measure caused by his unswerving dedication to settling high goals and to reaching for them. He has vision on which he bases his own objectives and sets his own goals. And he does this not simply on the basis of last year's results plus some growth factor, but on the basis of his own perception of his own capabilities and to satisfy his own needs.

Among other distinguishing attributes of entrepreneurship are a willingness to assume risk; a sense of acquisitiveness or unceasing curiosity; insight into the relationship between concepts, objectives, needs; and needs satisfaction; sound judgement as to what is central and peripheral to attaining his objectives; initiative and creativity: problem-solving ability; ability to marshall resources needed to achieve his objectives and goals; and the administrative ability to organize those resources to accomplish his goals and satisfy his minor needs.

The qualities and functions of entrepreneur's excellence generates effectiveness and efficiency in business.

ANNEXURE 1

ENTREPRENEUR SELF-ASSESSMENT PROFILE

Instruction

This questionnaire will help you look at your personal background, behaviour patterns, and lifestyle in relation to what is known about entrepreneurs. The questions were designed to represent some of the characteristics studies have shown, that entrepreneurs tend to exhibit. Put an X under the responses – **Rarely or No** or **Mostly or Yes** – that best represents your answer to each question. Be honest – there are no wrong answers. Complete all 50 questions.

	Rarely or No	Mostly or Yes
1. Do you worry about what others think of you?	________	________
2. Do you read books, watch television or play sports?	________	________
3. Do you take risks for the thrill of it?	________	________
4. Do you find it easy to get others to do something for you?	________	________
5. Has someone in your family shared the experience of starting a business with you?	________	________
6. Do you believe in organizing your tasks before getting started?	________	________
7. Do you get sick often?	________	________
8. Do you enjoy doing something just to prove that you can?	________	________
9. Have you ever been fired from a job?	________	________
10. Do you find yourself constantly thinking of new ideas?	________	________
11. Do you prefer to let a friend decide on your social activities?	________	________
12. Did you like school or college?	________	________
13. Were you a very good student?	________	________
14. Did you participate in school activities or sports?	________	________
15. Do you like to take care of details?	________	________
16. Do you believe there should be security in a job?	________	________
17. Will you deliberately seek a direct confrontation to get needed results?	________	________
18. Were you the first born child?	________	________
19. Was your father mostly present during your early life at home?	________	________
20. Were you expected to do odd jobs at home before ten years of age?	________	________
21. Do you get bored easily?	________	________
22. Are you sometimes arrogant about your accomplishments?	________	________
23. Can you concentrate for extended periods of time on one subject?	________	________

24. Do you, on occasion, need pep talks from others to keep you going? ________ ________
25. Do you find unexpected energy resources as you tackle things you like? ________ ________
26. Does personal satisfaction mean more to you than having money to spend on yourself? ________ ________
27. Do you enjoy socializing regularly? ________ ________
28. Have you ever deliberately exceeded your authority at work? ________ ________
29. Do you try to find the benefits of a bad situation? ________ ________
30. Do you blame others when something goes wrong? ________ ________
31. Do you enjoy tackling a task without knowing all the potential problems? ________ ________
32. Do you persist when someone tells you it can't be done? ________ ________
33. Do you take rejection personally? ________ ________
34. Do you believe that you generally have a lot of good luck that explains your successes? ________ ________
35. Are you likely to work long hours to accomplish a goal? ________ ________
36. Do you enjoy being able to make your own decisions on the job? ________ ________
37. Did you wake up happy most of your life? ________ ________
38. Can you accept failure without admitting defeat? ________ ________
39. Do you have a savings account and other personal investments? ________ ________
40. Do you believe that entrepreneurs take a huge risk? ________ ________
41. Do you believe that entrepreneurs must have advanced college degrees? ________ ________
42. Do you strive to use past mistakes as a learning process? ________ ________
43. Are you more people-oriented than goal-oriented? ________ ________
44. Do you find the answers to problems come to you out of nowhere? ________ ________
45. Do you enjoy finding an answer to a frustrating problem? ________ ________
46. Do you prefer to be a loner in your final decision? ________ ________
47. Do your conversations discuss people more than events or ideas? ________ ________
48. Do you feel good about yourself in spite of criticism by others? ________ ________
49. Do you sleep as little as possible? ________ ________

Reproduced with permission from "Beyond a Dream – An Instructor's Guide for Small Business Exploration." The National Centre for Research in Vocational Education.

ANNEXURE 2

ENTREPRENEUR SELF-ASSESSMENT PROFILE GUIDE

Instructions

The 49 questions have been grouped into three categories: personal background, behaviour patterns, and lifestyle. Each question addresses specific areas that relate to entrepreneurs; these areas are noted in the parenthesis following each question. The answers you see here are what studies show to be the responses commonly given by small business owners. You will want to compare your answers from the survey to what is shown here for similarities and conflicts.

Personal Background

	Rarely or No	Mostly or Yes
5. Has someone in your family shared the experience of starting a business with you? (family training)		
7. Do you get sick often? (attitude, energy, health)		
9. Have you ever been fired from a job? (displacement experience)		
12. Did you like school or college? (education)		
13. Were you a very good student? (average is common)		
14. Did you participate in school activities or sports? (need to achieve)		
18. Were you the first-born child?		
19. Was your father mostly present during your early life at home? (early responsibility)		
20. Were you expected to do odd jobs at home before ten years of age? (early experience)		

Behaviour Patterns

	Rarely or No	Mostly or Yes
1. Do you worry about what others think of you? (self-confidence, locus of control)		
3. Do you take risks for the thrill of it? (risk taking, internal locus of control)		
4. Do you find it easy to get others to do something for you? (leadership)		
6. Do you believe in organizing your tasks before getting started? (management, goal setting)		
8. Do you enjoy doing something just to prove that you can? (achievement oriented)		
10. Do you find yourself constantly thinking of new ideas? (creative, innovation)		
15. Do you like to take care of details? (impatience, risk oriented)		
16. Do you believe there should be security in a job? (internal locus of control)		

17. Will you deliberately seek a direct confrontation to get needed results? (determination, assertiveness) ________ ________
21. Do you get bored easily? (impatience, energy) ________ ________
22. Are you sometimes arrogant about your accomplishments? (self-confidence, independence) ________ ________
23. Can you concentrate for extended periods of time on one subject? (perseverance, determination) ________ ________
24. Do you, on occasion, need pep talks from others to keep you going? (self-starter, self-control) ________ ________
25. Do you find unexpected energy resources as you tackle things you like? (energy, resourcefulness) ________ ________
26. Does personal satisfaction mean more to you than having money to spend on yourself? (egoism) ________ ________
28. Have you ever deliberately exceeded your authority at work? (self-confidence, assertiveness) ________ ________
29. Do you try to find the benefits of a bad situation? (optimism, flexibility) ________ ________
30. Do you blame others when something goes wrong? (personal ability, problem solving) ________ ________
31. Do you enjoy tackling a task without knowing all the potential problems? (resourcefulness, risk taking) ________ ________
32. Do you persist when others tell you it can't be done? (optimism) ________ ________
33. Do you take rejection personally? (flexibility, self-confidence) ________ ________
34. Do you believe that you generally have a lot of good luck that explains your successes? (internal locus of control) ________ ________
36. Do you enjoy being able to make your own decisions on the job? (independence, responsibility) ________ ________
37. Did you wake up happy most of your life? (optimism) ________ ________
38. Can you accept failure without admitting defeat? (determination, optimism) ________ ________
40. Do you believe that entrepreneurs take a huge risk? (self-confidence, internal control) ________ ________
41. Do you believe that entrepreneurs must have advanced college degrees? (resourcefulness, initiative) ________ ________
42. Do you strive to use past mistakes as a learning process? (initiative, optimism) ________ ________
44. Do you find the answers to problems come to you out of nowhere? (foresight, perceptiveness, persistent) ________ ________
45. Do you enjoy finding an answer to a frustrating problem? (tolerance of ambiguity, initiative) ________ ________

Lifestyle

2. Do you read books, watch television or play sports? (time available) ________ ________
II. Do you prefer to let a friend decide on your social activities? (control, responsibility) ________ ________
27. Do you enjoy socializing regularly? (goal oriented, time management) ________ ________
35. Are you likely to work long hours to accomplish a goal? (persistence, determination) ________ ________
39. Do you have a savings account and other personal investments? (profit oriented) ________ ________
43. Are you more people oriented than goal oriented? (need to achieve) ________ ________
46. Do you prefer to be a loner in your final decision?
47. Do your conversations discuss people more than events or ideas? (idea oriented, creativity) ________ ________
48. Do you feel good about yourself in spite of criticism of others? (tolerance of ambiguity, self-confidence) ________ ________
49. Do you sleep as little as possible? (time management, energy) ________ ________

Reproduced with permission from "Beyond a Dream – An instructor's guide for small business, exploration." The National Centre for Research in Vocational Education.

LEADERSHIP WITHOUT BOSSING AROUND

"Followers raise real challenges for leaders because they are less and less leading through formal authority and are leading more through generating genuine excitement and meaningfulness of work."

— Prof. Harry Davis, Chicago Business School

5

Entrepreneurial Traits

Introduction

Entrepreneurial traits are an indispensable function of an efficient and effective management of an enterprise or an service units. The entrepreneurial traits thus form the rock foundation of the enterprise/ project. In short, these traits distinguish entrepreneurs from others. The entrepreneurs have some basic values, dreams, visions and responsibilities.

V.G. Siddhartha
Chairman, Amalgamated Bean Coffee Trading Co. Ltd.

Whenever we are looking around, we find certain entrepreneurs doing exceedingly well. They are managing their enterprises very well and are out to make them grand success. The various questions that normally arise are – who are they? What they possess? and various other questions related with their style of functioning. In their case there is a judicious mixture of knowledge, skill and personality. All these are called entrepreneurial traits or competencies. Knowledge refers to the collection and retention of information about any job or activity. Knowledge forms the basis for any action. Only knowledge cannot ensure success. Success depends upon the ability or skill of using the acquired knowledge for achieving desired results. Skill refers to practical application or use of the knowledge. Thus performance depends upon both knowledge and skill. Motivation is an inner urge in an individual which calls for action. According to Steneir "A motive is an inner state that energises, activates or moves and directs or channels behaviour goals." It is this inner urge in an individual to achieve his/her goal which David McClelland has termed as 'Achievement Motivation.' It is this stage to achieve goal which prompts the individual to perform better and better. Thus ion order to achieve success in any venture a person must possess a judicious combination of knowledge, skill and motive.

In this chapter, we shall examine the entrepreneurial traits.

Traits of a Good Leader

- Decision Making
- Leading by Example
- Setting Standards
- Multi Tasking
- Building Relationship
- Creativity
- Dedication
- Commitment
- Mission
- Vision
- Resolving Conflicts
- Team Player
- Approachable
- Appreciating Skills
- Integrity
- Trust
- Passion
- Compassion
- Capability
- Involvement
- Presence of mind
- Energy
- Clarity of thought
- Patience
- Daring to dream
- Sincerity
- Trust
- Honesty

The Way of the Future

The way of the future is to be able to generate enough from the ground floor to be able to built the first floor. Family businesses will be consolidated and professionalised, brands are built, customer focussed and strong entrepreneurship will become normal. Success rates must need to be spotty, but if some of them can expand their education and vision to encompass cutting edge technology, the returns will be the stuff of legends. A brief profile of six modern Indian industries is presented here as a measure of economic development in the 21st century.

In his book "Power Shift", Alvin Toffler had predicted that the landscape of tomorrow will be *terra incognita,* which implies that the future will be unknown terrain where the sheer pace of change will dictate uncertainty. Corporations will either plan or be forced to plan their future. An organisation choosing the volitional route will take control of its destiny through proactive initiative, the creative challenge will be to create marketing outfit that will be intelligent and will invite customers and partners to climb aboard and create an operating framework for sustained competitive superiority. This will be imperative as it is getting increasingly difficult to define what business an organisation is in and with which industry it is competing. Showing that we heartily subscribe to Charle Han's observation, "Winners are those who invest the future and not those who respond to it."

CHART I

Examples of three types of essential capabilities that help enterprises create benefits desired/appreciated by customers and also reduce cost of creating and delivering such benefits

1. Product specific capabilities visible to customers
   - Quality of the total product and also that of the individual components of the same
   - Performance features/attributes
   - Range/variety
   - New products/upgrades
2. Process specific capabilities – visible to customers (Transaction related)
   - Order fulfilment process
   - Pre and post sales services
   - Tendering process
   - Dealer management process
   - Order tracking process
   - Meeting special or emergency requirements (product/quality/volume/packaging)
   - Complaint handling process and for resolving customer's problem.
   - Documentation
3. Process specific capabilities – invisible to customers (leading to creating product transaction specific benefits (Ref. in (1) and (2) or helping in reducing the cost)
   - Creation and management of database on low cost and right quality inputs
   - Value engineering process
   - Selection process for sub-contractors/vendors
   - Purchase process
   - Material movement process (from suppliers to manufacturers to customers)
   - PPC process
   - Production process/set up process/methods
   - New product development process
   - Quality assurance process
   - Support services processing (*e.g.,* bill/processing, credit not issued etc.)

To deal with entrepreneurial skills is to concern oneself with a wide coverage of aspects of setting up an enterprise and its management. It is not confined to visualisation, planning, setting-up and risk-taking. The skills which an entrepreneur possesses include his ability to deal with new situations, organisations and social and economic forces as they emerge from time to time. The skills to deal with a situation, forevisualised or suddenly emerging, must be an essential characteristic of an entrepreneur.

The small entrepreneur must have the skill to elicit positive response from administrators, bankers, infrastructure institutions, clients and employees.

The entrepreneur is rarely a master of all management skills, and yet is usually directly responsible for all aspects of business. Often he or she has to be the general manager, production manager, purchasing manager, personnel manager, controller and research organiser for the business, all rolled into one, at least during its early years. The entrepreneur has, therefore, to have an understanding of marketing, quality control, finance, banking, commercial law, government regulations and procedures, traditionally trade-oriented families. Now there is emphasis on new classes of entrepreneurs. These would include women, tribals and young men from non-traditional families. For women entrepreneurs, special training facilities have to be provided owing to the special difficulties faced by them as compared to men. For tribal entrepreneurs, and human relations as each of them has a vital bearing on the health of the enterprise.

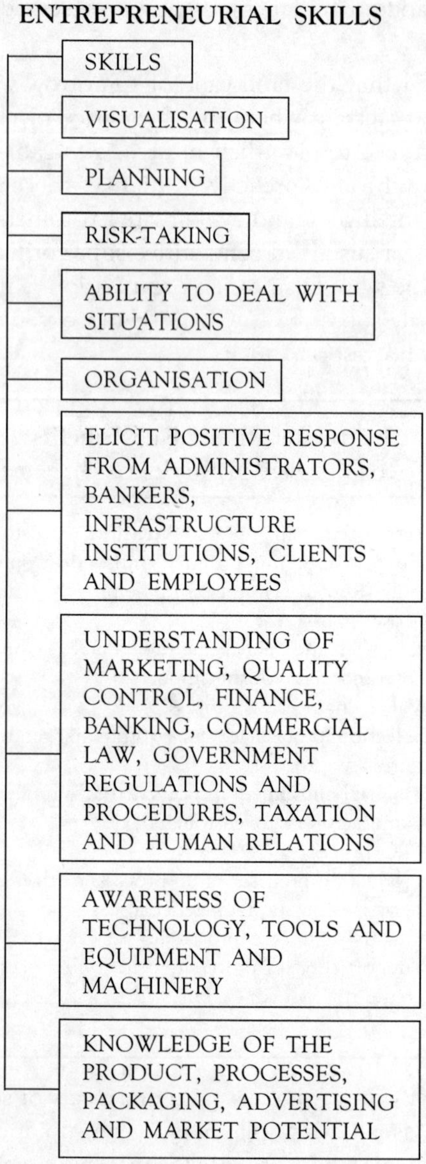

Fig. 1. Entrepreneurial Skills

Willingness to Change

Adding value requires willingness to change. Adding something innovative springs from nurturing attitudes. And as research and development build a critical mass, new products and services increasingly happen.

The journey of change is not without its obstacles. But it is also a journey that is full of rewards. The key to reaping the rewards and minimizing the breakdowns is to lead with your heart, not your head. Your heart is where you will find your willingness. Your head is where you will find resistance and fear.

When we begin to feel resistance and fear that it can be easy to lose touch with the willingness that we had at the beginning of the process. When this happens, we need to focus on reconnecting with the part of us that originally wanted make the change – the part that is excited about learning new things, facing new challenges, and bringing more joy and fulfillment to our life.

Adding value is not simply a matter of doing good – rather it is a synergistic process. It is a collaborative process of problem solving and of designing robust systems that produce goods and services that meet customer needs and specifications. It is a process of making thousands of moments of truth happy experiences for those involved.

Adding value is easier when we use the right tool for the job. Adding something new can come from the tool of stretch goals. Cutting waste, reducing failure costs, and delivery problems comes from tools of substraction, from employing the tool of simplicity. Intensification of effort can come from incentive tools, and from the tool of division – from focus of effort upon specific tasks. Adding value can come from teaming up to do a job, from enlisting others in a pyramid of effort.

Adding value goes beyond customer satisfaction to customer confidence. Trust is generated from honest relationships that are built into goods and services. It means being able to depend upon those who have earned that trust.

Add value to your life by self-improvement. The Japanese have a term for the kind of attitude and action they want their employees to nurture; it is kaizen. Kaizen means to continuously find small ways of improving yourself in whatever you do. It is an attitude that manifests itself in action. How does one do that? It is a matter of improving one's character, ones personality, one's relationships, and by increasing one's skill level.

At the company level, less rather than more, means finding ways to cut waste, cut costs, and to make one's product and service better fit one's customers: more durable, easier to use, more beautiful, and more accessible. Some gurus of quality refer to this as cutting failure costs – the aggregate cost of failure to do things right. Not doing it right costs in inspection, complaints, loss of customers, and rework. Less waste is more profit.

Need for Skills

We often talk of transfer of technology. As a matter of fact, the whole world is talking about it. There is hardly any international event at global and regional level where this subject does not come up for discussion. The poor nations demand technology and resources from industrialised and rich countries and rightly so. The developing countries would rather export semi-finished and finished products which are value added than export raw materials. The development of entrepreneurial skill must precede transfer of technology if we do not desire to keep such technologies and equipment serving such technologies idle. One has also to realise that technologies are developing very fast and skills also to match with this dynamic growth. The entrepreneur has to be made aware of the imperative needs of updated technologies, modern tools and equipments, processes and systems and skills. In this task, his whole organisation, however small it may be, has to join the exercise.

It is observed that in many least developed countries, sophisticated equipment and machinery imported at heavy cost, often under pressure of international financial institutions or aid agreements, are lying unutilised for want of trained hands. It is obvious that the accelerated development of human resources and appropriate training of manpower must be concurrent with the transfer of technologies which are relevant to the needs of each developing country. This will call for an inventory of existing manpower, degree of their present skills, arrangements for proper imparting and skills needed. This should have a relation to natural endowment and resources and their optimum utilisation.

Chart 2

The Skills Needed

- Individual skills
- Functional skills specific to jobs
- Knowledge skills
- Analytical skills
- Problem solving skills
- Negotiation skills
- Out of the box thinking skills
- Interpersonal skills/communication skills
- Business skills
- Management skills
- Behavioural skills
- Learning skills

Shital Kakkar Mehra

- Planning and implementation skills
- Ability to relate/understand disparate information/technology to develop new product/process service ideas
- Flexibility to work under unstructured/fast changing environment
- Risk Management skills

Group Skills

- Ability to work together
- Ability to learn together
- Ability to use task forces/project teams
- Ability to work in unstructured situation
- Ability to work with "tight" resource base

Technical Skills

- Writing
- Oral communication
- Monitoring environment
- Technical business management
- Technology
- Interpersonal
- Listening
- Ability to organize
- Network building
- Management style
- Coaching
- Being a team player

Business Management Skills

- Planning and goal setting
- Decision making
- Human relations
- Marketing
- Finance
- Accounting
- Management
- Control
- Negotiation
- Venture launch
- Managing growth

Personal Entrepreneurial Skills

- Inner control/disciplined
- Risk taker

- Innovative
- Change oriented
- Persistent
- Visionary leader
- Ability to manage change

Enterprise Skills

- Identify value creating processes and capabilities that leads to either differentiation or cost or both
- Market sensing skill
- Creating/setting new direction/vision
- Pulling in place a right organizational structure/systems/physical infrastructure
- Selecting the right people
- Inculcating ethics/principle centred management
- Encouraging subsidiaries/departments/functions to innovate
- Establishing networks and alliance
- Set clearly defined goals
- Never waiver in your belief that you can achieve them
- Manage your attitude and discipline
- Persevere when adversity strikes
- Learn to take risk and embrace change
- Love and be loved
- Make a difference whenever, wherever, and however, you can
- Behavioural skills
- Motivation
- Judgement
- Resilience
- Initiative
- Team working
- Self Management
- Self confidence
- Improvement reorientation
- Trust yourself
- Intuition taking

Communication Skills

- Be flexible
- Able to identify an opportunity to communicate
- Don't blow your own trumpet
- Put your intelligence into words

- Emphasise on the issue
- Communicate well
- Communicate with illustrations
- Interact effectively
  (*i*) Self-awareness
  (*ii*) Empathy
  (*iii*) Responsiveness
  (*iv*) Alertness
  (*v*) Timeliness
  (*vi*) Proficiency
  (*vii*) Clarity
  (*viii*) Focus
  (*ix*) Compassionation
  (*x*) Positive attitude
  (*xi*) Dissemination
  (*xii*) Presentation
  (*xiii*) Listen willingly

Listening Skills

- Listen without the intervention of any thoughts
- Pay more attention to others
- Establish rapport
- Actively listen

Soft Skills

- Using your knowledge effectively
- Clarity in expressions
- Read a lot
- Rapport building
- Be alive and alert
- Good knowledge of English
- Step out of the box, physically and mentally
- Taking lead

Call it a premonition, an instinct, a feeling – whatever you lable it, it's your intuition talking. Intuition by definition is quick and ready insight. The more you practice identifying, listening to, and acting on your intuition, the more you'll trust your instincts in the future, which is the first step to building the life you truly want. Once you know where you want to go intuition will show you how to get there. So, tune into your intuition and go with your gut.

A Learning Organisation

- Is an active philosophy; not merely an organisational system
- Believes that its only competitive advantage is learning
- Encourages people to learn to produce the results they desire
- Nurtures creative and innovative patterns of collective learning
- Develops fresh organisational capabilities all the time
- Never underestimate the power of belief when it comes to fulfilling your dreams.
- Belief fuels enthusiasm. Ride the wave of passion and manage your attitude. Continue to dream big dreams, but realise that short-term goals that take you to the next plateau are the real keys to success. Goals are dreams with deadlines.
- Tap your creative soul – imaging. Imagination is seeing things, not as they are, but as they could be. Have heroes. Failure is a big part of life, but it is how we react to failing that will determine our destiny. If we learn from it and move on, it can help to make us all we can be.
- To get what you have never had, you must do what you have never done. When you face adversity, be focused but patient, and the right answers will usually surface before you know it. Exercise to energise. Exercise is a small price.

The World Health Organisation defines life skills as the abilities for adaptive and positive behaviour that enable individuals to deal effectively with the demands and challenges of everyday life.

WHO categorises life skills into three components

- Thinking skills: self-awareness, social awareness, goal-setting, problem-solving and decision-making. To be able to think critically, information must be provided to make informed decisions and choices. Skills to think critically can be developed if teenagers are given the opportunity to look at different perspectives of an issue, the pros and the cons of making a decision over the other and making them realise the negative consequences of making hasty, unplanned decisions.
- Social skills: appreciating/validating others; working with others; understanding their roles; building positive relationships with friends and family; listening and communicating effectively; taking responsibility and coping with stress. These enable adolescents to be accepted in society and accept social norms which provide the foundation for adult social behaviour.
- Negotiation skills mean not only negotiating with others but with oneself. To negotiate with others, one needs to know what one wants in life; is firm on one's values and beliefs and can, therefore, say 'no' to harmful behaviour and risky temptations.

The Global Leader of the Future

- Thinks globally
- Anticipates opportunity
- Creates a shared vision
- Develops and empowers people
- Appreciates cultural diversity
- Builds teamwork and partnerships

- Embraces change
- Shows technological savvy
- Encourages constructive challenge
- Ensures customer satisfaction
- Achieves a competitive advantage
- Demonstrates personal mastery
- Shapes leadership lives and the values.

Your Skills are Integral to Growth

We attribute our achievements to the commitment and exceptional qualities of our people who drive the company forward.

- Analytical skills.
- Understanding of financial products and markets.
- Knowledge and exposure to data sources such as Bloomberg, Thomson, etc.
- Knowledge of Excel, Access and other databases.
- Quantitative modelling skills gained from advanced degree.
- Exposure to linear and non-linear programming.
- Knowledge of derivatives, options and statistics
- Basic programming skills (VBA, C++, Metlab, Mathematical).
- Programming skills in Oracle OLAP and SQL in a financial environment.
- Familiarity with equities, exchanges, Bloomberg. Experience of working with data sources such as MSCI, Dow Jones, FTSE would be preferred.
- Exposure to international environment.
- Thorough knowledge of English grammar and punctuation, British and American idioms.
- Ability to correct language without changing meaning, while retaining the original "tone" of research.
- Ability to understand and internet business figures and data.
- Time management, quick grasping power, a keen eye for detail, perseverance and ability to work with large numbers.

Good communication, presentation skills and experience in MS Office tools is a common requirement.

Types of Skills

Types of skills will vary according to location, products, clientele etc. In the rural areas, a small enterprise making goods for local consumption based on local raw materials would need relatively simpler skills. In urban areas, the product, processes, packaging, advertising have to match with the growing sophistication of consumer goods, preference of needs etc. They call for an intensification of effort to develop matched skills in all areas of entrepreneurial activity.

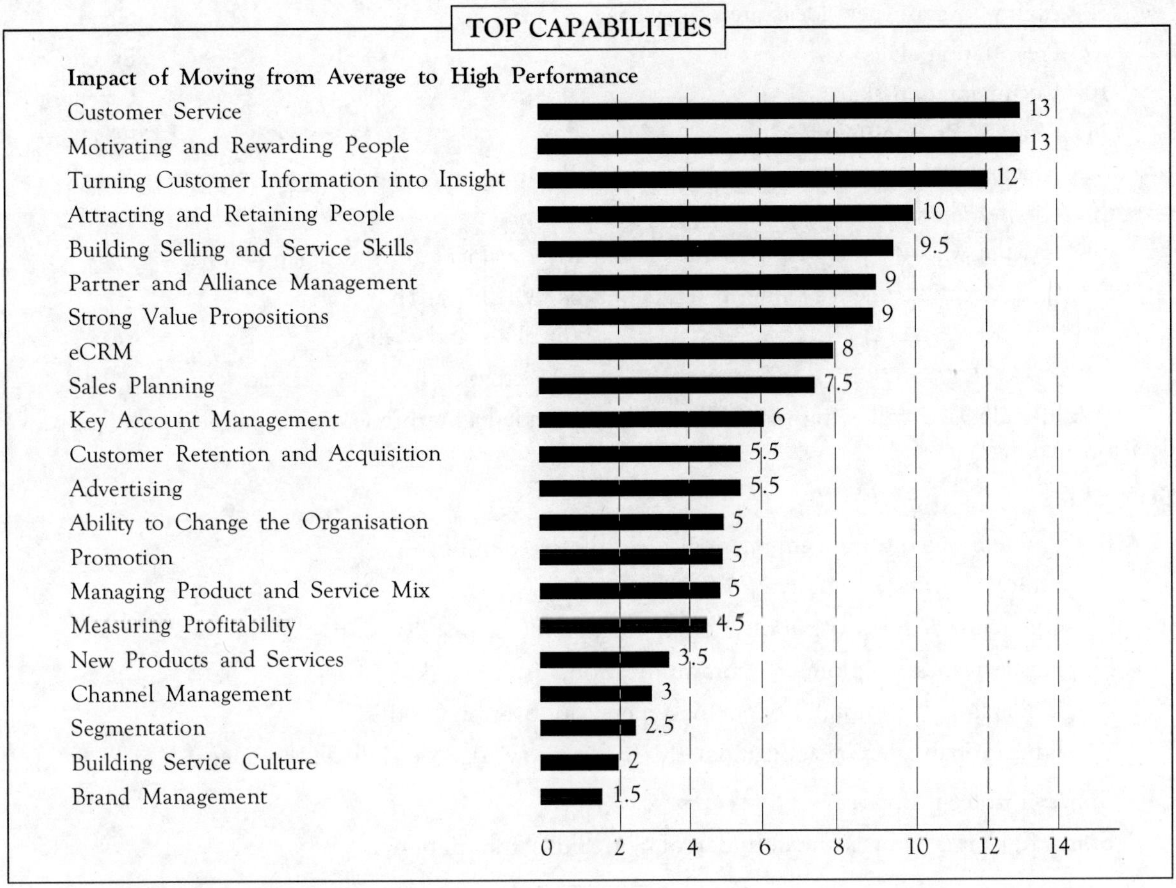

⏩ Soft Skill Appraisal

Fourteen soft skills to turn out the perfect executive needed by almost every organisation to-day.

Executives who can communicate, organise, present, sell, create, initiate, be team players and who add to the organisation's bottom line; because Corporates need to survive with competition, new technology and recession in the new world.

Given below is a performance appraisal of a executive after training.

	Rating *
1. Technical knowledge regarding the industry and the job he/she was involved	Good
2. Communication skills (*a*) Oral	Good
(*b*) Written	
(*c*) Listening skills	Good
3. Ability to work in a team	Excellent
4. Ability to take initiative	Excellent
5. Ability to develop a healthy long-term relationship with clients	Good
6. Ability to relate theoretical learning to the practical training	Good
7. Creativity and ability to innovate with respect to work methods & procedures	Good

8.	Ability to grasp new ideas and knowledge	Good
9.	Presentation skills	Excellent
10.	Documentation skills	Excellent
11.	Sense of Responsibility	Excellent
12.	Acceptability (patience, pleasing manners, the ability to instil trust, etc.)	Good
13.	His/her ability and willingness to put in hard work	Good
14.	In what ways do you consider the student to be valuable to the organisation?	
	Consider the student's value in terms of: (*a*) Qualification	
	(*b*) Skills and abilities	Yes
	(*c*) Activities/Roles performed	

Additionally, the following soft skills add to broaden enterpreneurial capabilities and improve decision making.

Soft Skills

P - Problem solving (judgement, logic, conflict resolution)

E - Ethics (courtesy, honesty, professionalism)

O - Open mindedness (flexibility, open to new ideas, positive outlook)

P - Persuasiveness (diplomacy, communication, listening skills)

L - Leadership (accountability, management, motivational skills)

E - Educational interests (continual thirst for knowledge & skill development)

Source: Infotech Enterprise

Shital Kakkar Mehra is the founder of Soft Skills International

Box 3

BUSINESS ETIQUETTES

The Art of Business Introductions

Making appropriate introductions is an important prerequisite to succeeding in the global marketplace. It helps you convey confidence and project a professional, well-networked image. According to Johann Kaspar Lavater, "In nothing do we lay ourselves so open as in our manner of meeting and salutation."

Here are some golden rules of making introductions:

- Identify the power base in the circle of individuals – Protocol for introductions is based on power and precedence; age/gender are less important. As a rule, Senior employees outrank juniors. Clients outrank every employee, even the CEO State officials outrank non-officials.
- Introduce the more important person first, using the phrase "I'd like to introduce to you ... " followed by an introductory phrase about him/her.
- Complete the process by introducing others to this key individual.
- When introducing diplomats or international dignitaries, use the word "present" instead of "introduce to you."

Improve Your Mingling Proficiency

Professional networking events are ideal opportunities to interact with others on a personal level and to develop profitable relationships. However, the prospect of entering a room full of strangers can be rather intimidating, and many fall in the trap of under-utilising this opportunity.

Some common self-imposed barriers are:

"I was not introduced to anyone in this room"

"I don't speak with strangers"

"I don't want to be seen as pushy/a job-seeker"

"My intentions may be misunderstood"

"I don't know what to say ...." Clearly, the goal is to meet people and to use this as an opportunity to improve your visibility in professional circles. Here are some tips to improve your mingling proficiency:

- Setting aside fear of failure, define how many new contacts you wish to make at the event.
- Have a ready set of conversation starters, e.g., "This is a growing industry ..."; "Are there others from your firm attending too?", "Seems like there is a lot of traffic in the city today."
- Keep business cards handy. They can be great conversation starters too – "You are in a very interesting industry ...", "Great logo."
- Scan the room for familiar faces ("connectors"), who could introduce you to others.
- Seek out the single person who makes eye contact/smiles at you.
- Pick the group of three or more people who are talking and laughing. Introduce yourself to everyone in the group and try to blend in with the conversation. This is not the time to change the topic to your company or personal agenda.
- Finally, ensure that you are equipped to mingle. Keep bags/folders to a minimum; wear appropriate business attire and present an open, confident persona, putting others at ease.

➧ Social Skill

The first three components of emotional intelligence are self-management skills. The last two, empathy and social skill, concern a person's ability to manage relationships with others. As a component of emotional intelligence, social skill is not as simple as it sounds, it's not just a matter of friendliness, although people with high levels of social skill are rarely mean-spirited. Social skill, rather, is friendliness with a purpose: moving people in the direction you desire, whether that's agreement on a new marketing strategy or enthusiasm about a new product.

Socially skilled people tend to have a wide circle of acquaintances, and they have a knack for finding common ground with people of all kinds – a knack for building rapport. That doesn't mean they socialize continually; it means they work according to the assumption that nothing important gets done alone. Such people have a network in place when the time for action comes.

Social skill is the culmination of the other dimensions of emotional intelligence. People tend to be very effective at managing relationships when they can understand and control their own emotions and can empathize with the feelings of others. Even motivation contributes to social skill. Remember that people who are driven to achieve tend to be optimistic, even in the face of setbacks or failure. When people are up beat, their "glow" is cast upon conversations and other social encounters. They are popular, and for good reason.

Because it is the outcome of the other dimensions of emotional intelligence, social skill is recognizable on the job in many ways that will by now sound familiar. Socially skilled people, for instance, are adept at managing teams that's their empathy at work. Likewise, they are expert persuaders – a manifestation of self-awareness, self-regulation, and empathy combined, given those skills, good persuaders know when to make an emotional plea, for instance, and when an appeal to reason will work better. And motivation, when publicly visible, makes such people excellent collaborators; their passion for the work spreads to others, and they are driven to find solutions.

But sometimes social skill shows itself in ways the other emotional intelligence components do not. For instance, socially skilled people may at times appear not to be working while at work. They seem to be idly schmoozing, chatting with colleagues or joking around with people who are not even connected to their "real" jobs. Socially skilled people, however, don't think it makes sense to arbitrarily limit the scope of their relationships. They build bonds widely because they know that in these fluid times, they may need help from people they are just getting to know today.

ATTRIBUTES OF ENTREPRENEUR

ATTRIBUTES OF ENTREPRENEUR
✦ PERCEPTIONS
✦ DEDICATION
✦ VISION
✦ HIGH GOALS/OBJECTIVES
✦ THRIFT
✦ VIGOROUS ENERGY
✦ HARD WORK
✦ CLEAN LIVING
✦ QUEST FOR NEW IDEAS
✦ WILLINGNESS TO ASSUME RISKS
✦ UNCEASING CURIOSITY
✦ RESTLESS URGE TO GET GOING
✦ SENSE OF ACQUISITIVENESS TO GET THINGS DONE
✦ INSIGHT
✦ GAMBLER'S INSTINCT
✦ INITIATIVE
✦ CREATIVITY
✦ ZEST TO EXPLORE THE UNEXPLORED
✦ PROBLEM-SOLVING ABILITY
✦ ABILITY TO MARSHALL RESOURCES
✦ TO ACHIEVE ONE'S OBJECTIVES AND GOALS
✦ ADMINISTRATIVE ABILITY

Fig. 2 Attributes of an Entrepreneur

For example, consider the case of an executive in the strategy department of a global computer manufacturer. By 1993, he was convinced that the company's future lay with the Internet. Over the course of the next year, he found kindred spirits and used his social skill to stitch together a virtual community that cut across levels, divisions, and nationals. He then used this *de facto* team to put up a corporate Website, among the first by a major company. And, on his own initiative, with no budget or formal status, he signed up the company to participate in a annual Internet industry convention. Calling on his allies and persuading various divisions to donate funds, he recruited more than 50 people from dozen different units to represent the company at the convention. Management took notice. Within a year of the conference, the executive's team formed the basis for the company's first Internet division, and he was formally put in charge of it. To get there, the executive had ignored conventional boundaries, forging and maintaining connections with people in every corner of the organization.

Is social skill considered a key leadership capability in most companies? The answer is yes, especially when compared with the other components of emotional intelligence. People seem to know intuitively that leaders need to manage relationships effectively; no leader is an island. After all, the leader's task is to get work done through other people, and social skill makes that possible. A leader who cannot express his/her empathy may as well not have it at all. And a leader's motivation will be useless if he cannot communicate his passion to the organization, social skill allows leaders to put their emotional intelligence to work.

The attempts to discover the secret of entrepreneurs' success has pre-occupied writers and analysts from a variety of disciplines. Biographies of successful entrepreneurs and businessmen, for example, frequently reflect the tendencies of the subjects of such studies in terms of simple virtues of thrift, hard work, and clean living. As an alternative to the biographical models are those studies that turn the entrepreneur into a superman, manipulating the complexities of an uncertain world with a sure and omnipotent touch. Thus emerges the notion of the "genius entrepreneur" whose success is in large measure caused by his unswerving dedication to setting high goals and to reaching for them. He has vision on which he bases his own objectives and sets his own goals. And he does this not simply on the basis of last year's results plus some growth factor, but on the basis of his own perception, of his own capabilities and to satisfy his own needs.

Among other distinguishing attributes of entrepreneurship are a willingness to assume risks; a sense of acquisitiveness or unceasing curiosity; insight into the relationship between concepts, objectives, needs, and needs satisfaction; sound judgment as to what's central and peripheral to attaining his objectives; initiative and creativity; problem-solving ability; ability to marshall resources needed to achieve his objectives and goals; and the administrative ability to organise those resources to accomplish his goals and satisfy his minor needs.

Not surprisingly, successful companies invest in Customer Relationship Management, or CRM and Financial Performance. Empirical research has demonstrated that CRM capabilities account for roughly half the difference between winners and the rest of the pack. In the very near future CRM will be the company's greatest strength.

Despite the uniqueness of each industry, our research revealed 21 capabilities that consistently appeared as producing the highest impact on financial performance (See graph). Of these 21 capabilities, two produce the highest impact on financial performance. They are, in order of impact: customer service, and motivating and rewarding employees. Achieving excellence in these areas is the factor most closely associated with high return on sales in every industry. Companies can significantly improve financial performance by improving performance in specific CRM capabilities.

Twenty-one different CRM capabilities were identified that could each add more per year to return on sales.

The five capabilities that have the greatest potential impact on financial return are customer service; motivating and rewarding, turning customer information into insight; attracting and retaining and building selling and service skills. And these improvements add. By making a 10 per cent improvement in the top 21 CRM capabilities identified in the study; a business unit can boost pre-tax profits. More aggressive improvements (i.e., moving from average to high performance) could triple this amount.

CRM capabilities are interrelated; how well a company performs in one area impacts the others. The interrelationship of the capabilities can be seen by looking at these five key areas.

Customer insight: Acquiring a unique, fact-based understanding of customer needs, expectations and value potential, and applying that insight to personalise the customer experience.

Customer offerings: Developing highly relevant, easily tailored offers to meet individual customer needs and create value in the eyes of the customer.

Customer interaction: Developing multi-channel interaction capabilities (*e.g.,* Web, phone or face-to-face contact) that are integrated seamlessly to deliver a consistent customer experience.

Highly-performing organisation: Developing, empowering and rewarding employees to influence the customer relationship positively and favourably.

Enterprise integration: Creating seamless intra- and extra-enterprise linkages to deliver on the commitment to the customer.

The most profitable companies are excellent at leveraging both technology and people. Technology influences 40 per cent of CRM impact across all capabilities. Put another way, technology may accelerate the impact of CRM by as much as two-thirds. People are critical and account for nearly one-third of the total impact across capabilities.

Attributes of Entrepreneurs

The attempts to discover the secret of entrepreneurs' success has pre-occupied writers and analysts from a variety of disciplines. Biographies of successful entrepreneurs and businessmen, for example, frequently reflect the tendencies of the subjects of such studies in terms of simple virtues of thrift, hard work, and clean living. As an alternative to the biographical models are those studies that turn the entrepreneur into a superman, manipulating the complexities of an uncertain world with a sure and omnipotent touch. Thus emerges the notion of the "genius entrepreneur" whose success is in large measure caused by his unswerving dedication to setting high goals and to reaching for them. He has vision on which he bases his own objectives and sets his own goals. And he does this not simply on the basis of last year's results plus some growth factor, but on the basis of his own perception, of his own capabilities and to satisfy his own needs.

Among other distinguishing attributes of entrepreneurship are a willingness to assume risks; a sense of acquisition or unceasing curiosity; insight into the relationship between concepts, objectives, needs, and needs satisfaction; sound judgement as to what is central and peripheral to attaining his objectives; imitative and creativity; problem-solving ability, ability to marshall resources needed to achieve his objectives and goals; and the administrative ability to organise those resources to accomplish his goals and satisfy his minor needs.

Developing Entrepreneurial Competencies

Entrepreneurial success depends upon entrepreneur's qualities or competencies. There are certain inborn qualities while certain others can be acquired through education and training. This fact has been amply demonstrated in Kakinda Experiments conducted by Prof. Davis C. McClelland. Competencies have direct bearing on human behaviour and performance. Various competencies can be cultivated or developed in the following ways:

1. Gaining first hand knowledge about Competencies: Various competencies cannot be cultivated without clearly understanding their meaning, significance and relevance. An earnest attempt must be made to understand at length the various competencies which are required for the efficient performance of the assigned task.

2. Competency Recognition: An individual's behaviour or performance depends upon the competencies he possesses. Therefore in order to get desired behaviour we should be in a position to know as to what are the competencies required in the individuals to perform in a particular manner. Under this step an effort is made to recognise the competencies.

3. Self Assessment: After getting clear cut idea about the competencies required for a particular type of behaviour, it is for the entrepreneur to see as to what extent he possesses these competencies and to what extent he is employing these competencies for achieving the desired goal.

4. Comparison of Competencies: The next step is to compare individual competencies with the competencies required for the desired performance. Wherever we find deficiencies an earnest attempt is made to find out the reasons for the same.

5. Developing Competencies and Feedback: Once it is realised that an individual does not possess a particular competency required for a particular type of behaviour, the next step will be to develop this competency. Assistance from various behavioural scientists may be taken for devising out ways and means for developing the required competency. In order to ensure that the required competency becomes part of the individual's behaviour, he is asked to practise the needed competency repeatedly. Lastly an attempt is made to know as to what extent change in individual behaviour has taken place due to acquiring of the requisite competency and to what extent it has been useful. It is through continuous application that one can ensure that the desired competency becomes part of his habit or personality.

6. Motivation: If the entrepreneur is to succeed and build an effective organisation to excell in global competitiveness, he should be motivated as well as motivate the team. "The ability to keep yourself and your team motivated is very important because it has a direct impact on individual and organisational productivity," says Edsil Coutinho who runs a logistical supply company and manages about 1000 people. "For example, there are times when you need people to put in long hours, often without the promise of a reward. During such times, it is important to keep them motivated. Even if the situation is bleak, the leader should take it upon oneself to motivate others and see the bright side of the problem." There are several motivational practices available at the hands of entrepreneurs.

- Most powerful motivators are rewards which in themselves include four types: membership and seniority, job status, competency and performance.
- Job design – the process of assigning tasks to a job – can be an effective tool to motivate employees. There are six approaches to job design: job rotation, job enlargement, job enrichment, social technical systems and ergonomics.
- DB Mod is based on the principle of law of effect. The principle states that repetition of a behaviour depends upon its earlier consequences.
- If consequences of the previous action are positive, the behaviour tends to get repeated. Being based on the principle of law of effect, DB Mod acts as a powerful motivator.
- Empowerment is another motivational practice. Empowerment makes employees believe that they own the jobs.
- Goal setting too is a powerful motivational practice. Performance goals, if properly set, will motivate: employees considerably.
- Problem employees need to be given one more chance, probably by shifting them to a new work environment. If they fail to respond, suspension of workers and firing of managers need to be resorted to.
- Flexi time, MBO, flexible benefits and other such practices also help motivate employees.

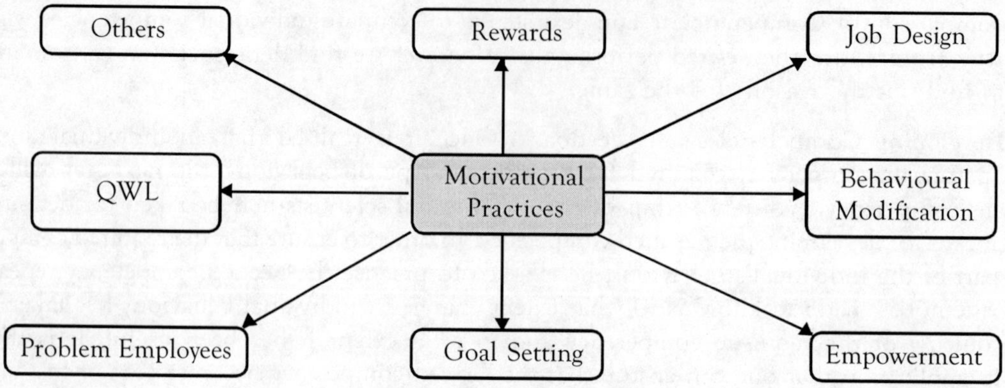

Fig. 3 Motivational Practices

Conclusion

Entrepreneurs play an important role in the development of society. For example, the use of Jeans in America has created the demand for it throughout the world. Similarly, Coca Cola has been accepted as a social drink. The introduction of colour T.V. has provided the society a means of information and entrepreneurs as Gillet, Wright Brothers, and Henry Ford. The inventions of these great entrepreneurs of the history has revolutionised the lifestyle of men in the society.

The role of entrepreneurs in economic development varies from economy to economy, country to country, depending upon its material resources, industrial climate and more importantly, the responsiveness of the political system to the growth of entrepreneurs. By and large, the entrepreneurs' contribution to development and growth is relatively higher in favourable opportunity conditions than in less favourable situation. The growth of an entrepreneurial society will bear fruitful results in a short span.

Entrepreneurship, the *de facto* barometer of overall economic, social and industrial growth has brought revolutionary changes in the society. It is the *sine quo non* of a nation's progress. It has facilitated large-scale production and distribution. It has widened the area and scope of the marketing of goods and services. Perhaps it is for these reasons that the small business sector has been given priority in our national development programmes for entrepreneurship flourishes when the size of business remains relatively small and viable.

Modern business studies have a distinct entrepreneurial discipline. The approach to the study of entrepreneurship is multi-disciplinary. It impinges on such areas as demography, economic anthropology, business history, politics, sociology, psychology, marketing and finance. That is why entrepreneurship development becomes an integral part of the overall economic, social and industrial development of a country. This is what makes the identification and management of entrepreneurial functions a highly complex exercise.

Apart from earning a livelihood and/or making profit, the entrepreneur is also motivated to fulfill his/her innate urge to achieve success in life, improve his/her social standing, gaining social recognition, to provide something to society. The motivational factor vary from place to place, time to time as well as entrepreneur to entrepreneur. Yet motivation moulds the different entrepreneurial traits. The traits and motivation are moulded by the socio, economic, political, cultural and psychological environment and varies from country to country.

The study of entrepreneurial traits and motivation is useful in developing a profile of a successful entrepreneur. It is indeed a positive approach in developing entrepreneurship and enterprise in country. Although, the entrepreneurial traits are complex, the goal of entrepreneur is to build enterprises to earn profit and serve the society.

ANNEXURE 1

RANKING ENTREPRENEURIAL TRAITS CENTRE

No single entrepreneur possesses all the traits or characteristics described earlier nor are all those characteristics needed to be successful. But which of the traits and characteristics are most commonly shared and most important for success?

In order to assess what you believe to be important entrepreneurial abilities, complete the following quiz. Rate the characteristics on a scale of 1 to 5. A rating of 1 indicates little importance, and a rating of 5 indicates great importance.

	Characteristics	Little Importance			Great Importance	
		1	2	3	4	5
1.	A strong need to achieve					
2.	A visionary					
3.	A need to associate closely with others					
4.	Ability to focus on people and process					
5.	Ability to get along with employees					
6.	Ability to motivate and build relationships					
7.	A willingness to tolerate uncertainty					
8.	Good physical health					
9.	A high level of energy					
10.	Singleness of purpose					
11.	A willingness to take risks					
12.	Drive to be ahead of others					
13.	Ambition					
14.	Self-confidence					
15.	Innovation					
16.	Ability to chart a course of direction					
17.	Ability to lead effectively					
18.	Patience					
19.	Ability to strive					
20.	A strong desire for money					
21.	Being well-organised					
22.	Thirst for knowledge and adequate reading habit					
23.	A desire to create					
24.	A desire to adopt active attitudes towards goals					
25.	A need for power					
26.	Perseverance					
27.	Commitment and hard work					
28.	Self-reliance					
29.	Abundant common sense					
30.	Desire and willingness to take the initiative					

31.	Competitiveness					
32.	Versatility					
33.	Desire to share knowledge/experience					
34.	Quality consciousness					
35.	Desire to add value					
36.	Honesty					
37.	Progressive approach					
38.	Flexibility					
39.	Ability to change					
40.	Uniqueness.					

Now that you have rated the various entrepreneurial characteristics, rank the characteristics in order of importance in you opinion under one of the following three categories:

(*a*) Most important for success (include those characteristics that you numbered 4 and 5)

(*b*) Important for success (include those characteristics that you gave a rating of 3)

(*c*) Least important for success (include those characteristics that you rated as 1 and 2)

Most Important	Important	Least Important

The idea is not just to work to finish a task but rather to work well and to savour each step you take up to the mountain you've chosen. Then, when you reach the top, you won't feel spent from all the effort. In fact, you won't even feel you've arrived. Instead, you'll feel refreshed and invigorated by what you've accomplished, and you'll find yourself looking for the next peak to conquer.

Taken together, mission, vision and a set of unique traits form the bedrock of entrepreneurship. They allow them to help shape their future. Mastering the discipline of innovation will require organisations to learn from one another.

Ranking entrepreneurial traits will definitely guide the entrepreneurs, particularly first generation entrepreneurs to recognize their deficiencies and move ahead with speed in this competitive environment.

THE IDEAL ENTREPRENEUR

Not a workoholic. Sure, you should be prepared to work long – and irregular – hours, but the freedom to choose priorities for free time is always at hand. If you cannot sleep at night, as long as there is a single file left underused, a memo unread, a number uncrunched, back off right now. Entrepreneurship isn't one-dayer. You must have the self-control to play for a long innings instead of burning yourself out.

The IT revolution burst into the most explosive business opportunities and Indians around the world especially in India seized them as they had never done before. The word was out; Indians were big on entrepreneurs in what was becoming the New Economy defined around the possibilities that the Internet was only now revealing. But what was more gratifying was that attention was shifting to domestic entrepreneurs, away from the bright ones in Silicon Valley or even the MNCs. India created its own MNCs be they Infosys or Reliance, Satyam or Ranbaxy to illustrate the point. Value creation is the core of ideal enterprise governance in the 21st century. Measurement of a enterprise's value should not be based solely on net profits but should include barometers like market capitalisation, economic value, customer satisfaction, deliverance of high quality products and services and shareholder value.

The key drivers to become a value grower as identified by a survey was a strong leadership combined with a well communicated vision, a focused strategy, a clear competence profile, customer satisfaction and investing in organisational excellence. Among the Indian value growers are Infosys, Wipro Infotech, Satyam, Mahindra & Mahindra, HLL, Telco, ITC, TVS Suzuki, Punjab Tractors, Gujarat Ambuja, Ingersoll-Rand, ABB, Cadbury's India, Castrol India, Berger, P & G, Indian Shaving Products, Reckitt & Colman, Hero Honda and Tisco.

Be warned, therefore: even when you are your own boss, long-term sustainability demands that you balance your professional and personal life. Only then can you truly make your own business sustainable in the long-term.

To Morph into an Entrepreneur

- Managers must be able to translate their career ambitions into specific business goals.
- Managers must use their people management skills to motivate and inspire their employees.
- Managers must capitalise on their skills to manage the financial aspects personally.
- Managers must turn their aggression in the workplace into a risk-taking approach.
- Managers must leverage their functional expertise when choosing their line of business.
- Managers must develop leadership qualities on the job before venturing out on their own.

Prepare, therefore, a mental checklist of the other side to the entrepreneur's job. Sure, your once-in-a-life-time innovative idea will convert customers immediately, but are you as prudent as a penny-pinching CFO? The diplomacy of the personnel manage? The doggedness of the door-to-door salesman? You'll need them all, in addition to that gem of an idea.

The entrepreneurship audit will judge individual capabilities to be an entrepreneur or not. Just try it.

THE ENTREPRENEURSHIP AUDIT

Do you measure upto the tough task of being your own boss? Assess yourself impartially and objectively your positive and negative points in becoming your own boss. If need be, negative points might be corrected by training and education. Take this test to find out:

	Yes	No
1. Do you enjoy taking big, even unwarranted, risks?	☐	☐
2. Do you plan ahead on most things you do?	☐	☐
3. Do you have a head for numbers and finances?	☐	☐
4. Do you make it a point to complete what you start?	☐	☐
5. Can you survive a drop in your standard of living?	☐	☐
6. Are you able to take decisions without dithering?	☐	☐
7. Are you free of major financial commitments?	☐	☐
8. Can you get along with different kinds of people?	☐	☐
9. Is your career path in your company flattening out?	☐	☐
10. Do you enjoy travelling on work?	☐	☐
11. Are you capable of leading people?	☐	☐

12. Do you have a clear vision about your dreams? ☐ ☐
13. Do you have innovative ideas about projects and services? ☐ ☐
14. Have you acquired specific skills to run the new venture? ☐ ☐
15. Do you plan your work methodically? ☐ ☐
16. Are you adaptable and flexible? ☐ ☐
17. Do you prefer working alone to teams? ☐ ☐
18. Do you find yourself envying entrepreneurs? ☐ ☐
19. Can you cope with punishing work schedules? ☐ ☐
20. Does your spouse support your plans? ☐ ☐

The Scoring

Give yourself 5 points for every YES, and 0 for every No.

TOTAL ☐

The Rating

0-35	You won't get far with I Inc. Be satisfied with what you already have in hand.
40-60	The passion as a self-starter is weak. You seek the *status quo* rather than a crisis.
65-100	All systems go. Greener pastures and challenges await you.

"Entrepreneur is a person who discovers new ideas and business opportunities, brings together funds to establish a business, organises and manages its operations in order to provide economic goods and services, for the public. Entrepreneurs have strong convictions, self motivation, the will to grow and prosper tremendously and also the courage to go bankrupt if they fail in their venture. But in majority of cases they start with nothing but entrepreneurial ability and end with positive results."

6

Types of Entrepreneurs

Introduction

In the previous chapter, we have analysed the concept of entrepreneurship and its understanding over the centuries, particularly in the post industrial revolution. In modern times entrepreneurial development has the thrust area of development planners, economic thinkers and policy makers. What is more, the entrepreneur has emerged as a kingpin of development.

M.S. Oberoi
(August 15, 1898 - May 3, 2002)

"For an entrepreneur, identifying a viable business opportunity is only half of the battle won. The real challenge lies in seizing the opportunity. Those who have identified a gap in the market often stumble because they can't scale their organisation to meet booming customer demand before competitors encroach. To use a military metaphor, a general must not only spot an opening in the enemy's defense, but also marshal the resources to execute an attack before the window of opportunity closes." He goes on to elaborate five key questions that entrepreneurs and managers must ask themselves before scaling a promising initiative. These range from identifying what you are really betting on, whether you have standardised what matters; to having the right "shock absorbers" in place to take the bumps along the way.

By and large, entrepreneurs are found in every economic system and in every form of economic activity as well as in other social and cultural activities. They are found amongst artisans, labourers, artists, importers, exporters, engineers, supervisors, bankers, industry, professionals etc. They are also found among farmers, fishermen, forest workers, tribals and so on. Some writers have also identified entrepreneurs among politicians, theologists, philosophers, bureaucrats.

This chapter attempts to analyse different types of entrepreneurs in business as well as in different faculties of understanding. On the basis of his study of American agriculture, Clarence Danhof classified entrepreneurs into four categories, namely, innovative Entrepreneur, initiative Entrepreneur, fabian Entrepreneur and drone Entrepreneur. The other classification is based on technology, economic activity and market economy.

▸▸ Economists' View

In economic analysis, entrepreneurial functions are supposed to be directed towards the materialistic objective of maximisation though its foundations may be of a high order such as spiritual, patriotic, social, psychological or ethnic. Entrepreneurial activity is a form-giving activity-giving form to the wishes of the society, to ideas, to the efforts of factors and to the raw material to be processed through.

J.S. Mill has listed three entrepreneurial functions:

1. Superintendence
2. Control, and
3. Direction

J. B. Say has stated that it is function of the entrepreneur to rationally combine the forces of production into a new producing organisation. J.S. Mill lists superintendence, control and direction as entrepreneurial functions. *Superintendence:* to assemble the means, turn out maximum at minimum cost and to supervise the work. *Control*: the flow of goods, use of finance, utilisation of machinery and the activities of the subordinates. *Direction:* he is a goal-oriented person; he has to keep the organisation constantly on the path of his objective. His is an activity of producing in present what the future will demand. Mill emphasises managerial and administrative functions. Organisation and superintendence are major functions of an entrepreneur. Organisation building capacity is the most critical skill expected of an entrepreneur.

Kirzener viewed the entrepreneur as a disequilibrating force. It is the alertness to unnoticed opportunities which creates a tendency of the ever-circular flow of equilibrium. Harvey Leibenstein states, "Entrepreneur is an individual or group of individuals with four major characteristics. He connects different markets; he is capable of making market deficiencies (gap-filling); he is input completer and he creates or expands time-binding, input-transforming entities (firms).

To Joseph, A. Schumpeter, innovation is the sole function of an entrepreneur. It covers the introduction of new goods, a new method of production, a new market, a new source of supply of raw materials or half-manufactured goods and a new organisation of any industry for the creation of a monopoly position or breaking it. The function of the entrepreneur is to reform or revise the pattern of production. So, Schumpeter has given a social context to the activity, a psychological objective to be attained and a functionality spearheading development of the community. Lazarfeld as also Meier and Baldwin concur with Schumpeter.

Frederick Fritz enumerates four functions : the undertaking or managing of risks and handling of economic uncertainty; planning and innovation; coordination, administration and control and routine supervision. Ability to build an organisation is, perhaps, Harbinson adds, the most precious of all entrepreneurial skills. Redlich's threefold division of function is: (i) capitalist – employing the factors and buying raw material, setting up the organisation; (ii) managerial – innovation, supervision and coordination of productive activities and (iii) entrepreneurial – decision-making. Benjamin Higgins lists seeing opportunities for introduction of new techniques, new products and exploitation of new resources and organising factors of production into an enterprise to take advantage of these opportunities as essential for economic development.

According to B.F. Hoselitz, "The primary function of entrepreneurship is the investment of time, capital and energy in economically significant pursuits; the emphasis is on decision-making on its various aspects." Another economist Harbinson enumerates four functions: in entrepreneurship the undertaking or managing of risk and handling of economic uncertainty; planning and innovation; coordination, administration and control, routine supervision. Ability to build organisation is, perhaps, Harbinson adds, the most precious of all entrepreneurial skills. Redlich's threefold division of functions are:

(1) Capitalist – employing the factors and buying raw material, setting up the organisation; (2) managerial – innovation, supervision and coordination of productive activities; and (3) Entrepreneurial – decision-making. Benjamin Higgins lists seeing opportunities for introduction of new techniques, new products and exploitation of new resource and organising factors of production into an enterprise to avail of these opportunities as they are essential for economic development.

B.C. Tandon discusses the functions of an entrepreneur in a developing economy in the context of economic, legal, political and cultural environment. Accordingly, the entrepreneur must possess *(a)* capacity to risk and have self-confidence; *(b)* technological knowledge, alertness to take existing opportunities, willingness to accept change and ability to initiate; *(c)* ability to marshall resources; and *(d)* ability of organisation and administration. He has to have tact, patience, sagacity, power of observation and ability of discriminating. He should have perseverance to overcome obstruction and fear, have the capacity to pick and choose associates and subordinates and wisely delegate authority to inspire loyalty. He must be able to develop "himself" effectively. Tandon describes entrepreneur as an "ideal-type" rather than as "social-type." Knight is said to have identified entrepreneurship with control and responsibility.

Economic functions described above isolate the entrepreneur from the economic environ, social milieu and political ethos in which he functions. Maximisation is taken as the pole star in his voyage. It seems to be conveniently assumed that he is abundantly provided with all the resources and the market readily absorbs what he puts into it. Reality is, however, full of bottlenecks and hurdles which are ignored in the above-mentioned works. Small industry is a natural habitat of the entrepreneur where his role is like that of a stoker who keeps the fire burning.

Sociology is intrinsically fascinating, as most sociological research seeks to explain prevailing social behaviour patterns and how they change over time. Some could be related to sex and gender, examining issues such as, 'Do men and women have different hiring, employment, and promotion experiences?' A sociologist could be asked to analyse which management styles increase productivity. A family sociologist could be researching whether children of divorced parents are more likely to divorce, or to reject marriage itself.

Any social phenomenon can be examined through different sociological standpoints. You can claim to be a sociologist if you have completed a master's level, ideally a Ph.D. too. Sociologists could be studying the causes of social problems like crime, poverty, patterns of family relationships, different living patterns in communities of varying types and sizes.

Sociologists provide insight into how people are affected by their families, schools, work. This gives professionals in the helping careers such as social workers, teachers and nurses some idea of what makes people behave the way they do.

Sociology gives you an advantage in understanding human behaviour on three levels: (*i*) how individuals behave in organisations, families, and communities; (*ii*) the ways in which these social units function as groups and (*iii*) the wider social, political, and economic contexts in which decisions are made and in which groups function.

⏩ Specialisations

Sociologists pursue diverse specialities in: families, adolescence, or children; the urban community; education; health and medicine; aging and the course of life; work and occupations; the environment, science and technology; economics, social inequality and social class; race relations, ethnicity, and minorities; sex and gender; sports; culture and the arts; politics, military, peace, and war; crime, delinquency, law, and justice; social change and movements; and any other area of human organisation.

⏩ Sociologists' View

Sociologists consider the entrepreneur as a role performer corresponding to the role expected by the society. Wishes of the society are exhibited through customs and taboos, rewards and restraints, ethnic values and child-rearing practices, nationalistic attitude and patriotic inculcations and protestant ethics. He is conditioned by the social milieu to which he belongs. According to Peter Marris, to assemble or reassemble from what is available, very concrete kind of imagination, to see what others have missed, sensitivity to business and social environment, zest in industrial development and entrepreneurial courage are the factors that make an entrepreneur. According to Flavia Derossi, coordination at every stage – inception, maintenance and expansion – is the function of an entrepreneur. She feels an entrepreneur needs two qualities: (1) An optimistic outlook that there is a possibility of change, the environment can be mastered and he himself can introduce the required change. He finds difficulties challenging and stimulating; he thrives on them. (2) In a sphere as dynamic as industry, new problems are seized upon as opportunities for testing one's own capabilities.

According to T.C. Cochran, the entrepreneur represents society's model personality. His performance depends upon his own attitudes towards his occupation, the role expectations of sanctioning groups and the occupational requirements of the job. Society's values are the most important determinant of attitudes and role expectations.

Arthur, H. Cole, states that entrepreneurship should not be studied by focusing on individual entrepreneur but rather by looking at the enterprise. Special attention was often paid to the social relations within the enterprise and to the relations between the enterprise and its surroundings.

Everett, E. Hagen also concluded that entrepreneurs have emerged from certain communities and castes.

Thus, Hagen disregard the complicated institutional environment that surrounds the entrepreneur.

⏩ Psychologists' View

Among psychologists, Frank young describes an entrepreneur as a change-agent. K.L. Sharma maintains that entrepreneurs are men who exhibit qualities of leadership is solving persistent professional problems; but those persons likewise demonstrate eagerness to seize unusual opportunities. They have a business gambler's itch. T.V. Rao and Udai Pareek describe entrepreneurship as a creative and innovative response to the environment. The entrepreneur is goal-oriented rather than means-oriented.

He must not only have a high capacity of risk-taking but must also have a high capacity of risk-sustaining which is a function of a high degree of self-confidence.

Joseph Schumpeter states that the entrepreneur is mainly motivated and driven by three things:

(*i*) 'the dream and the will to found a private kingdom';

(*ii*) 'the will to conquer';

(*iii*) 'the joy of creating.'

J. Schumpeter's formulation can be translated as:

(*i*) the desire for power and independence;

(*ii*) the will to succeed;

(*iii*) the satisfaction of getting things done.

According to him, money is not what ultimately motivates the entrepreneur 'Entrepreneurs', according to Schumpeter, 'are certainly not economic men in the theoretical sense.'

According to David McClelland, entrepreneurship has to do with an individual's so called need for achievement (referred to n-Achievement). He identified three features of entrepreneurs that were related to their need for achievement: (1) desire to accept responsibility for solving problems, setting goals and reaching the goals; (2) a willingness to accept moderate risks; (3) a desire to know the outcomes of their decisions. It was widely believed that a high achievement motivation has a strong likelihood of predicting entrepreneurial behaviour. Individuals with high achievement motive tend to take keen interest in situations of high risk, desire for responsibility and a desire for a concrete measure of task performance.

According to Fredrik Barth, entrepreneurship has essentially to do with connecting two spheres in the society, between which there exists a difference in value. Something which is cheap in one sphere, may be exdpensive in another sphere. Barth, one of the leading anthropologists of the world, states that entrepreneurial behaviour means to connect two different spheres in the society, between which there is a huge discrepancy in value.

In sum, the foregoing description of the functions of an entrepreneur presents the profile of a functionary. Economists present him as a perceiver of otherwise unnoticed opportunity, organisation builder, adaptor of new profitable activity and beneficiary thereof. Sociologists present him as a personality moulded by various practices of social enforcement and values imbibed in him. Psychologically, entrepreneurship is a vigorous application of the person's energies towards the long-cherished goals.

Business Entrepreneur: Business entrepreneurs are individuals who conceive an idea for a new product or service and then create a business to materialise their idea into reality. They tap both production and marketing resources in their search to develop a new business opportunity. They may set up a big establishment or a small business unit. They are called small business entrepreneurs when found in small business units such as printing press, textile processing house, advertising agency, readymade garments, or confectionery. In a majority of cases, entrepreneurs are found in small trading and manufacturing business and entrepreneurship flourishes when the size of the business is small.

Trading Entrepreneur: Trading entrepreneur is one who undertakes trading activities and is not concerned with the manufacturing work. He identifies potential markets, stimulates demand for his product line and creates a desire and interest among buyers to go in for his product. He is engaged in both domestic and overseas trade. Britain, due to geographical limitations, has developed trade through trading entrepreneurs. These entrepreneurs demonstrate their ability in pushing many ideas ahead to promote their business.

Industrial Entrepreneur: Industrial entrepreneur is essentially a manufacturer who identifies the potential needs of customers and tailors a product or service to meet the marketing needs. He is a product-oriented man who starts in an industrial unit because of the possibility of making some new product. The entrepreneur has the ability to convert economic resources and technology into a considerably profitable venture. He is found in industrial units as the electronic industry, textile units, machine tools or video cassette tape factory and the like.

Corporate Entrepreneur: Corporate entrepreneur is a person who demonstrates his innovative skill in organising and managing corporate undertaking. A corporate undertaking is a form of business organisation which is registered under some statute or Act which gives it a separate legal entity. A trust registered under the Trust Act, or a company registered under the Companies Act are example of corporate undertakings. A corporate entrepreneur is thus an individual who plans, develops and manages a corporate body.

Agricultural Entrepreneur: Agricultural entrepreneurs are those entrepreneurs who undertake agricultural activities as raising and marketing of crops, fertilisers and other inputs of agriculture. They are motivated to raise agricultural products through mechanisation, irrigation and application of technologies for dry land agriculture products. They cover a broad spectrum of the agricultural sector and includes its allied occupations.

▸▸ Entrepreneurs in Technology

The application of new technology in various sectors of the national economy is essential for the future growth of business. We may broadly classify these entrepreneurs on the basis of the use of technology as follows:

Technical Entrepreneur: A technical entrepreneur is essentially compared to a "craftsman." He develops improved quality of goods because of his craftsmanship. He concentrates more on production than marketing. He does not do much sales generation by and does not do various sales promotional techniques. He demonstrates his innovative capabilities in matter of production of goods and rendering of services. The greatest strength which the technical entrepreneur has is his skill in production techniques.

Non-technical Entrepreneur: Non-technical entrepreneurs are those who are not concerned with the technical aspects of the product in which they deal. They are concerned only with developing alternative marketing and distribution strategies to promote their business.

Professional Entrepreneur: Professional entrepreneur is a person who is interested in establishing a business but does not have interest in managing or operating it once it is established. A professional entrepreneur sells out the running business and starts another venture with the sales proceeds. Such an entrepreneur is dynamic and he conceives new ideas to develop alternative projects.

▸▸ Entrepreneurs and Motivation

Motivation is the force that influences the efforts of the entrepreneur to achieve his objectives. An entrepreneur is motivated to achieve or prove his excellence in job performance. He is also motivated to influence others by demonstrating his business acumen.

Pure Entrepreneur: A pure entrepreneur is an individual who is motivated by psychological and economic rewards. He undertakes an entrepreneurial activity for his personal satisfaction in work, ego or status.

Induced Entrepreneur: Induced entrepreneur is one who is induced to take up an entrepreneurial task due to the policy measures of the government that provides assistance, incentives, concessions

Table 1

CLASSIFICATION OF ENTREPRENEURS

According to the types of business

1. Business entrepreneurs
2. Trading entrepreneurs
   - (*i*) Wholesale trade
   - (*ii*) Retail trade
   - (*iii*) Mall trading
   - (*iv*) Exporters
   - (*v*) Importers
   - (*vi*) Stock trading
   - (*vii*) Real estate
3. Industrial entrepreneurs
   - (*i*) Large
   - (*ii*) Medium
   - (*iii*) Small and
   - (*iv*) Tiny Sector
4. Corporate entrepreneurs
5. Agricultural entrepreneurs
   - (*i*) Plantation
   - (*ii*) Horticulture
   - (*iii*) Dairy
   - (*iv*) Forestry
   - (*v*) Floriculture
   - (*vi*) Animal Husbandry
   - (*vii*) Poultry
   - (*viii*) Seeds
6. Retail entrepreneurs
7. Service entrepreneurs
   - (*i*) Repairs
   - (*ii*) Engineering
   - (*iii*) Beauty Parlours
   - (*iv*) Others
8. Re-engineering entrepreneurs
9. Health entrepreneurs
10. Fauzi entrepreneurs

According to the use of technology

1. Technical entrepreneurs
2. Non-technical entrepreneurs
3. Professional entrepreneurs
4. High-tech entrepreneurs
5. Low-tech entrepreneurs
6. Business process outsourcing
7. Knowledge process outsourcing
8. IT entrepreneurs
9. E-entrepreneurs
10. Legal processing outsourcing

According to the motivation

1. Pure entrepreneurs
2. Induced entrepreneurs
3. Motivated entrepreneurs
4. Spontaneous entrepreneurs
5. Forced entrepreneurs
6. Accidental entrepreneurs
7. Achieving entrepreneurs
8. Successful entrepreneurs

According to the growth

1. Growth entrepreneurs
2. Super-growth entrepreneurs
3. Aspiring entrepreneurs
4. Lifestyle entrepreneurs

According to the stages of development

1. First generation entrepreneurs
2. Modern entrepreneurs
3. Classical entrepreneurs
4. Generation-next entrepreneurs
5. Inherited entrepreneurs

According to area

1. Urban entrepreneurs
2. Rural entrepreneurs
   - (*i*) Artisans
   - (*ii*) Handlooms
   - (*iii*) Sericulture
   - (*iv*) Agri
   - (*v*) Khadi
   - (*vi*) Village industries
   - (*vii*) Handicrafts and
   - (*viii*) Rural service
3. Global entrepreneurs
4. Local entrepreneurs

According to organisation

1. Individual entrepreneurs
2. Group entrepreneurs
3. Institutional entrepreneurs
4. Private entrepreneurs
5. Public entrepreneurs
6. Government entrepreneurs

According to gender and age

1. Men entrepreneurs
2. Women entrepreneurs
   - (*i*) Young entrepreneurs
   - (*ii*) Old entrepreneurs
   - (*iii*) Middle–aged entrepreneurs

Unclassified

1. Professional entrepreneurs
2. Non-professional entrepreneurs
3. New Modern entrepreneurs
4. Trading entrepreneurs
5. Skilled entrepreneurs
6. Non-skilled entrepreneurs
7. Imitating entrepreneurs
8. Serial entrepreneurs
9. Social entrepreneurs
10. National entrepreneurs
11. International entrepreneurs
12. Bureaucratic entrepreneurs
13. Orthodox entrepreneurs
14. Immigrant entrepreneurs
15. Innovative entrepreneurs
16. Philonthropreneurs
17. Entertainment entrepreneurs
18. Creative entrepreneurs
19. Knowledge entrepreneurs
20. Education entrepreneurs

21. Intrapreneurs
22. Ultrapreneurs
23. Mompreneurs
24. Alterapreneurs
25. Altapreneurs
26. Joint entrepreneurs
27. Generous entrepreneurs
28. Promoter entrepreneurs
29. Multifaced entrepreneurs
30. Entrepreneur employees
31. Accidental entrepreneurs
32. Mentorpreneurs
33. Foodrepeneurs
34. Mobile entrepreneurs
35. Upcountry entrepreneurs

and necessary overhead facilities to start a venture. Most of the induced entrepreneurs enter business due to financial, technical and several other facilities provided to them by the state agencies to promote entrepreneurship. A person with a sound project is provided package assistance to his project. Today, import restriction and allocation of production quotas to small units have induced many people to start a small-scale industry.

Motivated Entrepreneur: New entrepreneurs are motivated by the desire for self-fulfilment. They come into being because of the possibility of making and marketing some new product for the use of consumers. If the product is developed to a saleable stage, the entrepreneur is further motivated by reward in terms of profit.

Spontaneous Entrepreneur: These entrepreneurs start business their by natural talents. They are persons with initiative, boldness and confidence in their ability which motivate them to undertake entrepreneurial activity. Such entrepreneurs have a strong conviction and confidence in their inborn ability.

Growth and Entrepreneurs

The development of a new venture has a greater chance of success. The entrepreneurs a new and open field of business. The customer's approval to the new product gives them psychological satisfaction and enormous profit. The industrial units are identified as units of high growth, medium growth and low growth industries and as such we have "Growth Entrepreneur" and "Super-Growth Entrepreneur."

Growth Entrepreneur: Growth entrepreneurs are those who necessarily take up a high growth industry which has substantial growth prospects.

Super-Growth Entrepreneur: Super-growth entrepreneurs are those who have shown enormous growth of performance in their venture. The growth performance is identified by the liquidity of funds, profitability and gearing.

Entrepreneur and Stages of Development

Entrepreneurs may also be classified as the first generation entrepreneur, modern entrepreneur and classical entrepreneur depending upon the stage of development. They are explained below:

First-Generation Entrepreneur: A first-generation entrepreneur is one who starts an industrial unity by innovative skill. He is essentially an innovator, combining different technologies to produce a marketable product or service.

Modern Entrepreneur: A modern entrepreneur is one who undertakes those ventures which go well along with the changing demand in the market. They undertake those ventures which suit the current marketing needs.

Classical Entrepreneur: A classical entrepreneur is one who is concerned with the customers and marketing needs through the development of a self-supporting venture. He is a stereotype entrepreneur whose aim is to maximise his economic returns at a level consistent with the survival of the firm with or without an element of growth.

Others

Innovating Entrepreneurs: Innovating entrepreneurship is characterised by aggressive assemblage in information and analysis of results, deriving from a novel combination of factors. Men/women in this group are generally aggressive in experimentation who exhibit cleverness in putting attractive possibilities into practice. One need not invent but convert even old established products or services by changing their utility, their value, their economic characteristics into something new, attractive and utilitarian. Therein lies the key to their phenomenal success. Such an entrepreneur is one who sees the opportunity for introducing a new technique of production process or a new commodity or a new market or a new service or even the reorganisation of an existing enterprise.

Innovating entrepreneurs are very commonly found in developed countries. There is dearth of such entrepreneurs in underdeveloped countries. A country with little or no industrial tradition can hardly produce innovating entrepreneurs. Such entrepreneurs can emerge and work only when a certain level of development is already achieved and people look forward to change and progress. Innovating entrepreneurs played the key role in the rise of modern capitalism through their enterprising spirit, hope of money making, ability to recognise and exploit opportunities, etc. Innovative entrepreneurs are creative and always bring in innovation in their work.

Imitative Entrepreneurs: Imitative entrepreneurship is characterised by readiness to adopt successful innovations by entrepreneurs. They imitate techniques and technology innovated by others. Thy are adoptive and more flexible.

Imitative entrepreneurs are also revolutionary and important. The importance of these humbler entrepreneurs who exploit possibilities as they present themselves and mostly on a small-scale must not be underestimated. In the first place, such adaptation requires no mean ability. It often involves what has aptly been called 'subjective innovation', that is the ability to do things which have not been done before by the particular industrialist, even though, unknown to him, the problem may have been solved in the same way by others. By western standards, an imitative entrepreneur may be a pedestrian figure, an adopter and imitator rather than a true innovator. He is more an organiser of factors of production than a creator. But in a poor country attempting to industrialise, he is nevertheless a potent change producing figure. He can set in motion the chain reaction which leads to cumulative progress. This humbler type of entrepreneur is important in undeveloped countries.

The reason for the backwardness of the underdeveloped countries lies in the fact that they are deficient in innovating and imitating entrepreneurs when they are found in abundance in developed countries. Men are needed who can imitate the technologies and products to the particular conditions prevailing in such countries. And at times there is a need of changing and adjusting the new technologies to their special conditions. Such countries, primarily need imitators who are responsible for transforming the system with the limited resources they possess.

Fabian Entrepreneurs: Fabian entrepreneurship is characterised by great caution and scepticism in practising any change. Such entrepreneurs have neither will to introduce new changes nor desire to adopt new methods innovated by the most enterprising entrepreneurs. Such entrepreneurs are shy and lazy. Their dealings are determined by customs, religion, tradition and past practices. They are not much interested in taking risk and they try to follow the footsteps of their predecessors.

Drone Entrepreneurship: Drone entrepreneurship is characterised by a refusal to adopt and use opportunities to make changes in production. Such entrepreneurs may even suffer losses but they do not make changes in production methods. They are laggards because they continue in their traditional way and in fields their product loses its marketability or their operation becomes uneconomical – they are pushed out of the market.

Aspiring Entrepreneurs: Aspiring entrepreneurs dream of starting a bussiness; they hope for the chance to be their own bosses, but they have not yet made the leap from their current employment into the uncertainty of a start up.

Lifestyle Entrepreneurs: Lifestyle entrepreneurs have developed an enterprise that fits their individual circumstances and style of life. Their basic intention is to earn an income for themselves and their families.

Growth Entrepreneurs: Growth entrepreneurs have both the desire and ability to grow as fast and as large as possible.

Opportunist Entrepreneurs: Opportunist entrepreneurs are those who have grabbed an opportunity which has come in their way.

E-Entrepreneurs: The new electronic or e-entrepreneurs are mostly concerned with "click-through schemes and capturing eye-balls." The e-entrepreneur comes in many modes. Young and ambitious, older and corporate based international and risk taking.

Mompreneurs: Homemaker entrepreneur is a mompreneur. Entrepreneurship is one way for women to get around corporate glass ceiling (not everyone can do an Indra Nooyi). It also gives them the flexibility to care for the home while avoiding barriers – and bosses – who come with traditional jobs, although there are bound to be other hurdles. For the 21st century women, there's no business like own business.

⏩ The New Kingmaker Entrepreneurs

The Indian economy is blooming and spreading its wings beyond its borders. To fulfill their growth aspirations there is need for corporate leaders to lead. With India Inc. in the throes of a top-level talent crunch, headhunters hold the keys to the corner office. A new breed of new kingmaker (headhunters) entrepreneurs have emerged.

⏩ Professor Entrepreneurs

It requires guts, motivation, inspiration, business sense, financial backing, among other traits to be an entrepreneur. A few characteristics are in-born and a few, taught. But somewhere down the line, the professors who play a vital role in the lives of the budding visionaries fade away and get lost in history books. What remains etched in our minds are the names of the people who stormed the world to set up vast empires of businesses. Ever thought of the people responsible behind the success of these entrepreneurs? Meet Prof. Radha Iyer, Prof. Suresh Rao and Prof. Arya Kumar who left their illustrious corporate careers and turned to academics to give direction to budding entrepreneurs. They are the pioneers in creating 'entrepreneurship' courses in their respective institutes thereby giving the visionaries a platform to hone and learn the skills to make the perfect kill!

▸▸ Intrapreneur

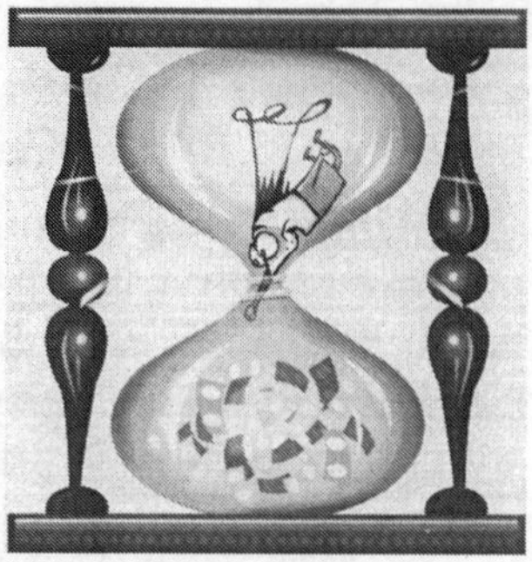

Tempted to point out a spelling error above? Wait a second! This exciting word is young but full of potential. Introduced by Gifford and Elizabeth Pinchot in 1973 as "intra-corporate entrepreneur" and later re-coined, the term "intrapreneur" was officially recognised in 1992 with this definition in American Heritage Dictionary:" A person within a large corporation who takes direct responsibility for turning an idea into a profitable finished product through assertive risk-taking and innovation."

Blend of the two terms intra+entrepreneur, intrapreneur embodies the same characteristics as the entrepreneur, conviction, passion, and drive. If the company is supportive, the intrapreneur succeeds. If it's not, the intrapreneur usually fails or leaves to start a new company. An intrapreneur thinks like an entrepreneur seeking out opportunities, which benefit the corporation. But there are, of course, a few things that are different between intrapreneurship and entrepreneurship. For starters, the intrapreneur acts within the confines of an existing organisation. The dictates of most organisations would be that the intrapreneur should ask for permission before attempting to create a desired future – in practice, the intrapreneur is more inclined to act first and ask for forgiveness than to ask for permission before acting.

The intrapreneur is also typically the intra-organisational revolutionary – challenging the status quo and fighting to change the system from within. This obviously creates a certain amount of organisational friction. A health dose of mutual respect is required in order to ensure that such friction can be positively channelled. One advantage of intrapreneurship over entrepreneurship is that intrapreneur typically finds a ready source of "free" resources within the organisation that can be applied to the opportunity being exploited.

To sum up the basic differences we could say firstly entrepreneurship involves huge amount of risk while there is no personal risk involved in case of an intrapreneurship. Secondly an intrapreneur is dependent on the organization in which he is working while an entrepreneur doesn't work in any confines, hence independent in every task he undertakes. While companies admire an intrapreneur who is an independent thinker, being too independent could cause problems. The biggest difference between intrapreneurship and entrepreneurship, according to Pinchot, is that an intrapreneur has to deal with authority figures. "So if you absolutely cannot stand to be told what to do by others, you may not do well as an intrapreneur," he says.

Intrapreneurship is more important now than ever before. No one needs to be told that the world is changing now faster than ever before. Organisations are finding it harder and harder to survive by merely competing. They are, therefore, increasingly looking towards their intrapreneurs to take them beyond competition to create new businesses in new markets.

▸▸ Conclusion

It should be noted that private entrepreneurship has to harmonise economic opportunities with social and moral responsibility. As our wise people have said, unless the pursuit of wealth is integrated with the pursuit of *Dharma*, there could be no lasting prosperity and peace, whether within a country or among nations. The highly developed countries have realised that aggressive entrepreneurship without an ethical base can produce more harm than good, more misery than happiness and more destruction than creation. *Harmonised planning of economic and moral values is a long-drawn-out process, but the goal has to be kept in mind constantly.* One should remain optimistic that entrepreneurship in India will develop on these lines – to promote India's economic development on a sound basis, as an integral part of the development of the economy. The burst of creativity and innovation in emerging teleological industries holds promise for economic development and growth of technology and business. When talent is linked with technology, people recognise and then push viable ideas and the entrepreneurial process is under way.

Liberalisation and the new economic policy have thrown open the doors for every entrepreneur to seek its own fortunes and thus contribute his mite to the growth of the economy. In a way, the new economic policy has been fostering the spirit of entrepreneurship. The human capital and infrastructure provide the two major assets in a global economy. The states are striving to provide a framework that will improve investment infrastructure, agriculture and industry. They have endeavoured to dovetail industrial growth with creation of employment and balanced development. The country has a vast pool of skilled manpower and there is no dearth of entrepreneurs.

In this time of rapid economic development and technological change, the entrepreneurial spirit can be a unique and of important advantage, but only if we learn to use it. The entrepreneurs are the agents of change and our hope for the future. In fact, the entrepreneur always searches for change, responds to it, and exploits it as an opportunity.

In this time of rapid socio-economic development and technological change, the entrepreneurial spirit can be of advantage but only if we learn to use it. The entrepreneurs are the agents of change and our hope for the future. In fact, the entrepreneur always searches for change, responds to it, and exploits it as an opportunity.

LEADER'S CHECKLIST

"The ultimate profile of a dynamic leader is someone who combines the learning and experience of someone who is 45 with the mental spark and open-mindedness of a 35-year old and the constant questioning and energy levels of a 25-year old." — ***Ronnie Screwvala, CEO, UTV***

7

Women Entrepreneurs

Introduction

The emergence of entrepreneurs in a society depends to a great extent, on the economic, social, religious, cultural and psychological factors prevailing in the society. In the advanced countries of the world, there is a phenomenal increase in the number of self-employed women after the World War II. In the U.S., women own 25 per cent of all businesses, even through their sales on an average are less than two-fifths of those of other small businesses. In Canada, one-third of small businesses are owned by women and in France it is one-fifth. In the U.K., since 1980, the number of self-employed women has increased three times as fast as the number of self-employed men.

Women are no longer confined to the hearth and home. The entrepreneurial capacity of women has made a mark in many areas and women have entered the industrial segment, too. It is time to foster and harness the entrepreneurship of women in a big way. According to the second census of small-scale industries, women entrepreneurs accounted for 7.7 per cent of the total small-scale enterprises in India. Though their share is less than 10 per cent, the heartening feature is that it is steadily increasing. A stage is set for social take-off for women from a low development path to an accelerated pace is achieving a higher level of self-sustaining economic growth. Women entrepreneurs have to graduate from a state of dependence of subsidies/concessions to that of seizing opportunities as they emerge in an open and competitive modern economy.

Women are now more cognisant about their existence, roles and rights. Women entrepreneurs are those who explore new paths of economic involvement and contribution. Women entrepreneurs have been making a significant impact in all segments of the economy in Canada, Great Britain, Germany, Australia and the United States. The areas chosen by women are retail trade, restaurants, hotels, education, cultural, cleaning, insurance and manufacturing. They have made their mark in business for the following reasons:

(*i*) They want new challenges and opportunities for self-fulfilment.

(*ii*) They want to prove their mettle in innovative and competitive jobs.

(*iii*) They want the change to control the balance between their family responsibilities and their business lives. Dina Lavoie, a Professor of Entrepreneurship, Montreal observes that, "women business owners hire an average of two or three employees, whereas men are more likely to have nine employees or more. Often, a micro-business fits a woman's lifestyle. Expansion might mean a loss of control or disruption in the amount of time she invests in other facets of her life. She may also want to oversee and control every aspect of her life. She may also want to oversee and control every aspect of her business and may feel she will lose that opportunity if she grows to the point where she cannot."

WOMEN OF SUBSTANCE

Sudha Murthy

Nita Ambani

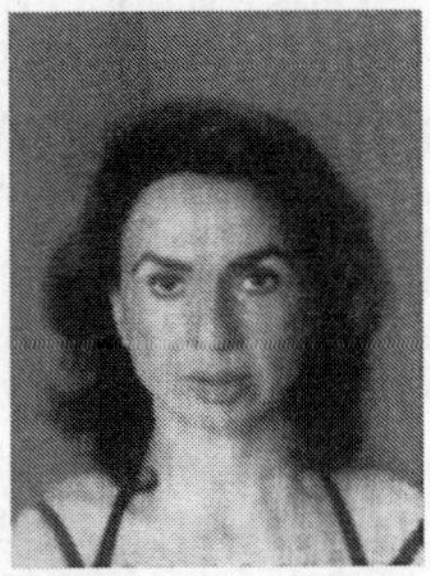

Parmesh Godrej

Priya Paul

Anita Kaul Basu

Malvika Sanghvi

Statistical Evidence

- Globally women own between one-quarter and one-third of businesses in the formal sector and are likely to play an even greater role in the informal sector.
- In Russia, women business owners are involved in international trade at a higher rate (19%) than in the US (13%).

- In Brazil, Mexico and Argentina, 22-32% of women business owners are involved in international trade.

In a recent study, economist Catherine Swift, has mentioned that women face tougher security requirements on their lines of credit than do men. However, she also explains that other identified differences such as higher interest rates, lower credit approval rates and espousal co-signature requirements are primarily attributable to the fact that women operate younger and smaller firms that are known to meet with such financing problems, whether they are owned by men or women.

⏩ Women Entrepreneurs

Women entrepreneurs represent a group of women who have broken away from the beaten track and are exploring new avenues of economic participation. A great many have chosen entrepreneurship because of the compelling sense of wanting to do something positive. Women have also become aware of their talents and abilities in business and industry. A great majority of women have taken up to run organised industries because of their skills and knowledge they acquire when the traditional society moulds them to play the role of housewives.

In a survey sponsored by the international Women's Forum, a number of interesting findings have emerged. In her article "Ways Women Lead", in the November-December 1990 issue of Harvard Business Review, Ms. Judy B. Rosener of the University of California points out that whereas men are more likely to use power that comes from their organisational position and formal authority, women use "interactive leadership." This means encouraging participation and utilising persuasion skills more than power. Inclusion is the core of interactive leadership. To facilitate inclusion, they use a conversational style that comes naturally to them. Women are more likely than men to say things that make people feel important and energised.

⏩ Supportive Style

The social background of women has for long helped them to exhibit quiet leadership, without making a show of it. In the process, they have learned to lead without formal authority. This is an advantage in the modern management set-up, particularly with the high educational level of the work-force which is more comfortable with a low profile leader who is supportive and helpful rather than a high profile leader who dictates to them. This supportive element is more strongly ingrained in women than in men. Of course, there can be quite a few exceptions.

Modern management theories abound with the concept of supportive rather than directive leadership. Particularly in the Indian context this element has a valuable contribution to make in understanding the practical difficulties people at lower levels face. Quite often at the working level, lack of right tools and lack of minor infrastructural facilities are common. These are not attended to in time and small grievances are allowed to build up. For example, a rack to keep tools or a proper space for files in the office which matters a lot for the person on the spot, is not considered important at a higher level. In such matters, women managers have a better appreciation of the problems and solve them immediately.

A study conducted by the Management Development Institute in collaboration with the National Institute of Entrepreneurship and Small Business Development has pointed out that a majority of women have a strong desire and ambition to venture into business. A pilot study conducted on Women Entrepreneurs in Delhi indicates that women have displayed confidence in starting manufacturing enterprise as compared to service industry and trade. The study also shows that the women entrepreneurs are as scientific as their male counterparts in product selection.

WOMEN ENTREPRENEURS

Poonam Soni
Signature Jewellery

Renu Garg and **Bela Agrawal**
Toys and Games

Anita Ramachandran
Cerebrus

Naina Javeri
Queen of Traditional Sarees

Mallika Srinivasan
Tractors

Waheeda Rehman
Cereal Making

Smita Bajoria
Watches

Kunti Shah
Handmade Ceramic Tiles

Anu Aga
Thermax

Sulajja Firodia
Kinetic

Kajal Gaba
Wall Paiinting

Kum. Hina Shah, Director, International Centre for Entrepreneurship and Career Development, Ahmedabad, has been training and developing women entrepreneurs for the past 15 years in different parts of our country. She reports that women have selected products in electronics (like printed circuit board, floppy disc), engineering items (armature winding, machine manufacturing), plastics (like injection moulding, film making), chemicals (golden paste, laboratory chemicals), food and allied products (like protein biscuits, cake mixture), rubber, pharmaceuticals, machinery and equipment, energy, fuel and others.

Empirical research studies indicate that several women are willing to become entrepreneurs due to various factors. They choose entrepreneurship as a challenge and adventure with an urge to do something new and to have an independent occupation. Women by nature are less aggressive and more objective regarding business matters. They learn fast the business intricacies and show patience in solving business problems. Psychologically, women are well-suited to become entrepreneurs. Entrepreneurship and leadership are in-built in their characters.

▸▸ Segments of Women Entrepreneurs

Four segments of women entrepreneurs exist: *Self-help groups:* Those who are well served and mentored by microfinance institutions.

Grassroots entrepreneurs: Those who are driven by a need to augment the family's finances especially to secure their children's future – tailors, flower sellers, STD booth owners, *paan* shops. With turnover aspiration of five lakh a year, they are very work focused, as they can see any increase in their earnings as directly impacting their children's lives. They are hungry for formal skills and training and can clearly articulate what they want to learn that will help them earn more. Domestic family support, financial support and better infrastructure and mechanisation is what they ask for.

Mid-rung entrepreneurs: They are driven by a need to build reputation, become known, and improve quality and satisfy creative instincts. Mostly graduate+, they typically have garments shops, poultry farms, export businesses etc., with turnover aspirations from Rs. 50 lakh to Rs. 1 crore. Fairly well supported by the family, their biggest need is for know-how to take the 'quality of their business' to the next level. However, they do not want to scale too much, because to them, there is an optimal level beyond which, they believe their children will get neglected.

Upper Crust: Drawn from the top-most social class, very well educated, with businesses like export houses, travel agencies, traders in pharmaceuticals, often adjuncts to their husband's businesses, they aspire to turnovers of more than Rs. 5 crore.

▸▸ Impact on the Economy

Women entrepreneurs have been making a significant impact in all segments of the economy in Canada, Great Britain, Germany, Australia and the United States. The areas chosen by women are retail trade, restaurants, hotels, education, cultural, cleaning, insurance and manufacturing. They have made their mark in business for the following reasons:

(*i*) They want new challenges and opportunities for self-fulfillment.

(*ii*) They want to prove their mettle in innovative and competitive jobs.

(*iii*) They want change to control the balance between their family responsibilities and their business lives. Dina Lavoie, a Professor of Entrepreneurship, Montreal observes that "women business owners hire an average of two or three employees whereas men are more likely to have nine employees or more. Often, a micro business fits a woman's lifestyle. Expansion might mean a loss of control or disruption in the amount of time she invests in other facets of her life. She may also want to oversee and control every aspect of her business and may feel she will lose that opportunity if she grows to the point where she cannot."

Becoming an Entrepreneur

The phenomenon of the growth of the women entrepreneurs in the world in general and in India in particular appears to be due to the growing economic development, importance of entrepreneurship, status enjoyed by women, education, development of financial institutions and cultural values. Women want more freedom outside the domestic environment, with birth control, declining birth rate, higher divorce rate and a changing social and economic environment. Over 70% of new entrants in the labour force in Canada are women. With a little job experience, they give up low-paid, dead-end jobs, to start their own business, providing greater flexibility for attending to family demands, upper level management and better utilisation of their talents, skills and knowledge.

Entrepreneurs are not born. Entrepreneurship is a highly personal process, when a "determining event" decides the starting of a business – a set of practices or skills developed out of dissatisfaction with the existing job, need for recognition, to gain independence or job security with economic gain. Men were drawn more by money and independence while women appear to be drawn more by recognition.

The start-up experience in a new business is little supported by business education, business training or business management experience. Learning to run your own business is by running it.

It needs distinct business knowledge regarding:

Size of the Business

Correct objectives growth/money/lifestyle. Acceptance of products in the market place. Appropriate contact – Government authority/Market. The most important start-up problems include:

Management cash-flow, internal financial control, management of employees and control of external factors which come only with practice, gaining confidence and market acceptance. Whether in bank or in the market place or facing a Government tender, the entrepreneur has to adopt any one of the three courses:

(*i*) Decide that being a woman makes a difference in her approach.

(*ii*) Behave as if sex makes no difference.

(*iii*) Send a male representative to cope with the situation for a male approach.

Government red-tape and stereotype attitudes of development officers cause major problems for women entrepreneurs. According to the United Nations, women earn one-tenth of the world's income and own one hundredth of the world's property. An international venture capital specialist says that women will never be a significant force in the venture capital.

A woman's life is characterised by distraction. She cannot give as much attention to her business as a man. The entrepreneur has to face the hard job starting the business by facing the human realities, that nobody cares for her success except herself, it is very easy to make mistakes when you are implementing a strategy, the markets are "closed to outsiders" and she must join the coterie. Conflicts arise with domestic partners/employees. Success brings considerable change in confidence, self-esteem, happiness, attitude etc.

Caution

It is essential to protect against foreign exchange fluctuations, never do business with a foreign company without a signed agreement, realise the pitfalls/dangers in separating personal life from business life, learn to be tough in bargaining and related business practices, and finally never tell the whole truth about your business; but you have to anyway.

Women have been doing well with languages, business skills, negotiations, conflict resolutions, research, presentation and confidence building. Experience in deal making is getting better.

Traditional business magazines are not capturing the interest of women. More contact between women entrepreneurs as a group has to be built up. The strength comes from exposure to strong role models. The repayment of bank loans by women entrepreneurs is much better than their male counterparts. Many women are now in second and third business venture and have learned how to build business. This illustrates tremendous progress.

"I am pleased and proud that we have 5 million more businesses than we did when I took office, that there are over 1.5 million new women owned businesses in that time, and that small business has been the major contributor in generating the nearly 18 million new jobs added to our economy since 1982. Small business owners are effective leaders in other areas as well. Increasingly, the voices of small businessmen and women are heard in public policy debates. Their concerns reflect not the narrow views of special interest groups, but broad perspectives on issues that affect all of us – the provision of health care for the uninsured, work place literacy and training, and international competitiveness ... alleviate regulatory paperwork or other burdens on small firms so that they will be free to do what they do best – create new enterprises, new jobs, and innovative products and processes... Government do a better job of paying its bills on time." President of the USA in his report transmitted to U.S. Congress, 1989.

According to the third census of the SSI sector for 2001-02, the total number of women enterprises in the SSI sector was 10.6 lakh. The number of enterprises actually managed by women is slightly less at 9.9 lakh units. Even though women own around 10% of the total enterprises in the small-scale sector, the gross output of these units is just barely 3.5% of the total output of the SSI sector. In contrast, in developed countries such as the United States, women own nearly 91 lakh small businesses and the number of women owned start-ups are growing at nearly twice the rate of their male counterparts.

The Census survey also shows that most of these enterprises are concentrated in few states including Kerala, Tamil Nadu, Karnataka, West Bengal and Uttar Pradesh. As high as 13% of the total women owned enterprises are concentrated in the state of Kerala. Moreover, in accordance with the trend in the SSI sector as a whole, the majority, that is nearly 87% of the women owned enterprises are unregistered units.

In the rural areas, Self-help group (SHG)-bank linkage have dramatically changed the face of rural India. Women groups account for nearly 95% of SHGs, who use these funds to take up and expand micro businesses. And the success of this model lies in the fact that the repayment rate is as high as 98%. "An important thing to remember is that when women have control over the finances, the first beneficiary is the child. Therefore, the true effect of this will be felt 20 years down the line" says Mr. Bhardwaj. However, penetration levels of these self-help groups is still very low.

In a study, Economist, Catherine Swift shows that women face tougher security requirements on their lines of credit than do men. However, she also explains that other identified differences such as higher interest rates, lower credit approval rates and espousal co-signature requirements are primarily attributable to the fact that women operate younger and smaller firms that are known to meet with such financing problems, whether they are owned by men or women.

Profile of a Woman Entrepreneur

Who is this Woman Entrepreneur? What are her qualities?

She is the child of a middle-class parents, at least one of whom is independently employed, she has a close relationship with her father and, after obtaining an undergraduate and subsequently a graduate degree in some area of liberal arts, marries, has children and starts her first significant entrepreneurial venture in the service area in her late 30s or early 40s. Her biggest problems at start-up and later in the venture reflect a lack of business training and generally are in the financial area.

With education and training, the women have gained confidence to do all work, which was the prerogative of man and do it excellently, rather better than men. Over the years, the educated women have become ambitious, acquired experience and basic skills, competency and self-assurance.

Table 1

PROFILE OF A WOMAN ENTREPRENEUR AND HER BUSINESS

First-born child of middle class parents
Father and/or mother in independent business
College-educated
Married
Early 30s for the first significant venture
Previous experience in new venture
Desires independence
Motivated by desire for independence and job satisfaction
Small and young business
Self-confident
Moderate risk-taker
High tolerance for ambiguity
High energy level
Biggest problems in start-up:
Lack of business training
Obtaining credit
Availability of Information
Obtaining seed capital
Marketing
Personnel management
Biggest problems in current operations:
Lack of experience in financial planning
Weak collateral position
Cash flow management
Taxation

Leadership Qualities

Some of the outstanding leadership qualities of women entrepreneurs are as follows:

Accept challenges
Adventurous
Ambitious
Conscious

Drive
Educated
Enthusiastic
Determination to excel
Hard work
Keenness to learn and imbibe
Patience
Experience
Industrious
Intelligent
Motivator
Perseverance
Skilful
Studious
Unquenchable optimism
Passion
Risk taking
Optimistic
Team builder
Team worker

Psycho-Social Barriers

Although some women entrepreneurs have excelled in their enterprise, the fear of success haunts women in general. Some psycho-social factors impeding the growth of women-related entrepreneurship are as follows:

(*i*) Poor self-image of women
(*ii*) Inadequate motivation
(*iii*) Discriminating treatment
(*iv*) Faulty socialisation
(*v*) Role conflict
(*vi*) Cultural values
(*vii*) Lack of courage and self-confidence
(*viii*) Inadequate encouragement
(*ix*) Lack of social acceptance
(*x*) Unjust social, economic and cultural system
(*xi*) Lack of freedom of expression
(*xii*) Afraid of failures and criticism
(*xiii*) Susceptible to negative attitudes
(*xiv*) Non-persistent attitude
(*xv*) Low dignity of labour
(*xvi*) Lacking in leadership qualities, *i.e.*, planning, organising, controlling, coordinating and directing.

▸▸ The New Thrust

Some recent researches conducted indicated that several women are now willing to become entrepreneurs due to various factors. These factors can be broadly classified under two headings, namely, "Pull factors" and "Push factors." Under the first category, the women entrepreneurs choose a profession as a challenge and adventure with an usage to do something new, liking for business and to have an independent occupation. The other category of women takes up business enterprises to get over financial difficulties and responsibility is thrust on them due to family circumstances. However, the latter category forms a negligible percentage of the total women entrepreneurs.

The thrust given to the process of economic development of the country by the new dynamic leadership has created an all-round enthusiasm and the new slogan of "March towards the twenty-first century" had gained popularity. But in this new enthusiasm every vital sector of the society which can contribute substantially towards the economic development of the country is not given enough attention.

And this vital sector is women entrepreneurs. In fact the Harvard School experts feel that the basic quality of efficient management is futuristic.

Empirical research shows that the primary motive for women to start a business is mainly to raise the present level of family income and the business units are largely under sole proprietorship. According to the Unescap study, a majority of the Indian women in SMEs fall within the age group of 25-40 years and most of them are married. The service sector units are generally not inherited and are started by the women entrepreneurs themselves. Moreover, priority is given to the ease of setting up the enterprise and availability of technical know-how. "In general it is also seen that women keep lower goals for themselves, which is why the size of the unit, too, tends to be smaller" says Mr. Bhardwaj.

With a growing number of women joining the workforce in larger cities, services such as day care centers are becoming very popular. Such services, in turn are providing an opportunity to women entrepreneurs. In general, services where there is an ease of entry and exit with very little capital investment and where the supply chain is short, are attracting women entrepreneurs in urban areas. Most of these services can also be operated from home, which increases the ease of operations for a woman who is required to balance her family life with her work.

Problems, however, are plenty for a female business enthusiast who wishes to start her own unit in the manufacturing sector. "In general, whatever problems that men might face in setting up a small-scale unit are accentuated in the case of women" says Mr. Anil Bhardwaj, secretary general, Federation of Indian micro and small & medium enterprises (FISME). If dealing with government officials and the process of registration is a difficult task for men, it's a nightmare for an average Indian woman. "Moreover, in certain businesses that are traditionally male dominated, women are looked at with suspicion on their seriousness of managing the business with a long-term perspective" adds Mr. Bhardwaj.

The root cause of the problem is the existing socio-cultural fabric and the broad mindset towards women entrepreneurs. According to a study on "Developing women entrepreneurship in South Asia Issues, initiatives and experiences 2005" by the United Nations Economic and Social Commission for Asia and the Pacific (Unescap), the traditional gender role expectations and patriarchal attitudes in countries such as India makes it difficult for women to relieve themselves of family responsibilities and inhibits their mobility, independence and confidence."

Family Business: Inheritor Woman Entrepreneur

Devita Saraf honestly believes she could sell ice to Eskimos. At age 11, when friends were loath to give up their Enid Blytons, Saraf, who would go on to become CEO of luxury brand Vu Technologies, was reading 'Handbook to Marketing'. "I loved it," she says. Seven years later when Saraf expressed a desire to study in the US her father, Zenith Computer's Raj Saraf relented only because he believed if there was one thing she could learn from the Americans, it was the art of marketing. "Every class I took in college was with the ultimate aim of coming back to immerse myself in the business whether it was a b2b marketing class or an e-commerce class," she says. The day she returned, she was made marketing director at Zenith. She was 21.

Young Saraf was a breath of fresh air at Zenith, setting about her tasks with alacrity. "1 took on what had been my father's mantra: 'Just do it'. "Never spend too much time analysing things, dive straight in," she says. "People think marketing is advertising, but it's so much more – it's understanding technology, it's channel meetings, it's sourcing, and also unfortunately sales (she isn't the biggest fan of the function)," she continues.

Then in 2006, not just satisfied with inheriting an IT giant from her father, Saraf followed every marketer's dream – to design something from scratch. "We could sense that there was a sizeable shift in customer taste so we set out to create a high-end Zenith brand" she says. And Saraf went from being the head of marketing to CEO.

While Zenith was mass technology focused, Vu was innovation based. "We wanted to be seen as a cool brand," she says. And Vu has come out with some 'firsts': a waterproof television, digital photoframe, and most recently, an "affordable" telepresence. Saraf though believes thought that no product sells itself; it needs to be branded or marketed right. "I'm always reiterating that our company's value lies in our brand equity; we are in the business of building brands."

Saraf has her work cut out for her in the largely opaque luxury market, especially since Vu is a new brand. She believes that wearing the customer hat is the best way to get into heads of consumers and have them reach for their wallets. "Americans are unafraid of new technologies but Indians are very cautious. The idea here is to get them to touch, feel and try before they buy." The other challenge is get the service proposition right. "The luxury culture has to be ingrained into everyone from the salesperson to the service engineer. This mindset creation in a country that has a history of frugality is tough," admits Saraf.

The internet is changing perceptions about marketing and Saraf isn't resisting it. Vu is redesigning itself around new marketing approaches made possible through web technologies – using social networks, YouTube, viral videos and blogs. Saraf says she still enjoys marketing more than any other

CEO function. "Marketing keeps you real because you're dealing with the customer, the channel operators. You see the business from the outside." Vu is still a year or two away from breaking even. "Building a brand is like building a reputation, it takes time," says Saraf "It's a lesson in patience."

Women Entrepreneurs` Enterprises

In 1988, for the first time, the definition of Women Entrepreneurs' Enterprise was evolved that termed an SSI unit/industry-related service or business enterprise, managed by one or more women entrepreneurs in proprietary concerns, or in which she/they individually or jointly have a share capital of not less than 51 per cent as partners/ shareholders/ directors of a private limited company/members of a cooperative society, as a Woman Enterprise.

Women entrepreneurs have been on the Indian business scene for quite some time now and have achieved remarkable success. However, their number in relation to the overall number of small-scale enterprises is still very small. One of the reasons for this is the initial hesitation and inhibition, both familial and social, due to the traditional perception of the women's role. Moreover, like any other entrepreneur, any first generation woman entrepreneur has to compete in the business against those already well established.

Women entrepreneurs, as a group, came into prominence in the late 1970s. The information contained in the Third All India SSI Census shows that about 25 per cent of the small enterprises were owned by women. Industry group-wise, the most popular activity of women entrepreneurs was food processing followed by garment making. Realising the great untapped potential, the Government has been making concerted efforts to channelise the skills and talent of women towards economic and business generating activities.

Table 2

COMPARISON BETWEEN MALE AND FEMALE ENTREPRENEURS

Characteristic	*Male Entrepreneurs*	*Female Entrepreneurs*
Motivation	Achievement – strive to make things happen Personal independence – self-image as it relates to status though their role in the corporation is unimportant Job satisfaction arising from the desire to be in control	Achievement – accomplishment of a goal Independence – to do it alone
Departure Point	Dissatisfaction with present job Sideline in college, sideline to present job, or outgrowth of present job Discharge or layoff Opportunity for acquisition	Job frustration Interest in and recognition of opportunity in the area Change in personal circumstances
Sources of funds	Personal assets and savings Bank financing Investors Loans from friends and family	Personal assets and savings Personal loans
Occuptional background	Experience in line of work Recognized specialist or one who has gained a high level of achievement in the field Competent in a variety of business functions	Experience in area of business Middle-management or administrative level experience in field Service-related occupational background

Personality characteristics	Opinionated and persuasive Goal oriented Innovative and idealistic High level of self-confidence Enthusiastic and energetic Must be own boss	Flexible and tolerant Goal oriented Creative and realistic Medium level of self-confidence Enthusiastic and energetic Ability to deal with the social and economic environment
Background	Age when starting venture: 25-35 Father was self-employed College education – degree in business or technical area (usually engineering) Firstborn child	Age when starting venture: 35-45 Father was self-employed College educated – degree in liberal arts Firstborn child
Support groups	Friends, professional acquaintances (lawyers, accountants) Business associates Spouse	Close friends Spouse Family Women's professional groups Trade associations
Type of business started	Manufacturing or construction	Service related – educational services, consulting, or public relation

Box 1

MAID IN INDIA

'Maid to order' isn't a pipe dream anymore. Surekha Kadapa-Bose chats up 'maid'en entrepreneur Dr. Manju Agarwal who's made a successful business out of taking care of mundane chores.

Hers is an interesting case of an academic becoming an entrepreneur. With a doctorate under her arm, Kandivali housewife Dr. Manju Agarwal got a job as a lecturer of Hindi in a city college but soon had to quit like many working wives do. The problem: "Like many others, I did not have a maid to care for my kids and house in my absence."

A month after she quit her job, Dr. Agarwal not only hired a maidservant for her home but became a 'social entrepreneur' too! But this 40-year-old mother of two prefers to call herself a "human resources consultant" and for ten years, has specialised in providing housemaids, governess, cooks and **housekeepers to thou**sands of homes in Mumbai and its suburbs.

Enterprising by nature, Agarwal saw a business opportunity in the situation and began scouring the slum localities on the periphery of Lokhandwala, namely, Damu Nagar, Kranti Nagar, Gautam Nagar and others for women who would want to work as maids. For two months every afternoon and evening, she visited them to slowly secure their confidence and soon got them jobs in the homes of local residents.

"I was touched by their misery as I came across housewives who supported their alcoholic husbands, wives abandoned by bigamous husbands and mothers-in-law thrown out by their daughters-in-law," says Dr. Agarwal. Over a decade into her vocation of "helping the helpless," Dr. Agarwal has provided maids to over 5,000 households located as far as Panvel, Kalwa and Virar, sourced from both the western and central suburbs.

Housemaids who have secured jobs in turn refer their relatives who come to work as maids from places as distant as Ratnagiri, Satara, Raigad and Alibagh. Little wonder then that her clientele has

grown by word-of-mouth publicity and includes film stars, industrialists, college lecturers, bank executives etc. On receiving a query, Dr. Agarwal's staff visits the client's house to make detailed enquiries and back it up with testimonials from neighbours and office bearers of co-operative housing societies. A trial period is offered to the client to try out the maid selected by the agency.

So does she ever get any complaints? "We do get complaints about the maid drinking milk on the sly, etc. On receiving the complaint, we counsel the maid and tell her that it is better to ask than to steal as this shakes the homeowner's confidence," informs Dr. Agarwal who soon plans to get a chawl in Dadar to shelter prospective maids coming from beyond Mumbai before they get their jobs.

Basic Problems of Women

The basic problem or difficulty of a woman entrepreneur is that she is a woman – this pertains to her responsibility towards family, society and work. With joint families breaking up, many women simply don't have the support of elders in the family. Women have been confronted by such dilemmas ever since they stated leaving home for the work place. On the other hand, the attitude of society towards women and constraints in which they have to live and work are not very conducive. In spite of the constitutional equality, in practice, the attitude of men is not only tradition-bound but even of those who are responsible for decision-making, planning and research is not of equality. They still suffer from reservations. This attitude of reservation creates difficulties and problems for women at all levels. Women in rural areas equally suffer. They have to face not only resistance or reservation from men but also from elderly women who are orthodox in their attitude. In rural areas joint families are still the norm. The overbearing presence of elders restrain even young men from venturing out; so one can imagine how much a young girl needs to put up to become economically independent. Though in rural areas women are working along with men since times immemorial, their contributions in monetary terms remains unaccounted for, or if at all accounted, it is given a very low value. They are mostly engaged in low-paid, heavy agricultural activities or act as helpers in handicrafts.

It is not that women do not have skills or capacity but they are not properly trained or initiated in craftsmanship because it is taken as a taboo – it is wasted because when she gets married, she takes the skills with her. Therefore, a woman was confined at home and not given many opportunities. She was not allowed to function independently. Training is basic for any entrepreneurship. Facilities are available, many institutions have been imparting training under various schemes but again social attitudes do not appreciate this independence and thus keep women away from them – both in urban and rural areas.

At the government level, the licensing authorities and labour officers and sales tax inspectors ask all sorts of questions like what technical qualifications you have, how will you manage labourers, how will you manage both house and business, does your husband approve your going out for working, etc.

The most important question is asked regarding strategies for marketing – both of raw material and of finished goods. To market her product, she has to be at the mercy of middlemen who go away with a big chunk of profit. Besides the middlemen try to exploit women entrepreneurs at both ends. They deny them discount or give the minimum discount in the purchase of raw material and on the other hand, try to extract maximum credit discount and commission on purchase of finished products from them.

If she decides to eliminate middlemen, it involves a lot of footwork. Secondly, in these days of stiff competition, a lot of money is required for using advertisement. If the product is targetted at a consumer, then it takes time to win people away from other products and make this product popular. And then there is a tendency to question the quality of the product produced by women entrepreneurs, though many agree that they are most sincere in maintaining the quality and time schedule.

New Awareness

The new Industrial Policy of the Government of India has specially highlighted the need for special entrepreneurship programmes for women entrepreneurs in the nature of product-process oriented courses – to enable them to start small-scale industries. It further adds that the objective of this course is to give representation to women in the field of small industry development with a view to uplifting their status in the economic and social fields.

Due to the aforesaid fillip, growth of industrialization, urbanization, education and democratic system in the country, the tradition-bound Indian society has seen a major technological change and the women are now seeking gainful employment in several fields in increasing numbers. The women entrepreneurship movement has taken off the ground and it is felt that the moment has crossed the state of transition. It is only during the last 15 years women have started becoming entrepreneurs and started industries and business and they have yet to go a long way to be on par with men. The fact however cannot be denied that women have to play a dual role as a home-maker and also as an income-earner. Thus arises a role conflict in many women, which prevents them from taking a prompt decision in entering business. Despite the modernisation and other factors mentioned above, the weight of tradition and the responsibilities of the family tends to slow down this movement. Further, occupational backgrounds of the families and the educational attainment of the husbands have a direct bearing on the development of women entrepreneurship. The development of kindergartens, day nurseries and creches and limiting the size of the family help the women entrepreneurs to some extent enter business in such a manner that their husbands' prestige is enhanced.

Some of the major conclusions and recommendations made at a seminar on "Woman and Rural Entrepreneurship" held at Madurai, Kamaraj University early in September, 1990 were: Women are not weak, but very strong; the industrial and business opportunities are many – electronics (printed circuit boards, floppy discs), engineering (winding, machinery manufacturing), plastic injection moulding, (film making), chemicals (golden paste and laboratory chemicals), food and allied products (protein biscuits and cake mixture); rubber, pharmaceuticals, machinery and equipment, energy, fuel etc.

A majority of women entrepreneurs are from the middle class families but have low technical education, less family responsibilities (owing to the joint family system) but desire to become entrepreneurs. This potential should be identified and tapped.

Adequate infrastructural support by one single coordinating or nodal agency to facilitate flow of adequate working capital, technology, electricity, land and marketing for rural women entrepreneurs may be helpful and mobile training centres should be opened. Post-training follow-up is vital for the success of entrepreneur development programmes.

Conclusion

Today, their is a greater awakening among women. Given an opportunity, they will deliver the results. In education, they have not only excelled but also become top makers. Likewise, in office and industry, many have shown brilliant results. Even in rural India with education, women have shown better performance. Educating women is absolutely essential in strengthening her personality. The need of the hour is to provide an opportunity in conducive atmosphere, free from prejudice and vengeance. The need for awareness motivation to be an active member of the society and courage to correct the faults of men, are greater challenges of this decade. It is, therefore, encouragement of the growing intensity of motivation amongst educated young women for coming in the entrepreneurial stream and extend support with scientifically designed package of the technical and financial assistance. The non-governmental organisations have bigger role in stimulating and nurturing the spirit of entrepreneurship amongst women. Towards this end, an integrated approach is necessary for making the movement of women entrepreneurship a success. For this purpose, both the Government and non-Government agencies have to play a vital role.

Entrepreneurship is certainly life's endurance test but it is also life's greatest platform to realise a sense of fulfilment. The entrepreneurial journey is one of building value every step of the way be it skills, knowledge, experience or wealth. Additionally, an entrepreneur builds value not only for him or herself but more importantly for society.

India is indeed witnessing the dawn of a new entrepreneurial era that is being populated by a new breed of entrepreneurs that include first generation entrepreneurs, women entrepreneurs and social entrepreneurs amongst others. This emerging paradigm is also about inclusive growth through self-employment opportunities that every strata of our society can access. This is influencing transformational change in corporate philanthropy where the "not-for-profit" charitable approach is making way for models that need to deliver self-sustaining profitability. Foundations like those of Bill and Melinda Gates, Bill Clinton and others are focused on research-linked activities that can finally translate into businesses that address affordable healthcare in the developing world. The profit-averse NGOs of yesterday are now focused on developing social enterprises along the lines of sustainable profitability.

Women are also transforming their social roles from being passive to active participants in the economic mainstream. Ela Bhat's SEWA, AWAKE (Association of Women Entrepreneurs of Karnataka) and others are helping to instil an entrepreneurial psyche amongst a wide cross section of women. First generation entrepreneurs like N.R. Narayana Murthy, Azim Premji and many others have set the stage for huge entrepreneurial opportunities in the technology segment and have created unprecedented wealth which has enabled India to earn global respect. These new entrepreneurs have created over a million jobs over the last five years and have set the tone for an entrepreneurial revolution that can deliver extraordinary results.

ANNEXURE

SOME SUCCESSFUL WOMEN ENTREPRENEURS

The role of women in manufacturing activity is quite sufficient. And, small-scale enterprises have been the breeding ground for women to prove their entrepreneurial activities, skills and contribute to the national development. Women entrepreneurs have entered all fields of manufacturing activities and are willing to experiment and change with time. She is characterised by a positive attitude and a healthy image, determination, experience, persistence and hard work. She accepts challenges and delights in her work. She is very task oriented and understands her workers. Women entrepreneurs both in rural and urban India are successful. Both young and old, trained and untrained, educated and uneducated are in the forefront of the industrial revolution in India.

The involvement of women entrepreneurs is spontaneous, far greater. The satisfaction and sense of achievement derived is major motivating factor and plus point.

Entrepreneurship is indeed an extremely challenging and exciting business. The promise and jubilation that lie ahead must surely outweigh the initial trials and tribulations. Overpowering the discouraging vicissitudes of the game, the entrepreneur sprints ahead to reap a rich harvest when the sapling that he nourished begins to bloom.

The successful women entrepreneurs come from different background. With initial training, they have scaled new heights and also provided employment opportunities to others. These success stories will inspire other women too.

1. Smt. Girija Venkatesh

Smt. Girija Venkatesh is a shining example of a successful woman entrepreneur. She was born in August 1961 and completed her B.Sc. with Physics, Chemistry and Mathematics in 1984 from Bangalore University. She is married to an engineer working in HMT watches, Bangalore.

SISI Bangalore gave her five month training in Lens Grinding and Polishing. She also attended a course on Decoration of Glass & Ceramic-ware at this Institute. As she was contemplating to start a unit for the manufacture of ophthalmic lenses, it was found that with prestigious watch manufacturing units like HMT, Titan, Befora coming in a large way for the manufacture of sophisticated watches, starting up a unit for the manufacture of mineral glasses and watch crystals was more relevant and challenging. With the added background of her husband already working in HMT watches the initiative was almost spontaneous. A visit by her husband to Japan and South-east Asian countries for survey-cum-study and also after finding out the latest machinery available at Japan for the manufacture of mineral glasses and watch crystals was very fruitful. The couple convinced HMT, Titan and Befora about their capability of manufacturing mineral glasses and watch crystals to absolute standards and decided to go ahead with the project.

As a result in the Electronics City at Bangalore, Smt. Girija Venkatesh along with a couple of more enterprising people have a unit on the flat allotted by M/s. Bangalore Mechactronics Pvt. Ltd., KSSIDX in 1990.

When they approached KSFC and State Bank of India both readily gave them financial assistance by way of term loan and working capital respectively. The cost of the project is around Rs. 60 lakh, out of which the advanced imported machinery from Japan is valued around Rs. 35 lakh.

Both thereafter selected suitable candidates including women and engineers and trained them at their unit so that the end-product sustains the rigid standards as demanded by the leading watch manufacturers. After facing the initial teething problems of quality, they have enforced rigid quality control at every stage. Nineteen people are now employed with them.

Through personal contacts, the unit is able to procure sizable orders and they don't envisage any problem for their products. Small Industries Service Institute, Bangalore is proud that one of its trainees has come in the Electric City of Bangalore.

2. Miss Savitha (Screen Printer)

Miss Savitha is an example of a young lady entrepreneurship who was very keen to stand on her own feet by taking up a self-employment venture. She worked for sometime as an accountant in various companies. Small Industries Service Institute, Bangalore identified and selected her for the screen printing course organised under the Nehru Rozgar Yojana. Miss Savitha has assisted with a loan of Rs. 12,000. In right earnest she set up her unit. She has since obtained good orders for screen printing from public sectors like HMT, LIC, Banks and other institutions apart from individuals. She is even making wedding cards, greeting cards also. She has paid back the bank installments, only one-third is outstanding. Owing to prompt repayment she is entitled for some special concessions, subsidies etc. After meeting all her expenses, she is able to have regular four figure income.

Small Industries Service Institute, Bangalore is satisfied with the quality of their training programmes which are found useful for the self-employment programmes.

3. Smt. Sujatha Bhaskar

Smt. Sujatha Bhaskar is a brilliant example of a woman entrepreneur who by sheer hard work and application has started a sophisticated unit for the manufacture of carbide tipped brazed tools. She was fortunate to have Shri Bhaskar as her husband who is a shop floor man and experienced in the line of carbide tipped brazed tools. With her management abilities and enterprising nature she started a small unit, viz., M/s. Rupa Engg. Works, 625, Medahali, Vigonagar, Bangalore-49 for manufacturing carbide tipped brazed tools.

Source of Inspiration

After seeing her capabilities and enthusiasm, officials of SISI Bangalore suggested that she should go in for a bigger unit with sophisticated machinery by getting the machinery on hire-purchase from NSIC. A suitable project report was prepared and put up to NSIC for consideration. NSIC and SISI officials together helped her get the machinery of Rs. 8.63 lakh sanctioned to her. She took a spacious shed measuring 2,500 sq. ft. on lease having all the required infrastructural facilities.

Smt. Bhaskar completed successfully the Export Management Course conducted by SISI and also a course on Management Development Programme organised by TECSOK and Canara Bank. She got permanent SSI registration from Karnataka Directorate of Industries, the registration number of KST and CST, Sub-contract registration issued by SISI Bangalore and GP registration from NSIC.

Canara Bank has provided her with working capital.

Her unit is having good orders from public sector undertakings like HMT, BEML, MICO apart from other large private sector units like Mitsubishi Corp., VST etc. Carbide tipped brazed tools have export markets also.

SISI Bangalore has helped Smt. Bhaskar right from the initial stage of identifying the entrepreneurs getting machinery on hire-purchase, in training programmes, and in various other Government facilities and is also trying to help her in marketing. SISI Bangalore is proud to be closely associated with the development of her unit.

4. Smt. Guna Mallara

Smt. Guna Mallara, a native of Chickmagalur and Managing Director of M/s. Toto Foods Pvt. Ltd., Baikampady, Mangalore, is one of the well-qualified entrepreneurs of D. K. District. Being the wife of a mechanical engineer, with her academic qualification winning a lucrative employment for herself would not have been a problem. But Smt. Guna Mallara chose to become an entrepreneur.

Since her college days as a social worker she was exposed to various problems faced by the women and children in the society. After her marriage she was in Nairobi (Kenya) along with her husband Shri S. Mallara who was looking after export and import business there. On return to India she nurtured a desire to establish and manage a small-scale unit in Mangalore. By doing so Smt. Guna thought she could fully utilise her knowledge and ability. Besides running a profit earning industry she wanted to contribute something useful to the industrially backward district of D.K. Giving shape to her plan with her husband's assistance, Smt. Guna decided to set up a small-scale unit at Baikampady to manufacture energy foods (weaning foods).

A little bit of market survey which she herself conducted, gave her the confidence to opt for this line of manufacturing.

Smt. Guna established her unit in the name and style of M/s. Toto Foods Pvt. Ltd. under self-employment programme employing 17 female and 15 male staff during 1989. The Karnataka Small Industries Development Corporation Ltd., Mangalore allotted two work-sheds to her in Baikampady industrial estate. Pursuing for term loan and working capital loan did not pose a serious problem to her as the Bank of Baroda, Mangalore extended Rs.23.5 lakh towards land and building and plant and machinery and Rs. 19 lakh towards working capital. She availed the technical assistance from the Central Food Technological Research Institute (CFTRI), Mysore. She supplies her products to Social Welfare Department and Integrated Child Development Scheme for the nutrition programme.

5. Smt. Manda Vilatkar

Smt. Manda Vilatkar had the ambition of becoming a business woman or an industrialist. So she joined entrepreneurship development programme conducted by SISI Indore in February 1990 which equipped her with necessary knowledge of management, accounts, taxes etc. As a result of this EDP followed up with the visit to The Plast India Fair in New Delhi, she set up Forrnoplast Pvt. Ltd. to manufacture disposable plastic containers. With loan from the MPFC for the purchase of machinery and working capital from Indore Paraspar Sahakari Bank Ltd., she purchased the machinery from Wonderpack Ltd., Mumbai. The unit took off in August 1991. The unit is running on single shift basis. Various products of her unit are cups of 50 ml., 100 ml., 1/2 kg. and I kg. capacity, tea and coffee glasses, boxes etc. with appropriate lids. Various Government dairies, ice-cream manufacturers, hostels etc. are some of the prominent buyers.

6. Smt. Saroj Sharma

On successful completion of the one-month entrepreneurship development programme on Food and Vegetable Preservation by SISI Karnal at NDRI Karnal in March 1991, Smt. Saroj Sharma started 'Swadist Vyanjan Centre' which gives training to the girls in cookery and vegetable and food preservation.

As part of the training programmes, Shri T.R. Sehgal, Director, SISI Karnal and his team had taken the participants around different units engaged in food and vegetable preservation, gave them tips in marketing. The participants, including Smt. Sharma, were later helped in introducing jam, jelly squash, pickles and murabbas in the market.

This has helped her in supplementing her income.

Women Entrepreneurs in Varied Fields

1. Jyoti Gogate – A dynamic industrialist from Pune and President of the Association for the Promotion of Plastics, a body with over 300 members.
2. Prerana Thakore – The 47 year old economic graduate is a capable entrepreneur – produces vitamin C.

3. Suman Gorwaney – An entrepreneur manufacturing wooden educational toys and games. "We decided to make wooden toys because the capital investment was low and this line gives a lot of scope for creativity and innovation."

4. Deepika Seth Dar – Proprietor of the fast expanding Hadimba creations. This seven year-old leather garments export company based in Madras, notched up a turnover of Rs. 20 crores during the year 1992-93.

5. Madhura Bhat – The Namaste Exports, the brain child of a bored housewife was literally born in a storage in Bangalore. She does not have a chequered educational and professional background. She is a school drop-out. In 1989, she received the "Best Entrepreneur" award from the Institute of Marketing and Management, New Delhi, in recognition of her outstanding contribution to the industry. The company which sold goods worth of Rs. 15,000 in 1979, notched up sales of Rs. 72 crore in 1992-93.

6. Shehnaz Hussain – Hussain began her beauty care business with a loan of Rs. 35,000 from her father.

7. Patricia Gokhale – Patricia Gokhale is an unusual kind of entrepreneur. She ventured into the not-too-profitable board industry and carved a niche for herself by manufacturing a differentiated product, which is environment friendly and whose key input is waste matter. And this was achieved in the process of fulfilling her primary goal of creating employment potential for rural women.

The most common product in the board industry and one with tremendous demand is grey board – commonly known as cardboard. The profit margins here are very low and only large-scale units, able to achieve economies of scale through volume production, are viable.

Aditi Speciality Boards started in 1989 with an initial capital investment of Rs.21 lakh.

Gokhale who has vast experience of rural areas was keen to provide income generating opportunities for women.

Today Gokhale is a happy woman. She has achieved most of what she set out to do.

WOMEN POWER

They are successful in business and they mean business when they talk.

The environment is now changing slowly and women are coming to the forefront. Earlier too, there were women entrepreneurs but were never as vocal or as visible as they are today.

Bunty Chand, Director, Asia Society

A woman entrepreneur should identify her passion, dream big, be passionate about her work and know her subject well. Let the client know you care and you will never look back.

Dr. Jamuna Pal,
Skin Specialist and Founder of Blushworld Clinics

Women make better entrepreneurs because they have an inherent ability to multitask, handle crisis logically and are better people managers.

Shailja Dutt,
Founder and MD, Stellar Search and Selection Pvt. Ltd.

For a woman entrepreneur, it is necessary to have great ambition and an urge to reach greater heights. They should not give up on their dreams. Instead, they should keep chasing it and never let go.

Anita Ramachandran,
CEO, Cerebrus Consultants

There is nothing that a man can and a woman cannot. Resilience factor is very high in a woman and that will go a long way in years to come.

Roopa Vohra,
Revivalist Couture Jeweller, Roopa Vohra

Entrepreneurship is not defined by gender. 'Continuous partial attention' is an adaptive behaviour that helps women balance both fronts, personal as well as professional.

Architect Krupa Zubin,
Principal Director, ZZ Architects

With a good balance of business acumen, emotional and humane approach toward subjects, women are well equipped to handle business situations.

Leena Mogre,
Director, Leena Mogre Fitness

Only a self-determining, independent personality, who can brilliantly balance her role as a creative team player, the number game with accounts, finance and administration can accomplish what I have achieved today as an entrepreneur.

Sucheta Khandwala,
MD, Hammer Plus Jewellery Pvt. Ltd.

There is still a tremendous need to identify and address problems that women face in setting up enterprises especially in the small-scale sector.

Sushma Puri,
CEO and Director, Elite Model Management

KNOWLEDGE POWER

"Power in the knowledge economy resides more with knowledge workers than with owners or managers. Serving the needs of those workers is a new leadership imperative. Research shows not only the characteristics of effective leaders but also the expectations that followers have of their leaders."

— Warren Bennis, Leadership Expert

8

Role and Importance of Entrepreneurs

▸▸ Introduction

The world is rapidly changing; and unless we are also able to change our attitudes and approaches there is a real danger that a country of India's size and potential will become peripheral in the context of world's economy. The process of development includes creation of infrastructure and setting up and management of public utilities. Non-conventional energy sources have to be developed on a commercial scale. Similarly, application of modern scientific techniques in agriculture and horticulture is essential for providing a sound base for a more rapid growth of employment and incomes. There is also a need for rapid growth of industries well distributed and in a multi-directional way. Apart from land, labour and capital, there is greater need for entrepreneurs to strive for growth on an ongoing basis. In this context an attempt has been made in this chapter to analyse the nature and importance of entrepreneurs.

Dhirubhai H. Ambani
(December 28, 1932-
July 6, 2002)

Entrepreneur plays a significant role in economic development of a country, Economic development greatly depends upon entrepreneurial and industrial development. In western countries, entrepreneurs have contributed a great deal in making their country developed. According to Harbison, entrepreneurs are prime movers of innovation and Sayigh describes entrepreneurship as a dynamic force. Indeed, entrepreneur is the person who perceives business opportunity and converts it into a viable business plan culminating into a business venture ultimately. The entrepreneur, therefore, not only launches a venture but also contributes to the objectives of employment creation, output growth, technological upgradation, improvement in the quality of production, export promotion, import substitution and supply of goods at a reasonable price to the customers.

Therefore, growth of entrepreneurship and development of entrepreneurial culture in underdeveloped and developing countries are imperatively needed not only for employment generation but also for infusing entrepreneurial culture in the society which is not so far exposed to it. Entrepreneurship may also help in skill formation and technological upgradation in developing countries. Efforts made by a group of entrepreneurs in motivating the youths to change their attitude for self-employment, thus, lead to further creation of wealth through enterprise creation. The important role that an entrepreneur plays are described in next sections.

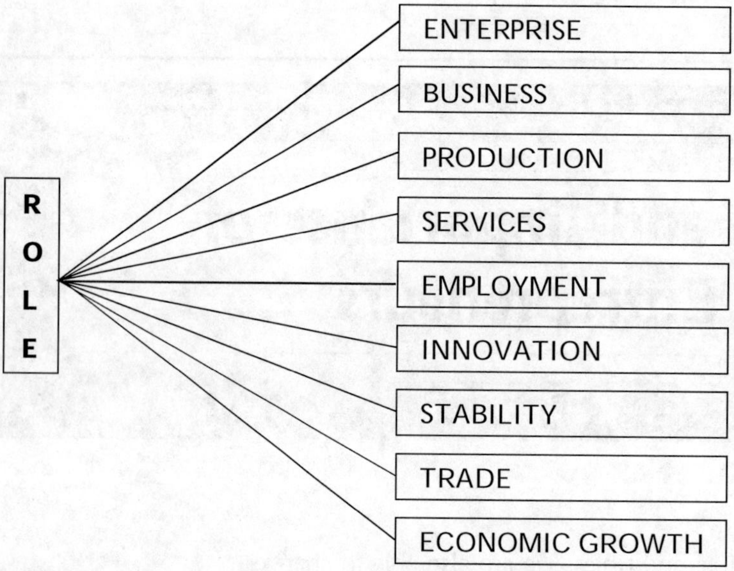

Fig. 1 Role of Entrepreneur

▸▸ Trends in Economic Development

There are twelve major trends affecting the direction of economic development:

1. Technology as a resource
2. Competition in domestic and international markets
3. The role of invention
4. Government as stimulator
5. Entrepreneurial and Intrapreneurial development
6. Innovative capital formation
7. Active financial sector
8. Innovative entrepreneurship
9. Progressive management

10. Quality as a goal
11. Supremacy of the customer
12. Collaborative relationships

Technology is more than a thing, stratagem or even a process. It is a self-generating resource that is not consumed in the process of use. Consequently, it is an important form of economic wealth.

Competition is forcing a reassessment of our individual and collective responses to the marketplace. Fierce domestic and international competition for scientific, technological, and economic pre-eminence, forcing communities and regions to leverage all their resources – human, technological and financial – to compete effectively for vibrant and diversified economies.

The countries are experiencing an unprecedented burst of invention. Myriad technological advances are occurring with incredible speed and frequency. The ability to commercialize these inventions will have direct and immediate economic consequences.

The governments are trying to find positive non-interventionist approaches to encouraging entrepreneurship and technological diversification. They seek to create jobs, provide benefits to the small business sector, and forward technology. The creation of an environment that promotes entrepreneurial activity has become a more important focal point in the government's policy on development.

People with raw energy and a proclivity for risk-taking built and sustained the countries. They are continuing to build it today – in new ways and with new approaches. These entrepreneurs and intrapreneurs are breaking tradition and providing a dynamic source of creative and innovative enterprises.

Innovative capital formation is providing the catalyst for the entrepreneurial process. Mechanisms for providing seed capital and venture capital as well as an expanding venture capital industry are helping to build new ventures. If the entrepreneurial process is to succeed, it is essential to continue to support and expand the formation of capital and its innovative utilisation in new business development.

Finally, creative collaborative relationships being formed between business, government, and academic are forging opening new opportunities for commercialisation and thus accelerating the technology transfer process.

▸▸ Lack of Entrepreneurship

Lack of entrepreneurship inhibits the process of industrialisation in the newly-developed countries. Although there is not such thing as a zero level of entrepreneurship, it is well recognised that entrepreneurs can be developed through appropriately-designed Entrepreneurship Development Programmes (EDP). These programmes broadly consist of three distinct stages: firstly, that of developing achievement motivation, and sharpening entrepreneurial trait and behaviour; second, that of project planning and development; and at the third stage, guidance is provided on industrial opportunities, incentives and facilities, rules and regulations and the development of managerial and operational capabilities. With the growth of technical manpower, it is necessary to organise entrepreneurship development programmes on a wider canvas to attract potential entrepreneurs to small business. While doing so, the characteristics of an entrepreneur have to be kept in the view.

Broadly, they are as follows:

– Development in any walk of life has always depended on individual qualities of entrepreneurship. A study of human history shows ample evidence of the role of individuals in the process of development.

- Industrial development in almost all countries has always started with individual enterprises.
- Even huge multinational and national corporations have mostly received their inspiration from one or a few individuals.
- In the case of small industries, the project is usually centred around a single individual.
- Small enterprises are mostly initiated, managed and developed by one or a few individuals.
- Qualities of entrepreneurship constitute one of the major resources in the promotion of an enterprise.
- An entrepreneur is someone who ventures out; prefers change as a means of growth; and is prepared to take calculated risks.
- While taking a risk, the entrepreneur is aware of the possibilities of success as well as the consequences of failure.
- He analyses the pros and cons carefully before making decisions.
- He is involved in the planning activities, both before and after the decision to start the enterprise.
- He is motivated by an urge to make a success of the project.
- He proceeds to accept the situation as a challenge.
- He equips himself with all the necessary tools.
- He is persistent and is full of perseverance for making a success of himself.
- Entrepreneurship is a product of interaction among a number of factors. Some of these factors are in the individual (psychological) and the rest are in the social, cultural and economic milieu.

In brief the ingredients for a successful entrepreneur are:

- He is confident in facing challenges and is eager to achieve.
- He identifies the product.
- He plans for a venture.
- He selects the technology commensurate with the means available and tuned to the social and economic environment.
- He is eager to improve quality.
- He is able to manage men and material.
- He finds markets.
- He is innovative.
- He is progressive.
- He always strives to climb up.
- He always imbibes new technology for improvement.
- He always strives for modernisation, diversification.
- He is well-informed.
- He strives to meet the changing needs of the customer or hold customer as king.

In India, a large number of institutions and organisations are engaged in the development of entrepreneurship, resulting in the speedy growth of industrial ventures.

The example of India is fascinating. During its First Five Year Plan, technical education was given importance. Industrial training institutes for low-level semi-skilled workers, polytechnics and prototype development and training centres for skilled workers and supervisors, engineering colleges for managers and institutes of technology for the higher managerial group were established all over the country. This resulted in India becoming the third largest technical power.

⏩ Sustaining Momentum of Change

The dynamics of change have wider implications. It is a continuous process. And, changes inside and outside the enterprise/organisation can move the goal posts.

Transforming an enterprise is not a science: there are no formulae for success. The enterprises studied were not following some masterplan; indeed, much of what the entrepreneur did was intuitive, almost an art form. Examining their experience yields valuable insights into creating a strategy that will realise the promise of transformation. By viewing an enterprise from three perspectives – how performance needs to change and how fast; a leader's aspirations and preference; and the sources of energy available to drive the change – we can gain insight into what strategy will work.

A successful strategy demands effective execution. Choose initiatives that link the sources of energy to the right performance levers. Grouping initiatives into four basic types – executive de-bottlenecking decisions, direction-setting or redesign task teams, mobilising and communicating and coaching – helps simplify the choice. Then, be sure to exploit the interdependent dynamics of the initiatives to keep the change moving ahead.

⏩ Importance of an Entrepreneur

Entrepreneur is one of the most important inputs in the economic development of a country or of regions within the country. Entrepreneurial competence makes all the difference in the rate of economic growth. In India, state and private entrepreneurship co-exist. The small-scale industrial sector and business are left completely to private entrepreneurs. It is, therefore, in this context that an increasingly important role has been assigned to the identification and promotion of entrepreneurs for this sector.

The need for a broad-based entrepreneurial class in India arises from the need to speed up the process of activating the factors of production, leading to a higher rate of economic growth, dispersal of economic activities, development of backward and tribal areas, creation of employment opportunities, improvement in the standard of living of the weaker sections of the society and involvement of all sections of the society in the process of growth.

Several factors go into the making of an entrepreneur. Individuals who initiate, establish, maintain and expand new enterprises constitute the entrepreneurial class. The socio-political and economic conditions, the availability of industrial technology and know-how, state of art and culture of business and trading, existence of markets for products and services and the incentives and facilities available for starting an industry or business, all have a bearing on the growth of entrepreneurship. A conducive environment is created through the policies and interest of the government in economic and industrial development.

It is now well recognised that entrepreneurs can be developed through appropriately designed entrepreneurship development programmes. These programmes broadly envisage a three-tiered approach: developing achievement motivation and sharpening of entrepreneurial traits and behaviour, project planning and development and guidance on industrial opportunities, incentives and facilities and rules and regulations, and developing managerial and operational capabilities. Various techniques and approaches have been developed and adopted to achieve these objectives, keeping in view the target-groups and/or target areas. The structuring of the programmes and training methodology also necessitate consideration of the specific target-groups and target areas. Methodology for selection of the prospective entrepreneurs as well as support services after training have a significant impact on the success of the entrepreneurs' development programmes.

⏩ A Catalytic Agent

An entrepreneur is one of the important segments of economic growth. Basically, an entrepreneur is a person who is responsible for setting up a business or an enterprise. In fact, he is one who has the initiative, skill for innovation and who looks for high achievements. He is a catalytic agent of change and works and looks for high achievements. He is a catalytic agent of change and works for the good of people. He puts up new grainfield projects that actually creates wealth, opens up employment opportunities and fosters other sectors.

The entrepreneur brings in overall change through innovation for the maximum social good. Human values remain sacred and inspires him to serve society. He has firm belief in social betterment and he carries out this responsibility with conviction. In the process, he accelerates personal, economic as well as human development. The entrepreneur is a visionary and an integrated man with outstanding leadership qualities. With a desire to excel, the entrepreneur gives top priority to Research and Development. He always works for the well-being of the society. More importantly, entrepreneurial activities encompass all fields/sectors and fetter a spirit of enterprise for the welfare of mankind.

⏩ Stimulants to Entrepreneurship

A variety of social, economic, political and cultural factors are stimulating entrepreneurial activity and thus generating more robust economic development. These stimulants are as follows:

1. An increasing focus on capital formation. Availability of capital is a stimulant to an entrepreneur to start a new firm and/or give birth to a new idea.
2. The ability to transform scientific and technical developments through new institutional development is a second factor.
3. A third stimulant is supportive government programmes.
4. Availability of required training and input is ranked fourth.
5. A collaborative relationship between business and research and their direct attempts to transfer technology to the market place may provide stimulus to a number of entrepreneurs who seek the opportunity to commercialise their ideas and
6. Finally, an endeavour to create an environment conducive to innovation will provide a much-needed stimulant to entrepreneurial activities.

The innovation centre provides technological evaluation, entrepreneurial assessment and other related levels of assistance to entrepreneurs.

⏩ Entrepreneur and Economic Growth

Economic development of any region is an outcome of purposeful human activity. A man assumes various roles in the development process, namely, as organiser of human capital, natural material resources, worker and consumer. He stands at the center of the whole process of economic development. According to Schumpeter, economic development consists of "employing resources in a different way", in making a new combination of the means of production. The entrepreneur locates ideas and puts them into effect in the process of economic development.

According to Baumol, an entrepreneur is a Shumpeterian innovator and something more than a leader. The entrepreneur, according to him, occupies a crucial place in the process of economic development.

Schumpeter further says that economic growth depends on the rate of applied technical progress (i.e., innovation) and rate of technical process in the economic field which in turn depends on the supply of entrepreneurs in society. Thus the entrepreneur becomes the agent of change in society.

In the Schumpeterian model, entrepreneur is an innovator and the supply of 'innovative entrepreneurs' depends on the necessary social and economic overheads. These economic and social overheads are very poor in backward regions which causes a shortage in supply of entrepreneurs. In this connection, we can refer to David McClelland who explained the development of entrepreneurship in terms of human motivation to achieve or need for achievement. McClelland's hypothesis is that a society with a generally high level of achievement will produce more energetic entrepreneurs, who, in turn, accelerate the princess of economic development.

In the Indian context, entrepreneurship has yet another dimension. An entrepreneur may not necessarily be an 'innovator' but an 'imitator' who would copy the organisation, technology, or products of innovators from other developed regions. His role as imitator is likely to be guided and controlled by the various constraints and conditions peculiar to this area of operation and the factors under which he conducts his minimal modest industrial activity.

Other social scientists, notably Max Weber, have talked of the importance of entrepreneurship and expressed the view that creative and entrepreneurial energies are generated by the adoption of exogenously supplied beliefs which in turn produce intense efforts in occupational pursuits and accumulation of productive assets leading to the manufacture of goods and services. According to him, entrepreneurs are a product of the particular social conditions in which they live and it is the society which shapes the personality of individual entrepreneurs.

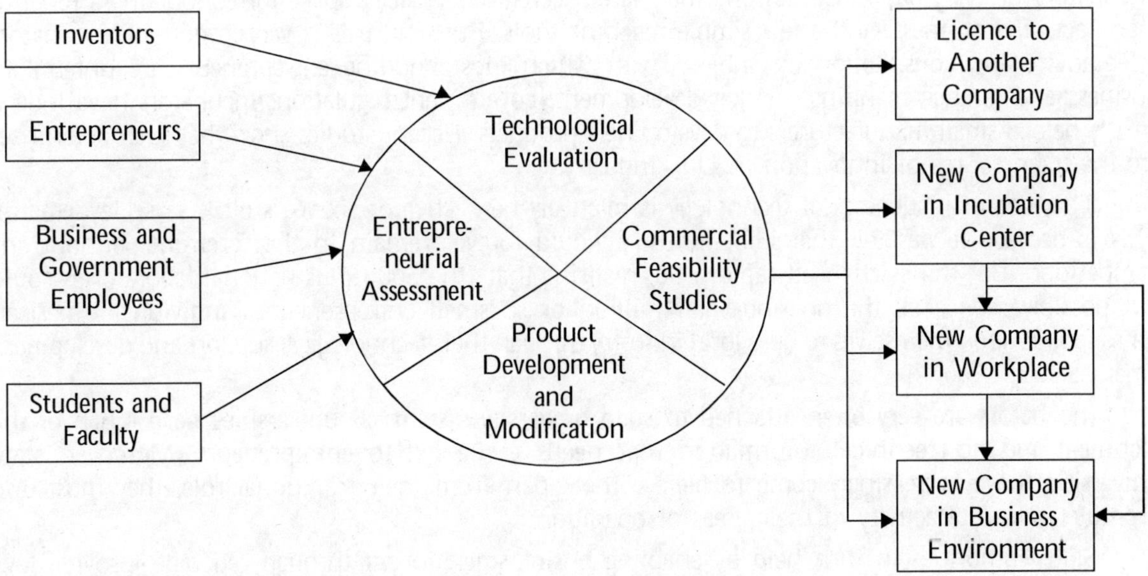

Fig. 2 Innovation Centre

John Kunkel believes that the behavioural pattern of individuals is important for development and such a pattern can be influenced by external stimuli so as to alter it in the manner we want it. In other words, if we want more people in society to behave as entrepreneurs, we can bring about such behaviour on their part by appropriate alterations in the social environment so as to influence them to take to entrepreneurial pursuits. Like Weber, Cochran and Young underscore the importance of society in shaping the entrepreneurial personality and consider that ingredients in the emergence of entrepreneurs are cultural values, role expectations, social tensions and inter-group relations in society.

Entrepreneurs are an important source of economic development. It is, therefore, suggested that there must be a motivational training programme to develop entrepreneurs and measures must to be taken to modify the environment to stimulate entrepreneurial behaviour among individuals. There are thinkers who believe that "Schumpeterian entrepreneurs are needed in underdeveloped countries for rapid economic development." Industries to promote rural industrial private enterprise, specifically to create a new class of indigenous industrialists throughout the countryside.

Small-scale industries play a useful role in regional development and industrial dispersal. Indeed, one of the pivotal problem confronting many countries in the world today in the task of social modernisation is how to disperse sources of economic activities so that development should become general, rather than concentrated in larger cities and capital. In a country that sanctions free enterprise, the movement of economic activities cannot easily be directed as the government would want it to be. Instead, we witness the tendency of capital to centralise itself in already developed areas.

⏩ Factors Influencing Entrepreneurship

Peter Heydemann, Science Counsellor in the U.S. Embassy here, is very much impressed with the role small business play in the process of innovation in the U.S. economy. He explained how 'incubators' are used successfully in the United States to encourage small entrepreneurs.

The problem is how best to help small entrepreneurs translate the results of laboratory research into marketable product, to transform a new scientific concept into a commercial product. Simply put, 'incubators' are very basic facilities offering shared secretarial services, space for conducting a retail or manufacturing business, and a few simple machine tools. But, and this is very important, incubators offer advice and consultation on subjects with which most budding entrepreneurs are unfamiliar: business and finance planning, market development, government regulation. Incubators have indeed greatly helped small manufacturers to develop new products. Recent studies show that such enterprises are the main source of innovation in U.S. industry.

The idea of incubators of technology is relatively new, "five or six years old", says Heydemann. This is because it was felt that U.S. industry would forever remain in the forefront, without any competition. But things changed rapidly. So, realising that "the 6000 plus national laboratories could not possibly service all the one-and-a-half million or so small entrepreneurs," individual American states took it upon themselves to help local industry through their technological support and development organisations.

Incubators are very often attached to state university systems as universities have much of the technical and non-technical information that needs to be fed to entrepreneurs. Moreover, state universities have increasingly come to believe that apart from their traditional role, they must also promote industrial activity in their areas of operation.

State authorities in turn help by enabling businessmen to cut through red tape, provide low-interest loans to develop prototypes, undertake market research and generally assist in bringing a new product to the consumer. "Some notion of the magnitude of this support can be had from the fact that last year alone, the federal and state governments together spent more than $ 2,000 million in encouraging small business." Many private sector companies also provide incubator facilities, though at a comparatively higher cost.

Another important aspect of incubators is that experts do not make any business decisions for their clients. They only provide guidelines and advice on product development, engineering, pilot production and in identifying markets.

Among the businesses in which incubators are making a significant contribution, says Heydemann, "are light manufacturing in matter technologies, retail and wholesale trade and, finally research and development in emerging technologies."

The success rate or incubators has been salutary in the number of new jobs created, the enlarged tax base for state revenues and in the export of manufactures. In short, incubators are bringing new vigour and vitality to America's industrial renaissance and are once more giving the country a competitive edge.

Entrepreneurs are to be innovators who must change the production function and bring about rapid development. It is only through entrepreneurs that substantial development can be brought about.

In a mixed economy, the government tries to remove the evil of monopoly capitalism by placing some restrictions. It may curb the growth of monopolies and introduce workable competition which is essential for the optimum use of the available resources. The mixed economy tries to solve the problem of distribution of goods and services in a better way than the capitalist economy. The government tries to level up the incomes of the poor people and level down those of the rich. This is done by fiscal measures, fixation of minimum wages and salaries and improvements in the environment of the people.

The role played by an entrepreneur is significantly important in a mixed economy as it permits the growth of both the public and the private sectors. In the private sector, the profit motive acts as an incentive to the entrepreneur and market mechanism plays its own role and this establishes the role of the entrepreneur in the mixed economy.

Entrepreneurship has great importance in various economic systems. It is all the more important under capitalism and mixed economy where not only are the responsibilities of the entrepreneur in production and distribution are recognized but the objectives of the growth of business and profit maximisation is also attained. Therefore, the importance of entrepreneurship stands beyond challenge in every economic system, except under socialism where it appears in a different form. Yet, entrepreneurship prevails in all economic systems in one form or the other.

⏩ Entrepreneur as an Innovator

The innovating entrepreneur introduces new products, new combinations of means of production, new services. This *inter alia* adds to rapid economic growth, rapid industrialisation, generation of employment, strides in trade, profit and prosperity.

As an innovator, entrepreneur performs the following activities:

1. Bringing about new combinations.
2. Pushes technical knowledge to achieve economic growth.
3. Utilising innovative talents/skills to initiate and improve the economy.

Innovation is self-replicating; the more you have the more you get. The founding chairman of Intel, Robert Noyce stated, "Innovation is everything, when you are in the forefront, you can see what the next innovation needs to be."

▸▸ Generation of Employment Opportunities

Entrepreneur plays a significant role in generation of employment opportunities. As we all know, entrepreneurship is a purposeful activity indulged in initiating, stimulating, promoting and maintaining economic activities for production and distribution of goods and communities, the person behind these economic activities is, therefore, a critical factor as well as a integral component of socio-economic transformation. The development strategy of our country confronts two important problems – unemployment and poverty of the masses. These problems can be effectively minimized by activating the latent human potential through entrepreneurship. This leads to the creation of self-employment and wage-employment avenues for large number of people.

The entrepreneur plays a key role in generation of employment opportunities by

1. establishing, tiny, micro, small-scale enterprises and service centres.
2. establishing industries in rural and backward areas.
3. utilising the surplus labour.
4. providing in training and fostering more small/tiny industries.

Peter Drucker has emphasized that this is the age of entrepreneurial society. Economic development and growth of a country depends to a great extent upon effective entrepreneurship. In his opinion, entrepreneur plays a crucial role for the creation of new small enterprises that energize the economic structure. Through constant creativity, new businessmen/entrepreneurs assure a strong economy and rising national income. Thus, the role of entrepreneur is important, as it not only complements but also supplements the economic growth of the country. To be more clear, entrepreneurs initiate, increase and sustain the economic growth in the following ways:

1. Generation of employment.
2. Capital formation.
3. Increase in per capita income.
4. Improvement in quality of life.
5. Improvement in standard of living.
6. Growth in infrastructural facilities.
7. Economic independence.
8. Backward and forward linkages.
9. Enhancing the basic skills.
10. Providing excellent products and services.

As such, entrepreneurs play a significant role in supplementing and complementing economic growth. To conclude with the words of Meir and Baldwin: "Development in an economy does not occur spontaneously as a natural consequence when economic conditions in some sense are right. A catalyst or agent is needed. This agent is entrepreneur."

Social Stability

Entrepreneur plays a crucial role in bringing about social stability and balanced regional development. In each and every country, entrepreneur is considered as a valuable human resource. The responsibility of social stability lies on his shoulders. Entrepreneur, as a catalyst of change, tries to bring about social stability in the following ways:

1. Absorption of work force in industries.
2. Glorification of self-help.
3. Widening self-awareness.
4. Deepening self-confidence.
5. Equitable distribution of income.
6. Creation of social infrastructures like schools, colleges, health care centres, vocational institutions, roads, homes etc.
7. Empowering women through enterprise.
8. Supply of qualitative goods.
9. Providing excellent services.
10. Alleviation of poverty through enterprises.
11. Promotion of arts through artists, handicrafts, etc.
12. Encouraging Creativity Balanced Regional Development.

The role of entrepreneur is also of paramount importance in bringing about balanced regional development. The following points justify this role of the entrepreneur:

(*a*) Setting up industries in rural and backward areas.

(*b*) Establishing agro-based industries to coordinate the dispersal process and development of agriculture.

(*c*) Utilizing indigenous technology for creation of enterprise in backward areas.

(*d*) Developing handicraft and cottage industries sector for eliminating regional imbalance and to bring about balanced regional development.

(*e*) Establishing industries in rural and backward regions and availing concessional finance, investment subsidy, transport subsidy, etc. provided by the government to reduce disparity.

The whole idea revolves round the need for simultaneity of investment in many and varied industries. However, to bring about balanced regional development, the role of entrepreneur is very much important as far as the creation of industries in backward areas is concerned. As small-scale industries bring about greater equality, it can stimulate the balanced regional development. Entrepreneurs can tap the local resources like raw materials, labour, idle savings, local talents, local experience and locally available technology to create enterprises in the backward areas. Thus, it will improve standard of living of the people in rural areas by creation of employment and income.

Export Promotion

Liberalisation, privatisation and globalisation have opened up a vista of export opportunities for entrepreneurs in India. The entrepreneurs have evinced their interest in setting up industries which are export-oriented in nature. They also find it more lucrative to establish industrial units which produce import substitutes thereby making India self-reliant. As such the role of entrepreneur is of fundamental importance as far as export promotion and import substitution are concerned. The rate of entrepreneur in promotion of exports are as follows:

1. Harnessing the available resources.
2. Exploration of new markets.
3. Export of handicrafts, handlooms, toys, apparels, gems and jewellery.
4. Minimisation of dependence on imports.
5. Earning foreign exchange.
6. Outsourcing services.
7. Lessening debt servicing.
8. Meeting balance of payments deficits.

⏩ Import Substitution

The role of entrepreneur import substitution can be viewed from the following view points:

(*i*) To achieve self-reliance in production of as many goods as possible.

(*ii*) To save foreign exchange for import of goods.

⏩ Foreign Exchange

The earnings of small-scale sector have been increasing at a faster rate and so also the forex earnings. Increase in exports brings about increase in foreign exchange earnings and thereby helping to achieve a favourable balance of payments. We all know that expansion of exports is the kingpin of any policy of solving the problem of deficit and increase of foreign exchange earnings. The entrepreneurs of small-scale units, therefore, play a great role in augmenting exports and thereby leading to earnings of foreign exchange reserve which is much needed for the development of a country like ours.

In order to earn more foreign exchange, entrepreneurs in India have come forward and motivated themselves to improve their exports and regulate their imports. The underlying aim of such export is to reduce the dependence on foreign assistance on any type and from any resource to the minimum. The balance of payments constraint is also eliminated.

⏩ Local Demand

The role of entrepreneurs is quite significant in augmenting local demand. Focus on entrepreneurs should spearhead towards production of items which are demanded locally and can be manufactured through indigenous technology, locally available skill, locally available resources and local experiences. Government should encourage entrepreneurs to create demand for the goods which are locally manufactured as the prices of goods are normally low because of low cost of production due to proper guidance, provision of adequate incentives in the forms of capital investment, subsidies, price preferences, tax exemption, tax holidays, electricity duty exemption, etc. provided by the government from time to time. Specific industries are being promoted to augment local demand as well as to compete with the products of large-scale enterprises.

While setting up enterprise, entrepreneurs should take into account the basic factors of the locality like size of customers for the goods to be produced, frequency of demand for the goods, tastes and preferences of the customers, pattern of demand for the goods, availability of substitutes whether the items are traditional or non-traditional items, etc. In order to expand the local demand, small-scale entrepreneurs in India are striving hard to expand at a faster rate than ever-increasing large-scale sector. They can be capable of expanding it further if production of innovative goods with the help of locally available resources, manpower, skill, technology, experiences can be made uninerruptedly by them so as to meet the increased demands of the local consumers. This will give rise to reduction of unemployment in the locality on one hand and generation of employment opportunities on the other; and consequent upon which the per capita income of the people will increase along with the increase in purchasing power leading in augmentation of effective demand of the people. Thus, the role of entrepreneur is of fundamental importance to a locality for augmenting local demand.

➧ Enriching Lifestyles

Of late, entrepreneurs are playing role in the field of media – paper, television, radio, entertainment, tourism, catering, courier, transport, communication, education and health care etc. These and associated entrepreneurial activities go a long way in enriching lifestyles, raises awareness, improves health and imbibes knowledge. In addition, social enterpreneurs are also playing a unique role in providing social services in the community.

➧ Small-scale Industries as Seed-beds of Entrepreneurship

Small-scale industries contribute significantly to the strengthening of the industrial structure, many articles can be produced economically on a small-scale, with some even more economically than on a larger scale. Efficient small-scale industries can be linked with large enterprises in complementary relationship, *e.g.*, sub-contracting. One of the most obvious benefits of such relationship is that it expands the industrial bases by efficiently utilizing resources, scarce or otherwise.

Also, small-scale industries may serve as seed-beds of entrepreneurship. They serve a newly industrialising country not only by their output of goods but also by functioning as a nursery of entrepreneurial and managerial talent. The almost infinite diversity of products and services that may be developed and produced by the small-scale industry sector also demands a commensurate development of skills – a desirable basis for long-term development of a diversified industrial structure in the region. Already skilled technicians, foremen and workers are induced, motivated and are often able to set up their own small-scale industrial enterprises. Generally, they offer the most promising means of promoting entrepreneurship among the people from different walks of life, especially those with limited financial resources and scant technical and managerial experience, thus establishing a wide base for rapid industrialisation. This role of small-scale industries is of decisive importance in any economy, where the industrial structure consists of a few large-scale and medium-sized industries (many of which are foreign-owned) on the one hand, and of large number of traditional industries such as artisans, handcrafts and cottage industries on the other.

The lack of a middle group of modern small-scale industries is a factor of an imbalance in the industrial structure. Such a lack also contributes to the stagnation of the economy as a whole. As a general rule, neither the government nor foreign investors are interested in owning and operating small-scale establishments.

➧ Conclusion

Entrepreneurs play an important role in the development of society. For example, the use of Jeans in America has created the demand for it throughout the world. Similarly, Coca Cola has been accepted as a social drink. The introduction of colour T.V. has provided the society a means of information and entertainment. The society has accepted the innovations of such entrepreneurs as Gillet, Wright Brothers, and Henry Ford. The inventions of these great entrepreneurs of the history has revolutionised the lifestyle of men in the society.

The role of entrepreneurs in economic development varies from economy to economy, country to country, depending upon its material resources, industrial climate and more importantly, the responsiveness of the political system to the growth of entrepreneurs. By and large, the entrepreneurs' contribution to development and growth is relatively higher in favourable opportunity conditions than in less favourable situations. The growth of an entrepreneurial society will bear fruitful results in a short-span.

Entrepreneurship, the *de facto* barometer of overall economic, social and industrial growth has brought revolutionary changes in the society. It is the *sine quo non* of a nation's progress. It has facilitated large-scale production and distribution. It has widened the area and scope of the marketing of goods and services. Perhaps it is for these reasons that the small business sector has been given priority in our national development programmes for entrepreneurship flourishes when the size of business remains relatively small and viable.

Modern business studies have a distinct entrepreneurial discipline. The approach to the study of entrepreneurship is multi-disciplinary. It images on such areas as demography, economic anthropology, business history, politics, sociology, psychology, marketing and finance. That is why entrepreneurship development becomes an integral part of the overall economic, social and industrial development of a country. This is what makes the identification and management of entrepreneurial functions a highly complex exercise.

ICONIC SUCCESS

Hard work, responsibility, clear vision, dynamism, creativity, enthusiasm, positivity, innovation, perseverance, integrity, commitment, spirit of enterprise, grit, determination, burning passion, teamwork, professional excellence, dedication, honesty, proactive inspiration, excitement, humility, focussed, learning, right motive, self-reliance, value system, a relentless spirit, high quality with value addition, hard work.

Being goal-oriented and driven by single-minded conviction, apart from humility and sincerity, is what defines these men. A clear-cut vision, intuitive streak and dedication besides a burning desire to reach loftier heights, is what we discovered to be the secrets of these achievers who got applauded for their efforts in an event that celebrate success.

UNIT : II

Entrepreneurship Theories and Development

- Theories
- Development
- Programmes
- Objectives
- Centres
- Policies
- Inputs

Many governments in developing countries recognise that small and medium-scale industries continue to play an important role in their socio-economic development. There is growing interest in developing programmes for stimulating and encouraging entrepreneurship development in these countries; with this the entrepreneur becomes the focal point in economic activities, especially in developing countries.

The most commonly adopted approach to entrepreneurship development is training.

Approaches to Entrepreneurship Development

There are various approaches to entrepreneurship development which policy makers, planners, trainers and other officials involved in development may choose. This development could be achieved within the conceptual framework in which the various strategies and policies of an entrepreneurship development programme are evolved or formulated. There is need for a thorough discussion of the various theories and their implications for the organisations' resources and capabilities. But however it is approached, entrepreneurship development should be viewed in the total perspective and should integrate entrepreneurial training, provision of incentives, consultancy services, sectoral development and other essential strategies of intervention. There are at least four major approaches:

1. Develop and arrange the course content by analysing needs and stating outcomes.
2. Choose the appropriate training methods.
3. Consider the subject area, the nature of learning, the trainee populations, the trainers themselves and time and material factors.
4. Achieve training objectives.

Training

Achievement motivation training is designed to increase the achievement orientation of the trainees with the idea that positive behaviour, such as striving for excellence, learning from feedback and moderate risk-taking, is initiated. Likewise, it strengthens the ability of an individual to generate alternatives as well as to solve problems creatively. It also develops the ability to define and set goals in life. As such, entrepreneurship development is viewed as behaviour-oriented. One of the factors contributing to the success of this training intervention in entrepreneurship development is that it is based on experience. In entrepreneurship training, learning by discovery is usually preferred. Here, one is able to learn from one's actions and behaviour in training, learning by discovery is usually preferred. Here, one is able to learn from one's actions and behaviour in training. Thus, the learning process becomes a positive reinforcement.

Although there are some variations of and/or models for this intervention, the overall objective of this aspect of training is making the entrepreneur more professional. The training intervention may also take the form of management skills development. Most entrepreneurs lack managerial skills and techniques needed to deal with the management problems of the enterprise. Therefore, for any entrepreneurship development programme to succeed, it is important not only to motivate the trainees but also to provide them with all the skills necessary to run their business successfully.

Designing an Entrepreneurship Training Programme

As mentioned earlier, designing the training programme involves setting training objectives, developing the course content and choosing appropriate training methods. The programme design is prescribed by the training needs of the target clientele. These objectives should be stated clearly, be trainee-centered, employ practically and be concerned with ends rather than means. When objectives are set, the course content can be developed. The elements of content are knowledge, habits, skills and control of emotion. The material to be included should be accorded priority according to the goal to be achieved.

GATEWAYS INTO THE CURRICULUM

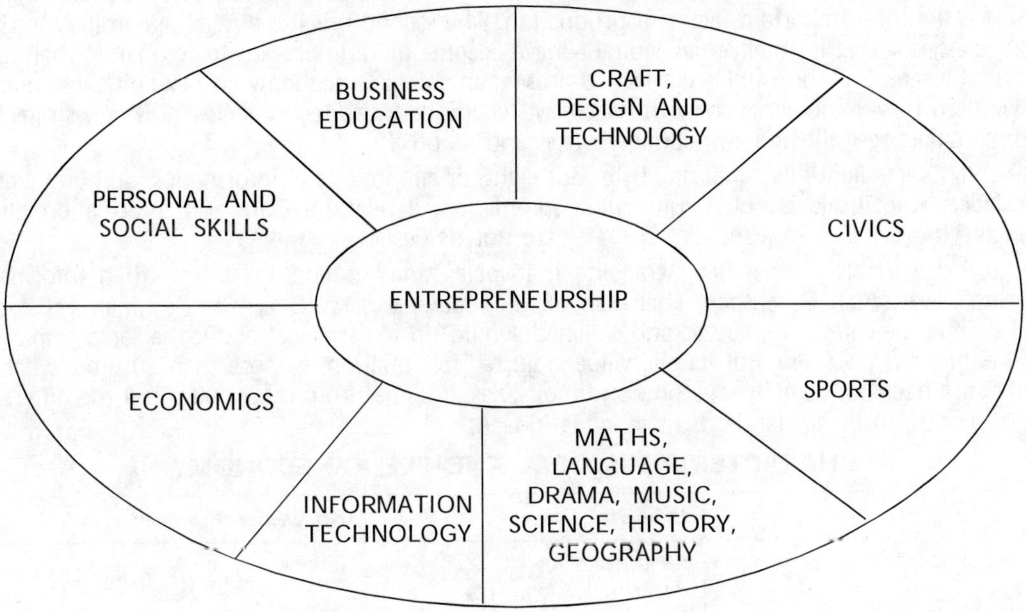

Role of Entrepreneurship Training Institutes

The training institutes which have accepted the responsibility of furthering entrepreneurial growth as well as the governmental agencies which have seen the need for entrepreneurial development jointly and independently should concentrate on the following:

- Public awareness programmes to let people realise the need, importance and advantages of entrepreneurial promotion.
- The entrepreneurial training programmes should focus on motivation, awareness, skill development, management, technology, laws etc.
- Focus should be on innovative organisation management, and research activities continuously.
- Helping trainees after they finish attending the training programmes in setting up their ventures.
- Offer counselling and guidance continuously to the entrepreneurs and help them to solve those problems which they cannot perhaps handle all by themselves.
- Follow up studies to validate the selection procedures adopted in identifying candidates for training periodically.
- Continuous evaluation of each and every training programme in terms of its objectives and the extent to which the "terminal behaviour" is in line with the programme objectives.
- Adopt a few enterprises and/or entrepreneurs every year and offer continuous support of every nature till they become self-reliant and sustaining.
- Encourage formation and development of 'entrepreneurial circles' where the membership is open to trainers in entrepreneurship officers of developmental and governmental agencies and entrepreneurs. These 'entrepreneurial circles' can monitor and guide information pertaining to entrepreneurial development in terms of short duration workshops and seminars.

Knowledge Economy

The knowledge economy stands on three pillars. The first: Knowledge has become what we buy, sell, and do. It is the most important factor of production. The second pillar is a mate, a corollary to the first: Knowledge assets – that is, intellectual capital – have become more important to companies than financial and physical assets. The third pillar is this: To prosper in this new economy and exploit these newly vital assets, we need new vocabularies, new management techniques, new technologies, and new strategies. On these three pillars rest all the new economy's laws and its profits.

In computers, eight bits equal one byte. But eight, or zillion, bits of information do not equal a byte of knowledge. Knowledge is not a sum but a summation, a relation. Data and information plug into knowledge: They are tiles in a mosaic, but they are not its design.

Knowledge involves expertise. Achieving it involves time. It endures longer than information – sometimes forever. Alan Greenspan, chairman of the Federal Reserve Board, has estimated that the US GDP, if it could be gathered together and weighed, would tip the scales at about the same amount today as it did a hundred years ago. But its real value, adjusted for inflation, is more than 20 times what it was. The difference does not come from atoms and molecules, it comes from intangibles. But the difference, in health, in wealth, in living standards, is tangible indeed.

CHARACTERISTICS OF A KNOWLEDGE ECONOMY

	Industrial Economy	*Knowledge Economy*
Objective of society	Basic needs for all through development	Empowerment
Education	Textbook, and formal teaching	Creative, interactive self-learning and informal with focus on values, merit and quality
Workers	Skilled, semi-skilled	Flexibly skilled, knowledgeable, self-empowered
Type of work	Structured & hardware driven	Less structured and software driven
Management style	Directing	Delegative
Quality of personnel	Performance based	Knowledge based
Impact on environment and ecology	Heavy	Strikingly less
Economy	Industrial	Knowledge driven

Source: Knowledge Society: Approach and Action Plan.

How many people actually become entrepreneurs?

The creation of the Global Entrepreneurship Monitor (GEM) in 1999 represented the first attempt to provide a regular annual review of the state of entrepreneurship around the world. The two principle measures of entrepreneurial activity cover start-up entrepreneurs (companies less than 42 months old), and individuals who are owners of established businesses. The 2006 report, covering 42 countries, found that the overall entrepreneurship rate including both measures expressed as a percentage of the total working population, varied widely.

The extremes were the Philippines at around 40% and Belgium at just over 4.5 %. The figure for the US stood at 15.5%. That for India was slightly higher at just over 16%.

According to the figures quoted in the 2005 GEM report, on average male entrepreneurs outnumber their female counterparts by a factor of around two to one. This is a surprisingly high ratio in the light of other figures. For instance, in 2002 a Canadian study reported that as of 2000, women were majority owners in only 15% of Canadian SMEs. And four years earlier, a study of the 500 fastest growing entrepreneurial companies in Europe included just 7% of companies run by women owner/CEOs. A likely explanation for the apparent discrepancy is that the GEM figures include both people who are opportunity-driven and necessity-driven entrepreneurs, and the report found that there tend to be higher shares of female necessity-driven entrepreneurial activity in countries where women have reduced access to established labour markets, thus pushing up the overall figure of women entrepreneurs.

> **"Embarking upon 'new combination' of the factors of production — which he succinctly terms innovation — the entrepreneur activities, the economy to a new level of development. The concept of innovation and its corollary development embraces five functions: (1) introduction of a new good, (2) introduction of a new method of production, (3) opening of a new market, (4) conquest of a new source of supply of raw materials and (5) carrying out of a new organisation of any industry...."**

9

Theories of Entrepreneurship

Introduction

The concept and theories of entrepreneurship evolved over more than two centuries have undergone major changes. Yet the concept of entrepreneurship is not clear. As the concept of entrepreneurship is complex in its content, it is influenced by not only economical aspects, but also by sociological, political, psychological, ethical, religious and cultural values. The concept also bears testimony to courage, creativity, determination, networking, hard working etc. Over the years the social scientists have interpreted the phenomenon of entrepreneurship differently in accordance with their perception and economic environment.

Keshub Mahindra
Ready for the Challenge

A coordinated and comprehensive theory of entrepreneurship is yet to come. Meanwhile let us understand the important theories of entrepreneurship propounded by social thinkers during the last two centuries.

The distinctive features of entrepreneurship over the years are:

1. Innovation,
2. A function of high achievement,

3. Organisation building,
4. Group level activities,
5. Managerial skills and leadership,
6. Gap filling,
7. Status withdrawal,
8. Entrepreneurial supply, and
9. Entrepreneurship – an emerging class.

Entrepreneurship as a process has and is undergoing changes in keeping with the continued 6 changes in different fields. In keeping with these changes, different theories of entrepreneurship have been evolved by different thinkers at different times. It is *a* continuously evolving process of *change.*

- Allow scope for flexible employment contracts to be negotiated, with remuneration arrangements and working conditions that arc well adapted to the needs of dynamic enterprises. Relax employment protection measures that inhibit restructuring or discourage entrepreneurs from taking on new workers.
- Examine the costs of complying with government-imposed administrative or regulatory requirements and identify where reductions could be made, either by removing the requirements to comply or by reducing the administrative burden involved (including through better coordination among various government agencies).
- Examine the overall effects of the tax system on entrepreneurship, and identify features that discourage entrepreneurs or the financing of entrepreneurial activity. Ensure that the tax system is transparent and that compliance is straight forward.
- Review and simplify the registration procedures required to create a business. Ensure that firms are able to close quickly should they wish to do so.
- Ensure that personal bankruptcy legislation provides an appropriate balance between encouraging risk-taking and protecting creditors.
- Re-examine the effects that social insurance provisions may have on encouraging or discouraging would-be entrepreneurs.

Ensure that specific programs designed to foster entrepreneurship operate as part of an integrated and coherent strategy that complements the framework conditions. In particular:

- Avoid policies that stem from a too-narrow definition of entrepreneurship (e.g., that entrepreneurship is only about start-ups or only about high-technology) and which may divert attention from getting the broader economic policy settings right.
- Widen the target population for entrepreneurship programs, where possible, to attract the participation of women, the young and minorities.
- Undertake regular and comprehensive evaluation of programs, and ensure that evaluation findings are acted on.

Improve the effectiveness of entrepreneurship programs by drawing on the knowledge of local level of government. In particular:

- Ensure that resources for programs to foster entrepreneurship are decentralised where appropriate in order to better tailor programs to the specific needs of an area and its business.

- Provide regular opportunities to exchange information at a national level on the experiences of local authorities in designing and implementing entrepreneurship programs.
- Seek to identify and implement low-cost and effective programs with minimal distortionary effects on market incentives. For example:
- Promote public awareness of entrepreneurship and examine the role the education system would play in developing entrepreneurial skills and attitudes.
- Increase opportunities for the unemployed to create their own jobs trough self-employment schemes.
- Facilitate networking among firms in order to foster a culture of mutual cooperation and risk-taking.
- Promote the entrepreneurial non-profit sector by contracting-out where possible the delivery of public service that meet pressing demands in economic and social development.

OECD, Fostering Entrepreneurship, 1998, pp. 28-30. Used with permission of OECD.

Entrepreneurship in Developing Countries

Among the many definitions of the entrepreneur, that which distinguishes him as a person who undertakes to organise, manage and assume the risk of running a factory is the one generally adopted in the region. Small enterprises, like entrepreneurship, cannot be defined specifically. The concept is variously understood in different countries depending on the prevailing economic and social conditions. Generally, the definition is based on two criteria: *quantitative*, which includes the size of the company in terms of number of workers, consumption of energy, capitalisation or value of sales; and *qualitative*, which refers to the organisation and management of the enterprise, methods of production or influence on the market.

A variety of social, economic, political and cultural factors are stimulating entrepreneurial activity and consequently generating economic development. These stimulants are as follows:

1. An increasing focus on capital formation. Availability of capital is a stimulant to an entrepreneur to start a new firm and/or give birth to a new idea.
2. The ability to transform scientific and technical developments through new institutional development.
3. The supportive government programmes.
4. Availability of required training and inputs.
5. A collaborative relationship between business and research and their direct attempts to transfer technology to the market place will be an opportunity for entrepreneurs who commercialise their ideas.
6. Finally, an endeavour to create an environment conducive to innovation will provide a much-needed stimulant to entrepreneurial activities.

Box 1

MOBILE MAN: AN ICON OF INDIAN ENTREPRENEURSHIP

Sunil Mittal has gone beyond cell phones to retail and more to realise his vision. He has fuelled ambitions and dreams and breathed life into promising business ventures. With his foresight and drive, he has risen as an icon of Indian entrepreneurship in the 21st century. It is a story of India's telecom to read or Sunil Bharati Mittal.

Sunil Bharti Mittal
Bharati Group
Net worth: $9.5 billion

Mittal landed at a trade fair in Taiwan, where he discovered an extraordinary device: the touch-tone phone. Months later he was selling the gadgets to customers in India under the brand name Mittbrau (short for Mittal brothers). But Touch-tone phones weren't on the government's list of products approved for Import. So he disassembled the phones in Taiwan, shipped the components through Kolkata, Delhi and Mumbai, and reassembled them in Ludhiana.

Market Cap

February 2002	Rs. 8,183 crore
February 2007	Rs. 1,38,702 crore

When he was 14, Sunil Bharati Mittal made up his mind that he was going to do something exceptional in life. He's not yet 50, but he's done it. Mittal is probably the most representative of the mobile revolution that has swept the country. It's not obvious yet. But future historians may well find this the single most important reason for India's economic miracle.

Bharati today has a turnover of Rs. 1,173 crore (2005-06). It is one of the leading private telecom companies in the country. It has the largest cellular footprint offering services in 23 states across India, fixed line operations in 94 cities, and voice service on international long distance. In the mobile business, it has a 21.8 per cent share in the telecom market (GSM and CDMA), and addresses "Today, Airtel is a household name in India and Bharati Airtel is the fifth largest enterprise in the country in terms of market cap. It has truly been a very rewarding and satisfying journey," says Mittal.

Mittal started his first venture at 18 with a capital of Rs. 20,000. He began in the small sector, manufacturing crank-shafts and cycle parts in Ludhiana.

The move into telecom did not happen till 1983, when the sector opened up and Bharati along with the Tatas and others got in. The privatisation of telecom in 1984 started the group's foray into the telecom terminal side.

When, in 1992, bids were invited for cellular service, Bharati – still a minnow – bagged Delhi despite other majors being in the fray. The success of the Delhi cellular business has been the foundation of the group. Real growth, however, came only after the National Telecom Policy in 1999.

Mittal has been at the forefront of consolidation by acquisition. In 1999, Bharati acquired a controlling Stake in JT Mobile, the cellular operator in Andhra Pradesh and Karnataka. This was followed by the acquisition of Chennai-based Skycell in 2000. The following year the company acquired Spice's Kolkata cellular operations.

"From 1983, telecom became an obsession," says Mittal. Now, of course, he is dialling a different number – he has retail and Wal-Mart on his menu.

Source: Business India.

Entrepreneurship and Economic Growth

Economic development of any region is an outcome of purposeful human activity. Men assume various roles in the development process, namely, as organiser of human capital, natural material resources, worker and consumer. He stands at the centre of the whole process of economic development. According to Schumpeter, economic development consists of "employing resources in a different way", bringing in a new combination of means of production. The entrepreneur looks for ideas and puts them into effect for economic development.

According to Baumol, entrepreneur is a Schumpeterian innovator and something more than a leader. The entrepreneur, according to him, occupies a crucial place in the process of economic development.

Joseph A. Schumpeter (1934) for the first time put the human agent at the centre of the process of economic development and assigned a critical role to entrepreneurship in his theory of economic development. According to Schumpeter "Entrepreneurship is essentially a creative activity or it is an innovative function. The process of innovation may be in the form of *(a)* Introduction of new product, *(b)* Use of new method of production, *(c)* Opening of new market, *(d)* The conquest of new source of supplying raw material or *(e)* A new form of organisation." Hence he depicted an entrepreneur not only a premier agent of production who brings together all factors of production but also provides a sound management and control for the survival as well as the growth of the production unit.

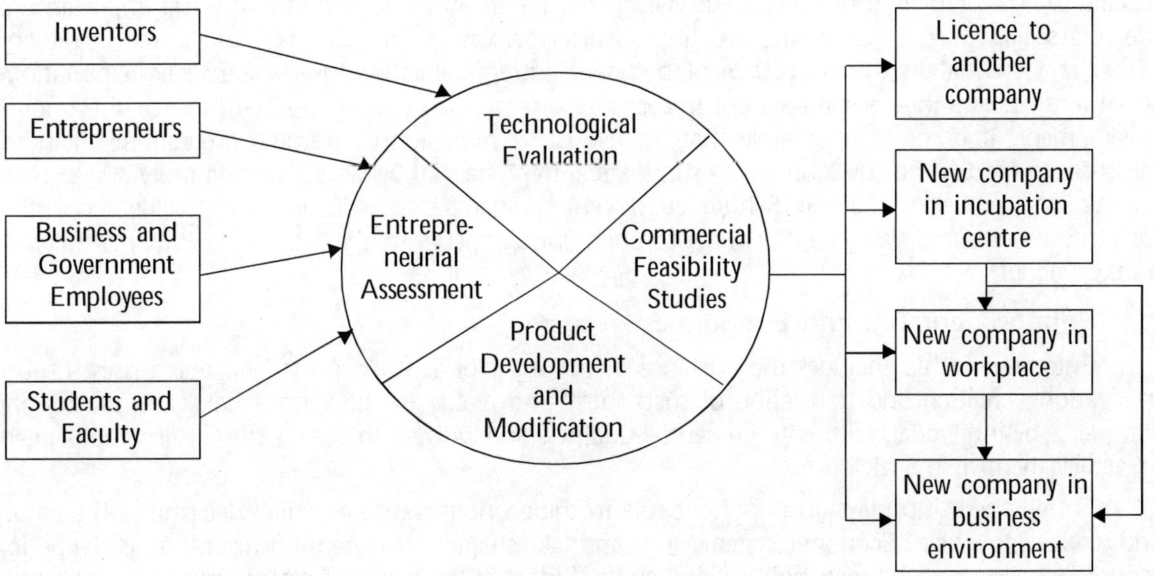

Fig. 1 Innovation Centre

Schumpeter further says that economic growth depends on the rate of applied technical progress (i.e., innovation) and rate of technical progress in the economic field which in turn depends on the supply of entrepreneurs in the society. Thus the entrepreneur is the agent of change in society.

In the Schumpeterian model, entrepreneur is an innovator, and the existence of "innovative entrepreneurs" depends on the necessary social and economic overheads. These economic and social overheads are very poor in backward regions which cause a short supply of entrepreneurs. In this connection, we can refer to David McClelland who explained the development of entrepreneurship in terms of human motivation to achieve or need for achievement (n Ach). His hypothesis is that a society with a generally high level of achievement will produce more energetic entrepreneurs, who in turn will accelerate the process of economic development.

In the Indian context, entrepreneurship has yet another dimension. An entrepreneur may not necessarily be an innovator "but an "imitator" who would copy the organisation, technology, products of innovators from other developed regions. His role as an imitator is likely to be guided and controlled by various constraints and conditions peculiar to his area of operation and the factors under which he conducts his minimal modest industrial activity.

Other social scientists, notably Max Weber, have talked of the importance of entrepreneurship and expressed the view that creative and entrepreneurial energies are generated by the adoption of exogenously supplied beliefs which in turn produce intense efforts in occupational pursuits and accumulation of productive assets leading to the manufacture of goods and service. According to him, entrepreneurs are a product of the particular social conditions in which they live and it is social conditions which shapes the personality of individual entrepreneurs.

John Kunkel believes that the behavioural pattern of individuals is important for development and such a pattern can be influenced by external stimulus so as to alter it in the manner we want it. In other words, if we want more people in society to behave as entrepreneurs, we can bring about such behaviour on their part by appropriate alterations in the social environment so as to influence them to take to entrepreneurial pursuits. Like Weber, Cocharan and Young underscore the importance of the role society plays in shaping the entrepreneurial personality and consider the scarce ingredients which are essential in the emergence of potential entrepreneurs' cultural values, role expectations, social tensions and inter-group relations in society. Entrepreneurs are an important source of economic development. It becomes imperative that there exists a motivational training programme including measures to modify the environment to stimulate entrepreneurial behaviour among individuals. There are thinkers who believe that the "Schumpeterian entrepreneurs are needed in underdeveloped countries for rapid economic development" is only through entrepreneurs that substantial development can be brought about.

⏩ Entrepreneurship and Economic Systems

Entrepreneurship includes the existence of the spirit of venturing into new enterprises through innovations, creation and translation of such spirit into reality in the various fields of industry and commerce by individuals with entrepreneurial qualities and with an intense desire for accomplishment or achievement in this field.

Entrepreneurship plays an important role in the economic system, which determines the nature and scope of this field. Economic systems grow and take shape under the influence of industrial policy, economic policy, and the socio-political and cultural ideas of the people. Entrepreneurship gives a fillip to new organisational forms and the economy has to adjust to these demands. However, changes in the structure of the economy bring about economic reforms which determine other factors affecting the economy. Economic systems is a basic structure of capitalism, socialism and mixed economy in which a certain level of entrepreneurship is found.

⏩ Capitalism

Capitalism has 'freedom' as its landmark. Free enterprise, freedom to save or to invest, free and healthy competition, lack of the dominance of central plan and consumer's sovereignty are the main features that distinguish capitalism from other economic systems. In a free enterprise economy, the problem of what to produce is solved by the price mechanism. The goods are bought and sold in the market at a price which is freely determined by the equality between demand for and supply of goods with reference to the cost of production. It is for this reason that entrepreneurship fully commands a price and market mechanism. On the basis of this, the entrepreneur also has the controls of the production and distribution of goods by mobilising the resources to maximise his profit. Profit motive is the main aim of the entrepreneur in a free market mechanism under capitalism. He also distributes the goods according to the different market conditions both in domestic and overseas markets and therefore, we find he is a competitor or monopolist or a monopolistic competitor in the home market. Besides he is a cut-throat competitor in the overseas market where he allocated the amount of goods and determines the price according to his capacity to unload goods – a special case of discriminating monopoly.

Socialism

Private entrepreneurship does not contribute much to an economic system but it becomes the responsibility of the economic and financial experts in the Central Authority to strategise the exploitation of resources and organise an equitable distribution of goods without any profit motive but for the social good.

Entrepreneurship exists in the form of a body consisting of the representatives nominated by the government to frame the plans for the proper mobilisation of resources, their allocation and re-allocation so that most of the resources channelised towards industries of national importance. It is therefore, for entrepreneur who has a complete control over the resources, the production of the goods according to the needs of the people and their distribution in the internal vis-a-vis external market. As socialism is contrary to capitalism or mixed economy, all such responsibilities are not shared by the private entrepreneur and hence his role under socialism is negligible.

Mixed Economy: The entrepreneurs also play an important role in the production and distribution of goods in a mixed economy. The basic characteristics of this economy is that the government undertakes the production of mostly capital goods while the production of consumer goods is left to the private enterprises and hence they are equally responsible for the uplift of the people because they produce not only luxuries and comforts but also goods of basic requirements of the people. Like a capitalist economy, mixed economy also tries to solve the basic problems with the help of the price mechanism. But where the price mechanism fails to achieve the desired result, the state tries to intervene in order to find a better solution to the various problems. When the problem of production is not solved satisfactorily by the private entrepreneur, the state tries to increase the production of essential goods and discourages that of less essential or non-essential goods. It does so by producing defence goods itself as also some basic goods like iron, steel and cement etc. and also by encouraging the private producers to increase the production of essentials like food, clothing, housing etc. In a mixed economy, the government does a good deal to encourage the production of most essential goods and in case their production still lags behind, it may itself undertake their production and increase it by giving it top priority in its economic programme.

In a mixed economy, the government also tries to remove the evil of monopoly capitalism through restrictions. It may curb the growth of monopolies and initiate workable competition which is essential for the optimum use of the available resources. Mixed economy tries to solve the problem of distribution of goods and services in a better way than the capitalist economy. The government tries to level up the incomes of the poor people and level down those of the rich people. This is done by fiscal measures, fixation of minimum wages and salaries and improvements in the environment by the people.

The role played by an entrepreneur is significantly important in a mixed economy as it permits the growth of both the public and the private sector. In the private sector, profit motive acts as an incentive to the entrepreneur and market mechanism plays its own role. This establishes the role of entrepreneur in the mixed economy.

Entrepreneurship has great importance in various economic systems. It is all the more important under capitalism and mixed economy where not only the responsibilities of entrepreneur in production and distribution are recognised but the objective of growth of business and profit maximisation is also attained. Therefore, the importance of entrepreneurship stands beyond challenge in every economic system except under socialism where it appears in a different form. Yet, entrepreneurship prevails in all economic systems in one form or the other.

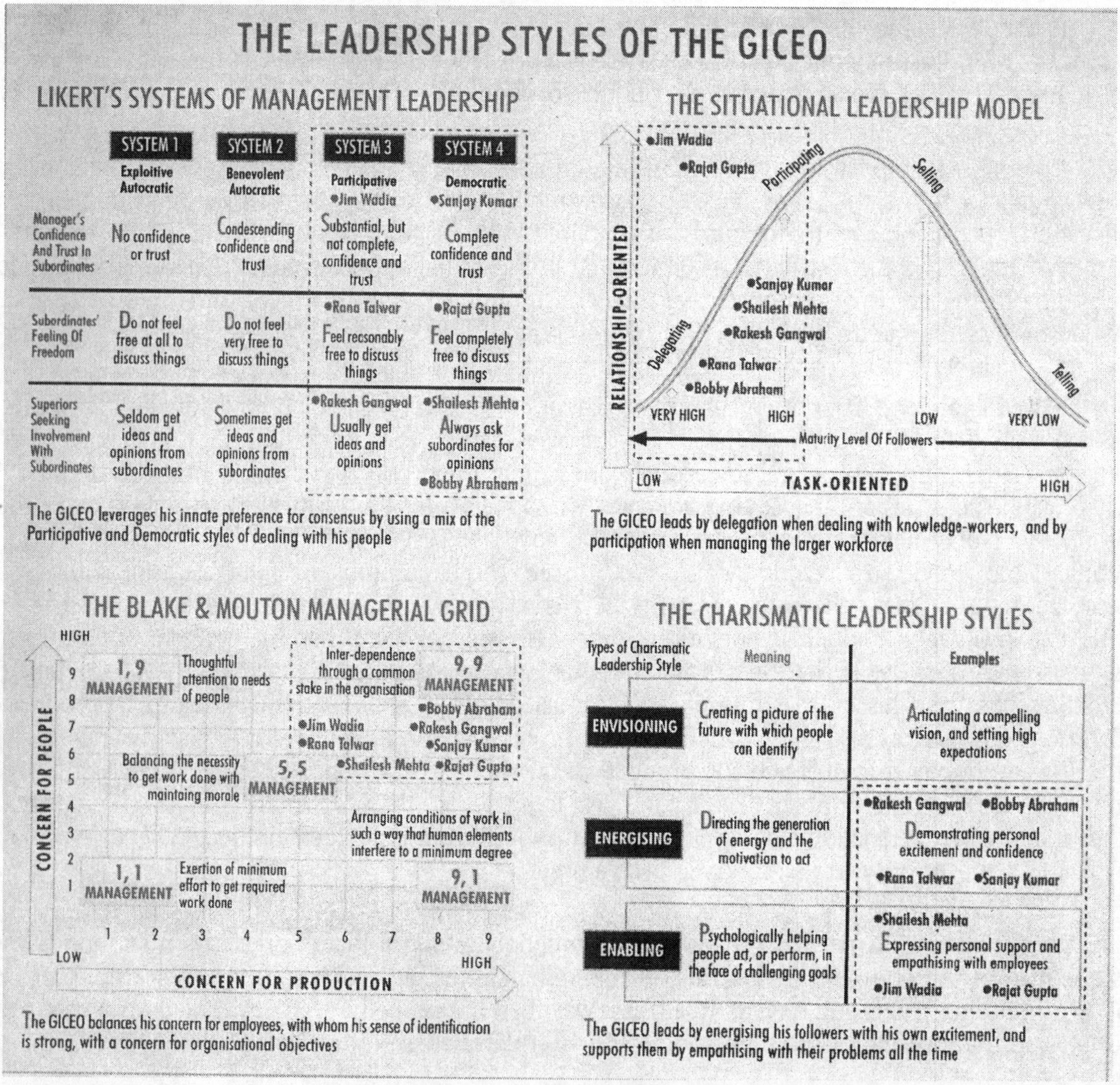

Theories of Entrepreneurship

Theories of Entrepreneurship are broadly classified into economic, psychological, sociological and cultural.

The static approach of the emerging Neo-classical school did not readily accommodate a concept with such dynamic connotations as entrepreneur. Alfred Marshall, for example, laid much more stress on the routine activities of management and superintendence than he did on the innovative activity of the entrepreneur.

The phenomenon of entrepreneurship development has been viewed, explained and interpreted differently by social scientists. Among those who have stressed on the routine activities of management and superintendence than he did on the innovative activity of the entrepreneur.

The phenomenon of entrepreneurship development has been viewed, explained and interpreted differently by social scientists. Among those who have stressed on the psychological aspects as contributing to entrepreneurial success are Joseph Schumpeter, McClelland, Hagen and Kunkal.

Entrepreneurship is inhibited by the social system, which denies opportunities for creative facilities. "The forces of custom, the rigidity of status and the distinct of new ideas and of the exercise of intellectual curiosity, combine to create an atmosphere inimical to experiment and innovation." The theories of Weber and Cochran in this context are mainly sociological in nature.

Briefly, the concepts of entrepreneur and entrepreneurship have been investigated from economic, social, political, cultural and managerial points. The development of this understanding is summarised in Table 1.

Table 1

DEVELOPMENT OF ENTREPRENEURSHIP THEORY AND TERM ENTREPRENEUR

4th BC Kautilya	:	Most successful enterprises owes to entrepreneurs ability to work in teamwork to achieve various goals in spite of ups and downs. Capable men, thus, will finally convert the whole idea into an 'amazing balance sheet.' The final leap may come in any manner – a big order, a turnaround client or a big financial investor. But one needs to carry on these trails – a hundred times. The word "entrepreneur" is derived from the French verb *entreprendre*. It means "to undertake" or go between. In the early 16th century, the French attributed this term to people who organised and/or led military expeditions. All those people who were responsible to find new land were also called "entrepreneurs."
Middle Ages	:	Actor and person in charge of large-scale production projects.
17th Century	:	Person bearing risks of profit (loss) in a fixed price contract with government.
1725: Richard Cantillon	:	Person bearing risks is different from one supplying capital.
1776: Adam Smith	:	Entrepreneur is an individual who undertook the formation of an organisation for commercial purposes. He is a person with unusual forcsight who could recognize potential demand for goods and services.
1797: Beaudeau	:	Person bearing risks, planning, supervising, organizing, and owning.

1803: Jean Baptiste Say	:	Separated profits of entrepreneur from profits of capital.
1848: John Stuart Mill	:	Elaborated on the necessity of entrepreneurship in private enterprise. The term entrepreneur subsequently became common as a description of business founders and the 'fourth factor' of economic endeavour in economic literature. The entrepreneur is one who possessed certain new economic enterprises, yet a person who had exceptional insight into society's needs and was able to fulfill them.
1876: Francis Walker	:	Distinguished between those who supplied funds and received interest and those who received profit from managerial capabilities.
1934: Joseph Alois Schumpeter	:	Entrepreneur is an innovator and develops untried technology.
1958: Haggen	:	An entrepreneur is an economic man who tries to maximise his profits by innovations.
1951: David McClelland	:	Entrepreneur is an energetic moderate risk taker.
1964: Peter Drucker (1909-2005)	:	Entrepreneur maximizes opportunities through systematic innovations.
1975: Albert Shapero	:	Entrepreneur takes initiative, organises some social-economic mechanisms, and accepts risk of failure.
1980: Karl H. Vesper	:	Entrepreneur seen differently by economists, psychologists, business persons, and politicians.
1983: Gifford Pinchot	:	Intrapreneur is an entrepreneur within an already established organisation.
1985: Robert D. Hisrich	:	Entrepreneur is the process of creating something different with value by devoting the necessary time and effort, assuming the accompanying financial, psychological, and social risks and receiving the results – rewards of monetary and personal **satisfaction.**
1985: Gartner W.	:	Creation of new organisations.
1989: Stevenson, H. Roberts, M. & H. Grousbeck	:	The pursuit of opportunity without regard to resources currently controlled but constrained by the founder's previous choices and industry related experience.
1990: Vasant Desai	:	The entrepreneur brings in overall change through innovation for the maximum social good. Human values remain sacred and inspires him to serve society. He has firm belief in social betterment and he carries out this responsibility with conviction. In the process, he accelerates personal, economic as well as human development. The entrepreneur is a visionary and an integrated man with outstanding leadership qualities. With a desire to excel, the entrepreneur gives top priority to Research and Development. He always works for the well-being of the society. More importantly, entrepreneurial activities encompasses all fields/sectors and fosters a spirit of enterprise for the welfare of mankind.
2004: Nandan Nilekani	:	In essence, entrepreneurship is about dreaming the impossible and helping followers to achieve the same. Moreover, the dream has to be built on sound and context-invariant values to sustain the enthusiasm and energy of people over a long time. Further, set direction to create a shared vision, encourage execution

		excellence, embrace inclusive meritocracy to build a globally best-in-class leadership team that delivers outstanding business value in every customer engagement.
2005: Sunil Bharati	:	For the Indian-bred entrepreneur, the path to sustained excellence is one that requires willingness to change, learn and excel. Most entrepreneurs exhibit a balanced combination of education and entrepreneurial drive with an eagerness to change and innovate. No doubt, they will be able to play a vital role in contributing to our country's development. As many more entrepreneurs spread their wings and explore new horizons, the fundamental focus must remain unchanged – seek the best in every domain and put to the service of the customer. Let this core thought continue to drive the spirit of entrepreneursip in India. If the economic environment becomes global oriented, it is certainly not difficult to achieve the dream and vision.
1006: N.R. Narayana Murthy	:	Entrepreneurship is an agent of change. Entrepreneurship built and sustained on the true set of value system is ready for the marathon race in the global economy. Innovation productivity, fairness, frankness, ethics on science and transparency are the core values of entrepreneurship.
2007: Richard Strozzi-Heckler	:	Entrepreneurial is a pracice that can be developed and trained for enterprise. An entrepreneur methodically build fluency and muscle through the regular exercise of disciplines that require simultaneous physical and mental effort.
Mansi Tiwari	:	As technology changes and global connectivity improves, entrepreneurship means that the entrepreneur not only has to ensure profits for all shareholders, he has to fix problems, tap new markets, bring cutting edge ideas to the table, and lead cross-cultural teams. The person has to be a passionate, empathetic, sharp and inspirational at the same time.

Entrepreneurship has taken on new meaning and greater challenges in the last decades. The real skill is learning how to influence through commitment, loyalty and trust rather than through mere compliance or, at worst coercion.

⏩ Economists' Viewpoint

Entrepreneur and entrepreneurship have been a point of interest to economics as early as 1755. The term entrepreneur seems to have been introduced into economics by Cantillon, but the entrepreneur was first accorded prominence by Say. It was variously translated into English as 'merchant', 'adventurer' and 'employer', though the precise meaning is 'the undertaker of a project.' James Stuart Mill popularised the term in England.

According to economists entrepreneurship and economic growth will take place in those situations where particular economic conditions are most favourable. Economic incentives are the main drive for the entrepreneurial activities. They firmly believe that a well development market and efficient economic policies foster entrepreneurship in a big way.

The static approach of the emerging Neo-classical school did not readily accommodate a concept with such dynamic connotations as entrepreneur. Alfred Marshall, for example, laid much more stress on the routine activities of management and superintendence than he did on the innovative activity of the entrepreneur.

Psychological Theories

The phenomenon of entrepreneurship development has been viewed, explained and interpreted differently by social scientists. Among those who have stressed on the psychological aspects as contributing to entrepreneurial success are Joseph Schumpeter, McClelland, Hagen and Kunkal. The main focus of the theories of these persons is as follows:

According to psychologists, entrepreneurship is most likely to emerge when a society has sufficient supply of individuals possessing particular psychological characteristics. The main characteristics are:

1. an urge to do something
2. to fulfill a dream,
3. an institutional capacity to see things in new ways (vision)
4. energy of will and mind to overcome fixed habits of thought
5. the capacity to withstand social opposition; and
6. the high need for achievement.

These characteristics motivate and drive people towards entrepreneurial activities.

Sociological Theories

Entrepreneurship is inhibited by the social system, which denies opportunities for creative facilities: The forces of custom, values, the rigidity of status and the distinct new ideas and of the exercise of intellectual curiosity, combine to create an atmosphere inimical to experiment and innovation. The theories of Weber and Cocharan in this context are mainly sociological in nature and worth mention.

Sociologists argue that entrepreneurship is most likely to emerge under a specific social culture. According to them, social sanctions, cultural values and role expectations are responsible for the emergence of entrepreneurship. Social cultural values channel economic action that gives birth to entrepreneurship.

"Embarking upon 'new combinations' of the factors of production which he succinctly terms innovation – the entrepreneur activates the economy to a new level of development. The concept of innovation and its corollary development embraces five functions: (1) introduction of a new good, (2) introduction of a new method of production, (3) opening of a new market, (4) conquest of a new source of supply of raw materials and (5) carrying out of a new organisation of any industry.

"The essence of entrepreneurship consists in the alertness of market participants to profit opportunities. A typical entrepreneur, according Kirzner (1979) is the arbitrageur, the person who discovers opportunity at low prices and sells the same items at high prices because of inter-temporal and inter-spatial demands ...."

The following theories of entrepreneurship enunciated by the social scientists from time to time are briefly discussed in the following pages:

1. An Economic Theory
2. Leibenstein's X-efficiency Theory
3. Dynamic Entrepreneurship Innovation Theory
4. Harvard School Theory
5. Theory of High Achievement
6. Theory of Change
7. Theory of Profit

THE INDIAN BRIGADE THAT RULES THE WORLD					
	CITI Group Vikram Pandit	**PEPSICO** Indra Nooyi, CEO	**VODAFONE** Arun Sarin, CEO	**HARTFORD FINANCIAL** Ramani Ayer, CEO	**ADOBE SYSEMS** Shantanu Narayen, CEO
Fortune 500 rank	8	63	95	82	NA
HQ	US	US	UK	US	US
Industry	BANKING	FOOD, DRINK & TOBACCO	TELECOM SERVICES	PROPERTY & CASUALTY INSURANCE	SOFTWARE AND SERVICES
Founded	1812	1965	1984	1810	1982
Operations	100 Countries	200 Countries	24 Countries	Japan, Brazil, Ireland, England, Canada	NA
Empoyees	Over 300,000	Over 168,000	Over 60,000	30,000	6,667
Turnover/Revenues	$147bn	$35bn	$51bn	$27bn	$3bn
Profits	$22bn	$6bn	$38bn	$3bn	$0.5bn
Assets	$1.9tr	$30bn	$22bn	$327bn	$6bn
Market Value	$247bn	$103bn	$147bn	$30bn	$23bn

8. Theory of Adjustment of Price
9. Theory of Market
10. Theory of Social Change
11. Theory of Entrepreneurial Supply
12. Theory of Personal Resourcefulness
13. Theory of Cultural Values

➧ An Economic Theory

Mark Casson, in his book, *The Entrepreneur – An Economic Theory,* presented a functional definition of the entrepreneur and considered why the entrepreneurial function is so valuable. He emphasised that the demand for entrepreneurship stems from the need to adjust to change, and that the supply of entrepreneurship is limited firstly, by the scarcity of the requisite personal qualities, and secondly, by the difficulty of identifying them when they are available. He suggested that there are four main qualities which are crucial for a successful entrepreneur of which one – imagination – is almost entirely innate. The other three qualities may be enhanced. The problems encountered in screening for these qualities, and in enhancing the ones that are deficient, have a number of important implications for the development of a successful entrepreneurial career.

Leibenstein's X-efficiency Theory

This theory, originally developed for another purpose, has recently been applied to analyse the role of the entrepreneur. Basically, X-efficiency is the degree of inefficiency in the use of resources within the firm: it measures the extent to which the firm fails to realise its productive potential.

For a given set of inputs, productive potential is identified with the point on Neooclassical production frontiers. X-efficiency arises either because the firm's resources are used in the wrong way or because they are wasted, that is, not used at all.

Leibenstein identifies two main roles for their entrepreneur. The first role is input completion, which involves making available inputs that improve the efficiency of' existing production methods or facilitate the introduction of new ones. The role of the entrepreneur is to improve the flow of information in the market.

The second role, gap filling, is closely asking to the arbitrage function emphasised by Kirzner Leibenstein provides a very vivid description of gap filling, visualising the economy as a net made up of nodes and pathways.

Dynamic Entrepreneurship Innovation Theory

A dynamic theory of entrepreneurship was first advocated by Schumpeter (1949) who considered entrepreneurship as the catalyst that disrupts the stationary circular flow of the economy and thereby initiates and sustains the process of development. Embarking upon 'new combinations' of the factors of production – which he succinctly terms innovation – the entrepreneur activates the economy to a new level of development. The concept of innovation and its corollary development embraces five functions: (1) introduction of a new good, (2) introduction of a new method of production, (3) opening of a new market, (4) conquest of a new source of supply of raw materials and (5) carrying out of a new organisation of any industry. Schumpeter represents a synthesis of different notions of entrepreneurship. His concept of innovation included the elements of risk taking, superintendence and co-ordination. However, Schumpeter stressed the fact that these attributes unaccompanied by the ability to innovate would not be sufficient to account for entrepreneurship.

Harvard School Theory

According to the Harvard School (Cole, 1949) entrepreneurship comprises any purposeful activity that initiate, maintain or develop a profit-oriented business in interaction with the internal situation of the business or with the economic, political and social circumstances surrounding the business. This approach emphasised two types of activities: the organisation or coordination activity, and the sensitivity to the environmental characteristics that affect decision making. Another exposition of the Harvard tradition is that of Leibenstein (1968) who emphasised activities such as searching and evaluating economic opportunities, mobilising resources necessary for the production process, connecting different markets and creating or expanding the firm.

Despite its stress on the human factor in the production system, the Harvard tradition never explicitly challenged the equilibrium-obsessed orthodox economic theory. This was challenged by the neo-Austrian School who argued that disequilibrium, rather than equilibrium, was the likely scenario and as such, entrepreneurs operate under fairly uncertain circumstances. The essence of entrepreneurship consists in the alertness of market participants to profit opportunities. A typical entrepreneur, according to Kizner (1979) is the arbitrageur, the person who discovers opportunity at low prices and sells the same items at high prices because of inter-temporal and inter-rspatial demands.

Theory of High Achievement

McClelland identified two characteristics of entrepreneurship, namely, doing things in a new and better way and 'decision-making under uncertainty.' He stressed the need for achievement or achievement orientation as the most directly relevant factor for explaining economic behaviour. This motive is defined as the tendency to strive for success in situations involving an evaluation of one's performance in relation to some standard of excellence. People having high need for achievement are more likely to succeed as entrepreneurs. McClelland explains the entrepreneur's interest in profits in terms of a need for achievement. People with high achievement (N-Ach) are not influenced by money rewards as compared to people with low achievement. The latter types are prepared to work harder for money or such other external incentives. On the contrary, profit is merely a measure of success and competency for people with high achievement need.

Theory of Change

Young conducted the Thematic Appreciation Test (TAT) on a group of entrepreneurs. The test revealed the tendency to describe the situation as a problem to be solved, an awareness of pragmatic effort required, confidence in their own ability, to solve the problem and a tendency to take the viewpoint of each individual in turn and analyse the situation as he might see it before suggesting an outcome.

Young's theory is a theory of change based on society's incorporation of reactive subgroups. A group becomes reactive when the following three conditions coincide:

(*i*) When a group experiences low status recognition;

(*ii*) When denied of access to important social networks; and

(*iii*) When the group has better institutional resources than other groups in the society at the same level.

Theory of Profit

Knight identifies the entrepreneur as a recipient of pure profit. Pure profit, according to him, with regard to the entrepreneur, is bearing the costs of uncertainty. He identifies uncertainty with a situation where the probabilities of alternative outcomes cannot be determined either by *a priori* reasoning or by statistical inference. *A priori* reasoning is simply irrelevant to economic situation involving a unique event.

Knight argues that business uncertainty can be reduced through 'consolidation.' Consolidation is to unceraintу what insurance is to risk; it is a method of reducing total unceraintу by pooling individual instances. The elasticity of the supply of self-confidence is the single most important determinant of the level of profit and the number of entrepreneurs.

Theory of Adjustment of Price

For Kirzner, the adjustment of price is the main role of the entrepreneur. If the wrong price prevails in the market, then an opportunity for profit is created somewhere in the market if a frustrated buyer or seller is willing, respectively, to pay a higher price or accept a lower one. Then, again, if different prices prevail in the same market, there is scope for profitable arbitrage between the two segments of the market.

According to Kirzner, alertness to disequilibrium is the distinguishing characteristic of an entrepreneur. Alertness enables some individuals to intervene in the market by changing the price while other individuals simply respond by changing their buying and selling plans in lieu of the new price.

Kirzner further maintains that the primary role of economic theory is to explain behaviour in terms of purposeful human action, and to consider to what extent purposeful human actions can interact to produce unexpected outcomes. To pursue the analysis of entrepreneurship further would be to go beyond the limits of the agenda of this piece. Anyone who believes that the entrepreneur is predictable has an incentive to himself intervene in the market process, and so become an entrepreneur.

To Kirzner, this provides a satisfactory basis for asserting the inherent unpredictability of the entrepreneur. It suggests that no predictor can be anything but an entrepreneur, and so makes a predictive theory of entrepreneurship impossible.

⏩ Theory of Market Equilibrium

Hayek's main contribution to entrepreneurial theory is to point out that the absence of entrepreneurs in Neo-classical economics is intimately associated with the assumption of market equilibrium. According to Hayek, the equilibrium postulate is equivalent to a postulate of full information; not full information in the sense of a complete information theory about every conceivable thing, but full information in the sense that no further information is needed in order to modify anyone's decisions.

For him, the empirical content of economics relates to the process of adjustment towards an equilibrium. This process involves the acquisition and communication of knowledge. He visualises a world in which there is a continuous process of discovery. Markets help people to communicate their discoveries to others and learn of discoveries, thereby moving towards a sale of equilibrium.

⏩ Hagen's Theory of Social Change

Everett Hagen, in his work "Theory of Social Change: How Economic Growth Begins" (1964), dictates on its psychological explanation. His creative personality is an individual characterised by a high need for achievement, order and autonomy. He views the entrepreneur as a creative problem solver interested in things in the practical and technological realm, and driven by a duty to achieve.

Hagen considers the withdrawal of status, of respect, as the trigger mechanism for changes in personality formation. Status withdrawal occurs when members of some social group perceive that their purposes and values in life are not respected by the groups in the society they respect, and whose esteem they value. Hagen postulates four types of events which can produce status withdrawal –

- Displacement of a traditional elite group from its previous status by another traditional supply physical force.
- Denigration of valued symbols through some change in the attitude of the superior group.
- Inconsistency of status symbols with a changing distribution of economic power.
- Non-acceptance of expected status on migration to a new society.

⏩ Theory of Entrepreneurial Supply

Another theory of entrepreneurial supply is the Behaviouristic Model propounded and elaborated by John Kunkal in 1965. His behavioural model is concerned with the overtly expressed activities of individuals and their relations to both past and present, and surrounding social structures and physical conditions.

The determinants of an individual's activities are to be found largely in the conditioning procedures, both deliberate and accidental, to which he has been subjected in the past and in the sets of reinforcing and discriminating stimuli which have become part of his behavioural claims and are part of the present social context.

The selected elements of social environment are amenable to change. Kunkel's theory is based upon experimental psychology, identifying sociological variables as the determinants of entrepreneurial supply.

Theory of Personal Resourcefulness

The root of entrepreneurial process can be traced to the initiative taken by some individuals to go beyond the existing way of life. The emphasis is on initiative rather than reaction, although events in the environment may have provided the trigger for the person to express initiative. This aspect seems to have been subsumed within 'innovation' which has been studied more as the 'change' or 'newness' associated with the term rather 'proactiveness.' This tendency to take initiative has been approached from different directions at various stages in the development of theory in entrepreneurship. For instance, Bygrave and Hofer (1991) talk of the importance of human volition, Carland *et al.* (1984) define an entrepreneur as one who 'establishes' an organisation, or Schumpeter (1949) talks of the agent who consciously disturbs the stationary process to take it in a new direction. They all reflect on the primacy of individual initiative. Studies of entrepreneurial traits related to this aspect of behaviour, such as internal focus of control (Brochaus, 1982), capability to take personal risks (Gasse, 1985) and positive approach to work and problems, without excessive fear of culture, seeming from strong belief in favourable future (Kuratko & Hodgetts, 1989) – all lend to a strong sense of personal resourcefulness (Kanungo & Misra, 1992) through which entrepreneurs take up and deal with non-routine tasks and situations. Hence, 'personal resourcefulness' in the context of this paper is the belief in one's own capability for initiating actions directed towards creation and growth of enterprises. Such initiating process requires cognitively mediated self-regulations of internal feelings and emotions, thought and actions as suggested by Kanungo and Misra (1992).

The theory of personal resourcefulness has got the following implications as far as the supply of entrepreneurs is concerned in the society:

1. Cognitive function: The present theory presupposes the activities undertaken by the individuals who require cognitively mediated behaviour like emotions, sentiments, inner feelings, thoughts and actions. In these situations, entrepreneur is fully appraised of the situation and knowledge which is shaded by risk and motivational involvement.

2. Human aspects of Psychology: Different authors have given their different opinions on human aspects of psychology.

Entrepreneurship is influenced by the following traits:

(*a*) will to power

(*b*) will to conquer

(*c*) will to excel

(*d*) will to achieve

(*e*) will to change

(*f*) will to innovate.

Thus, studies examining non-economic factors have brought out the fact that mere provisions of economic inputs may not itself guarantee success in entrepreneurial ventures, organisational and psychological factors also still remain a subject of further investigation.

Box 1

SUPPLY OF PERSONNEL TO GUIDE BUSINESS

The elevation of Nagpur-born Vikram Pandit as CEO of the world's largest financial institution has cast the spotlight on foreign-born head honchos in the American corporate world, with the conspicuous realization here that 15 of the Fortune 100 companies are run by foreign-born executives.

Even more striking is that three of the 15 are of Indian-origin, with perhaps an equal number in the larger Fortune 500. Pandit now heads the list as CEO of Citigroup, which is ranked 8th in the Fortune 100, followed by Indra Nooyi at Pepsico, which is ranked 63rd. Ramani Ayer is CEO of Hartford Financial Services, which is 82 in the Fortune 100.

All three were born in India and took the familiar route to the US to study – Pandit to Columbia University, Nooyi to Yale and Ayer to Drexel University.

The shift towards appointing foreign-born CEOs reflects, in part, the focus that companies place on foreign markets for growth.

Ironically, it even quoted a business school academic of Indian-origin reflecting on the trend.

It is absolutely nothing wrong with the US, but our population here is only 300 million. Imagine two billion people from the outside start getting a decent education and going through the pipeline. Well, we are going to encounter more of them who rise to the top.

Pandit, Nooyi and Ramani further the pioneering road taken by Vinod Khosla, Kanwal Rekhi and other Silicon Valley Indians who became the first CEOs of Indian-origin in the 1980s.

Most India-born executives readily acknowledge their debt of gratitude to a society that emphasizes industry and hard work and honed their survival skills if nothing else.

In contrast to the US corporations' worldwide search of the best executive talent with the suggestion that immigrants may have decisively broken the glass ceiling, Indian companies, many of them closely held, are still leery of hiring foreign CEOs.

Some of the more prominent examples of bucking the tradition is the hiring by Jet Airways of the Austrian Wolfgang Prock-Schauer as CEO. Another breakthrough is the Hawaiian Raymond Bickson, CEO of Indian Hotels, who has successfully expanded the Taj Hospitality business world-wide including in the US.

Source: Times of India, 13-12-2007.

Apart from these, some of the operational problems experienced in the course of implementing the entrepreneurship development programmes are listed below:

1. Past experience has shown that the supporting agencies/organisations either tend to be slipshod in the first phase or are less interested in the third phase which means that the programme fails to tape the entrepreneurial potential of the area or the trained entrepreneurs do not receive the support and counselling which they need most.
2. Most of the existing support organisations meant for maintenance operations are not for innovative functions. There is also an element of cynicism. A reorientation in the attitude of supporting organisations is called for.
3. Poor investment on the part of institutions as also trainees and wrong selection of target groups contributed largely to the failure of the number of entrepreneurship development programmes.

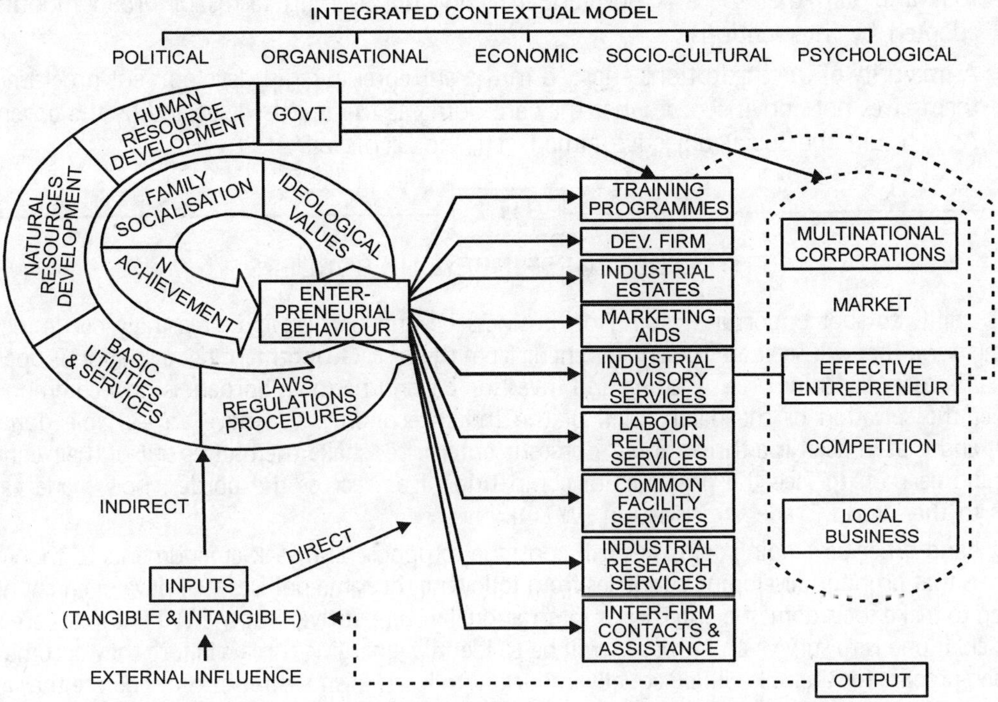

Fig. 3 A Model of Factors Influencing the Emergence of Entrepreneurship

Source: Adapted from Abdul Aziz Mahumud "Developing Effective Indigenous Entrepreneurs", *Malaysian Management Review,* April 1974, Vol. 9, No. 1.

4. Experiences reveal that entrepreneurial failures are mostly due to incompetence and poor management.
5. It is also said that there is an inability to identify the needs of institutions and differences of opinion prevailed amongst the practitioners and also amongst the trainees.
6. It is also stated that there is a low institutional commitment for local support to the entrepreneurs. There is also a very low level of involvement in the marketing of products of the units.
7. Non-availability of various inputs, *i.e.,* raw materials, power etc., and infrastructure support combined with poor follow-up by the primary monetary institutions resulted in the failure of the entrepreneurship development programmes.
8. It is also stated that there is ill-planned training methodology, inconsistency in the programme design, its content, sequence and theme and the focus of the programme is not clear.
9. Training institutions do not have much concern for the objective of identification and selection of entrepreneurs and the follow-up after training.
10. Some of the institutions are still debating whether to have a proper identification and selection of entrepreneurs for preparing successful entrepreneurs.
11. Those involved in and concerned with the selection and follow-up activities have either limited manpower support or a narrow linkage with other support agencies.

12. It is also said that there is no standard curricula even in terms of broad module being adopted by interventions.
13. A majority of the institutions engaged in the entrepreneurship development programmes are themselves not convinced of what they are doing as the task is delegated by the government. As a result, the social objective aimed at is not achieved.

Box 2

ENTREPRENEURSHIP BEYOND BORDERS

The ability to spot opportunities and do business beyond borders is increasingly becoming the defining trend that will separate the entrepreneur from the rest. Government de-regulation is opening national borders for commerce. Trading and investing beyond national borders is now common and is either the salvation or the death knell of the Indian economy. We have an enviable domestic market and that in itself is a threat unless domestic enterprises shake themselves out of their comfort zones and gear up to face the pressures of competition from across the border, now made easier, thanks to the World Trade Organisation (WTO).

India and other developing countries will continue to oppose and seek amendments to the WTO proposals that prohibit developing countries from following the same policies that developed countries pursued to make their domestic enterprises internationally competitive. But the WTO threats are real. The trick, if one is to survive and prosper, will be to identify emerging threats before they become real and then prepare for them. It will be equally important to learn to spot opportunities before they arise, and take advantage of them. Success comes to those who are able to take advantage of opportunity. Alexander Graham Bell said: "When one door closes, another door opens; but we often look so long and so regretfully upon the closed door that we do not see the ones that open for us." In business, opportunity knocks once; it usually does not lean on the doorbell.

Competition from across the border will affect high-cost producers, and perhaps even decimate entire industries, especially in the small-scale sector. India already finds itself in a situation of jobless growth. Where will new jobs be generated?

However, the alternative for job-seekers is to create their own jobs. Entrepreneurship in India (outside of family-controlled businesses) is largely necessity-based, not opportunity-driven. Entrepreneurs in this country have traditionally not been looked up to as role models. It is still widely believed that you cannot become a successful entrepreneur in this country without bending the rules. But this view is slowly changing, thanks to the success of Indian entrepreneurs in the infotech industry. They have fired the imagination of a whole new generation, and entrepreneurship is now a desired career option. Industries where entrepreneurship has flourished are IT, drugs, and pharmaceuticals.

The comparable advantage of developing countries will expand beyond low labour costs. This trend is a clear warning to those who are basking in the comfort of apparent demand for their products and services. If the industry is so complacent, then where is the opportunity for innovation?

▸▸ Maslow's Need Hierarchy Theory

Maslow felt that the needs have a definite sequence of domination. Second need does not dominate till first need is reasonably satisfied and third need does not dominate till first two needs have been reasonably satisfied. Man is never satisfied, if one need is satisfied the other will arise and so on. Maslow stated that human beings have five basic levels of needs, which they tend to satisfy in a hierarchial manner. The five needs are:

(*i*) **Physiological needs:** Food, water, air, shelter, clothing etc. These are basic or survival needs.

(*ii*) **Safety and Security needs:** Security of source of income, provision for old age, insurance against risks etc. These are aimed at making provision for future.

(*iii*) **Social needs:** It refers to belongingness or affiliation needs – needs for love, affection, warmth, friendship etc.

(*iv*) **Esteem needs:** These are egoistic needs – self-respect, self-confidence, recognition, apprecition, power, prestige and control.

(*v*) **Self-Actualisation or Self-Fulfillment needs:** Desire for personal achievement, realising one's potentials fully.

Alderfer's ERG Theory

Clayton Alderfer reformulated Maslow's need hierarchy theory. According to Alderfer, Maslow's five levels of needs can be regrouped under three heads, namely, Existence, Relatedness and Growth (ERG).

1. Existence Needs: These existence needs combine the physiological and safety needs of Maslow. These existence needs can be satisfied by material or financial incentives and include survival needs, physical and psychological safety etc.

2. Relatedness Needs: These include Maslow's social and esteem needs, which are derived from other people. These needs are satisfied by personal relations and social interactions.

3. Growth Needs: These include Maslow's self-actualisation needs. These needs will be satisfied only if an individual involves himself in activities of the organisation and is always on the lookout for new challenges and opportunities. Through creative efforts individual can realise his potential by making best use of the available opportunities.

For the proper development of entrepreneurship, Relatedness and Growth needs are more important. Alderfer theory assumes that different types of needs can operate simultaneously whereas Maslow's Theory follows a rigid need hierarchial order.

Daniel Kahneman
Behavioural Economist

The Prospect Theory

Psychologist Daniel Kahneman propounded the prospect theory. Human behaviour can be perplexing, the theory says. Emotions play a role. Guts count. Subjects when offered a choice formulated in one way might display risk-aversion but when offered essentially the same choice formulated in a different way, might display risk-seeking behaviour. And decisions under uncertainty are rarely explained by the classic 'utility function of wealth' model that has always guided economics. What matters, instead, are the attitudes to gains and losses – that too, defined in relation to a reference context. This contextualisation is natural. For, "immersing the hand in water at 20 degrees Celsius will feel pleasantly warm after prolonged immersion in much colder water, and pleasantly cool after immersion in warmer water."

There are several obstacles in defining entrepreneurship clearly. First, everyone has a personal opinion or understanding of entrepreneurship. Secondly, entrepreneurs are viewed as the new cultural heroes and are held in awe due to which critical examination of their characteristics is obscured. Thirdly, entrepreneurship is an abstraction, though entrepreneurs are tangible persons. Fourthly, well-

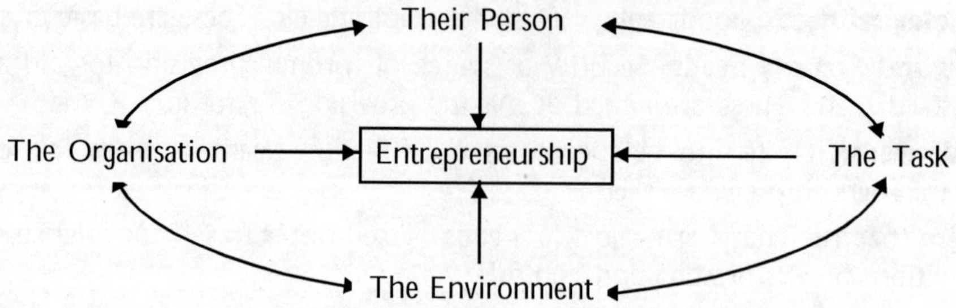

Fig. 1 A Conceptual Model of Entrepreneurship

designed and controlled research studies on entrepreneurship are very few. Lastly, when it is assumed that entrepreneurship is something opposed to or divorced from management defining entrepreneurship becomes difficult:

John J. Kao has developed a conceptual model of entrepreneurship. This model is presented in Fig. 1.

According to Kao, entrepreneurship and creativity result from the interrelationship of the following four elements.

- The person
- The task
- The environment
- The organisational context.

According to Kao, the most successful entrepreneur is one who adapts himself to the changing needs of the environment and makes it hospitable for the growth of his business enterprise. This ECO (Entrepreneurship, Creativity and Organisation) analysis framework developed and conceptualised by John J. Kao contribute a great deal to the emergence as well as sustenance of entrepreneurship and entrepreneurial talent in the prevailing business environment.

Kao's Conceptual Model

J. J. Kao in his book, *Entrepreneurship, Creativity and Organization,* has developed a conceptual model of entrepreneuship. The model is represented in Fig. 1. This is otherwise known as the ECO analysis framework (ECO stands for Entrepreneurship, Creativity and Organisation).

Element I: The most important element is the person. New ideas are not generated or implemented by organization or technology but come into being through effort of dedicated people. So, for entrepreneurial talent, it is important to understand people's personality, skills, motivation, levels of experience and psychological preferences.

Element II: The task is what a group of people or organization does. Tasks may be determined by an individual's personality or private vision. They are shaped by organizational strategy and influenced by the external environment. The task includes perceiving of opportunities, marshalling of resources and providing leadership appropriate for entrepreneurial growth.

Element III: The organizational context is the immediate setting in which creative and entrepreneurial work roles place. Factors like organizational structure and systems, the definition of work roles and group culture affect significantly the nature of the creative or entrepreneurial environment.

Finally, the above elements exist in an environment which refers to the outside world surrounding the organization. Environment includes in it the available resources, infrastructure, competitive pressures, social values, rules and regulations, state of technology. Environment too can facilitate or impede creative and entrepreneurial endeavour.

As such, the environment influences the enterprise creation significantly and the most successful entrepreneur is one who adapts himself to the changing needs of the environment and makes it hospitable for the growth of his business enterprise.

Theory of Cultural Values

The key elements in Thomas Cochran's theory are cultural values, role expectations and social sanctions. In his theory on the process of economic development, entrepreneurs are not seen as being deviant or super normal individuals but rather as representing society's modal personality. This modal personality is moulded by prevailing child-rearing practices and schooling common to a given culture. The performance of a businessman, according to him, will generally be influenced by three factors: (1) his own attitude towards his occupation; (2) the role expectations held by the sanctioning groups; and (3) the operational requirements of the job. The determinants for the first two factors are the society's values. Changes over time in such variables as population, technology, and institutional drift will impinge on the role structure by creating new operational needs.

Development in any walk of life has always depended, to some degree, on individual qualities of entrepreneurship. The success of planned efforts made by some countries in developing local entrepreneurs demolished the contention that an entrepreneur is a rare character; that entrepreneurship is not restricted to those who are gifted with certain qualities at birth. It can also be developed. It is precisely this conviction that has led to careful studies on entrepreneurship from economical, psychological and sociological perspectives, as well as steps to identify and develop entrepreneurship. As observed, every theorist has looked at the entrepreneur and entrepreneurship on the basis of his perception, and therefore, can, at best, provide only a limited view of entrepreneurial phenomenon. No view is right or wrong, or more or less; in fact, the various factors which cause the emergence of entrepreneurship are integral and not additive. They are interlocking, mutually dependent and usually reinforcing.

Factors Influencing Entrepreneurship

Peter Heydemann, the Science Counsellor in the U.S. Embassy here seems much impressed with the role the small business play in the process of innovation in the U.S. economy. He explained how "incubators" are used successfully in the United States to encourage small entrepreneurs.

The problem is how best to help small entrepreneurs translate the results of laboratory research into marketable products, to transform a new scientific concept into a commercial product. Simply put, "incubators" are very basic facilities offering shared secretarial services, space for conducting a retail or manufacturing business, and a few simple machine tools. But, and this is very important, incubators offer advice and consultation on subjects with which the most budding entrepreneurs are unfamiliar: business and finance planning, market development, government regulations. Incubators have indeed greatly helped small manufacturers to develop new products. Recent studies show that such enterprises are the main source of innovation in the U.S. industry.

Heydemann said that the idea of the incubator technology is "five or six years old." This is because until recently it was felt that the U.S. industry would forever remain in the forefront without any competition. But things changed rapidly. So, realising "the 600-plus national laboratories could not possibly service all the one-and-a-half million or so small entrepreneurs," individual American states took it upon themselves to help local industry through their technology support and development organisations.

Incubators are very often attached to state university systems as universities have much of the technical and non-technical information that needs to be fed to the entrepreneurs. Moreover, state universities have increasingly come to believe that apart from their traditional role, they must also promote industrial activity in their areas of operation.

State authorities in turn help by enabling businessmen cut through red tape, provide low-interest loans to develop prototypes, undertake market research and generally assist in bringing a new product to the consumer. "Some notion of the magnitude of this support can be had from the fact that last year alone, the federal and state governments together spent more than $2,000 million in encouraging small business." Many private sector companies also provide incubator facilities, though at a comparatively higher cost.

Another important aspect of incubators is that experts do not make any business decisions for their clients. They only provide guidelines and advice on product development, engineering, pilot production and in identifying markets.

Among the businesses in which incubators are making a significant contribution, said Heydemann, "are light manufacturing in mature technologies, retail and wholesale trade and, finally, research and development in emerging technologies."

The success rate of incubators has been salutary in the number of new jobs created, the enlarged tax base for state revenues and in the export of manufactures. In short, incubators are bringing new vigour and vitality to America's industrial renaissance and are once more giving the country a competitive edge. It remains to be seen how, useful it will be in the context of Indian entrepreneurs.

▸▸ For Illustration

Mr. Ashok Birla (1939-1990) displayed a restless urge to get going, to get things done. He was ever-sensitive to innovation with a quest for new ideas. His vigorous energy combined with a certain gambler's instinct, led him to pursue every potentially profitable venture. It was this zest to explore the unexplored which created an image of an unabashed entrepreneur willing to invest in risky off-beat ventures.

Always ahead of his time, he sensed the coming of a financial revolution and sought to be in its forefront by seeking to promote an offshore mutual fund – five years before the Unit Trust of India floated its first country fund. Foreseeing the national crunch in power generation, he introduced portable diesel-based gensets on which farmers and small shopkeepers could depend to tide them over critical periods of power shortages.

After a short training stint under the supervision of his uncle, Mr. Basant Kumar Birla, Mr. Ashok Birla built a cluster of companies into a dynamic Rs. 320-crore group.

The sales of Zenith Ltd., his flagship company, which was a mere Rs. 30 crore in 1977-78 when Mr. Birla took over, soared to Rs. 269 crore in 1989-90. Under Mr. Birla's leadership, the company changed from a single product manufacturer to a multiproduct, multi-dimensional conglomerate and became India's 74th largest company. Earlier, just out of college, he had nurtured Bharat Commerce from a Rs. 2-crore company into a Rs. 56-crore concern.

Mr. Rajan Pillai (1943-1997), London-based Indian engineer turned an entrepreneur, had brought in one swoop with this a group of four lucrative biscuit and snack food companies in Singapore, Hong

Kong, Malaysia and New Zealand under Pillai's belt. The group's combined sales are approximately Rs. 640 crore and net fixed assets in excess of Rs. 200 crore, which include Britannica Industries, India and English Biscuit Manufacturers, Pakistan. Rajan Pillai was an international success.

In 1973, Rajan and his father, who was by then one of the biggest exporters of cashew from India, decided that one member of the family should be abroad. Rajan was the one chosen. Relying on some 'contacts', Pillai embarked for Singapore to launch the 20th Century Foods, a salting operation using raw cashew nuts imported mainly from Kerala. But before leaving India, Rajan made a clean break – he redistributed amongst his six sisters and sole brother his inherited wealth, then amounting to about Rs. 5 lakh and relinquished all rights to the family business.

The 20th Century Foods was set in a joint venture with the Inchcape group. A food processing factory in the nuts and nut-related industry was set up in 1973, in the Jurong Industrial Estate, which was marshland in those days. Rajan secured financial assistance and land on easy lease terms from the Singapore Economic Development Board, being one of the first few to set up a factory there. Soon he started shipping branded consumer products (cashews in cans and pouches) to the neighbouring countries. Later, he extended the product line to peanut, pistachio and almonds to the markets to the Far East, Japan, the Pacific Rim and the Middle East, all in a span of five years.

The products sold under the 'Ole' brand name found wide acceptance. But this did not save the company from cash flow problems. The profits Rajan Pillai made went into paying off the loans from the Citibank and the Bank of India in Singapore. Clearly, working capital shortage and the bane of entrepreneurship threatened to wipe out the young fortune-seeker.

Cash losses started mounting and the company went into a tailspin. But Pillai's experience with the company laid the foundations for what was destined to be a rewarding career. "20th Century Foods is largely responsible for what I am today", he said. To combat the chronic shortage of capital, the young Pillai had started expanding the factory by taking in some local Singaporians as shareholders.

In spite of the trials and tribulations, the shift to Singapore was Pillai's big break.

Certainly he had not started with nothing in Singapore. On the contrary, by this time he was in a successful family cashew and shipping business. But there were other equally successful and rich businessmen in Kerala in the export trade. But no one had turned that base into an international, organised marketing and production company.

Pillai's success was due to the fact that he had clearly understood how business was organised and conducted in the West. This was the reason why he was able to capitalise on his base. In every instance, he had been able to merge his business into a bigger operation and eventually to gain control of the larger entity. It is this that had set him apart from most other Indian businessmen.

In 1978-79, Pillai convinced Standard Brands, a leading US public company and the largest nut producer, to join him in his venture. Pillai sold 74 per cent of his stake to Standard Brands. The company was renamed 20th Century Standard Brands and he became the working chairman, as is almost a custom in the West when a businessman merges his successful small company into a larger company. In 1980, Nabisco Foods merged with Standard Brands. After the merger, Pillai had sold out his balance holding. Once again, the new management retained Pillai as working chairman, "The senior people quickly saw in him an aggressive entrepreneurial trader", says an insider and in 1985 he was moved to London to head the Nabisco Commodities, a trading company.

Modern Concept

The term "entrepreneur" in the modern sense came into usage in the late 18th century with the advent of the Industrial Revolution in England. It was during this period that people developed inventions and made an appreciable amount of discoveries in a variety of productive occupations. Their innovative behaviour engaged them in doing new and useful things or old things in an improved way. The invention of colour photography and colour television, for example, were the responses of innovative efforts of the individual who conceived the idea, developed it and pursued it to its ultimate success. These innovators came to be known as entrepreneurs.

➧ Critical Analysis

From the above theories we can see that Schumpeter and McClelland have given primary importance to the individual. While Schumpeter has stressed on innovativeness or creativity of the individual as an important determinant of enterpreneurship, McClelland stresses more on the internal factors, specifically, the need for achievement. Though not according any importance to culture *per se,* however, he has dealt with one product of culture, viz., the need for achievement, extensively. Weber has touched upon the belief system which is part and parcel of culture and which has a great influence in determining the individual's behaviour in every aspect of his life – be it religious, social or economic. In Weber's view, certain belief system sanction economic endeavours, while others do not. Hagen views economic development as a process of technological change which is brought about by technological creativity of individuals in society. Granting the significance of psychic factors. Young lays greater emphasis on the nature of the groups, groups' assistance and coordination. Like Weber and McClelland, Cochran also speaks in different terms but explicitly, of cultural values and social structure (which include role expectations and social sanction) as playing a vital role in economic development. He identifies three important elements: (*a*) individual attitudes towards economic activity; (*b*) social sanctions; and (c) skills needed for the job (of a technical and social nature). While Young considers psychological factors and value system as passive, Kunkel argues that they do really matter and comes close to Cochran view of social structure as contributing to entrepreneurship development. By and large, the underlying current and emphasis in all theories seems to be the man and his personality, influenced by the culture in a given society.

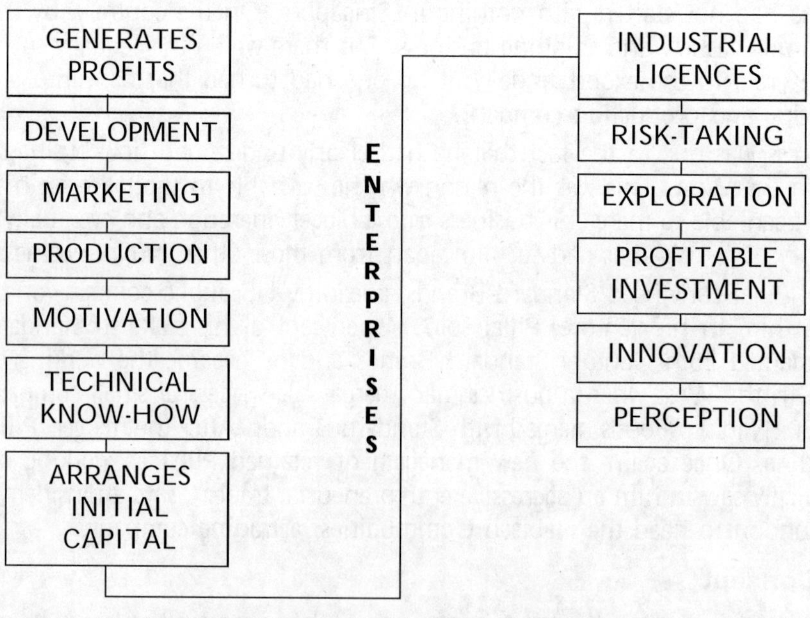

Fig. 2 Flow Chart of an Industrial Entrepreneur

▸▸ Conclusion

Major theories and expositions from Cantillon to Kirzner view the entrepreneur as performing various functional roles as risk taker, decision maker, organiser or coordinator, innovator, employer of factors of production, gap seeker and input completer, arbitrageur, etc. In spite of the diverse roles portrayed, certain common themes could be identified. All the theories ascribe a functional role to the entrepreneur in the productive process and entrepreneurial rewards are explained by the degree of success attained by fulfilling that function, rather than by a purely proprietary claim on income by virtue of mere asset ownership. Again, all the theories have been grounded against the backdrop of a capitalist society and as such the functional roles performed by the entrepreneur is determined within the capitalist paradigms of production and distribution.

A variety of models have evolved. Differences between cultures suggest that opportunity identification and entrepreneurial response to opportunity is culture-bound. Entrepreneurship should not be defined on the basis of opportunity, but rather cultural perception of opportunity should be considered; individuals from various cultures are culturally influenced in the perception of opportunity, and in turn react differently to that which may or may not (according to prevailing cultural values) be considered to be an opportunity for entrepreneurial behaviour. Therefore, a model which is successful in one environment cannot be expected to succeed as effectively in another culture. It is imperative for a model to reflect the culture of its host society.

There being multi-faceted dimensions of the problem, no simple theory can prove all the data or conceptual apparatus necessary to develop the "haffa lump" policy and programme. Planners may take this into account and devise suitable measures to identify the right type of person, give him the right type of training, provide effective institutional support, and also devise suitable modes of evaluating the impact of such efforts.

The varied theories evolved over more than two centuries have thrown up the concept of intrapreneur as a logical evolution of entrepreneurship in corporations. The intrepreneur is a professional with entrepreneurial skills. The concept of entrepreneurship will certainly undergo a change with the advancement of technology, information technology in particular. The evolution of entrepreneurship is a continuous process.

Each of the entrepreneurship theories discussed are interdisciplinary and are influenced by a multitude of factors. It is the integration of external environment, dream, ambition, passion, achievement motivation, commitment, integrity, zeal, honesty, sincerity, ability and hard work which largely determine whether an individual become an entrepreneur or not.

LEADER'S LADDER

"I don't think you need gurus standing in front of the class telling you what leadership is about. Leadership effectively is becoming yourself, and using the skills and unique capabilities that you have, in productive way. I think it's all about really becoming authentic."

— Prof. Harry Davis, Chicago Business School

10

Entrepreneurial Development Programmes

Introduction

Aparup Sengupta

An entrepreneur is one of the most important inputs in the economic development of a country or of regions within the country. Entrepreneurial competence makes all the difference to the rate of economic growth. In India, state and private entrepreneurship co-exist. The small-scale industrial sector and business are left completely to private entrepreneurs. Entrepreneurship development and small-scale industry development are the obverse and reverse of the same coin. The small-scale enterprise is a breeding ground for entrepreneurship. Conversely, that the rapid growth of small-scale sector is mainly due to the entrepreneurship development is also true. It is, therefore, in this context an increasingly important role has been assigned for the identification and promotion of entrepreneurs to this sector.

Peter Drucker, the well-known management expert, defines an entrepreneur as one who always searches for change, responds to it and exploits it as an opportunity. Entrepreneurs innovate and innovation is a specific instrument of entreprenruship, according to one definition that has emerged very recently, an entrepreneur is a person who senses opportunity for economic gains in the socio-economic spheres around him and initiates activity leading to production/distribution/service, through interaction of men and materials. Entrepreneurship involves taking risks or making investment under conditions of uncertainty and to innovate, plan and take decisions so as to increase production, productivity and profits. Growth-oriented development is the cornerstone of entrepreneurs.

The Entrepreneurial development is a key to achieve overall economic development through higher level of industrial activity. Emperial studies have shown that entrepreneurs are made. Entrepreneurial development is a process in which persons are injected with motivational drives of achievement and in sight to tackle uncertain and risky situations especially in business undertakings. The process of entrepreneurial development focuses on training, education, reorientation and creation of conducive and healthy environment for the growth of enterprises.

Entrepreneurial competence makes all the difference to the rate of economic growth – this calls for the entrepreneur's potential inputs to boost the economic development of India. In India, state and private entrepreneurships co-exist. The small-scale industrial sector and business are left completely to private entrepreneurs. Entrepreneurship development and small-scale industry development are the same coin. Small-scale enterprise is the initiation into entrepreneurship. Further, that the rapid growth of small-scale sector is mainly due to the entrepreneurship development is also true. It is, therefore, in this context that an increasingly important role has been assigned for the identification and promotion of entrepreneurs in this sector.

So, entrepreneurship involves taking risks or making investment under conditions of uncertainty and to innovate, plan and take decisions so as to increase production and productivity.

➧ The Meaning of Entrepreneurial Development Programme (EDP)

Entrepreneurial Development Programme (EDP) designed to help a person in strengthening and fulfilling his entrepreneurial motive and in acquiring skills and capabilities necessary for playing his entrepreneurial role effectively. Towards this end, it is necessary to promote his understanding of motives, motivation pattern, their impact on behaviour and entrepreneurial value. A programme which seeks to do this can qualify to be called a programmer. This has to be stressed here, because there are a number of programmes which aim at providing informational or managerial inputs or focus on preparation of a project. Although all these inputs are required by a new entrepreneur, a programme not touching entrepreneurial motivation and behaviour cannot be called an EDP.

Though EDP has been recognised as an effective human resource development tool, many a time there are very many expectations from a single programme, like removing unemployment, enhancing industrial development, promoting small-scale industries, developing industrially underdeveloped regions, etc.

EDP is primarily meant for developing those first-generation entrepreneurs, who on their own cannot become successful entrepreneurs. It covers three major variables: location, target group and enterprise (entrepreneurial activities). Any of these can become the focus or starting point for initiating and implementing an EDP. The remaining two then will follow by making proper synthesis with the first. As for example, if the objective is to promote women entrepreneurs, suitable location and proper entrepreneurial activities must match or if the objective is to develop North-East region, then the potential target group and feasible entrepreneurial ventures must follow.

EDP by itself therefore aims at achieving the specific objectives of the programmes and therefore cannot create any magical result. It is a continuous process of training and motivating them to set up profitable enterprises in large measure.

⏵⏵ Appropriate Design

It is now well recognised that entrepreneurs can be developed through appropriately designed entrepreneurship development programmes. These programmes broadly envisage a three-tiered approach: developing achievement motivation and sharpening of entrepreneurial traits and behaviour, project planning and development and guidance on industrial opportunities, incentives and facilities and rules and regulations, and developing managerial and operational capabilities. Various techniques and approaches have been developed and adopted to achieve these objectives, keeping in view the target-groups and/or to target areas. The structuring of the programmes and training methodology also necessitate the consideration of the specific target groups and target areas. Methodology for selection of the prospective entrepreneurs as well as support services after the training have a significant impact on the success of the entrepreneur development programmes.

Another important aspect of an EDP is the human factor. The human factor refers to the attitude, desire and motivation of the individual, his capability to perceive the environmental changes and opportunities as well as ability to solve the problems which he as an entrepreneur is likely to face. Training develops all these aspects of human factor, and also sharpens his skills, builds up a sound value system.

⏵⏵ Misconceptions about EDP

EDP is a catchword. But misconceptions about EDP prevail. Lack of understanding and clarity has limited its growth. EDP has yet to contribute much to the industrial economy of the country. Chandramauli Pathak has listed some of the prevailing common misconceptions about EDP. They are:

⏵⏵ Join an EDP, all your Problems are Solved

Joining an EDP is a privilege. It is indeed a valuable opportunity not available to all. But many a time an impression is created that joining EDP means assurance of finance, obtaining the required licences for business ventures and availing of the special incentives.

This misconception arises either because of lack of "honest" promotional efforts to get participants for EDP, or by attracting entrepreneurs by raising false hopes. It may also be a result of entrepreneur's expectations in gaining such advantages like finance, licences, raw material, quotations, etc. since most EDPs are state-sponsored. Unless this misconception at both ends (trainers and trainees) is not removed, EDP will only create more problems rather than solving them.

In reality, an EDP equips and makes them competent to anticipate and deal with a variety of problems that any entrepreneur may face. It prepares them to deserve and make good use of various forms of assistance.

⏵⏵ EDP means only Training

Any attempt to develop potential entrepreneurs through classroom training has been treated as EDPs.

In fact, training is only one of the segments in "the process" of developing entrepreneurs. The ED process starts from identifying the potential and right candidates, linking suitable projects with each one, training and developing managerial and entrepreneurial capabilities, counselling and motivating the entrepreneur and providing the required follow-up support to help him/her in establishing the venture. The whole process extends much beyond "training." Much of it is personal counselling and support.

Higher the Number, better the EDP

EDPs unfortunately have often been linked with statistical output rather than qualitative results. The quantitative dimension has forced manipulations in EDPs. It is taken that an EDP is a success with the maximum number of participants of responses.

The quality and impact of the EDP matters more than the quantitative dimension. Strategies to promote a particular target group, the nature of the non-traditional entrepreneurial activities and higher chances of success in new ventures go a long way in deciding the quality and impact of an EDP.

EDP Success is the Sole Responsibility of Trainer-Motivators

It is the responsibility of the Trainer-Motivator in most cases, to conduct the programme. However, many environmental factors challenge his role as a motivator.

The trainer alone cannot control or influence external factors which usually come in the way of 'start-ups' out of an EDP. EDP conducting agencies and the trainers alone cannot develop entrepreneurs and help them set up their enterprises since many other support agencies like Banks, SFCs, DICs, etc. are also involved to create better co-ordination and effective linkages with these agencies.

Such misconceptions prevail amongst EDP trainers or funding agencies, as also among entrepreneurs. We do hope that better awareness and clarity about the EDP process and strategy will help get EDPs their due importance and recognition.

Entrepreneurship Development Programme

Past experience has shown that industrial promotion by provision of facilities, technical assistance, management training, consultancy, industrial information and other services alone are not sufficient to develop entrepreneurs. It was concluded that the focal point should be aimed at the overlooked entrepreneurial spirit and entrepreneurial characteristics of the people to be developed. The EDP package was, therefore, launched. Over the years, the EDPs have become a vital strategy for harnessing the vast untapped human skills, to channelise them into accelerating industrialisation, in general and growth of the small-scale sector, in particular.

Of late, entrepreneurship development has become extremely important in achieving the goals of all-around development in the country. Consequently, many entrepreneurial opportunities are emerging in various fields. Be it electronic, medicine, engineering, agriculture, communication, atomic energy, telecommunication, food technology and packaging, entrepreneurial opportunities have surfaced at rapid pace in all these and many other areas. Such opportunities, however, become more perceptible and profitable to entrepreneurs when exposed to latest developments in the respective fields either in terms of technology, use or style of living. Accessibility and understanding of such information widens the base of opportunity sensing by potential entrepreneurs.

Objectives of the Programme

In line with the national programme for the promotion and development of small and medium industries in the countryside, the Industrial Service Institute (ISI) under the Department of Industrial Promotion (DIP) launched the EDP to give substance to the government's policies of stimulation of economic growth, dispersing industries to rural areas and promoting the processing of local raw materials. The EDP was considered a part of the industrial development policy which was articulated in the Five-Year National Economic and Social Development Plan.

The Programme had sought to develop entrepreneurial activities in the rural areas of Thailand as a vehicle for economic growth with the achievement of the following objectives:

(a) To promote the development of small and medium enterprises that would encourage self-employment among potential entrepreneurs;

(b) To provide, in the rural areas, special programmes designed to stimulate new ventures and encourage expansion of existing activities of small and medium industries;

(c) To generate employment and self-employment opportunities in the processing of indigenous raw materials for local consumption and for export;

(d) To develop entrepreneurial opportunities for potential entrepreneurs and upgrade managerial skills for existing entrepreneurs.

For a sound training programme for entrepreneurship development in India, the expert group constituted by the NIESBUD accepted that it must be able to help selected entrepreneurs to:

(a) Develop and strengthen their entrepreneurial quality/motivation;

(b) Analyse environment related to small industry and small business;

(c) Select project/product;

(d) Formulate projects;

(e) Understand the process and procedure of setting up of small enterprise;

(f) Know and influence the source of help/support needed for launching the enterprise;

(g) Acquire the basic management skills;

(h) Know the pros and cons of being an entrepreneur; and

(i) Acquaint and appreciate the needed social responsibility/entrepreneurial disciplines.

Some of the other important objectives of entrepreneurial training are:

(i) To let the entrepreneur set or reset the objectives of his business and work individually and along with his group for their realisation.

(ii) To prepare him for accepting totally unforeseen risks of business after such training.

(iii) To enable him to take strategic decisions.

(iv) To enable him to build an integrated team to fulfil the demands of tomorrow.

(v) To communicate fast, clearly and effectively.

(vi) To develop a broad vision to see the business as a whole and to integrate his function with it.

(vii) To enable him to relate his product and industry to the total environment, to find what is significant in it and to take it into account in his decisions and actions.

(viii) To enable him to cope with and coordinate all relevant paper work, most of which is statutorily obligatory.

(ix) To make him accept industrial democracy, that is, accepting workers as partners in enterprise; and

(x) To strengthen his integrity, honesty, and compliance with law, the key to success in the long run.

Evolution of Entrepreneurship Development Programmes

The various motivation campaigns or programmes taken up by the Small Industries Service Institute and SIET Institute in the sixties tried to fill the existing information gaps relevant for small entrepreneurs. The entrepreneurs required a lot of information and technological know-how for setting up a business and in that context, the contribution of these programmes was essentially in the area of disseminating knowledge on financial, technical and managerial aspects. To that extent, these programmes were in the nature of supportive programmes for the existing and new entrepreneurs.

Based on the above experience and in the context of the emergence of financial and industrial development corporations in the states, it was visualised that creation of all external facilities is not a sufficient condition for the promotion of entrepreneurship. Equally important are qualities of the individual who responds to the external opportunities (i.e., availability of funds, financial incentives, etc.). Also, social and organisational factors help people to perceive opportunities and learn to respond to them.

Experiences in EDPs Abroad

It will not be out of place to touch upon the experiences of some foreign countries in the area of entrepreneurship development. In a recent workshop organised by the East-West Centre Technology Institute, Hawaii, the EDP experiences of various countries were discussed which revealed that training made positive contributions in the performance of entrepreneurs. The non-entrepreneurial participants were motivated to start a business. The general conclusion was that EDPs could be developed as a valid substitute for natural institutions (i.e., business families). The experiences of other institutions like Development Technology Centre, Institute of Technology, Bandung Institute of Psychology, University of Indonesia, Jakarta also reiterate that EDPs have a great scope in increasing the number of new entrepreneurs to accelerate the process of industrialisation.

The basic features of the EDP programme has gone through several modifications over time as:

(*a*) Identification and careful selection of entrepreneurs for training;

(*b*) Developing the entrepreneurial capabilities of the trainee;

(*c*) Equipping the trainee with the basic managerial understanding and strategies;

(*d*) Ensuring a viable industrial project for each potential entrepreneur;

(*e*) Helping him to secure the necessary financial, infrastructural and related assistance; and

(*f*) Training cost is highly subsidised and only token fee is charged. A deposit is, however, taken to ensure commitment of participants.

Entrepreneurial Discipline

Entrepreneurs who are developed and promoted at social cost have a certain responsibility to the society that promotes and supports them. The society expects adequate returns from these people. Towards this end, entrepreneurs are expected to follow a certain discipline which is essential for entrepreneurial career. This covers subjects like:

1. Repayment behaviour.
2. Response to tax and statutory requirements.
3. Progressive outlook towards labour.
4. Care for ecology and environment etc.

1. Entrepreneurial education
2. Planned publicity for entrepreneurial opportunities
3. Identification of potential entrepreneurs through scientific method
4. Motivational training to new entrepreneurs
5. Help and guidance in selecting products and preparing project reports
6. Making available techno-economic information and product profits
7. Evolving locally suitable new products and processes
8. Availability of local agencies with trained personnel for entrepreneurial counselling and promotions
9. Creating entrepreneurial forum
10. Recognition of entrepreneurial skills.

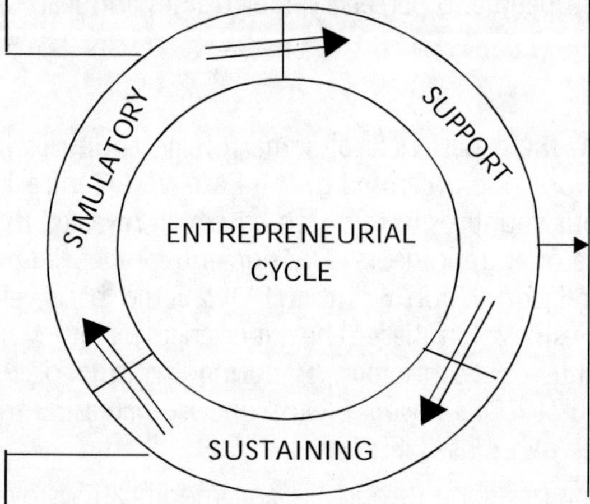

1. Registration of unit
2. Arranging finance
3. Providing land, shed, power, water, etc.
4. Guidance for selecting and obtaining machinery
5. Supply of scarce raw materials
6. Getting licences/import licences
7. Providing common facilities
8. Granting tax relief or other subsidy
9. Offering management consultancy
10. Help marketing product
11. Providing information

1. Help modernisation

2. Help diversification/expansion/substitute production
3. Additional financing for full capacity utilisation
4. Deferring repayment/interest
5. Diagnostic industrial extension/consultancy source
6. Production units legislation/policy change
7. Product reservation/creating new avenues for marketing
8. Quality testing and improving services
9. Need-based common facilities centre

Fig. 1 Entrepreneurial Development Cycle

Issues of EDPs

The development of EDP as a strategy contributing to the industrialisation and economic growth of backward and other areas needs a proper direction and organisation for making it more effective and purposeful. The contribution of EDPs is very uneven among regions for which definite programmes need to be chalked out to bring about some degree of uniformity and upgradation. Before this is tackled, some important issues need immediate attention. They are detailed below for consideration.

1. Structure and Composition of EDPs: The ED programme should have a practical content with inter-institutional organisational arrangement to make it a success. The successful EDPs have, at their base, the inter-institutional co-operation or an institution such as Gujarat Centre of the State Bank of India, which besides having conducted the programmes has also arranged for finance and other inputs for the entrepreneurs. The EDPs conducted in isolation would dissipate resources and talents. The issue, therefore, for effective functioning of EDPs is to have a financial agency strongly backing up efforts for entrepreneurial development. The place and role of TCOs need to be reviewed and their activities suitably accelerated. Who should conduct an EDP is an important issue.

2. Areas of Operation: As has been stated earlier, in North-Eastern Area, entrepreneurial development activities have not been benefiting from the support activities of financial institutions. In these areas, programmes have to be linked with support activities.

3. Fixing Priorities: Another area of fixing the priorities of EDPs is to consider their working in terms of efficiency and social need criteria. Evaluation of EDPs have revealed that those who have business experience, education and skills are proving successful entrepreneurs. This source should be tapped first and then go to the stratum to cover entrepreneurs from the non-traditional class, i.e., without business and industrial experience, but having the potential of becoming successful entrepreneurs. Next come the entrepreneurs belonging to backward and other communities who have to overcome many additional handicaps to become successful entrepreneurs. A proper course content of EDPs has to be developed to meet the specific requirements of each of these three strata of entrepreneurs in proper balance, without sacrificing the efficiency criteria.

4. Lack of Specialists' Support: Entrepreneurship has been an area of study requiring inter-disciplinary efforts by people from different disciplines. A large number of organisations/agencies engaged in entrepreneurship development in India do not have in the home all the specialists required and have to depend upon outside faculty. The number of specialists available in the country for developing small-scale industries is not very large. As a result, many a time organisations are unable to locate/avail services of experts. On the other hand, there are specialists who have time to spare in which they can render their services to the organisations.

This apart, the ED Programmes in India are afflicted with a number of operational problems. As such, though there are many a institution to train entrepreneurs, the growth of entrepreneurs is inhibited by these problems. The operational problems of EDP are as follows:

- Inherent inability,
- Diverse opinions,
- No proper strategy,
- Low institutional commitment,
- No local support,
- Non-availability of inputs,
- Poor follow-up,
- No adequate research facilities,
- Ill-planned training methodology,
- Inconsistent programme design,
- Perpetual ambiguity,
- No clear-cut objective,

- Lack of clarity in approach, and
- Lack of creativity and commitment.

1. There appears to be an inherent inability to identify the needs of the institution and differences of opinion prevailing amongst the practitioners and trainers.
2. There seems to be low institutional commitment for local support to entrepreneurs besides low involvement of marketing, voluntary and financial institutions in the programme, except for a few.
3. Non-availability of various inputs, i.e., raw materials, power, etc. and infrastructural support entwined with poor follow-up by the primary monitoring institution, results in failure of EDP.
4. There seems to be ill-planned training methodology, inconsistency in programme design, its content, sequence and theme and focus of the programme.
5. Training institutions do not show much concern for objective identification and selection of entrepreneurs and the follow-up after training.
6. Some of the institutions seem to be still debating whether to look for proper identification and selection of entrepreneurs for making successful entrepreneurs.
7. Those involved and concerned with the 'selection and follow-up' activities have either limited manpower support or a narrow linkage with other support agencies.
8. There does not appear to be standard course curricula even in terms of broad module being adopted by such institutions.
9. Majority of the institutions engaged in EDP are themselves not convinced of what they are doing as a task delegated by the Government of helping the policy in attaining its social objectives.
10. Perceptual ambiguity of the EDP objective seems to have percolated to grassroot level with a significant distortion both in terms of content and intent.

To conclude, it can be stated that many of the issues related to an EDP are conceptual in nature, many are practical and operational and many are in the borderline between concept and practice. Research and studies, building sophisticated skills and expertise, coordinating, collaborating, corroboration of ideas and actions are necessary strategies that should be continuously pursued to confront these issues.

In the post-independence period, the nation laid stress and put its faith in science and technology. The country has made tremendous investments in scientific institutions and scientific and technical manpower. These investments need to be harvested. We have learnt that the managerial skills necessary to harvest businesses are different from the skills required to create businesses. Similarly, to create technology enterprises we may also require a different breed of managers in our institutions. Development of technical entrepreneurship and the management of science and technology cannot be dealt with in mutual exclusion.

⏩ Development of Women Entrepreneurs

With a view to encouraging women entrepreneurs to take up industrial project, Industrial Development Bank of India (IDBI) has provided, under a special scheme, refinancing at a concessional rate of 9 per cent a year, the ceiling on the rate of interest on the loan being 12.5 per cent. A reduced minimum promoter's contribution of 15 per cent has been stipulated except for projects in the most backward districts where the minimum contribution is further reduced to 12.5 per cent. The IDBI also extends 100 per cent refinancing to SFCs in respect of proposals covered under the automatic refinancing scheme and 85 per cent if the proposals come under the normal refinancing scheme. For commercial banks, refinancing is extended at 75 per cent of the loan amount under both schemes. Over and above the financial assistance, organisations are being identified and encouraged to provide liaison, training, consultancy and extension support to women entrepreneurs: the cost of these services is being borne by the IDBI subject to a ceiling of Rs. 10,000 per beneficiary. While the support is need-based, it is envisaged that the subsidy will be broken down as follows:

Service	*Amount*
EDP training	Rs. 2,500.00
Feasibility/project report preparation and other consultancy services	Rs. 5,000.00
Follow-up and other extension services	Rs. 2,500.00

Training organisations have been advised to keep in mind the following:

(i) In the pre-training component, the need for identification of industrial opportunities consistent with the knowledge, skills and personal background of trainees.

(ii) The facility for the training part could include women trainers so as to help participants to open up and discuss their problems freely.

(iii) Women trainees should be motivated to set up modern small-scale units, for example, in electronics, engineering, plastics and chemicals, rather than conventional female enterprises.

(iv) The extension services should be tailored to the special needs and problems of women entrepreneurs, such as the long lead time invariably required by them to complete procedural formalities, arranging finances and tying up marketing arrangements.

(v) Apart from knowledge and skill inputs, demonstration of entrepreneurial initiative and exposure to actual industry operations through field visits should receive due weight.

(vi) Post-training escort services would be provided by the conducting agency till the projects taken up by women entrepreneurs reach their break-even stage.

The experience in conducting EDPs for women indicates that:

– Though women have the same potential as men to succeed as entrepreneurs, they suffer from two distinct disadvantages as compared to men and these entitle them to some special considerations. The first is solely internal and therefore, within their control to improve: Bring forth their initial confidence in their own abilities. The other is the long lead time required to complete all legal and procedural formalities in view of the various restrictions on their mobility.

– The majority of women entrepreneurs felt that discrimination was evident during the implementation stage but became less severe once the units were established.

– While carrying out the market survey during their training and in marketing their products after they had started their enterprise, some women entrepreneurs had to face the discouraging attitude of tradition-bound traders.

– Women coming from families in industrial and business activities could achieve success faster than most others. They easily assumed the role of independent decision-makers and had leadership qualities in the fullest measure.

– Young unmarried women were not found suitable for our programme as the course of their future life was not in their hands. Compared to them, married women in the age of 30-45 were found to be more reliable as their responsibilities towards their family were clearly defined and were gradually lessening.

– Today, 8 out of 10 working women forgo their careers for the sake of their family. We naturally do not expect women entrepreneurs to be free from this concern. We have seen that almost all successful women entrepreneurs had strong family support in the form of finance and business know-how, and enjoyed personal freedom. The family adjusted and rescheduled the normal house routine to suit them.

– Generally, women are considered less aggressive and more emotional. Initially, they get involved in the business situation where a man would usually remain cool. But, with a little experience, they quickly learn to be tough and remain objective.

– Their patience and gentleness make women sound personnel managers in small enterprises. They can generally understand the feelings of others and have a keen sense of justice and fairness.

⏩ Strategy for Entrepreneurship Development

Keeping this background in view, the following strategies of entrepreneurship development in India may be suggested:

(i) Public entrepreneurship should remain confined only to those industries and sectors where private enterprise, individual or corporate, is generally not attracted. Existing public entrepreneurship should be improved through better management and by putting relatively greater emphasis on research and development. There is need to streamline the R & D wing of public sector enterprises.

(ii) All possible efforts be made very seriously for the development of an industrial culture. It should be realised that the central core of entrepreneurship is the motive force since an appropriate, entrepreneurship implies positive action and initiative. Motivated individuals with combination of abilities and attributes can pursue their goal with enthusiasm. One can easily give examples of men like J.N. Tata or Ranchodlal Chhotalal who established their enterprises against heavy odds in the country under British rule. Without motivation, an individual cannot become a successful entrepreneur even though he may have access to finance. Individual qualities of vision, vigour, leadership and enterprise need be inculcated.

(iii) There is need to develop management education and industrial training. In modern times, management education is being viewed as an effective supplement to the development of entrepreneurship since entrepreneurial decisions have to be effectively supported by managerial decisions. Quite often, the entrepreneur functions a manager especially in small-scale industries where the entrepreneur is his own technician and manager. This fact justifies the route of formal education and necessitates the establishment of business schools and management institutes in the country, where relevant courses may be introduced. Happily, some such institutions have come up but they should further be strengthened and developed into first-class institutions comparable with their counterparts in developed countries. In addition, facilities should be provided on an increasing scale for sending talented young men and women to business schools abroad. But, strategies should be chalked out to give a conducive environment for them to come back to India and apply this knowledge in a suitable manner. Besides, industrial training programmes should be frequently organised. This will help in widening the mental horizon toward practical business and industrial problems. New industrial training centres well equipped may as well be established. Education and training will very much help in

developing and augmenting a race of new entrepreneurs needed to harness and utilise the scarce resources for economic development.

(iv) The development of backward regions/areas constitutes a new challenge. Programmes for their development be drawn up and should be effectively implemented. Such programmes await new entrepreneurs whose technical expertise and managerial competence would bring about the desired development and fulfil social needs.

(v) Adequate measures are a must for mobilising and fostering entrepreneurial talent in the country. In this context, it should be realised that entrepreneurs are not the gift of a particular class. For instance, in Japan, innovators came from the underprivileged classes as the affluent classes had hardly any incentive to innovate. "Innovating entrepreneurs have frequently come from those classes of people normally barred from advancement to status-bearing positions."

(vi) Economic administration by the State should be improved and made more effective so that objectives of economic policies may be fully achieved in the overall interest of the country's economy. Better economic administration would go a long way in ensuring and increasing entrepreneurship. Monopoly benefits to a few big entrepreneurs is an evil and must be checked. The general policy of encouraging the small entrepreneur will go a long way in activating and broadening the leadership potential. Improvement in business climate by the state through its well-designed economic policies, be it fiscal, commercial, industrial or agricultural will benefit the entrepreneurs in a changing technological society and thus facilitate healthy development of entrepreneurship.

(vii) Institutional framework should work towards meeting major industrial or economic needs or goals. Such framework, in addition to its several facets, must place entrepreneurial development and its objectives in a proper and meaningful perspective following which entrepreneurs may plan their business activities within the bounds of such a framework for the desired coordinated development.

(viii) Greater emphasis should be put on research relating to processes and enhancement of the value of indigenous techniques. This would have an encouraging impact on entrepreneurship and technology at the domestic level. As a general rule, Indianisation of entrepreneurship should be effected in place of foreign collaboration. However, general guidelines should be stated for cases in which foreign collaboration with well-known foreign companies may be allowed.

(ix) Financial institutions should provide adequate and timely credit and technical assistance, especially to small and medium-sized enterprises. They should also impart knowledge about the needs of the economy and they should file their massive data in terms of growth of new entrants or entrepreneurs in the field of industry. These may as well be dwelt upon at length in their reports and other publications. All this will go a long way in inculcating and sustaining entrepreneurial spirit in the newly-emerging classes.

(x) Now, special categories of entrepreneurs, viz., women, retired army personnel, handicapped persons, educated youths, Non-Resident Indians (NRIs), displaced persons etc., have appeared on the economic scene. Their emergence is more directly conditioned by economic and industrial factors and not only by social factors of caste, community and social approval or disapproval. Factors like access to capital, business experience, opportunity to acquire technical and managerial competence have played a crucial role. For instance, in the case of light engineering products, electronics, computers and in several other new products, the entrepreneurial source is generally not traceable to any specific caste or community background. The entrepreneurs in such fields are usually technologists and in their endeavour to establish manufacturing units, they reveal a multiple basis of entrepreneurship, viz., foreign collaboration, diversification, etc. Conducive working environment should be ensured for the

healthy development of such entrepreneurs in future. It is only then that their qualities of vision, vigour, leadership and enterprise can be well utilised for the industrial development of the country.

Entrepreneurship is not confined to industry and is needed in all activities. Its existence in agriculture among the cultivators, small and large, is seen by all today. The growing farm of today in many parts of the country is a proof of such entrepreneurship. The need for entrepreneurship is even greater in management of the Government, more so as it is the largest entrepreneur.

India has a proud record of entrepreneurship. Its present growing status in the industrial world is its proof. It has now to prepare itself for entrepreneurships of a different order. Tremendous advances of science and technology will have to be harnessed and incorporated requiring on the part of the people and the Government a more mature approach to be on par with advanced countries. Philips, Sony, Honda, Ford are the signposts of entrepreneurship today for all to emulate. Some of these have come up only in recent years and from small beginnings. In India, too, one sees glimpses of such entrepreneurship.

Conclusion

It is now well recognised that entrepreneurs can be developed through appropriately designed entrepreneurship development programmes. These programmes broadly envisage a three-tiered approach: developing achievement motivation and sharpening of entrepreneurial traits and behaviour, project planning and development and guidance on industrial opportunities, incentives and facilities and rules and regulations, and developing managerial and operational capabilities. Various techniques and approaches have been developed and adopted to achieve these objectives, keeping in view the target-groups and/or target areas. The structuring of the programmes and training methodology also necessitate consideration of the specific target-groups and target areas. Methodology for selection of the prospective entrepreneurs as well as support services after the training have significant impact on the success of the entrepreneurs development programmes.

More importantly, the Government and the financial institutions are in forefront in entrepreneurial development. However, it is said that various training programmes of these institutions work at training people for self-employment to acquire gainful employment. Thus the very purpose of developing entrepreneurial talent among the youths is defeated. This calls for a critical evaluation of EDPs and of personnel with conviction and commitment to undertake the task of planning, designing and implementing programmes in this area. More importantly, entrepreneurial programmes must be attuned to Indian economic environment and be made available in regional languages. The need of the hour is to develop genuine and not imitative entrepreneurs to accelerate the process of industrialisation. The need of the hour is for stimulating innovation and the entrepreneurial spirit to support the development of new ideas through new and mature enterprises.

The entrepreneurs themselves constitute the human factors and their needs as a human being must, therefore, not be overlooked. Being the kingpin in the whole small-enterprise development game, the human factors involved in the small- and medium-scale industry must be analysed, assisted to grow and develop.

The success of small industries depends upon the entrepreneurial and managerial capabilities of those involved in the business. Because of its size and unique operation characteristics, a small industry requires a management approach which is also unique. In general, small industries are managed in a personalized fashion. Their managers or entrepreneurs tend to know all the employees personally. They participate in all aspects of managing the business and there is usually no sharing in the decision-making process. As far as the scope and scale of operations are concerned, small industries, generally serve a local or regional market rather than a national or international one. They also tend to have a very limited share of any given market. These special characteristics must, therefore, be taken into account in the planning of small industries development on a national scale.

The human factor or the entrepreneur should also be considered. The entrepreneurial spirit, as mentioned earlier, involves not only a desire to gain monetary benefits but also an admixture of the characteristics of a high achiever, and social, family and service motives. Long-term involvement with a goal which the entrepreneur has set for himself creates the need to persist with an undertaking even in the face of difficulties.

Management and entrepreneurial skill must, therefore be blended in the small industry owner's total make-up as these will spell the difference between success and failure. The ideal would be to find a person who is both efficient and effective. Without the latter capabilities, a person may simply be a good manager. He still has to be developed into an effective manager by inculcating the entrepreneurial spirit in him. A small enterprise development programme, therefore, must take into consideration upgrading the managerial and entrepreneurial skills in the whole country in order to create a pool of enlightened entrepreneurs who can form a strong small industry sector in the business community of the country concerned.

CLARITY OF THOUGHT

"One vital aspect for being effective is to understand the diference between what is urgent and what is important. By having clear thinking and the right sense of balance, one is able to differentiate between these conflicting issues."

— Ravi Sharma, MD, Alcatel India

11

EDP Objectives

Introduction

The perception of entrepreneurship as a 'normal' career option can be helped enormously by the teaching of entrepreneurship. The principles of entrepreneurship can be taught. If they could not, that would make entrepreneurship the one and only human activity impossible to teach, which is an absurdity. In fact entrepreneurship education can help people understand how to go about validating an idea to determine whether it is a viable commercial opportunity, how to go about planning and launching a new company with all that this entails, and then how to run it including the pitfalls and danger areas and how to avoid them.

Dharmesh Mangwani

But it can do much more than this. It can positively influence an individual's perception of the risks entailed in becoming an entrepreneur so that he realises that the risks he/she perceives can be managed in such a way as to radically reduce them. This on its own is enough to make many people consider becoming an entrepreneur whereas before they would have been afraid to do so.

There is in fact empirical evidence of this, which demonstrates that education and training in entrepreneurship can help entrepreneurs increase their firm's chance of survival, and to a lesser extent, it can help make the resulting business more profitable.

For instance, it is important to know, as all entrepreneurs do, that the first stages of a new venture launch are often somewhat akin to white-water canoeing. You launch your carefully crafted business plan out on to the waters of reality like a kayak, and before you know it all hell has broken loose. Rocks (example, slower than anticipated sales growth) and boulders (example, longer than anticipated product development costs and lead times) emerge with frightening suddenness out of the spray, and all your energies and waking hours are devoted to keeping your fragile craft from getting smashed to pieces on them by the raging current that is remorselessly carrying you along.

During this time, you will experience the roller-coaster ride of any entrepreneur, but if you have some knowledge before-hand of what to expect and how to react, then your chances of survival will be greatly increased.

Training is an integral input of managerial development. The lack of adequate and skilled personnel is one of the bottlenecks in a developing economy. Staff training is essential for entrepreneurs and workers employed in small enterprises.

Entrepreneurship training provides a scientific and comprehensive approach to the development of entrepreneurship in the non-conventional communities and people. And, more importantly, it motivates individuals to become entrepreneurs to create wealth and offer new products and services to the community.

Training and Entrepreneurship Development

Entrepreneurship development and training is one of the key elements for development of micro, small and medium enterprises (MSMEs), particularly, the first generation entrepreneurs. The National Institute of Small Industry Extension Training (NISIET), Hyderabad, The Indian Institute of Entrepreneurship (IIE), Guwahati, and the National Institute of Entrepreneurship and Small Business Development (NIESBUD), NOIDA have been set up as national-level institutions for promotion of MSMEs through training and entrepreneurship development. To promote and assist entrepreneurship development in the country, the Ministry has also been implementing (in addition to the schemes of SIDO) two important schemes, namely, promotion of entrepreneurship development institutions (EDI) and scheme of National Entrepreneurship Development Board (NEDB). The main objectives of these programmes are (*i*) promoting entrepreneurship for creating self-employment through enterprise creation; (*ii*) facilitating creation of training infrastructure; and (*iii*) supporting research of entrepreneurship related issues.

What is Training?

Training is the systematic instruction of staff at all levels in new attitudes or new skills; random bits of continuing education or mere learning on-the-job cannot be called *training*: the term implies a scheme of instruction which is more-or-less formal and ongoing, which is planned systematic, consistent, pervasive and monitored to measure its effectiveness. Although it may be usually reactive to a response to a perceived demand or pressure, it should be developed to become proactive – an advance response, instigating new services, skills and methods, identifying unsuspected problems and leading the way towards an improved standard of service. As a term, it implies a trainer and a trainee; it suggests an institutional context, but it is in fact open to anybody to be a trainee and we should not mislead ourselves into assuming that an institution is essential.

All individuals have a need for training; new recruits need induction into the rationale and objectives of their jobs, besides being trained in specific skills and routines. New professional staff may need to undergo additionally programmes of training to enable them to improve their professional qualifications. Certain individuals may need training for a specific purpose, the development of a new service, taking on a new role in the organisation, preparing for retirement.

But, in a world where development and promotion happen more rarely, everyone still needs training, or rather needs it even more; if a job at any level becomes drudgery, then it cannot be effectively performed. The role of training is to develop the critical awareness of staff and prevent in-growth. An employee who can make some appraisal of her or his role, compare the situation of colleagues elsewhere, and feel that management promotes this process, is likely to feel satisfaction in the job, however great the constraints on achievement. And job-satisfaction is a clear way towards effectiveness; if individuals at all levels can contribute towards the formulation of goals – then those goals are more likely to be the most appropriate in the context.

⏩ Importance of Training

The importance of training employees has the following advantages:

1. It makes sure the availability of skilled workers at all levels of management.
2. It increases the potential abilities of workers and thus improves their performance to the maximum attainable level.
3. It enables workers to perform the work more efficiently and precisely so as to maintain the quality of products.
4. It minimises excessive scraps, defective outputs and wastage in the production process.
5. It minimises accidents said to be increasing as unskilled and semi-skilled workers are more to industrial accidents.
6. Training reduces fatigue.
7. Training enables the workers to work speedily and thus increases the earning of employees.
8. When the speed of production increases, overtime work can be avoided and therefore, the payment of overtime does not arise.
9. A trained worker does not feel the need to join other factories and thus reduces the labour turnover.
10. Training improves the good relations between employees and management.
11. New techniques can be easily adopted through trained employees.
12. Standardisation can be adopted in a factory where trained employees are available.
13. Team spirit and team work can be promoted when employment are fully trained.
14. Training enables employees to occupy higher positions of authority.
15. As trained workers do not require any consolation and because of less spoilage resulting from their performance, the supervision cost can be minimised.

⏩ Objectives of Training

The training programme is designed to subserve the following objectives:

(i) To impart basic knowledge about the industry, product and production methods;

(ii) To build the necessary skills of new entrepreneurs and workers;

(iii) To assist the entrepreneur/worker to function more effectively in his present position by exposing him to the least concept, techniques and information;

(iv) To build up second line of workers and prepare them to shoulder additional responsibility and/or switch on to the production of a new product, if there is any diversification;

(v) To expose the entrepreneur to the latest developments which directly or indirectly affect him;

(vi) To broaden the vision of entrepreneurs by providing them suitable opportunities for an interchange of experiences within and outside an industry;

(vii) To impart customer education;

(viii) To impart knowledge of the marketing of goods.

The Principles of training may be enumerated as under:

1. Training should be given in a proper atmosphere and that too systematically through duly qualified and trained instructors.
2. Training should be of reasonably long duration so as to enable the workers to understand the theory and develop skills for managing the job accurately.
3. Training should be given at all levels. This means training programme of a factory should include induction training, job training, training for promotion and refresher training.
4. The level of training should be high. It must be comprehensive and the participant should be made familiar with the latest trends in production technology.
5. Training should consist not only of theory; it should be supplemented by practical training and made interesting to all participants.

Methods of Training

The following are the important methods by which training may be imparted:

1. *Individual instruction:* Under this method, a single individual is selected for training. This mode of training is undertaken where a complicated skill is to be taught to an individual.
2. *Group instruction:* This mode of training is suitable for a group of individuals with a similar type of work and where general instructions are applicable to all are to be given.
3. *Lecture method:* Here the instructor communicates in theory the practice to be followed by the learners. Under this method, whenever there are any doubts, they may be clarified on the spot.
4. *Demonstration method:* Where the performance of work is to be shown practically by the instructor for better understanding, this method can be followed. This is more concerned with the practical than theoretical aspect.
5. *Written instructional method:* The medium of training is followed where a future reference is to be made by the learners. This method is mostly followed where a standardised production system is followed.
6. *Conference:* Conferences are frequently organised wherein experts in the field share their ideas and bring to the notice of learners new ideas and techniques to increase production.
7. *Meetings:* Meetings are a mode of training involving a group of people who discuss the various problems confronting them. They involve exchanging ideas and views and later on, coming to a firm conclusion based on the various proposals and alternatives.

Small-scale industries in India suffer from various handicaps one of the most important among these is the non-availability of technical and managerial personnel of the required calibre. On the contrary, large-scale industries can employ qualified staff specialised in different areas of production and management. Further, they can afford to retain from time to time their own supervisory personnel and workers. As against this, the small industrialist cannot afford to employ workers and supervisors having a sound educational background and the requisite experience in production and in trade. Besides, they do not have the equipment and resources to train their own staff. To meet this lacuna, the training of small industrialists and their workers has been taken up as an important part of the Industrial Extension Service rendered by the Development Commissioner, Small-scale Industries Organisations. The courses provided are designed to familiarise small industrialists and their workers with the latest tools and techniques in their respective fields. The object of the training of personnel for and from small-scale industries is to equip them with improved management/technical know-how and to apprise them of the kinds of assistance available from various Government organisations training programme of such personnel is suitably geared to the needs of individuals with different background and performing different functions.

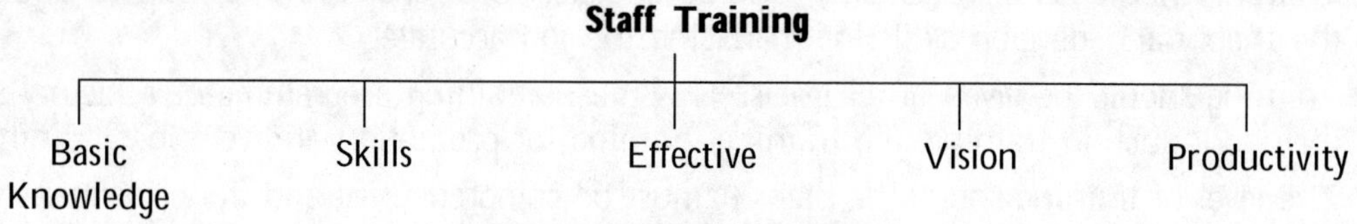

Fig. 1 Objectives of Training

The training of instructors at various levels was a *sine qua non* of the programme. Besides training officers of the DCSSIO, it became imperative that State Government officers, entrusted with the development of small-scale industries, should be given similar training, since the development of small industries is a State subject under the Constitution. Indeed, the training programmes of this organisation commenced within orientation training for its own officers in charge of the Pilot (industrial) Projects under the Community Development Programme, the small-scale Industries Organisation has extended the benefit of its training resources and programmes to other developing countries which, being interested in the development programme of small-scale industries, have been deputing their officers for participation in training programmes, study visits, etc., specially arranged by it for them.

In the post-independence period the nation laid stress and put its faith in science and technology. The country has made tremendous investments in scientific institutions and scientific and technical manpower. These investments need to be harvested. We have learnt that the managerial skills necessary to harvest business are different from the skills required to create businesses. Similarly, to create technology enterprises we may also require different kind of managers in our science and technology institutions. Development of technical entrepreneurship and the management of science and technology cannot be dealt with in mutual exclusion.

⏩ Training in Technical Trades

Regular ad hoc training courses in various technical trade are conducted by Small Industries Services Institutes, Branch SISIs, Extension Centres and Production Centres for Artisans, both skilled and semi-skilled, sponsored by small-scale industries for upgrading their existing skills and broadening their areas of competence to meet the specific requirements of small-scale industries.

⏩ Stage of Growth

The training contents will largely depend on the stage of growth of entrepreneurs. Entrepreneurs of the small industry and small business are usually owner-managers. In the beginning stage, they are

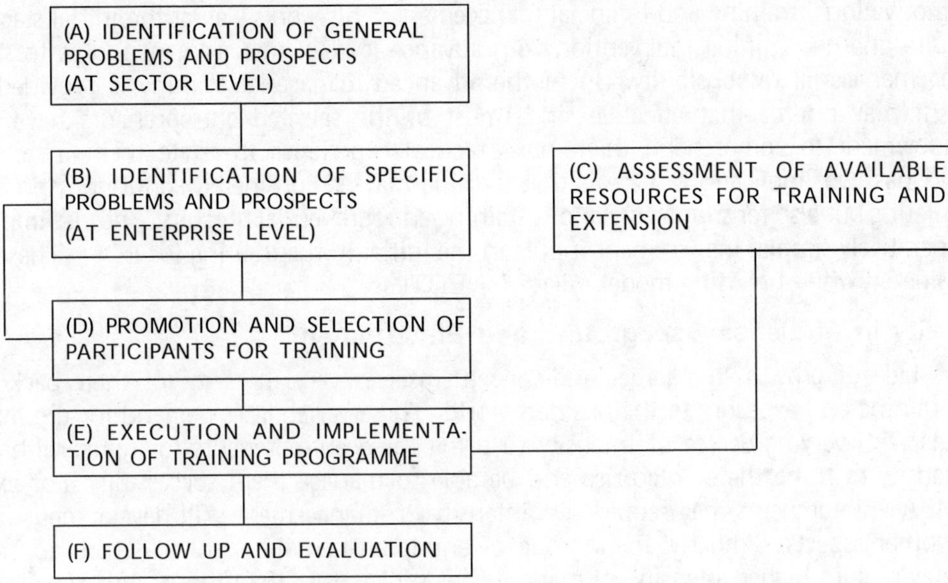

Fig. 2 Building up an Action-oriented Training Programme

more concerned with the start up work and at this stage they play the role of workers rather than that of a manager.

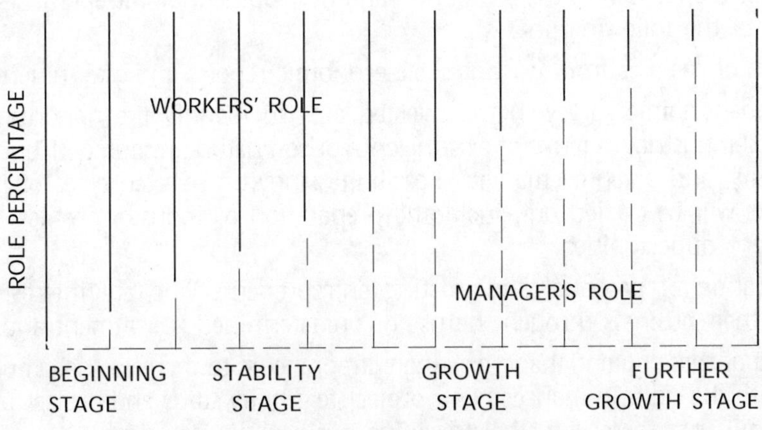

Fig. 3 Role of SSI Entrepreneurs

But as soon as the industry attains stability in terms of production/service, entrepreneur starts planning its growth and improvement. At this stage, his role as a worker gradually diminishes and proportionately the manager's role increases. Finally, with the growth of the industry, manager's role starts dominating. Thus, the role of small entrepreneur is a dynamic one and follows a continuum between worker's and manager's roles.

In order to maintain efficiency both as a worker at the initial stage and as a manager at the later stage, to those entrepreneurs who are the outcome of some planned programme, such preparations come mainly through training. Usually as the part of the entrepreneurship development programme, they receive motivational training and financial management. This works well at the initial stage. Later on, they require another training intervention with advance level of management inputs to shoulder the increasing managerial responsibility. But if the advanced managerial training is provided at the initial stage, it may not be that effective since most of the selected entrepreneurs have neither academic endowment to comprehend them nor practical experience to relate them in a real life situation. This has two implications. One is that training may be considered continuous process not only for stimulating but also for supporting and sustaining entrepreneurial pursuits. Another implication suggests comparatively simpler management inputs in the initial in the training for EDPs. These points must be considered while finalising model syllabi for EDTPs.

⏩ Variability in Audience Background and Environment

Besides stage of growth, the target audience themselves vary in terms of their background, experiences, training and exposure to the business world. These variabilities demand for the matching training inputs with varying degree of intensity to bring these entrepreneurs to inputs with varying degree of intensity to bring these enterprise and be able to manage them successfully. For example, a group of MBA entrepreneurs may require less intensity on management skill development input as compared to other aspects. Similarly, for a group of entrepreneurs who want to set up considerably larger units may require higher intensity on management skills rather than those who are going to set up comparatively smaller units. Therefore, while formulating training syllabi for EDPs, the variability in the audience background experience and training inclusive of economic and infrastructure development of the area deserve serious consideration.

⏩ Details of Project Implementation

As an integrated approach in the promotion and development of entrepreneurs in the rural areas, the EDP consists of the following phases:

(a) Selection of the area from existing socio-economic reports and government policy guidelines.

(b) A techno-economic survey in the selected area to identify the opportunities for new and expanded industries in terms of existing enterprises, natural resources, labour and raw material availability, and potential markets. Feasibility study on selected types of industry with good prospects will be carried out, including preparation of industry profiles for industries with investment opportunities.

(c) Identification of potential and existing entrepreneurs who are interested to diversify or expand their business through the use of predetermined recruitment and selection scheme.

(d) Training of these potential and existing entrepreneurs to increase their motivation and equip them with the skills in management, project feasibility study and project preparation, as well as to familiarise them with the prevailing business environment.

(e) Provision of follow-up and consultancy services in the areas of management, marketing, production, financing, technology, preparation of project, apply for loans, and upgrading of existing entrepreneurs by providing in-plant training.

⏩ Selection Scheme

(a) Historical development and rationale for selection: Before the EDP was launched, there was a programme to identify, select and include entrepreneurs to increase the likelihood of programme success. In undertaking EDP, the government has to provide considerable human and material resources. These expenditures are considered worthwhile in view of the significant role entrepreneurs play in the

economic development of their country. The proper identification and selection of participants for training is seen as an instrument to enhance the success of the EDP.

The EDP selection scheme is so designed that admission to the EDP is limited to the top 25-30 applicants who are presumed to process the traits or qualities of potential entrepreneurs.

The selection scheme was based on the assumption about the entrepreneurial characteristics which were considered to be generally accepted. The general and principal requirements to be met by an applicant for training are:

(i) *Biographical:* Demographic and socio-cultural data of the applicant to assess his readiness for the entrepreneurial role, such as age, educational background, work and business experience, type of business operation, financial resources, equity participation and labour intensiveness are essential.

(ii) *Motivation of the applicant* for attending the EDP, such as exposure to business, sibling position, reasons to go into business, source of encouragement and support to the entrepreneur, concreteness of plans, credibility and endurance.

(iii) *Psychological test* in the field of entrepreneurial traits such as risk-taking, need for achievement, and other relevant traits.

(b) Promotions and recruitment: In preparing the EDP training course, the information on the EDP is disseminated to entire public so that enough applicants are generated for screening. The assistance of local government agencies concerned in the development of the area, local banks, chambers of commerce, service clubs and some types of industrial forum are tapped in identifying target participants. The commencing of the training programme is usually announced by various means of advertisement, e.g., local radio, television, the local various means of advertisement, e.g., local radio, television, the local newspapers and posters. Brochures on the programme will also be distributed to local businessmen and individuals interested in going into business. They refer to the integrated package of assistance through the EDP, and is an opportunity for discussions with participants from other provinces who have benefited from EDP training.

(c) Selection procedures: The selection scheme consisted of a three-step process:

(i) Each applicant completes an application form which probes into his family background, education, work and business experience, business plans and financial resources.

(ii) The applicant is interviewed as to his motivation in becoming an entrepreneur, entrepreneurial potential, and desire to participate in the programme.

(iii) The applicant takes a psychological test which aims to measure entrepreneurial traits such as need for achievement, risk-taking, need to influence, optimism, and other relevant traits. Fig. 5 shows the process of selection.

A decision to admit an applicant to the EDP wholly depends on selection results. The number of participants to attend the training course are limited to a maximum of 30 persons per course.

Training Programme: Course Content and Curriculum

The EDP training will be set up according to the training needs of participants, who are both existing and potential entrepreneurs, and industrial prospects of the area. The training programme lasts for four weeks, and consists of six modules.

(a) *Introduction of entrepreneurship:* This module covers general knowledge on factors affecting small-scale industries, the role of entrepreneurs in economic development, entrepreneurial behaviour and the facilities available.

(b) *Motivation training:* Motivation training is a three-day live-in-module aimed at increasing the participant's level of achievement and confidence and developing the right attitude and behaviour toward business. Successful entrepreneurs are invited to speak about their experience in setting up and running a business.

(c) *Essentials of management:* This module is aimed at providing participants with basic management and technical know-how required to enable them to operate their business enterprise effectively and efficiently. It consists of the following subjects:

(i) General management.

(ii) Marketing management.

(iii) Production management.

(iv) Financial management.

(d) *Fundamentals of project feasibility study:* This ratio provides guidelines on the effective analysis of feasibility of the project in view of marketing, organisation, technical, financial and social aspects.

(e) *Organising the business:* The purpose of this module is to enable participants to know the environment in which they will operate their business. This covers such aspects as government incentives, industrial opportunities, policies, business laws and regulations, etc.

(f) *Plant visit:* Plant visits are necessary to familiarise the participants with real life situations in small business. Such trips also provide participants with opportunities, to learn more about an entrepreneur's behaviour, personality, thoughts and aspirations, including his plans and projects.

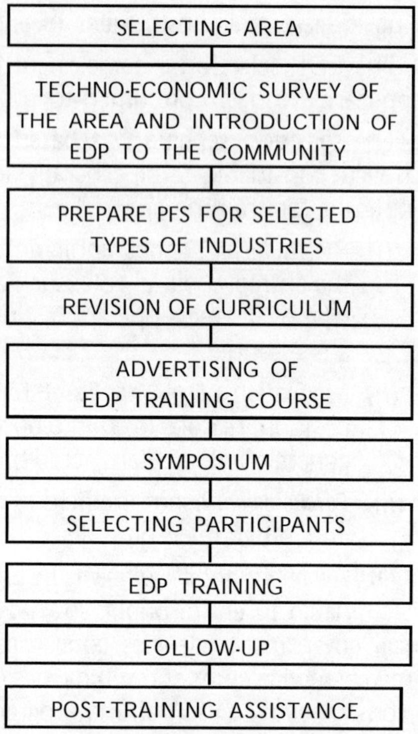

Fig. 4 EDP Flow Chart

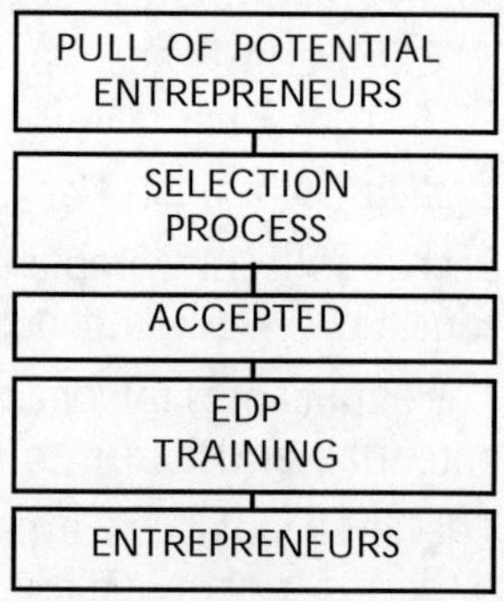

Fig. 5 Entrepreneur Selection Process

The training method is a combination of group dynamics, lecture discussions, case studies, actual preparation of project assignment, and workshop exercise.

➧ Course Duration and Schedule

The training programme is a 25-day course. Except for the achievement motivation training (a three-day live-in module), the daily programme consists of 2 sessions/day. The lecture sessions are conducted daily during the day or in the evening, depending on the opinion of people in the target area gathered during the industrial potential survey.

German Experience

The worldwide acclaim achieved by the German companies has been due to the rapid adaptation to change and restructuring the training accordingly. The common features of restructuring are:

1. Broadbased training to start with, followed by specialisation. This has led to a reduction in the number of trades.
2. Development of multi-craft skills.
3. Development of unique training modules and units.
4. Industry's lead and initiative in restructuring the training.
5. Change in complexion of the workforce leading to more skilled workers.
6. Retraining programmes for skill upgradation of the existing workforce, and
7. The overall personality development of the workforce through emphasis on 'key qualifications' which will equip the workforce with the ability to cope with change. This is illustrated in the diagram.

Two important recommendations emerged when there was an interchange of German and Indian experiences, through a workshop organised by the Confederation of Engineering Industry.

Multi-skill Concept

(1) The pattern of Indian training system needs to be overhauled. This is needed particularly in respect of offering broad training with limited number of trades and offering specialised modules in tune with the hitech requirements. Also, the multi-skilled concept which is fast emerging as a response to hitech needs would necessitate this approach.

(2) At the operational level, the modification of the existing training programmes to include the allied elements. In particular, the maintenance aspect has been much stressed, whether it be mechanical, electrical, electronics or the processing sector.

To make training successful, the German experiences point to the absolute necessity for developing good training materials and updating the instructors on their use.

Japanese Approach

In total contrast to the German approach, the Japanese place little accent on formalised institution training. On the other hand, tremendous emphasis is laid on "on-the-job" training. The primary objective of job training is to bring about a change – an increase in knowledge, the acquisition of a skill, or the development of confidence and good judgement. Job training is not successful unless the person can do something new or different or demonstrate a change in behaviour.

There are three dimensions in each job that an employee must master in order to perform effectively knowledge, skill and ability.

Knowledge refers to the information that is needed to perform a set of activities efficiently and effectively. Skill refers to the techniques, the approaches, and the styles of translating knowledge into action or practice. Ability refers to the intangible qualities or characteristics that are necessary for performance and are often referred to under the umbrella of 'motivation' or 'attitude.'

Job training is structured to consist of both formal and informal activities that address each of these three dimensions – knowledge, skill and ability – and the goals of training made clear enough so that the trainee understands what outcome or behaviour is desired.

In trying to solve job related problems, often the Japanese employees are encouraged to communicate their own training needs so that these can be arranged. This is in direct contrast to the practices prevalent in many factories here, wherein every one participates in determining the training needs of a person excepting the person himself.

For example, through the participation as members of Quality Circles, in the process of problem solving, the employees may identify specific skill needs to improve product quality. These are then arranged to be provided.

Table 1

NEW TRAINING TOOLS

No.	Level	Tool	Use
1.	Top & senior levels	ZOPP	Realistic organisational diagnosis and action plans to overcome problems.
2.	Middle level managers	Blockage concept	Identifying and helping to remove blockage to competency, "empowering" them for greater effectiveness.
3.	Workforce	Modular training	Adaptation to hi-tech integrated approach to Operation & Maintenance.
4.	Cross-functional	The New Seven tools of QC	To ensure better product quality and meeting customer expectations.

Entrepreneurship Development Programme Organisations

There are several organisations engaged in conducting entrepreneurship development programme in India. The lead in the matter was given by the Small Industries Development Organisation through its service centres. Entrepreneurial development in Gujarat has been conducted for a long time, and sophisticated selection techniques and training methodology have been developed. The programme has integrated identification and training of potential entrepreneurs, identification of viable industrial projects and developing managerial capabilities. Institutional support in the areas of finance, infrastructure, etc. is also linked with the programme.

Other organisations that have been actively conducting entrepreneurship development programmes are State Bank of India; financial institutions such as IDB; Entrepreneurial Motivation Training Centre in Northern-Eastern Region; Xavier Institute of Social Services, Ranchi; industrial consultancy organisations in various states; Centre for Entrepreneurship Development, Ahmedabad; State Financial Corporations; the Centre for Entrepreneurship Development, Hubli; Small Industries Extension Training Institute, Hyderabad; National Science and Technology Entrepreneurship Development Board etc.

The need for a national organisation to serve as an apex body to coordinate training programmes of various centres and organisations in the country, to train trainers and motivators in entrepreneurship development, to prepare model syllabi training for various target groups and target areas, etc. was felt, with a view to evolve an integrated national approach to this subject.

ENTREPRENEURSHIP DEVELOPMENT MODEL/PROMOTION

Pre-requisites for EDP

The entire infrastructure of an area should be reviewed. Entrepreneurs require a variety of assistance and support in arranging finance, plant and machinery, land, readymade sheds, power, raw materials and finally information relating to industry. The support activities provide nurturing and help

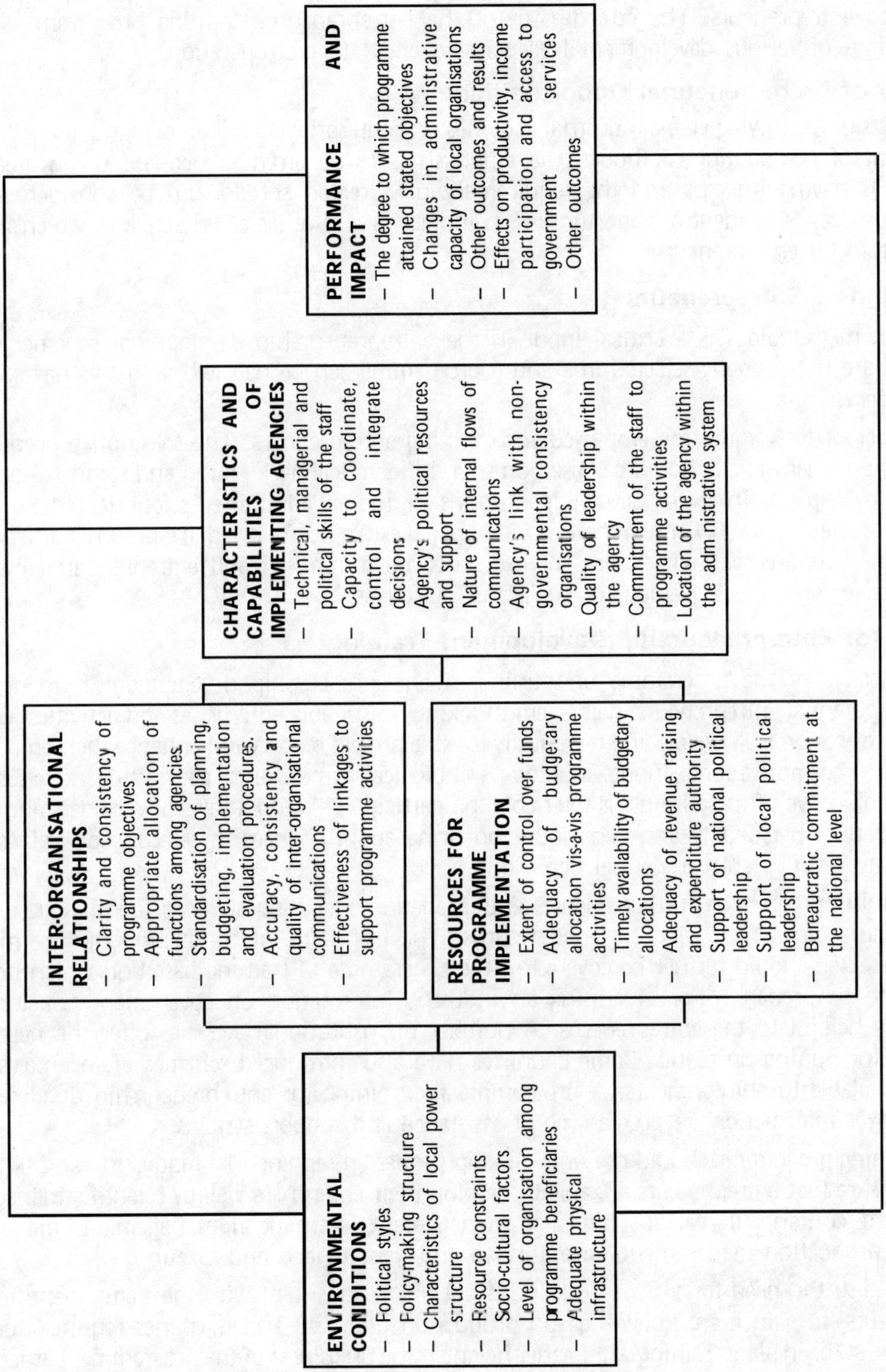

Fig. 6 Factors Affecting Implementation of Entrepreneurial Development

entrepreneurship to grow and survive. The inadequacy of support system may impede provision of timely help to entrepreneurs. The co-ordinator of the entrepreneurial training programme should arrange meetings of various developmental agencies to elicit their co-operation.

⏩ Survey of Entrepreneurial Opportunities

It consists of identifying viable industrial activities and enterprises based on demand and resources and the extent of competition. Although the emphasis is to be given to demand of an area, the adjoining areas having linkages and the requirement of a region should also be considered. The objective of a survey is to identify opportunities in industries and other allied activities which offer a promising future for entrepreneurs.

⏩ Selection of Entrepreneurs

Selection methodology is a critical input in the entrepreneurship development scheme. If the entrepreneurs are not properly selected, the entire programme can be defeated; and this has a direct bearing on success rate.

A number of techniques are employed for selecting entrepreneurs. The selection procedure to be adopted by an organisation should be based on sound theoretical background and standardised tests administered by experts. In India, several institutions of repute administer scientific tests such as Thematic Appreciation Test, Entrepreneurial Capacity Test, etc., followed by personal interviews. When entrepreneurs are selected, chances of drop-outs are minimised and entrepreneurial training becomes effective for the achievement of goals and objectives.

⏩ Inputs for Entrepreneurship Development Training

The objective of the programme of training in entrepreneurship development is to develop motivation of potential entrepreneurs, help them in taking up suitable enterprises and activities, enable them to prepare economically viable and technically feasible project reports and enhance their enterprise-building skills. The motivational inputs include psychological games, tests, goal-setting exercises and role play. The objective of these inputs is to enable the participants to do a self-study, understand their own entrepreneurial personality and behaviour and bring about changes in self-concept, values and skills, leading to positive entrepreneurial behaviour.

The training programme further enables entrepreneurs to develop skills in identifying suitable items for manufacture which will give good returns. The technique of conducting studies, market surveys and research should further be covered in the programme of training based on which project reports have to be prepared. For organising an industry, information on government policies and programmes is helpful to the entrepreneurs. A number of institutional agencies offer the necessary infrastructure for putting up plants. Some countries have also introduced schemes of incentives and concessions available to entrepreneurs. A programme for training for entrepreneurship development should also cover information on programme of assistance and support systems.

Any training programme should not only develop proper entrepreneurial motivation and skill but should also ensure that entrepreneurs are able to develop their enterprises well by scientific managerial techniques and contents in various fields of management – financial management, marketing management, production management, inventory control, labour laws and taxation.

There is also the need for visits to the industrial units, consistent with the items identified by the entrepreneurs, to gain more knowledge on production processes and machines required for the purpose. Facilities for in-plant training will further heighten the usefulness of the programme, particularly when the enterprises are very small or in areas where there is paucity of skilled personnel.

►► Support System

Individuals and organisations which provide assistance to entrepreneurs constitute a support system. Experiences in India have demonstrated that the calibre and willingness of a support system greatly influences the success of a programme. The various agencies of the support system should be involved in the training programme from the selection process to training and follow-up. The organisation conducting the training should be associated with these agencies to ensure that timely assistance is available to the entrepreneurs.

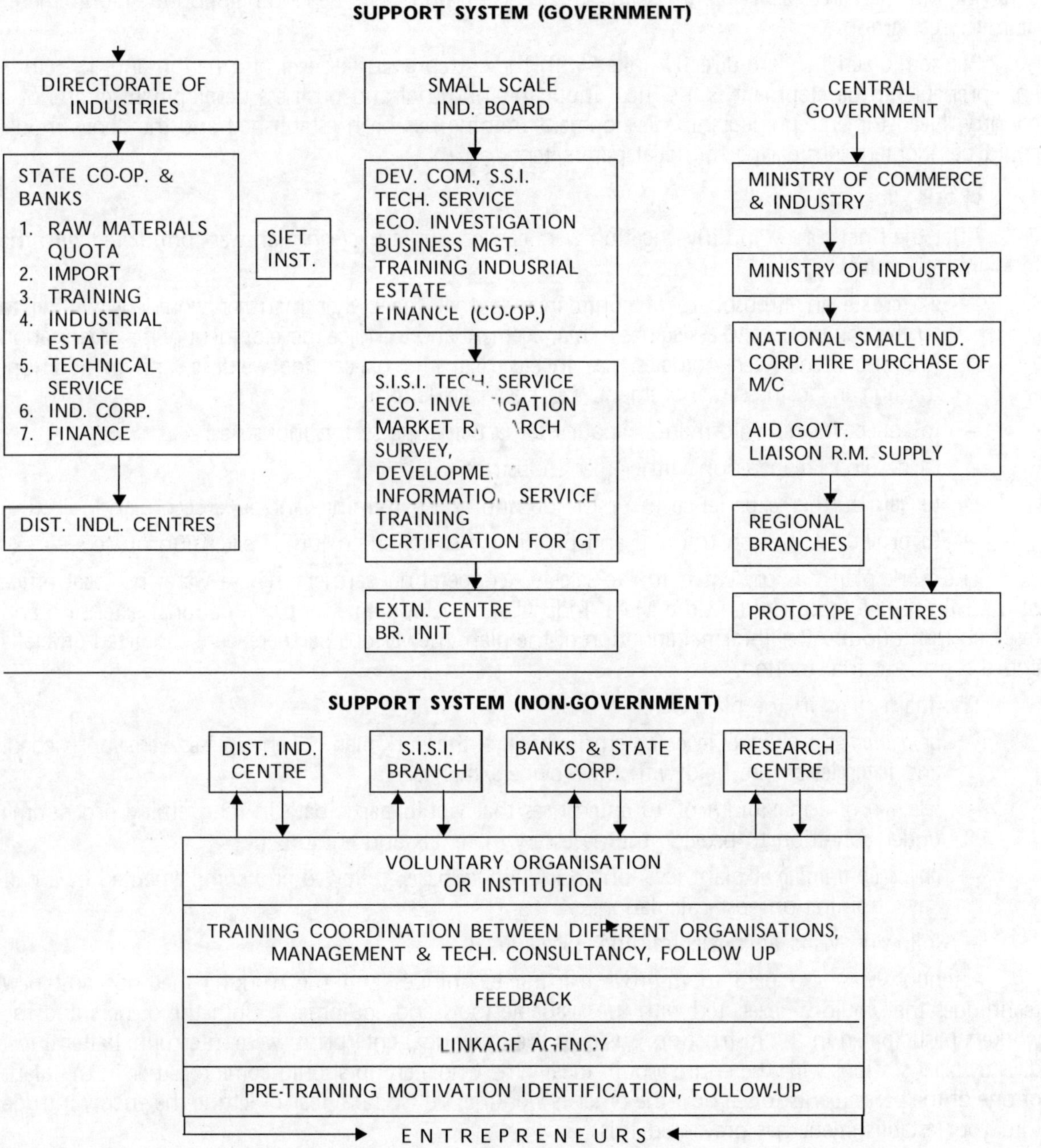

Fig. 7 Support System

Follow-up

It is as important to take up follow-up measures after conducting entrepreneurial development courses. Some of the institutions in the country have introduced cards for each trainee where progress is recorded from time to time. Project leaders contact the entrepreneurs by personal visits or otherwise to ascertain difficulties and to follow-up their needs with the appropriate agencies. Regular system of reporting should be developed to get feedback on the performance of entrepreneurs.

It has been envisaged that while the basic structure will remain the same, the degree of emphasis could vary in such areas as in-plant training, theoretical training etc. depending upon the requirements of the target group.

Economic activities are directly linked with the entrepreneurial level of a nation and, therefore, entrepreneurship development is a critical input for industrial and business development efforts of a country. Need for entrepreneurship development training has been established and the above model could be adopted considering the local parameters.

Work Plan

After the final survey and investigation were carried out, an action plan was formulated with the following objectives:

- To create an atmosphere of confidence so that the owner manager would be willing to receive comprehensive assistance in management and technical development of his organisation (training in new technologies, *i.e.*, in electrical and oxi-carbide welding, and in addition, training in business management, *i.e.*, cost calculation);
- to collect further information about the participating sector/industries;
- to develop co-operation with larger industries;
- to gain further experience in on-the-job and group training; and as a secondary objective;
- to provide on-the-job training and practical instruction to junior extension officers.

The work plan was presented to the selected cooperating partners. These were the local office of the Ministry of Industries and the Metal Industries Development Centre (a national extension and research institution). After informal adoption of the plan, the various partners were contacted officially and the plan set into motion.

The main steps in the plan were:

- *promotion* at individual level (enterprise level) of the work plan: 15 enterprises were approached, and interviews were held with their owners/managers;
- *selection* of a maximum of 10 enterprises that would participate in the training programme under condition to provide the necessary materials and equipment;
- *on-the-job training* at plant level on an individual basis, followed and complemented by a half day's training on cost calculation;
- follow-up visits after the training. (See Fig. 8)

Attention was also paid to improve existing techniques and the working methods and new techniques that could be executed with the available tools and equipment. Both the owners and the workers participated in the instruction. Visits to the individual enterprises were interrupted after a few days by brief sessions with the entire group. Ideally the whole group should come together in the plant of one of the participants to see how the other is working; but so far a fear of letting the enemy intrude into your establishment has prevented this.

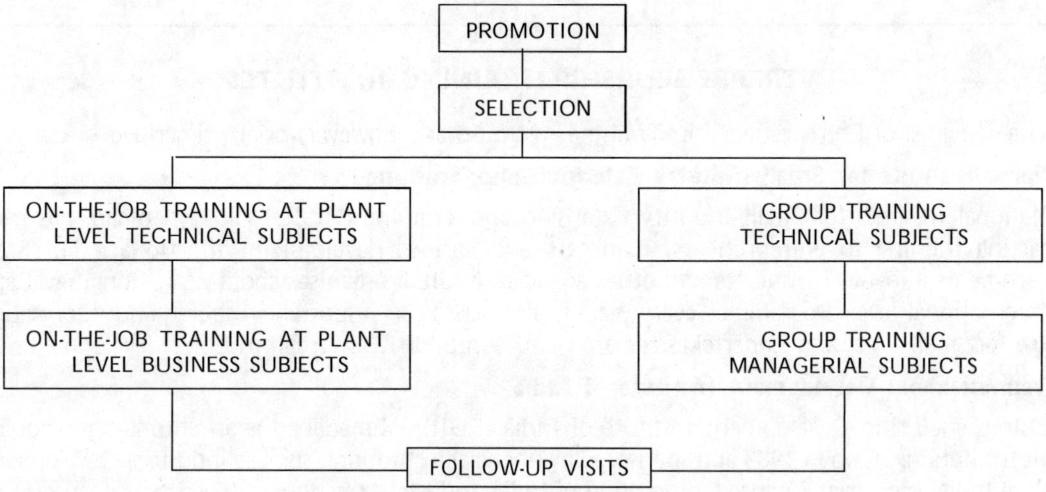

Fig. 8 Work Plan for Action-oriented Training

It was noteworthy that the common interests and common problems (encountered during the individual visits) contributed towards group cohesion during the group sessions characterised by open discussions. On this basis the group becomes more receptive to new ideas presented by the instructors (specialists in technical, management and financial fields).

The *training methodology* was oriented towards:

– building up a level of understanding with the entrepreneur and his business;
– discussions of problems and bottlenecks;
– training-cum-assistance in new techniques;
– introduction and practising of new techniques (also on repair of equipment);
– demonstration of related management concepts. Participants received half a day of classroom instruction and half a day on cost calculation;
– group instructions afterwards to discuss common problems, and aspects of a more general nature.

The follow-up visits to the participating enterprises form a logical complementary activity. Through such visits it is possible to guide the entrepreneur with the "translation" of all that has been presented to him into practical application. Follow-up visits take place shortly after the training sessions and after longer intervals (of 3 to 6 months) but on a regular basis. While the first visits are concerned with guidance during implementation, the later ones can be seen as evaluation visits.

⏩ Benefits of the Training Process

(a) The training: The combination of on-the-job training and consultancy with group training during rather a short time (three weeks) is an effective strategy.

– The entrepreneurs/participants demonstrate a willingness to improve existing working methodology and techniques and learned the possibilities or limitations in the use of equipment;
– They are more aware of the need to develop and introduce new products and production techniques; and relationship of theory to the situation in their workplace;

Box 1

ENTREPRENEURSHIP TRAINING INSTITUTES

The activities of Entrepreneurship Training Institutes are, however, briefly described below:

National Institute for Small Industry Extension and Training

National Institute for Small Industry Extension and Training (NISIET) at Hyderabad, has been imparting training to entrepreneurs, managers and various development functionaries of State Governments, Financial Institutes and other agencies. NISIET organises about 45 national level and 15 international level programmes every year. It also acts as an important resource and information centre for small units and undertakes research and consultancy for small industry development.

Entrepreneurship Development Institute of India

Entrepreneurship Development Institute of India (EDII), Ahmedabad is an autonomous not-for-profit Institution, set up in 1983 and sponsored by financial institutions, such as Industrial Development Bank of India, Industrial Finance Corporation of India, Industrial Credit and Investment Corporation of India, and the State Bank of India. The Government of Gujarat has also provided assistance for setting up of EDII.

EDII has been spearheading an entrepreneurship movement in the country and takes up activities like augmenting the supply of trained entrepreneurs, generating multiplier effect on opportunities for self-employment, improving the managerial capabilities of small-scale industries and producing trained motivators for entrepreneurship development. The Institute participates in institution-building efforts, besides promoting micro enterprises at a rural level. It has designed and implemented several national and international training programmes and workshops for the academic community and for the youth. The special training programmes that EDII organises include informal Micro Credit Delivery Systems, management programme for strengthening the participation of NGOs in the area of informal credit, etc. It organises trainers' meets and chief executives' meets to foster linkages among trainers and chief executives of entrepreneurship development organisations to facilitate experience sharing.

National Institute for Entrepreneurship and Small Business Development

The National Institute for Entrepreneurship and Small Business Development (NIESBUD), which started functioning from July 1983 is an apex body established by the Ministry of Industry, Government of India for co-ordinating and overseeing the activities of various institutions/agencies engaged in entrepreneurial development in small industry and small business. The activities of the Institute include: (*i*) Evolving effective training strategies and methodology, standardising model syllabi for training various target groups; (*ii*) Formulating scientific selection procedures, developing training aids, manuals and tools, facilitating and supporting Central State and other agencies in executing Entrepreneurship Development programmes; (*iii*) Conducting such programmes for promoters, trainers and entrepreneurs which are commonly not undertaken by other agencies; and (*iv*) Maximising the benefits and accelerating the process of entrepreneurship development.

Indian Institute of Entrepreneurship

The Indian Institute of Entrepreneurship (IIE), Guwahati was established in 1993 by the Ministry of Industry, Government of India to undertake training, research and consultancy activities in the field of Small-Scale Industries. SIDBI is a co-promoter of the Institute. IIE has adopted a multipronged approach in entrepreneurship development with a special focus in the northern region. The main activities of the Institute are: (*i*) To organise and conduct training for entrepreneurship development, (*ii*) To evolve strategies and methodologies for different target groups and locations and field to test them, (*iii*) To identify training needs and offer training programmes to Government and non-governmental organisations engaged in promoting and supporting entrepreneurship, (*iv*) To organise seminars, workshops and conferences, etc., for providing a form for interaction and exchange of views by various agencies and entrepreneurs; and (*v*) To conduct research to generate knowledge for accelerating the process of entrepreneurship development.

National Institute of Fashion Technology

The National Institute of Fashion Technology (NIFT), New Delhi was registered as an Autonomous Society in 1986. It is a Government funded institution under the Ministry of Textiles with Secretary (Textiles) as Chairman of the Board of Governors, besides the Chairman, there are 17 members on the Board of NIFT.

NIFT was established in collaboration with the Fashion Institute of Technology (FIT), New York. The genesis of the NIFT was in the idea of an apex institution to cater to the growing needs of India's evolving fashion industry. Over the years, NIFT has emerged as the premier training institute in India nurturing and creating a bright and able generation of professionals in different areas of fashion technology, meeting the human resource requirements of this vital industry. Its high level of interaction and collaboration with the leading fashion institutions of the world has enhanced the stature and scope for the fashion industry in India to meet the challenges of the industrial competitiveness on a global place.

- They demonstrate a growing awareness of the relationship between technical problems in their enterprises and management and control;
- During the group training, an opportunity is created to exchange experiences and problems and questions that were observed or arisen during the visits to the enterprises.

(b) Level of instruction: Through the mix of on-the-job training and group training, but mostly through direct contact between the entrepreneur and the instructor at the work floor of the former, the instructor usually speaks the language of the entrepreneur. The instructor had to adapt himself to the client, to the entrepreneur, and to think at his level while searching for new methodologies and solutions for problems observed. This contrasts with formal training programmes where the participants have to adjust themselves to the trainer and his environment, and where the participants are left afterwards with the burden of re-entry into their system with the new knowledge. The entrepreneur feels himself more at ease in his own environment where he is the boss; and with that self-confidence he often feels more comfortable in questioning the trainer/instructor about the things he himself considers to be of interest.

Table 2

COST ASPECT OF TRAINING THROUGH SUBCONTRACTORS VS. TRAINING BY THE INSTITUTION ITSELF

		Subcontracting arrangements		*Institutionalised operations*	
		Recurrent cost	*Incidental cost*	*Recurrent cost*	*Incidental cost*
1.	Professional manpower	Low	High	High	Low
2.	Administrative support	Relatively high	Low	Low	Low
3.	Logistic support	Low	Low	High	Low
4.	Material cost	Low	Low	High	Low
5.	Follow-up	High	Low	High	Low
6.	Staff training	Low	Low	High	High

(c) Mobilisation of resources: Within a limited time, the identification of the pertinent resources on contract terms for the training programme was initiated. Successful negotiation with a state technical training institute resulted in the contracting of three professionals for the three weeks of the course. This was mainly possible through the availability of a budget, and the possibility to decide on the use of that budget without approvals and endorsements of third parties or higher authorities. With this the mobilisation of resources through contracts approved at local level directly was made. Furthermore, the contribution of the larger industries was ensured, which resulted in the release of one instructor for a three-week period at no cost. Although his participation was of high value, his release by the large industry was a marginal cost, and was seen as a contribution to the development of the area (social investment by the large industry, also to improve their general image). Unfortunately, it was not possible to use the workshop facilities of a particular industry.

It became evident that even governmental services could be mobilised and integrated into the programme at the working level. Approaching the government at higher level for official approval and release would have been less attractive, because such activities are normally neither foreseen in annual plans and budgets, nor do the budget cater for such additional expenditures.

(d) Cost effectiveness: One of the major objections raised against the individualised training approach (albeit for a group of trainees) like the one described here, is related to the cost aspects. It is often claimed that the costs of group training alone (without consultancy and the like) are considerably less than the consultancy-cum-instruction technique. This, however, is not at all that obvious.

In the field of training in the small-scale enterprise sector, we see the following principles being adopted more and more:

- Training of entrepreneurs is seen more as a process of transfer of know-how;
- More attention is being paid to the process of adult learning instead of just setting university and college courses;
- Training programmes are more individualised, with special attention to the individual training needs;
- Training programmes are becoming more practice-oriented, with more attention being paid to on-the-job training aspects;
- Consultancy and extension are seen more and more as a part of the process of transfer of know-how; and
- More attention is being paid to ensuring active participation of both the entrepreneur and the "instructor."

▸▸ Conclusion

Training refers to the process of increasing knowledge and skill of an employee for doing a particular job. Soon after a worker is selected and inducted into a job, we may not expect full contribution from him initially in attaining the objective of the factory, as he is just a "raw" human resource. For ensuring satisfactory job performance, training is essential at all levels of management. Training serves not only the purpose of motivation but also as a means of developing various methods of work. The terms "training" and "development" are often synonymously used. But there is a difference between the two. While training is viewed as a process by means of which the aptitudes, skills, and capabilities of an individual employee to perform a specific job are enhanced, development implies the nature and direction of change induced in the employee through the process of education and training. Several factors have increased the adoption of training and development schemes of factories.

It is obvious that the achievement in rural areas is contingent upon the evaluation of a national training policy, the creation of a national training infrastructure, the formulation of suitable co-ordinative mechanisms at all levels, the acceptance of manpower planning and budgeting as the basis for training programmes, the developments of multiple skill courses, acceptance of area planning approach for training institutions at district and block levels, at the cutting edge level. Unless a massive training programme is organised to support ambitious rural development programmes, the goal of full employment may not be achieved within the stipulated time.

More importantly, the government and the development financial institutions are in the forefront in entrepreneurial development. However, experience shows that the various training programmes of these institutions are aimed at training people to take up self-employment and acquire gainful employment. Thus, the very purpose of developing entrepreneurial talent among the youths is defeated. This calls for a critical evaluation of EDPs and to develop personnel with conviction and commitment to undertake the task of planning, designing and implementing programmes for entrepreneurship development. More importantly, these programmes must be attuned to Indian economic environment and be made available in regional languages. The need of the hour is to develop genuine entrepreneurs accelerate the process of industralisation. The need of the hour is for stimulating innovation and the entrepreneurial spirit to support the development of new ideas through new and mature enterprises.

ANNEXURE-I

A PROGRAMME OF TRAINING SMALL INDUSTRY ENTREPRENEUR – MANAGERS

Types of Individuals to receive training	*Types of training measures required*	*Sources of personnel to staff training facilities*	*Means of Training the Trainees*
		FULL-TIME	
Typical managers of small factories or other planning to establish such factories.	Short courses	(*a*) Staff members of advisory services operated by Governments, associations or other bodies.	(*a*) Joint use can be made of facilities provided for manager training, *e.g.*, short courses, advanced management courses, self-educational measures.
Exceptional managers of rapidly expanding semi-modern factories.	Advanced Management Courses (either national, regional or international).	(*b*) Staff members of educational institutions, development corporations, banks,	(*b*) Specialised training can be given to management training personnel in the institutions – either national or foreign – designed for large industry; *e.g.*, in business, engineering or economics.
Manager candidates	Preparatory courses	(*c*) Foreign specialists.	(*c*) Internships may be possible in large industrial plants – national or foreign – to give practical training to prospective staff members.
		PART-TIME	
All types	Self-education measures	(*d*) same as (*a*), (*b*) or (*c*) above (*e*) Managers of modern small factories. (*f*) Managers of medium and large-sized factories, banks, Utilities, etc., (*g*) Government officials (*h*) Members of professions.	

BALANCING ACT

"The greatest danger to any business is the possibility of being overly conservative in order to avoid mistakes. It's important to understand and intelligently regulate our tendency to be conservative. The issue is how to best create a balance between aggressively implementing growth strategies and conservatively protecting the balance sheet."

— Barry Diller, CEO, InterActive Corp.

12

Selection of Centres by Target Groups

Introduction

Sunil Mittal

Since 1950, a substantial volume of study has gone into the different facets of entrepreneurial development in India to accelerate the process of industrialisation. The study showed that entrepreneurs are born and can also be made – their skills sharpened, quality of an enterprise improved and generated in good number. It is possible to identify individuals in all communities, in rural and urban areas, among men and women with entrepreneurial talent, to motivate and train them through properly organised programmes undertaking risk-bearing innovative activities for raising the growth rate in agriculture, in industry as well as in the service sector.

The Entrepreneurial Development Programmes (EDPs) thus became a new concept for harnessing the vast untapped human resources. The EDPs are presently one of the most talked about social development activities which many organisations have taken up in right earnest. It strikes a welcome note in respect of change in perception and recognition of the critical role the entrepreneurs play in industrial development by creating potential avenues for self-employment.

The diversity of entrepreneurs calls for special cells fostered to cater to the needs of the target groups, we examine a few in detail.

⏩ Entrepreneurship Development

Entrepreneurship development is recognised as a key element of small industry promotion imparting skills and strengthening the managerial capabilities of small entrepreneurs. Besides, small enterprises by their very nature are not able to attract professionally qualified persons.

⏩ Training

Training is one of the important industrial extension services rendered by the Small Industries Development Organisation through various Small Industries Services Institutes, Branch SISIs and Production Centres. The training courses organised by SIDO are meant for upgrading the skills of workers of the small scale industries as well as the managerial capabilities of their management personnel.

During the year 1996-97 (April-October, 1996), 88 Skill Development courses for workers of SSI and 50 Management Development Courses for supervisory personnel of Small Scale Industries were conducted benefiting 1,400 and 500 persons respectively. In the remaining period of the year (November, 1996 to March, 1997), it is proposed to conduct 152 Skill Development courses for workers of SSI and 70 Management Development Courses for workers of supervisory level personnel of SSIs for 1,170 and 2,100 persons respectively.

(i) Management Upgradation

Many of the small entrepreneurs running their units have had no opportunity for undergoing entrepreneurship development programmes formulated by professional agencies. Even those who had undergone such programmes would need to periodically update their knowledge and upgrade their skills to be successful in a changing economic and industrial environment.

(ii) Managers for Small Enterprises

A small entrepreneur has often to assume multiple responsibilities in areas of production, marketing or finance on account of inability to attract and retain professionally qualified persons. Recognising the availability of fresh graduates in the market, it was felt that a limited programme of orientation for fresh graduates to particular functional areas like finance, accounts and marketing could, over a period of time, build up a cadre of trained industrial managers whose services would be available to small scale units.

(iii) Marketing Skill Upgradation

With the emergence of semi-urban and rural market as important segments of marketing, SIDBI has identified the growing need for launching special training programmes for persons endowed with basic skills of good communication and acumen for salesmanship.

(iv) Artisans and Craftsmen

The need for supporting, preservation and development of skills of artisans and craftsman assumes added importance in the context of the contribution of Indian handicrafts to our export trade. With this objective in view, SIDBI has started extending support to KVIC and DGDC to train artisans and craftsmen. Apart from training support to artisans, SIDBI has extended its support to National Institute of Rural Development (NIRD) and National Institute of Small Industry Extension Training (NISIET) for training of officials of KVIC with special focus on development orientation.

(v) Rural EDPs

SIDBI has considered it necessary to promote rural entrepreneurs in the context of the renewed policy thrust on rural development. EDB has, accordingly, been commissioned to formulate rural EDPs keeping in view the special needs of prospective entrepreneurs from rural areas, type of SSI units that can be set-up and the problems associated with rural industrialisation. In formulating the programmes, has emphasized the need for simplifying the programme content and the delivery system to be tailored to motivate the entrepreneurs in rural areas. These rural EDEs will have a follow-up system to assess the success rate of entrepreneurs promoting new projects in rural areas and for extension of necessary escort services. Five such programmes have begun during the year.

⏩ Entrepreneurship Development Programme (EDP) and Barefoot Manager Programme (SEMA)

Identification and motivation of potential entrepreneurs, development of entrepreneurship through structural training programmes, follow-up of the trained entrepreneurs to enable them to set-up their own tiny and small scale industrial ventures with the assistance available from different development agencies, evaluation and reporting are the main objectives of the programme.

During the first half of 1996-97, 33 SISI/RTCs have been given sanctions for conducting 60 Motivation Campaigns, 147 EDP Courses and 3 programmes for Barefoot Managers.

⏩ National Entrepreneurship Development Board (NEDB)

Given the primacy of Entrepreneurship and Entrepreneurial ventures in the national growth processes, in general and commercial, industrial and agricultural sector in particular, it is essential to develop, sustain and maintain a forum for cohesive thought and action. For this purpose, the Department has constituted the National entrepreneurship Development Board under the Chairmanship of the Union Minister of State which will act as the apex body for entrepreneurship development in the country and will determine policy for entrepreneurship development. It will devise and recommend to the Government Schemes for promotion of Entrepreneurship for encouraging self-employment in small scale industries and small business. The Board will also recommend suitable facilities and incentives for entrepreneurship training. The Board will have powers to appoint Committees for specific purposes and will also have powers to invite persons to the meetings of the Board as and when necessary. The Board has so far recommended three studies.

⏩ National Institute of Small Industry Extension Training (NISIET), Hyderabad

National Institute of Small Industry Extension Training was set up at Hyderabad in 1962 to discharge functions of training of SIDO personnel in Small Industry Development and to undertake activities of Consultancy and Research for furthering the cause of Small Industries. Over the years, work of NISIET has expanded to include services to other agencies as well, such as Departments of Industries of State Government, Financial Institutions, Individual Enterprises in the private and public sectors etc. NISIET is a grant-in-aid institution, with part of its budget being covered by revenue accruing on account of course fee charged for participation in its training programmes for Development Professionals from Afro-Asian countries. Participation in International Programme is funded, in major part, by Ministry of External Affairs under ITED Programmes and Ministry of Finance under TCS Colombo Plan. Some of the participants are also sponsored by International Organisations such as UNDP, CFTC, AAR RO etc.

Highlights of the Institute's training schedule of 1996-97 are short-term programmes concerning Quality Circles, Tribal Entrepreneurship, Women Entrepreneurship, Pollution Control and Energy Management, among others.

During the year 1996-97 (upto October, 1996) 12 National Training Programmes were conducted, with 97 participants. In addition 14 unscheduled/sponsored/ outstation programmes were conducted with 949 persons benefiting from such endeavours. A special feature in these efforts had been that as many as 17 programmes exclusively meant for benefit to 484 PMRY beneficiaries were organised at different centres in the State. In the remaining period of the year 18 more National Programmes are expected to be taken up. Besides 10 International Programmes for 73 foreign participants are also conducted upto the end of September, 1996.

➧ National Institute for Entrepreneurship and Small Business Development (NIESBUD), New Delhi

The National Institute for Entrepreneurship and Small Business Development, registered as a society under the Societies Registration Act, was set up on 6th July, 1983 by the Ministry of Industry, Government of India, as an apex body for co-ordinating and overseeing the activities of various institutions/agencies engaged in entrepreneurial development particularly in the area of small industry and small business.

The major activities of the Institute include evolving model syllabi for training various target groups providing effective training strategies, methodology, manuals and tools, facilitating and supporting Central/State Governments and other agencies in executing programmes of entrepreneurship and small business development, maximising benefit and accelerating the process of entrepreneurship development, conducting programmes for motivators, trainers and entrepreneurs which are commonly not undertaken by other agencies and organising those activities that help in developing entrepreneurial culture in the society.

The Institute is envisaged to serve as apex national resource institute for holistic development of entrepreneurial activities throughout the country. The major activities of the Institute include:

(*i*) Evolving model syllabi for training various target groups;

(*ii*) Providing effective training strategies, methodology, manuals and tools;

(*iii*) Facilitating and supporting Central/State Governments and other agencies in executing programs of entrepreneurship and small business development; and

(*iv*) Conducting programs for motivators, trainers and entrepreneurs who are commonly not undertaken by other agencies and organizing activities which help in developing an entrepreneurial culture in the society.

During the year 2006, the Institute organised 62 Training Programmes having a participation of 1,510 persons belonging to different target groups. Out of these 5 Training Programmes consisting of 4 Grass Root Management Training (GMT) programmes and One Curriculum Development Workshop are organised under "Women Entrepreneurs Management Out Reach Programme" (WEMTOP) Project sponsored by Economic Development Institute (World Bank) with the basic objective of developing economic independence in rural women groups in India. This benefited 78 producer women and 14 Enterprise Support Teams. The period also saw the successful completion of the Second Trainers training programme for developing Small Enterprises Management Assistance (SEMA).

NIESBUD – DETAILS OF THE TRAINING PROGRAMMES

Sl. No.	Category of the Programme	April-Dec. 2006	
		No. of Programmes	No. of Participants
1.	Trainer's/Promoter's Programmes	20	322
2.	Small Business Opportunities & Development Programmes for Women/Weaker Section	11	348
3.	Entrepreneurship Continuing Education Programme	04	47
4.	Seminars, Workshops & Conferences	05	155
5.	EDPs	18	577
6.	International Training Programmes	04	61
	Total	62	1,510

One of the focus target areas of the training activities of the Institute during the period was organizing of Small Business Opportunities & Development Programmes for Women and Weaker Sections of the society. A total of 11 activities with 348 persons were organised towards this end.

The Institute has reached an understanding with the NSIC Ltd., for undertaking training activities under Small Enterprise Establishment Programme (SEEP) aimed at providing handholding facilities to existing/potential entrepreneurs. The initial two activities under the Programme have been initiated at Dehradun and Haldwani (Uttaranchal).

The Institute has been awarded the work of conducting of EDPs in the States of Delhi, U.P. and Haryana by the Ministry of Food Processing Industries.

The Institute organised a series of training activities (11) under Swarna Jayanti Shahri Rojgar Yojana of the Ministry of Urban Employment & Poverty Alleviation, Government of India, during the period.

The Institute has been performing the functions of a Technical Agency under the SFURTI – Scheme of Fund for Regeneration of Traditional Industries – Ministry of Agro & Rural Industries, Government of India.

▸▸ Centre for the Development of Glass Industry, Firozabad

In order to modernise the existing Glass Industry and to upgrade the technology for the manufacture of different type of glasses, a Centre for the Improvement of Glass Industry was set up at Firozabad, U.P. with the assistance of UNDP and Government of U.P. at a total cost of Rs. 10.04 crores. The first phase of the Centre has been implemented and it started rendering services in the field of physical and chemical testing of raw materials for glass and finished products. Specialised training programmes to upgrade the skill has also been started in the field of decoration and glass blowing. The experts at the Centre are providing advisory services to the small scale units to upgrade their technology and to resolve their day-to-day production problems. Workshops have also been organised during the year on packaging and export promotion. A number of UNDP experts have visited the Centre and provided expertise in the field of fumance design, refractory pot making, laboratory practices, design and decoration.

A prototype technology unit is being set up with UNDP assistance which will be used for the development of specialised glasses.

During the year 1995-96, the Centre earned a revenue of Rs. 2.50 lakhs. The Centre has earned a revenue of Rs. 2.37 lakhs during the year 1996-97 (upto October, 1996) and benefited 97 units by way of consultancy, testing and training.

Khadi and Village Industries Commission (KVIC)

Khadi and Village Industries occupy an important place in the Indian economy in generating income and employment to the rural labour force particularly to those living below the poverty line. These industries use local raw material and manpower, develop local initiatives and co-operation, promote the skill of the artisans and need low capital investment for generation of income and employment.

The Khadi and Village Industries Commission, established by an Act of Parliament (No. 61 of 1956) is mainly a service organisation engaged in the promotion and development of Khadi and Village Industries in rural areas. The main objectives of the KVIC include: (1) providing employment in rural areas, (2) skill improvement, (3) transfer of technology, (4) providing self-reliance among the people and to build up strong rural community base / spirit and (5) rural industrialisation.

Indian Institute of Entrepreneurship

The Indian Institute of Entrepreneurship (IIE) was established by the Department of Small Scale Industries and Agro and Rural Industries as an autonomous organisation in 1993 with its headquarter at Guwahati to take up training, research and consultancy activities in the field of small industry and entrepreneurship. The other sponsors of the Institute are the North Eastern Council, Shillong and Small Industries Development Bank of India. The Institute has started functioning from 1st April, 1994.

During the year 1996-97 (upto October, 1996) the Institute has conducted 15 training programmes having a participation of 367 persons. During the remaining part of the year the Institute will organise about 25 training programmes and complete the concurrent evaluation of PMRY for 1994-95 for Assam and Tripura and Study on effectiveness of EDP in the North East.

Role of NAYE (National Alliance of Young Entrepreneurs)

NAYE has been a pioneer in promotion and development of entrepreneurship among women. In keeping with the emerging trends, then NAYE had set up a Women's Wing in 1975, the internationally acknowledged Women's Year. NAYE convened a Conference of Women Entrepreneurs in November 1975 in New Delhi to discuss at length steps to be taken to make women self-reliant and to raise their status in the society. Since then three International Conferences and eight National Conventions of Women Entrepreneurs have been organised in different cities in the country.

Women's wing of NAYE assists women entrepreneurs in:

(a) getting better access to capital, infrastructure and markets;

(b) development of management and production capabilities;

(c) identifying investment opportunities;

(d) attending to problems by taking up individual cases with appropriate authorities;

(e) sponsoring delegations, participation in trade fairs, exhibitions, buyer-seller, specialised conferences, etc.;

(f) organising seminars, workshops and training programmes for giving them wider exposure to available facilities and developing their entrepreneurial capabilities;

(*g*) lobbying for them in Press, Parliament, State legislatures and other forums;

(*h*) advocating effectively for securing their rightful place in the Indian economy.

In addition, the Association of Women Entrepreneurs of Karnataka (AWAKE), Women Entrepreneurs Association of Maharashtra (WIMA) and Self-Employed Women's Association (SWWA) are not only fighting for their rights but also striving to promote entrepreneurship among women.

Set up in May 1985, WIMA – the Association of Women Industrialists/Entrepreneurs of Maharashtra has 400 members all over Maharashtra, with its head office in Pune, and branches at Mumbai, Aurangabad, Nasik and Dhulia. NAYE of which WIMA forms a part, presented the organisation with a national award in 1988 for promoting entrepreneurship among women. WIMA aims to help 1,000 women all over Maharashtra.

WIMA's main objective has been to provide a form for members and to help them sell their products. But making is their main problem. WIMA also has training programmes.

Having conducted approximately 20 exhibitions, the association held its first state level convention of women entrepreneurs of Maharashtra on its fifth anniversary in May 1990. "The women had good ideas for their projects." Observed a bank official who attended it, "but they needed guidance. Many, for example, did not know how to prepare feasibility reports, or of the existence of counselling centres, such as the ones run by Mahila Arthik Vikas Mahamandal (MAVIM)."

In 1989, the Industrial Development Bank of India (IDBI) set up the Mahila Udyam Nidhi (MUN) and Mahila Vikas Nidhi (MVN) schemes to help such entrepreneurs. The former had provided 15 per cent equity assistance for new units with project cost not exceeding Rs. 10 lakh. Eligible entrepreneurs were required to bring in a token contribution of 10 per cent, and allowed to retain central or state investment subsidies, if any, to meet working capital requirements. The MVN scheme extend aid to voluntary agencies in decentralised industries for training-cum-production centres and management and skill upgradation.

There were also a third scheme, under which indirect loans were given through State finance corporations and State industrial development corporations. In 1989-90, 563 units promoted by women were provided aid totalling upto Rs. 20.1 crore, as against Rs. 10.4 crore in the previous year for 323 units. The schemes have since been transferred to the Small Industries Development Bank of India (SIDBI), a subsidiary of IDBI set up on 2 April 1990.

Mumbai-based Sharayu Lele, one of WIMA's earliest members, was among those who benefited from IDBI aid. Ten years ago, with an initial investment of Rs. 5 lakh, she started a computer data centre with hand punches and hired IBM machines. With a Rs. 10 lakh turnover, she has acquired 20 Uptron data entry machines, and her initial clients were Air India, State Bank of India and Datamatics.

WIMA had received IDBI aid to the tune of Rs. 4 lakh in August 1988 for the development of the WIMA Bazaar in Pune. Of this, Rs. 1 lakh was in the form of a grant, and the rest, a soft loan.

There should be a curriculum change along with proper career guidance in women's polytechnics, which will shape the students to become capable entrepreneurs in future. There should also be some reservation for admission of women to disciplines like engineering, medicine, law, agriculture and architecture, with some concessions in regard to the qualification marks. It will be worthwhile to consider the institution of special scholarship schemes for meritorious women students. As far as the State and Central Governments are concerned, a scheme could be evolved for extending additional concessions for women entrepreneurs for setting up industrial units. As in the case of weaker sections of society, the financial institutions and banks should consider feasibility of waiving collateral security, because women do not possess any land or other property. Women should also be given property rights and an equal share in their fathers' property.

Although the rate of interest then charged by banks on loans extended to women entrepreneurs slightly lower than that charged on the normal loans, what is more important is further reduction and the reorientation by the Reserve Bank of India. In order to ensure that there was adequate credit flow to women entrepreneurs, a sub-goal was considered under the priority sector advances by the banks as is being done presently for advances to weaker sections and other special sectors. More importantly, the condition of a guarantor in the case of women entrepreneurs should be waived by the banks.

In order to ensure that development of women entrepreneurship takes place, as fast as possible, there is a case for setting up apex bodies at the State capital level and organisations at district levels which could be affiliated to the apex body. Separate industrial cooperative estates for women in different cities may be set up. And 15% to 20% of the purchases of the state governments should be made from women entrepreneurs.

Women entrepreneurs in rural and backward regions need special assistance and incentives from the Government and other associate agencies. What is more, training of lakhs of women entrepreneurs in the coming decade is a Herculean task for various agencies.

Although it is still in the growing stage, there is unquestionably a business revolution in the works across the nation – and women are a major part of it. Whether they opt to remain on a micro level, or move to expand on a major scale, they are making their impact felt on the society.

➧ Grooming Entrepreneurs

"The current economic crisis has led to the emergence of several start-up firms. Many entrepreneurs feel that the time now is right to initiate new ventures as enthusiasts have the time to think about innovations and even, evaluate the viability of it further," says Prof. K. Kumar, chairperson, N.S. Raghavan Centre for Entrepreneurial Studies (NSRCEL) at Indian Institute of Management Bangalore. NSRCEL was started with a vision to seed, nurture and promote entrepreneurship with emphasis on start-ups and existing organisations with growth potential. The centre takes up ventures based on the novelty of ideas, innovation, ability of the team/entrepreneur to build the business, etc. And the ideas are screened by a panel of industry experts, venture capitalists, etc. Soon after the review, an entrepreneur can start working on the idea. "The centre supports budding entrepreneurs by providing them with the essential infrastructure to get the idea evaluated, up and running. This includes allocation of cubicle space with computers and internet access, precision of facilities like photocopying, facsimile and telephone, access to the IIMB library and even access to expert advice and various external forums," says Kumar.

"The infrastructure is essential to maintain efficiency of the team; however, the mentorship component for a company like NextGen is equally essential where the average age of the team is 21 who are also currently pursuing their under graduation engineering courses. We are novices in the business world and at NSRCEL, we have professors whom we can approach and discuss our business strategy anytime with," feels Abhishek Humbad, a BITS-Pilani student and an incubate at NSRCEL who works on an energy and environment start-up (NextGen PMS Pvt. Ltd.) that helps companies across the entire green chain right from estimating their carbon footprints, benchmarking it to providing energy efficiency solutions to reduce it. "Simple things like time sheets, making proposals, making the right quotes, pricing, signing the right MOUs, building and training the best team, etc. are very essential and critical for a start-up's existence and success and NSRCEL offers just that to us," explains Humbad. A start-up venture can be in the IIMB campus for about 18 months. "Once the evaluated idea is built, tried and tested in local environments, NSRCEL will help the entrepreneur to network externally to take the fledgling business to the next phase of growth. The external parties could be venture capitalists, companies, industry experts and others," says Kumar. "The cell also helps in bringing in investments from outside," informs Kumar. According to Kumar, business schools must encourage entrepreneurs and must build in the value system that a start-up is also a great career option.

⏩ Nurturing Entrepreneurs

The Wadhwani Centre for Entrepreneurship Development at Indian School of Business (ISB), Hyderabad has started the 'entrepreneurs development' initiative to nurture entrepreneurship among its students. "There have been initiatives to encourage entrepreneurship in the past. We have realised the limitations of such initiatives and now, we are trying to revitalise our role in promoting entrepreneurship. We are taking a strategic view of what it takes to be a successful entrepreneur and the kind of ecosystem and mentoring framework required for becoming successful," says Dr. Krishna Tanuku, executive director, Wadhwani Centre for Entrepreneurship Development, ISB about the reasons for starting up the initiative. "ISB is encouraging ventures that have a significant social impact, which are self sustainable and more importantly, scalable over a period of time. We have taken about nine ventures of our students and our aim is to make them investment ready," explains Tanuku. ISB provides the entrepreneurs facility to stay in the campus, sustenance allowance, linkage to investment community and intellectual support like rigorous mentoring and guidance of the faculty members. "The entrepreneurs are full-time at the ISB campus and their main job is to make their ventures successful; the rest is taken care by the institute. This brings in a lot of energy and focus into the venture," believes Tanuku.

According to Deepesh Agarwal, founder of a start up GoCars and a management student at ISB, it is definitely an advantage for a start-up to be associated with a B-school. "At a B-school, you frequently get to meet people with diverse backgrounds, varied experiences and people who have been through this journey before. You get a lot of good advice and a lot of new ideas on solving problems of your own enterprise. You stay in constant touch with the VC community which is yet another advantage," explains Agarwal.

Such initiatives are providing excellent platforms to budding entrepreneurs by giving the much required support, mentoring and financial assistance thus realising their dreams into a reality.

⏩ Structuring Entrepreneurial Development Programmes

The above case studies bring out certain features important for the success of entrepreneurial development programmes. The training programme aims at identification and careful selection of entrepreneurs (using advanced series of psychological tests), developing the motivation and entrepreneurial capabilities of the trainees, equipping the trainees to identify viable industrial projects and to prepare project profiles or brief project reports, equipping the trainees with basic enterprise-building skills, imparting basic managerial skills required for the successful management of the unit and helping the trainees to secure the necessary financial, infrastructural and related assistance during the implementation of the project. Skill training formed a vital and major component of this programme.

⏩ Conclusion

Economic activities could be directly linked with the entrepreneurial level of a nation and, therefore, entrepreneurship development be considered as a critical input for industrial and business development efforts of a country. In this process, institutions play a catalytic role in entrepreneurship development.

Entrepreneurial development in India has now been conducted for a long-time, and sophisticated selection techniques and training methodology have been developed. The programme integrates identification and training of potential entrepreneurs, identification of viable industrial projects and developing managerial capabilities. Institutional support in the areas of finance, infrastructure, etc. is also linked with the programme.

The role of EDPs in accelerating industrialisation of a state or a region can hardly be over-emphasised. All those who are engaged in the administration of this programme must fully realise the enormous responsibility entailed in seeking to assist those without much influence, managerial ability or capability to bear risks. No tangible results can, therefore, be expected unless all the agencies involved in the task work with determination, zeal and a sense of dedication and commitment. Entrepreneur development is to be attuned to economic needs. It is, therefore, necessary to recognise the importance of entrepreneurship as an aspect of social life. Similarly, entrepreneurship education should be made more socially utilitarian. It is, nevertheless, imperative to restructure the entire curriculum – should identify the area of entrepreneurship and to motivate young people to start their own business at an early age in their chosen field of interest, for entrepreneurship exists in every profession, irrespective of its size. This will generate self-employment, which is always more satisfying than working for others.

A TEACHER'S GUIDE

In the early 1990s, the International Center for Entrepreneurial Studies, the University of Maryland's Dingman Center, and CIPE developed a core curriculum for Romanian trainers. The courses covered the essential elements needed to expose potential entrepreneurs to the realities of business life. The following list presents some of the subjects included in the core curriculum:

- **Introduction to Business and Economics**
  - Global economy
  - Wealth distribution
  - Relationship between government and industry
  - Regulation in a "free market" economy
  - Tax structure
  - Stock, bond, and futures markets
  - Bank and thrifts
- **Basic Concepts of Entrepreneurship**
  - Dynamics of change
  - Opportunities and resources
  - Entrepreneurial viewpoint and personality
  - Risk and risk/reward factor
  - Case histories

Venturing

- Innovation
- Objective analysis
- Creation of a team

Strategic Planning in New Ventures

- Business definition
- Market research and analysis
- Competition analysis
- Formulation of overall business strategy

Financial Planning in New Ventures

- Financial statements
- Financial projections
- Determination of funding requirements
- Debt and equity financing
- Valuation of company

Winning Business Plan

- Business plan objectives and targets
- Step-by-step guide to business plan preparation
- Presentation of business plans to financial community
- Operations plan from business plan

Raising Capital

- Fund-raising tools and team
- Financiers' considerations
- Sources of funding: equity and debt capital
- Negotiating the deal

Organisation for Success

- Company name
- Organisation forms
- Boards of directors
- Structuring the company organisation
- Attracting outstanding key employees
- Infrastructure without bureaucracy.

GOING BEYOND MEDIA HYPE

"We all suffer from being hyped up in the press. When people say things like, Bill Gates controls this or Malone conrols this or Ovitz controls that, I hope people don't really believe it. Because every day we're saying, how can we keep this customer happy? How can we get ahead in innovation by doing this, because if we don't, somebody else will? if anything, people underestimate how effective capitalism is at keeping even the most successful companies on the edge." ***— Bill Gates, Chief Software Architect, Microsoft***

13

Promotional Policies and Strategies for Small-Scale Industries in India

Introduction

The programme for the development of small-scale industries has been accorded a high place in India.

Amrita Patel
(November 13, 1943)

In India, ever since the days of Gandhiji, the Small Industry movement has been largely regarded as a vehicle for uplifting the weaker sections of the population. Whether it is the handloom weavers, the handicraft workers, the rural women doing spinning in their homes, the rural artisan or the urban craftsmen – all these sections of the population have been looked upon as needing specific support in being able to compete with the modern industrial sector. After Independence, when the problem of regional imbalances began to appear, small Industry was considered as the natural vehicle for correcting such imbalances. More recently, when the problem of unemployment has begun to take an acute form, the ability of the Small Industry to provide jobs at a comparatively lower cost made it an attractive pattern for the planner and the administrator.

In India, during the last decade, the extent of small-scale industries has grown very rapidly and occupy a position of vital importance in the national economy of the country. Small-scale and village industries taken together constitute about 55 per cent of the total industrial production and the contribution of industries falling under the purview of the Small Industries Development Organisation (SIDO) is about 35 per cent.

In India, Small Enterprises have been for long confined to manufacturing units and a few servicing activities such as auto-repair shops, agro-service centres etc.

Recently, however, service activities such as laundry, photocopying, repair shops, poultry etc., have been added but with a ceiling of Rs. 5,00,000 however, there is a marked reluctance to enlarge the scope of the definition to include trading activities – wholesale or retail.

The quantitative definitions of small industry in India envisages a capital investment on plant and machinery not exceeding Rs. 60 lakhs. While in the case of ancillaries, this limit could be extended to Rs. 60 lakhs in the case of the very small units (designated as 'tiny units) the capital investment is limited to Rs. 75 lakhs.

It is seen from the above that the definition of small industry in India relates primarily to capital investments and does not take into account the number employed or the location. The total number of units in the country which come under this definition is around two million which represent more than 96 per cent of the industrial units in the country. The total production of these units is about Rs. 1,60,000 crores which constitutes more than 55 per cent of the total production in the country. Exports from the sector exceed Rs. 10,000 crores. In terms of employment they provide jobs to as many as 13.5 million persons; these figures do not take into account the production or the employment provided by other sections of the decentralised sector such as the handlooms and the handicrafts. Together, tile total production is around Rs. 196,619.2 crores, employment provision of 45.7 million persons and exports exceeding over Rs. 25,971 crores. The significant growth of small-scale industries has been one of the striking features of planned economic development. The small industry sector, therefore, represents a very important element of the industrial economy of the country, both in terms of production, employment and exports.

▸▸ Policy and Measures

The year 1991-92 was momentous in the recent economic development scenario of the country marked by policy changes of an unprecedented nature for giving a major thrust to the country's developmental efforts. These policy measures, initiated in the backdrop of severe economic problems faced by the country, had special significance as they aimed at correcting the imbalances in the economy with due thrust on liberalisation, greater autonomy in decision-making and increasing degree of encouragement to the private sector through a process of elimination of controls and simplification of procedures. These measures, encompassing industrial, trade, fiscal, monetary and foreign exchange policies formed part of macro-economic management programme to facilitate transparency, greater competitiveness and productivity to sustain the growth process.

The policy formulations announced by government include those specially aimed at small-scale sector, but the other policy changes will have no less an effect on this sector. This policy aims at intensifying the efforts for the rapid and balanced industrialisation of the country to the benefit of the common people; at increasing the availability of goods at fair prices; creating more employment and improving the standard of living. The main aspects of the policy in relation to the small-scale industries are:

(*a*) Revision of the investment limit in plant and machinery for small-scale enterprises;

(*b*) More emphasis on the promotion of village industries;

(*c*) Correction of regional imbalances;

(*d*) Promotion of export-oriented and import substitution industries;

(*e*) Creation of new focal points of industrial growth and the establishment of nucleus plants and ancillary industries;

(*f*) Creation of buffer stocks of critical raw materials;

(*g*) Import and transfer of technology; and

(*h*) Improved capacity utilisation and modernisation of industries.

►► Policy for Small-scale Sector

The Government of India announced a package of policy measures in August 1991 for promoting and strengthening small, tiny and village enterprises. The primary objective of the policy is to harness this sector's full potential in industrial production, employment generation and exports. This objective is to be achieved through specific action programmes simultaneously with measures to free the sector from regulatory framework and procedures which hamper its growth potential. The policy seeks to shift the focus of this sector from subsidised or cheap credit to timely availability of credit while the more vulnerable segments of the sector will continue to get preferred treatment. The mechanism evolved is to ensure the increased availability of risk capital, access to technology, quality promotion, marketing, infrastructure, extension service and entrepreneurship promotion.

The population criterion linked to location of tiny units has been removed and industry-related services and business enterprises have been recognised as small industries with their investment limit conforming to the limit for tiny units, *viz.*, Rs. 5 lakhs. The scope of National Equity Fund (NEF) Scheme and Single Window Scheme (SWS) has been widened with the raising of financial limits. The policy permits non-SSI units to have equity participation up to 24% in SSI units; this is expected to facilitate ancillarisation. With the Over the Counter Exchange of India (OTCEI) becoming operational shortly, the relatively larger among the small-scale units might be able to have access to the capital market. Regulatory provisions of private limited companies have been proposed to be liberalised together with the introduction of Limited Partnership Act to the small-scale sector to facilitate supply of risk capital to SSI units. The Government of India also proposes to bring out a legislation for ensuring the prompt payment of the bills of SSI units by the purchasing organisations. Another important measure was introduction of factoring services for the benefit of SSI units by designated banks with the support of Small Industries Development Bank of India (SIDBI). The policy also envisages the setting up of a special monitoring agency to ensure that genuine credit needs of the small-scale sector are fully met.

A new scheme for Integrated Infrastructure Development for SSI sector with the active participation of Central and State Governments and SIDBI has been proposed to be implemented in a phased manner. Creation of Technology Development Cell, export Development Cell, development of component market, market promotion through cooperative, public sector and other professional agencies and a scheme for marketing of mass consumption items are a few other components of the policy announced. The policy gives special attention to quality promotion, creation of testing facilities and technology upgradation of specific industries through SIDBI. In the sphere of entrepreneurship promotion, the policy has underlined the need for having a larger number of trainers and motivators, simplified the definition of women entrepreneurs and proposed the creation of multi-disciplinary cadre of 'barefoot' managers.

A special thrust has also been given in the policy for extension of the required support services and other inputs for the orderly development of the handloom and handicraft sub-sectors and other village industries in recognition of their potential for employment generation and the need for improving the living conditions of those engaged in these activities. Reputed voluntary organisations have been assigned an important role in expanding training facilities and oilier support services to the traditional sub-sectors. Measures have also been suggested as part of the policy for systematic training of craftsmen, provision of essential inputs, supply of designs, technical guidance and creation of marketing channels to facilitate qualitative growth of these sub-sectors.

The general policy guidelines were supported by measures in specific areas some of which are:

(a) Financing for small-scale industries: The Reserve bank of India has given priority and special attention to the provision of credit for the promotion of small-scale industries sector. The Government has also approved the establishment of a national bank for agriculture and rural development for the promotion of agriculture and rural industries in backward areas;

(b) Programmes for small-scale industries: Policy guidelines and programmes for the development of village and small-scale industries have been incorporated in the Sixth Five Year Plan;

(c) Strengthening of SIDO: The technical expertise and the network of SIDO are to be strengthened for meeting the growing technical and technological needs of small-scale industries;

(d) Technical assistance for marketing and export promotion: This scheme has been formulated for rendering technical assistance to small-scale enterprises in product development, standardisation, quality control, marketing etc., keeping in view the demand and supply constraints and market changes, market potential, the control of prices, product specification etc. The different components of this scheme include the promotion of exports, trade delegations, market counselling, research etc.;

(e) Entrepreneurial development programmes are organised for motivating and preparing prospective or future entrepreneurs. In addition management training in different aspects of industrial management is also organised for the benefit of existing and prospective entrepreneurs;

(f) The development of ancillaries has been considered to be one of the main instruments for the promotion of the small-scale sector and also for the transfer of technology from the large-scale sector. With a view to achieving maximum ancillarisation, measures are taken to persuade the large undertakings to purchase their stores etc. from the small firms and to subcontract the manufacture of components and accessories to the latter. Subcontracting exchanges are in operation in an effective manner;

(g) A scheme has been taken up to *modernise small-scale industrial workshops and laboratories* by replacing the old and obsolete machinery and by equipping them with modern and sophisticated machines;

(h) Technical publicity and exhibitions of small-scale industry products are organised for disseminating information on government policies, programmes, facilities, concessions and incentives available to the small-scale entrepreneurs and the prospects of developing such industries in different parts of the country;

(i) There is the provision for making the much-needed consultancy services available to the small entrepreneurs. The scheme provides for subsidising the fees charged by private consultants from such entrepreneurs.

In India, small industries' development has been institutionalised through high-level agencies set up both at the Central as well as the State levels. On the whole, small industry development is the concern of the Ministry of Industrial Development through the Development Commissioner (Small-scale Industries). Setup in 1954, the Central Small Industries Organisation has grown to a vast network of about 25 Small Industries Service Institutes, 20 branch institutes and 41 extension centres spread throughout the country. The Small Industries Development Organisation (SIDO), as it is now called, in addition consists of specialised institutions dealing with the specific area such as Instrumentation, Tool Design and a network of tool rooms as well as test centres set-up in various parts of the country to provide specialised facilities to small industrial units, making it the largest promotion agency of its kind in the world. Associated with the Small Industry Development Organisation are the National Small Industries Corporation (NSIC), which is operated as a public sector undertaking, and a Small Industries Extension Training Institute (SIET) at Hyderabad which is the main centre for training personnel connected with the Small Industry.

At the National level, in addition to the Small Industries Development Organisation, there are organisations dealing with handlooms, headed by Development Commissioner (handlooms), and handicrafts headed by similar officials. In addition, a statutory body – Khadi and 96 other designated village industries, and operates a large number of schemes for the growth and development of those industries.

While the Small Industry Development organisation is with the Ministry of Industry, the handlooms and handicrafts are dealt with by the Ministry of Commerce. There are separate boards dealing with specific products such as Coir and Silk, both of which have tremendous potential for growth in the rural areas. This fragmentation of the decentralised Small Industries sector between several agencies spread over different ministries has lead, to problems of coordination, although, in actual practice, this is achieved through frequent meetings of the officials of the agencies concerned.

At the State level, the problem is much less since many of the subjects are dealt with by the Director (or Commissioners) of industry operating at the state level assisted by the Small Industries Development Corporations set-up in every state. In some states, there are special corporations assisting handlooms and handicrafts, and a Khadi & Village Industries Board which operates as a statutory body under the guidance of the Khadi & Village Industries Commission. At the district level, District Industries Centres have been set-up in most of the districts to cater to the growth of the industries in the region. The DIC programme was started on 1st May, 1978, as a centrally sponsored scheme. The main objective of this programme is to develop and promote small, tiny and cottage sector industries and to generate greater employment opportunities especially among rural and backward areas. The DIC Programme has been under implementation during the Eight period with the Government of India sharing its expenditure with the State Government on a 50:50 basis. DICs have been established in almost all districts of the country. The total number of approved DICs stands at 422 covering 431 districts.

Chart 1

STRATEGIES FOR SMALL INDUSTRY DEVELOPMENT

Strategy	*Japan*	*China*	*India*
1. Legislative Support	Systematic Legislation. A large number of laws have been enacted.	Legislation merely refers to the pattern of ownership	No specific laws enacted
2. Financial Support	Institutional Support: (*i*) People's Finance Corporation (*ii*) Small Business Finance Corp. (*iii*) Central Bank for Industrial Co-operatives	Agency controlling the unit	SIDBI, SFC, CB
3. Consultancy	The constitutional framework for providing consultancy is well-developed.	No formal consultancy organisation	SIDO
4. Technology	A number of technological institutes providing guidance and also generate technology suitable for SII	In-house on the "three-in-one" principle	National labs & regional research labs working under CSIR.

At the block level, which consists roughly of a population of 1,00,000 people, rural industry is part of an integrated programme of rural development. Attempts are now being made to develop greater linkages between industry and the main stream of rural development.

There has been no specific law constituted relating to the Small-scale Industry. For many years, Small Industry has been asking that a comprehensive legislation should be enacted which could bring together all the protective policy measures for the small-scale sector. In 1972, the Government of India appointed a Committee under the Chairmanship of Mr. Bhatt to advise them on whether such a legislation is considered necessary and if so, the important elements for such legislation. The Committee in its report identified the following areas for legislation: Definition, Restricted partnership. Reservation policy, Ancillary development, and Government purchase policy; so far however, no legislation has yet been enacted.

However, government has from time to time, formulated policies which are derived from the Industries (Development and Regulation) Act 1991. One such is to reserve products for exclusive production in small-scale sector.

➧ Reservation of Industries

The Policy of Reservation of Products for exclusive manufacture in SSI (now MSEs) was started in 1967. The objective of achieving socio-economic development, through development and promotion of small units all over the country. This was expected to counter the challenges of regional industrial imbalances, employment generation through self-employment ventures, increased productivity.

The Government continues to protect the small-scale industries through the policy of reserving items for manufacture in the small-scale sector. The policy of reservation was initiated in 1967 with 47 items exclusively reserved for production in small-scale units. Since then there have been additions to, and deletions from, the list including changes in nomenclature. After the introduction of the National Industrial Classification (NIC) codes, a decision was taken in 1978 to recast the reserved list by following codes adopted in the NIC. As a result, the list of reserved items expanded from 504 to 807 items in 1978. As on 31.3.1991, 836 items were reserved for exclusive manufacture in the small-scale sector.

Under the policy, creation of fresh capacities in the large-scale sector in the areas reserved for small-scale sector is not allowed except in cases where the large-scale unit gives an undertaking to export a minimum of 75% of new or additional production. Only the items which are technoeconomically suitable for manufacture in the small-scale sector are included in the reserved list. The reservation policy is constantly reviewed. The Government has constituted a high-powered Advisory Committee on Reservation under the Industries (Development & Regulation) Act, 1951, to review the list of items/products reserved for exclusive manufacture in the small-scale sector.

A policy has been formulated to assist the development of the ancillary units, particularly in the public sector for which purpose, a Government agency – the Bureau of Public Enterprises – has issued detailed guidelines to the public sector undertakings. Government has also formulated a suitable purchase policy so that the volume of purchases made from the small-scale sector is significant and commensurate with its share in the total national economy.

Consultancy is basically provided by the Small Industry Development Organisation through the Small Industries Service Institutes. Such consultancy is normally free of charge except for specialised services such as preparation of feasibility reports or techno-economic surveys. In addition, the National Productivity Council through the Local Productivity Councils and State Level Agencies like the Technical & Consultancy Organisations also provide service to small industrial units. In recent years, a large number of private consultants have also come up to offer their services for these purposes, but in many cases, their charges tend to be unduly high and the quality of services somewhat inadequate.

However, with the gradual opening up of the economy and policy of liberalisation, there has been progressive de-reservation of a number of items reserved for exclusive manufacture by the micro and small-scale sector. The objective of progressive de-reservation was to provide for opportunities for technological upgradation, promotion of exports and economies of scale, in order to encourage modernisation and enhance the competitiveness of MSEs in view of the liberalisation and globalisation of the economy.

Items were reserved/de-reserved in accordance with Section 29(B) of the Industries (Development & Regulation) [I(D&R)] Act, 1951, which, inter alia, provides for the constitution of an Advisory Committee under the chairmanship of the Secretary (SSI) [now Secretary (MSME)]. The Advisory Committee makes its recommendations on the basis of the laid down procedure in the I(D&R) Act, 1951 which relates to the economies of scale, the level of employment, the possibility of encouraging and diffusing entrepreneurship in industry, the prevention of concentration of economic power to the detriment of the common interest and any other issue which the Committee may think fit. After due consultation with the stakeholders, 125 items were de-reserved on 13 March 2007, 79 more on 8th February 2008 and the more on 10th October '08. The total number of items reserved for exclusive manufacture in micro and small enterprise sector now (2009) stands at 21 only.

▸▸ Technology

Technology development is undertaken primarily by the national labs and the regional research labs working under the Council of Scientific and Industrial Research, but the linkage between them and the small industrial units is still comparatively limited. Regional testing centres have been set-up under the Small Industry Development and Training Centres (PTC) are being operated by the NSIC. In addition, Process and Product Development Centres are proposed to be set-up at locations and in fields relevant to the Small-scale Sector.

⏩ Technology Support

(*i*) Small Industries Corporations of different States have been advised to acquire appropriate technology from R&D institutions for transfer to small-scale units/entrepreneurs in their States at a reasonable cost.

(*ii*) Under the Action Plan of Deptt. of I.D., a modernisation of dyestuffs industry was carried out during 1989-90. A Draft Report on the status and its potential for further development and modernisation of existing units was prepared and this has been circulated to all SISIs for comments.

(*iii*) A proposal for setting up a Process-cum-Product Development Centre for Polymers & Polymer based Industries at Haldia, Midiapur Distt., West Bengal has been drafted keeping in view that the Government of India has cleared Haldia Petrochemical Complex. Thus, there is a need for advance planning for setting up industries based on products/byproducts obtained by Haldia Petrochemical Complex. The proposal will be posed for consideration for assistance from UNDP.

(*iv*) Work relating to the setting up of Process & Product Development Centre on Essential Oils at Kannauj has been expedited since Memorandum of Understanding between Government of India and UNDP has been signed. The State Govt. of Uttar Pradesh has also finalised the working drawings of the proposed PPDC Complex and has sanctioned an amount of Rs. 52 lakhs during 1990-91 for construction of buildings. The Project has been cleared by the Standing Committee on schemes.

⏩ Energy Conservation

SIDO, through its network of SISIs has already initiated Awareness/Energy Conservation Programmes to be conducted throughout the country for the entrepreneurs at the operational level. The success of the Programme during 1989-90 encouraged further work during 1990-91 on Energy Management, Energy Audit, technical proposal of Energy Conservation at the Unit level, etc. During this period, many units got direct assistance on practical application of Energy Conservation methods at the unit level from the Technical officers of SIDO in the States/UTs.

SIDO has initiated special programme on Energy Conservation and Energy Audit for Steel Re-rolling Industry in SISI, Madras and Jaipur. The Energy Audit Study of the Re-rolling Mill through Jaipur office has been completed.

At SISI, Delhi, a special assignment has been undertaken under the Programme to analyse the design aspects of desert coolers and fluorescent tube choke of conventional design, both known to be energy inefficient. The re-designed and re-fabricated conventional fluorescent tube choke has already been put to tests and the results were found to be encouraging.

⏩ Ancillary Development

The ancillary development programme has received government support for many years at the highest levels. However, in actual practice, there have been many difficulties in the implementation of a vigorous ancillary development programme. Even in the public sector undertakings which are directly under government control there has been a marked reluctance for supporting the establishment of ancillaries and granting them a specific status as an "ancillary" which would guarantee 50 per cent off-take of their production. The purchase of the largest units from the small-scale suppliers have increased from Rs. 257.2 million in 1969-1970 to Rs. 1,500 million in 1978-1979. While this is encouraging, the large units prefer to deal with smaller units merely as suppliers and not in any special and contractual relationship. However, Government has been repeatedly advising the public sector undertakings to ensure that a large number of items are framed out for manufacture by the small-scale units, though with only modest success.

An important development in this area has been the establishment of Sub-contracting Exchanges at the Small Industries Service Institutes all over the country. These exchanges maintain up-to-date data on the capacities available in the small-scale sector which are then matched with the requirements of the large industry to enable the small-scale units to receive and execute job orders from the developed countries to the developing countries, is also being planned at present.

⏩ Financial and Extension Infrastructure

There is a wide network of institutional infrastructure for financing an extension service support to small-scale industries in the country. This network consists of State Financial Corporations (SFCs), Commercial. Co-operative and Regional Rural Banks (RRBs), National Small Industries Development Corporation (NSIC), State Small Industries Development Corporations (SSIDCs), Khadi and Village Industries Commission (KVIC), District Industries Centres (DICs), agencies meant for entrepreneurship development and consultancy support. National Bank for Agriculture and Rural Development (NABARD) and Small Industries Development Bank of India (SIDBI). While other agencies are serving the small-scale sector at the grass root level, NABARD has its focus on rural areas through linkages with the banking system. SIDBI has been set up as the principal financial institution for promotion and financing of small-scale sector and has functional linkages with the banking and institutional structure by providing refinance and other forms of resource support, besides organising extension services and coordinating their activities.

Setting up of Small Industries Development Bank of India (SIDBI) marked the fulfilment of a long felt need to have a separate institution at the national level to exclusively cater to the requirements of the small-scale sector in the country. The decision to set up SIDBI was announced by the Finance Minister while presenting the Union Budget for 1989-90 and the Bill for setting up the Bank is a wholly-owned subsidiary of Industrial Development Bank of India (IDUI) was introduced in the Parliament in May, 1989 and passed in October 1989. SIDBI became operational on April 2, 1990 with an initial paid-up capital of Rs. 250 crore and taking over the outstanding portfolio of IDBI relating to small-scale sector held under the Small Industries Development Fund (SIDF) as of March 31,1990 amounting to Rs. 4,200 crore. The authorised capital and paid-up capital of the Bank were subsequently raised to Rs. 500 crore and Rs. 450 crore respectively.

⏩ The Role

The SIDBI is designed to function as the principal financial institution for the promotion, financing and development of industry in the small-scale sector and to co-ordinate the functions of institutions engaged in similar activities. The role envisaged is wide-ranging. SIDBI's Statute allows considerable flexibility and empowers it to assist the entire spectrum of small, tiny, village and cottage industries in the decentralised sector. The range of assistance comprises promotional, financing an extension support, which will be made available through appropriate schemes to cover setting up of new projects and expansion, diversification, modernisation and rehabilitation of existing units.

⏩ Major Activities

The activities of SIDBI have been patterned to suit the requirements of the small-scale industries consisting of both modern and traditional ones. Broadly, these activities can be categorised as under:

(*i*) refinancing of term loans granted by banks and other eligible financial institutions;

(*ii*) direct discounting as well as rediscounting of bills arising out of sale of machinery/capital equipment by manufacturers in small-scale sector on deferred credit;

(*iii*) equity type assistance under National Equity Fund (NEF) and by way of seed capital to entrepreneurs;

(*iv*) rediscounting of short-term trade bills arising out of sale of product of small-scale sector;

(*v*) resource support to NSIC and other institutions engaged in supply of raw materials, marketing of SSI products, setting up of industrial estates, development of industrial areas and infrastructure, extension of hire-purchase and leasing facilities;

(*vi*) direct assistance for setting up and expansion of marketing outlets for SSI products and development of industrial areas for SSI units;

(*vii*) share capital and resource support to factoring organisations;

(*viii*) assistance for promotion of exports of SSI products; and

(*ix*) extension of technical and other related support services for promotion, development and growth of small-scale sector.

In consonance with the objectives envisaged in the Statute, the SIDBI has evolved new schemes of assistance while, at the same time, continuing the schemes of assistance hitherto operated by the IDBI for the small-scale sector under the SIDF. The SIDBI has also given special attention to liberalisation and simplification of existing schemes of assistance, simultaneously with extension and support services like modernisation and technology upgradation.

Credit for the small-scale sector is provided primarily by the State Financial Corporations for medium-term loans and through commercial banks for working capital. Various State Governments also provide loans for small amounts up to Rs. 10,000 under the State Aid to Industries Act. Concessional finance is provided by the financial institutions to the small-scale sector and in respect of loans below Rs. 25,000 no collateral is insisted upon. In practice, however, the problem of obtaining finances becomes increasingly acute as the size of the unit becomes smaller.

⏩ Fiscal and other Incentives

The small-scale sector enjoys certain fiscal and other incentives such as exemption in excise duty up to a specified limit, reservation of 836 items for the exclusive production in the sector, purchase and price preferences to SSI products in the stores purchase programme of the Government and preferential allocation of scarce and controlled raw materials. Besides, priority is accorded in extension of credit facilities on concessional terms both for fixed and working capital. The State Governments have also come out with package of measures for stimulating the growth of small-scale sector. A number of institutions in both Government and non-Government sectors, are providing extension and support services especially in the field of consultancy, technical assistance, entrepreneurship development and skill upgradation.

⏩ Small Industries Development Fund

The Small Industries Development Fund (SIDF) set up by IDBI in May, 1986 with a corpus of about Rs. 2,500 crores provides a focal point for coordinating financial assistance to the small-scale sector at the apex level. Now transferred to SIDBI. The SIDF provides assistance for development, expansion, diversification, modernisation and rehabilitation of SSI units and such assistance will be routed through SFCs, SIDCs, commercial banks and other eligible institutions. The fund also provides assistance by way of rediscounting bills and promissory notes arising out of sale or purchase of machinery by small-scale units on deferred payment terms. Besides, SIDF assists institutions engaged in the promotion, financing and providing extension services to the small-scale sector. Under the auspices of SIDF, a series of new measures to give a further boost to the small-scale sector have been launched by the IDBI. New schemes of assistance for setting up SSI units by women entrepreneurs. Ex-servicemen and for setting up in-house quality control facilities by SSI units have also been introduced. Ten model Quality Testing Centres for the benefit of SSIs will also be set up in different parts of the country.

The establishment of a separate Fund – SIDF – in IDBI is expected to provide a sharper focus to financial and non-financial assistance flowing to the small-scale sector in the years to come. Through the Funds, IDBI will increase the volume of assistance to the small-scale sector, to keep pace with its expected growth and development and also widen the spread of assistance to cover a large number of small and tiny units.

⏩ National Equity Fund

In August, 1987 Government of India introduced National Equity Fund Scheme aimed at providing support in the nature of equity assistance to tiny and small-scale industrial units which are engaged in manufacturing activities. Government of India has provided Rs. 5 crores towards the Fund and SIDBI an equal amount. The Scheme is administered by SIDBI through nationalised banks. State Bank of India and also SFCs/twin function SIDCs in the North Eastern Region and the hilly states of Himachal Pradesh and Jammu & Kashmir which act as agents of IDBI in regard to sanction and disbursement of assistance.

Assistance from the Fund is provided by way of seed capital in the form of soft loan to eligible small and tiny industries located in a village or town with a population not exceeding 5,00,000. However, in case of rehabilitation proposals for sick units the project could be located in towns/villages with population not exceeding 15,00,000. With the focus on the needs of smaller among small-scale units, the assistance is provided to manufacturing units having project cost not exceeding Rs. 5 lakhs. New units as also potentially viable sick units in the small sector, eligible for assistance under the Refinance Scheme of IDBI, get support out of the Fund. The assistance under the Scheme is made available upto a maximum of Rs. 75,000/- per project at a nominal services charge of 1% per annum. Units availing the assistance would be required to bring in a minimum cash contribution of 10% of the project cost. No security (including collateral) need be provided by borrowers for the assistance under the scheme. Assistance from the Fund enables the eligible tiny and small-scale sector units to bridge the gap in the required margin to obtain term loan assistance under various schemes.

⏩ SIDBI Single Window Scheme for Financing of Fixed Assets and Working Capital to Tiny and SSI Units

In order to overcome difficulties and delays experienced by tiny and small-scale units assisted by SFCs/SIDCs in securing working capital finance, SIDBI introduced in May 1988 a refinance scheme which enables SFCs and twin function SIDCs to provide through a single window both term loan for fixed assets and working capital to new tiny and small-scale units whose project cost does not exceed Rs. 5 lakhs. Besides, providing term loan for fixed assets, SFC/SIDCs will also now simultaneously provide working capital loans upto Rs. 2.5 lakhs.

Credit Guarantee Scheme

To encourage the financial institutions to lend liberally, a credit guarantee scheme is being administered by the Deposit Insurance & Credit Guarantee Corporation. The Corporation provides guarantee to a substantial extent in respect of loans granted to borrowers engaged in small-scale industrial activities. The existing monetary ceiling on the Corporation's claim liability is to be enhanced from (Rs. 10 lakhs per borrowing constituent) to Rs. 20 lakhs to be apportioned equally and separately between term loans (Rs. 10 lakhs) and working capital finance (Rs. 10 lakhs) in respect of eligible credit facilities extended on or after 1st April, 1989).

Marketing

Marketing has always been a major problem for the small industrial units although significant exports are being done. Small units suffer from lack of up-to-date market information and ability to make frequent visits abroad to contact potential customers. Even within the country, small units find it difficult to compete with large companies, particularly in respect of consumer goods where brand consciousness is an important criterion. Government has provided specific support programmes such as a purchase and price preference policy, but this has provided a limited assistance to the small-scale units, as seen by the fact that the share of the small units even in government purchases is still below 15 per cent. The problem is likely to become even more acute as small industrial units get established outside the metropolitan areas. The question of organisational support, which needs to be provided to the small units so as to make them able to compete on, equal terms with the large units, is under consideration of the Government.

Reservation of Items for Government Stores and Purchase

Government assists the small-scale units by procuring products manufactured by them. 409 items have been exclusively reserved for purchase from small-scale sector. Further, purchases upto 50% of the requirements in respect of 28 other items are also reserved for small-scale sector. Small-scale units were also accorded price preference upto 15% in case of items which are procured by them from large and small-scale units. The small-scale industries are also exempted from paying registration fee and the forms for registration are supplied free of charge. Security deposit upto a specified limit is also not taken from such units which are registered with NSIC under Single Point Registration Scheme and whose capacity has been certified by them.

The SIDO through its network of SISIs and Extension Centres provides assistance for promotion of exports of small-scale sector products. Packaging is an important component of modern marketing strategy both within the country and abroad. SIDO is conducting training programmes, seminars and workshops for packaging techniques for the benefit of small-scale industries. The aim of the programme is to generate packaging consciousness in the industry and to educate the entrepreneurs on the scientific packaging techniques.

Modernisation

Modernisation of the small-scale industry has been considered since the late sixties when a Government Committee identified five industries – machine tools, automobile ancillaries, domestic electrical appliances, foundry and hosiery – as being ripe for modernisation. Subsequently, more industries have been added to the list: and the Small Industries Service Institutes Operate a programme of modernisation under which studies are conducted to indicate the specific manner in which modernisation can be done. The basic weakness of the programme has been the lack of funds on soft terms to finance such improvements, however, the Industrial Development Bank of India is working on a plan to provide such funds and it is expected that once such a plan is implemented, the programme of modernisation may gather momentum.

Raw Materials

It has been the policy of the Government to help small-scale sector to get its due share of scarce raw material in time so that growth and progress are not affected. Small Industries Development Organisation (SIDO) maintains close liaison with the raw material suppliers such as primary producers, the canalising agencies like MMTC, MSTC, SSI Corporations etc., and helps in growth of the small-scale sector. With the liberalised import policy particularly in respect of raw material components and consumables by and large the raw material supply position was easy.

Conclusion

The government has been in the forefront in the development of small-scale industries. It has made multi-directional efforts to accelerate the process of industrialisation. The government has pursued a "mixed" policy not protecting and developing the small-scale industry, both as producer of consumer goods as well as a supplier of intermediate parts. Infrastructure development meets only the needs of a few. While a comprehensive credit delivery system has been built up to look after every kind of capital needs of small enterprises, it is quite lopsided. Market development is inadequate and there is a marked reluctance to introduce improved technology. At present, more than 66,000 institutions are assisting.

The system built up by the government to assist the small industries helps a few and the wrong units at the expense of the consumer and other smaller units. And the bureaucracy has only been catering to its vested interest rather than furthering the interests of the small-scale industries. On the contrary, corruption has made a big dent. There is much redundancy in the various programmes. The need of the hour is simplification for effective implementation. The entire gamut of strategies, policies and measures needs a change for the better.

"Entrepreneurship plays a key role in the economic development of a country."

14

Entrepreneurial Inputs

Introduction

Anil Ambani

There have been many attempts to shed light on what makes somebody want to become an entrepreneur, and there is still a widespread idea that entrepreneurs are, by and large, people who drop out of school when they are in their teens, go and invent something in the shed at the bottom of the garden, start a company, and go on to fame and fortune. Clearly, entrepreneurs with this profile do exist, but despite popular entrepreneur folklore, they are very much in the minority.

In fact, the only recipe that stands up to critical examination is that you are more likely to become an entrepreneur if someone in your environment is or has been one, your father for instance, or some other family member.

However, your environment includes more than just your family and so it can also be said that if there is a strong entrepreneurial community where you are brought up – your home town, or even a cluster of towns in your area – then this can also encourage you to think of becoming an entrepreneur yourself. It's not just a question of icons, or role models; it's more a matter of entrepreneurship appearing to you in those you see around you as a perfectly normal and widely practiced way of pursuing a career. In this chapter, we discuss the environmental influence on entrepreneur and entrepreneurship.

⏩ Entrepreneurship Inputs

Entrepreneurship inputs refer to the various facets within which enterprises – big, medium, small and others – have to operate. The enterprise or entrepreneurship is, therefore, influenced by the environment. By and large, entrepreneurship is influenced by an environment created by political, social, economic, national, legal forces, etc.

Entrepreneurial environment is broadly classified into six important segments, namely, (1) Political environment, (2) Economic environment, (3) Social environment, (4) Technological environment, (5) Legal environment, and (6) Cultural environment.

ENVIRONMENT

POLITICAL	ECONOMIC	SOCIAL	TECHNOLOGICAL	LEGAL	CULTURAL
POLITICAL ATMOSPHERE QUALITY OF LEADERSHIP	ECONOMIC POLICIES LABOUR TRADE TARIFFS INCENTIVES SUBSIDIES	CONSUMER LABOUR ATTITUDES OPINIONS MOTIVES	COMPETITION & RISK EFFICIENCY PRODUCTIVITY PROFITABILITY	RULES REGULATIONS	STRUCTURE ASPIRATIONS & VALUES

Fig. 1 Entrepreneurial Environment

⏩ Private Enterprise and Development

The existence of uncertainty in the economic environment means that there are limits to planning. These limitations stimulate entrepreneurs to play a leading role in the growth process.

Individual entrepreneurs, such as farmers and small businessmen and individual enterprises, such as manufacturing, construction, transport and wholesale enterprises and collective farms, continually face risks. Whether they are privately or publicly owned, they must take account of uncertainty. Private entrepreneur and managers of private enterprises take risks, despite the heavy costs of failure because of the possibility of high profits or large bonuses. In any case, they must run their business efficiently if they are to make a profit and survive. The problem usually arises because major industrial decisions which will affect the lives of thousands of ordinary people, are taken without proper planning and without public consultation. The result is that environmental activist have no choice but to fight a rear guard action. This often gives the impression that environmental activists are against all growth and industry. In fact, they are more than conscious of the need for a balanced approach to growth and industry. All they say is that industrial decisions ought to be taken after considering the impact on environment and also that the public has a right to know all details.

Environmental activists have repeatedly pointed out the havoc caused by some of our petrochemical, heavy chemical, dyestuff and other polluting industries, as also the environmental damage caused by large-scale open mining, quarrying and deforestation, which will take decades to reverse. For their dogged determination, these environmentalists deserve our gratitude.

At the same time, it is now clear that technology has advanced significantly to allow efficient and clean use of resources. Worldwide, industry has become conscious of the need to use renewable resources as far as possible and utilise non-renewable resources within planned limits. In fact, in India we have an advantage in that industry has not yet spread so far and wide. We can, therefore, learn from past industrial mistakes and ensure further growth, consistent with environmental protection.

In contrast, the manager of public enterprises (whether directly or indirectly, state-owned or collectively-owned) tend to be risk-alerters. Indeed, risk-aversion is usually, and perhaps inevitably, the emphasis of public service training. Entrepreneurs and managers of public enterprises must be offered incentives if they are to be efficient and take risks, yet they must also be penalised to discourage them from taking foolish risk or making too many mistakes. Devising appropriate incentives is very difficult. A variety of possible measures – some positive, such as bonuses for managers, and some negative, such as budget and operational controls can be used in the public sector; even so, the problem often remains intractable.

If an economy is made up of a large number of entrepreneurial units, risks can be spread among them; even though some enterprises may fail, others will be successful and the economy as a whole can grow rapidly. When inefficient units do not have access to subsidies or to other public assistance, they must improve their competitive position or disappear. Such failures need not be excessively costly because the economy's expansion creates job and income earning opportunities for political reasons. But allowing public enterprises to operate inefficiently will mean very heavy costs in the long run. It affects not only a country's ability to produce efficiently but also its capacity to save and invest for future production.

Private enterprises and entrepreneurs can function smoothly – and contribute to development – only in an appropriately public policy environment.

Entrepreneurial Urge

Entrepreneurship is the creative 'elan' of industrial development which for historical reasons is feeble in backward areas. It is wrong to expect entrepreneurial urge among people who live in poverty, illiteracy and ignorance. Conceptualisation of entrepreneurship in terms of self-confidence, optimism, achievement, motivation and other such attributes constituting the variable, residual non-marketed services receiving the residual profit income as payment (Kilby) does not have any meaning in backward areas; because these qualities themselves need a minimum of economic well-being below which the hard preoccupations with the basic needs of life leave no room for critical reflection and initiative necessary for any enterprise. Entrepreneurial qualities are not innate attributes of individuals which blossom inexorably against all odds and transform their situation; they are born of an environment through individuals' creative response to potential opportunities. An entrepreneur needs a clear perception of economic opportunities and the investment capacity to pursue these opportunities. In backward areas where the basic struggle for existence is so tough, per capital income so low and where illiteracy or low level of education prevents access to business information or ideas, there is neither perception of opportunities nor the capacity to exploit these opportunities. Not only the environment is timid without brisk activities or aggressive ideas but also men are too deprived to have an urge to know and grow. When we think of the development of backward areas, we must think of the ascent of these lowly men to the capacity to participate in the development process, into the cosmetic growth of the soil by outsiders' investment and outsiders' profit. No effort will be successful to convert such people into entrepreneurs unless we realise the basic symbiotic nature of entrepreneurship so inextricably integrated with their total life-situation and environment. Therefore, in developing environment and changing the life-situation, we take the first step to develop entrepreneurship.

Significance of Entrepreneurial Environment

A study of socio-political and economic environment has a great social and economic significance to the growth of entrepreneurship. Modern business is treated as a social and economic institution and is affected by the political, social and economic forces. The political environment, industrial policy, licensing policy, foreign exchange regulations, banking policy, technological development and social change form the framework within which an enterprise has to work. It is for these reasons that all business plans must be based on the environment prevailing around. An entrepreneurial plan cannot be framed and finalised for its implementation without its relevance to the political, social, economical and technological requirements. In fact, it is environment which regulates entrepreneurial activities. A study of socio-political and economic environment is essential for the growth of entrepreneurship. Business environment has a positive relationship with the development of entrepreneurship.

Political Environment

Political environment affects the entrepreneurial growth and accelerates the process of economic activity. Law and order is of high priority, followed by Government policies in regard to the promotion of entrepreneurship, followed by incentives, encouragement and right institutional structure will go a long way in fostering entrepreneurship.

Economical Environment

The entrepreneurial growth and development is also governed by the economic environment. It encompasses a wide spectrum of items, namely, land, availability of raw material, skilled labour, infrastructure, machinery, capital and so on.

Shortage of raw materials can much adversely affect the entrepreneurial environment and it has been affecting many industries. Shortage of raw materials, inferior quality, high price resulting in high cost of production are bringing bad name to the small industry. Without raw materials, no industry can run and no entrepreneurship would come up. The more favourable the conditions of raw materials are, better would be its influence on entrepreneurial emergence.

The role and importance of market and marketing should never be underestimated for the uprise of entrepreneurship. If the proof of pudding lies in eating, the proof of production lies in marketing. If the entrepreneur does not possess knowledge and various marketing techniques, he is unlikely to survive. The size and composition of market both influence entrepreneurship in their own ways.

The benefits of an improved and healthy market conditions in the environment of entrepreneurial growth are self-explanatory. Germany and Japan are examples where rapid improvement in market was followed by rapid entrepreneurial appearance.

A Brave New Marketing World

Markets have been changing faster than marketing. And marketing has to catch up with these changes. Today's customers are more price, quality, service and value sensitive. There's a proliferation of communication and distribution channels. There's a digital revolution affecting the speed with which we get information and the way we communicate.

Although the fundamental principles of marketing still apply marketers are also adding additional perspectives. They are recognising the great value of building strong brands. According to Interbrand, Coca-Cola is worth $77 billion, far more than its tangible plant and equipment value. Companies are focusing more on customer lifetime value, not just the immediate earnings from a transaction. Companies are inviting their customers to collaborate in the creation of value. They are putting their messages on newer media. They are developing new metrics and hoping to measure the ROI on marketing investments. Traditional marketing departments presumably are skilled in the basics of marketing research, advertising, sales promotion, and sales management. But in today's e-world, additional skills are needed in the marketing department. I would emphasise the following skills:

- Brand building skills and positioning skills
- Database management and data-mining skills
- Customer and partner relationship management skills
- Customer profitability measurement skills
- Public relations and buzz marketing skills

Philip Kotler would count the following as some of his contributions to the field of marketing:

- Making the customer and customer value central to the thinking of marketers. Telling companies to design their firm from the customer backward.
- Broadening the concept of marketing to include not only goods and services but also the marketing of ideas, causes, places, persons, and whole organisations.
- Developing the field of not-for-profit marketing to cover museums, symphony orchestras, theatre groups, and so on.
- Developing the field of social marketing to help change people's behaviours in positive, life-enhancing ways.

The 4 Ps remain a useful organising framework for marketing planning. There is nothing wrong with adding a few more Ps for emphasis, such as Packaging, People, Personnel, Politics, Public opinion, Product design positioning and Passion. All of these have been suggested. Those in services marketing have suggested three more Ps: people, process and physical evidence.

Even staying with the 4Ps I would advocate translating them into the four Cs which take a customer-based rather than a seller-based view. Product becomes Customer Value. Price becomes Customer Costs. Place becomes Customer Convenience, and Promotion becomes Customer Communication. Buyers want customer value, lower total costs, more convenience and honest communication.

Of course the starting point is not the 4Ps but Segmentation, Targeting, and Positioning (STP). STP is strategic marketing and the 4Ps is tactical marketing. The old marketing doesn't work any more and the outlines of the new marketing are barely emerging. New marketing will require getting closer to the customers, developing more customer insight, working with fewer but more partnered suppliers and distributors, finding newer communication vehicles, and moving to high-tech marketing without losing a high touch.

The Most Important Growth Drivers

- A sharply designed, ambitious and well-communicated **growth vision**
- A **strategic reach** that protects, leverages and stretches the core
- A **strong leadership** team with specific, diversified experience and skills
- A clear **competence profile** that can be leveraged and stretched
- **Organisational excellence** with growth-related structure, processes, measurement and incentive systems
- A **growth-embedding**, open and progressing culture

These growth drivers are propelled by vivid vision, leadership, communication, creativity, innovation fuel value building growth.

- Value-growers must pursue top performance, maintain stamina, redefine their businesses and markets, and continuously "push the envelope" even further.

- Profit seekers need to make a clean break from the profit trap-cost-cutting and control and refocus on market and growth-oriented investments. This begins by developing a vision and reassessing the company's culture and incentive system.
- Simple growers typically need to refocus on core competencies while maintaining growth momentum.

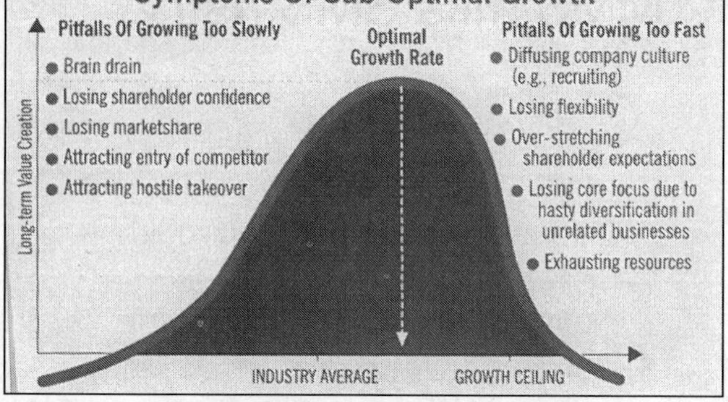

Symptoms Of Sub-Optimal Growth

- Underperformers may need fundamental restructuring and strategic reorientation.

➧ Social Environment

Social environment strongly affects the entrepreneurial behaviour which contributes to entrepreneurial growth. The social factors can be (*i*) family background, (*ii*) kith and kins (relatives, friends and teachers), (*iii*) religion, (*iv*) social status, (*v*) social mobility and (*vi*) social marginality.

Family background greatly affects the entrepreneurial environment and maintenance of social system. Joint family or nuclear families have their own benefits and disadvantages. There is more sentimental attachment of family members of joint family as compared to nuclear family. But even in nuclear families, sentimental association or emotional bonds are stronger in India as compared to those in the western countries where "out of sight out of mind" is the type of attitude of people. In the words of Desai, "the joint family is perhaps the most faithful in which he lays stress on generation depth and sentimental belongingness among the members of the family." The joint family according to him is a three and more generational group of lineal descendants.

The environment of the family also influences the entrepreneurship. If the father is a professional or a businessman or the like, the son is more likely to adopt the same occupation because of certain inherent advantages by virtue of his father being in the similar line.

The reference also affects the environment. A person is likely to adopt the guidelines or rules of the reference group to which he belongs. The reference group can be church groups, armed services and otherwise, informal circle of friends and relatives. The prospective entrepreneur would discuss his ideas with them and seek their advice while starting a new business.

Similarly, social status has its own role to play. Every human being aspires for a high social status and once he achieves a reasonable level, his aspirations and desires for it start getting multiplied. People, therefore, become quite responsible in the wake of protecting and developing their status. Chester Barnard said that the desire for improvement of status and especially the desire to protect status appears to be the basis of a sense of general responsibilities. People work hard to maintain their status as it also contributes to their entrepreneurial growth.

Caste and religion of entrepreneur are the contributory factors of entrepreneurial growth. History reveals that the entrepreneurial traits do not belong to a specific caste rather the entrepreneurs emerge from varied communities. James Berna conducted a study of 52 medium-scale manufacturing entrepreneurs and found that his firms had mostly grown from small beginnings and his entrepreneurs had come from a wide range of social and economic backgrounds. Many of his entrepreneurs had to face formidable obstacles but their enterprises did grow. But sociologists still claim that caste and religions do have an impact on the environment. For example, Parsis of Maharashtra, Jains of Rajasthan and Gujarat have been the mainsprings of entrepreneurial activity.

Social mobility involves the degree of social and geographical mobility and the nature of mobility channels within a system. There are varied opinions about the influence of social mobility on the entrepreneurial environment. Hoselitz and McClelland's need for openness of a system and flexibility in role relations respectively reveal an imperative role of mobility within a system for entrepreneurship development. Their viewpoint is that high degree of social mobility would help in the emergence of entrepreneurship. But Hagen's belief is that the lack of mobility possibilities promote entrepreneurship. Brozen's emphasis is that the system should neither be too flexible nor too rigid because the former would pull the entrepreneur away from his role and the latter would restrict the entrepreneur. However, social mobility does not work in the system in isolation but there are many other factors which influence the entrepreneurial environment.

Social marginality also positively influences entrepreneurship. Stauworth and Curran stress that a person belonging to a social group traditionally constrained to enter economic activity and barred from many other activities by the society is expected to choose the owner-manager role in a small industry.

⏩ Technological Environment

Technology represents the application of scientific knowledge for practical purposes. While the 20th century and certainly the 1st half upto 1950 gave us a massive industrial base, shift from agriculture and rural life to urban life, utilisation of energy and power for our benefit, the ongoing progress of technology through R&D efforts have led to more comfortable lifestyles. The last three decades of the 20th century brought in what we call an Information Revolution.

Technological advancement has become a catalytic agent in the promotion of entrepreneurship growth of industrial and allied services. Thomas DeGregori sets forth thirty operational principles demonstrating that technology creates resources and that with intelligent policies in science our society can be sustainable and will continue to invent new resource creating technologies. Conversely, he argues, "living within limits: is a course that, if followed, would lead to certain decline and destruction. The technological impact on agriculture, industry are immence. Further, technology bring in cultural changes as well as the quality of life. Technological development continues to give fillip to entrepreneurship in multi-facet manner, affecting the life of the entrepreneurs as well as the common man. The entrepreneur's endeavour is to stay ahead technologically in products and services with a penchant for quality. This will not only enhance profits, but also maintain balance in the ecosystem.

Next two decades will see a Knowledge Revolution, leading to large-scale adoption of new technologies in India. Most of them will be based on information technology using tools such as computer and mobile phones for processing, storage and transfer of data, internet communication and e-commerce. Many new industries, arising out of application of new technologies, will flourish in countries of Asia, depending on their stage of economic and technological development.

The Knowledge Revolution has made it possible to routinise processes – a shift from the traditional manual control of conventional machinery for using the computer brain to operate the machinery. Computer Software is an alternate way to reorganise traditional work processes, through application of overseeing knowledge aided by systematic, logical analysis.

⏩ Legal Environment

There are various rules and regulations applicable to different groups of industries, for various purposes. Some of them relate to:

Registration, licensing, pollution, location, acquisition, payment of wages and labour related laws, pollution and environmental rules, laws relating to organisation, product, patent, resource and taxes.

According to a recent study, there are over 150 legal requirements an entrepreneur has to take care of.

Some legal entity – may be a business, a government agency, or a large non-profit organisation – may well contain in its fold a network of diverse autonomous organisations. The old model of corporations is fast becoming obsolete and is being replaced by new ones. We are witnessing the operation of Schumpeter's doctrine of "creative destruction" in practice. Traditional geocentric way of industrial operations are being replaced by innovative, multi-location industrial operations tapping the synergies of "outsiders" from different countries. This is happening in China and India now; and in countries like Korea, Singapore, Thailand and Malaysia this process began almost a decade or two ago. Indeed Australia, being closely aligned to the Western countries, had the advantage of a headstart.

▸▸ Cultural Environment

Every organisation has an invisible quality – a certain style, a character, a way of doing things – that may be more powerful than the dictates of any one person or a formal system. This invisible quality 'the corporate culture' decides how effective the organisation is in the marketplace. Achieving cultural change to maintain a prime market position is the key preoccupation of every chief executive these days.

Max Weber emphasises that cultural factors have a crippling effect on entrepreneurial growth. Culture consists of (*i*) tangible man-made objects like furniture, buildings etc. (*ii*) intangible concepts like laws, morals, knowledge etc. (*iii*) values and behaviour acceptable within the society. America is a capitalist country, Russia followed a socialist pattern, democracy has no touch in China, but Indian culture encourages democracy and accepts mixed economy. At the time of Independence, India was in such a state that the economy could not be left in the hands of people. The government had to intervene and chalk out plans to take the country towards development. Culture of Hindus is to worship 'Ganesha' before undertaking any financial affair. Whether it is a superstition or not is a debatable point. While going on some long journey or on some special days or while tying up a nuptial knot, it is in our culture to seek the recommendations of priests, pandits or sufis.

Catalysing change in corporate cultures by managing people and talent better seems to be the new mantra on the Indian corporate landscape. Better people management is being recognised as the key to sustained success – from managing internal relationships to building corporate cultures that nurture talent. It is no longer enough to be a blue chip IIT-IIM manager, it is equally necessary to update one's EQ to become emotionally engaged with employee and customer need.

Gone are the days when the dictat ran down from the top and the words of boss were carved out in stone. In place of fear and distruct of management policies, is creeping in, slowly but surely, a culture of inclusiveness and openness which starts at the very bottom of the ladder. There is a growing understanding that it is people-driven strategies that sow the seeds of consistent growth.

Hence, there is a growing demand for change managers and culture interventionists who are putting in place a wide range systems and templates which handle issues from employee attrition rates to the business perceptions within the company, to nurturing talent by matching people with the right jobs and bringing in new talent.

And most often these are people who have been associated with that company either as employees and consultants but have since become specialists in one or more areas of change management. Take Ashoke Maitra, former head of Tata Share Registry whose focus is on organisational development and institution building.

Although he quit the Tata group years ago, today he is mentor to three top MDs and CEOs of the group and is actively coaching them on a one-to-one basis on a wide spectrum from intra-organisation relationships to developing organisational structures. "It is often lonely at the top. There is no one to look up to or discuss things with. Having a mentor helps because he or she is also a sounding board. And it is always better if it is someone who knows the company and its culture."

Besides demographic advantages, other factors that will contribute to the shifts in economic power are cultural traits, lifestyles, new technologies, and globalisation. Demographically young nations capable of efficient absorption and application of new technologies enabling sharper competition in business, will not only thrive, but will emerge as key drivers of globalisation.

The pace of India's ascendancy will be accelerated, when India move up the value chain, supplying high-value products and services in the global market. The emergence of the Internet will provide added thrust to the process.

▸▸ Infrastructural Network

It has, therefore, been argued sometimes that the development of industries be preceded by development of agriculture which introduces certain economic changes that culminate in industrial activities. "A developed mass agriculture is normally needed before you can have widespread successful development in other sectors" (Michael Lipton: Why Poor People Stay Poor?). But we cannot, perhaps, wait that long till a "developed agriculture sector provides wage goods and savings capacity" needed to support rapid industrialisation. If agricultural development does not first create savings for industrialisation, an industrial development process can be induced by substantial investments on certain selected nucleus industries, leading to a number of ancillary and other related industrial units. This method has gained wide acceptance. But before such nucleus industries are set up in backward areas, necessary infrastructural facilities have to be provided. Even the location of nucleus industries may not necessarily lead to a development process in which the poor people of backward areas whose development is the real development of the areas can successfully participate unless the choice of nucleus industries is such that it can utilise the available skills and capacities of a large number of small artisans or farmers. Otherwise, the entrepreneurial opportunities thrown up by such nucleus industries will be exploited by affluent entrepreneurs from outside who have the capacity to invest. It has been seen that entrepreneurs from developed areas have normally gravitated towards these backward areas which are contiguous to developed business centres with a view to availing themselves of the incentives and concessions. But each enterprise has not created any economic impact on the people of the backward areas except, perhaps, creating some negligible employment avenues.

It is, therefore, very important to ensure that the infrastructural facilities created to pave the way for nucleus industries are extended to cover a vast multitude of small artisans or farmers whose products can be processed in the nucleus industries. "An integrated infrastructural programme geared to the needs of small-holder farms and small-scale enterprises is the best means of promoting both types of productive activity." (J. Muller: *Promotion of the Manufacturer of Rural Implements in the United Republic of Tanzania*). For example, if there are a number of small dairy farmers, a central refrigeration plant can serve all the farmers in the area by an active network of communication. As a result, each farmer can get the benefit of an assured market and an enhanced income. If a large number of farmers are producing soybean, a central soybean processing unit would also bring about a pervasive growth of both. On the other hand, if a unit manufacturing some sophisticated machinery is the nucleus plant, its ancillaries would also need the precision or sophistication which will not be possible to achieve within the capabilities of the target-beneficiary group whom we want to develop through the development of backward areas. As Paul Streeten says, "Industry should produce the simple producer and consumer goods required by the people, the majority of whom live in the countryside, hoes and simple power-tillers and bicycles, not airconditioners or expensive cars and equipments. Much of the recent criticism of inefficient, high cost industrialisation behind high walls of protection and quantitative restrictions should be directed at the types of product and technique which cater for a highly unequal income distribution and reflect entrenched vested interests" (Paul Streeten: "Industrialisation in a United Development Strategy", World Development, January, 1975). What should actually be the simple goods to be produced depends on the character and potential of a particular backward area; and the infrastructure needed must be so developed that it would be capable of sustaining active linkages between the atomic units in the villages and the central unit.

➧ Environmental Analysis

This integrated approach which is the key to the development of backward areas implies a very careful environment analysis or a searching study of the target groups of beneficiaries, their activities and differential needs, and the practical modes of operation by which their activities and differential needs, and the practical modes of operation by which their activities can be linked with the covering enterprises. Unless these studies are made meticulously, the entire planning will go waste. Most of the development schemes fail to benefit the intended clientele because elaborate linkages are not identified and built up. An imaginative study should –

1. Identify the beneficiaries or target groups;
2. Analyse the environment to identify immediately feasible enterprises in an integrated manner;
3. Delineate the linkages and institutional arrangements; and
4. Recommend appropriate organisational structure to provide necessary promotional support.

Unfortunately, in most of the studies on backward areas, there is a tendency to make generalisations and ignore the specific details of really feasible projects. As a result, immediate perception of concrete opportunities by interested entrepreneur is left in confusion. Sometimes, "Area Studies" make a general statement of demand and resources and recommend certain enterprises which are not immediately feasible due to many other important reasons which are not taken into account in such studies. It is also normally not seriously contemplated whether the recommended enterprises are feasible within the capabilities and investment capacity of the target-group. In short, most of the studies tend to become general and fail to identify the concrete and specific needs of these endowments like resource, skill etc. to flourish. Enunciation of general objectives and generic beneficiaries tend to blur the distinct contours of one homogeneous group from the other; and extension of certain standard facilities or services does not serve their actual needs.

All this possibly happens because in such basic studies, we fail to identify clearly the target-groups and their specific problems, and make theoretical studies on resources and demand in an impersonal manner, as a result of which even the schemes devised on the basis of such studies tend to become too impersonal and rigid. Sometimes, the schemes become so inflexible on account of a standardised petrified approach that in some most genuine cases demanding a certain departure from the fixed framework, the scheme is incapable of giving requisite help. It is, therefore, absolutely necessary that any action plan for a backward area must first identify the target-group, identify the specific services they need for monitoring their enterprises and devise an appropriate structural support for comprehensive coverage of their needs.

The Green Arm of the Law

Three important Indian legislation presently enjoin industry to remain within the pollution control standards set by government:

1. **Water (Prevention and Control of Pollution) Act, 1974, with amendments made in 1988:**
   - Following the 1988 amendments, permission is necessary to set up any industry which is 'polluting' – one that uses or discharges any poisonous, noxious or polluting matter. Standards must be those set up state pollution boards. Industries set up prior to the amendment need to obtain clearance within three months of its coming into force.
   - State Pollution Control Boards (PCBs) have the power to obtain information regarding the construction, installation or operation of any process of the industry.
   - After the 1988 amendments, the PCBs can issue directions or order for closure or stoppage of electricity or water supply, if standards are not being met by the polluting industry.
   - Penalties for non-compliance have been increased to Rs. 10,000 for defaulting and Rs. 5,000 per day for continued default.
2. **Air (Prevention and Control of Pollution) Act, 1981, with 1987 amendments:**
   - The definition of air pollutant was extended from harmful solid, liquid or gaseous substances present in the atmosphere to include noise pollution.
   - Unlike the practice earlier, now all air polluting industries must have the sanction of their respective PCBs.
   - After amendments, powers have been given to PCBs to issue directions which include the closure, prohibition, stoppage of electricity etc., for violation of standards set.
   - Penalties are as those in the Water Act.
3. **Environment (Protection) Act, 1986:**
   - The Central Government has the power to take all such measures as it deems necessary or expedient for protecting the environment.
   - Section 3 of EPA empowers the Central Government to: (*a*) restrict areas in which any industry, operations, process or class of industries can be carried out under certain safeguards; (*b*) lay down procedures and safeguards for the prevention of accidents which may cause environmental pollution and remedial measures for them; (*c*) lay down procedures for handling hazardous substances; (*d*) examining manufacturing process and materials; and (*e*) widespread inspection powers.

- As in the order two Acts, the EPA gives the Centre wide powers to direct closure, prohibition and regulation of any industry if it contravenes the provisions of the Act.
- In addition, the Marpol Convention, pertaining to marine pollution control, was drawn up by the International Maritime Organisation, a United Nations agency, and ratified by India in 1978.
- The five annexures of this convention deal with: prevention of oil pollution; prevention of pollution by noxious liquid substance in bulk; prevention of pollution by noxious packaged substances; pollution from sewage and from garbage.
- The Indian government has ratified only the first two annexure. Thus a vessel can be penalised for oil or chemical pollution. But the remaining forms of pollution are unchecked.

▸▸ Instrumental Synergy

Comprehensive coverage of dynamic needs cannot be ensured unless there is comprehensive organisational support. In the development of backward areas, two things are of fundamental importance. Firstly, the needs of the entrepreneur or the target-groups are wider than those which are immediately related to an enterprise. Unless the complex structure of his private and social needs is understood, our assessment of his requirements which will have to be met to sustain him in a desired enterprise like a small industry or a farm will be unrealistic and lopsided. The amount spent on his enterprise tends to remain unproductive. Unless we support the man in all his needs and exigencies till his enterprise yields profit, entrepreneur are often coerced out of their enterprise during the initial years, because they have no power to absorb temporary shocks. In order to develop small enterprises and link small farmers in an integrated manner with an industrial project, the socio-economic conditions of these people have to be sympathetically understood to appreciate their needs, and appropriate loan schemes have to be devised. The weaker sections of the population are likely to benefit from a programme when its service is designed to meet the varying needs of beneficiary groups (*Development Programme for the Door: Do Strategies Make a Difference?* Samuel Paul and Ashok Subramaniam). Sometimes, even the consumption needs of the poor artisans have to be provided for in order to sustain them in their work.

Secondly, an integrated approach to rural industrialisation which has to deal with a complex structure of differential needs requiring regular monitoring and timely intervention of promotional agencies implies active coordination among institutions. "The more backward a country's economy, the greater was the part played by special institutional factors designed to increase the supply of capital to nascent industries and in addition to provide them with less decentralised and better informed entrepreneurial guidance; the more backward the country, the more pronounced was the coerciveness and comprehensiveness of these factors (A. Gershenkson: *Economic Backwardness in Historical Perspective*). In a backward place, the role of government institutions is of the highest significance. The institutions should not only cater to a variety of needs but also fulfil their role in the desired simultaneity or sequence so as to make the project work. This is what has been described by some as "synergistic effect or congruence." For example, small industrial units get term-loans from term-lending institutions but the working capital is not sanctioned at the right time or the desired amount is not sanctioned as a result of which the entire projections of the scheme go wrong. Similarly, if raw materials are not supplied for the essential utilities, the investment may remain idle, unproductive and eventually succumb to heavy accumulated liabilities. Various institutional supports must permit coverage in a synergy to make a success of an enterprise which needs all of them in a given order. In urban or developed areas, institutional synergy can perhaps be overcome by the resilience of the entrepreneur, but in backward areas, the staying power of the entrepreneur is so feeble that they quickly wear out with the smallest obstruction. Institutional patronage must, therefore, be comprehensive, continuous and synergistic.

➧ Training

It is only against this background that we can effectively plan for the development of entrepreneurship in the backward areas. The basic difference between a backward area and a developed area in this context is that unlike the latter, backward areas do not have a hidden reservoir of potential entrepreneur who through motivation, training and support can quickly become competent entrepreneur. Entrepreneurs from the backward areas have to be given comprehensive functional training based on the specific conditions of the entrepreneur and the choice of the enterprise. The entrepreneurship development programme must deal with the following:

1. On the basis of an elaborate Action-Plan based on environment analysis, various areas of entrepreneurial activities should be identified and specific projects formulated. These areas should be suitably assigned to artisan groups and high school drop outs, educated unemployed, farmers and men of other traditional skills or trade.
2. For each area of activity, institutional linkages should be clearly spelt out. Simultaneous attempts where necessary, should be made to build new institutions which are needed to give financial or marketing or other necessary support. For example, if we are promoting a large number of dairy farms, a central refrigeration plant in the area should simultaneously come up.
3. On the basis of institutional linkages, thus worked out, an interagency team should be constituted who should take up each identified group of entrepreneur for training. Since the product an entrepreneur of such a group is to manufacture is known, and his own socio-economic conditions are also known, a series of needs of each entrepreneur in implementing his project should be clearly identified and the agency to look after each need or group of needs should be assigned the work in a time-bound programme.
4. The training programme should briefly expose the entrepreneurs to a multi-disciplinary familiarisation course with the nature and problems of entrepreneurship in their context. But immediately after this brief exposure, the training programme should discuss their schemes and proceed with the implementation. No training is more effective than the actual experience in implementation, and all the agencies must ensure that the entrepreneur gets all assistance and guidance in the implementation of his project. This would eliminate inter-agency disputes and the consequent delay which prove fatal to many entrepreneurs.
5. There should be a nodal agency, preferably an agency which organises the training programme, to monitor the progress of the implementation of each trainee's project or scheme, and coordinate the functions of various promotional agencies in order to make its specific services available to the entrepreneur in right time.

Training programmes for entrepreneurship development which involve all promotional agencies and financial institutions have proved to be the most successful. Involvement in the training programme does create a continuing interest in the entrepreneur among these agencies to the advantage of the entrepreneurs. And since for backward areas, project-oriented training programmes have been considered indispensable, the multi-agency involvement in the training programme helps in a better appraisal and quicker implementation. These agencies should work in a manner as if they are escorting an entrepreneur right from the conception of a project-idea to the stage when the units starts production. Even after the stage, specific institutional arrangements have to be made to extend continuing marketing support.

Such a multi-agency "escort" approach compensates for many deficiencies which the entrepreneurs of backward areas are beset with by their birth and circumstances, and it slowly helps engender entrepreneurial qualities among them through practical experience.

➧ Artisans' Development

An integrated approach to rural industrialisation must attach the highest importance to the organised development of artisans. But this is a formidable task and the problems are not as simple as they often appear to be. They live in scattered places and do not constitute a homogeneous group. Their problems vary from place to place although the products may be the same. Their productivity is unremuneratively low, and the standard of their products is not always suitable for wider acceptability. Their inputs supply system in irregular and fragile, and the market is restricted. And above all, these underemployed artisans of the village live in so much of want that their socio-economic needs keep them permanently as wage-earners almost in bondage to some middlemen. Unless their consumption needs and other social exigencies are properly taken care of, they cannot really come up as independent entrepreneurs. Our incentives and assistance often fail because we fail to provide for the varying needs of the artisans. Many artisans just cannot attend design development training programmes because they cannot afford to stay out of daily wage-earning and starve their families. Sometimes, they sell their highly value added works of art at throwaway prices to middlemen because they cannot afford to wait for long nor can they take them to the right market. As a result they choose to work as daily wage-earners and the profit of their highly value-added items accrues to the middleman who employs the capital. What we need, therefore, is not a set of incentives or concessions but an enveloping support to the entrepreneurs in the backward areas which can reasonably cater to their varying private and social needs.

Besides providing for their needs, it is necessary to establish cooperative societies or government agencies to provide raw materials and help them in making their products. But since they stay scattered, it is not easy to organise rural market centres to supply raw materials and market their products on a regular basis. It is, therefore, necessary that the supplies from this sector should be given preferential status in marketing and if necessary, competition from big manufacturers has to be banned. In that case the total demand for such products in a region will have to be met from this artisan sector and more people can be inducted into this sector to increase output and even the underemployment of the existing artisans would disappear.

For example, if simple agricultural implements are only in the artisan sector, the total demand of a region can give so much work that the existing artisans cannot cope with it. The only problem is to organise this vast network to touch each atomic unit. But all this has to be done if the backward areas are to be easily awakened. "It is not argued that the village metalsmiths and tinsmiths should be promoted for any nostalgic or romantic reasons. On the contrary, these craftsmen, if supported, constitute a basis for rural industrialisation which will otherwise be wasted and by rural industrialisation is not meant the establishment of any industries in rural areas, it means the establishment of enterprises that are linked backward and forward to other productive activities within the rural communities." (J. Muller).

Appropriate technical and consultancy organisations must work constantly to introduce appropriate technological innovations to increase productivity without displacing labour. New designs and improvements can be introduced for decorative crafts to cater to sophisticated markets which are ever widening. It is just not enough to allow the artisans to survive. It is more important to make them increasingly relevant to our changing needs. If more efficient agricultural implements are available, no one would buy old-fashioned implements, simply because they are the products of the artisans. Nor would it be proper to upgrade their skill so as to enable them to produce more efficient equipments. Similarly, decorative handicrafts or metal works have to adopt the stylistic changes and needs. Otherwise, the market for these products would quickly shrink, decorative handicrafts or metal works have to adopt the stylistic changes and needs. Otherwise, the market for these products would quickly shrink. But it is not so easy to introduce these innovative changes among the illiterate or semi-literate artisans. In order to do this, we have to create active linkages between Research Organisations and these artisans on a permanent basis. Training programmes have to be organised which must expose their inadequacies and teach them to assimilate the innovative ideas. And this cannot be done unless their tradition, skill, quality of work, the use are studied in depth and an imaginative training programme is designed. Similarly, arrangements have to be made to market their products.

Organisations sponsored by government should initially buy their products in order to ensure quick payment to the artisans and then release the profit when the product is ultimately sold to the real customer.

⏩ Administrative Machinery with Passion

Developing entrepreneurship requires both short-term and long-term planning. Long-term planning consists in the spread of education, Development of human resources, growth of social infrastructure and the development of other related sectors of the economy. Since this is bound to be a slow process, we have to take short-term measures to promote entrepreneurship within a given time-frame in spite of all the obstacles that backwardness implies. The conditions of backwardness are so debilitating that none of the normal functions of an entrepreneur like exchange relations, political administration, management control and technology can be discharged by the new entrepreneur. He has to be guided by the promotional agencies in each one of these functions till he comes of age as an entrepreneur. There is possibly no alternative to guided entrepreneurship which casts heavy responsibilities on government institutions and officials. It is not only necessary to activate the existing artisans in a throbbing network of backward and forward linkages, but also to promote new industries through entrepreneurs of the backward areas in order to create a "demonstration" effect and impart some discontinuity to a stagnant environment. But such industries can only be promoted by the entrepreneurs of the backward areas if promotional agencies extend dynamic assistance.

⏩ Determinants of Entrepreneurship

The economic factors sometimes become more important determinants for flourishing of the entrepreneur rather than social or psychological factors. Access to capital needed for business and the opportunity to acquire technical training have indicated their significance more in the development of entrepreneurship than purely social factors, such as cast tradition and social approval or disapproval.

Since entrepreneurial activity involves multi-dimensional factors, the following factors promote entrepreneurship given the right socio-political and economic environment: (1) Financial assistance from institutional sources; (2) Accommodation in industrial estates; (3) Business experience in the same or related line; (4) Strong desire to do something independent in life; (5) Technical knowledge and manufacturing experience; (6) Heavy demand for the various products; (7) Availability of collaboration, both foreign and indigenous; (8) Availability of machinery on lease or hire-purchase; (9) Favourable attitudes of the government to help new units; (10) Protection of industries through increased import restrictions; (11) Encouragement from the already existing big business units; (12) Unsound units or sick units available at an economic price; (13) Adequate availability of finance from both government, and non-government sources; (14) The large objectives of industries being to help the unemployed and ill-educated youth; (15) Sufficient profit margin; (16) Sufficient encouragement from family, social and community groups for the entrepreneurial activities; (17) Adequate availability of indigenous raw materials; (18) Political influence for the purpose of economic activities.

The salient features of the important factors which influence entrepreneurial development according to the various researchers, are summarised in the Chart 1.

Chart I

SUMMARY OF FINDINGS OF VARIOUS RESEARCHERS

Authors	***Factors that contribute to development of entrepreneurship***
Schumpter, 1961	Suitable environment and intuition in grasping the essential facts.
Levine, 1966	Status mobility system where status is attained through outstanding performance, initiative, industriousness, foresight, through self-reliance and achievement training.
Hangen, 1971	Creative personality; High need achievement, need order and autonomy; Fairly widespread, creative problem-solving ability, and a tendency to use it; Positive attitudes towards manual and technical labour; and physical work.
Cochran, 1971	Attitude towards occupation, the role expectations held by sanctioning groups and the operational requirements of the job.
Nandy, 1973	Supportive community, self-image which gives meaning, value, and status to an entrepreneurial career.
Singer, 1973	Traditional system of occupational culture which facilitates the process of modernisation, special opportunities, motivations, experiences, training or knowledge and traditional belief and value system which are flexible to allow for reinterpretation with changing conditions.
Webro, 1980	"Professional Ethic" which emerged from the religious belief system of Calvinistic Puritanism and which is absent is oriental religious belief system.

Conclusion

Entrepreneurship, therefore, will flourish only in a right atmosphere which is conducive from the social, political and economic points of view. Even though the urge to excel others and to create something new is something which is inborn and psychologically oriented in the larger analysis, this urge to excel others will fail to blossom unless the right environment is available. Entrepreneurial environment, therefore, is one is which there is a high awareness of potential and enough source of capital, and also where there are sufficient number of individuals and institutions which provide adequate help and advice for the establishment and growth of industrial enterprises. But such help and encouragement required for the flourishing of the entrepreneurship can come forth only when the social, political and economic conditions are conducive.

Thus, since entrepreneurship involves a complex of economic and social behaviour, it can hardly survive under any given circumstances. It is only where conditions are ideal in terms of political, economic, social and ethical concerns, and when economic changes are free from restraints, that entrepreneurship can flourish to a considerable degree, for the benefit of all concerned.

An integrated approach to backward area development requires a unified administrative machinery, itself animated by a passion for distributive justice. And in no small measure, the proselytizing entrepreneurial zeal of the deprived and the downtrodden is a reflection of that passion.

Entrepreneurial behaviour, motivation coupled with ability leads to performance. Not only are employees motivated to perform allotted tasks, they look for better ways to do a job. This statement can apply for corporate strategists, and to production workers who are looking for better ways to do a job. When people actively seek new ways of doing things, they usually find them. It is the responsibility of managers to make employees look for better ways of doing jobs. An understanding of the nature of motivation is helpful in this context.

UNIT : III

Motivation and Behaviour

- **Behaviour**
- **Motivation**
- **Achievement**
- **Success**
- **Innovation**
- **System**

Sudha Murthy

What sets a leader apart from a manager is his all encompassing vision and his ability to communicate the vision to all levels in the organisation.

There is no definite route to success and a lot depends on how you define success. For me, a succesful person is one who is satisfied with what he or she has. Money is not a part of my idea of success. To be successful, one has to work hard and with integrity of mind and heart. You also need a portion of God's grace and a small element of luck. — *Sudha Murthy*

The need for a broad-based entrepreneurial class in India arises from the need to speed up the process of activating the factors of production, leading to a higher rate of economic growth, dispersal of economic activities, development of backward and tribal areas, creation of employment opportunities, improvement in the standard of living of the weaker sections of the society and involvement of all sections of the society in the process of growth.

Several factors go into the making of an entrepreneur. Individuals who initiate, establish, maintain and expand new enterprises constitute the entrepreneurial class. The socio-political and economic conditions, the availability of industrial technology and know-how, state of art and culture of business and trading, existence of markets for products and services and the incentives and facilities available for starting an industry or business, all have a bearing on the growth of entrepreneurship. A conducive environment is created through the policies and interest of the government in economic and industrial development.

Entrepreneurial *Behaviours*

- grasping opportunity
- training initiative
- solving problems creatively
- managing autonomously
- taking responsibility for, and ownership of things
- seeing things through
- networking effectively to manage interdependence
- putting things together creatively
- using judgement to take calculated risk

Entrepreneurial *Attributes*

- achievement orientation and ambition
- self-confidence and self-esteem
- perseverance
- high internal focus of control (autonomy)
- action orientation
- preference for learning by doing
- hard-working
- determination
- creativity

Entrepreneurial *Skills*

- creative problem-solving
- persuading
- negotiating
- selling
- proposing
- holistically managing business/projects/ situations
- strategic thinking
- intuitive decision-making under uncertainty
- networking

THE WEALTH OF KNOWLEDGE

Skills and knowledge have become the only source of sustainable long-term competitive advantage. Knowledge, which used to be tertiary – after raw materials and capital in determining economic success, is now primary. With this comes the need for more differentiated systems of determining who owns what intellectual property, better protection for whatever is owned and faster systems of dispute resolution when disputes arise.

Clear, easily enforceable, sellable ownership rights to intellectual property have to be established. Reverse engineering (the politically correct phrase for copying) is a way of life in the corporate world. But where should the limits be? Whatever the answer is not to be found in a patent system more than a century old.

It is not so clear, however what it means to own knowledge or how those ownership rights can be enforced. What part of their knowledge can employees take with them when they move to a new employer? How do employers stop employees from taking the employer's intellectual property when they go? Where is the dividing line between knowledge in the public domain and knowledge in the private domain? Without stronger systems of protection, companies will defend their economic positions by keeping their knowledge secret, but a recent study found that 73% of private patents were based on knowledge generated by public sources such as universities and non-profit government laboratories.

– Lester C. Thurow

WORK AS A TEAM

Make sure you're paying attention to people, being sensitive to the culture, and absolutely make sure that the organisation is working together as a team. It's critical for long-term success.

— ***John Thain,*** CEO, Merrill Lynch, in *Business Week*

15

Entrepreneurial Behaviour and Motivation

Introduction

Behaviour is a manifestation of what a person thinks, feels and acts. An entrepreneur is a creative person. Need for self-actualisation as manifested in the need for achievement forces him to create something new, a new product, a new way of doing things, a new source of raw material, a new market etc. Behaviour is always caused and is never spontaneous. Human behaviour is goal directed or is directed towards satisfaction of needs. Whenever a person feels any need, he feels uneasy and tension starts building in his mind. This tension provokes him to initiate some action which may lead to the satisfaction of the need. If that need is not satisfied that individual is required to resort to some alternate action for the satisfaction of the need. It is a systematic process which can be explained in the following manner:

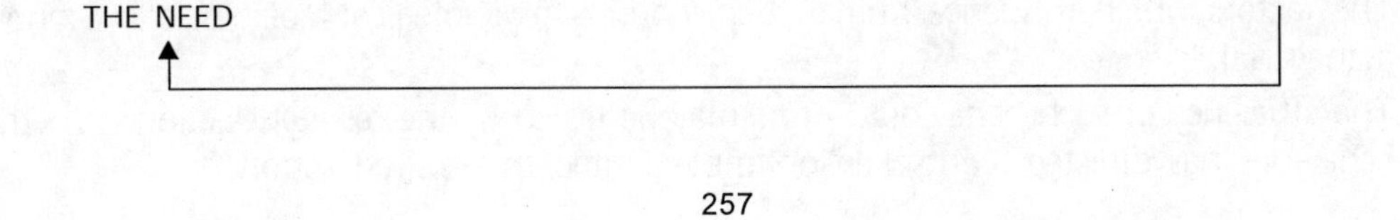

Entrepreneurial behaviour is the result of entrepreneurial motivation. Motivation refers to the inner urge that ignites and sustains behaviour to satisfy need. Motivation has been derived from the word 'motive' which implies the inner state of mind that activates, provokes and directs our behaviour towards the goal.

The attempts to discover the secret of entrepreneurs' success has pre-occupied writers and analysts from a variety of disciplines. Biographies of successful entrepreneurs and businessmen, for example, frequently reflect the tendencies of the subject of such studies in terms of simple virtues of thrift, hard work and clean living. As an alternative to the biographical models are those studies that turn the entrepreneur into a superman, manipulating the complexities of an uncertain world with a sure and omnipotent touch. Thus emerges the notion of the "genius entrepreneur" whose success is in large measure caused by his unswerving dedication to setting high goals and to reaching for them. He has vision on which he bases his own objectives and sets his own goals. And he does this not simply on the basis of last year's results plus some growth factor, but on the basis of his own perception, of his own capabilities and to satisfy his own needs.

Among other distinguishing attributes of entrepreneurship are a willingness to assume risks; a sense of acquisition or unceasing curiosity; insight into the relationship between concepts, objectives, needs, and needs satisfaction; sound judgement as to what is central and peripheral to attaining his objectives; imitative and creativity; problem-solving ability, ability to marshall resources needed to achieve his objectives and goals; and the administrative ability to organise those resources to accomplish his goals and satisfy his minor needs.

⏩ Motivation

Motivation is an indispensable function of management. When man is at work, he cannot be forced to work like a machine. He is a human being who has his dignity, self-respect, values, sentiments and aspirations apart from the economic status. Under such circumstances the efficiency of the enterprise is related not merely to the efficiency of sophisticated machines installed but more importantly upon the satisfaction and the spontaneous desire of man to put his mind and heart into the work. This spontaneous urge to involve in work is not merely related to monetary awards or assignment of position or the direction to perform the duty or even the fear of punishment but to the mechanics and system of motivation.

Motivation encompasses complex aspects of human behaviour to which contribution has been made by sociologists, social anthropologists, psychologists and business executives. This concept has its roots in motives within a person which induce him to behave in a particular manner. Generally speaking, the concept of motivation is by and large psychological which "relates to those forces operating within the individual employee or subordinate which impel him to act or not to act in certain ways" –

"Motivation refers to the way in which urges, drives, desires, aspirations, strivings or needs direct, control or explain the behaviour of human beings."

This is a deep-seated definition of Motivation. It includes three things:

(*i*) The urges, drives, desires, aspirations, strivings or needs of human beings influence human behaviour.

(*ii*) The factors which influence human behaviour – psychological, sociological, economic or managerial.

(*iii*) The efficiency of such behaviour – this may be tested by the resultant action. Whether this behaviour has directed, controlled or implemented the desired action.

If the entrepreneur feels motivated his behaviour will bring about the desired action.

Here, one reaches the most crucial point in the Regional or District Development Strategy of the underdeveloped regions. The development agency, with all the institutions concerned, will have to formulate a motivation programme and by continuous and ingenious methods, involve people in the process of development so that they acquire new attitudes and confidence to enter into new activities and to show the propensity of enterprise. Appropriate values will have to be inculcated and risk-taking capacity be cultivated. Unless this aspect is given its due weightage in the Development Plan, in spite of all the incentives, most of the projects will hardly make much progress. Development is the consequence of motivated people.

Motivational factors constitute the inner urge present in an individual which continuously demands from him to do something new and unique as also to perform better than others. The motivational factors again are comprised of three basic elements – entrepreneurial motivation, personal efficiency and coping capability. The achievement motivation is also termed *efficiency motivation*. McClelland and Winter have made considerable studies and concluded that what motivates a person to do something new or something to seek better is the inner urge which directs him towards such ends. This urge also force a person to use the resources efficiently than to be negligent of it. Also important is the power of motivation which is really the urge to have control over others and to direct their course of activities towards the end which one seeks to attain. These motivational factors induce the person to undertake entrepreneurial activities which relate to creating a new business where there was none. This also means to excel the performance in carrying out any activity by striving through persistent efforts unlike others who do not have sufficient capacity for hard work.

Box 1

A PLACE FOR EMOTIONAL INTELLIGENCE

Old ways of doing business no longer work: the increasingly intense competitive challenges of the world economy challenge everyone, everywhere, to adapt in order to prosper under new rules.

In the old economy, hierarchies pitted labour against management, with workers paid wages depending on their skills, but that is eroding as the rate of change accelerates.

Hierarchies are being replaced by networks; labour and management are uniting into teams; wages are coming in new mixtures of options, incentives and ownership; fixed jobs melt into fluid careers. As business changes, so do the traits needed to survive, let alone excel. All these transitions put increased value on emotional intelligence.

Jonathan Farrington is a business coach and mentor. He is a senior partner at the JF Consultancy based in London and Paris.

Competitive pressures put a new value on people who are self-motivated, show initiative, have the inner drive for out-doing themselves, and are optimistic enough to take reversals and setbacks in their stride. The ever-pressing need to serve customers and clients well and to work smoothly and creatively with an ever more diverse range of people makes the ability to empathise all the more essential.

At the same time, the meltdown of old hierarchies increases the importance of traditional people skills such as building bonds, influence and collaboration. And that is as true for employers as it is for employees.

The task of the leader draws on a wide range of personal skills. Research has shown that emotional competence makes the crucial difference between mediocre leaders and the best. Indeed, emotional competence makes up about two-thirds of the ingredients of star performance in general, but for outstanding leaders emotional competencies – as opposed to technical or cognitive cues – make up 80 to 100% of those listed by companies as crucial for success.

Star performers show significantly greater strengths in a range of emotional competencies, such as the skills of persuasion, team leadership, political awareness, self-confi-dence, and achievement drive.

Source: http://www.thejfblogit.co.ukl

The Five Components of Emotional Intelligence at Work:

	Definition	**Hallmarks**
Self-Awareness	The ability to recognise and under-stand your moods, emotions and drives, as well as their effect on others	Self-confidence, realistic self assessment, self-deprecating, sense of humour
Self-Regulation	The ability to control or redirect disruptive impulses and mood the propensity to suspend judgement to think before acting	Trustworthiness and integrity comfort with ambiguity openness to change
Motivation	A passion to work for reasons that go beyond money or status, a propensity to pursue goals with energy and persistence	Strong drive to achieve optimism, even in the face of failure, organisational commitment
Empathy	The ability to understand the emotional makeup of other people skill in treating people according to their emotional reactions	Expertise in building and retaining talent cross-cultural sensitivity service to clients and customers
Social skill	Proficiency in managing relationships and building networks an ability to find common ground and build rapport	Effectivess in leading change persuasiveness expertise in building and leading teams

It's not difficult to understand how and why a motivation to achieve translates into strong leadership. If you set the performance bar high for yourself, you will do the same for the organisation when you are in a position to do so. Likewise, a drive to surpass goals and an interest in keeping score can be contagious. Leaders with these traits can often build a team of managers around them with the same traits. And of course, optimism and organisational commitment are fundamental to leadership just try to imagine running a company without them.

Hierarchy of Needs

Most psychologists who study human behaviour and personality generally are convinced that all behaviour is caused, goal oriented and motivated.

There is a reason for everything that a sane person does. People constantly are striving to attain something that has meaning to them. Often we may not be aware of why we behave in a certain manner but we all have subconscious motives that govern the way we behave in different situations.

One of the most widely accepted theories of human behaviour is that people are motivated to satisfy certain well-defined and more or less predictable needs.

Abraham H. Maslow formulated the concept of hierarchy of needs. He maintained that these needs range from lower-level needs to higher-level needs in an ascending priority.

These needs actually overlap and are interrelated, and it may be preferable to consider them as existing along a continuum rather than as being separate and distinct from one another.

⏩ Maslow's Need Hierarchy Theory

Maslow's theory is based on human needs. He developed a conceptual framework for understanding human motivation. He was of the opinion that every individual has a complex set of exceptionally strong needs and the behaviour of an individual at a particular moment of time is usually determined by his strongest need. He defined a person's effectiveness as a function of matching man's opportunity with the appropriate position of hierarchy of needs. Process of motivation begins with the assumption that the behaviour, atleast in part, is directed towards the achievement or the satisfaction of needs. Maslow felt that the needs have a definite sequence of domination. Second need does not dominate till first need is reasonably satisfied and third need does not dominate until first two needs have been reasonably satisfied. Man is never fully satisfied, if one need is satisfied the other will arise and so on. Once a need or certain order of needs is satisfied, it ceases to be a motivating factor. Maslow stated that human beings have five basic levels of needs, which they tend to satisfy in a hierarchical manner. He proposed that human needs can be arranged in a particular order from the lower level needs to the highest level needs. This hierarchy of human needs can be shown in the following figure:

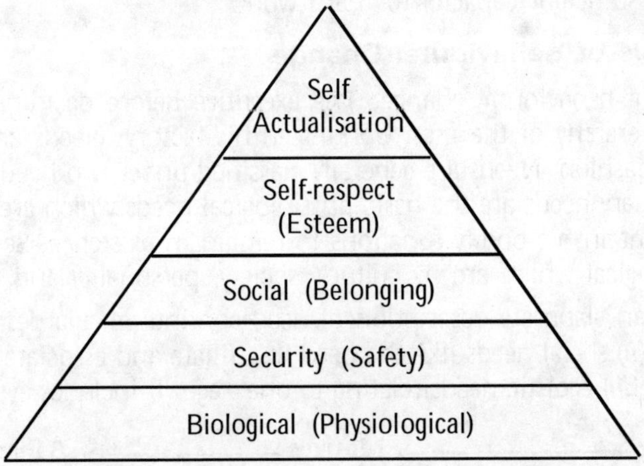

Fig. 1 Hierarchial Structure of the Needs

Various researchers are actively engaged in finding answer to one basic question, i.e., what motivates people? Or what makes them work? Various theories have been propounded by different experts to focus attention on this basic issue. Prominent and relatively more relevant to entrepreneurship are as under:

⏩ Theories of Motivation

Need is the starting point of motivation. A satisfied need does not motivate an individual. It is only the unsatisfied need which creates tension and stimulate drives within the individuals for the satisfaction of the need and reduction of tension. The efforts or actions initiated by the individual will yield results which will lead to satisfaction of need or removal tension. Classical theorists and scientific management thinkers were of the opinion that people were mainly interested in maximising economic gains as they were primarily concerned with satisfying their basic needs of food, water, air, shelter etc. Thus they tried to link up performance and productivity with monetary rewards or incentives. F. W. Taylor, father of Scientific Management proposed Differential Piece rate system for motivating workers to work at their level best. The traditional thinkers were mainly concerned with the monetary reward and were treating human beings as mere machines, which do not have any inner feelings or emotions. Under Hawthorne Experiments it was proved that there was no direct relationship between productivity and economic rewards. Money is an essential condition but not a sufficient one for motivating people to work. Human beings are not machines and they have also social and psychological needs.

Motivational factors constitute the inner urge present in an individual which continuously demands from him to do something new and unique as also to perform better than others. The motivational factors again are compressed of three basic elements – entrepreneurial motivation, personal efficiency and coping capability. The achievement motivation is also termed *efficiency motivation.* McClelland and Winter have made considerable studies and concluded that what motivates a person to do something new or something to seek better is the inner urge which directs him towards such ends. This urge also force a person to use the resources efficiently than to be negligent of it. Also important is the power of motivation which is really the urge to have control over others and to direct their course of activities towards the end which one seeks to attain. These motivational factors induce the person to undertake entrepreneurial activities which relate to creating a new business where there was none. This also means to excel the performance in carrying out any activity by striving through persistent efforts unlike others who do not have sufficient capacity for hard work.

⏩ Need of the Basis of Behavioural Change

Need is the basis of behavioural change. The executive before deciding a motivational model should study the need hierarchy of the man working in his factory. Needs are generally stated to be existing in a hierarchical fashion. Needs are generally classified under two heads: (*i*) Primary needs and (*ii*) Secondary needs. Primary needs are the basic physiological needs which are required to be fulfilled by the man so as to maintain his bodily functions to remain in existence. Secondary needs are both psychological and sociological which are by culture, society, personality and temperament.

Masan Haire gives an elaborate description of need continuum. He describes (*i*) physical needs similar to primary needs (*ii*) social needs like the need to affiliate and associate with others and to give and receive affection and (*iii*) egoistic needs relating to one's ego. It includes even the will to dominate.

⏩ Theories of Motivation

Need is the starting point of motivation. A satisfied need does not motivate an individual. It is only the unsatisfied need which creates tension and stimulate drives within the individuals for the satisfaction of the need and reduction of tension. The efforts or actions initiated by the individual will yield results which will lead to satisfaction of need or removal of tension. Classical theorists and scientific management thinkers were of the opinion that people were mainly interested in maximising economic gains as they were primarily concerned with satisfying their basic needs of food, water, air, shelter etc. Thus they tried to link up performance and productivity with monetary rewards or incentives. F. W. Taylor, father of Scientific Management proposed Differential Piece rate system for motivating workers to work at their level best. The traditional thinkers were mainly concerned with the monetary reward and were treating human beings as mere machines, which do not have any inner feelings or emotions. Under Hawthorne Experiments it was proved that there was no direct relationship between productivity and economic rewards. Money is an essential condition but not a sufficient one for motivating people to work. Human beings are not machines and they have also social and psychological needs.

Maslow's theory implies that people attempt to satisfy these needs in the order in which they are arranged. As one level of needs is satisfied to some extent, the individual focuses on the next level, which then becomes the stronger motivator of behaviour. Once a lower level of needs is reasonably satisfied, it no longer motivates behaviour, at least in the short-term.

Table 1 describes various types of needs under Maslow's need hierarchy theory.

Table 1

MASLOW'S NEED HIERARCHY

Nature of Need	***Description***
Physiological needs	Biological needs to pressure human life. These needs include food, clothing, shelter, drink, sleep, etc. These are the basic needs which are recurring in nature. They must be satisfied repeatedly on priority basis.
Safety needs	Human beings search for a protected environment. Safety and security needs kindle the urge for freedom from present and future physical and economic hazards. Though these needs are finite, still they may serve as motivators in case of arbitrary and unpredictable management action. Therefore people put by money in form of insurance, provident fund, etc.
Social needs	Man is a social animal and his desire to be loved and accepted by his near and dear ones is enormous. Thus, he seeks social affiliation and interaction with the people with whom he works together. In the home front, family members and the neighbours fulfil these needs.
Ego (esteem) needs	These needs arise after physiological, safety and social needs are fulfilled. Self-esteem, self-confidence, self-respect, competence, independence and achievement are vital elements in this process. They determine the entrepreneurial action of the human beings. A person desires to gain reputation, respect, status and appreciation from others.
Self-actualization needs	This desire arises after other needs are fulfilled. These are the needs for realizing one's full potential for continued self-development for being creative. These are aesthetic needs to attain moral maturity, contentment, authority, etc. It is an infinite growth need. This presumes man's inner urge for making the best use of his potentialities.

At the first level are the biological (or physiological) needs such as food, rest, shelter and recreation. The paycheck enables a person to purchase the necessities vital to survive as well some of the comforts of life.

Security needs include the need to protect ourselves against danger and to guard against the uncertainties of life. Job security, medical, retirement, disability and life insurance plans are benefits designed to satisfy safety needs of employees.

Social needs are those that people have for attention, for being part of a group, for being accepted by their peers, and for love. Many studies have shown that group motivation can be a powerful influence on employee behaviour at work in either a negative or a positive direction. Some employers provide off-the-job social opportunities for their employees as a means of helping them satisfy their social needs.

Self-esteem or ego needs are needs that people have for recognition, achievement, status and a sense of accomplishment. They relate to personal feelings of self-worth and importance. Managers should look for ways of satisfying these internal needs by providing variety and challenge in work tasks and recognizing good performance – if possible publicly.

Self-fulfillment (or self-realization) needs – the desire to use one's capabilities to the fullest. Managers can try to assign tasks that challenge employees to use their abilities more fully or allow them to use their creativity and resourcefulness.

The key for the manager is to recognize where each employee is in the hierarchy, what needs are currently driving the employee and then to design formal and informal rewards to motivate him.

It is formal for employees to expect good wages, generous benefit plans, and job security. For many employees (for example, those who see other employment option as being available in the market), these items may play a secondary role in day-to-day motivation. The key to longer-term, positive motivation of employees lies in better satisfying their higher level needs (social self-respect, self-fulfillment).

For some time now, employee surveys have been saying that money is not everything. According to a recent survey, one-third of the respondents place a positive work environment at the top of a list of factors for keeping employees satisfied.

Maslow was of the opinion that people put emphasis on lower-level needs and then proceed to higher-level needs in a step-by-step approach. Satisfied need ceases to be a motivator, while unsatisfied needs regulate an individual's behaviour.

Merits of the theory: The merits of Maslow's theory are as follows:

(*a*) This theory is easy to understand.

(*b*) This theory is generally applicable to a wide range of culture.

(*c*) This theory is capable enough to explain how needs influence human behaviour and motivate the human beings to chalking out their work plans.

(*d*) This theory gives an opportunity to the entrepreneurs and the managers to understand the needs of the people at different levels and to motivate them according to their needs.

Criticism: Maslow's Need Priority Model of motivation has gained extensive popularity because of its simplicity and logical explanation. This theory also explains how human behaviour differs in two similar situations. Nevertheless, there is little impartial support for it because its proposition could not be vigorously tested through empirical research. However, the theory is widely criticized for the following reasons:

(*a*) The theory does not give any scientific explanation or tool for measuring needs.

(*b*) The theory gives an oversimplification of human needs and motivation.

(*c*) Not everyone strives for higher-level needs.

(*d*) The hierarchy of needs is not always fixed. It varies from person to person, place to place and time to time. For example, in case of creative people like singers, artistes, etc., self-actualization need may be a dominant force, even before the lower-order needs are fulfilled. Similarly, the need priorities of the same individual may change over a period of time.

(*e*) Motivation and needs are not directly linked. The same need may lead to different types of behaviour in different individuals.

(*f*) Deprivation of needs may not necessarily motivate, it may cause depression also.

In spite of the criticism, Maslow's theory has a common sense appeal for all managers and entrepreneurs. The theory provides a deep insight into the concept of need and its relation of human behaviour.

▸▸ What Makes an Entrepreneur?

This is a frequent question. What makes an entrepreneur is the combination of various factors that have enabled the personality formation right from the childhood as also the psychological urge that exists intensively in the person.

These psychological processes which lead men to set up their own successful business enterprises begin in the very early life and have cumulative effect. The influences of early childhood and other social roles are determinant factors for the formation of that personality which motivates an individual towards becoming an independent businessman or entrepreneur.

In the case of persons who take up jobs, It has always been found that they have secured success in the established organisations. These people do not have a rejection towards the established institutions and neither do they attempt to rebel against the traditional path to success. On the other hand, an entrepreneur fails to achieve educational success through the established organisations and this is because of the general rejection of the established organisations at all levels. People who tend to like security and not uncertainty get more satisfied by taking up jobs which are less risk-oriented and hence are not motivated towards building up their own industrial enterprise.

Men who establish new business are men who have right from the childhood faced a different set of environment in their family, school and other social situations. Research studies have indicated that successful entrepreneurs identify a crisis before they venture into new Entrepreneurial activities. Even in their childhood most of them had threatening non-supportive and disgusting adult figures who had much say in their social and economic life. Most of these have a childhood of impoverishment and stress. Economic deprivation also works as a motivational factor towards creating something on their own and free oneself from the clutches of oppressing forces which attempt to kill their spirit of individualism. Thus it has been found that creating a successful new business is not due to an isolated incidence in the life of an individual but it has been as a result of learned response to their total social, emotional and economic environment.

Box 2

TEN QUESTIONS EVERY LEADER OUGHT TO BE ASKING

We are at our best when we catalyse progress – when we create environments that help people, teams and processes do great work together. Here are ten questions you can ask yourself and your team to get catalytic juices flowing:

1. What's the new opportunity that we are not seeing? How might we learn from other organisations, both competitors and non-competitors?
2. How might new trends in how people communicate and work open up new ways to improve our organisation?

3. When a meeting feels flat and perfunctory, what's going on? What's on people's mind that they are not saying?
4. What is "my best work" and how can I ensure I do that today? How can I enable my team to do their best work?
5. If we were starting this organisation from scratch, how would we design it?
6. What's the craziest idea that just might work?
7. What are the most irksome/damaging barriers facing me and my team right now and how can I reduce or obliterate them?
8. What is my manifesto (driving philosophy and passion) as a leader and how can I ensure my team understands it?
9. What's possible now that was not possible last year/month?
10. Do I have my team focused on doing the work that matters most?

We are leaders because we make things happen that would not happen without us. We are driven to create, model, and catalyse excellence. We do not maintain. We do not play the victim. We take the initiative to do whatever it takes to make a significant and positive difference and we have more opportunities to do this today than ever.

Source: http://www.managementcraft.typepad.com

The family plays an important role in developing the personality necessary for turning into an entrepreneur later in life. In family situations where security and non-risk bearing activities are encouraged right from childhood, the individual likes to be more security-oriented rather than attempt on his own in areas where adventures and uncertainty conditions prevail. Also in families where deep attachments and emotional relationship are encouraged, it has been seen that the child growing under such situations tends to take up activities which are more security-oriented than risk-oriented. Since in most of the middle class families attachment and security-oriented activities are encouraged despite seeking academic excellence, it itself does not help the person to develop the urge to be independent and create a framework required for enjoying autonomy.

As a result of this many bright graduates deviate from placing themselves in open positions. On the contrary they choose to stay in the established organisations because they have developed a favourable attitude towards the establishment. On the other hand, the entrepreneurial personality would rather face the impersonal forces of the economy than cope with enter-personal relations of the established organisations. Due to this characteristic of an entrepreneur, they tend to shift from job to job till they have finally found a field of activity in which they will ultimately have a say and also enjoy the happenings of events by their will, determination and efforts.

While people who take up jobs prefer to see success in the traditional and highly structured roles in the established undertakings, entrepreneurs, prefer to have a different approach toward success and be unique in their own way. They find more satisfaction in their creative faculties getting an opportunity to express themselves fully rather than submitting themselves to structured and rigid forces. The bright graduates may very often lack creativity and be unable to break through the undifferentiated mask of circumstance and make something of their own.

The entrepreneurs, on the other hand, find such situations extraordinarily challenging and attempt with determination and persistence to come out of this web of oppressing factors, which tend to keep him in the rigid framework. Thus we find entrepreneurial characteristics are formed through a combination of various social, economic and psychological factors to which the person becomes subjected to right from childhood. These factors reinforce in him urge to excel others and seek satisfaction in creating on his own a new enterprise instead of seeking a security-oriented job. In the absence of these reinforcing elements which go into the formation of the entrepreneurial personality, however successful a person may be in his academic life it does not guarantee that he would become a successful entrepreneur. Something more than mere academic excellence is a pre-requisite for becoming an entrepreneur of success and repute. These requisites are embodied in the various qualities that the entrepreneur must have basically within himself in order to establish himself a successful entrepreneur. But many graduates do lack in these qualities.

➧ The Motivating Factors

Several studies have been undertaken to identify the factors that motivate people to start their own enterprises. P.N. Sharma has identified nine motivating factors which are as under:

1. Educational background.
2. Occupational experience.
3. Desire to do work independently.
4. Desire to branch out to manufacturing.
5. Family background.
6. Assistance from government.
7. Assistance from financial institutions.
8. Availability of technology/raw material.
9. Accommodation in industrial estates.
10. Machinery on hire purchase.
11. Financial assistance from venture capital.
12. Encouragement from big business/MNCs
13. Availability of a franchise.
14. Heavy and sustained demand.
15. Profit margin.
16. Sick units available at a cheap price.

Entrepreneurs are tempted to enter industry because of the three main factors:

(*i*) They have strong desire to do something independent in life.

(*ii*) They have technical knowledge or manufacturing experience.

(*iii*) Availability of governmental and non-governmental assistance.

M. Chandra Sekhar and M. Gandhara Rao have classified factors behind entrepreneurial growth into three categories.

Other factors demand of the particular product, utilisation of excess money earned from contractual estate business, started manufacturing to facilitate trading/distribution business since the project was in short supply, unstable policy of the foreign government for non-residents and no chance for further promotion.

The above nine factors were grouped into two major categories – internal and external. First five motivating factors were termed as internal and the last four factors as external. The internal motivating factors like education, occupational experience, family background, the desire to do something independently together make the personality of the entrepreneur. These factors generate an inclination to adopt entrepreneurial activity. The presence of internal factor is a necessary condition for the entrepreneurial activity to take place. But entrepreneurial ideas cannot fructify or take real shape without a proper or conducive environment which provide support in terms of financial assistance, technology and raw material and infrastructural facilities. These facilities form external motivating factors and serve as a spark in igniting the entrepreneurial idea. These factors give a boost to the entrepreneurial activities.

Prof. R.A. Sharma has classified the factors which prompted entrepreneurs to enter industry as follow:

A. Factors Internal to the Entrepreneur

(*a*) Strong desire to do something independent in life.

(*b*) Technical knowledge and/or manufacturing experience.

(*c*) Business experience in the same line.

B. Factors External to the Entrepreneur

(*a*) Financial assistance from institutional sources.

(*b*) Accommodation in industrial estates.

(*c*) Machinery on hire purchase.

(*d*) Attitude of the government to help new units.

(*e*) Financial assistance from non-government sources.

(*f*) Encouragement from big business.

(*g*) Heavy demand.

(*h*) Profit Margin.

(*i*) Unsound units available at a cheap price.

It is clear from the above that majority of the new entrepreneurs were tempted to enter industry because of three main factors, viz.,

(*i*) They had strong desire to do something independent in life.

(*ii*) They were having technical knowledge or manufacturing experience.

(*iii*) Availability of governmental and non-governmental assistance.

Another study on entrepreneurial motivation by M. Chandra Sekhar and M. Gandhara Rao have classified the factors behind entrepreneurial growth into three categories as follows:

I. Entrepreneurial Ambitions

(*a*) To make money.

(*b*) To continue family business.

(*c*) To secure self-employment/independent living.

(*d*) To fulfil desire of self/wife/parents.

(*e*) To gain social prestige.

(*f*) Other ambitions – making of a decent living, self-employment of children, desire to do something creative, provide employment to others, circumvent Land Ceiling Act etc.

II. Compelling Reasons

(*a*) Unemployment.

(*b*) Dissatisfaction with the job so far held or occupation pursued.

(*c*) Make use of idle time.

(*d*) Make use of technical/professional skills.

(*e*) Others maintenance of large families, revival of sick unit started by father etc.

III. Facilitating Factors

(*a*) Success stories of entrepreneurs.

(*b*) Previous association (experience in the same or other line of activity.)

(*c*) Previous employment in the same or other line of activity.

(*d*) Property inherited/self-acquired/wife's.

(*e*) Advice or influence (encouragement of family members/relatives/friends.)

(*f*) Association as apprentices and sleeping partners.

Encouragement and moral support from near and dear inspires the entrepreneurs, reinforces his confidence and prepares him to lace the new challenges with courage.

According to McClelland, executive generally have higher need for achievement than men in other professions. He considers the need for achievement to the most critical to a nation's economic development. McClelland found that achievement motivation was lower amongst people of underdeveloped countries than those of developed countries. Overall better results can definitely be achieved by making people achievement oriented. According to McClelland achievement motivation can be developed through training and experience. Ambition is the lever of motives and nourishes achievement motivation. McClelland conducted Kakinada Experiment in Kakinada town of Andhra Pradesh. Fifty two persons from business and industrial community from the Kakinada town were selected. They participated in an orientation programme conducted by Small Industry Extension Training Institute (SIETI), Hyderabad. The experiment was designed to stimulate the imagination and encourage introspection into personal motivation and community goals. The achievement development programme consisted of the following steps:

(*a*) The individuals strived to attain concrete and frequent feedback.

(*b*) The participants sought models of achievement, i.e., watched those who have performed well and tried to emulate them.

(*c*) The participants imagined themseleves in need of success and challenge. They set carefully planned and realistic work goals.

(*d*) The trainees were asked to control day dreaming by thinking and talking to themselves in positive terms.

After two years the trainees were observed. It was observed that they performed better than those who did not attend the programme. McClelland concluded that the participants displayed a more active business behaviour and worked for longer hours. McClelland explains that people with low achievement motivation are prepared to work hard for money or other such incentives but the people with high achievement motivation work for status. He argues that people with the high need for achievement possess the following attributes:

(*a*) Prefer personal responsibility for decision.

(*b*) Are moderate risk takers.

(*c*) Possess interest in concrete knowledge of the results of decisions.

⏩ Challenge of Motivation

Since new employees and managers will be of a calibre selected with an eye on the future, they will all be of a high competence level, it will be a challenge to keep motivating them. It is conceivable that organisational structure will have to be looked into order to meet motivational needs of people and "position" them in jobs with the right type of responsibility.

Introduction of high technology and work groups operating without the traditional band of supervisors or inspectors will become more common. Such 'semi-autonomous work groups' will have to be trained so that they are motivated to take care of equipment and meet output targets and tough quality standards.

This will also demand leadership attributes of a high order on the part of people manning such decentralised operations.

V. Lakshmana Rao has aptly summarised the views of various experts on the sources of entrepreneurial supply and motivation as presented in Table 1.

Table 1

ENTREPRENEURSHIP: SOURCES OF SUPPLY AND MOTIVATION

Author	*Entrepreneurial Phenomenon*	*Source of Entrepreneurial Supply*	*Motive Force or Triggering Factor*
1. Schumpeter	Individual	Extraordinary individuals	Innate urge to achieve success
2. Weber	Status Groups	Extraordinary individuals	Religious beliefs Calninist ethic
3. McClelland	Religious and social groups	Individuals with high n-achievement, creative	Child-rearing practices and climate
4. Hagen	Subordinaed Groups	Individuals in the society driven by a duty to achieve	'Status withdrawal' and 'relative social blockage'
5. Cochran	Individual	Society's model, personality determined by its cultural values, role expectations and social sanctions	'Social Acceptance' of entrepreneurial role
6. Young	Homogenous	Relative subgroups (ethnic communities) occupational groups, or Politically-oriented factions.	Deviant view of the world strengthened by group solidarity
7. Kunkel	Group	Operant conditioning procedures in a society	Reinforcing stimuli and average stimuli
8. Hoselitz	Group	Culturally marginal groups	Gaining social recognition.

Source: V. Lakshmana Rao: *Industrial Entrepreneurship in India,* pp. 85-86.

Ideas to Motivate Self

The gap between knowing and doing is where great men and women are made or lost. Most of us know what we have to do to achieve our dreams but we have a 101 reasons not to act on our knowledge.

Application ideas to motivate yourself:

- Find satisfaction is your daily life, don't wait for your big break to come.
- Make a list of your 20 favourite things to do. Neglecting your personal happiness is a powerful de-motivator.
- Ground yourself with solid principles so you don't get distracted from your goal by trends or fads.
- Be able to readily identify the most common de-motivators like fear of failure, change in priorities, uncertainty, anger, jealousy, fear of the unknown and so on.
- Avoid identifying too heavily with what you currently are, it blocks your progress toward something new.
- You can have anything you want in life if you are willing to pay the price to achieve it.
- Never blame other people's action for your lack of action. Anyone can try to make you angry, afraid or depressed but your response to another person's actions will decide whether you are in control or being controlled.
- Rather than viewing life as an endless string of problems to be solved, view it as an unfolding mystery to be revealed.
- When minor failures occur, shift focus to the big goal and assess the impact of the failure on the whole and not only on the area of the failure.
- If you have trouble getting your work day started, choose the task you find most appealing and do it first everyday.
- Do something nice for someone else.
- Avoid comparing yourself to others.
- Don't give too much credit to other people's negative opinions about your goals.
- You have to start somewhere and there is no better time or place than here and now.

Entrepreneurial Behaviour

Achievement motivation and entrepreneurial behaviour are closely associated. Behaviour is a manifestation of what person thinks, feels and acts. Motivation is essentially the process of purposeful or goal oriented actions. The behavioural pattern of entrepreneurs is summarized below:

(*i*) An entrepreneur is creative. Need for self-actualization as manifested the need for achievement forces him to create something new – a new product, a new way of doing things, a new source of raw material, a new market, etc.

(*ii*) He acts out of desire not necessity. He is proactive not reactive in nature. He influences the environment rather than adopting to it.

(*v*) He is professionally very active but personally lazy. This is reflected in his casual dress and unkept hair. This casualness enables him to work with minimum physical facilities and constraints. His lower order needs are minimum.

(*vi*) He sets his own standards and acts as his own competitor.

(*vii*) He is not satisfied with the present and always looks ahead for more challenging jobs.

(*viii*) He is conscious about time and dislikes time wasters.

(*x*) He learns from his experience.

(*xi*) He is hopeful about future and sees opportunity in a crisis.

(*xii*) He accepts responsibility for his actions.

Entrepreneurship Leadership Style

An entrepreneur is a person who coverts an innovative idea into business. The word entrepreneur is generally associated with small-scale industry. What is an entrepreneurship leadership style? Based on both their personality characteristics, and the circumstances of operating a business, many entrepreneurs use a similar leadership style. The most notable features of this style are:

(*i*) Impatience and brusquences towards employees because the entrepreneur is always busy.

(*ii*) A heavy task orientation combined with a very direct-approach to giving instructions to employees.

(*iii*) A charismatic personality that inspires others to want to do business with him or her despite the impatience.

(*iv*) A much stronger interest in dealing with customers than employees.

(*v*) A strong dislike for bureaucratic rules and regulations.

(*vi*) Anxiety to consolidate business gains as quickly as possible.

Some of the styles described above will be referred to again later in different contexts.

Conclusion

The foregoing discussion highlights two major concepts of motivation. According to the first concept, people react to influences which are known as motivators. They are recognition, achievement, responsibility, development, etc., which have been discussed under the head "Developmental." Apart from motivators, sustaining incentives are also necessary. Whether sustaining or developmental is by and large the leadership factor.

Apart from earning a livelihood and/or making profit, the entrepreneur is also motivated to fulfill his/her innate urge to achieve success in life, improve his/her social standing, gaining social recognition, to provide something to society. The motivational factor vary from place to place, time to time as well entrepreneur to entrepreneur. Yet motivation moulds the different entrepreneurial traits. The traits and motivation are moulded by the socio-economic, political, cultural and psychological environment and varies from country to country.

Entrepreneurship is to a great extent the product of motivation. Motivation refers to the inner drive that ignites and sustains behaviour to satisfy needs. Behaviour is always caused and it is not spontaneous. In other words, human behaviour is goal directed or directed towards satisfaction of needs. A person's behaviour is shaped by several socio-psychological factors such as his goals, education level, cultural background, work experience, etc. When a person feels some need, tension arises in his mind until the need is satisfied. This tension motivates him to take action. If the action is successful, need is satisfied, otherwise the person changes the action until the need satisfaction occurs. Motivation implies an inner state that causes an entrepreneur to act towards the realization of his/her dream and the attainment of the goals.

The study of entrepreneurial behaviour and motivation is useful in developing a profile of a successful entrepreneur. It is indeed a positive approach in developing entrepreneurship and enterprise in the country. Although, the entrepreneurial traits, behaviour and motivation are complex, the goal of entrepreneur is to build enterprises to earn profit and serve the society. Thus, fulfilling his ambition, success, satisfaction, while shouldering social responsibility and earning profit, comfort, status and power. Finally, entrepreneurial behaviour and motivation result in fostering and nurturing entrepreneurship to accelerate the process of socio-economic development.

THE MOTIVATION AUDIT

Do you cultivate a positive environment for your team and bolster everyone's spirits? Take this audit to find out:

1. Do you rally your workers by treating them to special food, prizes, and cook-outs?	Yes	No
2. Do you prod people to express their appreciation for others through spoken praise or notices?	Yes	No
3. Do you look for ways to make jobs rewarding, such as training and friendly competitions?	Yes	No
4. Do you help your people laugh and bear adversity by giving them something to smile about?	Yes	No
5. Do you take advantage of scheduling flexibility by giving deserving workers extra time off?	Yes	No
6. Do you describe your group's achievements whenever you have a chance?	Yes	No
7. Do you support other groups within your company, and let them know about it?	Yes	No
8. Do you invest your group's time in being helpful to your customers, both internal and external?	Yes	No
9. Do you tell your team that you are committed to help it get the recognition it deserves?	Yes	No
10. Do you ask your team members what they need from you to get through the crunch?	Yes	No

THE SCORING

Give yourself 10 points for every YES and 0 for every NO

TOTAL

THE RATING

0-30	You are a miserable motivator. Learn to utilise your greatest asset: your people.
40-70	You are a mediocre motivator. Strive to improve your communication skills.
80-100	You are a master motivator. You know how to get the best of your people.

MIND FIELD

"For a leader, each hurdle coming his way should be thoroughly understood and methodically eliminated using all the means at his disposal. Howevr, care must be taken to see that these means stand up to scrutiny at a later date." ***— P.P. Chhabria, Chairman, Finolex Group***

16

Achievement and Management Success

Introduction

An entrepreneur is a creative person. Need for self actualisation as manifested in the need for achievement forces him to create something new – a new product, a new way of doing things, a new source of raw material, a new market etc. Human behaviour is goal directed or is directed towards satisfaction of needs. Whenever a person feels any need, he feels uneasy and tension starts building in his mind. This tension provokes him to initiate some action which may lead to the satisfaction of the need. If that need is not satisfied then that individual is required to report to some alternate action for the satisfaction of the need.

'Creativity'– the very mention of the word fills many of us with awe. It brings our minds, visions of great people – great by virtue of their masterpieces in art and literature, rare inventions and discoveries in science and technology and the like. Recent research indicates that creativity is not such an elusive quality after all. Scientific research is steadily chipping away at the mystery of the creative process – a process many believe is either a divine gift or a black art. And most important, the research is proving that creativity can be taught, in the sense that various techniques have been developed to facilitate creativity. Thus, creativity, innovation are to a greater extent influenced by human behaviour, many entrepreneurial behaviour. In this chapter, we shall examine the entrepreneurial behaviour and motivation.

If there is one trait that virtually all-effective leaders have, it is motivation. They are driven to achieve beyond expectation – their own and everyone else's. The key word here is achieve. Plenty of people are motivated by external factors, such as a big salary or the status that comes from having an impressive title or being part of a prestigious company. By contrast, those with leadership potential are motivated by a deeply embedded desire to achieve for the sake of achievement.

If you are looking for leaders, how can you identify people who are motivated by the drive to achieve rather than by external rewards? The first sign is a passion for the work itself such people seek out creative challenges, love to learn, and take great pride in a job well done. They also display an unflagging energy to do things better. People with such energy often seem restless with the status quo. They are persistent with their questions about why things are done the way rather than another; they are eager to explore new approaches to their work.

They say that success comes to those who believe in themselves and never give up; it comes to those who do not stop trying until they achieve their goals. Achievement is thus a benchmark of entrepreneurial activities. Achievement and entrepreneurship reinforce each other. In fact, achievement comes to those who dares and strives to reach their goals.

Achievement and management success is discussed in relation with successful management of enterprises. In this case, the students have to draw their own lessons from the case studies given in this chapter.

⏩ Recognition for Accomplishment

Recognition is ingrained in human psychology. If his work and his contribution have not been appreciated properly, he will lose interest in work because it is very difficult to sustain the will to work in the absence of proper recognition. Who recognises the work of the person will be determined by the status or designation of the worker. Herzberg states: "The source could be almost anyone; supervisor, some other individual in management, management as an impersonal force, a client, a peer, a professional colleague or the general public. Recognition may be a word of praise, a letter or a notice, to be published for the accomplishment of the worker. Sometimes, if the verbal recognition may not be there but when an employee gets a wage increase or promotion, they may be perceived as the elements of recognition.

It may, however, be pointed out that increase in wages or monetary awards may be motivating if perceived as award for recognition, otherwise they cease to be motivating. Recognition should be public. Man wants that others should know that he has done good work and, that the relevant agency has recognised his work. If he gets a cheque from the employer closed in the envelope, it may be motivating but not to the extent when even a token medal of one-tenth or of little value is awarded to him in public by the management in recognition of the work done by him.

Recognition should also include "negative recognition" – criticism, blame, reprimand. Even the element of criticism will satisfy his instinct of recognition by his bosses.

Recognition is related to the accomplishment of the challenging task assigned to him. Accomplishment includes "successful completion of a job, solution to problems, vindication and seeing the results of one's work." For instance, and when author finds his paper appearing in a recognised journal of repute or if he finds his book released in the market, he finds biggest satisfaction, though monetarily a writer, who has written a cheap note, may have earned more money.

David McClelland's Theory of Achievement Motivation

In the late 1940s, David McClelland and his associates developed the theory of achievement motivation, which was regarded as one of the best economic theories of entrepreneurial development. They concentrated mainly on the following three aspects:

- Need for achievement
- Need for power
- Need for affiliation.

1. **Need for achievement:** A strong need for achievement 'n Ach' is found within certain individuals, groups and communities. McClelland emphasized that the need for achievement or achievement orientation is the most important factor for explaining economic behaviour. People having this need are more likely to succeed as entrepreneurs. They strive incessantly for success in getting things done in an excellent manner. They try passionately to overcome any odd that comes on their way. They are so much self-confident that they do not believe in mere luck. They look upon money as the index of their achievement but basically they are not money oriented. Therefore, McClelland wrote: "Need for achievement is a desire to do well, not so much for the sake of social recognition or prestige, but for the sake of an inner feeling of personal accomplishment."
2. **Need for power:** This pertains to the desire by a person to be influential in a group. People with need for power 'n Pow' believe in position of authority. They seek leadership in politics, business, education or arts and feel satisfied having a great number of followers. All successful managers seem to have high need for power. They derive satisfaction to influence and direct authority.
3. **Need for affiliation:** The persons with high need for affiliation are sensitive to social relationship. They are keen on warm and interpersonal relationship. They are associated more with popularity, social support and friendship than with decision making. They love others and wish to be loved by others. This is not predominant among managers but this 'n Aff' greatly helps them in influencing their subordinates.

Thus, the theory of achievement motivation provides a deep introspection to the human behaviour in general and entrepreneurial behaviour in particular. It also glorifies the necessity of the Achievement Motivation Training (AMT) as an important tool for achievement of needs.

Keeping in view the above needs, 'n Ach', 'n Pow' and 'n Aff', David McClelland has pointed out that these factors, especially 'n Ach' are responsible for entrepreneurial development. The following analysis can reveal the impact of need for achievement in accelerating entrepreneurial urge among individuals.

Twin Characteristics of Entrepreneurship: McClelland pointed out the twin important characteristics of entrepreneurship that govern the economic behaviour of a person to become entrepreneurial. They are:

(*i*) Doing things in a novel and excellent manner.

(*ii*) Decision making under uncertainty.

Belief in Personal Accomplishment: According to this theory, 'n Ach' or need for achievement refers to the need for personal accomplishment by the person through excellence, This category of person is fond of shouldering personal responsibility. They are generally moderate risk lakers and try to be winners all the time. High achievers aim at personal achievement rather than the reward of success. Persons with high need for achievement behave in the entrepreneurial way.

Psychological Factors for Entrepreneurial Motivation: Need for achievement depends upon entrepreneurial motivation. This need motivates the persons to take risk. The following psychological factors are responsible for the growth of entrepreneurial motivation:

(*a*) Need for achievement through performance evaluation.

(*b*) Goal setting and problem solving.

(*c*) Strong desire to undertake calculated risk.

(*d*) Willingness for taking personal responsibility.

(*e*) Spirit to achieve success.

(*f*) Anticipating possibilities.

(*g*) Concrete measures of task performance.

(*h*) New instrumental activity.

(*i*) Feeling of personal accomplishment.

(*j*) Organisational as well as decision-making skills.

Inner Concerns as the Prime Movers: McClelland opined that inner concerns or motives are the prime movers of entrepreneurship. These forces drive the individuals to take risk, plunge into uncertainty where they find opportunity, discover new ideas, save more and reinvest the savings in the enterprise. According to him: "The internal factors are the human values and motives that lead the human being to exploit opportunities, to take advantage of favourable trade conditions."

'n Ach' Precursor of Economic Growth: McClelland applied his technique of 'n Ach' *to* study the relationship between achievement motivation and economic development. He found that it was the 'n Ach' factor which was a precursor of economic growth both in socialistic and capitalistic system of economy. Entrepreneurship, thus, becomes the pivot around which need for achievement and economic growth to revolve.

Lack of Ambition in Less Developed Countries: Ambition is the basis on which McClelland's 'n Ach' greatly depends. In less developed countries (LDCs), achievement motivation of people is lower than that of developed countries because of low level of ambition. Lack of ambition creates a great barrier for need for achievement and consequently leads to lack of enterprise in LDCs. So in order to bring about economic development, it is necessary that the level of ambition among the people should be high enough to pressurise the need for achievement in them. Then only entrepreneurial spirit can be generated and economic growth can be accelerated.

The 'n Ach' Model

Any behavioural model for entrepreneurial development must, therefore, take care of proportionate development of both Need for power and Need for affiliation in relation to the high priest – Need for achievement.

McClelland applied his technique of 'n Ach' to study the relationship between achievement motivation and economic development. He found that it was the 'n Ach' factor which was a precursor of economic growth both in socialistic and capitalistic system of economy. Entrepreneurship, thus, becomes the pivot around which need for achievement and economic growth to revolve.

Ambition is the basis on which **McClelland's 'n Ach' greatly depends. In less developed countries (LDCs) achievement motivation of people is lower than that of developed countries because of low level of ambition. Lack of ambition creates a great barrier for need for achievement and consequently leads to lack of the level of ambition among the people should be high enough to pressurize the need for achievement in them. Then only entrepreneurial spirit can be generated and economic growth can be accelerated.**

According to David McClelland, the role of 'n Ach' is the critical factor for entrepreneurial development, which, in turn, leads to accelerate the empowerment of economic development.

The model will thus look like the following:

$$M = \text{N–ach} + \text{N–Pow} + \text{N.Aff} \quad \text{... (1)}$$

Or Entrepreneurial motivation (Mo) is the additive function of three need variables. In this model N–Pow and N–Aff have fixed proportional relationship with N–Ach (which for sake of simplification may be denoted as M_{ea}).

Hence, N–Pow = $K_p.m_{ea} = m_{ep}$

and N–Aff = $K_f.m_{ea} = m_{ef}$

which means that if N–Ach (m_{ea}) score of an entrepreneur is 20 his N–Pow (or entrepreneurial power need - me_{dp}) should be 20 kp and N–Aff (or entrepreneurial affiliation need – m_{ef}) score will be 20 kf. The model can therefore be recast in the following form:

$$Mo = (m_{ea} + m_{ep} + m_{ef}) \quad \text{... (2)}$$

Need for achievement (m_{ea}) being the vital motivational ingredient of entrepreneur and the guiding force, its score shall be highest amongst all his motivational needs followed by the scores of (m_{ep}) and (m_{ef}), Constants kp for N–Pow and kf for N-Aff can be derived empirically from the study of motivational data of successful entrepreneurs, both present and past. The constants can also be established by Stochastic method and then tested for their validity.

As m_{ea} or entrepreneurial need for achievement is the biggest and guiding variable in terms of which both m_{ep} and mef are developed, theoretically the model can be presented in a right-angled triangle where m_{ea} is hypotenuse; m_{ep} is the base and m_{ef}– the perpendicular as below:

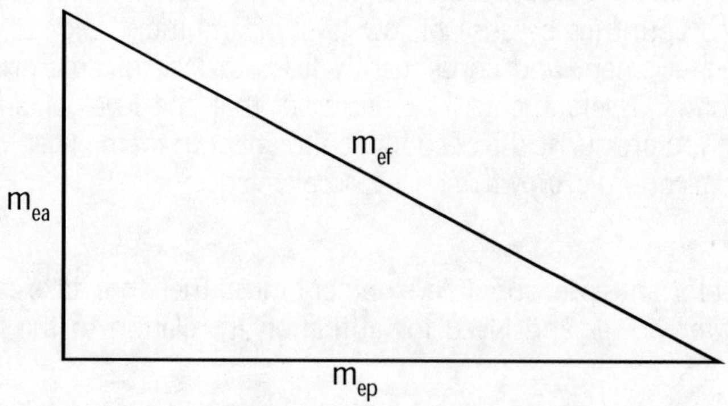

Then the control equations will be:

$$(m_{ea})^2 = (m_{ep})^2 + (m_{ef})^2 \quad \text{... (3)}$$

$$\text{and } k_{p2} + k_{f2} = 1 \quad \text{... (4)}$$

because k_p and k_f. are both proportional to hypotenuse m_{ae}.

Geometrically speaking, with a given hypotenuse there could be a number of such right-angled triangles and an ideal form can be determined for each class of entrepreneurs where $(m_{ep}) > (m_{ep}) > (m_{ef})$; – the base (m_{ep}) and perpendicular (m_{ef}) being determined automatically for the given hypotenuse (m_{ea}).

If the measurement scales reduced to one it will be further observed that:

$M_0 = m_{ea} + m_{ep} + m_{ef}$

The additive is less than three because it is difficult to find all the three motivational needs in equal degree in an individual and more so, it is an impossible psychological situation for a successful entrepreneur.

With the help of the model it will be possible to determine the degree of need for power and need for affiliation for a given score of need for achievement of a potential entrepreneur. Suitable training inputs can then be provided to increase or reduce the need variables to make the motivational profile of an entrepreneur effectively workable. For this purpose entrepreneurial motivational score (M) must satisfy all the conditions on the right hand side of the equation and none of the need variables will have any zero value.

Although, McClelland has shown, N-Ach of an individual can be increased, it can be increased only upto certain extent depending upon his past and present life situation, Theories of Motivation and his ability to put these to effective use in practical situations. Some of such situations and applications are given below:

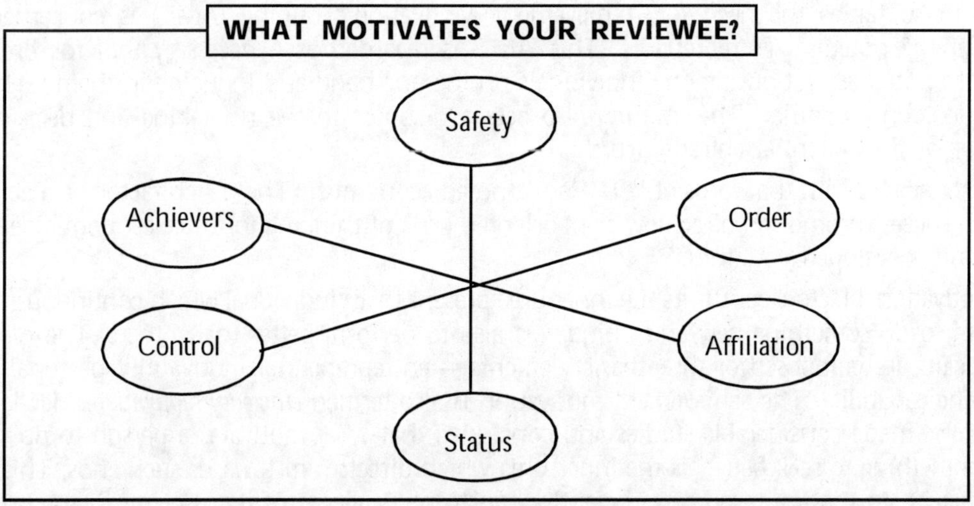

It is useful to 'put oneself in the reviewee's shoes' and think about what would motivate this person. McClelland categorised certain inner drivers that trigger responses. This identifies different priorities that individuals may have. These motivational drivers and their application in practical situations are discussed below.

➡ Experience at Kakinad

According to David McClelland, the role of 'n Ach' is the critical factor for entrepreneurial development, which, in turn, leads to accelerate the tempo of economic development. In order to prove this fact, he conducted several experiments with different groups of businessmen in America, Mexico, Mumbai and Kakinada in Andhra Pradesh. Through the experiments, he tried to induce the spirit of achievement motivation in adults and urged them to take up entrepreneurial ventures. Such an inducement was, in fact, essential to increase their level of aspirations and to give rise to confidence building character in them.

In January, 1964, a full-fledged training programme was organized by David McClelland at Kakinada with a total intake of 52 persons. The objectives of such programme were:

(*a*) To instill in them the quality of imagination.

(*b*) To encourage introspection and convert it into personal motivation and community goals.

The training was conducted at small Industries Extension and Training Institute (SIET), Hyderabad. The Achievement Motivation Training (AMT) included the following basics which were supposed to be accomplished by the trainees:

(*a*) Goal setting and goal achievement.

(*b*) Emulating the models of achievement by constant watch and alertness.

(*c*) Attainment of concrete and frequent feedback.

(*d*) Planning carefully the realistic goals through performance appraisal of their own.

(*e*) Converting ideas into opportunities using the positive self-concept and controlling day dreaming.

Thus, the training helped those participants in providing high degree of motivation and subsequently the need for achievement. They displayed a more active business behaviour and took enough stress to accomplish the job. As such, Kakinada experience was considered the most successful experiment so far as the need for Achievement Motivation Training (AMT) is concerned for the benefit of the potential entrepreneurs. This AMT is regarded as a necessary tool for breaking the barrier of limited aspirations among individuals on the one hand and inducing in them high need for achievement on the other. The training also acts as a boost to the risk-taking and decision-making behaviour of the potential entrepreneurs.

To conclude with the words of V.L. Rao, a noted economist: "The n Ach factor or n achievement approach suggest promotion of achievement-oriented ways of thinking to foster economic development in the underdeveloped countries."

Motivational factors constitute the inner urge present in an individual which continuously demands from him to do something new and unique, as also to perform better than others. The motivational factors again are composed of three basic elements – entrepreneurial motivation, personal efficiency and coping capability. The achievement motivation is also termed *efficiency motivation.* McClelland and Winter have made considerable studies and concluded that what motivates a person to do something new or something to seek better, is the inner urge which directs him towards such ends, This urge also force a person to use the resources efficiently than to be negligent of it. Also important is the power of motivation which is really the urge to have control over others and to direct their course of activities towards the end which one seeks to attain. These motivational factors induce the person to undertake entrepreneurial activities which relate to creating a new business where there was none. This also means to excel the performance in carrying out any activity by striving through persistent efforts unlike others who do not have sufficient capacity for hard work.

▸▸ Case Studies

The case studies in Management education have the same power to involve our minds, provided the narrative comes alive to us. A case tells the story of an organisation at a point in time. The organisation has a background – a past, an orientation towards the future (goal/s) and a present, which brings us to the moment of the story. The plot involves the key people in the organisation, who are engaged in the action plan in order to achieve the goal/s. The decision-maker is the tragic hero: like the winery-owner he ponders the issue – to pick or not to pick. Conflict is at the heart of the organisational narrative: an urgent goal that has to be achieved within a time frame and a persistent problem.

The case is more fascinating than a ready-made story because it is still evolving. The narrative acquires different shades of reality through case discussions in the classroom and students learn important lessons in creative problem solving. The analysis of the problem offers alternatives that would otherwise remain unexplored. The transformative power of the narrative holds immense potential to change our view of a problem and generate possible solutions.

The narrative approach provides the opportunity to explore multiple perspectives. Rather than be swayed by the views of one character, the analyst may take an objective approach and distance himself/herself from the scene. What if our Napa valley farmer were to meet an all-knowing fortune-teller who would tell him whether the welcome storm would hit or not? That would really make life so much easier, wouldn't it? But in its absence our hero would weigh the pros and cons of his choice objectively and plant a decision tree.

Clearly, this exercise in detachment is necessary to solve current problems in organisational and personal life situations. Action should be backed by logic. What if the Napa valley owner waited for the warm storm to hit and it never did? Imagine he has a niece who can give him definite scientific evidence of low pressure and high pressure cycles that can tell him the storm will come to his life, would he be willing to pay for that information? If yes, then the next question is: how much is the rich wine-producer uncle willing to shell out of his thick wallet? That is logical action for you!

Recent research shows that storytelling is one of the most effective tools leaders can use in organisations. Once the placements are over, the much sought-after MBA degree is in the bag, the student is suddenly in the position of the Napa Valley decision maker him/herself. While every problem-situation is like a fingerprint and finding a solution is by no means an easy task, a narrative approach can generate multiple options for the decision-maker and suggest unlimited possibilities.

A STUDY IN SUCCESS

MURUDESHWAR CERAMICS FORAYS INTO NEW AREAS

Inspiration and Early Beginning

Rama Nagappa Shetty would have been ploughing in his ancestral fields but for his father's inspiration. Today, he heads a rnulticrore empire, whose flagship company Murudeshwar Ceramics Ltd. is a study in success.

Shetty started off in the late fifties with some money loaned by his father. He ventured into construction and took up minor jobs like metalling and asphalting of roads. By 1961, he had become big enough io undertake construction of three major bridges on the Honnavar-Gerusoppa Road in North Kanara district. In 1996, he moved his operating base to Hubli and switched over to irrigation power works. Since then, Shetty has not looked back.

He has, over the years, executed major irrigation works like the Malaprabha, Ghataprabha and Upper Krishna projects. He has even completed the prestigious Varahi hydel power project, the first underground power house in Karnataka. Currently, Shetty has his hands full. He is also involved in the upper Krishna canal work and the Gerusoppa dam for the Sharavathi project – both financed by the World Bank.

⏩ Diversification

A natural offshoot of all this construction activity was the Murudeshwar Tile Factory, set up at Murudeshwar in 1977. Explains Shetty, "In North Kanara, we get a lot of clay suitable for manufacturing Mangalore tiles." Now, this is the biggest Mangalore tile factory in North Kanara district. A decade later, Shetty set up Murudeshwar Ceramics Ltd., a joint-sector undertaking with the Karnataka State Industrial Investment & Development Corporation, for the manufacture of ceramic glazed tiles. "In 1985, the KSIIDC was looking for a partner for a ceramic tile venture and my father, who showed an interest, was awarded the project."

⏩ Ceramics

A Rs. 13.45 crore project to manufacture 12,500 tonne per annum of ceramic tiles, the MCL project was financed by an equity capital of Rs. 4.50 crore and loans of Rs. 8.80 crore. The plant was completed in a record 14 months time. MCL is one of the major industries to have come up in the backward North Karnataka region. He selected Hubli for MCL because of its proximity to raw material sources and to the major consuming centres like Mumbai, Bangalore, Pune and Goa.

⏩ Turnover

In the first year itself, for a 11-month period in 1988-89, MCL achieved a turnover of Rs. 9.64 crores and posted a net profit of Rs. 42 lakhs. In 1991-92, its sales moved to Rs. 29.66 crores, while the net profit reached Rs. 4.79 crores. The EPS also moved from Rs. 0.94 in 1988-89 to Rs. 9.53 in 1991-92.

Over the years, MCL ceramic tiles marketed under the brand name "Naveen" have been well accepted in the ceramic tile market in spite of the tough competition from established players like Johnson Tiles, Somany, Pilkington and Spartek. Compared to Spartek, MCL has an edge in quality. It also enjoys an advantage in price since it enjoys a tax holiday between 1990 and 1993. And in spite of a large number of entrants in the market, MCL has managed to survive because of its higher capacity utilisation and cost control measures. Today, "Naveen" ceramic tiles are available in over 40 colours and shades.

⏩ Capacity Utilisation

In 1990 MCL doubled its capacity to 25,000 tpa. By January 1993, this will go up to 40,000 tpa at a cost of Rs. 17 crores. This should help them reach a turnover of Rs. 37 crores in 1992-93. Since the domestic market was growing slowly, MCL decided to concentrate on exports as well in 1991-92, MCL exported Rs. 45 lakh worth of ceramic tiles to the Middle East. This year, it has so far exported tiles worth Rs. 60 lakhs against a target of Rs. 1 crore.

⏩ Marketing

The domestic market has improved this year. And they are tapping the market aggressively with the help of 160 dealers most of whom sell only "Naveen" ceramic tiles. They have eight marketing offices and they will soon set up marketing offices in Pune, Vizag and Ahmedabad as well.

But it has not always been smooth sailing for MCL. The government has labelled ceramic tiles as a luxury item and clamped a 57.5 per cent excise duty on them. MCL's cost of production is less than mosaic tiles. But then they are bogged down with the excise duty.

In four years, MCL has notched up 9.3 per cent of the market share in ceramic tiles. It has recorded an impressive growth in the net sales (26.8 per cent), gross profit (31.3 per cent) and net profit (45 per cent). Its dividend went up, thanks to its excellent performance, from 16 per cent in 1990-91 to 20 per cent in 1991-92.

New Avenues

During 1971-72, Mr. R.N. Shetty promoted Seshank Sea Foods Ltd. at Bhatkal in North Karnataka for processing and export of sea foods. This year it hopes to achieve an export turnover of Rs. 25 crores. It exports to Japan (which is the major buyer), the US and France.

Mr. Shetty now plans to go in for aquaculture in a big way. For this purpose, he has already acquired 40 hectares of land near Kumta in North Karnataka and negotiations are on for another 60 hectares. This will be a Rs. 10 crore project.

TRANSFORMING DREAMS

Early Beginning

In 1966, a young electrical engineer, R.K. Parasuram, returned to his hometown Madras after working for General Electric Company, U.K., for 10 years, he dreamt of manufacturing world-class electrical transformers and selling them all over the world. Three decades later, his dream is coming true.

The Kappa group of companies (named after his wife Kamala Parasuram) – a bunchy of tiny private limited companies and proprietary firms with a turnover of Rs. 16 crore and an export turnover of Rs. 9 crore – manufacture almost the entire range of transformers. These are low-tech but essential items which require a lot of manual labour.

Having established his products successfully in the domestic market, Parasuram decided to go global. Exports in the early seventies really meant the rupee market. It was not easy to penetrate the European and American markets. So he looked towards South-East Asia which was a relatively easier hard-currency area.

No one had previously attempted to export products like transformers. Right from the outset, Parasuram's emphasis was on quality. The export products were produced to conform to the international standards prescribed by British Standards and International Electro-technical Commission. Due to the availability of cheap skilled labour, the cost of Kappa's transformers was very competitive.

First Order

In 1973, the company got its first export order from Dickson Primer, an engineering firm in Singapore, for 300 pieces of transformers worth Rs. 20,000. Singapore and Malaysia were the major markets then. By late 70s, Kappa decided to expand its activities to the Middle East. The focus was on Beirut. However, when the militarisation of Lebanon became complete in the early 80s exports to Beirut came to a grinding halt.

Parasuram was on the constant lookout for a big deal. Kappa's ability to produce transformers as custom-built original equipment fetched its first order from Siemens, Australia, in 1980. Siemens and Email-Westinghouse became their major buyers in Australia and New Zealand. A bulk of the company's international sales is to Asea Brown Boveri. Worth just Rs. 20,000 in the 80s, business with the Swedish-Swiss giant has grown to Rs. 60 lakh annually, Says Kamala, "With more and more enquiries from abroad, we opened an export office at Singapore in 1983."

In order to broad base exports, it was decided to trade in a wide range of current technology products not necessarily produced by the group. The relays produced by English Electric, semiconductor fuse and voltage transformer fuse links manufactured by S&S Power Switchgear Ltd. are some of the well-known products traded by Kappa Exports. Says T.V.G. Menon, general manager, relay division, English Electric, "We cannot export directly because of our agreement with our parent company. So we make our sales to Kappa who are doing a splendid job." Kappa has emerged as the biggest exporter of electrical goods from South India. Today 60 per cent of Kappa's export turnover is from trading.

Kappa's exports reached Rs. I crore in 1987. Since then, the annual growth rate has been phenomenal, around 40 per cent now. The main reason for this, according to Kamala, was Kappa's strategic move to become a single-window export house for all electrical engineering equipment. Parasuram is convinced that constant upgradation of technology is the only way for survival. Five per cent of the total turnover is being spent on R&D and another five per cent on technological upgradation. According to Kamala, the neglected but important area in exports is packaging. Says she, "Our special packaging efforts to withstand the wear and tear of the transit costs an additional three per cent."

To ensure quality. Kappa has invested about Rs. 1 crore in various imported testing equipment and this has now proved to be a great advantage as the group is gearing to enter the European market in a big way. Says the founder's daughter Miva Parasuram, an electrical engineer, "We are working with the Indian Statistical Institute to get the ISO 9000 accreditation. Our production systems already seem to conform to international standards. We have to only effect changes in areas like inventory, billing and accounting. We will get our accredition in the middle of 1993." Kappa wants to reach an export figure of Rs. 100 crore by the turn of the century and hence it is seriously studying the Middle East and African markets.

WHAT'S SIZE — IT ENTREPRENEURS

The new breed of IT entrepreneurs does not want to follow the venerated footsteps of Infosys, TCS, Wipro, Satyam. Instead, they are creating a new business model that takes them straight to the top of the value chain. The new companies have two things in common – a narrowly defined niche and a skew towards products. They are confident, ambitious, creative, innovative and raring to go.

We present FOUR varied examples from the new breed of entrepreneurs on the horizon.

AMRIT S. CHOPRA

HEALTH IS WEALTH

MEDICOM SOLUTIONS
Founder: Amrit S. Chopra
Niche: Healthcare Informatics
Revenues: Rs. 3000 lakh
No. of employees: 250

He is the only entrepreneur in this series who has grey hair. While we're in no way trying to underline the age of Amrit S. Chopra, the idea is to drive home the point that, unlike the others, Chopra turned entrepreneur late in his AMRIT S. CHOPRA career. He was with IBM till 1977, and also worked with Tata Burroughs for a while.

While in Oman, working for a firm called Oman Computing Services, he was asked by the Ministry of Health to advise on IT solutions for a hospital there. Not being satisfied with the given solution, he went to the concerned minister who told him to find a better solution. He found the answer in a Dutch firm, specialising in health-care. Purely by chance, that firm at the time was moving out of this area and so in 1992 along with OCS he founded Medicom.

The area has well-entrenched billion-dollar companies, so Medicom evolved a strategy that saw them working in the Middle East, South Asia and South Africa. Today the firm has already completed 140 implementations in 14 countries. Explains Ashwini Kumar, EVP Medicom: "We knew that the US was not our initial market, since India and Indians were not known for work at the high end. We therefore went to markets where there was more of a level playing field."

The Indian background came in handy in these regions. For example, in South Africa they were looking for a technology that could not only be scaled up but could also be scaled down. The bigger companies from the developed world assume a certain level of IT, and Medicom's versatility enabled it to bag the contract.

FITTING THE BILL

ANKUR LAL

INFOZECH

Founder: Ankur Lal
Niche: CRM, billing and settlement solutions for packet based converged networks
Revenues: Rs. 500 lakh
No. of employees: 50

Ankur Lal has never been one to let an opportunity go a-begging. The luckiest break he got was while studying electrical engineering at IIT Delhi. He managed an internship with a relatively unknown start-up in the US. He impressed them so much that the company gave him a project to take back to India. No wonder, when he finally graduated, a regular job was not what he wanted. And so in 1991 Infozech was born.

Lal still remembers the early days when he would pay money to make sure his firm appeared high on Google searches for offshore telecom software development. There was a time when 50 per cent of the firm's business was coming through the net. But with the dotcom bust, the profits made in 10 years of operations evaporated in eight months.

The big opportunity came while working on a telecom billing and customer care project. His firm decided to buy back from the client what they had developed and convert it into a product. With a little help from CDC, UK – $1 million to be exact – the product development work was taken forward.

Doesn't it worry him at all that his firm is in a sector that was hit the most in the IT downturn? Lal is quick to point out that the telecom domain is also the one that is rebounding the fastest. Today his firm has alliances with Microsoft and Osco, and these firms in turn refer Infozech to the system integrators that they work with.

OUT OF THE BOX

CHIRAG PATEL

NET4NUTS

Founders: Chirag Patel and Neerav Parekh
Niche: Wireless
Middleware Solutions Revenue: Rs. 50 lakh
No. of employees: 27

After studying and working in the US – like most scions of Indian business families – Chirag Patel returned to India to work in the family's edible oil business in Ahmedabad. However, he soon realised that his heart lay in technology. And so, along with an old classmate Neerav Parekh, a computer science graduate from Stanford, he formed NET4NUTS in 2000.

Their idea was simple – increasing dependence on the internet meant a lot of chaos in terms of managing various resources. Getting a Yahoo address book, Hotmail account and mobile to work in sync was quite impossible. It was (as Patel puts it) driving everyone 'nuts.' It was a problem they felt would only get worse, so they formed NET4NUTS with the idea of making these services complement each other.

By the end of 2001, with the $1 million funding they got from the World Bank – promoted GVFL, their product 'AVTAAR' was ready for launch. The timing could not have been worse – 9/11 happened ten days before the scheduled launch. The ensuing tech downturn meant there were no takers for their technology, which was seen as a next-generation product with long-term benefits, and not really a need of the times.

Patel says: "People had stopped investing in technology; no one had a cheque book ready." So they resorted to free trials but even that didn't prompt companies to invest. Finally, they came up with an ASP model where they implemented and ran the product for the client and got paid according to the end use.

TAKING A CALL

SUBHASH MENON

SUBEX SYSTEMS

Founders: Subhash Menon and Alex PJ
Niche: Telecom software solutions Revenues: Rs. 7000 lakh
No. of employees: 250

In 1992, Subhash Menon, along with classmate Alex PJ set up Subex with Rs. 20,000 loaned by an ex-employer. The two started by selling imported infrastructure products to cellular operators in India. That gave them a foretaste of what it means to compete against MNCs like Agilent (then part of HP). They graduated to software services and today develop their own products. Recalls Menon: "At that time it was difficult to get a Rs. 1 lakh loan from a bank. It was an uphill task with customers too, as we had no experience."

Once the company entered the product space, each customer was used as a stepping-stone. Menon explains: "Indian companies are not known for products in the advanced space. Also, telecom companies are conservative in choosing who they work with as they can't afford downtime." Even in

India they initially did not get a warm response, especially since big players like HP, Ericsson and Alcatel were well-entrenched.

It was the consistent focus on implementation that got them a foothold in the market. The first major breakthrough was with Hutch in Mumbai. Since then, there's been a build-up of credibility. From handling 70-80 mn transactions a day, their product today handles networks with 300 mn transactions a day.

Having gained experience in India, Subex has quickly expanded overseas. Today, only 10 per cent of revenues come from India. Their first product specialised in fraud management. Where once the two main products of the company were me-toos, today Subex is working on a new-to-the world product.

⏩ Peaks of Success

Fuelling ambitions and dreams. Breathing life into promoting business ventures. Charting the course of incisive business ideas. Providing foresight with a fine sense of direction. Helping insightful, imaginative business ideas glide smoothly over rough passages. Helping vision and enterprise sight the target and achieve it with pinpoint accuracy. Complementing acumen and enterprise with a steady flow of resources. Partnering enterprises on the move, till they reach the Peaks of success.

SUCCESS FACTORS FOR TODAY

- Total quality in manufacture, design, & delivery
- Lean organisation
- Focus on core competence (market segments)
- Productivity (new product development)
- Global player
- Total customer satisfaction

SUCCESS FACTORS FOR TOMORROW

- More of all the above
- Risk management
- Survival skills
- New organisation
- Learning organisation
- Creativity

MANTRAS FOR SUPER SUCCESS

⏩ Set Goals

Every success becomes a point of departure for new initiatives. Success should be measured in relation to goals. I believe that what has already been achieved, lies in the past. One should always look at the future and set new goals. I have set in my own mind, the goal of contributing, in a modest way, to the building of a resurgent India. I try to explore opportunities that will assist this goal by harnessing technological revolution taking place in a variety of fields – from information, communication, life sciences. India can realise its full potential only by assimilating the latest technological innovations. Given this goal, I have still a lot to do; many many more miles to cover.

⏩ Learn from Others

First and foremost, I owe my successes to all that I have learnt and imbibed from my father, Dhirubhai Ambani. He has taught us to think big, think long-term, to pursue excellence unflinchingly, and to trust people.

Secondly, I have also had the fortune of good counsel from a galaxy of well-wishers; eminent persons from various walks of life. In times of trials and triumphs, their advice and guidance have been a tremendous source of strength to me. It helped me look at the real issues and stay focused on the outcomes. Finally, I have been blessed with a large number of the dedicated colleagues, members of the Reliance family. It is on that pair of wings, their unswerving commitment to excellence and hard work – that Reliance has been able to fly to newer heights.

⏩ Create Opportunities from Obstacles

The most important lesson that I have learnt from doing business is to convert adversities into opportunities. Lessons drawn from adversities are invaluable. Reliance's history is marked with several encounters with obstacles and road-blocks. From every challenge, we have emerged that much stronger because for us, difficulty and obstacles are great teachers.

⏩ Conviction Counts

Proceed with conviction in what you do. Be passionate about achieving your goals. Combine a demanding environment with a humanitarian outlook. Most importantly, place trust in people.

⏩ Keep Track of Time

In any business dealing, there must be sincerity of purpose. Meaningful dialogues lead to positive business transactions. It is always helpful to be upfront and candid about the expectations, processes and deliverables because we regard time as a scarce resource. Money lost can be recovered. Time cost can never be regained.

Therefore, it is important to work in a time bound framework. This facilitates a purposeful and professional approach.

⏩ Fair Play Wins

In any business negotiation, it is important to make proposals that are fair to both parties and meet the aspirations of both. Success comes by marrying mutual interest and not by moves to outwit each other. Whenever I come across situations where the principle of fair play is not followed, I tend to take a hard line and attempt to strike a common ground.

⏩ Upgrade Standards

Success is a relative phenomenon. More than anything else, it sets a new standard for you to improve upon. So I always look at success as a base for future higher achievements.

⏩ Conclusion

Whether in small industry or large, problems always exist. Some face problems as if they are a challenge because that is the road to advancement. If there is no problem or challenge, we lend to feel complacent, which is the beginning of our degeneration. The problems of small industries should, therefore, be treated in this spirit. This, of course, does not mean that the government, the local bodies, financial institutions and banks should create unnecessary obstacles in the path of industrialists; nor that industrialists should function in isolation. Rather, they should be increasingly aware of the fact that they are a part of larger society, each section of which has its own strong and weak points.

In the post-independence period, the Governments as the Centre and the States have established a number of specialised institutions to cater to the varied needs of small-scale units. These promotional institutions assist all and sundry in setting up small units with a view either to fulfilling their objective or over-reach their target: but they do not ensure the provision of adequate working capital, raw materials, power supply; nor do they help them in developing marketing outlets for the sale of their products. This situation has arisen because of the absence of a meaningful co-ordination among the concerned agencies.

The entrepreneur needs to re-orient his attitude and develop special leadership qualities necessary for taking decisions based on wider implications rather than the narrow path of urge satisfying action alone. His problem, therefore, is one of growing from professional entrepreneur into a professional manager and finally into an administrator in order to successfully come out of the growth crisis which starts facing once his enterprise grows from a small business into a large enterprise.

The problems of entrepreneurs are multi-dimensional. These can be solved by the co-ordinated efforts of entrepreneurs, co-ordinated functioning of promotional agencies, and governmental assistance without red-tape or bureaucratic delays. The entrepreneur has to be educated: and he should have a proper naming in acquiring the necessary skill in running an enterprise. In fact, the entrepreneur is the kingpin of the industrial spectrum.

INTRAPRENEURIAL ACHIEVEMENT

Anjana Ghosh created a new identity to Bisleri by bringing innovaion to the brand and strategising the re-engineering of Bisleri from blue to green. She also tapped the premium brand in the water segment.

Anjana Ghosh, director of Ramesh Chauhan's Bisleri International Ltd. (BIL) joined the science stream to pursue a career in medicine, but her family could not afford it. In 1986, she had to take a detour and opted for management studies at the S.P. Jain Institute in Mumbai. "I have no regrets," she says.

Today, she looks after new business development and heads sales, marketing and brand strategy at BIL, besides carrying the responsibility for capacity planning and implementation processes. She is driving the packaged water company closer to the consumption centres. Under her stewardship, Bisleri has touched a record sale of one crore cases in 2008-09 in Mumbai, the highest by any bottled water brand in one city. Aquafina at 45 lakh cases was a far second. Her brand strategy and marketing leadership ensured that Bisleri touched 3.24 crore cases in the last fiscal year.

Ghosh has always stayed away from the rut, doing things differently. From the time she got into management studies, unlike the crowd that looked at majoring in marketing, finance or IT, she chose to go in for project planning. Her first job, via campus recruitment, landed her in a position where she had to plan and prepare feasibility reports on the potential of the market in wildlife resorts and tourism for Indian Adventures Ltd. "I always wanted to do something different. I had the option to join pharma and finance companies, but I did not," recalls Ghosh, whose first job saw her earn a stipend of Rs. 1,000 a month. "It was the magical four digit figure that lured me, the rest were below that."

In the early 1990s, three years into her wildlife job, not seeing much of a future for tourism, she spent the next three years setting up chemical intermediaries (for pesticides) in Chamundi Chemicals, then moved on to something she could not relate to – steel. "I just do not know how, but I ended up putting in over a decade in this industry; setting up plants and implementing projects across various companies In the steel industry," says Ghosh. In the steel sector she worked with companies like Graham Firth Steel, Rajendra Steels and MAN Industries.

One fine day, in 2006, she felt she had enough of steel. She sat home for two months before being headhunted for the Bisleri job. Recruited at the DGM level.

The Journey from Blue to Green

"I started to question myself. Am I at the right place and should I continue. But in my heart, I wanted a challenge," recalls Ghosh, who joined the company when the sales graph was south-bound (2004 to 2006) and Bisleri's sales was Rs. 150 crore. During this period, there were many new local brands that were being launched; Bisleri was just one amongst them. Kinley, Aquafina, etc. had also come to India. "They were all coming out with blue packaging. There was absolute turmoil in the market," says Ramesh Chauhan. "Ghosh was primarily responsible for bringing innovation to the brand and strategising the re-engineering of Bisleri from blue to green. She played an important role in the peculiar novel green we have today. Getting that shade on plastic, metal and paper is not easy. The change has been an historical and fantastic move for Bisleri," recognises Chauhan. However, after the brand re-engineering, the new and young image of a vibrant Bisleri ensured that the company's sales zoomed ahead by almost 60 per cent. In three years, sales had doubled to Rs. 380 crore (March 2009).

The journey from blue to green saw a revolution of change in the perception and demand of the brand. Realising that Bisleri did not have a presence in the natural mineral water segment despite being the first company to launch bottled water, Ghosh decided to tap this premium water segment. Thus Bisleri Mountain natural mineral water was launched with a bottling plant at Rudrapur.

Now as part of the strategy to grow the brand, Ghosh is working on market penetration through a combination of backward and forward integration. While consolidating the brand presence in the metropolitan and Class-A cities, she ensured that the brand penetrated from metros and satellite cities to B & C class cities, districts, towns and rural markets. "To increase growth we are increasing the number of bottling plants from 35 to 52 and investing Rs. 1,000 crore by 2011-12," adds Chauhan, targeting a 40 per cent growth this fiscal.

"Given the unavailability of clean drinking water, an increase in water contamination and health awareness among consumers has led to the growth of the mineral water segment. In the wake of the rising consumption of mineral water, even in the rural hinterland, there is huge opportunity for growth in India. We will tap it," concludes Ghosh, as Bisleri continues to lead in the Rs. 1,200-crore organised, mineral water market with a 60 per cent market share.

Lancelot Joseph

Source: Business India, September 20, 2009

EMPIRICAL STRATEGY

"Strategy comes from clever people who can synthesise a lot of information. you don't get strategy through analysis; it evolves out of efforts and experiments and tasks, where little ideas grow into big initiatives."

— Henry Mintsberg, Management Guru

17

Entrepreneurial Success in Rural Areas

Introduction

Promotion of rural industries and has been the central objective of many strategies adopted to bring about an equitable distribution of income through raising the productive capacity of rural people and increasing their participation in the process of development. Rural industrialisation is inter-linked with the agricultural activity.

The Concept

Rural enterpreneurship is defined as entrepreneurship emerging in villages in India. A variety of endeavours such as rural artisans, self-employed shoppers/traders, agro-based industries, khadi and village industries, cottage industries. Even farmers engaged in horticulture, floriculture can be included as rural entrepreneurs.

What is a Rural Industry?

Rural industry embraces different kinds of village and small industries. The cottage industries are an important component of rural industries. By the term "rural industry" is meant industry appropriate for the rural areas as demarcated by the census records. The concept here has a special demographic undertone. The rural industry serves the requirements of rural people as well as other markets. By and large the financial needs of rural industry are small. More, importantly, they function in the absence of infrastructural facilities and are environmentally friendly.

The term village industries has been defined as "any industry located in rural area which produces any goods or renders any service with or without the use of power and in which the fix capital investment per head of artisan or worker does not exceed Rs. 50,000 or such other sum as may be specified by Central Government from time to time." All activities which do not appear in the negative list circulated by KVIC are eligible for financing under the scheme.

Main Objectives

- To generate employment in rural areas.
- To develop entrepreneurial skill and attitude among rural unemployed youth.
- To achieve the goal of rural industrialisation.
- To facilitate participation of financial institutions for higher credit flow to rural industries.

Rural Entrepreneurs

The entrepreneur who brings in overall change through innovation, new ideas for the maximum social good in rural areas is a rural entrepreneur. Thus, the rural entrepreneur is one of the segments of rural growth. Basically, he is a person responsible for effecting change, add value to art and crafts.

In rural areas, accept agricultural labourers all are entrepreneurs with a degree of differences. Rural entrepreneurship sustains in agriculture, agricultural related activities, micro industries, small business, rural artisans and others. However, rural entrepreneurship is in a dormant stage for lack of awareness, encouragement and training.

Rural entrepreneurs are broadly classified into:

1. Agricultural Entrepreneurs
2. Micro Entrepreneurs
3. Small Business Entrepreneurs
4. Rural Artisans.

Rural Artisans

Rural artisans are creative workers living in rural areas, playing a key role in the growth of the rural economy. An artisan is a doer, skilled craftsman of either gender.

He may be a machinist, operator, driver, mechanic, minder, or simply a craftsman.

An artisan has been defined as an "artmaster", designer or draftsman. He may be an artificer, tradesman, technician, skilled or semi-skilled worker or a pastmaster.

He may be proficient, journeyman or an apprentice. The categories of craftsmen specifically mentioned are: turner, potter, joiner, cabinetmaker, carpenter, carver, woodworker etc. He can be an architect, mastermason, housebuilder, bricklayer, smith, blacksmith, coppersmith, to name a few.

Benefits of Rural Industrialisation

1. Rural industries provide additional employment opportunities, raise production and improve economic conditions in rural areas.
2. Rural industries are labour-intensive. They provide additional employment to men and women. Ensure decentralisation of economic power and elimination of monopolistic exploitation.

Originally started as a part time activity in rural areas, handicrafts have now transformed into a flourishing economic activity

3. Decentralised production through network of well-knit rural industries obviates the necessity of complicated managerial and competitive marketing techniques, thus reducing the costs on account of overheads.
4. Rural industrialisation leads to the development of rural areas thereby lessening the disproportionate growth in large cities, reducing the growth of slums, social tensions, exploitation and atmospheric pollution.
5. Rural industries will strive to build up village republics and human resources development.
6. Rural industrialisation provides ample scope for the promotion of artistic achievement and creativity that has been suppressed in rural areas.

Although, agriculture is the main stay of the rural economy, rural industry is a complementary industry. The pressure of population on land is already high and increasing. In the process, it has resulted in a large surplus of labour, both educated as well as uneducated in rural areas. Agriculture alone cannot absorb the entire surplus force and hence the need for rural industries. If we consider

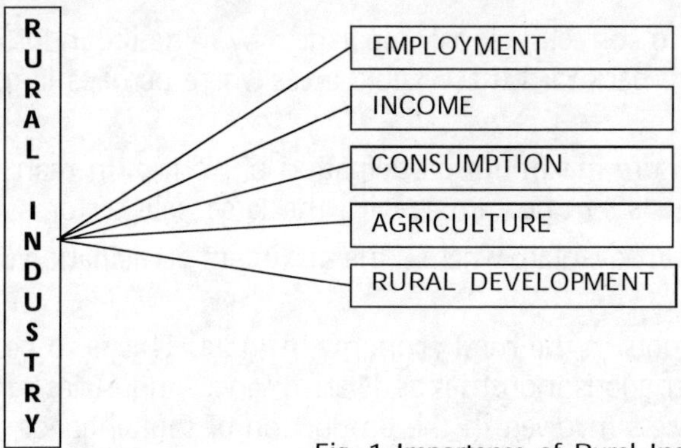

Fig. 1 Importance of Rural Industry

rural industry as a main stay, agriculture is an important part of this process. Rural industrialisation aims at the maximum productive employment of local resources, revival and development of traditional industries and skills, establishment of new units and integration of agricultural and industrial development to local prosperity, progressively narrow down the disparities between urban and rural incomes, prevent migration of rural population. More so, rural industrialisation has been assigned a crucial role in the development of industrially backward areas in rural India.

▸▸ Types of Rural Industries

By and Large, rural industries are inter-linked with agricultural activities, rural development and service sector. They may also be grouped into Small-Scale Industry/Tiny Industry and Rural Artisan (Self-Employed). The scope for process industry is vast and unexplored. The need of the hour is to propel organisation of rural industries and integrate them into the rural ethos and development.

▸▸ Importance of Rural Industrialisation

Rural industrialisation is important not only as a means of generating employment opportunities in the rural areas with low capital cost and raising the real income of the people, but because it contributes to the development of agriculture and urban industries. Without rural industrialisation, it would be considerably more difficult to solve the problem of agricultural unemployment and widespread underemployment. Rural industrialisation promotes rural industry. The development of rural industries increases the level of income in rural areas, and tends to break down the old self-sufficiency of the family and lessen its cohesiveness, creating opportunities for youth, women and the able bodied as well in changing the pattern of leisure and work. Rural industrialisation should be looked upon not merely as way of containing the rural workers and stopping them from migrating to urban areas by providing them some kind of remunerative employment in the villages, but as a dynamic element in process of raising the productivity and income levels of the workers in areas.

The main characteristics of these industries are to develop local initiative cooperation and spirit of self-reliance in the economy and at the same time, help in utilisation of the available manpower for processing locally available raw materials by adopting simple techniques.

These are capable of offering employment opportunities at the place of residence to a large section of population.

The village industries are an antidote to the widespread problems of disguised unemployment or underemployment.

These decentralised industries require less gestation period on the one hand and produce goods of common necessities on the other.

These industries have the capacity to correct regional imbalances by initiating industrial activities on dispersed basis in the most neglected, backward inaccessible areas where perhaps large-scale sector is unable to penetrate.

Being small, these activities can ensure maximum participation of workers in management thus ensuring a feeling of involvement which is so uncommon with the large-scale sector,

These industries possess an additional advantage wherein the maximum participation of womenfolk can he ensured.

Rural industrialisation has taken roots in the rural economy in India. This is so because simple forms of manufacture typical of consumer goods industries and varied service industries, are everywhere developed before the more complex process involved in the production of capital goods, and because the size of the home market at the time of industrialisation prohibits the establishment of optimum-sized plants in the production of certain capital goods.

Towards Rural Prosperity

Rural industrialisation is a key to rural development and rural prosperity. It constitutes a significant link in the process of socio-economic transformation of rural areas. Primarily, it provides additional opportunities of employment, income, better standard of living and thereby enriches the cultural heritage of the various social structures in rural areas. Rural Industries programme should not be drawn in isolation. It should be drawn up keeping in mind the long-term industrial development plan under a broad framework for developing not only manufacturing industries but also industry related activities to generate income and employment in the country, particularly for the vulnerable section of the society in backward regions. The development of rural industries should also take into account of enriching the environment, particularly the eco-system in the rural hinterland. Yet another policy measure adopted and implemented shall be to use products manufactured by rural industries in preference to imported goods, particularly in urban market segment. This will open up a vast market both in urban as well as rural areas for the goods manufactured by rural industries and pave the way for its rapid growth in the coming years.

Table 1

DETAILS OF RURAL INDUSTRIES PROGRAMME

States	***Districts***	***Agency***
Madhya Pradesh	Betul & Dhar	Centre for Entrepreneurship Development, Madhya Pradesh (CEDMAP), Bhopal
Chattisgarh	Raipur	Centre for Entrepreneurship Development, Madhya Pradesh (CEDMAP), Bhopal
Jharkhand	Hazaribagh & Koderma	Nav Bharat Jagriti Kendra (NBJK), Hazaribagh
	Palamu	ACIL Navsarjan Rural Development Foundation (ANARDE Foundation), Mumbai
	Ranchi	Society for Human Ability and Right Endeavour (SHARE), Ranchi
Bihar	Bhagalpur	Science & Technology Entreprcneurship Development Project (STEOP), Bhagalpur
	Buxar	Asian Society for Entrepreneurship Education & Development (ASEEO), New Delhi
	Vaishali & Muzaffarpur	EDA Rural Systems, Gurgaon
Orissa	Mayurbhanj, Balasore, Bhadrak & Jaipur	Organisation for Social Change and Rural Development (OSCARD), Bhubaneshwar
	Nayagarh & Keonjhar	Centre for Development Research & Training (CENDRET), Bhubaneshwar
Uttar Pradesh	Mirzapur	Asian Society for Entrepreneurship Education & Development (ASEED), New Delhi
	Pratapgarh	Society for Entrepreneurship, Environment & Human Resource Devclopment (SEEHURD), New Delhi
	Etah	Integrated Management Group (IMG), Lucknow
	Ghazipur	Purvanchal Grameen Kalyan Sansthan (PGKS). Ghazipur
	Varanasi (Rural) Jaunpur	IEDUP, Lucknow

Tamil Nadu	Salem & Namakkal	Industrial and Technical Consultancy Organisation of Tamil Nadu Ltd. (ITCOT), Chennai
Rajasthan	Alwar Bharatpur Jaipur, Ajmer & Dausa Jhalawar	Matashree Gomati Devi Jan Seva Nidhi, Fort Road, Rajgarh, Alwar Lupin Human Welfare Research Foundation (LHWRF), Bharatpur EDA Rural Systems, Gurgaon Shri Pramod Paliwal, Indian Institute for Rural Development (IIRD), Jaipur
Karnataka	Bijapur & Shimoga Dharwad & Hassan Udupi	"Association of Women Entrepreneurs of Karnataka (AWAKE), Bangalore Centre for Entrepreneurship Development of Karnataka (CEDOK). Dharwad Rural Development and Self Employment Training Institute (RUDSETI). Ujire, Karnataka
Assam	Barpeta	Indian Institute of Entrepreneurship (IIE), Guwahati, Assam
Himachal Pradesh	Kangra & Kullu	Himachal Consultancy Organisation Ltd. (HIMCON), Shimla
Andhra Pradesh	Anantapur, Warangal, Chittoor, Karimnagar, Vizianagaram & East Godavari Nellore	Andhra Pradesh Industrial Technical Consultancy Organisation Ltd. (APITCO). Hyderabad Shri M.V. Ramanan, Principal Director, Andhra Pradesh Productivity Council, Hyderabad
West Bengal	Maida & Murshidabad Howrah Midnapore	Shri Sanjay Sinha, Director, EDA Rural Systems, Gurgaon West Bengal Consultancy Ltd. (WEBCON), Kolkata Midnapore Planning & Development Society (MPDS), Midnapore
Sikkim	East & South District	Sikkim Consultancy Centre (SICON)
Gujarat	Bhachau region of Kutch District	Shri Pramod Paliwal, Indian Institute for Rural Developmcnt
Jaipur	West Tripura District	Tripura Industrial Development Corporation (TIDC)

Source: SIDBI.

⏩ A Mass Movement

The programme for rapid growth of rural industries should be launched like a mass movement, with the emphasis on rural brand. Efforts should be made to carry the message of rural development to the rural people. This apart, a sure market is created for the rural consumer goods. And, the urban and international markets are developed for artistic works. The rural industrialisation is an integral part of the overall rural economy and it will hasten the integrated rural development.

The traditional village industries and crafts continue to play a pivotal role in providing new markets, particularly in case of handicrafts, handlooms and other varied crafts. However, till today, the rural potential has not been effectively utilised. Besides, a number of industrial activities have begun to play a significant role in the generation of employment and income in rural areas. Most of these activities have been economically more rewarding than the traditional ones, and have been providing remunerative employment and shown a relatively better growth potential. The emerging pattern of rural industries and their relative performance, therefore, indicate that rural industrialisation is an effective means for the generation of growth and employment in rural areas by utilising the potential new industries and of the traditional ones.

Need for Rural Entrepreneurship

The need for developing rural entrepreneurship is to promote rural development in the country. This is justified as follows:

1. Rural industries being labour intensive serve as an antedate to the widespread problems of rural disguised unemployment and underemployment stalking the rural areas.
2. The development of rural industries by providing jobs to rural unemployed helps in reducing disparities in income between rural and urban areas.
3. These industries promote balanced regional development by dispersing industries to rural areas.
4. Development of rural industries serves as an effective means to build up village republics.
5. Rural industries also help preserve the age-old rich heritage of the country by protecting and promoting art and creativity.
6. Rural industrialisation fosters economic development in rural areas. This checks migration from rural to urban areas, on the one hand, and lessens the disproportionate growth in the cities, reduces growth of slums, social tensions, and atmospheric pollution, on the other.
7. Rural industries also lead to development without destruction of the environment.

Box 1

ON FOR A TRANSFORMATION

SourcePilani, a rural enterprise in Pilani, Rajasthan provides high quality, low cost backoffice services in the areas of medical transcription, form processing, lead generation/tele-surveys and vernacular voice services. SourcePilani was founded in 2007 with a vision of bridging the digital divide and to generate employment and wealth among the rural masses.

"I did my studies from BITS Pilani and knew the rural dynamics very well. There is abundance of talent which goes untapped in Pilani. The business model made a lot of sense since we were extending the BPO industry landscape into rural India to be more competitive in the market in terms of pricing. Also, we provide an opportunity to corporates to engage in a transformed CSR activity by outsourcing to an organisation like us employing a 100% rural workforce," explains Manoj Vasudevan, CEO, SourcePilani.

Even though Vasudevan managed to source the seed capital from the Goenka Group, there were other challenges for him. "One of the biggest challenges was the telecom infrastructure problem. The only internet service provider in Pilani was BSNL and we applied for an office broadband connection in the first week of our inception. But they made delays and we did not have an internet connection for three whole months. This was in spite of one of our person going to their regional office in Jhunjhunu (50 kms away) everyday. Finally, we wrote to the Union Telecom Minister complaining about this issue and within a week, the connection was up and running," I explains Vasudevan about the initial hiccups. He believes that things like this can really deter the passionate entrepreneur and it's really important to weather out the storm whenever you encounter one.

According to Vasudevan, it is much harder to execute a rural venture rather than a venture in a city. We need to take into account the rural dynamics rural people have, special set of needs and aspirations which have to be nurtured and protected. The employer-employee relationship can become very volatile since we are bringing employment to their doorsteps. Also, rural areas are majorly politicised environments which mean having to deal with emotionally charged people. "With recession kicking in, I think there will be more focus on greener ideas and ideas that focus on social entrepreneurship," believes Vasudevan.

Mahatma Gandhi said the soul of India lies in the villages and these entrepreneurs are going by his words and are trying to provide better lives for the millions in small towns, thereby benefiting the country at large.

KHADI AND VILLAGE INDUSTRIES

The development of village and khadi industries provides opportunities for work, albeit part-time work, in certain cases, and thereby helps to mitigate the severity of rural unemployment and underemployment. With this end in view, the Khadi and Village Industries Commission (KVIC) was established in April 1957, under the Khadi and Village Industries Commission Act, 1956.

Under the guidance of Mahatma Gandhi, provisional activities of Khadi were started in 1922, when they were symbolic of the "Fight for Freedom." The Khadi Programme was thus closely linked with the struggle for freedom. The All-India Congress Committee, then known as the All-India Spinners' Association (AISA), was established in 1925 to organise hand-spinning and hand-weaving. This was followed by the establishment of another organisation in 1935, called the All-India Village Industries Association (AIVA), to look after other village industries such as hand-pounding of paddy, ghana oil, palm gur, bee-keeping, hand-made paper, etc. The establishment of the Khadi Commission was the culmination of the efforts to organise cottage/village industries during the freedom movement. In 1951, the Saiva Seva Sangh took over the work of AISA and AIVA, as a part of an integrated plan for rural industrialisation.

The Government of India evolved a general policy frame for the development of these industries. In the First Plan, these industries were treated as an integral part of agriculture; and the emphasis was on local consumption. In the Second Plan, on the advice of the Village and Small-Scale Industries Committee (Karve), 1955, and in consonance with the Industrial Policy Resolution of 1956, Khadi and Village Industries programmes were made an integral part of the whole plan for the country's industrialisation. The Third Plan retained the emphasis on these programmes while highlighting the need for an integrated approach. In the successive plans, the emphasis unit policy were shifted from one of protection of such industries to positive forms of assistance, such as improving skills, supplying technical guidance, better equipment and adequate credit with a view to increasing productivity and reducing cost.

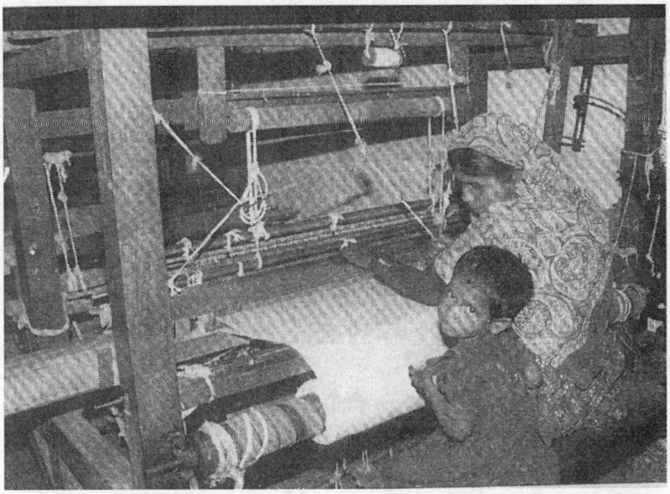

The Government is committed to the encouragement of the production of textiles and textile products in the khadi sector. Considering its large employment potential, it would be the endeavour of the Government to make the products of this sector more competitive and of better quality.

The infrastructure for the distribution of controlled cloth, particularly in rural areas, will be strengthened and streamlined. State Governments will be encouraged to open more rural outlets and exercise stricter control over distribution.

Functions of KVIC

The functions of KVIC also comprise building up a reserve of raw materials and implements for supply to producers, creation of common service of facilities for processing, marketing and training.

- To promote the sale and marketing of Khadi products of village industries or handicrafts, the KVIC may forge lines with established marketing agencies wherever necessary and feasible.
- The KVIC is also charged with the responsibility of encouraging and promoting research in the production techniques employed in the khadi and village industries sector and providing facilities for the study of the problems relating to it including the use of non-conventional

energy and electric power with a view to increasing productivity eliminating drudgery and otherwise enhancing their competitive capacity and to arrange for dissemination of salient results obtained from such research.

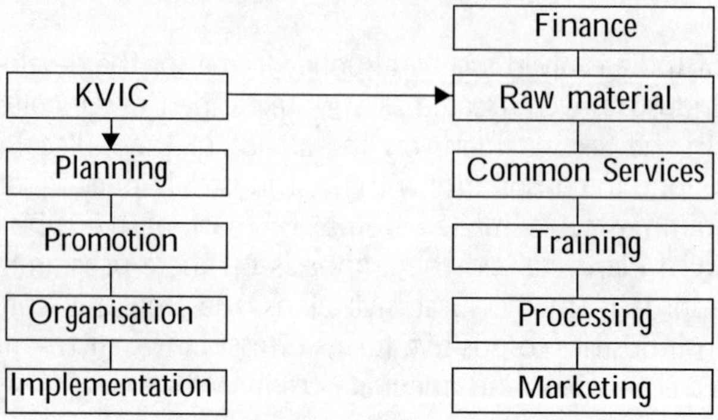

Fig. 2 Functions of KVIC

- Further, the KVIC is entrusted with the task of providing financial assistance to institutions or persons engaged in the development and operation of Khadi and Village industries and guiding them through supply of design, prototypes and other technical information.
- In implementing KVI activities the KVIC may take such steps as to ensure genuineness of the products and to setup standards of quality and ensure that the products of khadi and village industries do conform to the standards including issue of certificates or letters of recognition to the concerned.
- The KVIC may also undertake directly or through other agencies studies concerning the problems of khadi or village industries besides experiments or pilot projects for the development of khadi and village industries.
- The KVIC is authorised to establish and maintain separate organisations for the purpose of carrying out any or all of the above matters besides carrying out any other matters incidental to its activities.

Strategy of Rural Industrialisation

The framework of a strategy of rural industrialisation should consist of attempts towards rejuvenation of traditional village industries by bringing improvement in their technology, dispersal of modern manufacturing activity in the countryside with or without a linkage to the existing village industries as also production of any type of commodities that would cater to the needs of the country's population and that may or may not be based on the local resources. The rural industries would continue to be supplementary source of income as well as part/full time employment activity for the rural artisans, landless labourers, women and educated unemployed. Progressive expansion and modernisation of rural industry could be best brought out by the establishment of small industrial units along with (the necessary services in large villages and small towns located all over the country.

The non-traditional industries also seem to be capable of breaking the caste-industry nexus and reducing the rigidities of social stratification in rural areas. Their entrepreneurs come from a wider cross-section of rural society, while the caste-industry identification has been more or less complete in the traditional industries. In fact, the growth of rural industries, based primarily on traditional occupations, may well accentuate the social distance among the caste groups, despite the betterment they may bring about in the economic conditions of artisans and craftsmen. No doubt, even non-traditional activities exhibit concentration by social groups, though to a smaller extent than the traditional industries; but such concentration is primarily based on class distinction in terms of ownership resources, rather than on the traditional caste-occupation association.

Most rural industries, however, have a limited capacity for generating even as subsistence income for those engaged in them and have not shown a very encouraging record of growth in the recent past. Only blacksmith, carpentry and handloom have shown a good promise in so far as the value added per worker and their dependents. The new industries – wire-meshing, lampshade and hub-brush manufacturing – meet the criterion easily; and food and oil products, the two old industries but run on modern lines and on a larger scale, have brought prosperity and affluence to their entrepreneurs.

The basic reason for their low income-generating capacity lies in their tiny size in terms of their physical volume of output. Most units are run on a household basis, and do provide full employment to all the household workers. Low level of productivity, prevalence of traditional technology, lack of knowledge of the new innovations and development in the field of production, inadequate infrastructure, inadequate finance, absence of marketing skills, lethargy, inefficiency, non-availability of skills and entrepreneurial ability, administrative snags have been enumerated as the constraints in the task.

The supply of raw materials, which mostly are a free gift of nature, has already started posing a problem, and is likely to taper off with the passage of time. It is, therefore, essential to concentrate on the development of such traditional rural industries as have a positive income elasticity of demand for their products and are not faced with the danger of inevitable extinction, such as have potential for the technological flexibility which is necessary before they are able to cope with the changes in the demand pattern. Blacksmith, carpentry, handloom and leather products fit quite well in this category. In order, however, that rural industrialisation becomes an effective tool for the development of rural areas as well as for the better integration of the rural and urban sectors, equal emphasis should be laid on the development of non-traditional industries in this areas. Many of them may not be linked with rural areas in terms either of use of local materials or of having a local market, but would be effective in providing productive employment to rural labour.

Rural industrialisation should be looked upon as a dynamic process in raising the productivity and income levels of people in rural areas. It should also be looked upon as means of rural development. The first issue relates to the treatment of rural industrialisation is an aspect of industrial location or as a programme primarily for the development of rural areas. The long-term strategy of rural industrialisation would require not merely the development of traditional rural industries, but also a programme of infusing increasingly a larger component of modern consumer and other industries in rural areas. The promotion and development of 'dynamic' rural industries, no doubt, needs emphasis, but in the interest of long-term growth on a sustained basis, rural industrialisation should be looked upon as an integral part of the programme of rural development. It means effective linkages with the medium and large industries in urban areas.

Further, it is important not only to accelerate development of rural area, but also to reduce the economic and technological gap between rural and urban areas, and seek to achieve a greater degree of integration between the two. The development of low technology and low productivity industries located in rural areas should generate not only linkages, to the extent possible, in the villages, but become a link in rural-urban integration. Besides reducing the income gap between the two sectors, it is also desirable that rural industries use technologies which are in line with the technological pattern of the emerging industrial structure in the country as a whole. The upgradation of relatively modern-technology industries in rural areas alone are likely to make rural industries an integral part of the industrialisation process in the country. The technology used in rural industries varies terms of the use of machinery, equipment, non-human energy, and, therefore, of capital intensity; but, by and large, the activities in which mechanical devices and capital equipment are used yield a reasonable income only to those who are engaged in them. At the same time, the use of such devices and equipment neither turn these industries into "capital intensive" nor reduce the employment potential. It only makes employment more effective in terms of income generation.

One of the reasons which accounts for the fact that the productivity and income aspects of rural industries have received less attention than employment creation lies in the assumption that these industries are subsidiary activities on the part of the households, for which agriculture or some other activities is their main occupation; and therefore, they only reduce underemployment and supplement their income from their major activity. In fact, however, this assumption is not valid. For the households and workers engaged in rural industries, their occupation in them is their sole or at least the main source of income. Most of them do not even have another activity as a subsidiary occupation. These industries will, therefore, have to be seen as the effective means of providing full employment and as the only source of income for those engaged in them. The need for industrial employment on a full-time basis is likely to increase, for the development of agriculture, even if rapid, will absorb only a part of the increasing rural labour force.

It is necessary to spell out the concept of rural industrialisation. It begins with the assessment of resources, human and material, locally available in a selected area. Assessment is also made of the pattern of demand. Present and future and an area-wise production plan is formulated for ensuring minimum needs of the people by using local resources, skill and appropriate technology.

As rural industries play an important role in national economy, particularly in rural economy, modernisation and improvement of efficiency of these industries has assumed greater importance. A main element in the success of the modernisation programme is to train and bring awareness about the new technology to the people who will implement it. As rural industries increase in progress, in number and diversity, and as their share of industrial production begins to grow, it becomes even more important that they improve efficiency in their operations. Five main elements in the success of these programmes are: the orientation of the rural entrepreneurs and rural artisans to a more forward-looking approach and flexibility of loan basis to meet the cost of modernisation and the role of appropriate technology and marketing in modernisation and improvement efficiency of rural industries. The basis objective of the programme is to set the rural industries – traditional and non-traditional – on a path of growth so that they are able to complete, on more equal terms, with the urban industries.

New Initiatives

- Decentralisation of the implementation of the scheme by making payment of margin money through State Offices and State KVI Boards.
- Fixation of targets for projects and Margin Money for all field offices based on Rural Population of the State.
- Financing of units based on coir as raw material was allowed.
- Financing of auto-rickshaws in Andaman and Nicobar Islands, house boat, shikara and tourist boat in Jammu and Kashmir were also allowed under rural transport, keeping in view the special requirement of these States.
- For providing information/guidance to the new entrepreneurs, REGP helping counters were opened in all the field offices of the Commission and the State KVI Boards.

Box 1

PROBLEMS FACED BY RURAL ENTERPRISES

Small-scale enterprises quite often face distinctive problems. These are:

1. Difficulty in obtaining credit from commercial banks because of their general inability to provide security.
2. Inability to offer liberal credit terms in the sale of their products.
3. Absence of management expertise. Often management is by one person who performs a number of functions usually with no formal training.
4. Difficulty in competing with imported products due to high production costs.
5. Difficulty with competition from other local entrepreneurs in the same line of business competing for the limited local market.
6. Difficulty in obtaining industrial land in towns and cities. The shortage of industrial land is giving rise to more and more backward operations.
7. Under capitalisation.
8. Difficulty in identifying appropriate technology and technical assistance.
9. The manner in which both the needs of the economy and linkage with existing industry can best be served.
10. Bureaucratic red tape and regulations.
11. Surveys of the material and human resources of the countries to identify the regions or areas for the development of small-scale and medium-scale industrial enterprises.
12. Identification of industrial projects for development.
13. Project preparation and evaluation.
14. Financial or credit support and investment promotion.
15. Consultancy and counselling services.
16. Technology development and applications such as, the designing of proto type machines for products identified according to country resources and requirements.
17. Development of infrastructure of various kinds in the appropriate areas.
18. Entrepreneurship development.
19. Industrial training and skill formation.
20. Linkages between large industries and small industries and the creation of sub-contracting facilities at the national, regional and international levels.
21. Quality control and testing facilities.
22. Market promotion, both domestic and export.
24. Scientific and industrial research.
25. Information collection and dissemination on technology, markets etc.
26. Identification of and assistance to enterprises which are experiencing difficulties.
27. Management and reorganization or restructuring of small- and/or medium-scale enterprises through various schemes.
28. Productivity increases through modernisation.
29. Incentive measures, by industry and by area.
30. Local initiative.
31. Creation of institutions and changes in prevailing institutional arrangements.
32. Regional and international technical and financial assistance.
33. Co-operation among the developing countries.

- For payment of margin money besides 33 States KVI Boards, 346 number of model branches of Public Sector Banks were identified. They were provided margin money in advance on quarterly basis.
- Training to all KVIC/KVIB's field offices staff was provided to acquaint them with the implementation of the programme.
- Extensive publicity programme was made through workshops, awareness camps, exhibitions etc.
- A system of awarding best banks, field officers and the staff for their contribution to the programme was introduced. Awards to Punjab National Bank, Central Bank of India and Oriental Bank of Commerce have been given under this scheme. Awards to KVIC Officers and staff were also given in recognition to their active performances in implementation of the REGP scheme.

Steps to Boost Rural Enterpreneurship

The following measures have to be taken to give a fillip to rural entrepreneurship:

(*i*) Promoting rural industries in a big way.
(*ii*) Give a fillip to rural artisans.
(*iii*) Widening rural business and trade.
(*iv*) Modernising rural indusrial sector.
(*v*) Upgrading rural skills.
(*vi*) Continuous supply of raw materials.
(*vii*) Training rural entrepreneurs.
(*ix*) Instilling self-confidence.
(*x*) Providing adequate and timely finance.
(*xi*) Exploring new domestic and international markets for their products.
(*xii*) Imbibing professional management skills.
(*xiii*) Simplifying licencing provisions.
(*xiv*) Feeding them with new ideas/products collected through market reserch/surveys.
(*xv*) Popularising their products through fairs and exhibitions.
(*xvi*) Establishing common marketing complexes in every block.
(*xvii*) Give stress on vocational awareness.
(*xix*) Popularise various self-employment.
(*xx*) Initiate creative interaction.

Necessary Corrective Action

Rural industrialisation constitutes the key link in the process of socio-economic transformation of underdeveloped rural areas as well as social structures. In view of its importance and problems, it is necessary to take some corrective actions to rejuvenate rural industries and rural artisans to play a pivotal role in the development process.

Some of the necessary ingredients of successful rural industrialisation may be briefly stated as follows: (1) The industry should be based on locally available resources. (2) There should be rural-urban, local-national, and, wherever possible, even foreign trade, linkages. The concept of "village republics" is no longer valid. (3) There should be comprehensive planning, especially with regard to the availability of ready markets. (4) There should be a nationwide organisation, with separate sections for each product or group of products which are produced in the rural industrial sector. The existing organisations like the Khadi and Village Industries Board, Handlooms Board and Handicrafts Board can be utilised for the products which they are already handling. (5) Up-to-date technology should be used so that the industrial units can be competitive; obsolete technologies should not be adopted in the name of "appropriate technology" etc. (6) While the government may provide necessary benefits, the units should be set up on a cooperative basis or through individual enterprise, and not by government departments.

Conclusion

The programme of rural industrialisation has endeavoured to take industrial and manufacturing activity to the rural areas through a process of dispersal as also developing on sound footing the existing traditional units thereby creating an industrial climate in the countryside. For effecting this creation of growth centres and provision of infrastructural facilities in the rural areas should be planned carefully. Setting up of nucleus plants in districts or potential block level will promote as many ancillary, small and cottage units, as possible. The interlinkages will strive for integrated industrial development in rural area. Development of focal points in specific regions by providing different kinds of complementary facilities on the lines of Punjab is considered worth emulating. This will facilitate better balancing, greater optimal use of resources, better control and higher productivity and profitability. And, setting up of agro-industrial services complexes and non-traditional industries in planned manner will lead to gradual urbanisation of the rural areas. This will in turn stop migration from the villages and may enable return flow of skilled manpower to rural areas. Rural industrialisation is, therefore, integral part of rural development. A 'cluster of villages' approach would also be beneficial if adopted sagaciously and without undue interference of exogenous elements. Thus, rural industrialisation provides the necessary impetus to rapid rural development.

Initiating an entrepreneurial venture in rural area or a small town is a daunting task. But today, the number of entrepreneurs tapping the opportunities available are on a steady rise. The will power to overcome challenges and a strong passion to make a difference in the lives of thousands residing in rural areas is making these entrepreneurs strive for excellence. The growth of entrepreneurship in rural areas provides answers to innumerables ills prevailing in rural areas and placing it on growth path.

In short, entrepreneurial success in rural areas will assist in eradicating rural poverty, increase employment opportunities, raise the per capita income level and improve living standards significantly.

RE-ENGINEERING INGENUITY

"It takes a long time for a new idea to penetrate organisations and to be turned from theory into reality. Even companies continue to extend the idea of re-engineering to apply it to new areas, to get new kinds of benefits from it. Re-engineering today is much bigger, broader and deeper than it was ten years ago." — ***Michael Hammer, Re-engineering Guru***

18

Innovation and Entrepreneur

Introduction

Entrepreneur, entrepreneurship and innovation are not born characteristics. These are competencies that an organisation can learn. The crux of the issue is to combine managerial practices with the acts of innovation to create entrepreneurs and institutionalise entrepreneurship.

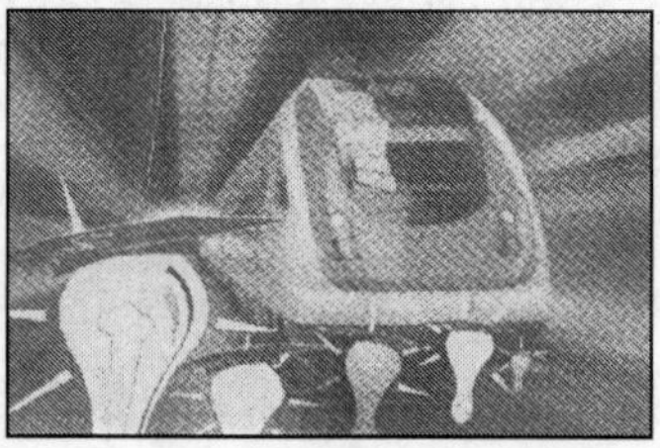

Innovation has been a key to the success of practically every entrepreneur. Essentially, entrepreneurs are innovators. Peter Drucker in his famous book 'Innovation and Entrepreneurship' says, "Innovation is the specific instrument of entrepreneurship. It is the act that endows resources with a new capacity to create wealth." That's about the crux of it.

In a highly competitive business environment, firms – particularly SMEs – need to maintain their competitive edge. They need to keep upgrading their speed and quality continuously. And SMEs have to do it with limited resources. This is where innovation comes into play. "SMEs need to counter the advantage of size and scale, that big companies have, by showing an ability to innovate and respond at a faster pace than others," says Sashi Reddi, Founder CEO of AppLabs.

However, innovation is more than the transforming an idea into a product. It has to be based on market understanding and be backed by appropriate management skills, technology and of course by money flow. Moreover, it is not only about improving a product; it can also be applied for improving a process.

When Henry Ford introduced his famous assembly line production, it was actually a process innovation. "Optimal utilisation of the resources is the only way that these organisations (SMEs) can address the competition and growth challenges. It calls for adopting newer technologies to improve the process and system around those resources," says Biswa B. Das, Country Sales Manager, Blue Star Infotech. In fact, as Mr. Das adds, "Information technology can be a great business enabler" by which an organisation can gear up its processes to meet the challenges of a competitive market.

Innovation can never happen in isolation. It is a dynamic force that is moved by the ideas and requirements of the world that we live in. Many times, innovations bring about a big change and many times innovations happen as a reaction to change. The invention of television shook up Hollywood. But one man saw opportunity in it. His name was Walt Disney. The advent of television inspired him to build the world's first media company that transformed his cartoon creations into money making toys. Little wonder that Walt Disney 'believed in being an innovator.'

Look at some of the biggest success stories back home in India and you would see that it is all about innovation. From Jamshedji Tata to Dhirubhai Ambani and from Laxmanrao Kirloskar to Azim Premji, the word innovation occurs in their story in bold letters. These are big names. But they all started small and built their empires through innovation.

Many SMEs too are today dreaming big because they believe in their dreams, and in innovation. For example, Mumbai based Intelligent Business Systems (IBS) brings innovation through artificial intelligence (AI). In fact, it is the only company in this space in the country as of now. Co-founded by Dr. Kautubh Chokshi, IBS develops AI based enterprise solutions. "We provide analytic applications" or business, incorporating cutting-edge AI technologies," says Dr. Chokshi. "Our latest innovation is called Shadow, an intelligent inventory management system," he adds. The innovation lies in the fact that Shadow goes beyond inventory management; it also helps in asset and document management.

Innovation and entrepreneur are two sides of the same coin. Both are intimately interrelated and correlated to each other. Innovation is the crux of entrepreneurship. It helps in developing entrepreneurial base of the country through application of newly-created things into practical use. According to Schumpeter, entrepreneurship is a creative activity and entrepreneur is essentially an innovator. Innovation manifests itself in problem-solving activities wherein entrepreneur acts as a problem solver. He is the person who converts the problems into opportunities. His role is to do the things in a novel and better way. It is a fact that a businessman who behaves in traditional ways hardly becomes an entrepreneur. Thus, in Schumpeter's opinion, the dream and the will to establish a private kingdom, will to conquer and finally the joy of creating, getting things done or simply exercising one's energy and ingenuity are the motives that inspire the innovative entrepreneur to undertake innovator.

Innovation implies doing new things or doing of things that are already being done in a new way. It includes introduction of new products, creation of new markets, application of new method of production, discovery of new and better sources of raw materials and developing a new and better form of industrial organisation. Innovation may be leased on the application of knowledge produced by research. Innovation is different from invention. Invention implies discovery of new ideas, new products and new methods whereas innovation refers to the application of inventions to make new combinations and thereby produce satisfaction and profit. Invention may facilitate innovations but invention is of little use to mankind unless it is marketable. An invention becomes an innovation only when it is embodied in a product or service that can be successfully sold in the market. Entrepreneur exploits the invention commercially and thus produces newer and better goods which give him profit and satisfaction.

Innovation means "doing new things or the doing of things that are already being done in a new way." It includes new processes of production, introduction of new products, creation of new markets, discovery of a new and better form of industrial organisation. Risk-bearing means making provisions for capital in order to enable the entrepreneur to establish and run the enterprise. An important function of an entrepreneur is to reduce uncertainty in his plan of investment and expansion of the enterprise. Thus innovations may occur in the following forms:

1. Introduction of a new good, that is, one which consumers are not yet familiar with or of a new quality of a good.
2. Introduction of a new method of production, founded upon a discovery scientifically new and can also exist in a new way of handling a commodity commercially.
3. Opening of a new market, that is, a market into which the particular branch of manufacture of the country in question has not previously entered, whether or not this market has existed before.
4. Conquest of a new source of supply of raw materials or half-manufactured goods, irrespective of whether this source already exists or whether it has first to be created.
5. Carrying out of the new organisation of any industry, like the creation of a monopoly position (for example, through trustification) or the breaking of a monopoly position.

Before coming to other functions, it is necessary to clarify how innovation differs from the two other notions with which it is sometimes confused: research and invention.

The aim of research is to produce knowledge, that of innovation to produce objects which work and can be sold. Since it is inspired by different objectives, innovation can be completely independent of research. It is not based on the same skills. Even the relevant information required on markets, on patents and on management has title to do with research. Innovation may be based on the application of knowledge produced by research but it may also be purely empirical: indeed practice often precedes theory and innovation may open the way to research (the steam engine for thermodynamics, or the computer for programming). Moreover, many innovation are not based on research but on ingenious combinations of existing materials and components.

Invention too, is different from innovation. An invention becomes an innovation only when it is embodied in a product which can be successfully marketed. History abounds in examples of bankrupt inventors whose brainchild took hold years later. The innovator, on the other hand, is the person who comes on the scene at the right moment to find the missing element in an invention which will make it eminently marketable. Thus, it is always difficult to identify the true innovator.

Several individuals or organisations may simultaneously claim the authorship of ideas or inventions which have given rise to innovation.

Innovation cannot be confined to a simplistic scheme. Facts show that small and medium firms, at least in some countries, can make a very significant contribution to technical prosperity. For instance, it is estimated that firms of less than 1000 workers and individual inventors were responsible for more than 40 per cent of the major innovations appearing in the United States in the early 1970s. This innovation potential can be explained by the advantages enjoyed by small firms over large ones.

Box 1

WHAT IS INNOVATION?

Global competitive pressures, emerging economies, saturated domestic markets and demanding customers have brought companies to a dire crossroad – innovate or die. As companies embark on their innovation journcy, some adopt innovation is a tag line in their advertising; others appoint executives in charge of innovation. Nearly any and every action taken by a company is now loosely labelled as innovation. However, very few companies actually innovate!

To begin with, innovation is not incrementalism. Given the hypercompetitive marketplace, there is nothing called incremental innovation. There is just innovation and it is radical! Either you innovate or you don't. Innovation is not a management fad, but a philosophy that should permeate throughout a company. Innovation should be disruptive to the company's core, competition and industry – but not disruptive to its customers. A company can tell it has embarked on true innovation when its efforts net abnormal rate of return on investment.

Innovation is not invention either. A lot of smart companies are very good at developing new offering in the hope that the customers will buy them. This "engineering-friendly" view of "build and they will come" innovation is no longer going to cut it. Customers demand products that suit their notion of what is valuable. This requires engaging the customer in the product/service design process and observIng how they would use the "potential" innovation in their context. Some of the best innovations meet not only the needs expressed by customers, but also their unexpressed needs.

Nor is innovation just new products. Often companies restrict their view of innovation to introduction of new products and services. There are several types of innovation possible. At the foundational level is the process innovation – delivering same products and services in a more effective and efficient way or creating new products and services. Experimental innovation involves allowing customers to consume offerings in a context that is unique (example, Starbucks). These types of innovation in conjunction with each other are the building blocks for the highest form of innovation – business model innovation – whereby a company changes the rules of its industry or creates a whole new industry.

Innovation is not complexity. Often companies equate innovation with coming up with even more complex products and scrvices – the Swiss army knife effect. However, customers demand products and services that are intuitive and meet their needs. Instead of cramming more features into products that don't do anything well, companies should be creating "simple and easy" offerings that do a few things really well. Innovation also requires a design mindset that ensures that the "potential" innovation fits with the life processes of customers rather than have customers adjust their life style to the innovation. The less pain caused to the customer, the more is the gain from the innovation.

Innovation is not just R&D's domain. Companies spend inordinate amount of resources on R&D and have a very poor success rate to show for it. The thinking that R&D is responsible for innovation stymies and stagnates a company. To be honest, R&D is geared towards improving what they have already developed in the past. Coming up with something "radically" new would be admitting that the previous product/service was flawed. Innovation is everyone's business in a company (especially those closest to the customers) if it is to be seriously pursued. Further, "in"novation (inside the company) has to give way to "ex"novation (including external constituencies in the innovation process). In order to satisfy customer needs, companies have to look for solutions (help) from business partners and sources that are not exclusive to the company. Innovating is a complex process (mind you, that does not mean that the innovation has to be complex). The more help and sources of ideas, the better the chances of market success.

THE DISCIPLINE OF INNOVATION

We live in a period of very rapid change. That also means that the opportunities for improving, for getting results, are changing very fast.

The discipline of innovation means having a clear mission. It means defining what you mean by results. It means the ability and willingness to abandon where you don't get results. And then – when you find the real opportunity, the unique opportunity where you can make the greatest difference, zone in on it, and reassess and reassess and reassess. This is a discipline. This is not being brilliant, it's being conscientious. This is not looking at needs alone, it's looking at need and opportunity. We need to define what results we are after, and to assess and stress what we're doing and how we're doing it constantly to make sure that we put our scarce resources of people and money where we get the most for them.

In a rapidly changing society innovation is badly needed because the problems are changing. All societies need the community organisation that is out to make a difference, the organisation that works on the local level with local volunteers and gives them opportunities to contribute. These volunteers are successful people, but they need significance and to have results, especially results that show all of us that we can make a difference, we can change things .... This is what the discipline of innovation is all about.

⏩ Steps to Improved Innovation

Innovation means differently to different people. For some it means new product ideas or new manufacturing processes that lower delivered costs. The manager may define it broadly as a strategic and profitable management of change. Still others think in terms of developmental stages: idea, implementation and diffusion throughout the market place. Many entrepreneurs appreciate the need for innovate thinking and implementation in every area, from human resources management to transportation. All these require special planning, implementation, and control. More importantly, the entrepreneurs today recognise that careful management of innovation can go a long way towards assuring real growth, competitiveness and profitability.

Box 2

ON INNOVATION

There are innovators who are 'kissed by the Muses,' and whose innovations are the result of a 'flash of genius' rather than of hard, organised, purposeful work. But such innovations cannot be replicated. They cannot be taught and they cannot be learned .... But also, contrary to popular belief in the romance of invention and innovation, 'flashes of genius' are uncommonly rare. What is worse, I know of not one such 'flash of genius' that turned into an innovation. They all remained brilliant ideas. The purposeful work of innovation resulting from analysis, system, and hard work is all that can be discussed and presented as the practice of innovation.

The extraordinary performer in innovation, as in every other area, will be effective only if grounded in the discipline and mastery of it. Purposeful, systematic innovation begins with the analysis of the seven sources of opportunity: the organisation's own unexpected successes and failures, incongruities, process needs, changes in market structures, changes in demographies, changes in meaning and perception and new knowledge. All sources of innovative opportunity should be systematically analysed and studied. It is not enough to be alerted to them. An innovation, to be effective, has to be simple and it has to be focused. It should do only one thing; otherwise it confuses. If it is not simple, it won't work. All effective innovations are breathtakingly simple. Indeed, the greatest praise an innovation can receive is for people to say, 'This is obvious. Why didn't I think of it?' – *Peter Drucker*

Arthur Young and the Institute For Innovation have created a group of powerful analytical tools that assist the entrepreneurs to innovate and change. The ten steps to improved innovation management area are as follows:

STEPS	**INNOVATION MANAGEMENT**
ONE	UNDERSTANDING
TWO	RECOGNITION
THREE	ANALYSIS
FOUR	REVIEWING
FIVE	MEASURING
SIX	EVALUATION
SEVEN	DETERMINATION
EIGHT	IMPROVING
NINE	DEVELOPING
TEN	IMPLEMENTATION & MONITORING

Fig. 1 Ten Commandments of Improved Innovation Management

Step One: Understanding what Innovation Really Means

Innovation encompasses every phase of business activity from new products to internal controls and management. Innovation can be divided into 'producer innovation' and 'user innovation.' Perspective innovation can also be viewed as a continuous sequence from idea to implementation and to diffusion in the external market place or within the organisation.

Step Two: Recognising Innovation in a Small Organisation

Small enterprises are more likely not only to possess the skill but also depend on it for competitive survival. Whereas the large enterprises find it difficult to recognise innovation in the organisation. Invariably large enterprises acquire the innovative ways of smaller, entrepreneurial companies.

Step Three: History — Analysing Past Innovation Successes and Failures

While innovation successes are interesting, failures can be interesting too. Analysis of the corporate innovation record needs to be comprehensive and unflinchingly candid: what are the strengths and weaknesses in research, product, quality control, price, market positioning, distribution, human resources management, etc.? A tough retrospective analysis is a crucial investment in the future.

Step Four: Reviewing the Innovation Avenues

Innovation management relies on effective use of Innovation Avenues within both the parent corporation and unit operating environments. These are:

- Research & Development
- University R&D
- New Product Development
- Internal Entrepreneurship/Venturing
- Venture Capital
- Technology Transfer
- Entrepreneurial Acquisitions
- Specialised Joint Ventures.

Only a handful of companies pursue all the eight; some engage in half or more; every company is involved in at least one. A majority of companies would benefit from utilizing a greater number of Avenues to Innovation. Learning to link the Avenues into an interactive network – a total innovation strategy – is important. Commonality of climate, techniques, procedures, and incentives creates efficiencies. And the Avenues should run parallel to each other, with plenty of communicating pathways in which people and ideas can easily mingle.

Step Five: Measuring in Terms of the Innovations Success/Failure Factors

The Innovation Audit supersedes the typically subjective way in which most companies evaluate innovation management between the birth of an idea and its ultimate diffusion into the company or the economy.

Combined with the Twelve Requirements (see Step Six), Success/Failure analysis gives a highly structured, comprehensive view of the state of innovation management today in a company and/or its operating units.

Step Six: Evaluating Performance in Terms of the Twelve Requirements for Corporate Innovation Management

Graphically represented is the second of the AY/II diagnostic tools, the Twelve Requirements for Corporate Innovation Management.

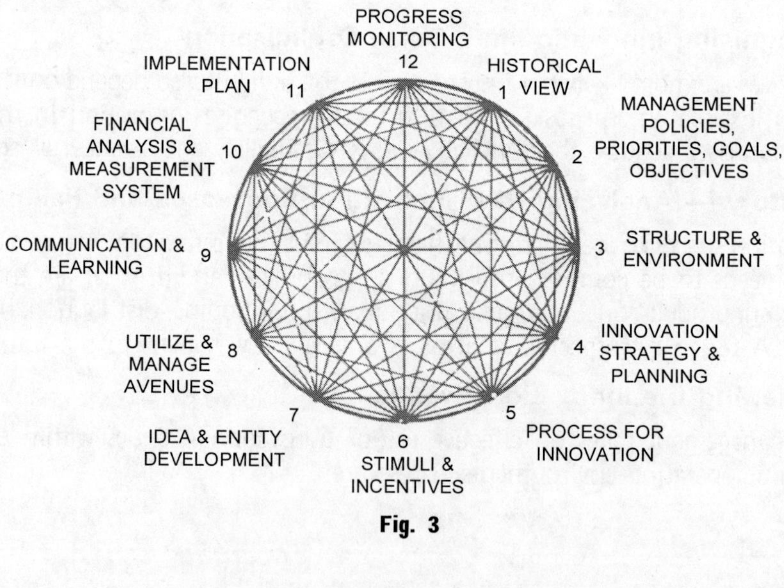

Fig. 3

This diagram indicates the key elements that call for regular management attention, and it suggests intensive interaction. Neglect of any requirement will affect the others and frustrate innovation. Innovation cannot be managed piecemeal, as it is today in at least eight of every ten companies with sales of over $100 million. Bits-and-pieces innovation management is a sure path to under-achievement or outright failure.

Step Seven: Determining the Impact of Innovation on Existing Strategic Goals

Typical, improved innovation management car, impact market, share, product margins, distribution, marketing, white collar productivity, training and development, financial controls – in fact, any and every area where change is desired or necessary.

Step Eight: Defining What Must be Done to Improve Innovation Management

When the desired contribution of innovation leverage to existing strategic goals has been agreed upon, specific innovation goals and sub-goals can be set.

In some areas, prudent risk-taking will need to be encouraged in order to build a more conducive entrepreneurial environment. In others, training may be necessary in the patterns of innovative thinking and entrepreneurial leadership. In still other units of the company, the need may be for greater organisational flexibility; innovation roadblock analysis and demolition; revised financial measurement systems for innovation; new incentives; better implementation; stronger top management commitment or involvement.

Step Nine: Developing an Innovation Strategy and Plan

Few companies, however, develop a separate innovation strategy and plan that encompasses the entire corporation vertically and horizontally. Such a strategy and plan must be a working agenda that closely aligns innovation management with the overall business strategy (Step Seven) and extensively outlines the means for achieving company/business unit innovation goals (Step Eight).

This comprehensive innovation strategy and plan must address the following issues:

1. The desired degree of innovation commitment, priority, and continuity.
2. The required balance between innovation management (managing the new) and traditional management (managing ongoing business) in terms of structure, process, culture, and motivation.
3. Realistic short-term and long-term perspectives in relation to innovation, supported by a plan for communicating them and fostering their acceptance throughout the organisation.
4. Precise innovation needs and objectives.
5. Definition and prioritisation of efforts needed to:

   (*a*) improve targeted Success/Failure Factors, (*b*) fulfill the Twelve Requirements and

   (*c*) manage and coordinate the Innovation Avenues.
6. Specific company/business unit innovation tactics and performance expectations.
7. Assignment of individual responsibilities for implementation of all innovation plans, including barrier analysis and demolition.
8. Predetermination of the reporting system to be used to monitor (re-audit) implementation.

Step Ten: Implementing and Monitoring Innovation Management

The secret of implementation is the disciplined follow-up or monitoring. Constant monitoring proves to be a tool in refining the complex process of implementation.

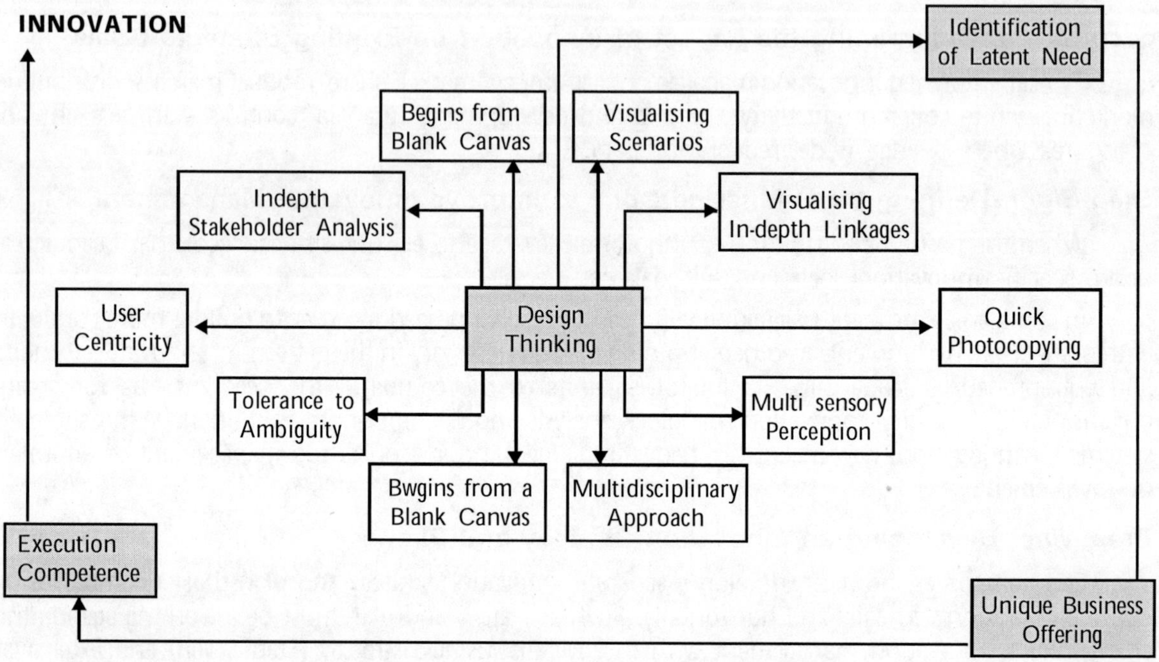

⏩ Innovations from Different Quarters

Here it may be pointed out that a radically different school of thought holds that competition through innovations may come from any quarter, procedures in similar lines of business as well as those in entirely different ones. This view is based on conclusions drawn from numerous different studies.

- Cooper (1983), from a study of KB industrial firms, concluded that the relationship between R&D spending and innovations is not as obvious and linear as might have been assumed (p. 22).
- Freeman (1983), too concludes that there was no strong systematic evidence that larger or smaller firms or R&D departments were more or less successful. He also points out that he found no relationship between success and the number of scientists and engineers on the main board of the innovating company, although this proportion varied considerably (p. 117, 123).
- Schmookier (1957) in his study on "Inventors Past and Present", concluded that a large proportion of inventors are not college-trained (p. 325).
- Van Deusen (1954) concluded that "truly significant innovation generally are the work of outsiders, individuals far enough removed from an industry to have a fresh viewpoint on its problems" (p. 133). Examples quoted are those of the anatomist Galvani discovering the electrical properties of metals, the patent-attorney Chester Carlson conceiving the idea of xerography, the physician Chairman Takeshi Mitarai innovating the canon in the photo

industry, two musicians inventing the Kodachrome, a watchmaker working with brass casting coming up with the process of continuous casting of steel, dye-making chemists developing synthetic detergents after soap-making chemists turned the project down as uninteresting.

- Scherer (1980) also emphasises that outsiders and newcomers contributed a disproportionately high share of all really revolutionary new industrial products and processes. Among them are lighting (Bruch), the incandescent lamp (Edison) alternating current (Westiaghouce) etc.
- Masifield (1975) also notes that the laboratories of major petroleum firms were not responsible for the radical inventions that occurred prior to World War II. In the pharmaceutical industry too about one-half of the major innovations during 1935-62 were based on discoveries made outside the established laboratories (p. 318). The list is endless.

J. Schumpeter says that an entrepreneur is basically an innovator as he introduces something new in the economy. According to Schumpeter the introduction of new combination of factors of production, in any one of the five forms.

1. The introduction of new products with which consumers are not yet familiar or introduction of a new variant of an existing product.
2. The introduction of new method of production that has not yet been tested by experience in the branch of manufacture concerned.
3. The opening of a new market, that is a market into which the new-product of the company has not yet entered, whether or not this market has existed before.
4. The discovery of new source of supply of raw material, irrespective of the fact as to whether that source already existed or it has been created now.
5. The carrying out of new organisation of any industry by creating of monopoly or the breaking up of it.

Thus entrepreneur can be defined as a person who creates something new, organises production and undertakes risks and handles economic uncertainties involved in enterprise.

According to Paul H. Wilken various types of changes initiated by entrepreneur are:

1. **Initial Expansion:** Original production of goods.
2. **Subsequent expansion:** Subsequent changes in the amount of goods produced.
3. **Factors Innovation:** Increase in the supply or productivity of factors.
   (*a*) *Financial:* Procurement of capital from new source or in new form.
   (*b*) *Labour:* Procurement of labour from new source or new type, upgrading of existing labour.
   (*c*) *Material:* Procurement of old material from new source or use new source or use of new material.
4. **Production Innovations:** Changes in production process.
   (*a*) *Technological:* Use of new production process.
   (*b*) *Organisational:* Change of form or structure of relationship among people.
5. **Market Innovations:** Changes in size or composition of the market.
   (*a*) *Product:* Production of new products or change in the quality cost of existing product.
   (*b*) *Market:* Discovery of new market.

Entrepreneur is different from a manager. According to Schumpeter manager is one who deals with day-to-day affairs of the business whereas an entrepreneur is the owner and makes policies and takes decisions. According to him "everyone is an entrepreneur only when he actually carries out new combinations and loses that character as soon as he has built up his business, when he settles down in running it as other people run their business."

Rogers and Shoemaker have summarised their findings concerning the tributes of an innovator and these are:

(*i*) More educated.

(*ii*) Higher in social standing.

(*iii*) Less dogmatic.

(*iv*) More emphatic.

(*v*) Better equipped to deal with abstraction.

(*vi*) More receptive to risk in general.

(*vii*) Higher in achievement motivation.

(*viii*) Higher in social participation.

(*ix*) More cosmopolitan.

(*x*) More often engaged in inter personal communication.

(*xi*) A more active information seeker.

(*xii*) More knowledgeable about innovations.

(*xiii*) An opinion leader.

(*xiv*) More in contact with persons outside the social system.

Some thinkers believe that innovations can be carried out only by big business houses. Their opinion is based on the assumption that big business houses have more financial resources, better organisational structure and management skills. But in reality most of the innovations are attributed to small scale businesses. It is due to their in-built flexibility, small firms can respond to new demands without any loss of time and can easily exploit new ideas. A large firm operating under the constraints of size and competition tend to achieve perfection in existing lines of production in order to survive and increase profits. Small firms on the other hand can adjust promptly as per requirement and can exploit the opportunities as and when arise. Small firms are not forced to engage on expensive conversions and can launch themselves on new, narrow or risky markets.

Schumpeter for the first time in 1934 assigned an important role of innovation to the entrepreneur. He did not equate entrepreneur with an inventor. An inventor creates a new product while Schumpeter entrepreneur exists if factors of production are combined for the first time. Schumpeter theory is based on the following assumptions:

(*i*) Existence of sufficient availability of capital.

(*ii*) Existence of developed banking system.

(*iii*) Existence of high level developed technology.

(*iv*) Existence of private initiative and broad based entrepreneurial process.

The above assumptions hold good more in case of developed economy and may not be suitable for underdeveloped economies. The path of innovativeness in underdeveloped countries is blocked by scarcity of capital and other bottlenecks. Schumpeter innovating entrepreneur represents the most vigorous type of enterprise. But this type of entrepreneurs are rarely found in developing countries. The type of entrepreneur who exploits opportunities as they present themselves within a limited time horizon and mostly on a small scale can only produce limited results. Society must produce innovators with a long time horizon and who are capable of achieving substantial transformations.

Schumpeter's views are more relevant to developing countries where innovations need to be encouraged. The transformation of an agrarian economy in an industrial economy requires a great deal of initiative and changes on the part of businessmen and managers. Innovating entrepreneurs are found in abundance in developed countries whereas there is dearth of such type of entrepreneurs in underdeveloped countries. A country with little or no industrial tradition can hardly produce innovating entrepreneurs. Such entrepreneurs can emerge and work only when a certain level of development is already achieved and people look forward to change and progress. Innovating entrepreneurs have played major role in the rise of capitalism, through their enterprising spirit, urge to do something different, hope of making money and ability to identify and exploit opportunities as and when these arise. Imitative type of entrepreneurs are characterised by readiness to adopt successful innovations initiated by successful innovating entrepreneurs. Imitative entrepreneurs do not initiate the changes themselves, they only imitate techniques and technology innovated by others. Such entrepreneurs are more important for underdeveloped economies as they assist in accelerating the pace of development and growth of these countries. Imitative entrepreneurs help in the adjustment and adoption of new technologies in the context of conditions prevalent in underdeveloped countries. The importance of these imitative or humbler entrepreneurs who exploit possibilities as they present themselves and mostly on a small scale must not be underestimated. Such adoption requires no mean ability and it is called subjective innovation. It is the ability to do things which have not been done before. Imitative entrepreneur acts as a potent change producing figure. He can set in motion, the chain reaction which can lead to cumulative progress or development of the country.

⏩ Management Innovation

In a market where talent is largely a commodity and can be bought anywhere, the secret sauce is creating an environment in which you push that frontier out, in which you can steadily raise the returns on human capital. The combination of technology and talent is a powerful catalyst for value creation, but to take advantage of the web's capacity to help us aggregate and amplify human potential in new ways.

The opportunity is substantial. Against the backdrop of the digital age's dramatic technological change, ongoing globalisation, and the declining predictability of strategic-planning models, only new approaches to managing employees and organising talent to maximise wealth creation will provide companies with a durable competitive advantage.

Gary Hamel

Research on management innovation has suggested the following a few important factors. There's something intriguing about the phenomenon of management innovation. Almost by definition, it is hard to do.... But when a company does have the courage to innovate in this way, the very same qualities are what makes the innovation hard for competitors to copy.

Become a management innovator: Just as you need a physical R&D lab to do technological innovation, you need awareness and dedicated resources to take management innovation seriously. Very few companies do this at the moment.

Create a problem-solving culture: When employees are faced with an unusual problem or challenge in the company, what is their typical reaction? Do they resort to a standard solution that has already been endorsed by competitors? Or do they look deeper, see the problem in new ways and start to hypothesise about new ways of solving it? Only the latter path can lead the company toward management innovation.

Seek out analogies and exemplars from different environments: If your challenge is to become more resilient, try looking at highly resilient social systems, such as parliamentary democracies, cities or faith systems. If the problem is one of increasing the motivation of employees, then look at the Scouting movement, or Open Source software. Benchmarking your competitors is not going to do the job.

Build capacity for low-risk experiments: Rather than letting new and questionable ideas loose on the entire organisation, try an experimental approach where each innovation can be tested with a limited number of people and for a limited period of time. We have seen companies run one-day experiments with genuinely valuable outputs.

Make use of external change agents to explore your new ideas: While you need to own your innovation activities, there is value in selectively making use of outsiders as sources of new ideal analogies, and as sounding boards and sense-makers.

Conclusion

Innovation, in fact, takes many forms and the search for new or existing need applies to all functions – research, production, distribution, advertising and salesmanship. Innovation is not just about new ideas, welcome though these may be. It is also about minor improvements in products, range extensions, slight differences which can make considerable differences and also unsuspected spin-off.

While innovation is one facet of technology development process, discoveries and innovation also play a significant role. Innovation is distinctly different from invention. Invention is an "act of insight", going beyond the exercise of normal technical skill. When, where and how it will occur is unpredictable and it may be a dramatic breakthrough or an unexciting consequence which draws little attention.

Many a time, scientific discoveries precede invention. In fact, considerable time may elapse between the discovery of a new scientific principle and its applications as a practical technology. But a study of the scientific innovations and discoveries of five very important technological innovations has shown that non-mission oriented pure basic research is the source of technological innovations. According to the findings of this study, a period of twenty to thirty years elapsed between pure research and the realization of its fruits in technological innovations.

Invention and innovation are the two wheels on which the advancement of technology runs. Scherer found this to be true in the case of the study of the Watt-Boulton steam engine venture. Development of a fundamental principle into an economically advantageous machine is a necessary prerequisite in the process of technological change. This investment is necessary for innovation and development and it is possible that all three follow from scientific curiosity and a fortuitous combination of change factors without any direct stimulus from profit expectations or such public policies as the granting of patent monopolies.

As entrepreneurship and innovation reinforce each other An Entrepreneurship Policy (EP) automatically puts innovation high on the economic and social policy agenda. As a by-product, it also drives regional development and guarantees social inclusion by offering opportunities of creating one's own businesses regardless of location or social background.

EP also looks at entrepreneurship as a phenomenon governed by similar processes, be it in the rural areas or in the knowledge hub of a metropolis. It can effectively address the issues of welfare at the bottom of the pyramid by combining developmental schemes with entrepreneurial initiatives. In view of the experiences of several countries, following initiatives are needed to give our economy an entrepreneurial focus: (*a*) integrate entrepreneurship into welfare and other social developmental efforts of the government both in the rural as well as urban sectors; (*b*) deploy workforce and community development systems to support and promote entrepreneurship; (*c*) use the education system for harnessing entrepreneurial talent at all levels; (*d*) incubate entrepreneurial companies by providing incubation services through physical and virtual incubators and also through remote incubation options for rural areas; (*e*) invest in diverse sources of risk capital for the nation's entrepreneurs and growth companies through the development of a rich base of early-stage capital options; and (*f*) focus on payback quality rather than on collateral in bank lending.

SYNCHING VISIONS

"Often the source of conflict and misalignment in implementation of vision is that people are working off different mental pictures about where things are going. One person's idea of success may be global, and another's may only be qualitative. The inevitable operational conflict can only be solved by a conversation and an agreement at the level of vision." — *David Allen, Expert on Organisational Productivity*

19

Establishing Entrepreneurial System

Introduction

In the changed environment, establishing an entrepreneurial system is quite crucial and timely.

Industrialisation is one of the important means to usher in economic and social transformation in the developing countries. More so when agriculture cannot sustain the burden of the population growth, it is the industry and service sectors which have to shoulder the responsibility to sustain as well as, accelerate the pace of growth. So industrialisation is indispensable for survival and growth.

Industrialisation results from the interaction of technological change, innovation, entrepreneurial growth, specialisation and trade. Good transportation and efficient communication system and an educated labour force help promote the rapid development of industries. Well-defined rules reduce the costs of transactions as specialisation increases and economies become more complex.

Large industrial units and business houses also play an important role in developing and sustaining new entrepreneurship. For, it should be noted that while the growth of entrepreneurship in India in the last 25-30 years have been remarkable, entrepreneurship is still a comparatively scarce factor in India, as indeed in all developing countries. In spite of our fairly good economic progress, India is one of the poorest countries in the world. On the other hand, our natural and human resources are such that we can be a fairly prosperous country. So, what we require is more entrepreneurship on the part of the government and the private sector.

Entrepreneurship is a core sector which can be developed in a big way. What with so many technological and management institutes in India, it should not be difficult to develop thousands of entrepreneurs every year. In this connection, economic policies of the government leave an important impact on the growth of entrepreneurship. Sometimes, the government gives the impression that the private sector will only be tolerated. This impression should be removed and there must be a formal recognition of the fact that in a country like India, we require entrepreneurship at various levels and of various sizes – Central Government, State Government, large, medium and small private sector units and also foreign entrepreneurship.

The entrepreneurship development movement in India had received significant attention; this is borne out by the fact that the small manufacturing enterprises have made phenomenal progress during the last three decades and today occupy an important position in the industrial economy of India.

To overcome the very many hurdles in enterprise success, the entrepreneur can only lift himself by adopting a project approach for development. In this context, project management forms a strategic tool of economic growth.

The strategic issue for organisations in the 21st century will be how to balance their activities: what to put in the core and what to put in the space around it. For example, an organisation has to be small enough to be human and flexible, but, at the same time, in some areas, it has to be big because you need a certain clout in the market place; you need research or global reach. That's why, anywhere

CHANGE STRATEGY: CHARACTERISTICS

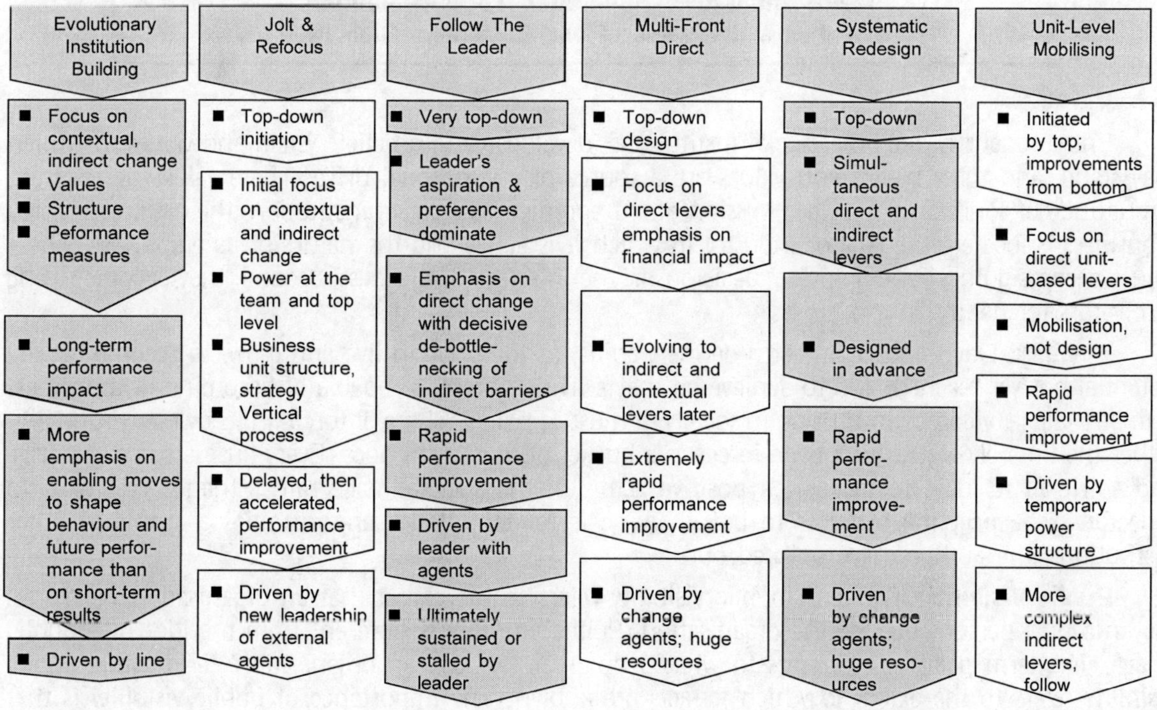

we look today, we see organisations grappling with the need to decentralise and centralise at the same time.

⏩ The Modern Concept

The modern concept of entrepreneur is, thus, a very broad one. Entrepreneur is viewed as a subsystem of the total social system. According to Davis and Blomstorm, "our modern view of society is an ecological one. Ecology is concerned with the mutual relations of human populations or systems with their environment. It is necessary to take this broad view because the influence and involvement of entrepreneur are extensive. Entrepreneurs cannot isolate itself from the rest of society. Today the whole society is a business's environment.

Davis and Blomstorm point out that, in taking an ecological view of business in a systems relationship with society, three ideas are significant in addition to the systems idea. The three ideas are values, viability and public visibility.

VALUES

Continuously improve our Products & Services to become preferred Partner of our Customers.

Own the process of delivering Results with entrepreneurial Spirit and Joy of working in an empowering environment.

Enhance Stake Holders' Value through Profitable Growth in Sales & Earnings.

Enhance our Family Bond with the Employees and Business Partners through fair and equitable dealings as well as Constant Communication.

Provide Innovative, Application Focused Solutions to enhance the Value of our Customers Globally.

⏩ Values

Entrepreneur is like other social institutions, develops certain belief system and values for which they stand, and these beliefs and values are a source of institutional drive. These values derive from a multitude of sources, such as the mission of entrepreneur as a social institution, the nation in which a business is located, the type of industry in which it is active and the nature of its employees. These values become guides for employees' decisions in the interface of business. Second, they become strong motivators for people in a business.

Viability: Davis and Blomstorm define viability as the drive to live and grow, to accomplish the potential not yet reached, and to achieve all that a living system is capable of becoming. If a business is to be a viable, vigorous institution in society, it must initiate its share of forces in its own environment, rather than merely adjust to outside forces as a bucket of quicksand docs. Every business needs a drive and spirit all its own to make it a positive actor on the societal stage rather than a reactor or a reflector. To expect the business to be otherwise is to deny it the opportunities available to other institutions, the authors have pointed out.

Public Visibility: The term public visibility refers to the extent that an organisation's activities are known to persons outside the organisation. Public visibility is different from the idea of a public image. The term *public image* refers to what people think about an organisation's acts, while public visibility refers to the extent to which its acts are known. The importance of public visibility is that it subjects business activities to public examination, discussion and judgement. If acts are not known, they cannot be judged.

In short, according to modern thinking, entrepreneur is an integral part of the social system. It is a social organ to help accomplish the societal goals. Its activities and attitudes are, therefore, subject to public judgement, which may have far-reaching implications. A business enterprise shall make profit only by accomplishing the socially accepted goals and by satisfying society. Indeed, entrepreneur and society are very intricately interwind, acting and reacting upon each other. And, both are part of the cultural ethos that govern the varied activities in the world.

Entrepreneurial Ethics

Entrepreneurial ethics is concerned with the relationship with the customer, environment and the society. Briefly, entrepreneurial responsibilities.

Many people identify ethics with vague feelings of approval or disapproval, it should be noted that ethics does not rest on feelings but on the careful examination of the reality around us. It may be unpleasant to fire a man, but ethics may demand just this. It may be hard to do the right thing in the face of strong disapproval and at great personal cost, but principles and not emotions should guide us. With all of these things in mind, we can now make some more positive statements about the nature of ethics.

Ethics is the science of judging specifically human ends and the relationship of means to those ends. In some way it is also the art of controlling means so that they will serve specifically human ends. From this point of view, ethics involves the use of any human knowledge whatsoever which has something to tell us about the relations between men or about the suitability of the available requirement. As an art, moreover, it involves techniques of judging and decision-making as well as the tools of social control and personal development. Thus ethics really is or should be involved in all human activities.

Business ethics is concerned primarily with the relationship of business goals and techniques to specifically human ends. It studies the impacts of acts on the good of the individual, the firm, the business community, and society as a whole. While it does not concentrate on the obligations which man has as a private individual and a citizen, these enter in, since the businessman is not three separate persons. This means that business ethics studies the special obligations which a man and a citizen accepts when he becomes a part of the world of commerce.

The social dimension of business ethics must not be overlooked since many major problems arise from the relationship of business to the broader society. Often, as we shall see towards the end of this book, business is involved in social situations which harm men or breed injustice even though business alone is not responsible for this. Unless we recognise this social dimension from the very start, there is danger of reducing business ethics to a study of only individual relationships between men. This would simplify the work at hand, but only by robbing business of its full human significance.

The Six Pillars of Enterprise Governance

In this global age, leaders in the business world can come from anywhere. The best ideas will dominate, regardless of their national origins. It is in this competitive global regime that the best hopes and aspirations of India rest.

A well-run enterprise embraces and practices a sound Predictability-Sustainability-Profitability-De-risking (PSPD) model. A good forecasting system for sales based on data gathered ensures predictability.

Sustainability is achieved by motivated sales people who make sales happen; by production people ensuring that quality products are delivered on time; and by billing and collecting on time.

Every enterprise must focus on high profitability in order to ensure the best returns for its shareholders. Indeed, profitability is crucial for the long-term success of a corporation.

The enterprise must have a good de-risking approach that recognises, measures and mitigates risk along every dimension. Take them you must, but carefully thought-out risks.

Enterprise governance is focused on maximising shareholder value while ensuring fairness to all stakeholders. In these days of free flowing global capital, in order to attract capital, corporations have to adhere to the best global standards of enterprise governance.

The foundation of enterprise governance philosophy is the belief that it is better to lose a crores of rupees than to act in ways that make one lose a night's sleep.

It is a good practice to under-promise and over-deliver. It is best to deliver bad news to the stakeholders proactively. This creates goodwill, as they understand that ups and downs are inevitable in every business. What they value is honest and open managements.

Quick progress comes in an environment that respects competence, where there is competition and where there are no prejudices. Infoscions have respect for our competitors and a sense of humility about what we have achieved. The success is, generally, ephemeral. We are only as good as the results we produce and we believe in a long-term approach; our strategies and policies reflect that.

The enterprises have an important duty to contribute to society. No enterprise can sustain its progress unless it makes a difference to its context.

The six Pillars of enterprise governance are:

- I want to emphasise the importance of being trustworthy in your dealings. It is on such foundations that great organisations are created.
- Fear is natural, but do not let your actions be totally governed by it. Just as fear may sometimes be the voice of your institution, it might also be an invitation to explore yourself and the world.
- A supportive family is the bedrock upon which lives and careers are built.
- Learn how to manage yourself, separating the merits and demerits of a decision from the accompanying feelings. Infusions call this being transaction oriented.
- Live your life and lead your career in a way that makes a difference to your society.

Follow your bliss. All else will follow.

So, choose a worthy dream for yourself. Go after it confidently. But always, ensure that you are following your bliss.

▸▸ Entrepreneurial Culture

The key to growth is to foster entrepreneurial culture and play a pivotal role in deepening in the enterprise/organisation, so that, it will contribute to the success of the enterprise.

Indian entrepreneurs will have, therefore, to draw up their futuristic vision by way of redefining their purpose and mission and resetting their attainable objectives, and developing long-term strategy against the background of emerging opportunities and impending threats inherent in domestic and global environments on the one hand and competencies and weaknesses, on the other.

While charting out its future course of action the Indian entrepreneur will have to remember that to get a competitive edge over its rivals on a sustainable basis five things are essential – increased productivity, improved quality, innovation in the market, a deep understanding of customer needs and delivery of world class service and only one factor that could provide all these capabilities is 'knowledge' and human beings are the drivers of the knowledge juggernaut. As such, primary focus of the strategic management approach of any organisation has to be on effective and efficacious utilisation of human resources. It will, therefore, be imperative to set new paradigms for managing an enterprise and its people so that the human resource function, forms an integral part of enterprise policy and strategy and the entrepreneur plays a pivotal role in management of men and in progressive integration of conceptual values with operational values.

The entrepreneurial culture is the rock bed of economic growth and development. It fosters the growth of enterprises/businesses with a vision and accountability for the betterment of a society.

Entrepreneurial culture implies a set of values, norms and traits that are conducive to the growth of entrepreneurship. It is the corporate culture that focuses on the emergence of new opportunities, the means of capitalising on item, and the creation of the structure appropriate for pursuing them. Entrepreneurial culture should be differentiated from administrative culture. Administrative culture is the corporate culture which focuses on existing opportunities, organisational structures and control procedures. An ideal administrator would ask such questions as "what resources do I control? What structure determines our organisation's relationship to its market? How can I minimise the impact of others on my ability to perform? What opportunity is appropriate?" On the contrary an ideal entrepreneur would ask very different questions such as 'Where is the opportunity? How do I gain control over them? What structure is best?"

An ideal entrepreneur is one who combines values in the market economy; that profits do not somehow preclude ethical behaviour; that growth is possible even if political patronage is not used to bend rules and cut corners, and quite simply that pursuit of wealth can be grateful and mannerly one. He takes with him the interest of his people, his country, his natural resources, the ecology and sees that his enterprise becomes a catalytic agent of development. There is thus a need of true entrepreneurs, who do not wait for incentives, infrastructure, government support; but build their enterprises, harness the resources and develop. They adopt a responsible value-driven corporate philosophy for their enterprises and/or business activities. As such, there is no dispute among economists and social thinkers about the urgent need for the emergence of an entrepreneurial society as a forerunner of accelerated development of the economy in an integrated manner.

In short, the entrepreneurial culture develops entrepreneurial focus while the administrative culture develops administrative focus.

The most important characteristics of entrepreneurial focus are:

(*a*) Strategic orientation, that is, the entrepreneurial kind of managers will be driven by perception of opportunity.

(*b*) Commitment to seize opportunities they will be revolutionary with short duration.

(*c*) Commitment and control of resources, effective utilisation of resources.

WORK CULTURES OF THE PAST AND THE FUTURE

Work Culture of the Past	Work Culture of the Future
→ individualism	→ communitarianism
→ independence	→ interdependence
→ autocracy	→ democracy
→ humanity against nature	→ humanity part of nature
→ unsustainable production	→ sustainable production
→ unsustainable consumption	→ sustainable consumption
→ patriarchy	→ gender equality
→ intercultural intolerance	→ intercultural tolerance
→ interreligious intolerance	→ interreligious tolerance
→ conflict resolution by confrontation	→ conflict resolution by negotiation
→ reliance on defence	→ reliance on security
→ reliance on rational intelligence	→ reliance on emotional intelligence

Ten Steps to Change Entrepreneurial Culture

Changing entrepreneurial culture doesn't require magic. What it needs is down-to-earth action that will set a good example at the top. The following ten steps will help an entrepreneur to create a culture supportive of change:

1. Start at the top. Lead the enterprise.
2. Attune to a culture of innovation.
3. Remove the hidden obstacles.
4. Create an integrated enterprise culture.
5. Create a marketing culture.
6. Create a listening environment.
7. Absorb competing technologies and involve people.
8. Do not let product innovations fool you.
9. Be flexible and open for diversification and new ideas.
10. Always be ready to change cultures.

No matter what culture your enterprise has settled into profitably and comfortably, change will eventually come along the jerk your business into a new environment. Be ready for it constantly scanning the developments, the markets and the society for trends, opportunities and innovations (Technological and management), and do not be hesitant to use them when the time comes.

Human Resource in Industry

India's physical resources have many dimensions.

Fertile crop lands, immense reserves of minerals, great rivers, a long coast line and a diversified industrial base are only a small sample.

The greatest of all our assets, however, are our human resources. These are abundant, inexhaustible, and more important, can be developed and channelled to meet the equally colossal problems confronting our country. However, for these resources to be productive, they must be of a high calibre.

Many types of resources are necessary to manage an industry, capital, technology, and goodwill in the form of property in brand equity. But the mere existence of these resources is not a sufficient condition for entrepreneurial activity; it needs human resources to make them come alive.

Human resources are to be channelised into productive activities. Many of them have to be motivated to direct their energies fruitfully.

A key ingredient of this process lies in training, in particular in-plant training.

These programmes include skill courses of wide variety, *e.g.*, sales skills courses which provide the sales teams a broader picture of a changed market and adapting to the competitive environment; courses for computer applications; workshops for sharpening commercial skills, amongst many others.

Training programmes have a clear objective: to make the workforce do their job better through minimising wastage; maintaining plant and equipment and sharing corporate concern for quality, cost effectiveness and safety. Such programmes are run at individual unit level.

Training is often proactive and anticipates the need for a new range of knowledge or skills arising out of perspective business plan, for instance, in the application of information technology, logistics and energy conservation.

Another dimension of training is its 'people' orientation. The annual appraisals of employees usually suggest special areas that need attention in terms of training inputs. These inputs are particularly regular for supervisory and managerial personnel.

Training is a continuous process and we find that it is most effective when it occurs on the job or is closely allied to it. In this way, training is made relevant to meet business needs as well as to improve performance and productivity.

With continuing liberalisation, competition will be intense and the people manning industry will have to deliver products of significantly better quality and value to the consumer. Given the flux and rapid pace of change, reactions to developments in the market place will have to be swift. So employees at all levels will have to be better trained, more educated and technically competent.

Another area where perhaps industry in general will have to focus more sharply is the availability of the right calibre of people. This will require industry to initiate suitable linkages with academic and technical institutions. This is a step needed not only to enhance the number of people available for managing businesses in the future but also to make them competitive with products and services of international calibre. This is turn will equip the country with the capacity to exploit the opportunities in international trade, an area that will grow in importance.

⏩ Training Intensity

One of the major issues is training. Since shortage of the right type of people is likely to be a fact of life, the standards of internal training systems will have to be so moulded as to enhance the promotability potential of an increasing number of people from within.

Since the pace of change in technology and consumer preferences will be more rapid, employees will have to keep learning newer and newer fillings to cope with the demands of change. So nimbleness of mind needs to be cultivated through the acquisition of new knowledge and skills and hands-on training will be of a very different order. People in charge of HRD will have to recognise this right from the stage of selection of employees so that making people respond and adapt to change in a business environment becomes an integral part of business strategy.

Ensure that specific programs designed to foster entrepreneurship operate as part of an integrated and coherent strategy that complements the framework conditions. In particular:

- Avoid policies that stem from a too-narrow definition of entrepreneurship (e.g., that entrepreneurship is only about start-ups or only about high-technology) and which may divert attention from getting the broader economic policy settings right.
- Widen the target population for entrepreneurship programs, where possible, to attract the participation of women, the young and minorities.
- Undertake regular and comprehensive evaluation of programs, and ensure that evaluation findings are acted on.

Improve the effectiveness of entrepreneurship programs by drawing on the knowledge of local level of government. In particular:

- Ensure that resources for programs to foster entrepreneurship are decentralised where appropriate in order to better tailor programs to the specific needs of an area and its business.
- Provide regular opportunities to exchange information of a national level on the experiences of local authorities in designing and implementing entrepreneurship programs.
- Seek to identify and implement low-cost and effective programs with minimal distortionary effects on market incentives. For example:
- Promote public awareness of entrepreneurship and examine the role the education system could play in developing entrepreneurial skills and attitudes.
- Increase opportunities for the unemployed to create their own jobs through self-employment schemes.
- Facilitate networking among firms in order to foster a culture of mutual cooperation and risk-taking.
- Promote the entrepreneurial non-profit sector by contracting out where possible the delivery of public service that meet pressing demands in economic and social development.

(*OECD, Fostering Entrepreneurship,* 1998, pp. 28-30. Used with permission of OECD.)

⏩ Towards a New Order

There is an increasing disenchantment with ideologies which put the onus of development on the state apparatus; and which believe that a centralised ownership, regulation and operation of economic activity was the best way for rapid and balanced development. It is now increasingly being realised that while the State must continue to play a crucial role in macro-economic management of the system, it is far more effective to permit market forces and private initiative to determine investment priorities and to raise resources for the purpose. There is considerable discussion nowadays about throwing open to the private sector or joint sector areas which traditionally were 'reserved' for the State. This includes creation of infrastructure and setting up and management of public utilities. There are increasing constraints on resources available to the public sector and there is also a growing skepticism about the efficiency as also probity of public expenditures. It is in this context that one will have to view the possibilities of the so-called 'privatisation' in order to augment the resources available and also to ensure that they are utilised efficiently.

The world is rapidly changing: and unless we are also able to change our attitudes and approaches, there is a real danger that a country of India's size and potential will become peripheral in the context of world's economy. Several countries which not so long ago were less developed as compared to India have in recent years overtaken us in terms of quality of their infrastructure, the level of sophistication of their industry and the quality of life for their people. In the process they have also been able to attract substantial additional resources for investment from abroad. If instead of looking ahead and aligning ourselves to cope with the massive changes that are taking place in the field of science and technology, we choose to hark back to the past or remain prisoners of dead dogmas, we will have missed a great opportunity.

The coming decades hold for us both challenges and opportunities. In order to meet the challenges of the future and to exploit the opportunities, the Government and the entrepreneur have to chalk out a plan of action to play their rightful role in the future industrial development of the county. For this purpose the entrepreneur has to introduce innovations, update technology, raise the necessary financial resources, improve skills, introduce management concept and even more importantly, spares awareness of development.

⏩ Vision for Future

The entrepreneurship that contributes in a modest way to critical economic and social needs of the country and always strive to attain global leadership in all of its major initiative. This is the vision for future.

Pursuing this vision, over the next few years, entrepreneurs will pursue a strategy of:

- Reinforcing competitive advantage of existing business through new capacities and synergistic acquisitions.
- Scaling sizeable opportunities in the core sectors.
- Forward integrating into retailing transportation fuels and creating new customer experiences.
- Addressing the significant information and communications market opportunity in India and in the world.
- Leveraging its strong balance sheet, cash flows and managerial capacity to create value by adding new capacities, acquisitions and turnaround of under performing assets.
- Developing strategic alliances in technology and product-market domains with global majors.
- Fostering new higher education institutions for knowledge creation and sharing.
- Leveraging its formidable strengths beyond Indian borders.
- Reorienting the best practices to enhance productivity and quality (Q).
- In addition to manufacturing products venture into developing manufacturing systems.
- From having a manufacturing orientation to providing technical solutions.
- From being an intermediate goods producer to being a final goods and services provider.
- From licensing technology to developing technology.
- From being an intellectual property user to an intellectual property creator.
- In addition to operating in India to being a global company.
- From building financial equity to fostering social equity.

This change will entail creating new organisational competencies such as:

- Creating a customer-centric organisation.
- Developing new products and technologies.
- Exploring and producing new products to meet the new generation's expectations.
- Fostering and sustaining globally oriented management talent.
- Training the human resources to harness the opportunities.

- Encouraging intrapreneurship.
- Focusing on Research and Development for sustainable development.
- Imbibing new technology to enhance the value of the product.
- Focusing on business ethics in managing the enterprises.
- Managing customer-oriented supply chains.
- Developing and protecting intellectual capital.
- Managing strategic technology and product-market relationships.

Managing diversity in business, technologies, export, innovation and people are the primary challenges to the entrepreneur, as he marches ahead in realising his vision for future.

⏩ Entrepreneurial Society — A New Goal

The winds of change sweeping all over the world are bound to affect us and unless we re-orient ourselves to the new realities, we are likely to miss a great opportunity to improve the quality of life of our people.

It is, in my view, essential that there should be a national debate on the manner in which we are going to reshape our economic policies, keeping the global perspective in view. It is not enough to have debates. We must quickly put the agreed consensus into operation. The essence of this consensus, in my view, would be an environment supportive of growth and poverty alleviation; an environment in which the Government's main function would be to govern and not to underwrite losses of public sector undertakings, an environment in which the Government facilitates and encourages entrepreneurs.

The process of industrialisation will have to be harmoniously integrated with the development of industrial centres, both in urban and rural area. The process of linkages has also to be harmoniously blended with quality as well as productivity.

The future belongs to the entrepreneurs. They will continue to be the prime-movers of the new phase of industrial development in India. In the coming years, entrepreneurial society will blossom and spread entrepreneurial culture among all sections of the society. The vision that sustains entrepreneurs must certainly contribute to the growth of viable enterprises, make profit and contribute to a better quality of life. The country should develop in an integrated way. This depends upon the right kind of visionary entrepreneur.

⏩ The New Credo at Levi Strauss Behavioural Change

Management must expemplify "directness, openness to influence, commitment to the success of others, and willingness to acknowledge our own contributions to problems."

⏩ Diversity

Levi's "values a diverse workforce (age, sex, ethnic group, etc.) at all levels of the organisation.... Differing points of view will be sought; diversity will be valued and honestly rewarded, not suppressed."

⏩ Recognition

Levi's will "provide greater recognition – both financial and psychic – for individuals and teams that contribute to our success... those who create and innovate and those who continually support day-to-day business requirements."

Ethical Management Practices

Management should epitomise "the stated standards of ethical behaviour. We must provide clarity about our expectations and must enforce these standards throughout the corporation."

Communications

Management must be "clear about company, unit and individual goals and performance. People must know what is expected of them and receive timely, honest feedback...."

Empowerment

Management must "increase the authority and responsibility of those closest to our products and customers. By actively pushing the responsibility, trust, and recognition into the organisation, we can harness and release the capabilities of all our people."

In a new entrepreneurial system, the entrepreneur takes with him the interest of his people, his country, his natural resources, the ecology and sees that his enterprise becomes a catalytic agent of development. There is thus a need of true entrepreneurs, who do not for incentives, infrastructure, government support, but build his enterprises, harness the resources and develop. They adopt a responsible value-driven corporate philosophy for their enterprises and/or business activities. As such, there is no dispute among economists and social thinkers about the urgent need for the emergence of an entrepreneurial society as a forerunner of accelerated development of the economy in an integrated manner.

The Success Audit

Take the success audit for enterprise success:

1. Do you contribute creatively to any business function other than your own? Yes No
2. Do you consciously attempt to network with other professionals in your field? Yes No
3. Do you have an overall perspective of the industry you are in? Yes No
4. Do you understand your company's business goals, and how your job fits into them? Yes No
5. Do you understand the needs and constraints of the different business functions? Yes No
6. Can you cope with upgraded software packages without professional help? Yes No
7. Would you volunteer for a challenging long-term overseas assignment? Yes No
8. Do you make a conscious effort to keep abreast of international trends in your field? Yes No
9. At a pinch, can you take over for a colleague in the event of his sudden illness? Yes No
10. Do you often enrol for courses that deal with subjects that are supplementary to yours? Yes No

The Scoring

Give yourself 10 points for every YES, and 0 for every NO.

Total

The Rating:

0-30	Take those blinkers off. Else, you could get left behind in the career stakes.
40-70	Wishy-washy. You have the potential, just get more focused.
80-100	Congrats! You're in pole position in the corporate grand prix.

Conclusion

It should be noted that private entrepreneurship has to harmonise economic opportunities with social and moral responsibility. As wise people have said, unless the pursuit of wealth is integrated with the pursuit of Dharma, there could be no lasting prosperity and peace, whether within a country or among nations. The highly developed countries have realised that aggressive entrepreneurship without an ethical base can produce more harm than good, more misery than happiness and more destruction than creation. Harmonised planning of economic and moral values is a long-drawn-outprocess, but the goal has to be kept in mind constantly. One should remain optimistic that entrepreneurship in India will develop on these lines, to promote India's economic development on a sound basis, as an integral part of the world economy. The burst of creativity and innovation in emerging technological industries holds tremendous promise for economic development and technological business growth. When talent is linked with technology, people recognise and then push viable ideas and the entrepreneurial process is under way.

Liberalisation and the new economic policy have thrown open the doors for every entrepreneur to seek his own fortunes and thus contribute his mite to the growth of the economy. In a way, the new economic policy has been fostering the spirit of entrepreneurship. Human capital and infrastructure provide the two major assets in a global economy. The states are striving to provide a framework that will improve investment, infrastructure, agriculture and industry. They have endeavoured to dovetail industrial growth with creation of employment and balanced development. The country has a vast pool of skilled manpower and there is no dearth of entrepreneurs.

In this time of rapid economic development and technological change, entrepreneurial spirit can be unequal and important advantage, but only if we learn to use it. The entrepreneurs are the agents of change and our hope for the future. In fact, the entrepreneur always searches for change, responds to it and exploits it as an opportunity.

An ideal entrepreneur is one who combines values in the market economy; that profits do not somehow preclude ethical behaviour; that growth is possible even if political patronage is not used to vend rules and cut corners, and quite simply that pursuit of wealth can be grateful and mannerly one. He takes with him the interest of his people, his country, his natural resources, the ecology and sees that his enterprise becomes a catalytic agent of development. There is thus a need of true entrepreneurs, who do not need incentives, infrastructure, government support; but build their enterprises, harness the resources and develop. They adopt a responsible value-driven corporate philosophy for their enterprises and/or business activities. As such, there is no dispute among economists and social thinkers about the urgent need for the emergence of an entrepreneurial society as a forerunner of accelerated development of the economy in an integrated manner.

The ethos of entrepreneurial culture runs through the business society in the 21st century. Indeed entrepreneurial culture lays a strong foundation for a well regulated, sustainable and environmentally friendly society.

FIVE KEYS TO SUCCESS

Shared goals : The whole organisation should know where it is going and everyone must be involved in developing the vision. But it must happen gradually – to rush is to court disaster.

Shared culture : Staff should be managed to ensure everyone understands the company's values, not just towards customers but also to suppliers.

Shared learning : Neglect staff at your peril. Unwilling, unresponsive and unskilled workers can undermine the best strategies, but well-founded career and development plans increase loyalty.

Shared effort : Teams are the building blocks of innovative businesses. Training is vital. Don't let teams compete. Over time, encourage them to lose rigidity, to adopt a looser, more flexible more efficient "teaming" approach.

Shared information : Tell the truth at all times, without undue optimism or pessimism. Avoid corporate bureaucracy and excessive meetings.

Table 1

COMPARISON BETWEEN THE ENTREPRENEURIAL CULTURE AND ADMINISTRATIVE CULTURE

	Entrepreneurial Culture		***Administrative Culture***	
Dimensions	***Characteristics***	***Pressures***	***Characteristics***	***Pressures***
1. Strategic orientation	Driven by perception of opportunity	Diminishing opportunities Rapidly changing technology, consumer economics, social values and political rules	Driven by controlled resources	Social contracts Performance measurement criteria Planning systems and cycles
2. Commitment to seize opportunities	Revolutionary, with short duration	Action orientation Narrow decision windows Acceptance of resources risks Few decision constituencies	Evolutionary, with long duration	Acknowledgement of multiple constituencies Negotiation about strategic course Risk reduction Co-ordination with existing resource base

3. Commitment of resources	Many stages with minimal exposure at each state	Lack of predictable resource needs Lack of control over the environment Social demands for appropriate use of resources Foreign competition Demands for more efficient resource use	A single stage, with complete commitment out of decision	Need to reduce risk incentive compensation turnover in managers Capital budgeting systems Format planning systems.
4. Control of resources	Episodic use or rent of required resources	Increased resource specialisation Long resource life compared with need Risk of obsolescence Risk inherent in the identified opportunity Inflexibility of permanent commitment to resources	Ownership or employment of required resources	Power, status and financial rewards Co-ordination of activity Efficiency measures. Inertia and cost of change Industry structures.
5. Management Structure	Flat, with multiple informal networks	Co-ordination of key non-controlled resources. Challenge to hierarchy Employee's desire for independence	Hierarchy	Need for clearly defined authority and responsibility Organisational culture. Reward system. Management theory.

Source: Howard H. Stevenson and David. E. Gompert, "The Heart of Entrepreneurship," *Harward Business Review* (March-April, 1985).

**"Being a leader is a thought,
a mission with a strong vision....
Some are born leaders,
some attain leadership...
and there are few,
who inspire others to become leaders...."**

UNIT : IV

Search for Ideas

- Ideas
- Sources
- Processing
- Inputs
- Financing
- Assessment
- Assistance
- Marketing
- Sickness
- Remedies
- Feasibility
- Formalities

IDEAS SUPER POWER

India is a nation of ideas, a super power. The ideas have changed the outlook. People see us as a happening market and Potential Super Power in the world. This perceptual shift is preordained. Two leaders who contributed to this change are:

THE COMPLETE MANAGER

Infosys Chairman made Indian software, even industry, respectable.

N.R. Narayanamurthy
Founder, Chairman, INFOSYS TECHNOLOGIES
Entrepreneur, Global Manager, Mentor

If the world cannot seem to have enough of Nagavara Ramarao Narayana Murthy, it's because he was the very antithesis of the typical (and stereotypical) Indian entrepreneur: austere, willing to share wealth with employees, governance-oriented, and focused on building a global brand and corporation. The result is a company that has, to its credit, a seemingly unending list of firsts: Infosys was the first Indian company to issue stock options, host analyst meets, list on NASDAQ – essentially, the first Indian company to grab Western eyeballs. Murthy lavished money and attention on the company's Bangalore campus; he wanted overseas visitors to take back the message that Infosys was no sweatshop. And he splurged and hosted customer meets at the best hotels in the US: one year, the setting was New York's famed Waldorf Astoria. Infosys was the immediate beneficiary, but then, the rest of the Indian IT industry and, eventually, all of India Inc. gained from Murthy's efforts. Not surprisingly, rumours abound about his appointment to public office. The man belongs there.

THE FATHER OF CODERS

The founder of TCS engendered India's most global industry, software.

F.C. Kohli
Former Deputy Chairman, TCS, Technocrat, Manager, Visionary

If you are an Indian, goes prevailing logic, you must be a good software engineer. The image of Indian coders going at it in Silicon Valley, the heart of the world's technology industry, has become so ubiquitous that mainstream American media is no longer excited by once-novel disclosures about a canteen at Oracle serving *sambhar*. Attribute that to one man: Fakir Chand Kohli. In the early 1960s, Kohli, now 77, was a director on the board of Tata Electrical Company, one of the six utilities in the world to be digitised; in the late 1960s, when the Tata Group decided that Tata Consultancy Services (TCS) would focus on technology solutions, he was a natural choice to head it. Kohli was convinced India could exploit the global market for software and for warm bodies familiar with code. The discipline of software engineering wasn't around in those days, so TCS decided to recruit engineers and masters in science in any discipline and train them. By 2000, an estimated 20,000 TCS-trained engineers were working for other companies. Body-shopping gradually gave way to offshoring but as early as 1974 TCS developed a healthcare system for Burroughs out of India. And the body-shopping boom had its positives: how else would the world have learned about Indian IT?

"Market: An abstract concept that encompasses the trading arrangements of buyers and sellers that underlie the forces of supply and demand. A market may be quite narrow (for example, the market for razor blades). Alternatively, it is sometimes useful to aggregate diverse goods into a single market, such as the market for 'consumer goods.' There is also a broad range of sophistication among markets. The New York Stock Exchange is a highly computerised market in which buyers and sellers who never formally meet exchange each weekday shares of corporate ownership worth billions of dollars. In contrast, the neighbourhood market for lawn-mowing services may be highly informal, since it brings together buyers and sellers primarily by word of mouth." (from James D. Gwartney and Richard L. Stroup, *Economics: Private and Public Choice*, Harcourt Brace Jovanovich, 1990).

"Marketing is the business process by which products are matched with the markets and through which transfer of ownership is effected." **– Cundiff**

"Marketing is the total system of business activities designed to plan, price, promote and distribute want satisfying goods and services to present and potential customers." **– W. J. Stanton**

"Marketing is the response of business men to the need to adjust production capabilities to the requirements of consumer demands." **– McCarthy**

"Marketing includes all activities involved in the creation of place, time and possession utilities. Place utility is created when goods and services are made available at the places they are needed, time utility when they are needed and possession utility when they are transferred to those who need them."

– Hugey and Mitchell

"Marketing is the process of planning and executing the conception, pricing, promotion and distribution of ideas, goods and services to create exchange that satisfy individual and organisational objectives."

– American Marketing Association

"The marketing concept holds that the key to achieving organisational goals consists in determining the needs and wants of target markets and delivering the desired satisfaction more effectively and efficiently than competitors." – **John B. McKitterick**

"Selling focuses on the needs of the seller, marketing on the needs of the buyer. Selling is preoccupied with the seller's need to convert his product into cash; marketing with the idea of satisfying the needs of the customers by means of the product and the whole cluster of things associated with creating, delivering and finally consuming it." **– Theodore Levitt**

"Marketing Management focuses on managing the marketing activities. It takes place when at least one party to a potential exchange gives thought to objectives and means of achieving desired responses. 'Marketing (management) is the process of planning and executing the conception, pricing, promotion and distribution of ideas, goods and services to create exchanges that satisfy individual and organisational objectives." **– AMA**

"Marketing is a social and managerial process by which individuals and groups obtain what they need and want through creating, offering and exchanging products of value with others." – **Philip Kotler**

"Marketing is not concerned solely with tangible goods, it also plays a similar role in connection with the services." **– J. M. Rathwell**

PROCESS OF MANAGEMENT

Planning	***Organising***	***Directing and Motivating***	***Controlling***
What is to be done? When? And how? Where, when and how is it to be done? Bridging the gap from where we are to where we want to reach. Planning deals with setting of goals or objectives for realisation, prescribing the future course of action on the basis of past and present knowledge, laying down policies, programmes, schedules, procedures, etc., to achieve the goals and fixing the budgets of all planned work, Aniticipated future possible problems, modify policies and programmes and modify your plans in the light of control results. Planning – Look before you leap. It is intelligent forecasting of the future based on accurate knowledge.	Who is to do what? With how much authority'? Under what physical conditions? Organisation is a tool or mechanism **enabling people to work** together effectively and realize the plans. It deals with physical equipment and facilities for best work performance, i.e., organisation of things. It also deals with staffing, *i.e.*, selection, training, promotion and development of people working in the organisation. It is an important device to exercise all managerial functions. Organisation is developed for the people. Adjust the organisation in the light of control results. People, materials and machines are brought together for joint adventure.	Here we consider: 1. Leadership 2. Co-ordination and communication, 3. Process of Motivation of employees to raise employee's morale, i.e., willingness and co-operative spirit to achieve teamwork. Employee's participation in management proper employee communication devices, democratic managerial style, financial and non-financial incentives offered to the employees, and best coordination of efforts – are some of the tools for best direction and motivation of the employees in their work-performance. Revise motivation and direction in the light of control results.	Here, Manager is interested to follow-up the work performance of the employees and ensure that the planned work is being properly carried out and if not, manager has to apply proper remedial measures. He can adjust controls in the light of results. Things are controlled by controlling what people do. Under Controlling – 1. Performance standards are established. 2. Work in progress is measured. 3. Results are interpreted. 4. Corrective actions are taken in time. Effective control ensures realisation of plans. Effective control ensures cost reduction and maximum efficiency.

Note: Each fundamental function of management is influenced by innovation, decision-making and co-ordination.

DOS AND DON'TS WHEN **PITCHING YOUR IDEA**

- Be organised, clear and concise. KISS is the rule – Keep It Short and Simple.
- Don't make things up. If you don't know something accept it and say you will get back with details.
- Be polite but confident. Acknowledge what the mentors/investors are saying and politely put your point across. Ask questions.
- Have a positive body language throughout. Team dynamics are very important and investors notice it.
- It's important to get the positioning of the company right
- Make sure you are able to convey the core points of your agenda within the allotted time.
- Apart from the technology, make it clear who the product is targeted for and how you plan to sell it.
- Have pictures and some interaction in your presentation. Plain text can bore the listeners quickly.
- If there are shortcomings in the team, be frank. That's where the mentors/investors can help.
- Make comparisons – mentors/investors understand better with analogies.

> 
>
> **EQUITABLE ECONOMICS**
>
> **"We have a world that has enough resources for everybody to live a very high standard of living and participate in a very productive vital economy. I think our responsibility is to move in directions that help us to do that as quickly as possible."** ***— Danny Hills, Inventor and Disney Fellow***

20

Search for Business Ideas

Introduction

Industrialisation is widely recognised not only as one of the important means to usher in socio-economic transformations and achieving industrial self-sufficiency but also for the accelerated development of agriculture, transport, trade, services and other potential sectors through the forward and backward linkages. It is a process which accelerates economic growth; effects structural changes in the economy, particularly in respect of resource utilisation, production functions, income generation, occupational pattern, population distribution and foreign trade; and induces social change. Jawaharlal Nehru had emphasised that "Real progress must ultimately depend on industrialisation. Throughout the world, industrialisation has indeed become the magic word of the mid-twentieth century."

Dr. K.K. Birla

Late Shri G.D. Birla

Industrialisation is brought about by well-trained entrepreneurs. Entrepreneurship is one of the most important factors of industrialisation in the process of economic growth.

Choosing an Idea

Establishing yourself as a successful entrepreneur depends, in part, upon choosing a good idea. That idea must not only be good for the market, but good for the project and good for the entrepreneurs. It should also be manageable by you without much dependence on others. Importantly, the idea should give satisfying results to you.

As an entrepreneur, when you are searching for an idea worthy of your commitment, don't pursue one idea at a time. Develop five or ten in parallel until one emerges so appropriate that it begins to dominate your thoughts and fantasies. To adopt one idea at a time has several disadvantages. First, because you are constantly receiving random information from what you read and from people you talk to, having a number of back-burner ideas gives you a greater likelihood of finding uses for information you pick up. Secondly, if you are pursuing a single idea by feigning commitment before you feel it, you may put yourself into a tight corner. It is very hard to be objective when you are down to your last idea.

Choosing an idea is quite difficult and the entrepreneur has to weigh objectively his intrinsic capabilities in finalising an idea.

In the idea stage, suggestions for new products are obtained from all possible sources: customers, competitors, R & D, distributors, and company employees. Frequently, one of the creative problem-solving techniques discussed below are used to develop marketable ideas. The suggested ideas need to be carefully screened to determine which are good enough to qualify for a more detailed investigation. Established objectives and defined growth areas provide a basis for developing these criteria.

PRODUCT IDEA

It had been an exhausting day. Mansukhbhai had spent all morning cycling to and fro, hawking his home made goods in the lanes and bylanes of the crowded city. Now he sat outside a pan shop, trying to snatch a few minutes rest before starting another round.

As he sat there, he noticed how the customers at the pan shop kept growing, in number and impatience. Mansukhbhai saw the time it took to make each pan, the panwallah trying to attend to a dozen people at the same time. It occurred to him that if pan could be packaged and sold, it would instantly find a ready market.

And an idea was born. A man of the masses, with only his native shrewdness to guide him, had hit upon a marketing idea in a million. The kind that takes a genius to think of. That man was Mansukhbhai Mahadevbhai Kothari. The man behind Pan Parag Pan Masala.

An Illustration: Choice of a Product

Sanitary Napkin: The product was first introduced in the late 60s, and the concept of a sanitary napkin was popularised through the 70s while the 80s introduced new variations like the beltless napkin and tampons.

Since the very concept of a sanitary napkin was so new to India, one realised that conventional retailing alone was not enough to sell the product. What was important was educating women about the product and about personal hygiene, so the manufacturers started schools, screening firms on menstruation and how to cope with it. This was followed up by free sampling.

The market leaders and pioneer in the field is undoubtedly Johnson and Johnson with Carefree, Stayfree, OB tampons and now, Freshday, Pantyliners. As things stand, the consumer does not yet have a real choice in terms of wide price variations, for instance. But the market is poised for a boom and even smaller manufacturers who admit that they earn 50 per cent of their income from his one product category alone are doing well, though they are not advertising or retailing their product.

Starting with the base, which is still the belted napkin, the pyramid narrows to the apex consisting of products like tampons (3 per cent of the market share) and pantyliners. There is still a tremendous potential for expansion even at the base. The women population needing sanitary napkins is estimated to be around 20 crores, of which 5 crore lives in urban centres. There is thus scope for (Rs. 840 crore industry) 500 crore pieces alone in urban centres. At that time, big cities were prime targets for expansion and the huge rural market remained untapped. Given this scenario, the 90s will see many new brands and consequently more brand wars, hopefully resulting in the ideal napkin at the right price, for the consumer. And this is what is happening in this industry.

⏩ Observations

With the constant awareness campaign, the entrepreneurs have targeted the consumers and made an impact on them. The product has a ready market. Technology is available. Raw material is in plenty. With the widenings of the market the demand for the product has increased manyfold. It is profitable. It is healthier, comfortable and socially accepted. Market is vast but tricky. The product is tempting entrepreneurs/manufacturers to step into this field.

⏩ Projects Ideas — Scanning of Business Environs and Identifying a Project

Project ideas could originate from various sources or due to different reasons like the success story of a friend/relative, experience of others in manufacture/sale of product, demand for certain products, chances of producing substitute of an article imported for which there is good demand etc., and of course, the motivation, background and skill of the entrepreneur and his associates.

One major aspect while choosing a project idea should be to ascertain the extent of the marketability of the product proposed to be manufactured, its general use, industries which use it, its end-use and its buyers. You should, therefore, study the demand and supply of the product over the last few years to estimate its future demand based on the past trend. While doing so, it would be necessary to take into consideration the anticipated changes in fashions, technology and levels of income of the people. If the product proposed to be manufactured has a market throughout the country, the study should take into account the demand and supply of the product for the whole country. However, if the market for the product would be confined to one/two state/or a region. Many units function as ancillaries to major industries. In such a case, their fortunes being very closely dependent and linked to that of the 'parent unit', it is very important that detailed analyses are made on the various areas before the decision to become an ancillary is made, i.e., areas like: will the unit be totally dependent on the parent unit, the potential for reasonable profit and future growth, the experience of similar ancillary units, whether there are any problems in obtaining payments or supportive know-how, whether the investment in fixed assets will be such as to facilitate easy branching off into a new product line in case the ancillary arrangement does not yield the anticipated benefits, etc.

It will be equally important to judge the market demand even when you are setting up a 'general purpose' workshop or service industry. In such cases, it will be necessary to have a clear idea of the industrial environment, the type of job orders you may obtain, whether they will be repeated, who will be giving them local competition, whether there are any large projects/establishments which promise a potential for assured orders, whether your unit will have specialisation in a particular type of work which will give an edge over your competitors, etc.

An import-substitute products basically should have a good market in view of the general policy to encourage indigenous production. It would, however, be necessary to have a clear idea of the government's import policy, present demand, the landed price of the imported item and how your price will compare with it, quality differences, etc.

In order to arrive at reasonable estimates ot the future demand for and supply of a product, information relating to the capacity of existing units manufacturing that product, the extent of its utilisation, the capacity of the units that have already been granted licences but are in the process of being established, import and export potentiality of the product etc., should be taken into consideration.

Although it is difficult to arrive at a precise forecast for demand and supply of a particular product, specially since reliable and up-to-date information is difficult to obtain, on the basis of the available data it should be possible to decide on the future prospects of the item proposed to be selected by you. Towards this, capacity utilisation of the existing units could be taken as a broad indication of the market for the product. Similarly, under utilisation of the existing capacity could be taken as a signal for little or no scope for setting up a new unit.

An SSI unit generally enters the market which is localised and already has existing manufacturers. The success of the new unit in competing with the existing manufacturers would depend on a combination of its capability to identify and approach its targeted customer group and its marketing features like price, quality, delivery schedule, sales promotion, etc.

➧ Importance of Project Identification

Project identification is often of great importance for the following reasons:

1. They become the catalytic agents of economic development.
2. They initiate the process of development – production, employment, income generation and so on.
3. They have consequences which are long-term in nature.
4. Projects provide the framework of the future activities of the enterprise.
5. They also shape the future pattern of services.
6. Projects usually involve substantial financial outlays.
7. They also initiate development of basic infrastructure and environment.
8. Project commitments cannot be easily reversed.
9. Project identification brings the necessary changes in society in course of time.
10. Projects accelerate the process of socio-cultural development.

➧ Selection of Product

At this stage, the entrepreneur is concerned with identifying a particular product that he hopes to market successfully at a reasonable profit. Therefore, the selection of the right product is very essential for being successful in the business venture. The right product here means that which can be marketed at a reasonable profit which will go towards growth business. Various factors influence the entrepreneur in selecting the right product. These decisive factors are: *(i)* Whether import restrictions or the items selected are banned items would considerably weigh favourably or otherwise in the selection of the products. This is because in the case of banned items the domestic market offers considerable scope for selling as the demand for such a product would not be met by import. Thus, if the item selected fall in the category of banned import items, the entrepreneur would favour it and in the case of unrestricted import of the items, he would definitely not show his favour for selecting such a product. *(ii)* If the entrepreneur himself or his partners have gathered, substantial amount of experience in the manufacture and marketing of certain products, then the selection of such a product would be to their advantage. Therefore, most often the items selected are of those lines of products in which the entrepreneur or his colleagues have gathered enough experience. The line in which they are not experienced obviously would not be favoured much as it will entail uncertain situations very often. *(iii)* The selection of the product will also be based upon the degree of profitability that generally rules in the market. Such information can be obtained from the banks or the financial corporations or the market itself. The selection, therefore, will depend upon the information compiled for the particular line of product for its profitability. *(iv)* Many concessions are available from the government for producing a product which serves as an import substitute or even essential item, hence if a particular product enjoys a substantial amount of incentives, concessions, liberal taxation policies, obviously the entrepreneur will select that item to enjoy these advantages conferred on the production of this particular type of product. *(v)* Many products belong to the priority industries or small-scale sector also; certain products are listed by the Government for purchasing exclusively from the small-scale sector. As a result if a particular product belongs to this category, the selection of such a product would be advantageous for the entrepreneur; therefore, these factors also must receive due consideration before the selection of a product. *(vi)* The market for the product also plays a significant role in the selection of the product. If the product also has an export market, it widens the scope of marketing, hence such a product has its own advantages in the success of the enterprise. *(vii)* Certain products are permitted for production only if the licence is obtained from the appropriate authority while others belong to the de-licensed category. In the case of a licensed product, obtaining a licence would be a difficult proposition or the capacity required for the entire industry may also have been created fully by the government. As a consequence, impossibility of seeking further permission for the production of such a product. A product belonging to licensed category or de-licensed category also is considered before selecting the product. *(viii)* Many products enjoy specific advantages in regard to the scale of manufacture or carry locational advantages, e.g., if produced in a free trade zone or in the backward areas with special incentives and concessions which are made available for manufacturing such a product. Selection of a product therefore depends upon these factors. *(ix)* If a product belongs

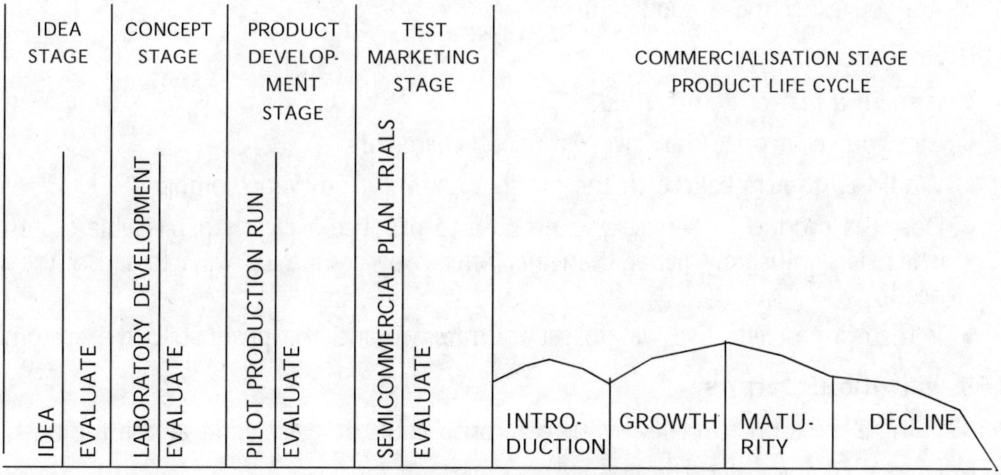

Fig. 1 Product-Planning and Development Process

Source: Adapted from Robert D. Hisrich and Michael P. Peters, *Marketing Decisions for New and Mature Products.* (Columbus, Ohio: Charles E. Merrill Publishing Co., 1984).

to an ancillary unit and serves as a major component for the parent industry, it provides a ready demand, hence selection of this type of product entails easy marketability.

Finally, at this stage, the selection of product would also be weighed in favour or against depending upon whether or not the machinery and the raw materials required would be imported or indigenous. Similarly, the section would also be based upon the skill and unskilled labour position as well as the technical know-how which is available indigenously or would require foreign collaboration.

The study of the project idea is the starting point of the feasibility analysis. The study is undertaken to identify the logic of the project, the tasks which must be performed for achieving the objectives, and the inputs, outputs and process involved in each activity. The ultimate aim is to identify the characteristics of the project. A project idea poses a problem, on the one hand and seeks a solution of the problem, on the other. In order that the solution may be an appropriate one, it is necessary to examine and appreciate the nature and extent of the problem and to clearly identify its dimensions.

CHECKLIST FOR CHOOSING IDEAS

Fit with your skills and experience

- Do you believe in the product or service?
- Does the need it fits mean something to you personally?
- Do you like and understand the potential customers?
- Do you have experience in this type of business?
- Do the basic success factors of this business fit your skills?
- Are the tasks of the enterprise the ones you will enjoy doing yourself?
- Are the people the enterprise employ will enjoy working with and supervising?
- Has the idea begun to take over your imagination and spare time?
- Is the idea innovative to the extent of social benefit?
- Are you expecting a good return?

Fit with the Market

- Is there a real customer need?
- Can you get a price that gives you good margins?
- Would customers believe in the product coming from your company?
- Does the product or service you propose to produce a clearly perceivable customer benefit which is significantly better than that offered by competing ways to satisfy the same basic need?
- Is there a cost effective way to get the message and the product to the customers?

Fit with the Enterprise

- Is there a reason to believe your enterprise could be very good at the business?
- Does it fit the enterprise culture?
- Can you imagine who might sponsor it?
- Does it look profitable (high margin – low investment)?
- Will it lead to large markets and growth?

What to do when your idea is rejected?

Frequently, as an entrepreneur, you may find that your idea has been rejected and/or is not successful as envisaged. There are a few things you can do:

1. Give up and select a new idea.
2. Listen carefully, understand what is wrong, improve your idea and your presentation, and try again.
3. Find someone else to whom you present your idea by considering:
   – Who will benefit most if it works and can they be a sponsor?
   – Who are the potential customers and will they demand the product?
   – How can you get to the people who really care about entrepreneurial ideas?

All India financial institutions like ICICI, IDBI, SIDBI and IFCI, State Industrial Corporations and leading nationalised banks, have jointly promoted the Industrial and Technical Consultancy Organisation Ltd. (ITCO). Its objective is to provide high quality technical, managerial and marketing consultancy to new as well as existing entrepreneurs. Major services included in its sphere of operations are as under:

1. It helps entrepreneurs in scanning out various project opportunities and ultimately selecting a suitable one.
2. It helps aspiring new entrepreneurs to choose a good profitable industrial project opportunity. If one has one's own project idea, ITCO will test the same for its overall viability.
3. ITCO's technical, marketing and financial experts will prepare a comprehensive project report which would be more than sufficient for applying to the respective financial institutions for financial assistance.
4. ITCO also undertakes exclusive market surveys, regional or all-India, for small, medium or large projects.
5. For entrepreneurs who have all basic details ready with them, ITCO can assist by way of preparing "Loan Application", at a very nominal charge.
6. It provides a comprehensive project finance services, especially for medium and large-scale projects, by way of preparation of term-loan application and documentation,

EFFECTIVE MANTRA

"Effective leadership is putting first things first. Effective management is discipline, carrying it out." — Stephen Covey, leadership expert.

21

Sources of Ideas

Introduction

Economic growth, profit and satisfaction are the main concerns of entrepreneurs. This concern with economic growth is linked to a keen interest in the ideas. It is the idea that succeed. It is the ideas that indeed contribute to products, industries, services contribute to economic growth.

In the previous chapter we have discussed about search for ideas and we shall discuss the sources of ideas in this chapter.

Sources of Ideas

A business idea/project idea may be discovered from several sources. The ideas also originate in several forms:

A government-owned laboratory filing the most parents in the country; the chief of another government-owned laboratory defecting to the private sector; a resurgence in venture capital activity in the country, this time focused around the creation of

IP (Intellectual Property); a continuation of the trend of multinationals putting down research laboratories and development centres in India; and a significant growth in patent-filing activity by Indian companies. Like all good ideas it grows and grew till it acquired a life of its own.

Early on in the making of this, BT's Twelfth Anniversary Issue, it became evident that this wasn't just about multinationals setting research-shop in India.

Project identification is concerned with collection, compilation and analysis of economic data for the eventual purpose of locating possible opportunities for investment and with the development of such opportunities.

Opportunities according to Drucker are of three kinds: *additive, complementary* and *breakthrough.* Additive opportunities are those opportunities which enable the decision-maker to better utilise the existing resources without in any way involving a change in the character of business. These opportunities involve minimum disturbance to the existing state of affairs and hence the least risk. Complementary opportunities involve the introduction of new ideas and as such do lead to a certain amount of change in the existing structure. Breakthrough opportunities, on the other hand involve fundamental changes in both the structure and character of business. These opportunities involve minimum disturbance to the existing state of affairs and hence the least risk. The element of risk is greater in the case of complementary opportunities and is greatest in the case of breakthrough opportunities. As the element of risk increases, it becomes more and more important to precisely define the scope and nature of the project objectives and to select the best possible approach so as to minimise both resource consumption and risks and to optimise the return or gains.

Human mind has an infinite capacity to observe and to innovate and deduct. Observation is one of the most important sources of project ideas. The observant mind continuously comes across situations which can be utilised to develop investment opportunities. The observation may be made during the course of one's routine occupation or otherwise. The dearth of a particular article or service may for instance lead to the development of an industry which can provide the article or service in short supply. The availability of a specified type of raw material or skill may lead to yet another type of industrial activity. The observant mind is always on the look out for opportunities which can form the basis for the development of new project ideas. Observation of the existing processes can sometimes lead to new opportunities and financially beneficial project ideas.

This would for instance be the case when a processing unit decides to manufacture machines which it has so far been using for processing purpose only. The process of deduction is on many occasions used to supplement and rationalise project ideas based on pure observations. In innovative units, it often becomes necessary to depend upon the deductive process for the development of new approaches to the solution of existing problems.

Trade and professional magazines provide a very fertile source of project ideas. The statistics and information given by these magazines and reports and records of professional bodies often reveal opportunities which can be eventually developed into investment propositions. It is very important for every person who is involved in the development of new investment opportunities to remain in touch with the latest developments in his own field of specialisation. It is also necessary for him to keep in touch with developments in order fields which may be horizontally or even vertically liked with his own line of specialisation. Study of technical and professional literature, besides keeping a person all in a running attitude (courant), also stimulates thinking and helps in the process of development of new project ideas.

Bulletins of Research Institutes are also a very fertile source of information for new project ideas and opportunities. These bulletins generally give the broad outlines of the new processes or products developed by research institution. However, the information made available in the research Bulletin may not be adequate for concretisation of ideas. Further correspondence with the research institute may become necessary.

In most developing countries where planned development has been accepted as an approach towards the removal of poverty, the plan document published by the Government provides a very useful source of project ideas. The plan document generally analyses the existing economic situation in a country and also pinpoints the investment opportunities which fit into the overall planning effort. Considerable information can, therefore, be gathered from the plan document.

Departmental publications of various departments of Governments also provide useful information which can help in the development of new project ideas. These publications are either periodical in character or are issued on special occasions. The census document which is a periodical publication is a very useful source of information about the economic structure of the society and various trends in the growth of economy and purchasing power and can be used to develop new ideas.

The project idea is a user friendly concept of what a project should be like. It is the raw expression of the desire of the project sponsoring body to achieve something. The exact form in which the project idea is expressed is immaterial. In order to avoid unnecessary communication between the project sponsoring body and the project formulation team, the project idea should indicate broad objectives of the sponsor and limit these in time, space, function and structure. In case no limitations are envisaged, the sponsoring body should state so and leave the project formulation team in no doubt about it.

(i) Observing Markets: Careful observation of markets can reveal a business idea. Market surveys can also reveal the demand and supply position for various products. It is necessary to estimate future demand and to take into account anticipated changes in fashions, income levels, technology, etc. In this connection, it will be useful to ascertain whether the demand is elastic or inelastic and whether the product is repeat purchase or not. Attempt should be made to determine the trend of demand and the composition and pattern of potential users of the product. A survey of the available channels of distribution should also be made so that the selling campaign can be properly planned well in advance of the production. Advice of professional experts like dealers, commercial consultants, bank managers, advertising agencies may also be obtained to supplement product analysis and market surveys.

Competition and price trends can also be found through market surveys. From the data collected through market observation, one can identify the products/industries which are in demand and which require increase in supply. A promoter can then find out the most profitable line of business. For example, the scarcity of edible oil prompted many firms to enter into the production/supply of edible oils in India.

(ii) Prospective Consumers: Consumer knows best what he wants and the habits/tastes which are going to be popular in the near future. Contacts with prospective consumers can also reveal the features that should be built into a product/service. These days good business firms generally conduct a survey among prospective consumers before choosing the product to be manufactured. These firms also conduct a market test of the prototype product before launching it into the market. The customer is the foundation of a business and it is he who keeps it going. Therefore, data on consumer needs and preferences must be collected. Initially, a new enterprise should concentrate on one or a limited range of products. More products can he added to complete the line later on as the business becomes well established.

(*iii*) *Developments in other nations:* People in underdeveloped countries generally follow the fashion trends of developed countries. For example, video, washing machines, micro ovens, etc. which are now the 'in things' in India were being used in the United States and Europe before the eighties. Therefore, an entrepreneur can discover good business ideas by keeping in touch with developments in advanced nations. Sometimes, entrepreneurs visit foreign countries in search of ideas for new products/processes. Trade delegations of various chambers of commerce, etc. visit foreign markets to explore foreign collaborations and other types of business ideas.

(*iv*) *Study of project profiles:* Various Government and private agencies publish periodic profiles of various projects and industries. These profiles describe in detail the technical, financial and market requirements and prevailing position. A careful scrutiny of such project profiles is very helpful in choosing the line of business. Technical and other types of experts may be employed to carry out a specialised study of project profiles and to suggest the most promoting projects/industries for further evaluations.

(*v*) *Government organisations:* Several Government organisations nowadays assist entrepreneurs in discovering and evaluating business ideas. Development banks, state industrial development/investment corporations, technical consultancy organisations, investment centres, export promotion councils, etc. provide advice and assistance in technical, financial, marketing and other areas of business. Government also identifies the priority sectors for investment through five year plans, industrial policy resolutions and guidelines for industry. In this connection government publications on trade and industry can also be helpful in discovering business ideas. Items reserved for small sector will also indicate the potential areas.

(*v*) *Trade Fairs and Exhibitions:* National and international trade fairs are a very good source of business ideas. At these fairs, producers and dealers in the concerned industry put up their products for display and/or sale. A visit to these fairs provides information about new products/machines. Negotiations for the purchase, production, collaboration, dealership, etc. may also be made at these fairs.

(*vii*) *Attending Motivation Campaigns:* Entrepreneurial programmes are organised periodically by the Public Sector Commercial banks, Industrial and Technical consultancy organisations, Small Industries Service Institute and the District Industries Centres individually and in association with one another where also advice and guidance are made available to the Interested participants/potential entrepreneurs.

►► Creativity

You need creativity initiatives for all business purposes. We all have a tendency to look for creativity in products and to forget about its importance in processes, practices, and perceptions. Such myopia can lead only to disaster. No business today can afford to neglect the need for continual renewal of its marketing, its recruiting, its accounting, its planning processes, and so on. Ditto for pedagogic creativity: improvement in the methods by which a company passes on old skills to new employees and teaches new skills to old employees. Even the realm of corporate values should support a certain kind of creativity. Businesses are not traditional societies that, with involuntary efficiency, disseminate their values through, as it were, everyone's mental DNA. The values that companies work by, and do business by, must be consciously and deliberately – that is, creatively or uncreatively – established.

Mr. P.E. Vernon says that creativity involves novel combinations or unusual association of ideas which must have theoretical or social values or make an emotional impact. Creative thinking has a theme, is rational and is problem-oriented. The problem, however, is not dealt within a routine manner. Solution to the problem involves innovative thinking, which produces either better, more ingenuous, or more aesthetic results than usual. 'originality' in that original thought merely means something new or different, without the value or utility implied in creativity.

Creativity is seldom a single flash of intuition. Instead, it is a process that generally involves extensive analysis of a number of places of information and a separation of the irrelevant from the significant. Much creativity results from analyzing a variety of combinations and searching for new relationships. Ideas do sometimes come after a sudden burst of insight. Usually, however, the individual has been working on the problem for some time.

Recent research shows that creativity is also the ability to use different modes of thought. Howard E. Gardner, Co-director of a long-term study at Harvard University, on creativity development in children theorizes that humans have at least seven distinct capabilities: logical, linguistic, musical, spatial, sensitivity to bodily sensations, self-understanding, and the understanding of others. No one intelligence is intrinsically creative. Creativity requires honing one or more of these intellectual processes to a high degree.

THE CREATIVE PROCESS

The basic steps in the creative process include the following:

1. Desire: A creative idea can be discovered by accident. More frequently, however, the individual either from within or as a result of an external request has a personal need or desire to solve a problem. Thus conscious or unconscious motivation is usually present to begin the thought process.

2. Preparation: Most creative ideas come only after an intense period of preparation. This involves gathering information and laying a foundation as also trying to see new and meaningful relationships among ideas that are already familiar. The originality of the creative idea is usually a direct result of the amount of data gathered and the information available. The more alternatives available, the more potentially creative the solution.

3. Experimentation: This stage involves trying out various alternative solutions to the problem.

4. Incubation: Here the problem is mulled over, either at a conscious or an unconscious level.

5. Illumination: A flash of insight – an event that often occurs during the incubation period – may lead to the solution. At other tunes, however, the individual may need to gather new data and conduct new experiments to get this illumination.

6. Refinement: Usually the new idea is only tentative, needing to be polished and improved. At other time, little or no work need be done on refinement, particularly if the innovation is a simple one.

7. Implementation: After the discovery is made and polished, it need to be adopted and put into practice.

However, these steps may or may not take place sequentially; for example, experimentation may sometimes follow the development of the creative solution.

Many of the characteristics and qualities that make up an individual's internal creative climate are listed below. There may be others, and the ones noted here probably overlap to some extent. Nevertheless, these 19 characteristics should be fairly representative of the factors involved:

Curiosity: Creative individuals are always searching for explanations and need to discover answers by themselves.

Independence: Creative people are free thinkers; they maintain a strong sense of their own identity. Their freedom from convention enables them to break away from the traditional constraints imposed on problems and view things with new eyes.

Ability to Defer Judgement: Many people react instinctively and attack new ideas with their most negatively critical opinions. In contrast, people who have developed their creative potential have learned to give new ideas a chance to breathe and grow.

Willingness to Test Assumptions: Adept creative problem solvers know that the most important phase of the process is defining the problem by testing all possible assumptions about the problem situation.

Optimism: Creative people view the world with bright, positive eyes. This does not mean, however, that they see everything through rose-coloured glasses; however, they tend to maintain an attitude that things can be done, that the problem can be solved.

Humour: Humorous people are capable of taking life and twisting it around to produce new ways of looking at themselves and others, a trait unvaluable to creativity. Humour acts as a catalyst to creativity by helping to unleash subconscious information useful for making connections and producing creative insights.

Self-confidence: Being creative requires a certain amount of belief in oneself, and creative people believe that they have the abilities needed to produce unique problem solutions.

Openness to Ideas: Most creative people are aware that being creative is not a static condition but a dynamic, ongoing process of growth and development; thus they are constantly vigilant for any new ideas they might use or build on.

Persistence: Creative problem solving isn't easy, and luck doesn't help much. Persistence does much to ensure that a solution will be achieved.

Concentration: Because of their hard-to-solve nature, most unstructured problems require intense periods of concentration, which usually isn't hard for most creative people, since they become so immersed in the problem that little disturbs them. Most creative people have learned, however, to switch occasionally to another problem or an unrelated activity. Then, when they return to the original problem, they can resume their intense concentration with fresh energy.

Tolerance for Ambiguity: People with a relatively poor internal creative climate usually have trouble dealing with ambiguity, which characterises most unstructured problems. Creative people, in contrast, tend to view people and situations in different shades of gray. Rarely will a creative person stereotype people or situations.

Self-awareness: Most problems are portions of situations onto which we project a little of ourselves. As an extension of yourself, a problem situation will be easier to solve if you know why you are perceiving it in a particular way.

Commitment: Because unstructured problems do not bring with them any easy recipes that will guarantee a solution, solvers of such problems must develop an attitude that nothing can deter them, that it is their problem, and that they have dedicated themselves to developing a workable solution.

Flexibility: Creative problem solvers have to stand loose. A person needs mental flexibility to develop new perspectives when defining a problem as well as to generate different types of solutions.

Willingness to Take Risks: People who engage in creative problem-solving must be prepared to assume certain risks in their quest for solutions. Otherwise, they may not be able to view the problem in a way that makes creative solutions possible.

Discipline: There is no such thing as a "correct" approach in creative problem solving. Rather, the essential factor is the extent to which progress is made in working toward a solution – regardless of the approach used. And making progress requires discipline to stick with a problem and approach it from many different angles.

NEW BUSINESS CONCEPT GENERATION AND GESTATION PROCESS

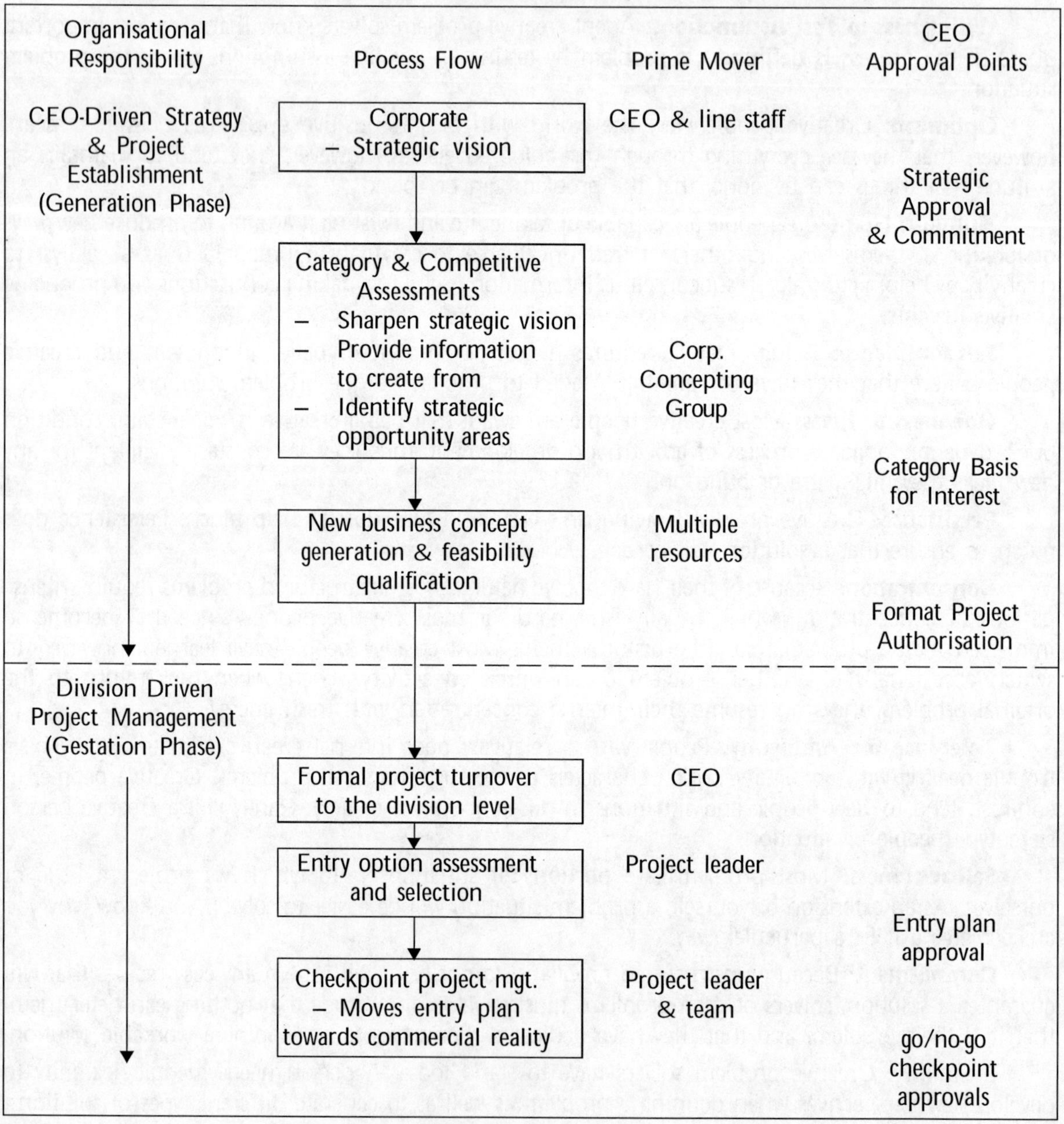

Fig. 1

Ability to use Imagery: We all develop visual images of problems. Unfortunately, many fail to use imaginary when it would be most helpful. By developing mental images of problems at the appropriate times, a person can often produce unique solutions with less effort than might be required using a more analytical procedure.

Ability to Toy with Problems and Ideas: Playing with an object helps children understand it better. The same can be true when we deal with ideas. Creative people play with problems and ideas before taking action; it is only by toying with their problems that many people can truly understand and deal with them.

Impulsiveness: Creativity also benefits from intuitive and impulsive leaps of the subconscious, which frequently result in a remote association that you wouldn't have made if you had been more deliberate in your approach.

INCREASED INNOVATION

Innovation will provide the basis for the sustainability of an organisation. Richard Foster in his book Innovation has sketched the curve of performance versus effort for technological progress. The result is an S-shaped curve that moves from infancy to explosion and then a gradual maturation. The key to sustainability is the ability to glide through successive such S curves, in other words, the ability to continually innovate. 3M, on account of its constant innovation (it has something like 60,000 products in its stable) has been able to glide smoothly through many successive S-curves and thus has built an incredible amount of staying power in the market.

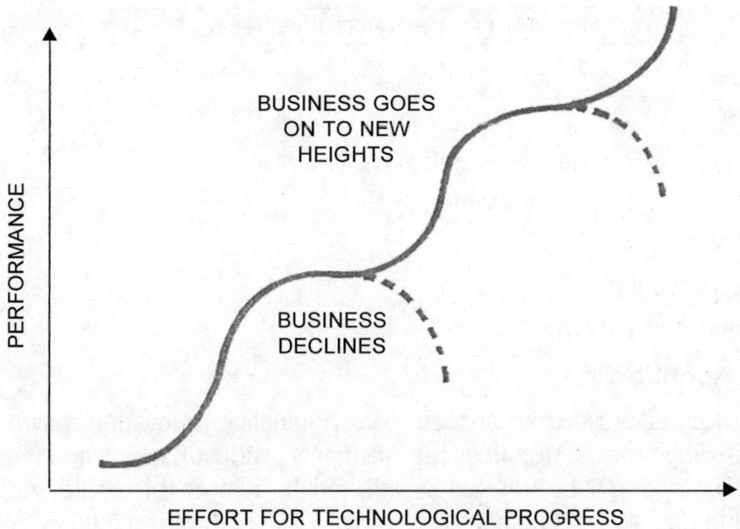

Fig. 2 The Successive S-Curve

Implicit in continuous innovation is the importance of cannibalisation. Intel is one of the few organisations that has perfected the art of cannibalisation. As the market of a processor begins to mature, Intel launches a superior processor, and tries to make the market graduate to its new offering. This not only pre-empts imitators, but also keeps margins high for Intel. In fact, with its continual innovation and cannibalisation, Intel has been able to create an artificial monopoly for itself.

Though there are no set rules, Rosebeth Moss Kanter, a Professor at Harvard University has suggested six characteristics of innovation:

- Uncertain
- Knowledge intensive
- Controversial
- Crosses boundaries
- Changes work relationships and hierarchical arrangements
- Conditions for organisation and innovation are different from those of adoption and diffusion.

Thus, "if innovation is uncertain, fragile, political and imperialistic (reaching out to other territories)," she adds, "then it is most likely to flourish where conditions allow flexibility, feedback, quick action and intensive care, coalition formation, and connectedness." Here Kanter also hints at the organisational environment that surrounds the entire process.

THE STEP THEORY

Attraction of new customers

Innovation of products and services

Innovation of value-delivery system

Acquisition and/or consolidation

Expansion into new geographies

Step outs into new competitive arenas

Current Business

Fig. 3

The innovation process involves at least five generic stages:

- Idea generation and concept definition
- Model development
- Limited/test production
- Full production and growth

Diffusion and Adoption

Innovation cannot be divorced from change. A technological innovation may bring a change in the materials, manufacturing process, stop-floor management, product packing and marketing strategies too. This change may be opposed by the people affected by it and this could initiate a debate or opposition which is seldom objective. Often restructuring in an organisation follows a major innovation or breakthrough. It is important to ensure that a minor innovation that could possibly take place at such a time is not ignored.

Conclusion

All the essentials to make India a great power are embedded in the richness of our civilisation already. These are: the tradition of lifelong intellectual quest, respect for wealth creation and work excellence held in high esteem.

A variety of favourable factors have arisen in the 20th century to nurture these seeds and help them grow into a mighty force. These include a critical mass of educated and skilled young men and

Chart I

SYSTEM OF POLICY MEASURES TO PROMOTE THE USE OF INFORMATION SYSTEMS

1. Promotion of the use of computers by small and medium of firms
   - (Survey-Studies)
     - Research on the development of new small and medium retail businesses
     - Research on the wider use of microcomputers (Institute of the Japan Small Business Corporation)
   - (Training)
     - Activities — Training activities on information processing and related matters (Institute of the Japan Small Business Corporation)
     - Preparations — Facilities for training (Institute of the Japan Small Business Corporation)
   - (Consultation, Guidance)
     - Consultation to promote the introduction of computers
     - OA System Center for Small and Medium Enterprises
   - (Development of technology)
     - Activities to promote the use of information systems in small and medium firms (Subsidies from the Information Technology Promotion Agency, Japan)
     - Research on the programme for small and medium firms
     - Development of a general-purpose programme for small and medium firms
     - Technology development for the uses of computers in small and medium firms
   - (Promotion of the introduction of equipment and programmes)
     - Activities to lease computer equipment (Structural strengthening)
     - System of programme credit insurance
     - Loans for the modernization of equipment of smaller enterprise (Applied to the acquisitions of computers)
2. Establishment of an information service system enterprises
   - (Small Business Information Center — Collection and dissemination of information
   - (Small and Medium Enterprise Regional Information Centres) — Establishment of information activity system of Regional Information Centers
   - (Local Public bodies) — Research on regional information system of network systems of small and medium
   - (Promotion Centers of Local Industries) — Activities to upgrade information functions
     - Activities to collect and disseminate information
3. Establishment of intensive information system in guidance organizations.
   - (Small and Medium Enterprise Agency), Bureau of International Trade and Industry — Commission on payment monitoring system to sub-contractors
   - (Comprehensive Guidance Center) — Installation of computers (15 stations)
   - (Federations of Small Business Associations) — Model Federation of intensive information operations (one federation)
   - (Societies of Commerce and Industry. Chambers of Commerce and Industry)
     - Commission on research to develop an information processing system for the management of small-scale firms
     - Expenses to promote computerization of book-keeping
   - (Association for Sub-contracting Enterprises Promotion) — Rental Fee of OA Environment

women, strong institutions of science and technology, a new sense of self-confidence amongst professionals, and last but not least, the unleashing of the private sector's productive energies. Indians are set to climb new peaks of innovation and creativity. These forms the continuous source of ideas on an ongoing basis.

India has a momentous opportunity to leverage the power of her people and build on the promise of her potential to emerge as a global superpower. realise this potential, we need to focus on the following:

- Empower young inspiring leaders in all walks of life to stimulate over a billion people in a resurgent wave.
- Invest in professional resource development to bridge people power and global opportunities.
- Nurture innovation to differentiate and promote indigenous initiatives that could define the future.
- Develop infrastructure to bring people, resources and opportunities together, in an inclusive eco-system.
- Foster information and communication technologies – powerful tools of the knowledge age – to pervade the economy and society in a ubiquitous manner.

Innovation has the potential to distinguish India from other nations. We have one of the largest education infrastructures in the world. We have one of the largest science and technology manpower bases in the world. We have a strong institutional framework in science and technology. The cognitive ability of Indians is legendary. We now need to bring about a dynamic partnership between creators of wealth, producers of goods, providers of services and people engaged in generation of ideas.

ATTITUDINAL ISSUE

"Creating a culture of consumer trust is the single most important aspect of the successful adoption of CRM. It has nothing to do with software, it has everything to do with attitude." — ***Don Peppers, Guru of CRM***

22

Idea Processing

Introduction

A business idea germinates and to convert into a business opportunity it is to be scrutinised carefully.

1. Preliminary Evaluation and Testing of Ideas

Once business ideas are discovered, screening and testing of these ideas is done. The following considerations are significant in the evaluation and testing of business ideas.

(a) Technical feasibility

It refers to the possibility of producing the product. Technical feasibility of an idea is judged in terms of availability of necessary technology, machinery and equipment, labour skills and raw materials. The advice and assistance of technical experts may be necessary to judge the technical feasibility of various business ideas.

(b) Commercial viability

A cost-benefit analysis is required to ascertain the profitability of the ideas. An elaborate study of market conditions and prevailing situation is made to assess the viability and prospects of the proposed project. This is known as feasibility study of the project. A number of calculations have to be made about the likely demand, expected sales volume, selling price, cost of production, break-even point, etc. The services of market analysis and financial experts may be necessary for this propose.

There is a difference between a business idea and a business opportunity. While the idea for a product or service may be workable (technically feasible), the proposed business built on this may not be profitable. It is normal for an entrepreneur to have several ideas that have to be rejected before finding one that is not only workable but worthwhile. In order to judge the workability and profitability of the proposed business, feasibility analysis has to be conducted.

2. Detailed Analysis

After preliminary evaluation of the idea, the promising idea is subjected to a thorough analysis from all angles. Full investigation is carried out in the technical feasibility and economic viability of the proposed project. Financial and managerial feasibility of the idea are tested. At this stage a lot of information is required. Consultations with experts in various areas of the industry may be necessary to carry out the detailed analysis. Due care should be exercised at this stage because the idea is finally accepted or rejected at this stage.

After the evaluation of a business idea is completed, the findings are presented in the form of a report known as 'feasibility report' or 'project report.' This report helps in the final selection of project. It is also useful for procuring licences, finance, etc. from governmental agencies.

3. Idea Selection

The feasibility report is analysed to finally choose the most promising idea. Generally, the following considerations influence the selection of idea for a product or service:

(*a*) Products whose imports are banned or restricted by the government.

(*b*) Products which can be exported easily and profitably.

(*c*) Products whose demand exceeds their supply so that there exists ready demand.

(*d*) Products in which the entrepreneur has manufacturing and/or marketing experience.

(*e*) Parent ancillary relationships, *i.e.*, the product is to be manufactured for a parent company.

(*f*) Products which showed high profitability.

(*g*) Products based on the expansion or diversification plans of existing forms of the family/friends/relatives.

(*h*) Products which ensured specific advantages. The advantages might accrue because of the scale of the industry or the location of the factory or technology of manufacture.

(*i*) Products favoured by the country's industrial/licensing policy, *e.g.*, delicensed industries.

(*j*) Products for which incentives and subsidies are available.

While considering these various factors – market, owner's own experience, policy and incentives – an entrepreneur would generally come across a mix of some encouraging and some discouraging factors with reference to every product. It therefore, becomes necessary to analyse and compare the pros and cons. A selection matrix may be prepared for this purpose. In the selection matrix given in Table 1, a comparison is made between Project A and Project B.

Table 1

ENTREPRENEURIAL SELECTION MATRIX

Data	***Project A***	***Project B***
1. Product	Priority industry	Reserved for small industry
2. Raw material required	Imported	Indigenous
3. Machinery	Imported	Indigenous
4. Market	Defence Ministry	Local
5. Technical Know-how	Foreign trained personnel	Indigenous
6. Location	Free trade zone	Backward area
7. Profitability	High	Low

Source: H.N. Pathak – Project Planning in Udai Pareek and T.V. Rao – Developing Entrepreneurship, Learning Systems, New Delhi, 1971, 16.

Many more items can be added for such comparison. The matrix indicates the type of diverse data that needs to be collected for each project. It also throws light on how each item can hold out some encouraging and some discouraging factors. The entrepreneurial selection needs to take all these factors into account.

4. Input Requirements

Once the promoter is convinced of the feasibility and profitability of the project, he assembles the necessary resources to launch the enterprise. He has to choose partners/collaborators, collect the required finances and acquire land and buildings, plant and machinery, furniture and fixtures, patents, employees, etc. Decisions have to be made about the size, location, layout, etc. of the enterprise. The form of ownership organisation has to be selected. According to Shubin "the firm is launched by assembling and organising the physical facilities, developing operation and production processes, advertising its product and initiating a sales promotion campaign, recruiting labour and accumulating inventories."

The Adoption Process

The adoption of an innovation demands planned management of change (overcoming the resistance to change). An adoption process is a process bringing about a change in a buyer's attitudes and perception. Consumer adoption process covers the steps that a consumer usually goes through in determining the feasibility of buying new products: (1) Awareness, (2) Interest, (3) Evaluation or mental trial, (4) Trial (physical), (5) Adoption.

1. ***Awareness:*** A person learns about a new idea, product or practice. He has general information about it, *e.g.*, through advertisement. He has, however, limited knowledge about special qualities, usefulness, performance, etc., regarding the innovation. He merely knows about its existence.

2. ***Interest:*** He now develops an interest in the innovation. He demands more detailed information about the new product, its utility, its performance, and so on. He listens with interest to Jingles on the radio or TV ads, reads press ads, and learns more about it from others, and is now inclined to actively seek the desired information from sales-persons, opinion leaders, peers, friends, etc.

3. ***Evaluation:*** The accumulated information and evidences are weighed by the person in order to assess the basic soundness or worth of the innovation. He tries to weigh the value of the new product and the extent to which it is good for him. In a sense, he conducts a mental trial of the new product.

4. ***Trial:*** The person now is ready to put the idea into practice. Competent personal assistance is necessary to put the innovation to use.

5. ***Adoption:*** It is the final stage in which he makes a decision to buy. The person now decides to adopt the new idea, product or practice for continued use. If post-purchase experience is good, he becomes a repeat buyer and a talking advertisement of the innovation.

➧ Product Innovation

The innovation attitude of the marketer is expressed in the watch word "innovate or die." Such an attitude must be an integral part of the marketing concept. P. Drucker recognised the equal importance of innovative attitude and marketing concept. He said, "Because it is its purpose to create a customer, any business enterprise must have only two basic functions: *marketing* and *innovation.* All growth industries have an important role for innovation in their marketing and market penetration plans. Innovation alone assures growth and survival while customers' orientation assures survival. The evolution of new products is a practical business function and it is described as a process product management. The new product programme must be organised and controlled if it is to be effectively managed. The process of product planning and development is always adopted for product innovation. Product development is a general term covering the search for new products and new innovations as well as the improvement of existing products.

METHODS OF OBTAINING PRODUCTS

1 Internal Development	2 Licensing	3 Acquisition
Discovering and developing new products by the firm itself. Desirable means.	Securing right to produce the product from a patent holder – Contractual arrangement, *e.g.,* Coca Cola.	Buying the firm that developed or patented the product. Costly means.

Note:
1. Internal product innovation implies no payment of profits to inventor or developer.
2. Licensing obviates the possibility of internal discovery and may inevitable or preferable, e.g., complex products like electronics.
3. Acquisition is very costly but gives exclusive rights.

Fig. 1

➧ Product Planning and Development Strategy

Marketers have four alternative ways of bringing about an increase in sales and profits: (1) Market penetration; (2) Market development; (3) Product development; and (4) Product diversification.

	EXISTING MARKETS	NEW MARKETS
EXISTING PRODUCTS →	MARKET PENETRATION A	MARKET DEVELOPMENT B
NEW PRODUCTS →	PRODUCT DEVELOPMENT C	DIVERSIFICATION D

Fig. 2 Four Basic Types of Opportunities for Sales Growth

Market Penetration: It involves the expansion of sales of the existing products in the existing markets by selling more to present customers or gaining new customers in the existing markets. The firm can market its present products to existing markets. This is done through a more aggressive marketing mix. Customers from rivals or potential buyers can also be attracted. Existing buyers may be induced to increase their rate of use. We may have a temporary price cut to raise the volume of sales and penetrate the market in a big way.

Market Development: In market development, a present product is introduced to a new market or segment. Market development is the creation of new markets by discovering new applications for existing goods, e.g., Mini-bus may be made available for goods or passengers. The firm can offer its existing products to new markets. This is another alternative to expand market opportunity, prolong product life cycles, profitability and survival.

Product Development: Product development occurs when a firm introduces new products into a market in which it is well established. Product development is the introduction of new products in the present market, e.g., new synthetic fibres for known textile products. The firm may decide to create new products for the existing market. Established firms with high customer patronage may have new product additions upon existing market successes. The firm by offering new or improved products to present markets can satisfy the present customers better and stand assured of their loyalty.

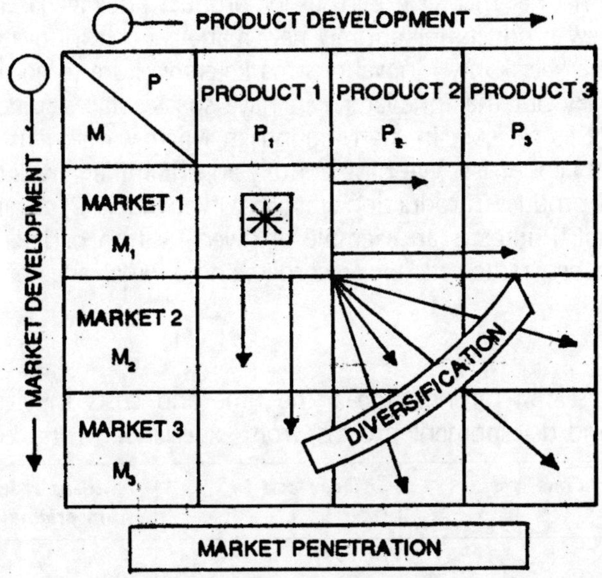

Fig. 3 Relationship between various Marketing Strategies

Note:
1. We have four marketing strategies to achieve growth: (1) Market Penetration, (2) Product Development, (3) Market Development, and (4) Diversification.
2. Market penetration, *i.e.,* penetrating the current market for higher usage rate is a conservative choice.
3. Diversificaiton by entering a new market with brand new product is the most radical choice. It is the most difficult strategy as the firm has no market expertise and no product knowledge. Many firms fail in their diversification straegies.

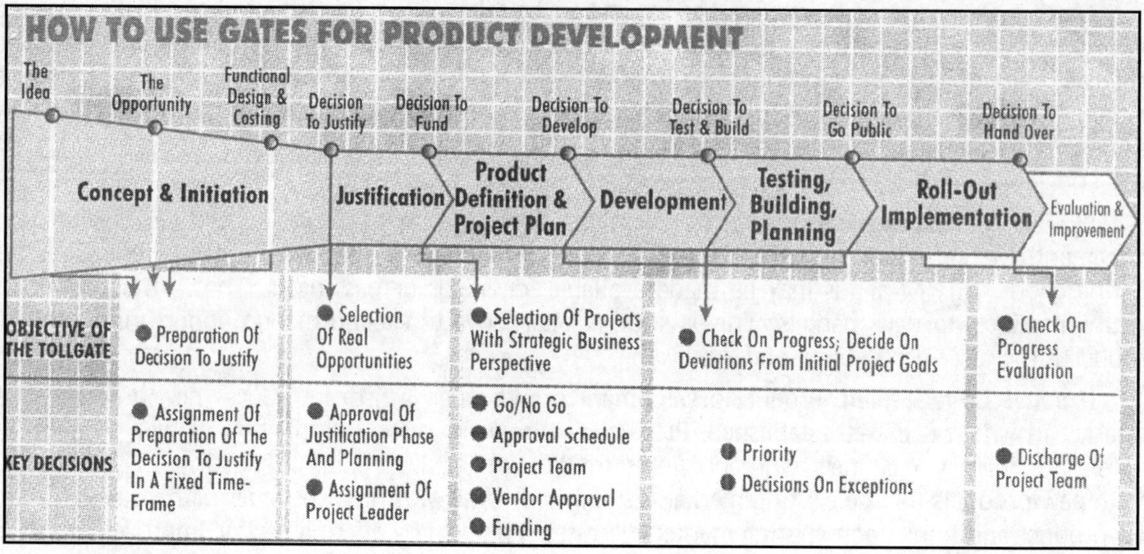

Diversification: Diversification occurs when a firm seeks to enter a new market with a completely new product. Such a firm has neither market expertise nor product knowledge. The firm may adopt a daring strategy by creating new products for entirely new markets. The innovations are introduced for the first time in the new markets. Only innovations marketers venture to go in for diversification of products. The strategy is risky but the innovator can have spectacular results. In 1960, polaroid camera and television were in this category in many countries. Micro-wave ovens and digital watches are novelties even today in many countries. We have entirely an unfamiliar product for an unfamiliar market. Factors rating for a new product introduction are: (1) marketability, (2) durability, (3) Productive ability, and (4) growth potential. Philips is an example of diversification or lateral integration: light bulbs, radio lamps, television tubes, radio sets, tape-recorders and a wide range of luminaries or lamp shades.

▸▸ New Product Idea

Excluding the continual search for new ideas, the time and costs involved in the activities relating to product planning and development process, from experience in the U.S.A., is as follows:

Stage	***Time***	***Money cost***	***Ideas reduced from original 60 to***
1. Screening	3 p.c.	2 p.c.	12
2. Business Research	12 p.c.	7 p.c.	7
3. Development	40 p.c.	31 p.c.	3
4. Testing	20 p.c.	15 p.c.	2
5. Commercialisation	25 p.c.	45 p.c.	1 (One successful new product)

Note: 1. Development, testing and launching are the most expensive stages.
2. They take more than 50 per cent of total time involved in the process.

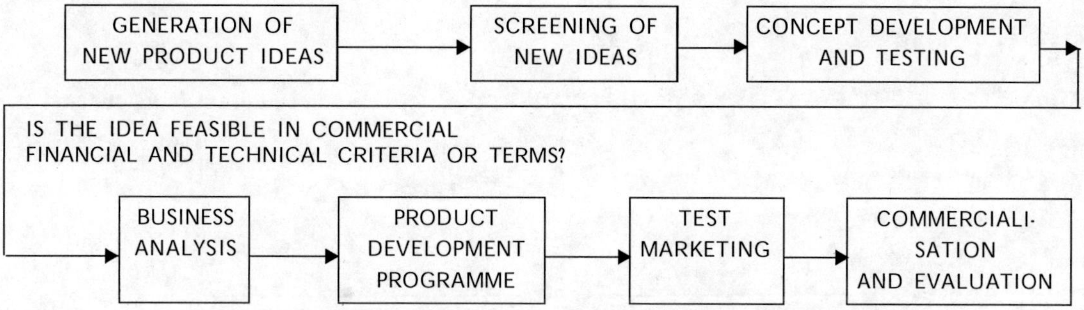

Fig. 4 New Product Development Process (Innovation Management)

Note. 1. Product life cycle requires the product development programme for new products and new profit opportunities.
2. New product development must be carefully planned and managed.
3. Special organisational wing is necessary to stimulate, collect, screen, evaluate, develop, test, and commercialise new product ideas.
4. Business analysis is the crucial stage. It concentrates on demand analysis, cost analysis and profitability analysis. It also considers social responsibilities of marketing new product.

Many innovative ideas are needed to find one good idea worth for commercialisation and many new ideas fail to pass the screening stage. Few ideas are compatible with the corporate resources and goals. Finally, five ideas are eliminated for lack of profit potential. Finally, having profitability, only one new product idea becomes eligible for market introduction and officially enters its life cycle.

⏩ Product Planning and Development Process

There are seven steps in the planning and development of a new product:

1. ***New Product Ideas:*** We visualise the detailed features of a model product. Ideas may be contributed by scientists, professional designers, rivals, customers, sales force, top management, dealers, etc. We may need sixty new ideas to get one commercially viable product.

2. ***Idea Screening:*** We have to evaluate all ideas and inventions. Poor or bad ideas are dropped and through the process of elimination, only the most promising and profitable ideas are picked up for further detailed investigation and research.

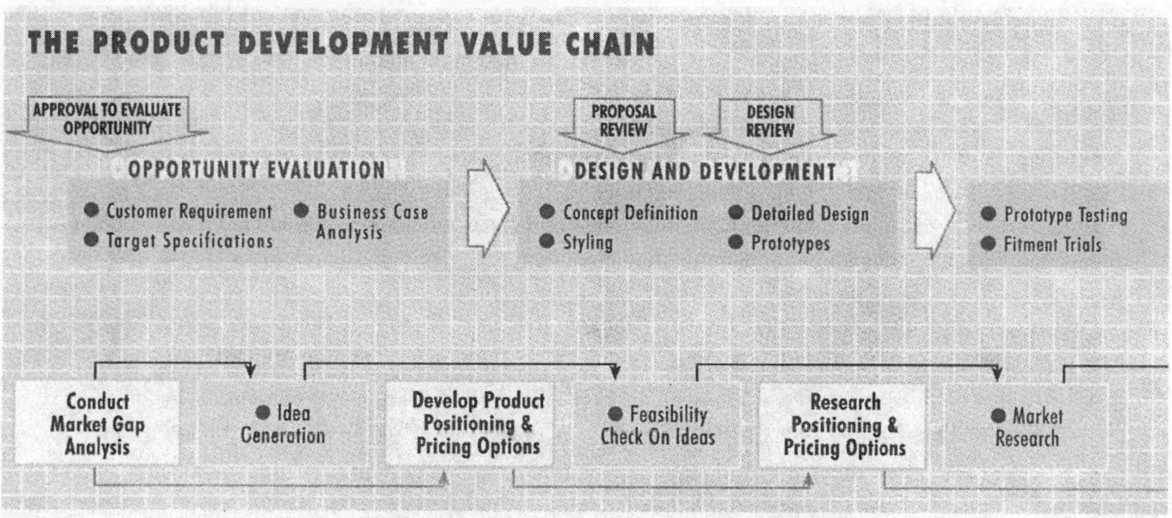

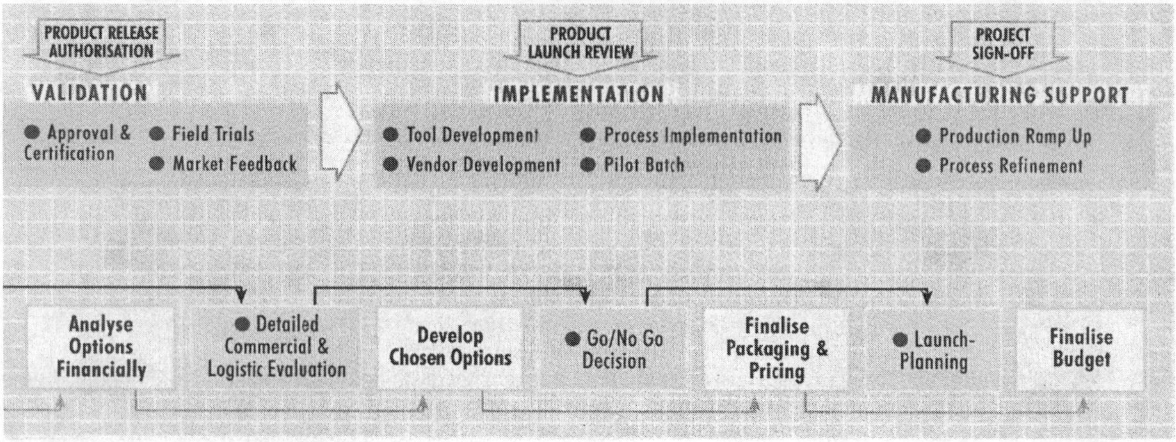

3. ***Concept Development and Testing:*** All ideas that survive the process of screening (preliminary investigation) will be studied in detail. They will be developed into mature product concepts. We will have a precise description of the ideas and features of the proposed product. At this stage, we can incorporate consumer preference into our agenda for concept development and testing product ideas. Concept testing the company to choose the best among the alternative product concepts. Consumers are called upon to offer their comments on the precise written description of the product concept, viz., the attributes and expected benefits.

4. ***Business Analysis:*** Once the best product concept is picked up, it will be subjected to rigorous scrutiny to evaluate its market potential, capital investment, rate of return on capital, etc. Business analysis is a combination of marketing research, cost-benefit analysis and assessment of competition. We have demand analysis, cost analysis and profitability analysis. Business analysis will prove the economic prospects of the new product concept. It will also prove the soundness and viability of the selected product concept from a business viewpoint. Now we can proceed to concentrate on product development programme. The proposed product must offer a realistic profit objective.

5. ***Product Development Programme:*** We have three steps in this stage when a paper idea is duly converted into a physical product: *(a)* Prototype development, giving a visual image of the product; *(b)* Consumer testing of the model or prototype; and *(c)* Branding, packaging and labelling. Consumer testing of the model product will provide the ground for the final selection of the most promising model for mass production and mass distribution.

6. ***Test Marketing:*** The entire product marketing programme is tried out for the first time in a small number of well-selected test markets, *i.e.,* test cities or areas. Test marketing is necessary to find out the viability of a full marketing programme for national distribution. Customer reactions can be tested under normal market conditions. It helps the company to learn through trial and error and to get additional valuable clues for product improvement and for modifications in our marketing mix. We can use test markets for testing the effectiveness of all ingredients of our marketing mix. Test marketing can answer such questions as: Is the new product labelled and packaged properly? Is the new product liked by the consumer? Is the firm justified in spending large sums on productive capacity? Has the communication (promotion) programme been right? Positive answers will reassure marketers.

7. ***Commercialisation:*** Once the test marketing gives the green signal for the product with or without expected modifications, the company can proceed to finalise all features of the product. Now marketing management can launch a full-fledged advertising and promotion campaign for mass

distribution. Mass production will start and all distribution channels will be duly organised. The product is now born and will start its life cycle in due course.

Conclusion

The search for a business idea is a continuous process. The entrepreneur will have to undertake constant checking of the new product through its life cycle. And, keep a constant tap on the markets, consumer needs and their changing styles, research and development as an ongoing source of information regarding business idea as well as appropriate technology.

Chart 1

Examples of three types of essential capabilities that help enterprises create capabilities desired/appreciated by customers and also reduce cost of creating and delivering such benefits.

1. Product specific capabilities visible to customers

- Quality of the total product and also that of the individual components of the same
- Performance features/attributes
- Range/variety
- New products/upgrades

2. Process specific capabilities — visible to customers (Transaction related)

- Order fulfillment process
- Pre and post sales services
- Tendering process
- Dealer management process
- Order tracking process
- Meeting special or emergency requirements (product/quality/volume/packing)
- Complaint handling process and for resolving customer's problem
- Documentation

3. Process specific capabilities — invisible to customers (leading to creating product or transaction specific benefits (Ref. in (1) and (2) or helping in reducing the cost)

- Creation and management of database on low cost and right quality inputs
- Value engineering process
- Selection process for sub-contractors/vendors
- Purchase process
- Material movement process (from suppliers to manufacturers to customers) PPC process
- Production process/set up process/methods
- New product development process
- Quality assurance process
- Support services process (*e.g.,* Bill processing, credit not issued etc.)

Willingness to Change

Adding value requires willingness to change. Adding something innovative springs from nurturing attitudes. And as research and development build a critical mass, new products and services increasingly happen.

The journey of change is not without its obstacles. But it is also a journey that is full of rewards. The key to reaping the rewards and minimixing the breakdowns is to lead with your heart, not your head. Your heart is where you will find your willingness. Your head is where you will find resistance and fear.

When we begin to feel resistance and fear that it can be easy to lose touch with the willingness that we had at the beginning of the process. When this happens, we need to focus on reconnecting with the part of us that originally wanted to make the change – the part that is excited about learning new things, facing new challenges, and bringing more joy and fulfillment to our life.

Adding value is not simply a matter of doing good – rather it is a synergistic process. It is a collaborative process of problem solving and of designing robust systems that produce goods and services that meet customer needs and specifications. It is a process of making thousands of moments of true happy experiences for those involved.

Adding value is easier when we use the right tool for the job. Adding something new can come from the tool of stretch goals. Cutting waste, reducing failure costs, and delivery problems comes from tools of substraction, from employing the tool of simplicity. Intensification of effort can come from incentive tools, and from the tool of division from – focus of effort upon specific tasks. Adding value can come from teaming up to do a job from enlisting others in a pyramid of effort.

Adding value goes beyond customer satisfaction to customer confidence. Trust is generated from honest relationships that are built into goods and services. It means being able to depend upon those who have earned that trust.

Add value to your life by self-improvement. The Japanese have a term for the kind of attitude and action they want their employees to nurture; it is Kaizen. Kaizen means to continuously find small ways of improving yourself in whatever you do. It is an attitude that manifests itself in action. How does one do that? It is a matter of improving one's character, one's personality, one's relationships, and by increasing one's skill level.

At the company level, less rather than more, means finding ways to cut waste, cut costs, and to make one's product and service better fit one's customers: more durable, easier to use, more beautiful, and more accessible. Some gurus of quality refer to this as cutting failure costs – the aggregate cost of failure to do things right. Not doing it right costs in inspection, complaints, loss of customers, and rework. Less waste is more profit.

LEADING EDGE

"In a knowledge economy, leaders cannot command employees to work harder, smarter, or faster. Knowledge workers, if they are earning their pay, know more about their work than the CEO does, and are in great demand. Without leaders who can attract and retain talent and manage knowledge, an organisation's future is in jeopardy."

— Warren Bennis, Leadership Expert

23

Input Requirements

Introduction

The development of small-scale industries has been one of the most significant and characteristic features of industrial development in India. One of the distinctive characteristics of small-scale sector is that, the development of these industries would create broader employment opportunities, assist in entrepreneurship and skills development, and ensure a better use of scarce financial resources and appropriate technology. Furthermore, they can play a main role in the achievement of national economic and socio-political objectives. The gestation period is very short and they need smaller amount of capital to start. It also helps in the dissemination of productive capacity unlike the large-scale industries which tend to concentrate in a few hands. This part, establishment of such industries in rural areas and small towns helps to check the influx of population into bigger towns.

Anjali Bansal
CEO, Spencer Stuart

Basic Objectives

The basic objectives underlying the development of small and medium scale industries are the increase in the supply of manufactured goods, the promotion of capital formation, the development of indigenous entrepreneurial talents and skills and the creation of broader employment opportunities. In addition, they include socio-economic goals such as the decentralisation and dispersal of manufacturing

Steps of the ladder the entrepreneur (Small) has to climb.
It is a continuous process of industrialisation.

34. ANCILLARY DEVELOPMENT
33. GROW BIGGER
32. COMPETE WITH OTHERS
31. MODERNISATION
30. DIVERSIFICATION
29. PLOUGH BACK PROFITS
28. KEEP UP-TO-DATE
27. SELL
26. PRODUCE
25. PLAN OUT RECORD-KEEPING
24. ORGANISE MARKETING
23. DECIDE ON PRICING POLICY
22. TRAIL RUN
21. RECRUIT PERSONNEL
20. PROCURE MATERIALS
19. INSTAL MACHINERY
18. PLAN BUYING
17. APPLY FOR MATERIALS (IF IMPORTED OR CONTROLLED)
16. PLACE ORDER FOR MACHINERY (PREFERABLY ON HIRE-PURCHASE)
15. PLAN SOURCES OF MACHINERY
14. PLAN FINANCE
13. OBTAIN CLEARANCE FROM CENTRAL, STATE & LOCAL AUTHORITIES AND SSI REGN. NO.
12. MAKE SURE WHAT LAWS WILL PARTICULARLY AFFECT YOU
11. ARRANGE THE WORKSHEET WITH FACILITIES (PREFERABLY ON RENT)
10. DECIDE ON LOCATION AND SITE
9. OBTAIN THE PROJECT REPORT FROM SISI OR ELSEWHERE OR PREPARE IT YOURSELF
8. DECIDE WHETHER TO PURCHASE A GOING CONCERN OR TO START A NEW ONE
7. DECIDE ON FORM OF OWNERSHIP [SOLE-PROPRIETARY/PARTNERSHIP/COOPERATIVE/ COMPANY (PRIVATE/PUBLIC)]
6. CHOOSE A LINE
5. DATE WITH YOURSELF FOR A DECISION
4. DISCUSS WITH ALL AROUND YOU AND WITH SISI & D.I. OFFICE
3. CONSULT PUBLICATIONS AND AGENCIES
2. DATE WITH YOURSELF FOR NEWER IDEAS
1. ANALYSE YOURSELF AND YOUR OBJECTIVES

Note: This is a bare outline. The next chapter contains some details and suggestions for step-by-step planning.

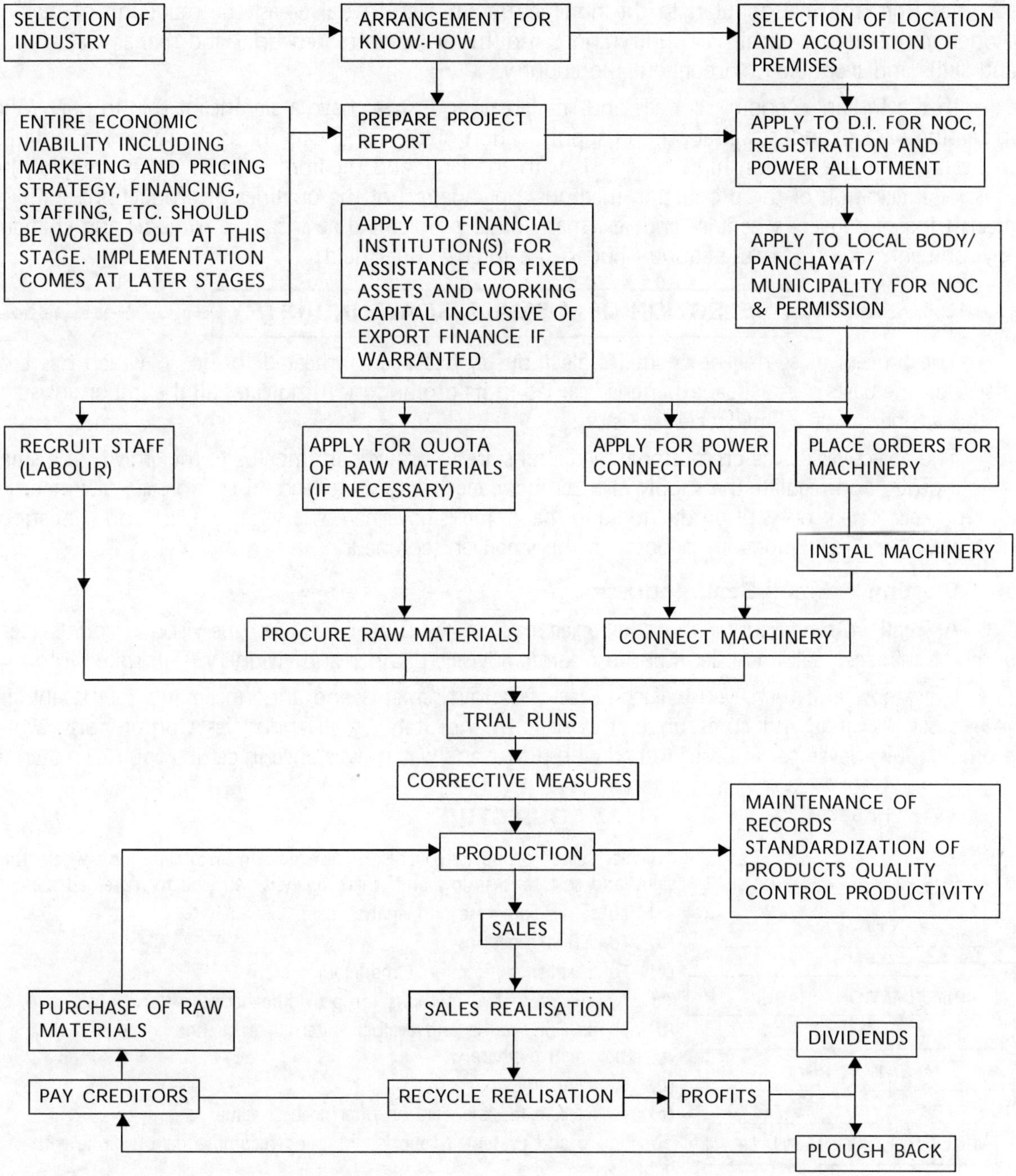
SELECTION OF INDUSTRY
ARRANGEMENT FOR KNOW-HOW
SELECTION OF LOCATION AND ACQUISITION OF PREMISES
ENTIRE ECONOMIC VIABILITY INCLUDING MARKETING AND PRICING STRATEGY, FINANCING, STAFFING, ETC. SHOULD BE WORKED OUT AT THIS STAGE. IMPLEMENTATION COMES AT LATER STAGES
PREPARE PROJECT REPORT
APPLY TO D.I. FOR NOC, REGISTRATION AND POWER ALLOTMENT
APPLY TO FINANCIAL INSTITUTION(S) FOR ASSISTANCE FOR FIXED ASSETS AND WORKING CAPITAL INCLUSIVE OF EXPORT FINANCE IF WARRANTED
APPLY TO LOCAL BODY/ PANCHAYAT/ MUNICIPALITY FOR NOC & PERMISSION
RECRUIT STAFF (LABOUR)
APPLY FOR QUOTA OF RAW MATERIALS (IF NECESSARY)
APPLY FOR POWER CONNECTION
PLACE ORDERS FOR MACHINERY
INSTAL MACHINERY
PROCURE RAW MATERIALS
CONNECT MACHINERY
TRIAL RUNS
CORRECTIVE MEASURES
PRODUCTION
MAINTENANCE OF RECORDS STANDARDIZATION OF PRODUCTS QUALITY CONTROL PRODUCTIVITY
SALES
SALES REALISATION
PURCHASE OF RAW MATERIALS
DIVIDENDS
PAY CREDITORS
RECYCLE REALISATION
PROFITS
PLOUGH BACK

Fig. 1

activities from the metropolitan to the non-metropolitan and rural areas, the reduction of regional economic imbalances within a country and the diffusion of entrepreneurial and managerial abilities and skills and technology throughout the country.

In the Indian Economy, cottage and small-scale industries have a significant role to play. With increasing pace of industrialisation and sophistication of the large-scale industries, a new orientation is inevitable in the relationship of the SSIs with the large and medium industries. This relationship calls for integration of the production methods, upgradation of the qualities of production, ability to meet stringent delivery schedules and very many other problems that arise in a dynamic and changing environment not only in the country but in the international field.

SELECTION OF A SMALL-SCALE INDUSTRY

The process of setting up a small-scale industry has been indicated in Fig. 1, which has been drawn on the basis of practical experience gained in its promotion. It indicates all the important stages in the setting up of a small-scale industry.

The objectives of the promotional regulations are to provide an impetus to the growth of a small-scale industry and regulate the supply of machinery, electricity, water, premises, finance, raw materials and markets. The process of production and marketing is governed by a series of rules and regulations. In a way, these regulations are a boon to the small entrepreneur.

Starting a Small-Scale Industry

A small entrepreneur is the chief executive of his unit, its floor supervisor, accounts clerk, purchase manager, salesman, legal and economic adviser, planner and visionary – all rolled into one.

Every now and then, you will come across advertisements and announcements in the enticing you to set up small industries under the aegis of the State Small Industries Corporations, which promise a fully developed industrial shed with power and water, assistance in getting you raw materials,

PHASES

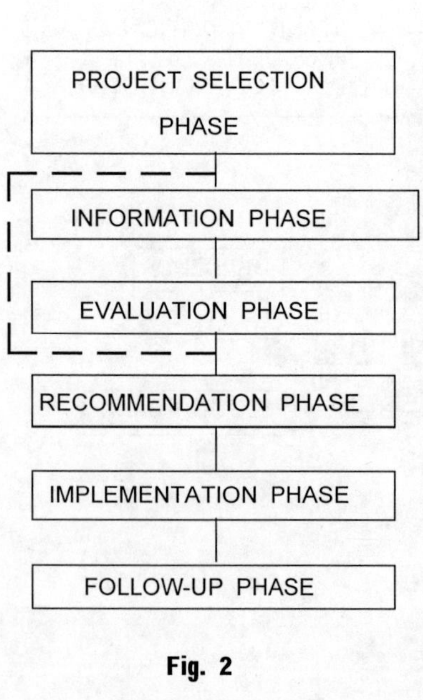

OBJECTIVE

To select those products, processes or systems in an organisation where the value and cost ratio is low and where analysis will lead to increased benefits:

(*a*) To gather, organise and analyse data.

(*b*) To define functions.

(*c*) To establish a functional monetary value.

To generate alternative methods for providing necessary functions:

(*a*) To develop, refine and evaluate alternative methods generated during the creative phase.

(*b*) To determine the cost.

(*c*) To select a feasible method offering best value.

To prepare and present a report containing recommendation along with benefits:

(*a*) To establish a plan of action for implementation of the selected method.

(*b*) To obtain approval.

(*c*) To perform all other actions necessary to put the proposal into effect.

(*a*) To follow-up and audit actual results.

(*b*) To resolve problems, if any, during proposal implementation.

Fig. 2

machinery on hire-purchase basis, common services facilities, training facilities and facilities in the marketing of your product. Assurance term loans on attractive terms and working capital in time and at concessional rates. In backward areas, a number of additional subsidies are available.

An entrepreneur may be a qualified engineer. Even so, he should not dream of becoming a small entrepreneur unless he is confident of meeting the following twelve essential requirements:

(i) The entrepreneur should be fully conversant with the product line. It is not enough that he knows the method of manufacture; he has to know how to operate the machines, etc.

(ii) He should have adequate shop floor experience to guide the machine operators in fool-setting techniques or the die-maker on the specific needs of his press tools.

(iii) He should be familiar with the raw materials he requires, their specifications, how to ensure their quality and where to get them at reasonable prices.

(iv) He should know how to keep accounts, how to maintain stores, how to prepare the balance sheet, etc.

(v) He should have knowledge of marketing channels, distribution network, agency practices, transport intricacies, and the economic of packaging.

(vi) He should know how to ensure the stipulated quality of his product.

(vii) He should be well-versed in taxation and other laws governing SSIs.

(ix) He should be willing to put up with bureaucratic regulations and insults, and be fractional under any circumstances.

(x) He should know how to avail himself of the various benefits available to the SSIs.

(xi) He should possess expertise, shrewdness, resourcefulness and, most important, perseverance in his business dealings. There is no substitute for hard work.

(xii) He should have the guts to withstand the high pleasure climate in which he has to build his unit.

OBJECTIVES

Any entrepreneur desirous of starting a small-scale industry should have a clear picture of the objectives of his project. It is advisable to prepare a comprehensive check list. Such a list, embracing all the important matters, has been given below for the guidance of prospective entrepreneurs. Students will get an insight into the various processes of a small-scale industry.

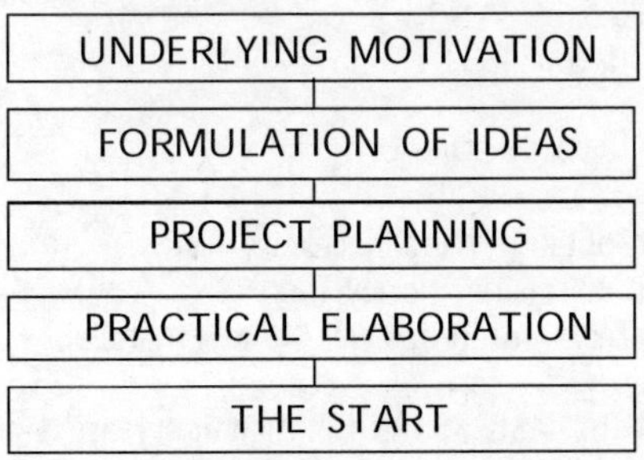

Fig. 3 Process of Starting a Small Enterprise

CHECK LIST

Does your industry have scope for development? Yes – No

(Consult Director of Industries)

Is there enough demand for the item you propose to manufacture? Yes – No

Do you have some experience of

(*a*) Manufacturing? Yes – No

(*b*) Marketing? Yes – No

Have you studied the viability of your scheme? Yes – No

(Consult the Small Industries Service Institute)

Is factory space available

(*a*) In the industrial Estate? Yes – No

(*b*) In an Industrial Area? Yes – No

(*c*) In some other approved place? Yes – No

Have you obtained the necessary licence from the Municipality or the Local Body? Yes – No

Are the necessary raw materials available

(*a*) Indigenously or are they to be Yes – No

(*b*) Imported? Yes – No

Are facilities available for

(*a*) Tooling, Yes – No

(*b*) Quality Control? Yes – No

Is necessary labour available

(*a*) Of skilled workers, Yes – No

(*b*) Of semi-skilled workers? Yes – No

Have you the necessary technical background for

(*a*) The erection of the machinery, Yes – No

(*b*) Operations? Yes – No

Have you studied your product in respect of

(*a*) The manufacture of the various parts, Yes – No

(*b*) Production Planning, Yes – No

(*c*) Inspection and Quality Control, Yes – No

(*d*) Assembly, Yes – No

(*e*) Packaging, Yes – No

(*f*) Diversification? Yes – No

Have you the necessary finance?

(*a*) Are you a client of any bank? Yes – No

(*b*) Has any bank offered to lend you –

(*i*) Short-term loans? Yes – No

(*ii*) Long-term loans? Yes – No

(*c*) Have you any assets? Yes – No

(*d*) Are your assets adequate for obtaining the necessary funds? Yes – No

(*e*) Have you other sources/ways of raising money? Yes – No

(*f*) Have you approached the Director of Industries/State Financial Corporation for financial help? Yes – No

(*g*) Do you propose to approach the NSIC/SSIC for machinery on hire-purchase basis? Yes – No

(*h*) Have you adequate cash/bank arrangement to furnish the earnest money required by the NSIC? Yes – No

What are your markets?

(a) Local, Yes – No
(b) Countrywide, Yes – No
(c) Export? Yes – No

How would you market your product(s)? Through

(a) Retailers, Yes – No
(b) Wholesalers, Yes – No
(c) Agents? Yes – No

Are the necessary transportation facilities available by

(a) Road, Yes – No
(b) Rail? Yes – No

Have you attended a course on

(a) Production, Planning and Control, Yes – No
(b) Purchasing and Marketing, Yes – No
(c) Finance and Cost Control, Yes – No
(d) Personnel Management, Yes – No
(e) General Industrial Management? Yes – No

Have you entered into a foreign collaboration agreement for

(a) Technical Know-how,
(b) Royalty/Commission on sales? Yes – No
(c) Has your agreement been approved by the Government? Yes – No

Once the industry is identified, the SISI prepares a feasibility report and project report, giving one a comprehensive idea of an industry's prospects and profitability.

(1) LICENCES

An impression seems to have gained ground among some people that there are some restrictions on the getting up of small-scale industrial units and that licences from either the Central or State Governments have to be taken out before an entrepreneur to set up an industrial unit in the small-scale sector; no formal permission from the State or Central Government is necessary for this purpose. Also, industries employing less than 100 workers and having fixed assets of less than Rs. 10 lakh need not obtain any licence under the Industries (Development & Regulation) Act.

Small-scale units have, however, to conform to the rules and regulations prescribed by State or local authorities under the Factories Act, Commercial Establishments Act, Town Planning Rules, and rules made for the issues of quotas of raw materials, etc.

However, powerlooms do not come under the purview of the small-scale industries programme. For installing powerlooms, the prior permission of the Textile Commissioner, Government of India, Mumbai is required.

▸▸ Registration of Small-scale Industries

In their own interest, all existing small-scale units or intending entrepreneurs employing more than 10 workers should get themselves registered with the Director of Industries in their State. A copy of this application for registration should be sent to the Director of Small Industries Service Institute in the concerned State. Such registration with the Director of Industries and the Small Industries Service Institute will be of considerable help to small-scale unit in obtaining financial assistance from the government and for obtaining machinery on hire-purchase basis from the National Small Industries Corporation. Assistance in the supply of controlled raw materials, specific certificate for imported raw materials and components, and facilities for export promotion, would then be easily made available to small-scale units registered with the State Director of Industries. The registration number is now required to be quoted while submitting import applications.

DOING BUSINESS

So, how has India fared in the Ease of Doing Business Index? Well, here's the breakdown.

Ease of ...

	Economy Rank (India)	***Best Performer***	***Worst Performer***
Doing Business	116	New Zealand	Congo, Dem, Rep.
Starting a Business	90	Canada	Angola
Dealing with Licences	124	Palau	Tanzania
Hiring and Firing	116	Palau	Burkina Faso
Registering Property	101	New Zealand	Nigeria
Getting Credit	84	United Kingdom	Cambodia
Protecting Investors	29	New Zealand	Afghanistan
Paying Taxes	103	Maldives	Belarus
Trading Across Borders	130	Denmark	Iraq
Enforcing Contracts	138	Norway	Timor-Leste
Closing a Business	118	Japan	West Bank and Gaza

Starting a Business (2005)

The challenges of launching a business in India are shown below. Entrepreneurs can expect to go through 11 steps to launch a business over 71 days on an average at a cost equal to 61.7 per cent of gross national income (GNI) per capita. There is no minimum deposit requirement to obtain a business registration number.

Indicator	***India***	***Region***	***OECD***
Procedures (number)	11	7.9	6.5
Time (days)	71	35,3	19.5
Cost (% of income per capita)	61.7	40.5	6.8
Min. capital (% of income per capita)	0.0	0.8	41.0

Dealing with Licences (2005)

The steps, time and costs of complying with licensing and permit requirements for ongoing operations in India are shown below. It takes 20 steps and 270 days to complete the process, and costs 578.5 per cent of income per capita.

Indicator	***India***	***Region***	***OECD***
Procedures (number)	20	15.7	14.1
Time (days)	270	195.3	146.9
Cost (% of income per capita)	678.5	385.9	75.1

▸▸ Hiring & Firing Workers (2005)

The difficulties that employers in India face in hiring and firing workers are shown below. Each index assigns values between 0 and 100, with higher values representing more rigid regulations. The Rigidity of Employment Index is an average of the three indices. For India, the overall index is 62.

Indicator	*India*	*Region*	*OECD*
Difficulty of Hiring Index	56	41.9	30.1
Rigidity of Hours Index	40	35	49.6
Difficulty of Firing Index	90	42.5	27.4
Rigidity of Employment Index	62	39.9	35.8
Hiring cost (% of salary)	12.3	5.1	20.7
Firing costs (weeks of wages)	79	75	35.1

▸▸ Registering Property (2005)

The ease with which businesses can secure rights to property is measured below. In India, it takes six steps and 67 days to register property. The cost to register property there is 7.9 per cent of overall property value.

Indicator	*India*	*Region*	*OECD*
Procedures (number)	6	6,9	4.7
Time (days)	67	124.0	32.2
Cost (% of property value)	7,9	6.3	4.8

OECD Organisation for Economic Co-operation and Development.
The index ranks economies from 1-155. The ranking on each topic is the simple average of the percentile rankings on its component indicators.

(2) INFRASTRUCTURE

The Director of Industries and/or the SISI in the State can be approached to provide you with built-up factory space in an industrial estate, or develop the factory site, power, etc. After the initial clearance from the State Director of Industries, the Municipality or the Panchayat issues a "No Objection Certificate."

The mechanics of putting up a new factory in Greater Mumbai are:

(i) Apply to the Industries Commissioner, Industries and Labour Department, Government of Maharashtra, and obtain a "No Objection Certificate." (NOC)

(ii) With a copy of the above NOC, apply in Factory Form "A", to the Ward Engineer of B.M.C.

(iii) Clarifications and submission of further details on the information supplied in Form "A" may follow.

(iv) The sub-engineer will inspect the premises and submit Form No. '2' to his assistant engineer.

(v) The assistant engineer will scrutinise and confirm if the applicant's activity conforms to the zone and will intimate to the applicant in Form No. '3' if there is no objection or in Form No. '4' if there is any objection.

(vi) Form 'B' will be received by the applicant if Form No. '3' is issued to him. This form should be filled in and submitted.

(vii) Within 21 days after the submission of Forms 'A', 'B' and the factory plans in triplicate, the assistant engineer will issue Form No. '5' and '6' in which he will specify:

(a) The electric power sanctioned (thereafter, the BEST provides current);

(b) Adequate water facilities provided;

(c) The various requirements, requisitions and conditions for operating the factory, including those required by the chief inspector of factories.

Form 'C' will also be issued along with these forms. (Upon complying with the stipulations in Form 'B', the BMC should be informed thereof in writing.)

Subsequently, permission to commence production will be given.

(3) MACHINERY

The small entrepreneur needs the requisite type of machines for production. He can get the necessary machinery from the National Small Industries Corporation under a hire-purchase scheme.

The scheme for the supply of indigenous and imported machines on hire-purchase basis was launched in March 1956 to enable small entrepreneurs without substantial means to avail themselves of assistance. The scheme is different from the credit operations scheme for entrepreneurs. The NSIC has acquired the necessary experience and expertise in the procurement of machines from the right sources. It also takes care of the problems up to the stage of delivery of machineries to the entrepreneurs. Also, while financial institutions plan to look mainly to the creditworthiness of entrepreneurs, the NSIC would look primarily to the motivation of the individual applicant, his capacity, his technical competence and his managerial ability to run the enterprise.

The small entrepreneur should enlist himself as a member with the NSIC. His application form should be accompanied by the Registration Certificate and report of the Director of Industries. The application for obtaining machines under the hire-purchase scheme of the NSIC is quite comprehensive. The small entrepreneur has to provide full details along with the relevant documents.

The application form for hire-purchase of machinery calls for information regarding the organisational set-up of the unit, its programme of production, and the marketability and profitability of the enterprise. It also calls for additional information regarding the cost of production, the infrastructural facilities available for the unit, the technical capability of the entrepreneur, etc. The details in the application are self-explanatory.

(4) RAW MATERIALS

The raw materials required by SSIs may broadly be classified as under:

(i) Raw material components and spares, both indigenous and imported;

(ii) Non-ferrous materials – both indigenous and imported;

(iii) Iron and steel – both indigenous and imported; and

(iv) Chemicals – indigenous and imported.

Under the liberalised scheme, the actual users are provided with adequate foreign exchange to meet their justifiable requirements of imported items of industrial materials. The "*priority*" industries are assured of an adequate supply based on requirements by way of grant of rotational licences.

Small-scale units should apply directly to the Regional Licensing Authority, and not through the sponsoring authority, for import licences for raw materials, components and spares after utilising the previous set of licences to the extent of 90% by way of opening their own credit or 60% by way of actual import, covering six month's requirements of the unit. New units should submit their applications through their respective sponsoring authority.

The State Director of Industries allocates indigenous non-ferrous metals. Some of the non-ferrous items are canalised through the State Trading Corporation of India (STC). The raw materials imported by the STC are given to the SSI units in accordance with the recommendations of the Director of Industries concerned.

The same applies to iron and steel raw materials are canalised through the MMTC.

In times of difficulties, the decontrolled chemical raw materials are canalised through the DGTD in accordance with the recommendation of the State Director of Industries. Indigenous controlled chemicals are allocated through the State DIS/SICs. Imported raw materials are canalised through the STC.

In short, controlled and imported raw materials are to be obtained through the State DIS, SICs (SSI).

(5) FINANCE

The financial function in a small-scale industry is similar to the financial function in any other organisation, but with this essential difference – that there are a host of banking and insurance regulations to be strictly adhered to and quite a few precautions to be taken.

The areas where finance would be needed, after the small-scale industrialist fixes the land accommodation, are:

(i) Purchase and installation of machinery;

(ii) Procurement of raw materials and components and the manufacture of products;

(iii) Working funds;

(iv) Availability of funds until the realisation of sales.

The State Director of Industries provides loans for block capital under the Industries Act. One should apply through the sponsoring authority. State Financial Corporations provide long-term credit for the purchase of fixed assets. The application should be submitted to the SFCs along with the following documents:

(i) Project Report; *(ii)* Copy of Registration; *(iii)* Cash-flow Statement; *(iv)* Stock Statement.

In some states SFCs and the banks agreed to process the common applications for loans. Up to an amount of Rs. 2 lakh, a commercial bank provides medium-term instalment credit. It also provides loans for meeting needs for working capital for the purchase of raw materials as also for day-to-day requirements.

In order to get a loan from a commercial bank, the entrepreneur has to fill in an application form as per the specimen provided by the financial institutions including banks and submit it to the bank along with the following documents:

(i) Authentic copies of Balance Sheets and Profit and Loss Accounts (if the industrial concern is a limited company or an industrial co-operative society).

(ii) A statement of total assets and liabilities in the prescribed form in the case of partnership and proprietary concerns.

(iii) Perform statements in all other cases.

(iv) Copies of the affidavit in regard to the size of the unit.

(v) Technical Feasibility Report from the Small Industries Service Institute, the Director of Industries, if obtained, may also be closed.

(6) MARKETING

The rationale of the Government Purchase Scheme of the Corporation lies in the fact that the Government of India is the largest single buyer, and by channelising these purchases in favour of small-scale units, it gives a tremendous boost to the marketing of their products.

The salient features of the scheme are:

(a) The small-scale units, desiring to avail themselves of assistance, have to enlist themselves with the NSIC;

(b) Instead of purchasing tender sets from the DGS & D, the small units enlisted with the NSIC automatically get them from it and its branches free of cost;

(c) If their prices are acceptable to the DGS & D they are not required to pay a security deposit on the issue of a competency certificate by the NSIC;

(d) Price preference up to 15% over the quotations of large-scale units is considered by the Purchasing Agency, depending on the merits of each case;

(e) Wherever they feel that injustice has been done to them, the NSIC takes up their cases with the DGS & D and other Government Departments such as Defence, the Railways and the P & T in order to find out the reasons for non-placement of contracts with the units, and tries to redress their grievances.

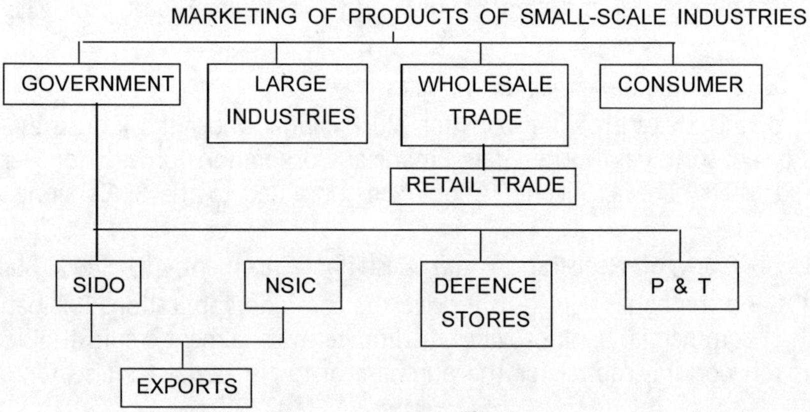

Fig. 4

In the beginning, purchases in respect of only 16 items were reserved exclusively for the small-scale sector; the number of such items has steadily increased to 409 items in 1995-96.

Besides, in respect of 13 items, purchases upto 75 per cent and in respect of 28 items, purchases upto 50 per cent of the requirements are earmarked for the small-scale sector.

The Corporation also helps small-scale industries in securing contracts from other Government Departments such as the Railways, Posts and Telegraphs, etc.

Hitherto, the purchase programme has been restricted purely to Central purchase houses like DGS & D, the P & T and the Railways. It is proposed to extend the base further to cover State Government Departments such as the State Electricity Boards, PWDs, etc. and provide liaison offices at each of the principal centres of the State.

(7) INCENTIVES

For availing the various incentives, it is advisable to seek the help of the SISI and/or the Director of Industries.

Small-scale industries are the industrial units having an investment in fixed assets in plant and machinery not exceeding Rs. 10 lakhs. The ancillary units are those having an investment in fixed assets in plant and machinery not exceeding Rs. 15 lakh and they are engaged in the manufacture of parts and components.

The Small Industries Development Organisation (SIDO), Ministry of Industry, Nirman Bhavan, New Delhi, co-ordinates policies and programmes at the national level and provides a comprehensive range of extension services through its network of sixteen Small Industries Service Institutes, nineteen Branch Institutes and forty-five Extension Centres.

At the State level, organisation like State Directorates of Industries, Small Industries Development Corporations and Finance Corporations cater to the needs of small industries; these needs include land, sheds, credit, power, raw materials, etc.

The National Small Industries Corporation (NSIC), Okhla, New Delhi, has been providing machines and equipment on hire-purchase basis to entrepreneurs, assists units to participate in stores purchase programmes and provides training and prototype development facilities.

Registration with NSIC entitles the units to obtain facilities from Central or State Government organisations. New units have to apply to the respective State Directors of Industries for provisional registration, which is given within a week. It enables the party to take the necessary steps to bring the unit into existence, i.e., apply for sheds in industrial estates or on developed sites, for water and power connections, and for credit facilities. After the party has taken all the steps, it can apply for registration.

SIDO provides technical consultancy on improved technical processes, use of modern machines and equipment and technical assistance on all aspects of production. Each SISI has attached workshops for common facility services, training of workers, demonstration of modern machines and processes, making of tools and dyes, etc.

The Central Institute of Tool Design (CITD), Hyderabad, has been specialising in the provision of technical consultancy and tool facilities training in the design and manufacture of tools.

The Institute for the Design of Electrical Measuring Instruments (IDEMI), Mumbai, provides technical knowhow and testing, calibration, laboratory, workshop and training facilities to manufacturers of electrical measuring instruments.

The Prototype Development and Training Centres (PDTCs) at Okhla, Rajkot and Howrah develop prototypes of machine tools and other machinery provide assistance to units in the manufacture of prototype machines, technical consultancy and training.

The Product and Process Development Centre in glass and ceramics, Ranchi has been developing new products, viable processes, new designs of product and machines, consultancy services and training.

Under the modernisation programme for selected industries guidance and assistance are provided to small-scale units to adopt modern production and management techniques with a view to improving their productivity and competitive strength.

Technical assistance guidance in a wide range of industries is provided by specialised institutions and experts. Testing facilities are available at the Regional Testing Centres in New Delhi, Calcutta, Mumbai, Madras and also at SISI Workshops.

Industrial Management, Consultancy and Training

SIDO offers consultancy services in a variety of fields – technical, managerial, marketing, quality control, production, finance, labour laws, solving problems through special training programmes, in-plant studies, open-house discussions and seminars.

A panel of consultants, consisting of reputed engineers, technologists and scientists in every branch of technology, has been drawn up for such jobs or products for which expertise is not available with SIDO. In 246 backward areas, small-scale units can avail themselves of the services of these consultants, and the entire expenditure is borne by SIDO. In other areas, the units have to bear 75% of the cost, while the rest is borne by SIDO.

Technical training facilities are available in a wide range of trades with the SIDO, CITD, IDEMI, PDTCs and a number of training centres of the Ministry of Labour and Employment and of State Governments.

The Small Industry Extension Training Institute (SIETI), Hyderabad, has been giving training in industrial management and other aspects of small industries development, also undertaking feasibility and research studies, collecting and disseminating technical information through its documentation centres.

Under the Assistance to Young Engineers Programme, training is provided through specified agencies, and an interest subsidy, i.e., the difference between 7% interest rate and the normal rates charged by financial institutions, is provided, subject to a maximum of Rs. 20,000 per annum for a period of five years in backward areas and 3 years in other areas.

Backward Areas Development

Special incentives and facilities are available for the development of small-scale industries in 246 selected backward districts. These include credit facilities on concessional terms, i.e., lower rates of interests, extension of initial grace period for the commencement of the date of repayment of the loan, reduction in service charges and margin of security; income tax deduction of 20% from profits and gains is allowed while assessing income tax for a period of ten years.

The Rural Artisans Development Programme, which has been in operation in forty-one districts, is also covered by the Rural Industries Projects (RIP) programme. The main features of the programme are special training facilities for artisans and the supply of improved tools and equipment at subsidised rates.

Machinery on Hire-Purchase basis: The NSIC and several SSICs supply machines chosen by the entrepreneur on hire-purchase basis on liberalised terms. The full title to the machinery is transferred to the entrepreneur on payment of the last instalment.

Government Stores Purchase: Two hundred and forty-one items have been reserved for the exclusive purchase by the Government purchasing agencies from small-scale units. A price preference, extending up to 15% offered to small-scale units against medium and large-scale units for purchase of all other items. The NSIC verifies the competence of the unit to execute government orders and enlists them for participation.

Exchange: Ten sub-contracting exchanges at the SISIs in Mumbai, Kolkata, Hyderabad, Bangalore, Channai, Ahmedabad, Jaipur, Kanpur, Ludhiana and New Delhi are entrusted with providing information, enlisting and assisting small units in obtaining contracts from medium and large-scale units for parts, components, sub-assemblies, etc.

Export Promotion: Export promotion facilities, subject to certain conditions, include cash compensatory support in the export of specified non-traditional products; liberalised export credit for pre-shipment advances, and general permission by the Reserve Bank to exporters to enter into negotiations for the export of capital goods; liberalised schemes for the registration of export contracts

Box 1

ADVICE TO STARTUPS

- Develop a unique proposition.
- Critique it with potential customers and thought leaders.
- Prototype the proposition and build vigour in execution.
- Search for innovation and improvements in biz model.
- Be flexible as the business evolves and be resilient.
- Never think that it is easy because the market is huge and getting a small piece of the cake won't be difficult.
- Be prepared for eventual hiccups. You may have to bear losses and even humiliation in the first couple of years. But hang on.
- Before launching your business, carry out foolproof research on every aspect of the business – product, technology, competition, market size, product quality, operations, et al. It shouldn't be like I have got an idea, so here I am.
- Do it only if you are passionate about the idea.

  Trivia: Parle got its name from Ville Parle in Mumbai where the Chauhan family lived. It's not the other way around.
- An idea should impact the society for the better. It should change the way people live.
- An entrepreneur should not be bound by his/her ideas. You should have the ability to change course when required
- Great ideas alone are not enough. You should surround yourself with great people. An entrepreneur has to make people buy into his dream. When you live that dream, other people will follow you.
- Passion, commitment and energy are more important than capital. Also, if money is the motive, you will fail. Money will come as a consequence of your actions.
- Many entrepreneurs fail because of indecisiveness. You should have the courage to decide with speed.
- What will separate you from the rest is your attitude.
- An entrepreneur is excited by the opportunity element.
- Keep reinventing yourself from time to time.
- Learn to compete on 'unlevel' playing fields.
- Whatever role life gives you, play it big.
- Growth your belief and dreams. Keep on pursuing it.
- You must realise whether you have the ability to think beyond.
- Everyone cannot be an entrepreneur.
- You need to know if you are comfortable with getting into uncharted territory.
- Walk on the path not tread by others. Never say NO.
- Be an entrepreneur only if you have the passion.
- Be prepared for the brickbats and the downfalls.
- Be thorough about the regulatory environment.
- Lead by example ... do it yourself before you delegate.

for cash assistance; liberalised procedure for the payment of cash assistance claims of exporters; exemption of fifty-four specified raw materials imported for export production against advance from customs duty payment; simplified payment procedure for cash assistance. Exporters are paid 95% of their claims on a preliminary scrutiny within a fortnight and the balance on detailed scrutiny.

The Export Credit and Guarantee Corporation Ltd. (ECGC) has been authorised to issue an export promotion guarantee covering bid bonds up to 90% in specified cases; offer protection against fluctuations in foreign exchange in specified cases; and issue blanket permits for export promotion tours. Exporters receive assistance for sales and marketing promotion from the Marketing Development Fund and package assistance for export promotion and marketing by the Trade Development Authority in addition to liberalised facilities for the import of raw materials, capital goods, parts, components and technical samples.

⏩ The Winning Edge

The opening up of the Indian small industry sector to competition as well as the increase in the need to cater to the global market, demands fresh perceptions to respond to the radical changes in the 90s. Consequently, this sector must change first to survive as well as restructure itself to meet the new challenges through a critical evaluation of the forces of free global trade and increased competition. These events demand quantum strategic changes in terms of industry culture, flattening of the organisation structure, employee empowerment as well as team building. Only those organisations which can respond to these changes will be able to survive and retain a winning edge.

Some of the important characteristics that differentiate the successful organisations from the unsuccessful ones are:

1. The most important aspect of successful business is leadership. It calls for clear vision, goals and objectives, well defined mission, dash and employees' participation.
2. Adequate but well-orchestrated control. Constant feedback of results as well as setting and adherence of high standards give an organisation a cutting edge over others. Planning, foresight and analysis are other important qualities.
3. To able to extract the best from its employees through total involvement, the organisations put a lot of emphasis on proper internal communication and on training employees.
4. The successful organisation is one which is very close to the market place. The process of systematic market is used to develop products or process of systematic market research is used to develop products or process and to provide value for money to the customers. This helps to gain the market share.
5. The next most important characteristic of a winning business organisation is "Zero Basing" or sticking to the last – knowing what business the company is in swiftly recognising and preventing when it has diverted into an unsuitable path and preventing risks.

⏩ Biz Mantra

- A sense of purpose, hard work and commitment.
- Integrity is important specially as money is our raw material.
- Believe in the potential of people. Create leaders.
- Excel in customer service by offering value-added solutions.
- Provide customers an experience they cannot forget.
- Open door policy helps. Share information with colleagues.

- Inspire people to make a difference in their own lives.
- Commit to the purpose.
- Lead by example.
- Motivate the organisation to excel.
- Encourage new ideas.
- Share knowledge, wealth etc.
- Learn to listen, the best ideas come from other people.
- Passion and commitments are musts.
- Innovate always.
- Focus on your strengths and build on them.
- The successful running of a business is based on a strong foundation of values and ethics. Never compromise on principles of fair play, ethics and value for the customer.
- It is also important to make your customers your partners in progress so that they also gainfully share in the benefits of the business.
- Another important guiding principle has been that two wrongs don't make one right. Therefore, believe in trying to amend laws and change them for the better rather than bending or deviating from laid down norms and laws of the land.
- Enjoy whatever you are doing and be contented with it. Otherwise, you will not be able to do justice either to your own needs or to the profession you are pursuing.

CASE STUDY

Haryana

Area	44,222 sq. kms.	
Population	21.15 million	
Urbanisation	29.1%	
Literacy	67.9%	
Large and medium Industries	1,347	
Small-scale Enterprises	90,550	
Employment	5,10,080	
Fixed Investment	Rs. 1,532.60 crore	
Production	Rs. 3,801.70 crore	
Gross Industrial output	Rs. 21,290	
Per capita value added (2001-02)	Rs. 3,043	
Net Domestic Product	Rs. 57,937 crore	
Per capital income	Rs. 26,632	
Outstanding Advances to:		
	No. of Accts.	*Amount Rs. crore*
Agriculture	4,24,097	3,479
Small-Scale Industries	46,710	2,360
Transport	10,086	109

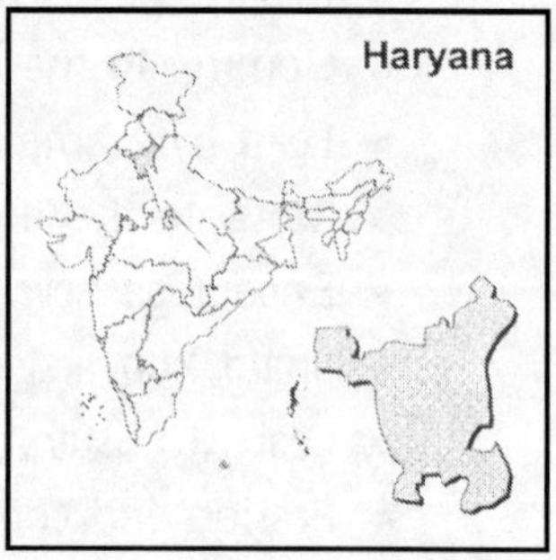

Branches	
Rural	699
Semi-urban	429
Urban	511
Total (March, 2009)	2,183
Deposit	Rs. 36,892 crores
Credit	Rs. 19,163 crores
Population per office	11,000
Per Capita Bank Deposits (March-2005)	Rs. 17,270
Deposit per office	Rs. 2212 lakh
Bank Credit per office	Rs. 1149 lakh
Credit-Deposit Ratio	68.4 per cent
Investment Plus Credit Deposit Ratio	70.7 per cent
Kisan Credit Cards Numbers	23,48,000
Amount	Rs. 18,358.50 crore

Major Industries:

Repairing services for capital goods, cement, sugar, paper, cotton textiles, glassware, brassware, cycles, tractors, motor cycles, metal products, canvas shoes, wood, furniture and agro-based industries.

Major Exports: Rice, Electronics, Handloom, Readymade garments, Gual gum

Industries in Haryana are concentrated in the Faridabad and Ballabgarh areas. The Planning Commission has notified Mohindergarh, Bhiwani, Jind and Hissar districts as backward, eligible for concessional financial assistance. Of these, the districts of Mohindergarh and Bhiwani and a few contiguous blocks from the other 2 districts are eligible for the 15% Central Subsidy. For purposes of various incentives, the State has been divided into 3 regions depending upon the level of industrial development. These are: developed regions limited to Faridabad and Ballabgarh, developing areas covering rest of the State, and backward areas. The duration of the various incentives in the above three regions is 3, 5 and 7 years respectively. Incentives are available only to small-scale units in the developed regions, to units with an investment up to Rs. 50,000 in developing areas and to units requiring an investment up to Rs. 1 crore in backward areas.

INDUSTRY — HARBINGER OF PROGRESS

Haryana today rightly harnesses the progressive thrust of industrialisation of steering, pacing and channelising it with tried and tested innovative techniques. By instituting new infrastructural and organisational set-ups, Haryana has become the paradigm state in modern India.

Backed by a clear vision and an immense practical sense of Chief Minister Bhupinder Singh Hooda, Haryana has turned into an industrial giant ushering in an era of equity and social development. During the last four and a half years, Haryana has emerged as the first choice of investors worldwide. The base for this massive industrial development has come from the highly-developed agriculture sector and its sturdy farmers, peaceful environment, excellent law and order, best infrastructure, cordial labour relations, availability of intellectual and skilled manpower and its hardworking people. All this makes Haryana the first choice of investors. The face of India is changing fast and Haryana

is today the embodiment of a progressive state that means business. Industrial development is at its peak and the state has witnessed a boom in this sector.

The industrial scenario in Haryana looks promising and the statistics speak for themselves. This has come about because investors have found that state a promising location and the industries present have benefited from the facilities and incentives provided to them. Some of the companies that have set up shop at the industrial estates at Bawal and Manesar are Mitsubishi Electric Automotive Ind., Napino Auto & Electronics, Pricol, Toyota Kirloskar Motor Systems Pvt. Ltd., India Japan Lighting Pvt Ltd., and Caparo Maruti.

Out of the countrywide production of cars more than 55 per cent such vehicles, 55 per cent motorcycles and 25 per cent tractors are produced in Haryana. The number of big and medium scale industries from a meagre 162 in the year 1966 has taken a quantum jump to 1,347 in December 2009. Further the State fosters nearly 80,000 small scale industries. During the nine month span from March 2005 to December 2005 of the incumbent government, the State has attracted fresh industrial investments of Rs. 230 crore in the form of new 20 big and medium industrial units and 682 .small scale industries. At present 69 industrial entrepreneurship memoranda with a gross investment of Rs. 2,245 crores are being actively implemented. After the declaration of a new industrial policy by the Hooda Government, the State has received fresh industrial proposals worth more than Rs. 10,000 crores.

To promote industry in the state, the Industrial Assistance Group has been converted into Investment Promotion Centre and will be further strengthened to take up the task of providing Single Window Services. This centre will act as an operational unit to High Powered Clearance Committee and State Level Clearance Committee.

This Investment Promotion Centre has been set up in Delhi and Chandigarh to act as a Single Point Contact Agency to provide information, guidance and hand holding services for venture location by prospective entrepreneurs particularly with regard to various sanctions/approvals needed for implementation of the projects, availability of land and present level of infrastructure in the State and to assist entrepreneurs in submission of applications for approvals/registration to different organizations. This Centre will have complete database on availability of land, water, power, finance etc. and norms, rules and regulations of all the institutions engaged in industrial development. This agency would showcase Haryana as an ultimate destination for investment.

ON THE HIGH-TECH HIGHWAY

The Hooda Government has realized that there are unlimited possibilities of employment generation and exports in the field of information technology. Under the new industrial policy the Government is according top priority to information technology, information communication technology and IT enabled services. This is proved by the fact that the Haryana Government web portal has won a merit citation award at the 7th National Conference on eGovernance. At present Haryana's software exports are the third highest in the country.

The State Government recognises the role of IT as an effective tool in catalysing economic activity, in efficient governance and in developing human resource. The IT policy encourages the replacement of traditional delivery system of public services by IT driven system of governance that works better, is economical and is capable of serving the citizens' needs with ease.

The state aims to achieve its IT vision through a process of modernisation and rationalisation of the administrative set up for an efficient, cost effective and responsive government. The Hooda government has encouraged IT literacy and education to generate IT related employment opportunities. IT plans to encourage private sector initiative in IT industry and IT related infrastructure and services to increase the share of IT in the state GDP.

In Northern India, Gurgaon has emerged as the favoured town of entrepreneurs seeking to establish IT units. The Hooda Government has undertaken all efforts to maintain this avant garde position of Gurgaon by developing and upgrading the available infrastructure. Other parts of the State, especially the economic hubs to be developed along the Kundli-Manesar-Palwal Expressway and Panchkula will be fostered as IT corridors.

The Department of Information Technology is the nodal agency for clearing and monitoring IT parks projects. The private sector and public-private joint ventures are being encouraged in establishing and maintaining IT parks and other infrastructure facilities. The State Government will facilitate the process of establishing research and development labs in public, private and joint domains. In this concern due efforts will be made to attract foreign direct investment.

The government has also developed a package of incentives for the IT industries. This includes infrastructure facilities like preferential allotment of land, uninterrupted power supply, single window clearances, relaxation in floor area regulation (FAR), changes in land use, various rebates and concessions on Sales Tax. IT has also been designated as a priority sector for lending by state level lending institutions, is exempt from the pollution control board and various incentives have been provided for mega projects. To this effect, the state government shall be establishing reliable, adequate and efficient telecom and communication infrastructure in all the districts in Haryana.

At the IT Park being developed on 140 acres of land in Manesar by Haryana State Industrial Development Corporation, 12 big IT companies including HCL, Bharti, Galilo, e-Clark. KLG Systels,

Agilent Technologies, Shapurji Polanji and Co. have been allotted land. Another IT corridor on similar lines is being developed on 250 acres in Panchkula. Haryana State Industrial Development Corporation has already allotted 97 acres of land for this purpose.

The Government has envisaged a project to introduce E-Disha civic amenities in all the villages, development blocks and district headquarters in a phased manner. Under this project, service centres will be established where information pertaining to different departments and corporations will be made available.

A Statewide Zonal Network to take IT services to the village level has been planned and an on-line payment gateway is planned. The results of the 2005 Haryana State School Board were made available on internet and a software system, which was the first of its kind in the country, was prepared to analyse the results.

REACHING MILESTONES

Haryana produces 50 per cent of the total cars being manufactured in the country and 50 per cent motorcycles and 25 per cent sanitaryware. Every fifth bicycle being manufactured in India is from Haryana.

- In the last 40 years, the state had a capital investment of Rs. 40,000 crore whereas after the Hooda government came to power, investment proposals of Rs. 40,000 crore have been implemented. Investment proposals worth Rs. 90,000 crore are also in the pipeline.
- Haryana has a per capita investment of Rs. 78,500, the highest in India.
- Under the present Hooda government, the state received a foreign direct investment of Rs.9,000 crore whereas it had received only Rs. 3,500 crore in the last 40 years.
- The plan outlay budget which was Rs. 2,236 crore in 2004-05 has been raised to Rs. 10,000 crore in 2009-10. The state government implemented the new industrial policy to attract an investment of Rs. 2 lakh crore and generate employment for 10 lakh people.
- A petro-chemical hub is being set up in Panipat over an area of 5,000 acres at a cost of Rs.35,000 crore. It will employ 50,000 people and facilitate the setting up of 3,500 auxiliary units.
- There is a proposal to set up 97 SEZs with an investment of Rs. 2 lakh crore to promote exports. As many as 64 of these SEZs have been accorded a formal approval. More than 21 lakh people will get employment as a result of these SEZs.
- The exports from Haryana touched the Rs. 30,000 crore mark in 2007-08 and estimated to touch Rs. 40,000 crore in 2008-09. The software exports alone have touched the Rs. 18,000 crore mark.
- A footwear and leather garment park is coming up at Bahadurgarh.
- A Central Institute of Plastic and Engineering Technology is coming up at Panipat.
- The HSIIDC has undertaken the development of the KMP Expressway. New integrated townships will come up along the expressway.
- During the tenure of the present government, 98 new big and medium scale and 7,683 small scale industrial units have come up with an investment of Rs. 5,465 crore.

Policy Shapes Growth

To give further impetus to industry, the government has adopted the New Industrial Policy, which came into effect in June 2005. A multi-faceted approach has been adopted to provide the best of the infrastructure, simplification of rules and regulations governing industry, efficient institutional mechanism and incentives to the industry in the backward areas of the state. The policy has also envisaged boosting service sector, including information technology, bio-technology and tourism. The government has identified agro-based and food processing industries, electronics and information technology, automobiles and automotive components, handloom, hosiery, textile and garment manufacturing, export-oriented units and footwear, leather garment and accessories' industries as thrust areas for the economic development of the state.

Destination Par Excellence

To strengthen industry-related infrastructure and improve connectivity, a six-lane, 135-km-long Kundli-Manesar-Palwal Expressway is coming up, which will facilitate in a better connectivity of Haryana with other parts. Economic hubs will be developed around this expressway and these will generate large economic activities and employment. The expressway will pass through major towns from Kundli in Sonipat on NH-11 to Palwal in Faridabad on NH-2 via Jhajjar, Bahadurgarh and Manesar. The expressway will be built on BOT basis at a cost of Rs. 1,200 crore for construction and Rs. 630 crore as the cost of land. The project has been awarded to Madhucon-Apollo-DSC Consortium with a concession period of 24 years. The process of acquiring about 3,450 acres of land for the project has been completed. Haryana Financial Corporation is playing a fundamental role in providing much-needed finances to the entrepreneurs. The procedure for getting loans has been simplified. Consumer meets are organised at regular intervals at the district level to facilitate setting up of new industries and expansion of the existing ones, says Dheera Khandelwal, MD, Haryana Financial Corporation.

Rapid Strides

Under the leadership of Mr. Bhupinder Singh Hooda, Haryana has taken rapid strides on the development front. Since its inception in November 1966, it has taken a big lead in social and economic advancement. The state stands out for its progressive policies which have led to an improvement in the quality of life for its residents through focused development of agriculture, industries, commerce and trade, and creation of excellent social infrastructure. It is recognised as a state trying to orchestrate improvement in every parameter involved in guiding investment decision. The government firmly believes that there is a need for rapid industrial growth on a sustainable basis to achieve the twin objectives of economic development and generation of adequate employment. The government has formulated a fresh industrial policy to streamline the procedure of allotment, transfer and leasing of industrial plots and to ensure better utilisation of infrastructure and speedy industrialisation. Haryana stands second in terms of infrastructure development, according to a CMIE report. It also enjoys the distinction of being among the top investor-friendly states, with an unmatched track record in law and order and responsive administration.

⏩ Conclusion

Starting a small-scale industry is not easy. It is ninety per cent perspiration and hardly ten per cent profit. It calls for vision, perseverance, co-operation and hardwork. The entrepreneur has a uphill task in coordinating multifarious activities and turn into a viable enterprise. It calls for a thorough business plan and prompt implementation. The entrepreneur needs a number of skills to set up a small industry, which will grow into a giant in coming years. Many of the giants of today, viz., Kirloskar, Honda, Escort, Camlin, Reliance were started small. It calls for a missionary work with a purpose. Then the joys of fulfillment is like a beautiful rainbow.

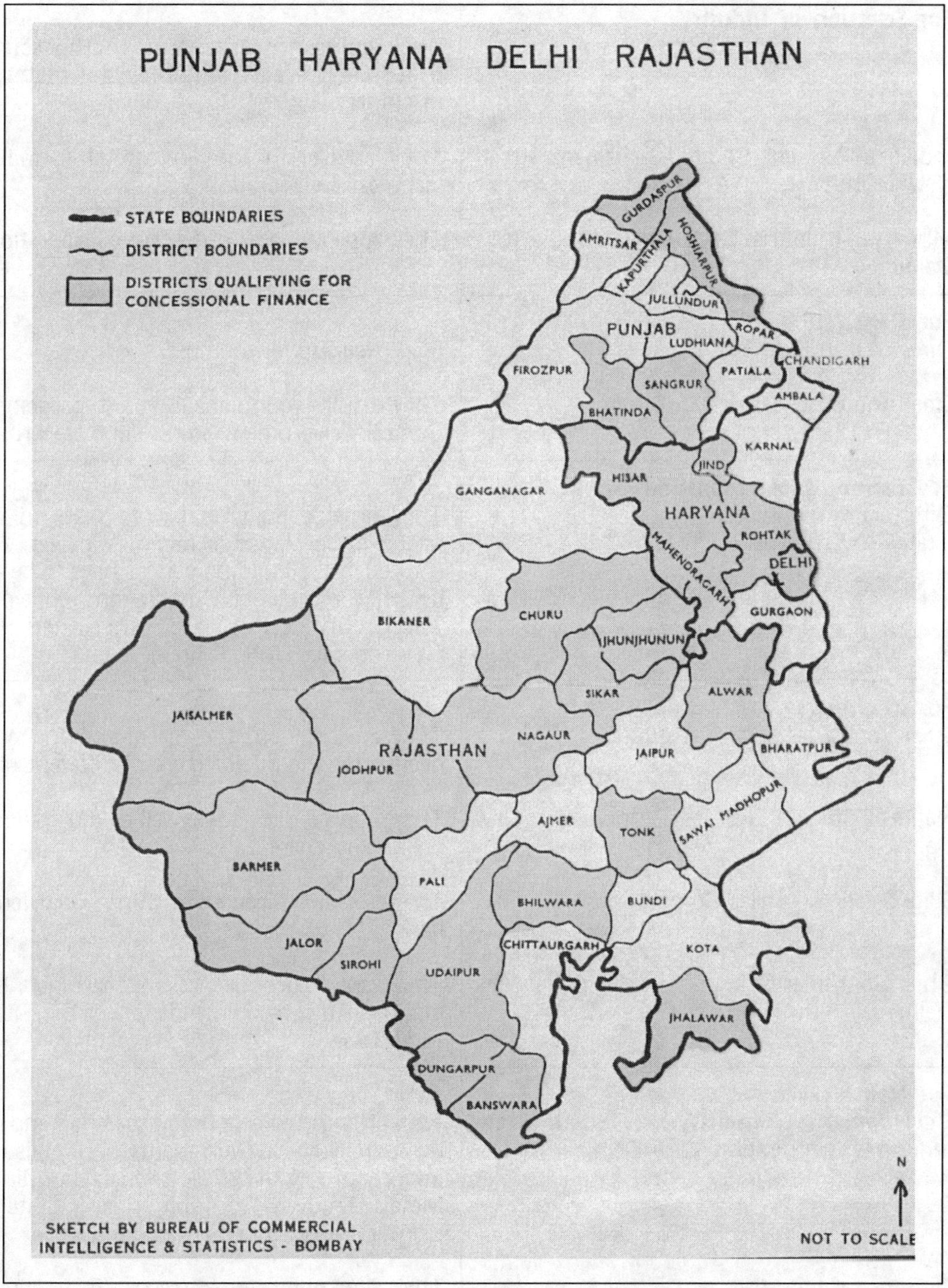
PUNJAB HARYANA DELHI RAJASTHAN
STATE BOUNDARIES
DISTRICT BOUNDARIES
DISTRICTS QUALIFYING FOR CONCESSIONAL FINANCE
GURDASPUR
AMRITSAR
KAPURTHALA
HOSHIARPUR
JULLUNDUR
PUNJAB
LUDHIANA
ROPAR
CHANDIGARH
FIROZPUR
SANGRUR
PATIALA
AMBALA
BHATINDA
KARNAL
JIND
HISAR
GANGANAGAR
HARYANA
ROHTAK
MAHENDRAGARH
DELHI
GURGAON
BIKANER
CHURU
JHUNJHUNUN
SIKAR
ALWAR
JAISALMER
NAGAUR
RAJASTHAN
JODHPUR
JAIPUR
BHARATPUR
SAWAI MADHOPUR
AJMER
TONK
BARMER
PALI
BHILWARA
BUNDI
JALOR
SIROHI
UDAIPUR
CHITTAURGARH
KOTA
JHALAWAR
DUNGARPUR
BANSWARA
N
SKETCH BY BUREAU OF COMMERCIAL INTELLIGENCE & STATISTICS - BOMBAY
NOT TO SCALE

ANNEXURE 1

WHOM TO APPROACH FOR WHAT (A DIGEST)

1. For Selection of Industry	
Small Industries Service Institutes	They guide entrepreneurs in the selection of industries, areas, suitable raw materials and machinery.
Indian Investment Centre, Parliament Street, New Delhi-1.	They advise on foreign capital formation and technical collaboration.
Ministry of Industrial Devt., Govt. of India, New Delhi.	They approve cases of foreign collaborations.
2. For Registration	
Director of Industries	S.S.I. Registration number.
Small Industries Service Institutes	They register you to enable you to participate in the Central Government Stores Purchase Programme.
3. For Factory Accommodation	
Directors of Industries (State Government)	They provide built up factory space in industrial estates of developed factory sites, power, water, etc. (Although the building designs have to be approved by the Municipalities/Corporations, while power and water connections are sanctioned by State Governments/Undertakings).
4. For Machinery	
Small Industries Service Institutes	They advise about the machinery and equipment needed for the manufacture of different products.
National Small Industries Corporation, New Delhi.	They supply indigenous as well as imported machinery on hire-purchase basis.
State Small Industries Corporations	They provide indigenous machinery on deferred credit basis.
Chief Controller of Imports and Exports, New Delhi.	They issue import licences for machinery of foreign origin on the recommendation of the Directors of Industries.
5. For Raw Materials	
Development Commissioner, Small Scale Industries Organisation, New Delhi.	They arrange indigenous raw materials and distribute through State Governments. They also arrange imports of raw materials through the Minerals and Metals Trading Corporation and State Trading Corporation of India.
Directors of Industries	They allot quotas of scarce raw materials.
State Small Industries Corporations	They supply raw materials.

Chief Controller of Imports and Exports and its Port Offices.	They issue licences for import of raw materials.
6. For Finance	
Small Industries Development Bank of India (SIDBI)	SIDBI has been set up as a principal financial institution for the promotion, financing and development of industry in the tiny and small sector and co-ordinate the functions of institutions engaged in similar activities. SIDBI provides finances for new projects, expansion, diversification, modernisation, rehabilitation. In addition, it provides refinance assistance to other institutions engaged in similar activities.
State Financial Corporations	They provide long-term credit for purchase of fixed assets.
State Directors of Industries	They provide loans under State Aid Industries Act/Rules for block capital.
State Bank of India and its Subsidiaries	They sanction medium-term and instalment credit loans for purchase of machinery and construction of factory buildings. They also provide working capital for purchase of raw materials and meeting day-to-day requirements.
Commercial Banks	They sanction loans for meeting working capital needs.
Small Industries Service Institutes	They furnish technical reports to the State Bank of India on the applicant units.
7. For Technical Know-How	
Small Industries Service Institutes	They prepare improved designs and drawings for the products. They assist in making tools, dies, jigs and fixtures. They help in the optimum utilisation of men, material and machinery through technological and management consulting. They train managers and supervisors in industrial management. They train workers to upgrade their skills. They demonstrate modern technical processes.
National Small Industries Corporation, New Delhi	They give advanced training in their Prototype Production-cum-Training Centres in the operation of modern machines.
Council of Scientific and Industrial Research, New Delhi.	They develop new technological processes and disseminate the same to industry.

Productivity Councils	They train the factory owners in getting higher productivity.
Small Industry Extension Training Institute, Hyderabad	They give full-time management training to the managers/proprietors of small industry sector.
8. For Standardisation	
Small Industries Service Institutes	They provide technical guidance in the production of goods according to prescribed standards.
Indian Standards Institution	They prescribe specifications for the products and give ISI marks.
Directors of Industries	They prescribe standards and give 'Q' Mark to the small industry's products.
9. For Marketing	*Internal*
Small Industries Service Institutes	They conduct distribution and surveys for the benefit of small industrialists.
	They enlist the units for participation under Central Government Stores Purchase programme.
	They issue competency certificates to the units receiving Government orders.
	They promote ancillary relationship with the large and medium-scale units in the Public as well as Private Sectors.
National Small Industries Corporation, New Delhi.	They secure contracts from the Director-General of Supplies and Disposals, Railways, and Defence for supply of manufactured goods on behalf of small-scale units.
State Small Industries Corporations	They secure orders from the State Governments and other semi-Government organisations for the supply of stores.
	Export
Small Industries Services Institutes	They enlist small units for participation under Export Aid to Small Industry Scheme of the State Trading Corporation of India.
	They render technical counseling for satisfactory execution of export orders.
	They disseminate information about the items having export markets.
	They maintain close liaison with specialised agencies like Export Promotion Councils to have up-to-date knowledge about the products having export markets.

Chief Controller of Imports and Exports, New Delhi	They issue licences for export of products to foreign countries.
Directorate of Export Promotion, Udyog Bhavan, New Delhi	They collect and supply information on foreign markets.
	They carry out market studies for particular products.
Export Promotion Councils	They publish Trade Directories, Brochures and Bulletins.
	They organise exhibitions and show rooms.
	They maintain close liaison between Indian exporters and foreign buyers.
	They settle commercial disputes.
	They frame special export promotion schemes.
State Trading Corporation of India, New Delhi	They register units for participation under Export Aid to Small Industry Scheme.
	They held the small-scale units in the preparation of sales leaflets, price lists, etc.
	They secure export orders for small industries.
10. For Inventions The Inventions Promotion Board, 39, Ring Road, Lajpat Nagar IV, New Delhi-14	They promote workable inventions of practical utility, through financial assistance and other incentives.
11. For Miscellaneous Problems The Federation of Associations of Small Industries of India, Rohtak Road, New Delhi	They represent the problems faced by the small industries to the Government.

DREAM TEAM

"Nothing can beat a good team that works together like a well-oiled machine. And making that happen is one of the toughest challenges for any manager." — *Shekhar Dasgupta,* *MD, Oracle India*

The growth objective of the financial system is to achieve the structure and rate of growth of various financial assets and liabilities in consonance with the optimal characteristics of real capital stock. The more efficient composition of real wealth is obtained through the promotion of such financial assets which provide incentives to savers and the public to hold a growing part of their wealth in financial form. Increasing rate of savings correlates well with the increase in the proportion of saving held in the form of financial assets relative to tangible assets. There is a direct correlation between growth of the economy and the growth of the financial assets. Investment in the real sector depends on the functioning of the financial sector, as the latter collects and channels savings into investment which is necessary for growth. It would be pertinent to note here that economic growth is function of the level of investment, capital-output ratio in each activity of productive process, the level of investment, determines the increase in output of goods and services and incomes in the economy.

24

Criteria of Financing

►► Introduction

Finance is a key input of business – industry, trade, infrastructure – to accelerate economic growth. We discuss the issue of criteria of financing in this chapter.

It is well-known that resources are the key inputs of development. The development bank plays an important role in providing not only development finance needed at different stages of development, but also extending professional, and promotional assistance on an ongoing basis. In fact, the contributions of the various inputs to the productive transfer into:

(*i*) Rapid growth in output,

(*ii*) Change in the structure of the economy, and

(*iii*) Accelerated overall socio-economic growth.

Economic development is achieved by increasing both the inputs of resources and the productivity of those inputs, *i.e.*, resources. Productivity enhances the recycling of resources in an accelerated manner.

Among other things capital also plays a crucial role in the growth process. The process of economic development involves savings to create a surplus for capital formation and further boost savings and investments, prudentially and productively.

Development Finance

Finance is one of the basic requirements of a project. The entrepreneur needs capital to start with and he needs financial assistance at every stage of the project. Product finance is both for short-term and long-term. The sources form which the entrepreneurs can meet their financial needs for their projects are: *internal source* and *external* source. Besides, the entrepreneur raises his finance by availing of available subsidies, state aid to industries, etc. Project finance, therefore, is very crucial for the success of a project. Here, the various facets of project financing will be discussed.

"One of the key problems of planning, therefore, is where to strike this balance between giving enough credit for the small man to develop and not giving him so much that there have to be large write-offs every year."

Finance is one of the constant problems, and if the economy has to develop in the way the Government policy hopes, various segments such as agriculture, industry, transport etc., must have adequate credit. Credit is available on the basis of the creditworthiness of the entrepreneur. In regard to capital structure and working capital management, substantial differences between large, medium and small-scale industries exist. However, finance is the catalytic agent for development.

Finance is the life-blood of any business. Its management is an art and merits special attention. The financial function of management is to:

(*a*) Ensure fair returns on investments;

(*b*) Generate and build-up surpluses and reserves for growth and expansion;

(*c*) Plan, direct and control the utilisation of finances so as to ensure maximum efficiency of operations and build a proper relationship with suppliers, financiers, workers and members; and

(*d*) Co-ordinate the operations of the various departments through appropriate measures to ensure discipline in the use of financial resources.

A growing economy needs the support of a financial structure which is responsive to the needs of development. In India, in the process of financial deepening, commercial banks had to shoulder special responsibilities for meeting the financial needs of diverse sectors of the economy, at various stages of development. In the process, they have evolved various modes and instruments of financing, fashioned various organisational innovations, moved away from traditional commercial banking and evolved into development banks, responsive to socio-economic needs.

Finance is now made available to entrepreneurs on a totality basis by commercial banks, except in cases where the State Financial Corporations and other similar financing agencies step in to meet their medium-term requirements. An appropriate type of credit is granted for the construction of the factory building, the purchase of plant, machinery and equipment, and for working capital requirements. In deserving cases, loans are advanced for the expansion, renovation and modernisation of plant and machinery. Banks and financial institutions provide the export finance provide needed by small industries for letters of credit, issuance of guarantees and extension of pre-shipment and post-shipment credit facilities. The interest rate structure is generally graded on a slab basis, with a favourable bias towards the smaller loans.

Types of Industrial Finance

Depending upon the nature of the activity, the entrepreneurs require three types of finances, viz., *short-term, medium-term* and *long-term* finances. The distinctive features of these are emulated below:

Short-term Finance

Short-term finance usually refers to funds required for a period of less than one year. These funds are usually required to meet variable, seasonal or temporary working capital requirements.

Borrowing from banks is a very important source of short-term finance. Other important sources of short-term finance are trade credit, instalment credit and customer advances.

Technicians Scheme: Technically qualified or experienced professionals — upto Rs. 7.50 lakhs.	**Equipment Finance:** For procurement of new machinery/equipment by existing industrial units — upto Rs. 90 lakhs.
Special Capital Scheme: Soft loan assistance up to Rs.4 lakhs is available on soft terms along with term loan for technically qualified or experienced persons.	**Quality Control Equipment:** 100% assistance for setting up quality control facility by existing and new SSI units — up to Rs. 7.50 lakhs.
Seed Capital Scheme: Assisatnce towards equity on soft terms up to Rs.15 lakhs along with term loan for technically qualified or experienced persons.	**Assistance to Ex-Servicemen:** Term loan up to Rs. 9 lakhs and seed capital up to Rs. 1.80 lakhs for gaining self employment.
Composite Loan Scheme: Both equipment finance and working capital up to Rs. 50,000 for artisans and rural industries.	**Single Window Scheme:** Both term loan and working capital together to new tiny and small-scale industrial units up to Rs. 7.50 lakhs towards term loan and up to Rs. 375 lakhs towards working capital.
Disabled Entrepreneurs: 100% finance up to Rs. 50,000 to disabled entrepreneurs.	**Tourism Related Facilities:** Up to Rs. 90 lakhs available for tourism related business ventures.
Modernisation: For replacement/renovation of equipment for successful units which are in existence since 5 years assistance up to Rs. 90 lakhs.	**Mahila Udyam Nidhi Scheme:** To set up new industrial projects in SSI sector by women entrepreneurs.
Electro-Medical Equipment: For qualified Doctors/private nursing homes — up to Rs. 90 lakhs.	**National Equity Fund Scheme:** Assistance towards equity for new projects of tiny and small-scale sector — up to Rs. 75,000.
Nursing Homes/Hospitals: Assistance for full-fledged nursing homes and hospitals — up to Rs. 90 lakhs.	**Assistance for Marketing:** (a) Maximum assistance upto Rs. 3 lakhs per sales van, not exceeding six vehicles per borrower (b) Assistance up to Rs. 7.50 lakhs for setting up new sales outlets

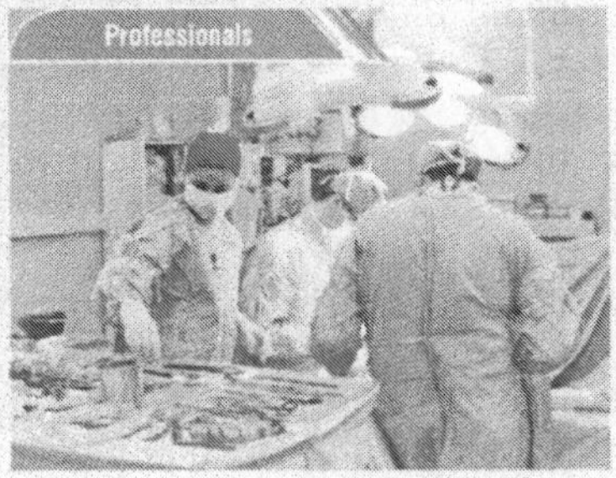

Medium-term Finance

The period of one year to five years may be regarded as a medium-term. Medium-term finance is usually required for permanent working capital, small expansions, replacements, modifications, etc.

Medium-term finance may be raised by (*i*) issue of shares; issue of debentures; borrowing from banks and other financial institutions; and ploughing back of profits (by existing concerns).

Long-term Finance

The period exceeding 5 years is regarded as long-term. Long-term finance is required for procuring fixed assets, for the establishment of a new business, for substantial expansion of existing business, modernisation etc. (Chart 1).

The important sources of long-term finance are similar to the medium-term finance to industry.

Short-Term	***Medium-Term***	***Long-Term***
(*i*) Bank credit (*ii*) Trade credit (*iii*) Instalment credit (*iv*) Customer advances	(*i*) Issue of shares (*ii*) Issue of debentures (*iii*) Loans from banks and other financial institutions (*iv*) Public deposits (for existing concerns) (*v*) Ploughing back of profits (for existing concerns)	(*i*) Issue of shares (*ii*) Issue of debentures (*iii*) Loans from financial institutions (*iv*) Ploughing back of profits (for existing concerns)

Fig. 1 Types of Finance for Entrepreneurs

Sources of Finance

A characteristic feature of small-scale units is that the personal funds of entrepreneurs form a substantial proportion of the total assets. Most of the units are not corporate entities. The owners of small units, therefore, run a considerably higher risk than those of corporate units. The sources that usually provide the working capital requirements are commercial banks, special agencies like SIICOM, GIIC, and co-operative banks. Indigenous bankers, and moneylenders also advance loans for working capital needs. The fixed capital needs are usually met by State Governments (under the State Aid to Industries Acts/Rules), SFCs, NSI which machinery on hire-purchase basis, Corporations (SSICs), (SIDCs), the State Bank of India and subsidiaries, and other commercial banks.

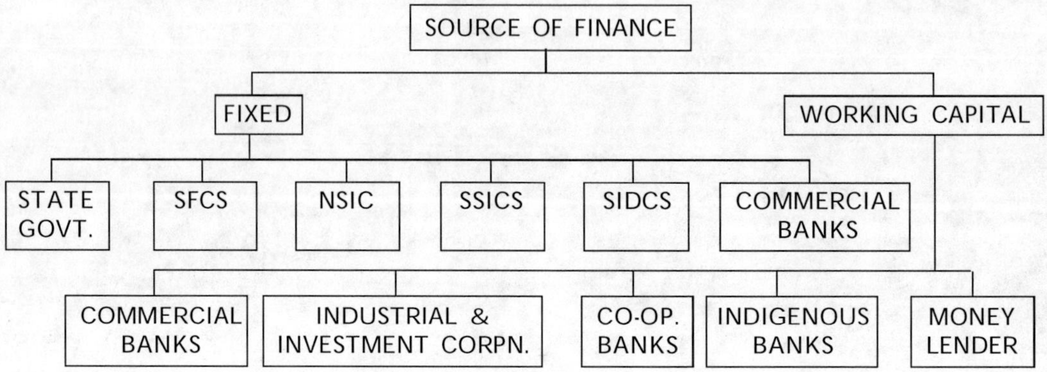

Fig. 2 Sources of Finance for Small-Scale Sector

Working Capital	***Fixed Capital***		***Venture Capital***
Commercial Banks	IDBI	NSIC	STATES
SFCs	SIDBI	UTI	Venture Companies
Co-operative Banks	IDCI	NABARD	Mutual Funds
Finance Companies	ICICI		Commercial Banks
Indigenous Bankers	LIC		SFCs
Money Lenders	GIC		Finance Companies
	NSIC		SIDCs
Refinance	KVIC		RCTFC
	SFCs		RCTFC
IDBI	SIDCs		TDICI
SIDBI	Commercial Banks		TFCI
NABARD	EXIM Bank		
EXIM BANK	SSIDCS		

⏩ The Metamorphosis

Post the unlocking of financial controls on the economy since 1991; Indian companies have had increasing access to capital from various sources. Over time, as private equity funds have started gaining attention, companies have realised that they are a viable source of funding for several reasons:

- Funds can be raised in far less time than it takes to get listed or to raise a loan
- A PE fund brings a lot of expertise and networking contacts to the table
- The fund can be tapped for subsequent rounds of resource raising

Raising resources through PE gives growing companies the impetus they require to accelerate their growth while allowing them sufficient time to build sustainable value in their businesses. A company with a reasonably long track record of growth and profitability, with a sustainable competitive advantage which has been nurtured and proven stands a far better chance of attracting high valuations than one which goes public without reaching its "critical mass."

A Key Role of Private Equity

Private Equity can play a very important role in the development of the SME space in the country, beyond that of providing capital. Many private equity funds deploy members of their team on the boards of directors of their investee companies and take active part in their governance and activities. This brings in more accountability, transparency and corporate governance in companies which were usually run as autocracies (albeit run well). The portfolio companies get exposure to global standard practices in operations, human resources management, financial planning, reporting and investor relations. Many funds are also able to leverage the capabilities of their other investee companies or their existing relationships in industry to synergistically enhance value across their portfolio. This transforms companies into organizations.

Synopsis

- PE Funds – viable source of funding
- Funds can be raised in far less time than it takes to get listed or to raise a loan
- A PE fund brings a lot of expertise and networking contacts to the table
- The fund can be tapped for subsequent rounds of resource raising
- Provide impetus to accelerate their growth
- A vast range of industries have successfully tapped into the PE stream
- Larger amounts are now accessible through the PE route
- Very important role in the development of the SME space, beyond that of providing capital.

Broadly speaking, the various sources from which an entrepreneur can raise funds are enumerated in its balance sheet. These sources may generally be grouped under the following heads:

I. Internal

A. Paid-up Capital

(i) Ordinary shares
(ii) Preference shares
(iii) Deferred shares
(iv) Forfeited shares

B. Reserve Surplus

(i) Capital reserve
(ii) Development rebate reserves
(iii) Others

C. Provisions

(i) Taxation (net on advance of income-tax)
(ii) Depreciation.

II. EXTERNAL

D. Borrowings

(i) From banks
(ii) From term-lending institutions like IDBI, IFCI, ICICI, Industrial Development Corporations, etc.
(iii) From government and semi-government agencies
(iv) Others

E. Trade Dues and Other Current Liabilities

(i) Sundry creditors
(ii) Others

The share distribution of source and of all companies and profit-making companies is as follows:

Table 1

Sources	*All Companies (505)%*	*Profit-making Companies (450%)*
A. *Internal Sources*	34.2	35.5
1. Paid-up capital	0.5	0.5
2. Reserves and surplus	17.2	18.9
3. Depreciation	16.5	16.1
B. *External*	65.8	64.5
4. Paid-up capital	2.1	1.8
5. Long-term Borrowings	31.0	31.1
(a) Debentures	9.6	9.8
(b) From Financial	14.8	14.6
(c) Banks	–	–
(d) Others	6.6	6.7
6. Bank borrowings for working capital	7.7	7.3
7. Trade dues and other current liabilities	21.3	20.4
8. Non-current liabilities	3.7	3.9
Total A & B	100.0	100.0

Table 1 indicates that the companies' dependence on financial institutions and banks is to the extent of 40 per cent of its total funds for development. Even to some extent companies depend heavily on banks to recover their trade dues for development. Thus, financial institutions' involvement is nearly 60 per cent as far as finance alone is concerned. This apart, their promotional consultancy and other related services go a long way in the process of economic development. It is true that industrial development may or even the entire process of economic development is dependent on the financial institutions and their innovative assistance on an ongoing basis.

The funds which an industry can raise depend on its productive activity and the uses to which these funds are put:

(i) Gross Fixed Assets: Land, building, plant and machinery – these are by and large, met out of market borrowings or term loans from financial institutions, including banks.

(ii) Working Capital: This includes inventories – raw materials, components, finished goods, works in progress and operating expenses – wages, salaries, lighting and other running expenses. All these expenses are met out commercial bank loans in the form of hypothecation credit or pledge loans.

(iii) Funds are also required for *(a)* making loans and advances in the course of day-to-day purchase-and-sale operations; *(b)* sundry debtors – that is, for sale on credit basis; *(c)* investments; and *(d)* building up other assets.

F. Miscellaneous

All these sources of finance are not available to all the small units. Much would depend on the status, character and the period of time the units have been in operation. For example, a new small unit has no reserves to provide for depreciation. These are built up in gradual stages out of the funds set apart in the course of current operations.

QUICK GUIDE TO SOURCES OF FINANCE

A firm wants...	Temporary working capital: bridging finance; capital to meet seasonal fluctuations; finance for short-lived assets.	Finance for assets with a medium-term life, *e.g.*, plant and machinery; general working capital; overdraft funding.	Finance for long-life assets, *e.g.*, buildings; 'permanent' working capital; corporate acquisitions.
So it needs...	Short-term finance Upto 3 years	Medium-term finance 3-10 years	Long-term finance More than 10 years
Main sources...	Clearing banks	Clearing banks	Accepting houses and issuing houses
	Accepting houses	Merchant banks	Insurance companies
	Finance houses	Leasing companies	Pension funds
	Discount houses	Finance houses	Specialist organisations including ICFC and FCI
	Factoring companies	Specialist organisation including ICFC and FCI	Other British and foreign banks
	Invoice discounting companies	Other British and foreign banks	NEB and other public sector agencies
	Other British and foreign banks	NEB and other public sector agencies	
	Leasing companies		

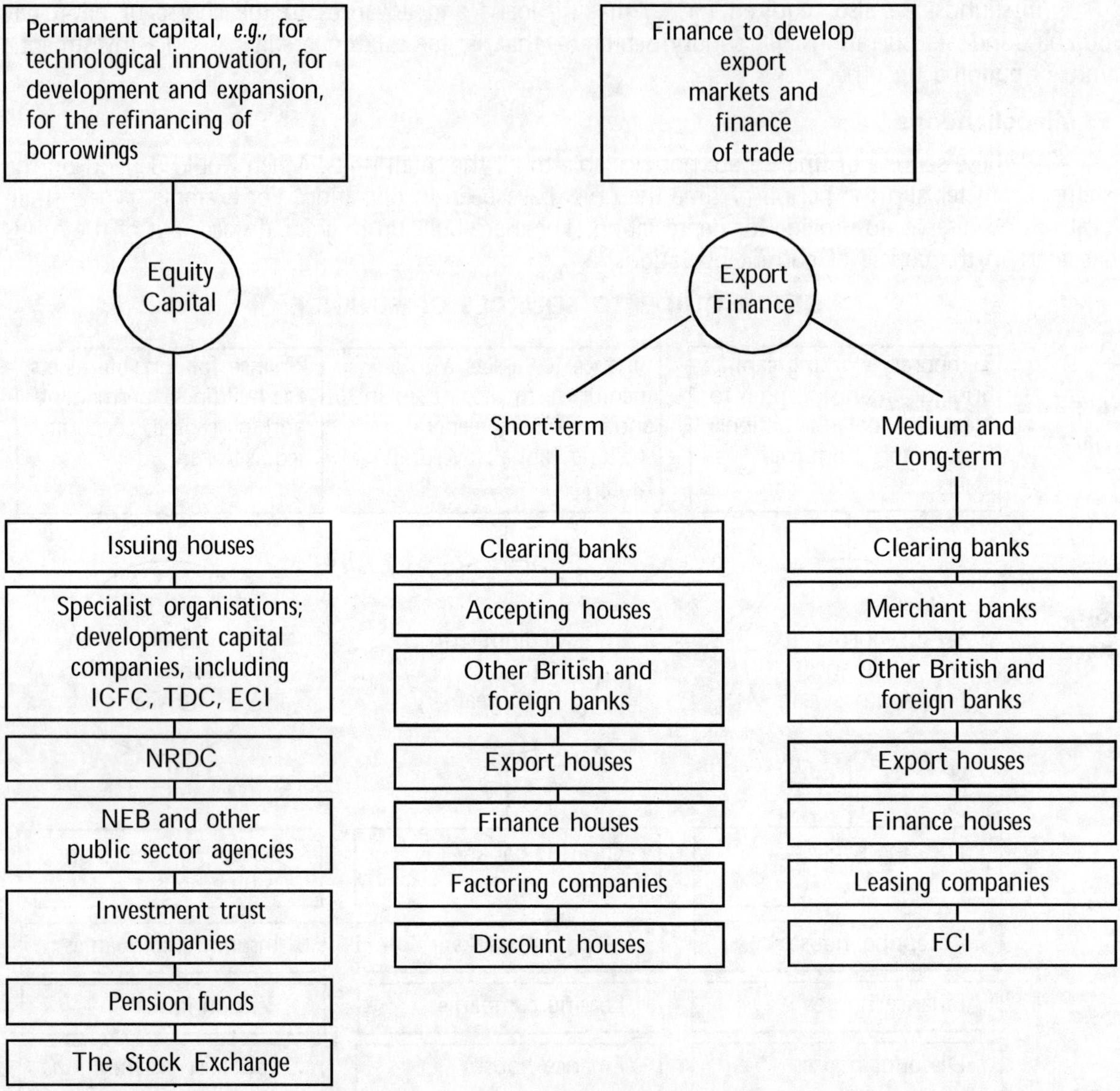

Moreover, the funds a small-scale industry can raise depends upon the character of the company, its productive activity and the substantial uses to which these funds are put – irrespective of it being a private limited or a proprietary concern. Some of the uses are:

(i) Gross Fixed Assets: Land, building, plant and machinery – these are by and large, met out of market borrowings or term loans from financial institutions, including banks.

(ii) Working Capital: This includes inventories – raw materials, components, finished goods, works in progress and operating expenses – wages, salaries, lighting and other running expenses. All these expenses are met out of commercial bank loans in the form of the hypothecation credit or pledge loans.

(iii) Funds are also required for *(a)* making loans and advances in the course of day-to-day purchase-and-sale operations; *(b)* sundry debtors – that is for sale on credit basis; *(c)* investments; and *(d)* building up other assets.

Sources of Credit to the MSE Sector

The principal source of institutional credit of MSE sector is the public sector banks. Besides, credit is extended to this sector through the private sector banks (both new as well as old generation) and foreign banks operating in India. The RRBs and LABs supplement the efforts of the SCBs to some extent. Credit to this sector is also provided by UCBs, State and District Central Co-operative Banks, State Financial Corporations, NBFCs and Small Industries Development Bank of India (SIDBI).

Flow of Credit to the MSE Sector

(i) Policy Announcements

On the basis of the Policy Package announced by the Union Finance Minister on August 10, 2005, PSBs were advised to fix their own targets for funding MSEs in order to achieve a minimum 20 per cent year on year growth in credit to MSEs. The objective is to double the flow of credit to the sector from Rs. 67,600 crore in 2004-05 to Rs. 1,35,200 crore by 2009-10, *i.e.,* within a period of 5 years. This target was surpassed in the financial year ending March 2008 itself.

The outstanding credit to the MSE sector as at the end of years 2006-07, 2007-08 and 2008-09 by public and private sector banks and foreign banks is provided in the Table.

(ii) Refinance Facilities and Funding Support for MSEs

In the context of the global developments and the knock on effects in the domestic credit markets. Reserve Bank has taken several measures to enhance credit delivery to the employment intensive MSE sector. One of the measures was that a refinance amount of Rs. 7,000 crore was provided to the SIDBI under the provisions of Section 17(4H) of the Reserve Bank of India Act, 1934 on December 6, 2008 to enhance credit delivery to the sector. This refinance will be available against: (*i*) the SIDBI's incremental direct lending to MSE; and (*ii*) the SIDBI's loans to banks, NBFCs and State Financial Corporations (SFCs) against the latter's incremental loans and advances to MSEs. The incremental loans and advances will be computed with reference to outstandings as on September 30, 2008. This refinance facility will be available up to March 31, 2010. The utilisation of funds will be governed by the policy approved by the Board of the SIDBI. The outstanding amount of refinance availed by SIDBI stood at Rs 6,095 crore as on June 30, 2009.

Table 2

THE OUTSTANDING CREDIT TO THE MSE SECTOR

As March 31 of	*Public Sector on Banks*	*Private Sector Banks*	*Foreign Banks*
2007	1.02.550 (24.40)	13.136 (26.05)	11.637 (38.04)
2008	1.51.137 (47.38)	46.912 (257.12)	15.489 (33.10)
2009 P	1.91.307 (26.58)	47.916 (2.14)	18.138 (17.10)

P: Provisional.

Note: Figures in brackets indicate the percentage growth as compared to the previous year.

Source: Reserve Bank of India.

In pursuance of the announcement made in the Union Budget 2008-09, MSME (Refinance) Fund and MSE (Risk Capital) Fund were set up with SIDBI in June 2008. Contributions to the Funds were made by SCBs which failed to achieve their priority sector lending targets. The present corpus of the MSME (Refinance) Fund stood at Rs. l,600 crore and MSE (Risk Capital) Fund stood at Rs. 1,000 crore. Taking into account the need to ensure the growth momentum in the employment-intensive sectors of micro and small enterprises and as announced by the Governor, on November 15, 2008, a series of measures were taken for liquidity management and improving credit flow. The corpus of MSME (Refinance) Fund, 2008-09 was enhanced by Rs. 2,000 crore.

(iii) Special Refinance Facility

In order to provide liquidity support to SCBs (excluding RRBs), a special refinance facility was introduced on November 1, 2008 under Section 17(3B) of Reserve Bank of India Act 1934, whereby banks were advised to draw up to 1 per cent of their NDTL as on October 24, 2008, for a period of 90 days. Banks were encouraged to use this facility for the purpose of lending to MSEs. This facility has been extended up to March 31, 2010.

(iv) Focused attention in 388 Identified Clusters

Earlier, as part of the "Policy package for stepping up of credit to MSMEs", banks were advised to treat cluster based approach for financing MSE sector as a thrust area. The Reserve Bank's Annual Policy Statement for 2007-08 announced that banks were required to review their institutional arrangements for delivering credit to the MSE sector, especially in 388 clusters identified by United Nations Industrial Development Organisation (UNIDO) spread over 21 States in the country.

(v) Working Group on Rehabilitation of Sick MSEs

In recognition of the problems being faced by the MSE sector, particularly with respect to rehabilitation of potentially viable sick units, the Reserve Bank constituted a Working Group under the Chairmanship of Dr. K.C. Chakrabarty. The Working Group, in its report submitted in April 2008, dealt with the entire gamut of issues and problems confronting the sector. The Group recommended setting up of several funds namely (*i*) Rehabilitation Fund, (*ii*) Fund for Technology Upgradation, (*iii*) Marketing Development Fund and (*iv*) National Equity Fund by the Government of India to facilitate credit flow to the MSE sector. These recommendations have been forwarded to the Government of India and SIDBI for their consideration and necessary action. Banks were' advised to put in place Loan Policy on extension of credit facilities, restructuring/rehabilitation policy and non-discretionary OTS to the MSE sector.

(vi) Formulation of "Banking Code" for MSE Customers

The Banking Codes and Standard Board of India (BCSBI) has formulated a Code of Bank's Commitment to Micro and Small Enterprises. This is a voluntary Code, which sets minimum standards of banking practices for banks to follow when they are dealing with MSEs as defined in the MSMED Act, 2006. It provides protection to MSEs and explains how banks are expected to deal with MSEs for their day today operations and in times of financial difficulty. The Code is expected to (*a*) give a positive thrust to the MSE sector by providing easy access to efficient banking services, (*b*) promote good and fair banking practices by setting minimum standards in dealing with MSEs, (*c*) increase transparency, (*d*) improve understanding of business through effective communication, (*e*) encourage market forces through competition, to achieve higher operating standards, (*f*) promote a fair and cordial relationship between MSEs and banks, (*g*) ensure timely and quick response to banking needs, and (*h*) foster confidence in the banking system.

Credit Guarantee Schemes

Availability of bank credit without the hassles of collaterals/third party guarantees would be a major source of support to the first generation entrepreneurs to set up MSE of their own. Keeping this object in view, Ministry of Micro, Small and Medium Enterprises (MSME), Government of India launched Credit Guarantee Scheme (CGS) so as to strengthen credit delivery system and facilitate flow of credit to the MSE sector. To operationalise the scheme, Government of India and SIDBI set up the Credit Guarantee Fund Trust for Micro and Small Enterprises (CGTMSE).

The main objective of the scheme is that the lending institution should give importance to project viability and secure the credit facility purely on the primary security of the assets financed instead of insisting the secondary collateral. Any collateral/third party guarantee free credit facility (both fund as well as non-fund based) extended by eligible institutions, to new as well as existing micro and small enterprises, including service enterprises, with a maximum credit cap of Rs. 1 crore, are eligible to be covered under the CGS. For the unit covered under CGTMSE and becoming sick due to factors beyond the control of management, assistance for rehabilitation extended by the lender could also be covered under the scheme provided the overall assistance is within the credit cap of Rs. 1 crore.

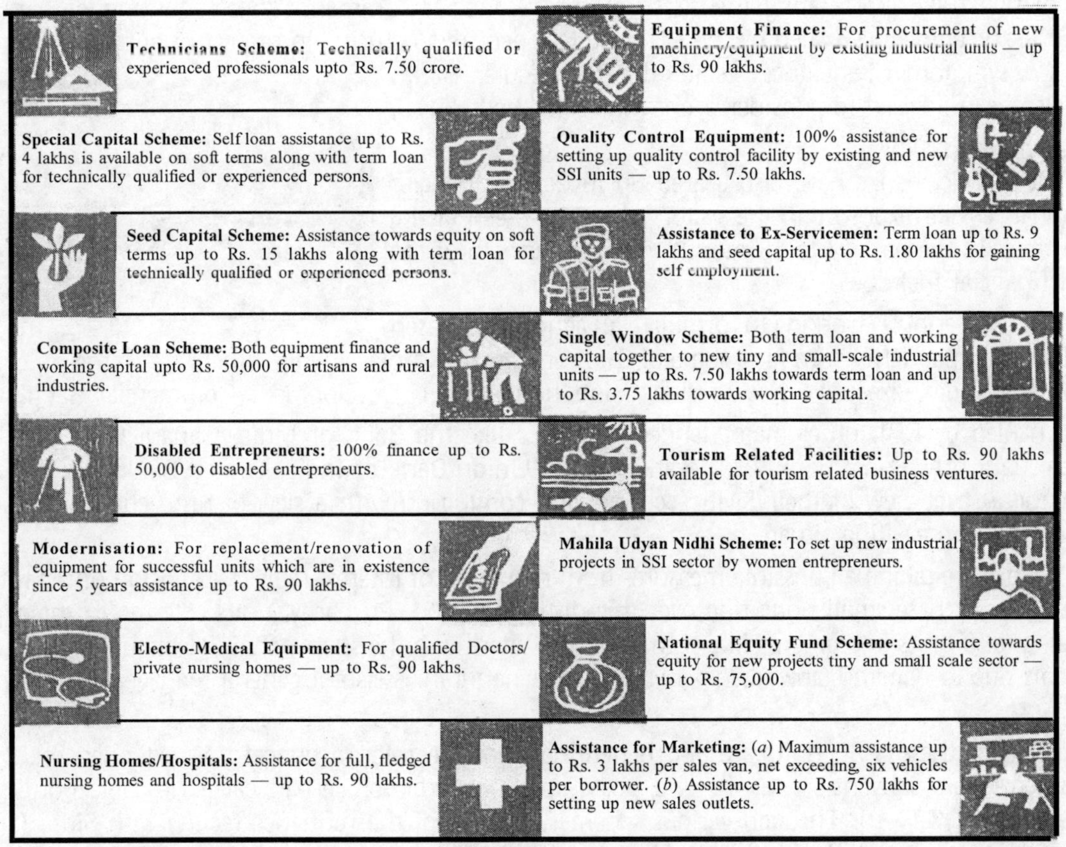

Fresh Approach

Banks are in the process of creating various innovative lending devices to increase their credit flow to small and medium enterprises.

Following the Reserve Bank of India's (RBI's) revision of provisioning norms in December 2008, banks have recently restructured around Rs. 10,000 crore worth of loans advanced to small and medium enterprises (SMEs). The country's largest bank, the State Bank of India (SBI), with Rs. 100,000 crore worth of exposure to this emerging space, has restructured over 41,500 accounts. According to an estimate, about one lakh accounts require some kind of restructuring to avoid becoming non-performing assets (NPAs).

"Such restructuring has become imperative, else it may force many of these units to shut down their operations, as demand has declined considerably in recent months," states N. Narsareddy, general manager, priority sector, Canara Bank.

Besides, RBI has been asking public sector banks to enhance credit flow to fund-starved SMEs in a time-bound manner, given the prevailing market conditions. The central bank has asked banks to prepare an action plan based on the recent recommendations made by the Working Group on Rehabilitation of potentially viable sick units in the SME sector. As per the recent RBI circular (May 2009), banks have been asked to submit an action taken report to the apex bank by 31 June 2009. Apart from timely detection and remedial action with respect to incipient sickness, the Group has recommended the rehabilitation of sick units which can be revived.

"While fully appreciating the sense of the Group's recommendations, attention of banks is invited to the guidelines issued by the RBI on SME debt restructuring in respect of borrower accounts that show symptoms of stickiness," states the RBI circular. Banks have also been advised to consider a one-time settlement (OTS) scheme for the sector.

Meanwhile, banks have also geared up to devise strategies and enhance their exposure to the sector, which has been facing tough times in the past 12 to 18 months in the aftermath of the global financial meltdown.

"We are seriously working to formulate an action plan based on RBI recommendations. In fact, some of these are already in place, while others are in the pipeline," says K.S. Ramdas, executive vice president and head (SME), Development Commercial Bank.

Enabled by RBI, other major lenders to SMEs like the Bank of India, Canara Bank, Bank of Baroda, Punjab National Bank, Corporation Bank, Union Bank of India, United Bank of India, etc., are taking a strict view of their SME accounts and coming up with a slew of restructuring measures to address the prevailing situation.

"Banks are taking all possible measures from reduction of interest rates to extension of repayment period to help these small units tide over this difficult period. Primarily, units catering to the export market, as also units in segments like auto ancillary, catering to the supply chain of big units, are facing problems due to demand slowdown," says K. Ramachandran, assistant general manager, Corporation Bank.

Many of these SME units are also benefiting from the interim budget that extended the 2 per cent interest rate subvention in pre- and post-shipment credit for certain categories of exporters up to the end of Q2 FY10. Through various schemes, the size of the refinance facility with Sidbi (Small Industries Development Bank of India) has effectively been increased by Rs. 10,000 crore.

Moreover, the Credit Guarantee Trust for Small and Medium Enterprises (CGTSME) scheme, that is designed to give comfort to banks to extend collateral-free loans to SMEs, has also been bolstered. RBI's Working Group on Rehabilitation has recently recommended further review of the scheme as it has been narrow in its reach so far.

Most banks have also set up special SME care centres to service their existing accounts. A monitoring cell with the Union SME ministry is at the disposal of SMEs which have a credit-related problem lasting two weeks or longer.

Even as banks have geared up to restructure their existing portfolio of stressed accounts, the RBI has instructed banks to improve their credit flows to fund starved units, which has seen sluggish growth in recent times. "Banking institutions need to improve their credit assessment capabilities to improve the flow of credit to SMEs. It is necessary to scientifically assess the small-scale enterprises and not to equate SSIs with high risk," the RBI states in its 'Currency and Finance' report. "On the whole, agriculture, large corporates and the retail sector benefited from credit expansion, while credit growth to the SME sector remained tepid until recently," it adds.

Ramdas
Taking actions

Although banks are allowed to fix their own targets for funding SMEs in order to achieve a minimum 20 per cent year-on-year growth, the government's objective has been to double the flow of credit to the SME sector by 2009-10 from Rs. 67,600 crore in 2004-05. Since January 2009, there has been a marked improvement in the credit offtake of banks. Moreover, credit risk in the SME sector is widely dispersed and banks get better yield from SME advances, as against the traditional advances, where the spread is getting gradually reduced.

Some Issues

In order to align bank credit to the emerging needs of the society, the scope and definition of priority sectors have been fine-tuned by including new items. Priority sector comprises agriculture (both direct and indirect), small scale industries, small roads and water transport operators, small business, retail trade, professional and self-employed persons, State sponsored organisations for Scheduled Castes/Scheduled Tribes, education, housing (both direct and indirect), consumption loans, micro-credit, small loans to the software, and food and agro-processing sector. As part of this process, the following measures have been initiated.

First, the ceiling on credit limit to farmers against pledge/hypothecation of agricultural produce (including warehouse receipts) was increased from Rs. 5 lakh to Rs. 10 lakh under the priority sector. Second, the limit on advances under the priority sector for dealers in agricultural machinery, including drip/sprinkler irrigation systems was increased from Rs. 20 lakh to Rs. 30 lakh and for distribution of inputs for allied activities from Rs. 25 lakh to Rs. 40 lakh. Third, banks were permitted to extend direct finance to the housing .sector up to Rs. 15 lakh, irrespective of location, as part of their priority sector lending. Fourth, investments by banks in the mortgage backed securities (MBS) have been classified as direct lending to housing within the priority sector lending subject to certain conditions. Fifth, loans advanced to distressed urban poor to prepay their debt to non-institutional leaders, against appropriate collateral or group security, have been classified as advances to weaker sections within the priority sector. Sixth, investment limit in plant and machinery for seven items belonging to sports goods, which figure in the list of items reserved for manufacture in the small scale industries (SSI) sector, was enhanced from Rs. 1 crore to Rs. 5 crore for the purpose of classification under priority sector advances. Seventh, banks were urged to make efforts to increase their disbursements to small and marginal farmers to 40 per cent of their direct advanced under Special Agricultural Credit Plans

(SACP) by March 2007. All private sector banks were also asked to formulate SACP targets from 2005-06 with an annual growth rate of at least 20-25 per cent of credit disbursements to agriculture. Eight, investment by banks in securitised assets representing direct lending to the SSI sector have been classified as their direct lending to the SSI sector under priority sector lending, subject to certain conditions.

CGTSME SCHEME

In the absence of collateral or third-party guarantee, access to adequate and timely finance at reasonable rates of interest to entrepreneurs having viable business proposals in the SME sector has been a major bottleneck. Recognising this weakness, the government of India (GOI) and the Small Industries Development Bank of India (SIDBI) set up the Credit Guarantee Trust for Small and Medium Enterprises (CGTSME) in August 2000 to provide guarantee support to banks and lending institutions for their exposure to the SME sector. This is the only credit guarantee institution in the country exclusively set up for the benefit of entrepreneurs in the SME sector.

Vinod
Guaranting
Finance

Though the coverage of loans under the scheme has increased over the years, the pace of growth has been slower than expected. "With all our efforts, there has been a significant improvement in coverage under the scheme. Banks have been proactive in sanctioning credit facilities to SMEs. The Trust, on its part, is making an all-out effort to spread awareness of the scheme amongst entrepreneurs, bankers and industry associations through a series of awareness programme," says O. S. Vinod, CEO, CGTSME.

During FY09, the Trust extended 53,708 credit guarantee approvals aggregating Rs. 2,200 crore, registering a 77 per cent growth in number and 108 per cent growth in amount of guarantees approved over the previous year. Cumulatively, the Trust had, as on 31 March 2009, approved 1,50,034 guarantees amounting to Rs. 4,824 crore. The trend is expected to continue, with 10,983 guarantees worth Rs. 552 crore being approved during the first two months of the current financial year. As many as 21 banks/lending institutions have been registered with the Trust as new member lending institutions during FY09, and the member base of the Trust has increased to 96 banks/lending institutions so far.

The Trust has taken a number of initiatives to boost collateral-free credit flow to the SME sector. Some of the recent measures include enhancing the ceiling of eligible credit facility for guarantee cover under the scheme from Rs. 50 lakh to Rs. 1 crore. The extent of guarantee cover has been increased to 85 per cent for credit facility up to Rs. 5 lakh in respect of micro enterprises. In addition, the Trust has brought down the cost of guarantee cover by reducing the guarantee fee from 1.5 per cent to 1 per cent, and service fee from 0.75 per cent to 0.50 per cent in respect of micro enterprises for credit facility up to Rs. 5 lakh. Simultaneously, the lock-in period for claim settlement under the scheme has been brought down from 24 to 18 months.

Meanwhile, the RBI's Working Group on Rehabilitation of the SME sector has recommended a review of the scheme to make it more effective in the wake of changing market conditions.

As the Credit Guarantee Scheme of CGTMSE has not picked up, it was announced in the Reserve Bank's Annual Policy Statement for the year 2009-10 that the Standing Advisory Committee on MSEs will review the CGTMSE scheme so as to enhance the flow of credit to the MSE sector. Accordingly, a Working Group (Chairman: Shri V.K. Sharma) has been constituted to review the present CGTMSE scheme, identify the weaknesses and suggest measures to simplify the existing procedures for obtaining cover and lodging of claims under the scheme and to examine the feasibility of introduction or a whole turnover cover for the micro and small enterprises and modalities for the same. The Working Group is expected to submit its report shortly.

Additionally, banks earn a better spread on loans to SMEs than to larger corporates. For instance, a large corporate with a strong balance sheet, by the virtue of its sheer size can at times manage a rate below or around the bank's benchmark prime lending rate (PLR), while even a very strong SME can at best get 100-150 basis points above the PLR. Banks look forward to not just lending, but earning a variety of fee-based income from different avenues. For instance, some offer cash management services, while others offer fee-based products like credit guarantees and other business advisory services.

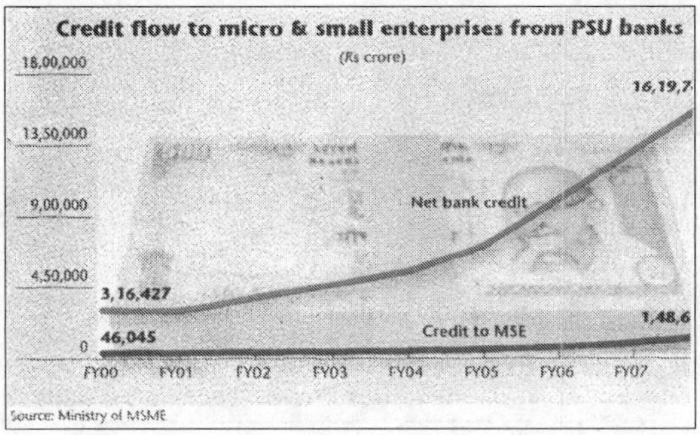

▸▸ Criteria of Finance

The main criteria of finance are:

1. Production
2. Employment generation
3. Modernisation
4. Infrastructural development
5. Upgradation process, technology and product
6. Export-orientation
7. Import-substitution
8. Improvement
9. Creating demand for consumer durables
10. Promoting handicrafts, gem-jewellery
11. Searching of new avenues
12. Strengthening Research and Development
13. Filling up innovation
14. Giving boost to creativity.
15. Giving fillip to outsourcing activities.

In the process, earn a steady income, improve profits and raise the standard of living of people.

In short, the criteria of finance is:

- Entrepreneurship
- Entrepreneurism
- Employment
- Economic Development

- Economic Growth
- Enrichment
- Education, and
- Sustained social development.

From the financial institutions (Banks, SFC, Cooperatives, NBFCs) the principle criteria are:

- Investment
- Income Generation
- Generating profits
- Expanding services
- Fostering and strengthening entrepreneurship and ensuring sustained social development.

Thus, the criteria of finance helps the entrepreneur, enterprise and the financial institutions to grow together and accelerate the pace of socio-economic growth.

R.M. Malla, CMD, Small Industries Development Bank of India (SIDBI)

ENSURING CREDIT FLOW

Small Industries Development Bank of India: SIDBI is the principal financial institution for SMEs, introduced several schemes for SMEs, especially for micro enterprises. SIDBI has formulated a special refinance scheme to augment the credit to micro enterprises. Under the scheme, an amount of about Rs. 4,400 crore was sanctioned to public sector banks, with the condition that they will grant credit to the extent of double the amount (Rs. 8,800 crore) to micro enterprises with a base date of 30 September 2008. Thus, through this scheme, further credit has flowed to micro enterprises.

R.M. Malla,
CMD, Small Indusries Development Bank of India (SIDBI)

The bank recorded its highest-ever credit disbursements of Rs. 28,273 crore – an increase of more than 87 per cent. The outstanding portfolio grew by 50 per cent, which would probably be the highest in percentage terms achieved by any bank/financial institution during the financial year 2008-09. The number of branches also grew by 27 during FY09, taking the total network to 100 branches.

Under SIDBI's micro credit scheme, disbursements made during FY09 were Rs. 1,721 crore, which is more than the cumulative figure for the preceding nine years of operation of the scheme. The total portfolio under micro credit rose to Rs. 2,137 crore as of end FY09, from Rs. 950 crore as of end FY08, i.e., a growth of over 125 per cent. Our subsidiaries and associates .also performed very well.

The highlights of the year would be incomplete without mentioning the awards conferred on SIDBI by the Association of Development Financing Institutions in Asia and the Pacific (ADFIAP), which invites nominations annually from its 110 member institutions from around 40 countries. SIDBI was honoured to receive three awards – Outstanding CEO of the Year, Best Website and Setting up of ISARC under SME Development category.

In addition to the schemes to ease liquidity requirements, SIDBI, with a view to promote energy-saving investments in the SME sector, will introduce a special scheme to offer assistance to SMEs at concessional rates for taking up energy-saving projects. We have also entered into structured arrangements with a few original equipment manufacturers (OEMs), where SMEs are provided assistance for procurement of capital equipment from OEMs as per simplified processes and OEMs, in turn, extend a buyback arrangement, corporate guarantee, etc. Under our Risk Capital Scheme, we have already committed Rs. 380 crore and will be looking forward for proposals from SMEs for equity and equity type assistance.

The SIDBI has entered into an arrangement with Faridabad Small Industries Association (FSIA) to provide pre-approved limits to well-performing SME members of FSIA to meet their small, unforeseen capital expenditures. This arrangement allows FSIA members to avail of financial assistance from SIDBI in a faster manner. We are also exploring similar tie-ups with others.

As regards suggestions for SMEs, there is a need to reduce cost to improve quality, improve the inventory management and adopt lean manufacturing processes. Incorporating the latest technology into their production processes would enable SMEs to achieve a competitive edge. Energy efficiency is another area where SMEs need to focus on. The SME exporters may also attempt to diversify their export destinations and explore new markets, including the untapped domestic markets, which by themselves, may be very large. SMEs must also widen their information and knowledge base.

▸▸ Credit Linked Capital Subsidy Scheme (CLCSS)

The Ministry of Micro, Small & Medium Enterprises (MSME) is operating a scheme for technology upgradation of Small Scale Industries (now MSEs) called the Credit Linked Capital Subsidy Scheme (CLCSS). The Scheme aims at facilitating technology upgradation by providing upfront capital subsidy to SSI units (now MSEs), including tiny, khadi, village and coir industrial units, on institutional finance (credit) availed by them for modernisation of their production equipment (plant and machinery) and techniques in specified sub-sectors/products approved under the Scheme.

The ceiling for eligibility of loans under the Scheme is Rs. 1 crore and rate of subsidy is 15 per cent. Further, in the light of the experience gathered through implementing the Scheme, certain modifications have been made in taking up technology upgradation on a larger scale.

The Scheme is monitored by the Governing and Technology Approval Board (GTAB) of the CLCSS. The Secretary (MSME) is the Chairperson of the Board with the Additional Secretary & Development Commissioner (MSME) as its Member-Secretary. The GTAB also periodically reviews the functioning of the Scheme. There is a Technical Sub-Committee under the GTAB to consider inclusion of new sub-sectors/products and Well Established and Improved Technologies under the Scheme.

Nodal Agencies: The Scheme is being implemented through eligible Primary Lending Institutions (PLIs) which include Scheduled Commercial Banks, Scheduled Cooperative Banks [including urban cooperative banks co-opted by the SIDBI under the TUFS of the Ministry of Textiles], Regional Rural Banks (RRBs), State Financial Corporations (SFCs) and North Eastern Development Financial Institution (NEDFI). The capital subsidy is released to SIDBI and NABARD for onward disbursement to the beneficiary units through eligible PLIs. An advance of Rs. 5 crore and Rs. 3 crore has been placed with SIDBI and NABARD respectively for operationalising the Scheme.

Box 1

FACTORING: AN EMERGING OPTION FOR SMES

A substantial portion of the SME sector neither have the security required for conventional collateral-based bank lending, nor is it attractive to venture capitalists and other investors. In addition, our credit markets are characterised by deficient information, limiting the effectiveness of financial statement-based lending. Due to these factors, factoring is an alternative finance option that is becoming increasingly popular with SMEs. Factoring removes the waiting period for SMEs by converting their short-term trade receivables into cash.

Factoring receivables is an ideal financial solution for new and emerging firms without strong financials. This is because creditworthiness is evaluated based on the financial strength of the customer (debtor). Hence, these companies can leverage on the financial strength of their customers. Factoring is a financial option for the management of receivables. In simple words, it is the conversion of credit sales into cash.

"It is time for the SME sector as a whole to look at supplementing bank finance with a factoring facility to avoid facing a major liquidity crunch again. A factoring facility will improve liquidity by unlocking the cash tied up in their trade receivables," says Arvind Sonmale, managing director, Global Trade Finance (GTF), a major player in the Indian factoring space with more than 50 per cent market share. Over the years, GTF has made rapid strides in the trade-receivables finance landscape in the country.

One of the major attractions of factoring is that it relies on the customer's credit standing, and not that of the SME. Factoring is particularly suited for a company with good earnings profile, but not so good cash flow. Earnings are not a record of actual money received by a company. A company can show positive net earnings (on the income statement) and still not be able to pay its debts. Factoring boosts the cash flow of a company by converting trade receivables into cash. This boost in cash flow helps the company to finance its daily operations effectively. Flexible credit limits mean that the factoring facility essentially grows with the business. Apart from finance, factoring takes care of debt collection, sales ledger management and bad debt protection.

Keeping in view that there is a big spectrum of SMEs in India and most of them will not be candidates for assistance from VC funds, the policy framework also provides for SIDBI to directly provide risk capital to a larger number of its SME customers and other banks using simpler risk capital products, based on successful risk capital practices in other parts of the world. In this regard, SIDBI has already developed mezzanine products based on long-term subordinate debt (sub-debt).

"SIDBI is also looking to finance start-ups and early stage enterprises using the risk capital fund; wherein it provides risk capital to SMEs with the help of a mentor network," says Harsh Kaul, CEO, SIDBI Venture Capital.

"With mounting stress in the financial markets – domestic as well as global – these alternative sources of financing are also facing some kind of constraint. Banks, therefore, remain a major source of funding for SMEs," says Kaushal Sampat, chief operating officer, Dun & Bradstreet India.

Most Indian SMEs are family-managed and lack of professionalism is a major challenge. Managing exits is one of the most challenging issues facing investors in the Indian SME space due to small sizes of Indian SMEs, lack of adequate platform for accessing capital markets and relative lack of second round/strategic investors, compared to developed markets. Promoter issues play an important part in such investments, as most Indian promoters are reluctant to dilute control over their companies. "In the absence of proper exit routes, VC/PE players have been unable to increase their exposure to Indian SMEs," feels Kaul.

A stock exchange purely dedicated to SMEs could be the next big thing.An SME-focussed stock exchange is likely to boost the confidence of SMEs planning to tap the capital market to raise low-cost capital.

Some examples of SME-dedicated stock exchanges include AltX, Africa's first alternative exchange for SMEs, a partnership between the Johannesburg Stock Exchange Ltd. and the Department of Trade and Industry; and AIM, a sub-market of the London Stock Exchange that allows smaller companies to float shares with a more flexible regulatory system compared to the main market.

The decision to set up a dedicated bourse for SMEs has been mooted some time ago. Sebi is, in fact, toying with a fresh idea to set up an exclusive exchange for SMEs, even as its past exercise – Over The Counter Exchange of India (OTCEI) – failed to take off.

This will facilitate access to capital markets for small units which do not currently qualify the stringent norms of stock exchanges. Apart from credit needs, it will also boost adherence to corporate governance norms, which is receiving less attention from small family-owned enterprises. While this will increase attractiveness of the Indian SME sector to private equity investors, increased liquidity brings with it the challenge to control volatility in foreign investment.

▸▸ Credit Penetration in SMEs

Small and Medium Enterprises (SMEs) are not able to exploit their potential due to the low credit penetration into the segment. Almost 90 per cent of the units are not registered and close to 95 per cent of them do not have access to any kind of formal institutional credit. According to the Third All-India Census of Small Scale Industries, only 17.9 per cent had availed of credit. Of these, 14.9 per cent could have had access to institutional credit. The report of the Committee on Financial Sector Assessment (CFSA) points to both a decline in the share of credit to SSIs and a widening of the credit gap to unreasonable levels. Further, the SME sector is underserved especially in terms of working capital and trade-finance.

The CFSA report goes a step further and points out that even in cases where credit is available for investment, the loan tenures are far too short to payoff any sizeable investment. Also, small-scale units do not have access to competitive rates, which are usually reserved for blue-chip companies. The practice is that when banks lend to SSIs, banks charge a commission for the additional risks and apply tougher screening measures, which drive up costs.

The CFSA has made an attempt to gauge the extent of the credit gap by assuming the credit that would have been available, if the share of small scale credit in total bank credit remained at 13 per cent, its average share during 1998-2007. Figures show that credit gap expressed as a per cent of the actual lending to SSIs has steadily increased from 9 per cent in 2002 to nearly 100 per cent in 2007, the average gap being 69 per cent during the period.

The report cites three reasons for banks' increasing reluctance to lend to SSIs. One, banks consider them high-risk borrowers, as they have insufficient assets, high vulnerability to market fluctuations and high mortality rates. Second, there are issues related to high transaction costs, as the small amount of credit used by each unit raises administrative costs. Third, there are difficulties in assessing the creditworthiness of the units, due to the lack of accounting records or financial statements.

The third factor is especially relevant in the Indian context, where the growing sophistication of lending technologies has become a barrier to accessing credit for small units, which are dependent on relationship lending – where decisions are based on soft information gathered by the lender on the borrower.

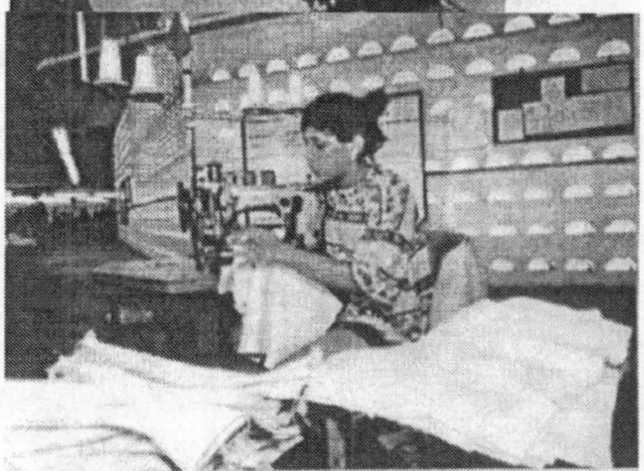

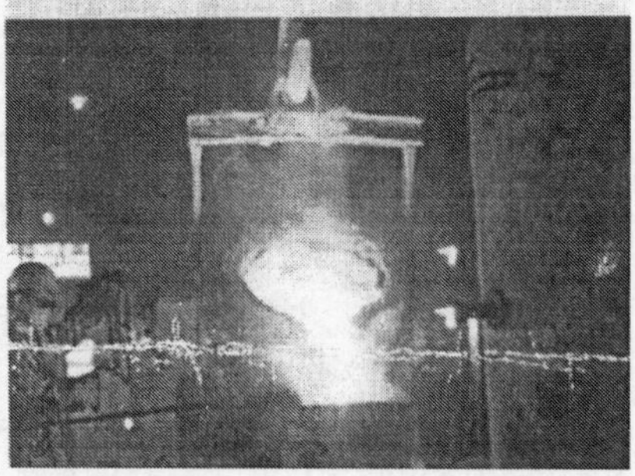

In relationship lending, the banker has personal knowledge of a borrower's managerial skills and business strategy of the loanee firms over a period. This substituted for transparency of records. But as lending technologies of large banks become dependent on quantifiable transactions-based information, which is electronically stored and communicated across the institutions, the credit flows based on relationship lending are bound to fall, states the report.

Experts have stressed on the need to regenerate SME financing. According to *Firm Size and Business Environment in SME Financing*, a World Bank study, SMEs across the world face similar problems, due to inversely related factors, the problem areas being financing and regulatory policies.

Financing agencies are focussing on a cluster approach to achieve the twin objectives of their own business growth and development of the SME sector. The objective is to ensure that the fruits of development are spread across a vast majority of entrepreneurs and community and balanced regional development.

Regenerating SME financing in India is essential as the sector serves as a greenfield for nurturing entrepreneurial talent. An increased focus by Indian banks and financial institutions on providing micro finance, factoring assistance, etc., at reasonable costs will go a long way in making SMEs domestically and globally competitive, leading to economic growth.

Going forward, to ensure better accessibility of credit by SMEs, banks' ability to quickly evaluate the creditworthiness of small and medium enterprises will be critical. Due to limiting factors of financial statement lending and asset-based lending, credit scoring lending, long used in consumer lending, may be considered by banks in the case of SMEs. To make this a more effective option, it may be combined with relationship lending, universally the most popular lending technique for SMEs, where information and documentation are quite inadequate. Under relationship lending, a lenders decision in substantial part is based on the proprietary information about the firm and its owner, acquired by the loan officer through a variety of sources.

SMEs are now forced to get rated and provide their credit scores to the banks for further processing of their credit applications, whereas they are not provided with any independent rating or information about the expertise and performance of their prospective bankers. If banks and SMEs are partners in the business then both must have enough information to make informed decisions about the choice of their partners. Entrepreneurs must be provided with independent rating of individual branches of banks, and even better, of individual credit appraisal officers. Ratings by reputed rating agencies reflecting the abilities, expertise and performance of individual branches of banks will allow the entrepreneurs to make the right selections of their bankers.

With relationship lending becoming the most preferred choice of lending to SMEs the world over, proper selection of the bank and its branch is quite vital for any cash-strapped entrepreneur. Once the entrepreneur, on the basis of independent rating, identifies an appropriate branch of a particular bank for his project finance, he can start making investments in time and money to establish high bandwidth interaction (such as personal or face-to-face interactions, invitations to special events, sites, etc.) for creating a meaningful relationship with the potential banker. Relationship developed through high bandwidth interactions, as opposed to low-bandwidth communications (such as e-mail, fax and letters) will ultimately create a high level of confidence and trust between both the parties. Therefore, the system must initially provide reliable data of the entrepreneurs on performance of individual bank branches and their appraisal officers, similar to the credit information available to the bankers on the firms and/or entrepreneurs.

FDI NOT ENOUGH

Small Enterprises Need Local Equity

The government has clarified the ambiguity over foreign direct investment (EDI) norms for micro and small enterprises (MSEs). They can have foreign investment upto the applicable sectoral limit. Though this opens another option for this generally capital starved sector, a rush of FDI is unlikely anytime soon. What is needed is some way of revitalising the smaller exchanges, which would allow MSEs to raise risk capital from local investors who are likely to be more appreciative. Most micro or small enterprises lack access to any sort of formal funds, and are forced to rely on costly informal credit. Ironically, this is largely because organised lenders do not find them creditworthy, as many of them would not have the balance sheet strength to meet the basic eligibility conditions. The truth is functional MSEs are meeting the far more exacting terms of informal credit. If this informal credit could be substituted by FDI, small and micro enterprises would see a sharp jump in their profitability. The large interest component on their profit and loss account would disappear and minus the debt, the balance sheet would look good too. The ability to plough back profits would allow them to expand and reap economies of scale. However, for the very reason MSEs cannot access formal credit, they are unlikely to interest some investor in an overseas country. The FDI that they may attract is likely to be venture capital type, which is very expensive and therefore may entail huge dilution by the promoter.

Micro and small enterprises need smaller local exchanges where they can raise capital easily from investors who are likely to appreciate them better because of proximity. Access to the bigger national exchanges is difficult for smaller enterprises and they are also unlikely to get a good valuation. Despite SEBI's efforts, the regional exchanges have been a non-starter. The next best solution is for existing profitable exchanges to develop the regional markets or invest in the regional exchanges and put in place a viable business model for them. The obvious way of doing that is to allow more equity exchanges. The competition would encourage product innovation and diversification.

⏩ Conclusion

The opening up of the banking sector and greater disintermediation have facilitated the access of these SSI units, particularly the larger among them, to a variety of financial services. Private sector banks are also in the process of evolving special innovative schemes to attract the more efficient SSIs especially the export-oriented units. The pattern of financing these small scale units is gradually changing in favour of specialised, target-specific financial services, with the introduction of new financial products. The financial institutions including SFCs/SIDCs and public sector banks are preparing themselves to provide a diversified range of services to various target groups including venture capital, leasing, equipment finance, export finance, factoring services, etc. and private sector banks are carving out niche areas within the sector to give specialised services with innovatively designed financial instruments. The access of SSIs to the capital market has also improved with the formulation of bought-out deals on Over The Counter Exchange of India by merchant bankers, providing yet another avenue to them for raising resources. Strategic alliances between institutions, banks and professional bodies of industries would also enable to SSIs to receive specialised non-fund based services, e.g., technology tie-ups, quality improvements, etc. as well as finance, under a common umbrella. These would result in speedy project appraisals and better project monitoring

Finance is available for a project. But there is need for prudent financial management. All along, there is need for planning the flow of funds for the smooth functioning of a project. A successful project is one which generates its own finances to a greater extent and finances its diversified activities. Internal resources will serve as a backbone of a project.

The generation of internal resources not only benefit the enterprise, but also the entrepreneur, shareholders and the society. Above all, a prudent of internal resources may also assist the natural growth of the capital market.

Finance, which has been aptly described as the 'life-blood' of industry, is a pre-requisite for the mobilisation of real resources to organise production and marketing. Depending upon the nature of the activity to be financed, business requires short-term, medium-term and long-term finance.

Criteria of finance and financial management forms an integral part of industry and ranks equally in importance with other key components like production and marketing. Capital and finance form the bed rock foundation for industrial development They are provided by a number of financial institutions, The saga of industrial development in the post-independence period is the story of these core institutions.

To make finance available for a project there is need for prudent financial management. All along, there is need for planning the flow of funds for the smooth functioning of a project. A successful project is one which generates its own finances to a greater extent and finances its diversified activities. Internal resources will serve as a backbone of a project.

The generation of internal resources not only benefits the enterprise, but also the entrepreneur, shareholders and the society. Above all, a prudent management of internal resources may also assist the natural growth of the capital market.

Finance, which has been aptly described as the "life-blood" of industry is a pre-requisite for the mobilisation of real resources to organise production and marketing. Depending upon the nature of the activity to be financed, business requires short-term, medium-term and long-term finance.

A new chapter for business finance is being hammered out. And with it, the flexibility for the entrepreneur to design the financing mix to suit every need. To use an assortment of financial products that both lowers financing costs and minimises risks. In short, to evolve a financing strategy that dovetails with the enterprise's competitive strategy tomorrow.

With deregulation, entrepreneurs will find it cheaper to access the markets directly. The phenomenon of disintermediation is interwined with securitisation, or the tendency of enterprises to raise capital by issuing securities rather than on relying on direct loans. While short-term working capital needs can be met by the issue of commercial paper, long-term project finance requirements can be partially serviced through debenture offerings. In fact, in the more developed capital markets, funds are raised by even scrutinising the regular cash-flows generated by receivables.

Fierce competition among the leaders will transform once standard working capital or term-loans for the entrepreneurs. The lenders will be forced to assume higher credit risk. Project financing will, increasingly, be of the non-recourse variety while a rising proportion of working capital finance may be extended on an unsecured basis. Since credit risk will be transferred in full to the financial intermediary, that intermediary will be much involved in monitoring the loan. So, while securitisation moves towards more impersonal forms of financing, lending will become more intimate.

Financial management is an integral part of industry and ranks equally in importance with other key components like production and marketing. Capital and finance form the bed rock foundation of industrial development. They are provided by a number of financial institutions. The saga of industrial development in the post-independence period is the story of these core institutions as well as market participation.

ANNEXURE-1

REQUIRED DOCUMENTS FOR PROCURING BUSINESS LOANS

Sole Proprietorship/Partnership Firm

- Proof of identity (Copy of Sales Tax/VAT/Service Tax/PAN ID/IT Return of the Concern/Water/Electricity/Municipal Tax Bill in the Name of the Concern)
- Proof of individual identity (Copy of Passport/Voter's identity Card/Photo PAN Card/Driving License/MAPIN Card)
- PAN Number/Form 60 of the Concern Financial Documents (Copy of P&L Account and Balance Sheet for last two years, audited by a CA and Copies of IT returns for the last two years)
- Proof of residence address (Copy of Passport/Voter's Identity Card/Driving License/Ration Card/Life Insurance Policy/Electricity Bill/Telephone Bill)
- Bank Statements for last 6 months
- Partnership deed (Required only in case of Partnership Firm)
- Two passport size photographs
- Proof of place of business

For Private Limited Company

- Proof of Identity (Copy of Sales Tax/VAT/Service Tax/Excise Registration or Registration under Shops and Establishment Act or PAN ID/IT Return of the Concern or Water/Electricity/Municipal Tax Bill in the Name of the Concern)
- Memorandum and Articles of Association (Copy of Certificate of Incorporation)
- Board Resolution (Copy of Annual Return establishing the shareholding pattern)
- Proof of Individual Identity for the authorised signatories and 2 directors, including the Managing Director (Copy of Passport/Voter's Identity Card/Photo PAN Card/Driving License/MAPIN Card)
- List of Directors
- Copy of Form 32 filed with ROC
- PAN Card/Form 60 of the Concern
- Financial Documents (Copy of P&L and Balance Sheet for last two years, audited by a CA, and Copies of IT returns for the last two years)
- Bank Statements for last 6 months
- Proof of Place of Business
- Two passport size photographs

Steps to Obtain a Business Loan

1. **Gather Information:** Obtain information on the documents so that the lending institution can evaluate your financial status and your ability to repay.

2. **Application and assessment:** Submit the required documents so that the lending institution can evaluate your financial status and your ability to repay.
3. **Approval:** On approval of the loan, you will receive a Facility Offer Letter.
4. **Receiving the money:** The approved amount will be deposited into an agreed bank account.
5. **Making payments:** Instalments will be deducted directly from a designated bank account.

According to the Code of Bank's Commitment to Micro and Small Enterprises, once the loan is sanctioned, the Bank has to supply authenticated copies of all the loan documents executed along with a copy each of all enclosed documents quoted in the loan document and the list thereof.

IT'S IN THE ATTITUDE

I've never run into a guy who could win at the top level in anything today and didn't have the right attitude; didn't give it everything he had, at least while he was doing it; wasn't prepared and didn't have the whole programme worked out. — *Ted Turner, American Media Mogul*

25

Fixed and Working Capital Assessment

Introduction

During the pre-independence period, financial constraints had hampered the rapid development of industries in the country. After independence, the Government built up a network of specialised financial institutions with a fairly big capital base to provide financial assistance to all types to industries, including small-scale industries.

Sridharan
Tapping New Businesses

A growing economy needs the support of a financial structure which is responsive to the needs of development. In India, in the process of financial deepening, commercial banks had to shoulder special responsibilities for meeting the financial needs of diverse sectors of the economy, at various stages of development. In the process, they have evolved various modes and instruments of financing, fashioned various organisational innovations, moved away from traditional commercial banking and evolved into development banks, responsive to socioeconomic needs.

Finance is now made available to entrepreneurs on a totality basis by commercial banks, except in cases where the State Financial Corporations and other similar financing agencies step in to meet their medium-term requirements. An appropriate type of credit is granted for the construction of the factory building, the purchase of plant, machinery and equipment, and for working capital requirements. In deserving cases, loans are advanced for the expansion, renovation and modernisation of plant and machinery. Banks and financial institutions provide the export finance needed by small industries for letters of credit, issuance of guarantees and extension of pre-shipment and post-shipment credit facilities. The interest rate structure is generally graded on a slab basis, with a favourable bias towards the smaller loans. Institutional support and economic factors are stimulating entrepreneurial activity and thus generating more robust economic development.

⏩ Miscellaneous

All the sources of finance are not available to all the small units. Much would depend on the status, character and the period of time the units have been in operation. For example, a new small unit has no reserves to provide for depreciation. These are built up in gradual stages out of the funds set apart in the course of current operations.

Moreover, the funds a small-scale industry can raise depends upon the character of the company, its productive activity and the substantial uses to which these funds are put – irrespective of it being a private limited or a proprietary concern. Some of the uses are:

(i) Gross Fixed Assets: Land, building, plant and machinery – these are by and large, met out of market borrowings or term loans from financial institutions, including banks.

(ii) Working Capital: This includes inventories – raw materials, components, finished goods, works in progress and operating expenses – wages, salaries, lighting and other running expenses. All these expenses are met out of commercial bank loans in the form of the hypothecation credit or pledge loans.

(iii) Funds are also required for *(a)* making loans and advances in the course of day-to-day purchase-and-sale operations; *(b)* sundry debtors – that is for sale on credit basis; *(c)* investments; and *(d)* building up other assets.

⏩ Analysis of Financial Ratios

The financial data of small units are usually worked out in terms of some of the important conventional ratios. Most of the ratios, however, do not indicate any definite relationship with credit facilities. A detailed discussion of this aspect has been undertaken in the technical volume. It will be sufficient to mention here that comparatively high inventory-to-sales ratios were recorded by units which received institutional credit facilities. The average net working capital needs of small units, which are also given, show that the units which received credit facilities need a comparatively high average working capital. A major proportion of the net working capital, however, was accounted for by inventories. The figures in the statement do not, by themselves, point to any firm conclusions regarding the place of inventories among the factors to be taken into account by banks while examining the credit proposals of small-scale units.

Balance Sheet of Institutional and Non-Institutional Borrowings

The survey also gives information on the balance sheet of both institutional and non-institutional borrowings of small units. It shows that institutional borrowings per unit varied from one unit to another, and were the highest in the case of the following categories of units:

(i) Units whose assets exceeded Rs. 10 lakh;

(ii) Units which manufactured electronic and electrical goods;

(iii) Units of 6 to 10 years standing;

(iv) Units which employed 101 and more persons;

(v) Public limited companies;

(vi) Units which were registered; and

(vii) Units located in industrial estates.

It may be pointed out here that those units which had high savings per unit institutional borrowings recorded high inventory ratios. The average non-institutional borrowings per unit in respect of respective classifications were the highest in the case of units which –

(a) Borrowed from banks/co-operatives;

(b) Whose assets were above Rs. 10 lakh and which employed 101 or more persons;

(c) Were private limited companies, registered units and located in industrial estates; and

(d) Belonged to the manufacturing group, including chemicals, dyes, etc.

It is also known that both large and small units borrow from institutional and non-institutional sources. However, the extent of reliance on non-institutional sources was lower in the case of large units than in that of small units. At the same time, even the smaller units obtained a major portion of their credit needs from institutional lenders. Further, the average non-institutional borrowings formed a major proportion of average borrowings (institutional and non-institutional) on the part of units which did not approach any commercial bank/co-operative for credit or which did not get any institutional credit even though they asked for it. It has been mentioned above. Clearly, the reliance on institutional sources was relatively high on the part of modern younger and larger small-scale industrial units.

Table 1

SOURCES AND USES OF FUNDS OF 1,125 SELECTED SMALL PRIVATE LIMITED COMPANIES

(1)	(Rs. Crores) (2)	% share in the total (3)
Sources of Funds		
Internal Sources	468	22.52
A. 1. *Paid-up capital*	9	*0.43*
B. Reserves and surplus	13	0.58
2. Capital reserve	5	
3. Development rebate reserve	16	
4. Others	2	

C. Provisions	446	21.46
5. Depreciation	408	19.63
6. Taxation (net of advance of income-tax)	17	0.82
7. Other current	10	0.48
8. Non-current	11	0.53
External Sources	1,610	77.48
D. Paid-up capital	100	4.81
9. Net issues	100	4.81
10. Premium on shares	–	–
E. Borrowings	898	43.21
11. From banks	543	26.13
12. From Industrial Finance Corporation and State Financial Corporations	–	–
13. From other institutional agencies	27	1.30
14. From Government and semi-Government agencies	5	0.24
15. From others	323	15.54
F. Trade dues and other current liabilities	611	29.40
16. Sundry creditors	575	27.67
17. Others	36	1.73
G.18. *Miscellaneous non-current liabilities*	–	–
19. Total	2,078	100.00
Uses of Funds		
H. Gross fixed assets	710	34.17
20. Land	31	1.49
21. Buildings	140	6.74
22. Plant and machinery	420	20.21
23. Capital works in progress	2	0.10
24. Others	116	5.58
I. Inventories	514	24.73
25. Raw materials, components, etc.	290	13.96
26. Finished goods	193	9.29
27. Works in progress	27	1.30
28. Others	59	2.84
J. Loans and other advances and other debtor balances	744	35.80
29. Sundry debtors	598	28.77
30. Others	146	7.02
K. 31. Investments	37	1.78
L. 32. Other assets	7	0.34
M.33. Cash and Bank Balances	80	3.85
34. Total	2,078	100.00

According to a study of small private limited companies, conducted by the Reserve Bank of India some time back, the small private limited companies relied on external sources for financing assets. Of the total resources of Rs. 2,078 crores, external sources contributed as much as Rs. 1,610 crore (77.5 per cent) to asset formation. Of this amount, borrowings constituted more than 55.8 per cent, while trade dues and other current liabilities contributed about 38.0 per cent. Bank borrowings, in particular, accounted for more than one-third of the total external resources. Among the internal resources, depreciation provision amounting to Rs. 408 crore constituted the main source. It represented 87.18% of total internal resources.

While assessing the resources of a concern, we have to bear in mind whether it is a new concern or a long-established concern; whether it is a private company or a proprietary concern; what is the nature of activity – is it manufacturing or trading; whether the purpose of raising resources is modernisation and expansion of business, or the establishment of a new concern, or increase in turnover.

The expansion or diversification of business involving an addition to plant and machinery should be met out of owned funds – that is, out of depreciation and provisions – or out of increase in capital, out of term loans. The ability of a concern to raise resources from all or some of these sources depends upon its strength, character and standing in the market. If the purpose is a mere increase in the turnover of the business which involves a larger inventory and increased operating expenses, the additional funds should be raised by way of bank loans.

From a banker's point of view, there are well-established guidelines for assessing the credit requirements of a concern. A banker analyses the balance sheet and evaluates the turnover of funds, sales and other operating results in assessing the viability of a unit.

There are certain established ratios. For example:

(a) The debt equity ratio;

(b) Turnover to net worth;

(c) Return on capital employed;

(d) Net profit as a percentage of net worth;

(e) Dividend paid to shareholders;

(f) Ratio of current assets to current liabilities.

A banker has to go behind these figures and assess the technical and managerial competence of a management, and the integrity of the men running a concern, in order to decide whether credit should or should not be advanced.

Credit is a very important element in the process of economic development. It stimulates economic activity, particularly in countries which are short of capital and entrepreneurial talent. Because of the dearth of these two basic elements in the process of development, bankers who create credit have been assigned a vital role in stimulating the process of development.

⏩ Norms for Inventory and Receivables

For an efficient management of assets, the Tandon committee suggested norms for raw materials, stock-in-process, finished goods and receivables. These norms represent the maximum levels of holding inventory and receivables in each industry.

Coverage: These norms are made applicable to all industrial borrowers, including small-scale industries, with aggregate limits from the banking system in excess of Rs. 10 lakhs and extended progressively to small borrowers.

Objective: The norms for the four kinds of current assets are related to consumption/cost of production/cost of sales/sales, respectively. If the carryover of any one kind of asset is higher than the relative norm level, the surplus is treated as "excess" carryover to be shed off, failing which an amount equivalent to the value thereof would be treated as excess borrowing. Again, such excess holding cannot be set off against any shortfall in the holding of other assets, for the norms represent the maximum permissible levels of holding; and they are not entitlements. Lending banks are expected to scrutinise the periodical stock and receive statements to determine whether the borrows comply with the aforesaid stipulation.

Experience shows that while norms are reckoned in sanctioning credit limits, these are not uniformly complied with subsequently through the medium of monthly stock statements. Although both Tandon Committee and the RBI had hoped, while introducing the report, that excess current asset holdings would be adjusted in two months, this has not happened. In fact, RBI itself has had to adopt a flexible approach by permitting, *inter se,* adjustments of norm levels of different assets, raising norm levels, etc.

Given the manufacturing cycle of a borrower, starting with raw materials to stocks-in-process, and further to finished goods, it is only logical to think of a combined norm for all the three items in relation to the value of output. A lending bank ought to scrutinise the levels of each kind of current assets in the ordinary course of its vigil on the borrower's operations but to treat any of them as excess holding even as the overall level is considered reasonable and consistent with production is to make things unnecessarily complicated; and this serves no worthwhile purpose. It is said that combined norms may be developed for different industries from the RBI studies on company finances. These may be revised from time to time to meet the objectives of national economic policies and/or bring them in tune with the policy by individual industry groupings. Thus, the suggested modification of laying down a combined norm for inventories in relation to the value of output, and receivables to sales as at present, would make things pragmatic, without jeopardising the interests of lending bank and without hurting any macro economic objectives.

The suggested norms are as follows:

SUGGESTED NORMS FOR INVENTORY AND RECEIVABLES

Industry Raw materials (including stores and other items used in the process of manufacture)		***Stocks-in-process***	***Finished goods***	***Receivables* and bills purchased and discounted***
(1)	(2)	(3)	(4)	(5)
(i) Cotton and Synthetic Textiles	Cotton 2 (Mumbai and Ahmedabad areas) 2 Eastern areas – Bihar, Orissa, West Bengal and Assam) 2½ (Other than the above areas) 2 Other raw materials	¾ (Composite textile mills) ½ (Other mills)	- 2¼ -	
(ii) Man made Fibre	½	½	- 1¾ -	

(1)	(2)	(3)	(4)	(5)
(iii) Jute Textiles	2½	¼	1 (For domestic sales) and 1½ (For exports)	1½
(iv) Rubber Products	2	¼		- 1¾ -
(v) Fertilisers *(a)* For nitrogenous plants	¾ (Units near refinery) ½ (Units away from refinery)	Negligible	1 (where stocks are in plant site) ½ (Where stocks are also in upcountry centres)	1¼
(b) For phosphatic plants	2 (Units in port areas) 3 (Units away from port areas)	Negligible	1 (Where stocks are in plant site) 1½ (Where stocks are also in upcountry centres)	1¼
(vi) Pharmaceuticals	2¾	½	2	1¼
(vii) Dyes and Dyestuffs	2¼	1	¾	2¼
(viii) Basic Industrial Chemicals	2¾	¼	1	1¾
(ix) Vegetable and Hydrogenated Oil	1	Negligible	¾	
(x) Paper	2-6 Bamboo and Wood (to be built up in stages from November to May and thereafter to be brought down) 2¼ Chemicals		1 (For controlled sales) and 3/4 (for free sales)	¾
(xi) Cement	2¼ Gypsum ¼ Limestone 3/4 Coal ½ packing material	½	- 1 -	
(xii) Engineering Automobiles & ancillaries	2¼	¾	- 2½ -	
(xiii) Engineering Consumer Durables	2	¾	- 2½ -	

(1)	(2)	(3)	(4)	(5)
(xix) Engineering Ancillaries (other than Automobile ancillaries) and Component Suppliers	2	¼	- 2½ -	
(xv) Engineering machinery manufactures Capital Equipment Suppliers (other than Heavy Engineering)**	2¾	1¼	- 3½ -	

Notes:

(i) Raw materials are used in so many months.

(ii) *(a)* Stock-in-process are expressed as so many months' cost of production.
(b) In individual cases, the bank may deviate from the norm for Stock-in-process if it is satisfied that the actual process time involved in any particular unit, say, in view of the nature of production, past experience and technology employed, is more than the suggested norm.

(iii) *(a)* Finished goods and receivables are expressed as so many months' cost of sales and sales respectively. These figures represent only the average levels. Individual items of finished goods and receivables may be for different periods, which may exceed the indicated norms so long as the overall average level of finished goods and receivables does not exceed the amounts as determined in terms of the norm.
**(b)* The norm prescribed for receivables relates only to inland sales on short-term basis (i.e., excluding receivables arising out of deferred payment sales and exports).

(iv) Stocks of spares are not included for norms, since in financial terms they are not significant in many industries. Banks will ascertain the requirements of spares for individual units. They should, however, keep a watchful eye to ensure that spares do not exceed 5% of the total inventories.

***(vi)* Heavy Engineering will include the supply of whole or substantial plants involving a long manufacturing period, i.e., sugar, cement, steel and textile plants.

Source: Report of the Study Group, RBI, 1975, pp. 20 & 21.

Illustration

ABC Industry

Estd. 1969

Manufacturer of automobile spare parts & nuts & bolts

Investment in Plant & Machinery	Rs. 15 lakhs
Bankers	Bank of Bombay
Capital	Rs. 5 lakhs
Reserves	Rs. 3 lakhs
Net Worth	Rs. 8 lakhs

(Rs. in lakhs)

Current Liabilities		*Current Assets*	
Creditors for Purchase	55	Raw Materials	120
Other Current Liabilities	25	Stock-in-progress	20
		Receivables	30

	80	Finished goods	40
		Other current assets	10
Borrowings	120		
(i) Long-term	50		
(ii) Short-term	70		
	200		220

1st Method		*2nd Method*		*3rd Method*	
Total Current assets	220	Total Current assets	220	Total Current assets	220
Less: Current Liabilities other than bank borrowing	80	25% from long-term sources	55	*Less:* Core current assets	55
Working capital gap	140		165		165
25% of above form long-term sources	35	*Less:* current liabilities other than bank	80	25% of above from long-term sources	41
Maximum bank borrowing permissible	105	Working capital gap	85	*Less:* current liabilities	80
			140	Other than bank borrowing	44
		Maximum bank borrowing permissible	85	Working capital gap	140
				Maximum bank borrowing permissible	44
Excess Borrowings	15	Excess Borrowings	35	Excess Borrowings	96
Current ratio 1.19:1		Current ratio 1.33:1		Current ratio 2.12:1	

▸▸ Working Capital

In simple terms, working capital is the amount of funds which a small-scale enterprise must have to finance its day-to-day operations. It is a short-term finance. An effective utilisation of working capital results in the maximisation of productivity and profits. A proper management of working capital synchronises the cash receipts and cash outlay, and a unit may function with minimum cash reserve.

THE PARADIGM SHIFT IN WORKING CAPITAL

	The Old	***The New***
Bank Finance	• Maximum Permissible Bank Finance • Rigid Receivables Norms • Loan & Cash Credit Component • Fixed Prime-Lending Rates	• Current-Ratio Financing • Cash-Flow Financing • Flexible Norms • Increasing Loan Component • Variable Prime Lending Rates • Short-Term Foreign Currency Loans

Non-Bank Finance (Short-Term)	• Trade Credit • Bill Discounting • Inter-Corporate Deposits • Public Deposits • Commercial Paper	• Trade Credit • Bill Discounting • Inter-Corporate Deposits • Public Deposits • Commercial Paper • Euro-Commercial Paper • Factoring
Non-Bank Finance (Long-term)	• Non-Convertible Debentures • Equity	• Non-Convertible Debentures • Equity • Floating Rate Notes • Note Issuance Facility • Revolving Underwriting Facility • Dutch Auction Notes

To obtain working capital, entrepreneurs should approach one of the commercial banks (State Bank of India or any of its subsidiaries, other nationalised banks, private sector banks, etc.)

Banks provide credit facilities to meet working-capital requirements to facilitate production as per the manufacturing needs of the industrial unit.

Broadly speaking, working-capital facilities could be classified as:

(*i*) Lock and key pledge of stocks;

(*ii*) Factory /Mundy type/hypothecation advances (pending statement on stocks held by the unit to be intimated to bank);

(*iii*) Advances against stock-in-process;

(*iv*) Advances against bills (when finished goods are supplied on credit);

(*v*) Clean advances (contingent needs);

(*vi*) Packing credit to exporters to execute export orders.

As already stated earlier, banks provide both term-loan and working capital together in composite loans and also give small loans. Some entrepreneurs also depend on friends, relatives and other sources for their increasing requirements of working capital.

In order to get a loan from a commercial bank, the entrepreneur has to fill in an application form as per the specimen provided by the financial institutions, including banks and submit it to the bank along with the following documents:

(*i*) Authentic copies of Balance Sheets and Profit and Loss Accounts (if the industrial concern is a limited company or an industrial co-operative society).

(*ii*) A statement of assets and liabilities in the prescribed form in the case of partnership and proprietary cencerns.

(*iii*) Proforma statements in all other cases.

(*iv*) Copies of the affidavit in regard to the size of the unit.

(*v*) Technical Feasibility Report from the Small Industries Service Institute, the Director of Industries, if obtained, may also be enclosed.

The total cost of the SSI project is computed as under:

(*i*) The cost of fixed assets proposed to be acquired.

(*ii*) Total working capital requirements (for the first year of production).

(*iii*) Preliminary and pre-operative expenses. Provision should be made for escalation of costs.

The following are the sources for meeting the above cost of the project:

(*i*) Your own capital, seed capital assistance from State Government/Development Corporations.

(*ii*) Loans/Deposits from your friends and relatives, which can be held for long periods say, three years.

(*iii*) Medium-term loans (for fixed assets) from the banks/term-lending institutions.

(*iv*) Working capital loan from the bank.

(*v*) Credit on purchases.

(*vi*) IDBI bill discounting for purchase of machinery on deferred payment guarantee.

Profitability estimates may be worked out using the format placed at in Annexure 3. The schedule of repayment proposed to be adopted should be based on the profit accounts. The format at Annexure 4 would help the working out of cash flow estimate. Cost over-run and time over-run are common in most 551 units. Careful planning must be done to overcome them.

⏩ The Working Capital Cycle

The operating cycle begins with the arrival of the stock, and ends when the cash is received. The cash cycle begins when cash is paid for materials, and ends when cash is collected from receivables.

It has been rightly stressed that the small-scale enterprises will have to learn to manage with a lower level of current assets to be globally competitive. Efficient working capital management techniques are those that compress the operating cycle. The length of the operating cycle is equal to the sum of the lengths of the inventory period and the receivables period. Besides, innovative financial instruments can also be deployed to churn over the current asset portfolio with greater speed. The entrepreneur may resort to bill discounting, factoring etc.

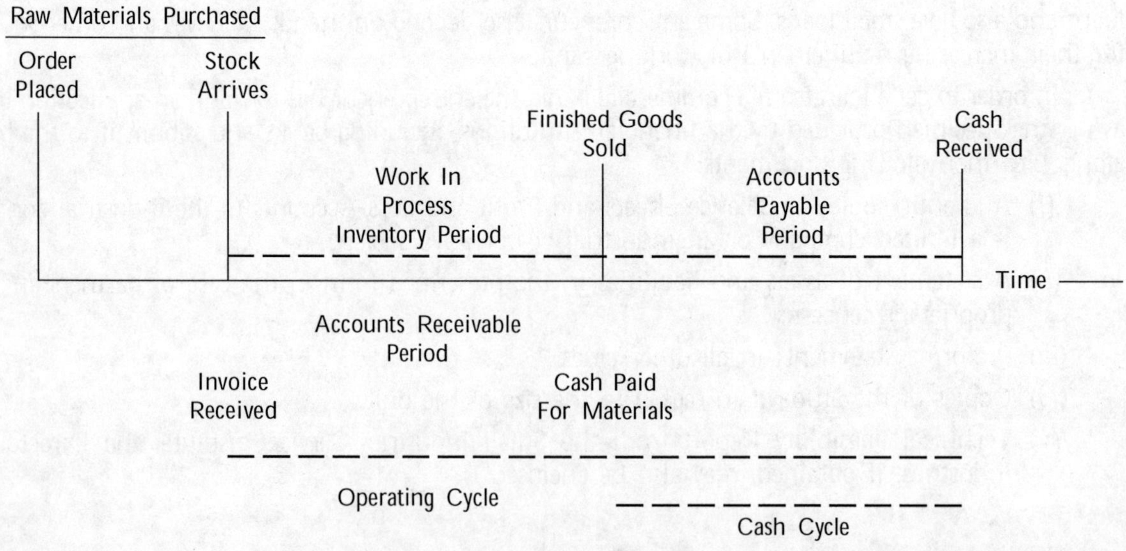

Both core and variable working capital are supported by a mix of spontaneous current liabilities (trade credit and provisions for taxation), short-term financing (bank finance and short-term marketable securities), and long-term financing (long-term, debt and equity). Since trade credit and accruals for tax payments are determined by exogenous factors, the crucial aspect for any working capital financing strategy is determining the proportion of current assets that is to be funded by short-term sources of finance.

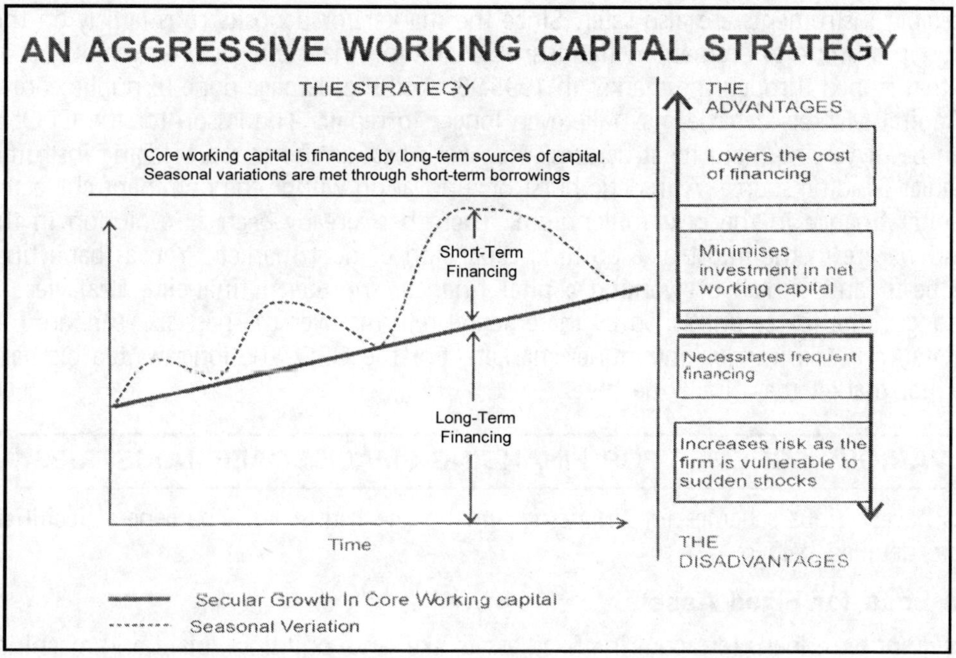

Current Ratio Financing: Obviously, the liquidity of the enterprise – that is, its ability to meet its obligations in the short run – will loom large in credit risk appraisals. Since the most common, and convenient, measure of liquidity is the ratio of current assets to current liabilities, future methods of estimating working capital finance will be predicated on the current ratio. To fund the gap between production and receivables, banks will continue to examine the production cycle and the recovery process.

While this may look suspiciously like the old system, there are vital differences. The acceptable current ratio – and, therefore, the ratio of bank funds to own funds – is now a matter for negotiation between the corporate and the bank. Plus, there will be greater flexibility as to what qualifies as a current asset. For instance, under the MPBF norms, marketable investments were not counted as current assets. Now, corporates can lobby for the inclusion of such investments, thereby lowering the amount to be brought by the promoters.

Cash-Flow Financing: The need for working capital arises essentially because of the asynchronous, and uncertain, nature of cash flows. This is because cash outflows to meet production expenses do not occur at the same time as cash proceeds from sales are realised. They are uncertain because sales and costs are not known in advance. By projecting future cash receipts and disbursements, the cash budget enables the corporate to determine its cash needs, and plan their financing accordingly. Clearly, bank finance based on the submission of periodic, say, quarterly – cash-flow statements would fit smoothly into a firm's cash cycle.

Cash-flow financing imposes its own brand of discipline. To determine the quantum of bank finance, banks must evaluate cash flow risks, forcing them to be more involved in the day-to-day operations of the borrower. Once the bank has appeared the cash budget, ad hoc requests for more funds will not be entertained. This will demand sound resource planning, receivables management, purchase planning, and management of inventory.

Marketable instruments are also safer. Since the market for deposits runs largely on the oxygen of credibility, it is prone to dramatic deflations; ICD volumes have still not recovered from the spate of defaults that ripped through the market in 1995-96. And the damage done to public confidence by the CRB Capital Markets debacle may take even longer to repair. The lesson for the CFO: although deposits can be of varying maturity structures, they work best as short-term bridging instruments and not as a regular funding source. A frenetic burst of innovation will be the dominant characteristics of working capital finance in the next millennium. There has already been a revolution in the equity markets, and we are in the midst of a bustling expansion of debt markets. Yet, as bank finance was simply the be-all and end-all of working capital finance, short-term financing strategies remained static. No longer, the forces unleashed by incremental reforms over the past six years are freeing the price of capital, and the interlocking money markets. For the CFO, the long-awaited big bang in the working capital market may finally be here.

VARIOUS SCHEMES FOR FINANCING SMALL-SCALE INDUSTRIES

Banks have various schemes for financing Small Scale Industries. The general facilities offered by banks are detailed below:

Term Loan for Fixed Assets

Banks grant term loans for acquiring fixed assets like land, buildings, plant and machinery. Such loans are repayable in stipulated instalments ranging between three and seven years linked to profit accruals. A suitable moratorium period is granted for the commencement of repayment depending upon the lead period necessary for the first batch of products to reach the market.

Cash Credit

Working capital loans are granted in the form of cash credit, i.e., running accounts in which drawings are allowed within the limits sanctioned in proportion to the value of goods pledged/ hypothecated.

Bills Purchased or Discounted

Banks purchase demand bills accompanied by invoices and documents like railway receipts or lorry receipts evidencing the despatch of goods, and discount bills maturing after a specified period mentioned thereon. Banks also grant advances against book debts arising out of trade transactions.

Export Finance

Banks grant pre-shipment and post-shipment finance to units engaged in exports:

(*i*) Pre-shipment credit which is also known as packing credit, is granted to a unit where an irrevocable letter of credit in its favour have been received or a firm order has been secured by the unit from an overseas buyer/export house. This credit helps the unit to purchase raw material, pack/manufacture the goods ordered and export the goods.

(*ii*) Post-shipment credit is granted to an exporter after the shipment of goods, against export bills.

Letters of Credit

Banks establish letters of credit in favour of an exporter in another country when their clients have to import machinery, equipment or raw materials.

Clean Overdrafts

Banks also grant clean overdrafts to units to help them tide over their temporary difficulties.

Deferred Payment Guarantees

Banks accept the liability to pay periodical instalments of term loans granted to units for purchase of machinery and issue deferred payment guarantees.

Financial Assistance to Technically-Qualified Persons

Most banks have schemes under which technically-qualified persons or those who have proven skills/experience in the line of activity they propose to undertake and who are not able to introduce the required capital of their own are eligible for 100 per cent finance so long as their schemes are viable.

Consultancy Services

Some banks have Consultancy Cells and Technical Officers whose services can be utilised by those desirous of setting up small-scale units for drawing up their projects or for ascertaining whether any areas in the projects already drawn up by them require any toning up.

Equity Fund Scheme

Some banks have schemes under which those who are unable to meet the usual margins from their resources are offered interest-free assistance to supplement the capital they can introduce, provided they do not have any other unit and do not borrow from any other bank. The amount of assistance is repayable on a long-term basis.

Many State Development Corporations have capital subsidy schemes.

Assessment

The working capital management is an integral part of overall management of small-scale industries. There is a need for greater co-ordination between small-scale industries and financial institutions. Towards this direction, the Small Industries Development Bank of India (SIDBI) is shaped to provide a strong support to small-scale industries.

It is essential that financial institutions should safeguard their interests with adequate security. At the same time, small industrial concerns should not, as far as possible, be denied the assistance they deserve or need. Lack of finance is often not the cause but the result of difficulties in other areas. In such cases, what is needed is measures to set right those factors which would render financial assistance fruitful. It is common knowledge that the small-scale sector needs non-financial assistance – marketing assistance, technical guidance and training in management, etc. In order to assist it, the Government has already established special institutions like the Small Industries Service Institutes, the National Small Industries Corporation, and industrial estates with necessary facilities. It has also arranged training programmes for small entrepreneurs; but the scope of operations of these need to be expanded. Above all, there is need for greater co-ordination at all levels between the financial and non-financial institutions and agencies engaged in the promotion of small-scale industries.

In the present Indian context, the socio-economic obligations of a banker include identification of project ideas, formulation of projects, location of managerial talent and provision of technical and managerial guidance to new ventures with a view to broad-basing entrepreneurial talent and assisting in the creation of more employment opportunities in the country. The banker who controls credit is a "supply leader" as opposed to his erstwhile role of a "demand follower." He is no longer a "wholesale" banker sitting in an ivory tower. His new role as an agent of economic development is to assist in the development and growth of economic activities.

Planning and control of working capital centres around, sound cash planning which includes setting of cash policies and procedures and the control over cash and credit. The working capital has, therefore, to be managed properly, especially by the small-scale industries, because over or under circulation may create volatile problems.

➤➤ Scientific Approach to Working Capital

A scientific approach to working capital involves a study of the factors which affect the need for working capital – the terms offered by suppliers, the terms offered to customers, the average period of lead time for various inventory items, the seasonal fluctuations in sales, the production cycle, the level of stock and other influencing factors. These factors may be used to relate the balance sheet items to sales volumes. The relationships yield measures which may serve, among other things, as tools for the prediction of future working capital needs.

For a scientific study of the working capital problem, a mathematical model may be developed to state the important quantitative relationships among different variables. In order to construct such a model, it is necessary to make an objective study of the situation. In the case of working capital, the relevant factors which should be studied are the relationship that exist between the amounts of the current assets and current liabilities, and the volume of sales.

In developing the model, the first step is to analyse the relevant factors of a company's situation. This involves an examination of the records, a study of actual procedures and a consultation with company officials.

The suggested method of forecasting working capital needs is an improvement on the methods which are currently employed by companies. The use of the model would result in a more accurate forecast, allow for improvement through observation and experience, and act as a useful tool for the assessment of the size of the working capital.

The use of the working capital model is appropriate for many types of businesses. In companies which manufacture different types of products involving different materials or different processes, separate sub-models may be constructed, and these may be combined in the final analysis. Where conditions are changing rapidly, the effects of the changes can be estimated objectively.

As long as the general pattern of the production and financial process does not change substantially, the model will hold good. When any change occurs, a re-study of the pertinent items would be sufficient.

In most cases, this type of working capital model can be developed easily. It would enable managers to forecast the level for each working capital item and ensure that the necessary resources are available. In addition, the model could establish working capital standards. A comparison of the actual with the standards would provide a measure of the efficiency of financial management.

Management

Effective financial management is based on three factors: analysis of past performance; planning for future activities; and control of current activity. Control is achieved by implementing decisions in accordance with agreed plans. Accordingly, financial planning is of crucial importance in a small unit.

An effective working capital management calls for an understanding of cash requirements at varying stages of design, development, production and marketing. The overall efficiency of the working capital is judged by the annual result it produces.

The working capital management is an integral part of overall management of small-scale industries. There is need for greater co-ordination between small-scale industries and financial institutions. Towards this direction, the Small Industries Development Bank of India (SIDBI) is shaped to provide a strong support to small-scale industries.

It is essential that financial institutions should safeguard their interests with adequate security. At the same time, small industrial concerns should not, as far as possible, be denied the assistance they deserve or need. Lack of finance is often not the cause but the result of difficulties in other areas. In such cases, what is needed are measures to set right those factors which would render financial assistance, good returns. It is common knowledge that the small-scale sector needs non-financial assistance – marketing assistance, technical guidance and training in management, etc. It has also arranged training programmes for small entrepreneurs; but the scope of operation of these need to be expanded. Above all, there is need for greater co-ordination at all levels between the financial and non-financial institutions and agencies engaged in the promotion of small-scale industries.

In the present Indian context, the socio-economic obligations of a banker include identification of project ideas, project formulation, managerial talent and provision of technical and managerial guidance to new ventures with a view to broad-basing entrepreneurial talent and assisting in the creation of more employment opportunities in the country. The banker who controls credit is a "supply leader" as opposed to his erstwhile role of a "demand follower." He is no longer a "wholesale" banker sitting in an ivory tower. His new role as an agent of economic development is to assist in the development and growth of economic activities.

Planning and control of working capital centres round sound cash planning which includes setting of cash policies and procedures and the control over cash and credit. Cash is of course a very sensitive component of working capital. The working capital has, therefore, to be managed properly, especially by the SSIs, because over or under circulation may create volatile problems.

Financing of Industrial Estates

Financial institutions have commenced extending estimated direct assistance for financing of industrial estates. Such ventures estimated at Rs. 300 lakh are covered under the IDBI's re-finance scheme where primary lending is effected through the SFCs, SIDCs and commercial banks. Industrial estates costing beyond Rs. 300 lakh are extended direct financial assistance by the all-India financial institutions.

The main aspects considered in proposals for setting up of industrial estates are the suitability of the location, availability of power, water, raw materials, skilled and unskilled labour, transport and communication facilities, market for the products of industries to be set up in the estate and the potential for overall economic growth. Significant emphasis initially is, therefore laid on physical survey of the site and its proper designing.

Size of Industrial Estate

The size of the estate should preferably be not less than 15 acres of land where the cost is up to Rs. 300 lakhs and not less than 25 acres of land where the cost is more than Rs. 300 lakhs. This size results in individual units deriving the advantage of some economy in overhead expenses and sharing of some common facilities. However, it may not always be practical to insist on the minimum size of land and the financial institutions may, under such circumstances, relax the minimum area where the estate is in urban areas or if the estate is proposed in a multi-storeyed building.

The institutions also desire that the project acquires adequate reserve land at the beginning itself as the cost of acquiring adjacent land at a later date might become prohibitive. Twice the estimated initial capacity for sheds booked/expected to be booked is considered a fair reserve area over the present requirements. This is not, however, taken as an inflexible norm and for large estates, particularly in urban and semi-urban areas, the reserve may be less, say, equal to the area initially required.

Conclusion

To make finance available for a project there is need for prudent financial management. All along, there is need for planning the flow of funds for the smooth functioning of a project. A successful project is one which generates its own finances to a greater extent and finances its diversified activities. Internal resources will serve as a backbone of a project.

The generation of internal resources not only benefits the enterprise, but also the entrepreneur, shareholders and the society. Above all, a prudent management of internal resources may also assist the natural growth of the capital market.

Finance, which has been aptly described as the "life-blood" of industry is a pre-requisite for the mobilisation of real resources to organise production and marketing. Depending upon the nature of the activity to be financed, business requires short-term, medium-term and long-term finance.

A new chapter for business finance is being hammered out. And with it, the flexibility for the entrepreneur to design the financing mix to suit every need. To use an assortment of financial products that both lowers financing costs and minimises risks. In short, to evolve a financing strategy that dovetails with the enterprise's competitive strategy tomorrow.

With deregulation, entrepreneurs will find it cheaper to access the markets directly. The phenomenon of disintermediation is interwined with securitisation, or the tendency of enterprises to raise capital by issuing securities rather than on relying on direct loans. While short-term working capital needs can be met by the issue of commercial paper, long-term project finance requirements can be partially serviced through debenture offerings. In fact, in the more developed capital markets, funds are raised by even scrutinising the regular cash-flows generated by receivables.

Fierce competition among the lenders will transform once standard working capital or term-loans for the entrepreneurs. The lenders will be forced to assume higher credit risk. Project financing will, increasingly, be of the non-recourse variety while a rising proportion of working capital finance may be extended on an unsecured basis. Since credit risk will be transferred in full to the financial intermediary, that intermediary will be much involved in monitoring the loan. So, while securitisation moves towards more impersonal forms of financing, lending will become more intimate.

Financial management is an integral part of industry and ranks equally in importance with other key components like production and marketing. Capital and finance form the bed rock foundation of industrial development. They are provided by a number of financial institutions. The saga of industrial development in the post-independence period is the story of these core institutions as well as market participation.

A DIFFERENT VIEWPOINT

When you're the first person whose beliefs are different from what everyone else believes, you're saying, "I'm right, and everyone else is wrong." That's an unpleasant position to be in. It's at once exhilarating and at the same time an invitation to be attacked.

— Lawrence Joseph Ellison, Oracle Corporation, Founder and CEO

26

Technical Assistance

Introduction

Technology is an evolutionary process. Industrial technological capabilities include the ability to acquire or select imported or indigenous technologies, assimilate or adapt new technologies, disseminate new technological knowledge and improve the existing production processes and develop new technologies through investment in R & D. The dynamic process of combining technologies to create new technologies or borrowing technologies is greatly facilitated by freedom of thought and freedom of action. It is a combination of innovation and adaptation. And, this could be achieved by good management of technological innovation.

Hugh Sandeman

A broader goal of technological innovation is to upgrade existing industrial infrastructure to sustain long-term economic growth. An indirect benefit is to spur the manufacturing sector which is expected to be the lynch-pin for future growth. By managing technological innovations relating to industrial technology, it is expected that the country will be better able to assimilate, adapt and develop technology.

The impact of technological change and innovations has only just been fully realised and appreciated within the realms of Office Management and Administration. Presently, the focus of attention is on the development and utilisation of new information technology within the office. Theorists and practitioners suggest that the introduction of this new technology will have a tremendous impact on the productivity of the office worker. Administrative and office work has been classed as labour-intensive but the introduction of new technology will shift the emphasis towards being more capital intensive.

India has approximately 32 million small and medium enterprises (SMEs), which form the lifeline of the country. The business performance of the SMEs directly impact the economy. In the past few years, SMEs' dependence on and use of technology have increased dratically. SMEs now operate in a challenging business environment, with complex technology infrastructure models and the inherent business issues associated with it. However, their access to sophisticated technology is still fairly limited.

⏩ The SSI Sector

The SSI sector in India is widely dispersed and heterogeneous in character having units ranging from household to modern enterprises using latest technology, sound managerial practices and good infrastructural facilities. SSI units have major concentration in industries like food processing, chemicals, hosiery, garments, plastics, paper, leather and leather products, wood, metal, non-electrical machinery parts, software and service oriented sector. Clusters of SSI units have emerged over the years, which are manufacturing a range of products and having strong forward and backward linkage.

The SSI units can remain competitive in the era of globalisation and liberalisation only through adoption of state-of-the-art technologies. The sources of technologies for SSIs are (*i*) indigenous (government sponsored R&D or in-house R & D – which is very rare) and (*ii*) acquisition, adoption and assimilation of imported technologies. The SSI units import technology only when there is a wide gap between indigenous technologies and contemporary technologies abroad. The import of new technologies is constrained due to royalty payments, commitments of patents, unsuitability of local skills/raw materials, difficulties in sourcing cheap and useful technologies abroad, etc.

SSI units normally go in for new technologies in the following cases:

- Introduction of new machine tools/equipment used in production.
- Use of alternative/new raw materials.
- Introduction of new products/designs.
- More efficient methods of production.
- Changes in the manufacturing processes leading to improvement in quality.
- Demand of the parent organisation for new products/sub-assemblies/parts with high standards and specifications.

Technology is not a static concept but is of dynamic nature. Continuous upgradation goes on in improvement of level of technology. Introduction of new energy efficient, cost reducing manufacturing processes, alternative raw materials, upgradation of quality parameters, specifications, etc., bring changes in technology.

Technology changes critically depend upon the user's ability to respond dynamically to changes in domestic skills, production needs, demands, market etc. The techniques and technologies of production at the shop-floor are becoming more and more skill and knowledge based. Unlike the large scale units, SSIs are afraid to adopt new technologies due to factors like uncertainty of use of new technology in an untested market and fear of adjustments in production process, marketing, input supply and profits.

Further, the SSI units do not have sufficient financial resources (either accrued from internal resources or capability of borrowing from banks/financial institutions) for technology upgradation and modernisation. Absence of venture capital funds for SSIs also inhibits technology upgradation and modernisation.

The SSI units are lacking knowledge about technology sourcing, evaluation and demonstration facilities, absence of design centres, non-availability of specific surveys and feasibility studies, non-availability of pilot plants for trials and absence of insurance cover in case of failure, etc. A number of R & D results developed by national scientific laboratories involve huge investment and most of the time, these are not successfully established through demonstration.

STAGES OF TECHNOLOGY DEVELOPMENT – A MODEL

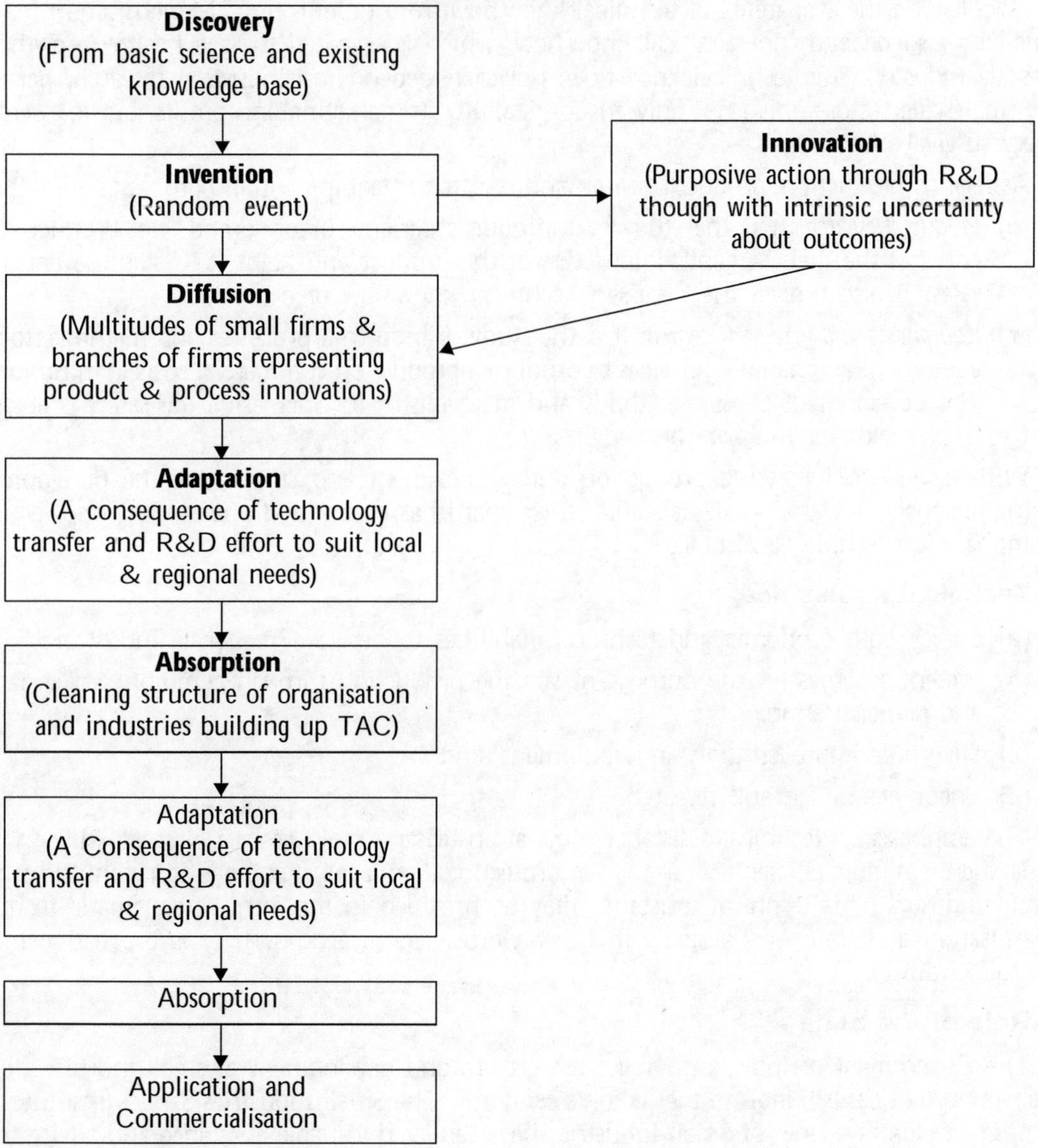

The Study feels that to commercialise process/product know-how, it is necessary to have first demonstration followed by feasibility studies, plant layout, detailed engineering, streamlining of production processes, etc. The Study Group has also felt that cluster approach would be the best for adopting new technologies. In the clusters of SSIs, demonstration of new technologies would start a chain reaction and as success is seen by other units, they would follow the line to adopt new technologies.

Many SSEs acquired the needed technology displaying ingenuity in adopting the technology to local conditions. On a broad estimate, about 70 to 80 per cent of the SSI units have acquired or developed technology/ know-how not through any formal contracts but on their own and only 20 to 30 per cent SSI units have acquired technology through external sources. Direct dependence of SSI units on foreign sources for technology is minimal.

In constantly changing marketing conditions, the production of quality goods at a minimum cost depends solely on the availability of technical know-how from time to time. Modernisation for higher productivity also depends on technical know-how, which is essential for the healthy growth of the small-scale industry. This technical know-how, however, depends on industrial research, particularly in the small-scale sector, which not only ensures stability in marketing and profits, but is essential for the very survival of a unit.

As regards production, product research and research in equipment and processes are important.

(*a*) *Product Research:* It is the study of a product's design, colour, brand, etc. Product research enriches the management's knowledge of the product and helps it to stabilise and expand sales. It also evolves the necessary technical know-how of a product.

(*b*) *Equipment and Process Research*: It is the study of industrial processes and methods, tools and equipment and handling devices to produce a product on commercial basis at minimum cost. The development of new methods and mechanisms for increasing the safety processes are fertile fields for this type of study.

With a view to increasing production and employment and stimulating the development of industrial co-operatives, the Small-scale Industries Board has constituted a working group, which has laid emphasis on technical assistance.

Technical Assistance

(*a*) Survey both economic and technical viabilities to develop small-scale industries;

(*b*) Present schemes for the purpose of starting production through common service facilities, and demonstration;

(*c*) Distribute improved tools and equipment; and

(*d*) Encourage design and research.

The emphasis on technical assistance aims at ensuring a rapid growth of small industrial units and making them more efficient rather than at protecting them against competition from the organised sector of industry. This technical assistance may be provided in the form of systematic techniques, standardisation and improved designs. In other words, technical know-how is the bed-rock of the small-scale industry.

Role of the State

The Government of India encourages the growth and development of small industries because of their important contribution to the nation's economy. The Small Industries Service Institutes of the Development Commissioner of Small Industries have rendered valuable assistance and advice to small industrialists because the latter, unlike the big industrialists, cannot afford the financial cost of their own staff of qualified specialists. In order to make this service as complete and comprehensive as possible, a Design Cell was set up in each of the four Regional Institutes at Kolkata, Delhi, Mumbai and Chennai. The object of setting up of these Cells was to study and improve the designs of the products of small industries. In August, 1959, in order to improve its services, the Design Cell was centralised in one office at New Delhi because common workshop facilities were available there for purposes of experiment and building actual prototypes. Today, the Design Cell is attached to the Small Industries Service Institute, New Delhi, and is housed in a modern building with attached workshop consisting of a Tool Room, a Machine Shop, a Heat-treatment Shop, a Ceramic Shop and Laboratories for chemical and electrical research and a reading room and library containing many books on industrial designs.

The Industrial Design Cell

Since the setting-up of the Industrial Design Cell, the small-scale industry in India has made tremendous progress in the field of technology and marketing.

To cope with the constant demand for improvement in the products, the Industrial Design Cell has been engaged in evolving new designs which are suitable for production in the small-scale sector with its limited resources and mechanical and technical ability.

The principal function of an industrial design is to create a product which is functionally perfect and has a strong aesthetic appeal, besides being economical and convenient to manufacture. The designer studies the capability of the manufacturer in order to determine how a product should be designed. He also considers the colour, material and finish which should be combined in such a way that the product acquires a form which clearly expresses its function.

From the manufacturer's point of view, the most important purpose of industrial designing is to render the production of his products economical and convenient. A good design means significant savings in skilled labour, reduction in the number of production operations and better utilisation of raw materials. These savings cannot be brought about at the cost of the utility and function of a product; this can best be accomplished when the designer has a good understanding of the machines, workers and the existing production methods of the manufacturer.

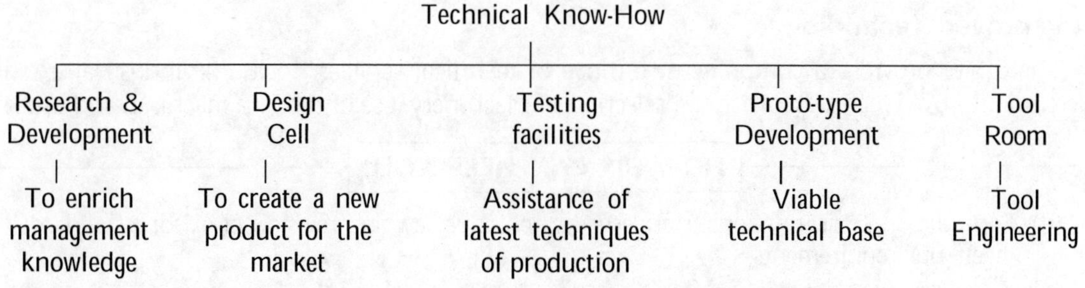

Fig. 1 Areas of Technical Know-how to Small Industry

Some of the precepts of a modern industrial design and what it tries to accomplish may be summarised here.

A modern design should fulfil the practical needs of modern life. It should express the spirit of our times and should also take advantage of new materials and techniques and develop the familiar ones. It should develop the forms, textures and colours that spring from the direct fulfilment of requirements in appropriate materials and techniques, and should express the purpose of an object and techniques, and should also indicate the methods used to make an object, not disguising mass production as handicraft or simulating a technique which has not been used. At the same time, it should be simple; its structure evident in its appearance and it should avoid extraneous enrichment.

A modern design should muster the machine for the service of man and should serve as wide a public as possible, considering modest needs and limited costs no less challenging than the requirements of pomp and luxury.

The Industrial Design Cell has played a vital and significant role in helping the small-scale sector in product designs. Till recently most of the products manufactured in the small-scale sector were either imitations of imported products irrespective of any consideration of suitability to Indian conditions, or were functionally bad. The Industrial Design Cell has made efforts to overcome these shortcomings and has helped the small-scale sector to improve its product design and its viability. At present the Industrial Design Cell specialises in designs for the following industries:

(*i*) Cutlery and Domestic Utensils;

(*ii*) Domestic Electrical Appliances;

(*iii*) Furniture and Woodwork;

(*iv*) Ceramics;

(*v*) Leather Goods;

(*vi*) Builders' Hardware; and

(*viii*) Plastic Goods.

It also conducts studies and developmental work in some of the newer subjects and has contributed significantly to the development of small industries.

A considerable number of the designs developed by the Industrial Design Cell have been commercially manufactured. However, the use of the designs which have been developed is a continuing process, and it takes several months before a design can be fully used for production purposes. This is so because its use involves different stages, such as the manufacture of prototype, the designing of dies, jigs, tools and fixtures for full-scale production.

➧ Improved Technology

The SIDO provides a comprehensive range of technical services, including industrial extension services on improved technical processes, selection of machinery, use of modern machines and processes,

HOW BIS CAN HELP YOU?

(*a*) Formulation of new national standards as well as review and revision of existing standards to meet your requirements.

(*b*) Improving the quality of goods manufactured through its certification scheme which provides a third party quality assurance.

(*c*) Providing consultancy and training for developing company standardization.

(*d*) Training for establishment of Quality System as per IS 14000/ISO 9000 series.

(*e*) Training in Statistical Quality Control.

(*f*) Training of laboratory personnel for operation of Certification Scheme.

(*g*) Providing information on various national and international standards.

preparation of factory layouts and designs, material handling and guidance in production. This is done through its network of 25 Small Industries Service Institutes, 20 Branch Institutes, 41 Extension Centres, 4 Regional testing Centres, one Product and Process Development Centre, 3 Footwear Training Centres and 5 Production Centres. Common facility services are offered to small-scale industries by its workshops and laboratories attached to the Institutes and Extension Centres.

⏩ Technical Literature

The SIDO brings out a great deal of technical literature – model schemes, blueprints, drawings, etc. – for benefit of existing and prospective entrepreneurs. During the year 1990-91 about 26,000 technical schemes, blueprints, drawings, designs and prototypes were supplied to entrepreneurs.

⏩ Modernisation of Selected Industries

Modernisation programmes involved an integrated approach, for it was felt that it would not be possible to tackle and solve individual problems connected with modernisation because of the prevailing imbalances in the production set up. To obtain optimum results, a package programme was considered necessary. The basic aim of the modernisation programme was, therefore, to achieve overall production efficiency and bring the small-scale industries abreast of the latest information on production processes, product, designs, technical developments, training facilities by the provision of an effective technical consultancy service and other forms of assistance. The programme of modernisation of selected industries was initiated in 1975-76. The salient features of the programme were:

- Modernisation of management techniques, including the modernisation of the attitudes and skills of the personnel at all levels;
- Modernisation of products in terms of designs and standardisation;
- Modernisation of organisation structure;
- Modernisation of machinery and equipment; and
- Modernisation of technology in the sense of identification and use of low cost technology which is, at the same time, consistent with economy, efficiency and quality.

The programme involved two major tasks. First, the conduct of motivational contact programmes through seminars, workshops, industrial clinics, modernisation media, etc. Through this, it was expected that small industries would be motivated to modernise their units voluntarily. Second, the conduct of intensive and quick plant studies for selected small-scale units and assisting them in implementing the suggestions made in the studies. This involved the services of field teams, consultants and the assistance of various agencies dealing with technology, management, training, sales, finance etc. The various inputs included the training of managers, supervisors or workers, facilities to entrepreneurs for visiting various industries relevant to their line of production and arrangement of visits of experts to the modernised units with a view to studying specific problems of the industry as a whole and the units in particular, and suggesting suitable solutions. It was proposed to provide comprehensive assistance, including in-plant studies, technical consultancy services, managerial assistance, interest subsidy and industry-wise workshops, industrial clinics, modernisation courses, etc.

- Innovation for improvement in Coffee roaster equipment for rural women's employment and income in Kerala.
- Project on modification and manufacture of 80 Nos. of improved "Vimla Loom" used for making table mats from banana and palm fibre.
- Project on developing appropriate skill-oriented technologies in screen printing.

- Training and upgradation of existing technology for women and youths in rubber goods production.
- Technology upgradation of processing various kinds of medicinal plants materials.
- Upgradation of existing technology of coir products and introduction of income generating activities among women of fishermen community.
- Dissemination of technology of RDO Loom in North East Region of India.
- Implementation of Appropriate Technology schemes to implement 5 small projects for upgradation of rural industries in Mysore for upliftment of rural artisans.
- Manufacturing of machines for leaf cup and plate for Tribal population.

Some study projects like Status study of small scale industries manufacturing toys in the country and technological assessment of Dindigul Lock Industries have also been completed during the year.

APPROPRIATE TECHNOLOGY

The Appropriate Technology Unit of the Department of Small Scale Industries and Agro and Rural Industries provides assistance in upgrading the technology of rural, village and cottage industries and disseminating it to the artisans at the field level through reputed NGOs/Research Institutions. With improved technology, the sustainability and economic viability of these industries increases and they are able to compete in the market.

Some important technologies developed with the assistance from A.T. Unit are as follows:

- Yarn making machine (Coir, Sabaigrass, Moonj and Sunhemp)
- Lacquereware toys making machine
- Akik stone processing machine
- Medicinal plant processing machine
- Turmeric plant processing machine
- Bamboo product making machine
- Looms for shawl and carpet weaving
- Equipment for brass and bell metal industry
- Conversion of Hand operated charkhas and sewing machines into power operated ones
- Development of technology for processing Dodi Oil.

The upgradation of technology through development of the machines and its distribution amongst the artisans has substantially increased the productivity and income of the artisans. The technology so developed helps in reducing the drudgery, fatigue and disease which were caused by the traditional methods of production.

Out of 19 Project proposals amounting to Rs. 196.42 lakhs received during the year, 10 projects amounting to Rs. 52.09 lakhs have been approved by the Screening Committee. In addition to the ongoing projects the following new projects have been undertaken :

- Upgradation of Technology for Processing of Dodi Oil by rural artisans.

►► Modernisation for Productivity

The Government of India launched a programme for the modernisation of 40,000 small industrial units falling under 40 selected industries with a view to rendering them direct and indirect assistance during the Fifth plan period. The programme, initiated in 1975, aimed at raising the productivity of small-scale industries and improving their competitive strength. The productivity was sought to be improved by improvements in the quality of the product and by reduction in costs.

The Small Industries Development Organisation implemented this programme through its network of 25 small industries service institutes and branch institutes. Criteria for the selection of the units for the modernisation programme were laid down. These criteria included quantum of exports by a unit, export potential, production for defence, management ability and creditworthiness. The suitability of a unit for modernisation was also examined on the basis of a fair use of raw materials by the concerned unit.

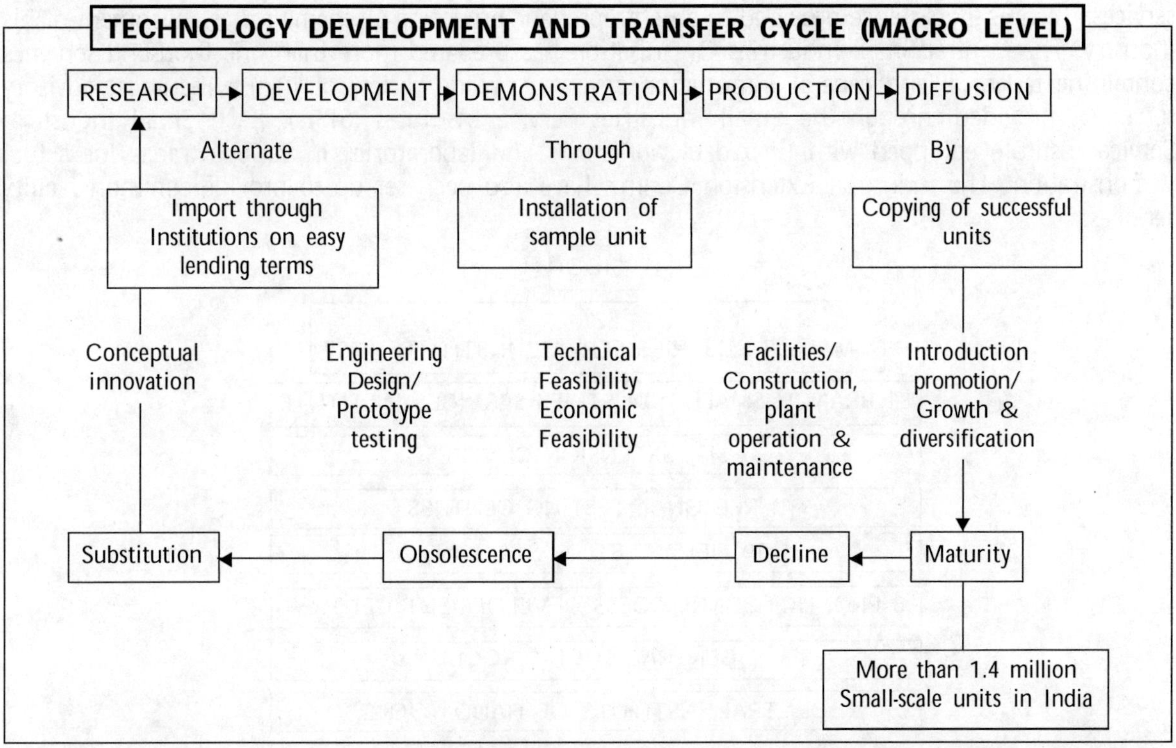

In Maharashtra, the Small Industries Service Institute at Mumbai implemented the modernisation programme. A state level committee was formed in 1976 to co-ordinate the programme and draw up future lines of action. In the first phase, 10 industries were selected for the modernisation programme. These included: foundry, leather goods, domestic electrical appliances, storage battery and components, hand tools, scientific glass instruments and automobile components.

The programme launched by the Small Industries Service Institute also aimed at motivating entrepreneurs to go in for modernisation. Group discussions were held to arouse and hold their interest in the modernisation programme in the small-scale sector. Another important aspect of the programme was to get an assessment of the existing status of the industry. Status report on small-scale industries have already been completed. Quick studies of individual units were undertaken to chalk out the modernisation programme on an individual basis. The SIDO has allotted a target of 60 units to the SISI Mumbai. Quick studies have already been completed and action has been implemented on more than 50 units.

Industrial consultants have been associated with the modernisation programme. Management techniques, products and organisational structure have been modernised. Modernisation of technology, by identification and using low cost technology consistent with economy, efficiency and quality has also been considered and equipment has been modernised.

This apart, there are 77 common facility workshops attached to SISIs Branch SISIs. Extension centres having workshop facilities for technical disciplines like General Engineering, Tool Room, Heat Treatment, Electroplating, Glass and Ceramics, Forging, Chemical Labs, etc.

Technical know-how is provided to small-scale industries by several agents with a view to upgrade the skills of workers, increase the productivity, and improve the quality of their products and services. Technical assistance provided to an entrepreneur preparing a scheme for establishment of his industry. The Central Small Industries Organisation has prepared more than one thousand schemes containing technical and general information covering a wide variety of items. Technical advisory service is provided through the Small Industries Service Institutes (SISIs). Each Small Industries Service Institute equipped with up-to-date workshops and laboratories in various trades for actual demonstration. The Industrial Extension Centres have also been set up to provide common facility services.

SIDO

27
SMALL INDUSTRIES SERVICE INSTITUTE (SISI)

31 BRANCH SMALL INDUSTRIES SERVICES INSTITUTE

37 SISI EXTENSION CENTRES

4 REGIONAL TESTING CENTRES

19 FIELD TESTING STATIONS

3 PRODUCT-CUM-PROCESS DEVELOPMENT CENTRES

2 CENTRAL TOOL 1 ROOMS

CENTRAL INSTITUTE OF HAND TOOLS

4 PRODUCTION CENTRES

Fig. 2 institutional support relating to technical know-how to small-scale industries

Management and technical services are rendered through the agency of Small Industries Services Institutes and Extension Centres of the Central Small Industries Organisation. A number of technical officers socialised in different trades are stationed in the Small Industries Services Institutes and Extension Centres, while the officers of the Central Office are engaged mainly in co-ordinating the programme in different lines, the officers on the field are engaged in what is called "Extension Service." The problems of the small-scale industries are studied by these offices with a view to provide solutions. Keeping in view the fact that the main aims are maximum productivity and improvement in quality. Management and technical consultancy services are provided to the small-scale industries.

The Study Group on SSI has recommended following measures for technology upgradation and modernisation of SSI units:

- Setting up of a Technology Bank for collection and dissemination of information about technology sources.
- A Technology Upgradation & Modernisation Fund of Rs. 5,000 crore with an interest subsidy of five per cent.
- Accelerated depreciation on plant and machinery installed for technology upgradation and modernisation.
- Five per cent custom duty on capital goods with import obligation and five per cent interest subsidy as recommended for technology modernisation.
- Need to encourage co-operation among SSI's and R & D institutions to transform their innovations into practical propositions. To start with, incubation facilities may be set up in about 50 technical institutions in the country.
- A Technology Mission is to be established to promote awareness, coordination, incubation, transformation, encourage R & D and motivate SSIs' to obtain BIS/ISO certification.

TECHNOLOGY FOR SMALL BUSINESS

Technology implies the know-how, design and intellectual input of doing things. It refers to the practical application of the principles of science to day-to-day industrial and commercial use. In the modern era, technology is changing very fast. Enterprises with superior technology often have an edge over their competitors.

Appropriate technology is the technology that best suits the resources and requirements of an enterprise. For example, the most modern sophisticated technology which is employed profitably in a giant steel mill may not be appropriate for a mini-steel plant. The choice of an appropriate or relevant technology is a very crucial decision as it is bound to have a long-term and lasting impact on the future of the enterprise. The choice of appropriate technology depends upon several factors:

(i) Nature of Product: For some products, *e.g.*, safety matches, detergents, etc., low technology may still be appropriate. On the other hand, for manufacture of high precision watches and advanced process control equipment high technology has to be employed. As new and more sophisticated products are being introduced, high technology is becoming necessary.

(ii) Volume of Production: Desired volume of output depends on the size of the market. In case of small scale firms, the market is often local and therefore low tech plants are sufficient. For example, a small steel rolling mill may use simple technology and yet be successful. But large firms producing large volumes need automatic plants.

(iii) Investment Capacity: High technology requires large capital investment which is often beyond the capacity of most small scale units. Therefore, small scale firms often depend on manual operations.

(iv) Manufacturing Strategy: Choice between general purpose and special purpose machines depends on the manufacturing strategy of the enterprise. Two small scale firms in the same industry may adopt different technology due to differences in their manufacturing strategy.

(v) Engineering and Technical Evaluation: Process requirements, design considerations and engineering feasibility influence the choice between high tech and low tech.

(vi) Economic Evaluation: While choosing appropriate technology considerations of cost per unit and return on investment are important. Risk associated with investment should also be considered.

(vii) Social Considerations: Environmental, legal and cultural aspects and employees' attitudes are significant. As the public is becoming more concerned about industrial pollution, need for anti-pollution technology is increasing.

Testing Facilities for Small-scale Industries

Small-scale units cannot afford to have all the testing facilities in their own premises. However, such testing facilities as are not within their means have to be obtained by them either from established testing houses or laboratories set up in various regions, including engineering colleges. The Government Test House at Alipore in Kolkata, the Indian Standards Institution's Laboratory at New Delhi and the national laboratories under Central Scientific and Industrial Research Organisations have played a significant role in offering testing facilities to small-scale units. The DCSSIO has also paid special attention to this aspect of the needs of small units; and through the industries in every State, common facility services and testing facilities are provided to small units for the following:

(i) Hardness testing and heat treatment;

(ii) Stand testing, carbon silver determinator and other testing equipment for metallurgical goods;

(iii) Tensile testing and other testing for metals;

(iv) Chemical laboratories for testing vegetable and essential oils fats, and soaps;

(v) Electrical testing laboratories.

Even though small-scale units have been getting a good deal of assistance for quality control, a great deal more needs to be done. There is need for a proper inventory of training, testing and other facilities available in the country and making these facilities known and available to small units. A "source-book" of this type would go a long way in making several facilities available to small units and help them to ensure quality control.

Conclusion

Technology has transformed the small and medium enterprises sector. Today, there is need for SMEs to look into technology transformation as a whole, to costs and increase efficiency.

SMEs in India, which constitute more than 80 per cent of the total number of industrial enterprises, are still in technological backwaters. They suffer from problems of suboptimal scales of operations and technological obsolescence.

"While most of the large companies have financial as well as technical capacity to identify technological sources and evaluate alternate technologies that would suit their requirements, unfortunately, this capacity is missing in the case of most SMEs," Anil Bhardwaj secretary general, Federation of Indian Small and Medium Enterprises (FISME)

In the given situation, SMEs primarily need access to new technologies. Apart from poor financial situations, low levels of R&D; poor adaptability to changing trade trends, non-availability of technically trained human resources, lack of management skills and access to technological information are some of the reasons that are blocking the growth of SMEs.

"Small and medium enterprises are the back-bone of India's economy. They have to now work hard to get out of this impending scenario. There has to be a major change in policy on how they are operating," says Kaushal Sampat, chief operating officer, Dun & Bradstreet India. "SMEs have to put in more effort on research and development and on ways to use technology at par with the international standards."

Recognising the importance of technology, the RBI's Working Group on Rehabilitation of potentially viable SME units while recommending to the government, says, "There is little availability of funds with the promoters for technological upgradation. Hence, the department of science and technology, which is actively working for development of new technologies for the small and large industry, may also consider adaptation of technology developed in other countries to the needs of the Indian SME sector for making the sector more cost effective and dovetailed to the requirements of the customer."

Further, the group adds, "It is necessary that all stakeholders extend financial support to engineering colleges/IITs for undertaking research for technological upgradation in micro, small and medium enterprises. In order to encourage R&D towards upgradation of technology for micro, small and medium enterprise units, the group pro-poses that Section 10(21) of the Income Tax Act may be amended to allow 150 per cent deduction for contribution made towards funding of R&D work in engineering institutes."

The government, says the group, should introduce industry-specific interest subsidy scheme for SMEs along the pattern of TUFS for technology upgradation and for setting up new units with latest technology. It has also asked the government to consider setting up more ITIs, tool room training centres, etc., for training the workforce on the latest technology, especially in the command areas of the user industry.

Technical assistance made available for the various technical institutions specially set up by the government cater to the varied needs of the small-scale sector set up in urban and metropolitan centres. However, Small-Scale Industrial units are at a disadvantage compared to large-scale industries. Mainly because of poor development and extension of research and development in this sector.

There is a need for rendering tool room assistance and design assistance to industries located in rural and semi-urban areas, so that they may also benefit from modern technology and improve their productivity; for no one can discount the fact that the availability of technical know-how accelerates the growth of small-scale industries.

THE TECHNOLOGY AUDIT

Just how do you use the latest business technology to reduce costs and lead times at your workplace? Take this audit to find out.

1. Do you keep abreast of the new technologies that could benefit your business? Yes No
2. Do you install systems that don't boost productivity, but increase expenses? Yes No
3. Do you believe in installing business-specific equipment, or think anything will do? Yes No
4. Do you agree that communicating through fax is not only economical, but also time-saving? Yes No
5. Do you think an automated phone attendant renders better service than a live operator? Yes No
6. Do you seek feedback about your telephone system to make it more efficient? Yes No
7. Do you examine the software applications before buying the hardware? Yes No

8. Do you believe in weighing the pros and cons before investing in pagers and cellphones? Yes No
9. Before installing new technology, do you discuss it with those who already have it? Yes No
10. Do you familiarise yourself with the technology that you wish to adopt? Yes No

The Scoring

Give yourself 5 points for every YES, and 0 for every NO.

TOTAL

The Rating

0 - 30	Business has been taken over by technology – and you've missed the bus.
40 - 70	You're almost there. Just take care of technology applications.
80 -100	You sure believe in making technology drive your business for you.

FACTORS IN COMPARATIVE TECHNOLOGY DEVELOPMENT

Factors	*Timing factors*		*Accumulation factors*	*Overall factors*	
	Time and environment	Social system and policy	Economic, industrial and technological traditions and bases	Natural and geographical conditiions	National character
Supply factors	Contemporary level of world technology development – innovations active or inactive? Competition with neighbouring countries. Competition with advanced countries.	Social system and government leadership – led by the government or the private sector? – Centralised or decentralised?	Level of indusrialisation – quality and quantity of technical manpower – development or ancillary industries and small firms. Presence of traditional technology relation to agriculture	Resource endownments Land area and climate – closed or open to sea? – transport conditions?	Values – labour: experience logic? – aesthetic senses – inward or outward lookiing? Behaviour principle? – group or individual?
Demand factors	Contemporary state, the world state of – growing or stagnating? International commercial relations	Linkages with market	Market size – income level and distribution population. Market characteristics? – quality of demand? – export oriented?	Markets – homogeneous or regional?	Characteristics of demand – conservative or progressive? – aesthetic sense.

ANNEXURE 1

PRODUCTION CENTRES

Production Centre, Ettamanur - 686 631 Kottayam Dist. Kerala.	General Engineering
Production Centre, Manjadi, Tiruvalla, Alleppey - 689 105 Kerala.	Production of Electric motors
Extension Centre Attingal - 695 104 Trivandrum Dist. Kerala.	Aluminium and Stainless Steel utensils
Extension Centre Muvattupuzha, Ernakularn Dist. Kerala.	Tin can making and tin printing

CENTRAL FOOTWEAR TRAINING CENTRES

Central Footwear Training Centre,
428, Kaushalpura, Agra Bypass Road,
Agra - 282 005.

Central Footwear Training Centre,
65/1, G.S.T. Road, Guindy,
Chennai - 600 032.

TOOL ROOM CENTRES

Central Tool Room & Training Centre, Bon Hoogly Industrial Area. Kolkata - 700 035	Tool Design and Toolmaking
Central Institute of Tool Design, Balanagar, Hyderabad - 500 037	
Central Tool Room A -5, Focal Point, Dhandari Kalan, Ludhiana - 141 010.	- do -
Central Institute of Hand Tools, G.T. Road, By Pass. Jalandhar - 144 044	Hand tool designing
Hand Tool Design Development & Training Centre, Industrial Area, Nagaur - 341 001 (Raj.)	- do -

PRODUCT & PROCESS DEVELOPMENT CENTRES

Product-cum-Process Development Centre, Kumhartoli, II Lane, Purulia Road, Ranchi-834 010.	Glass & Ceramics
Product-cum-Process Development Centre Sports Goods Complex, Delhi Road, Meerut.	Sports Goods
Product-cum-Process Development Centre, F-166, Kamla Nagar, Agra - 282 006.	Foundry and forging

TECHNOLOGY IN RURAL INDUSTRY

Industry	***Market***	***Technology***	***Location***	***Infrastructure and Institutional support required***
Agro-based Rice Hulling				
(*i*) Superior variety	Village/Town/City	Power operated dehusker	Central village/town	Power, transportation facility, credit
(*ii*) Coarse variety	Village/Haat	Hand operated dehuskar	Village	–
Dal Mill	Town/City/Haat/ Village	Dall Milling	Central village/town	Power, transportation facility, credit
Gur/Khandsari	Village/Haat/Town/ City	Gur-pan etc.	Village	Transport, credit
Sugar Factory	Town/Countrywide market	Sugar machinery	Town	Power, transportation facility, credit
Cotton Ginning and Pressing	Town/City	Ginning and pressing machinery	Central Village/town	-do-
Weaving	Village/Haat/Town/ City	Handloom, powerloom	Village	Yarn supply, marketing, credit
Oil Pressing	-do-	Power/bullock operated village ghani	Village	–
Solvent Extraction	Town/City	Solvent extraction process	Town	Power, transportation facility, credit.
Soap	Village/Town/City	Simple technique	Town	-do-
Forest-based				
Saw mills	Village/Town	Bandsaw machine	Central village/ Town	Power, transportation, credit
Furniture	Village/Haat/Town	Skill-based	Village/Town	Marketing assistance, transportation credit

Bidi-making	-do-	-do-	Village	–
Artistic Wood Work	Town/City/abroad	-do-	Village/Town	Marketing supply, marketing assistance, credit
Mineral-based				
(*i*) Black Smithy	Village/Haat/Town	Crude technique	-do-	–
(*ii*) Copper Smithy	Village/Haat/Town	-do-	-do-	–
(*iii*) Artistic Metal Ware	Town/City/Abroad	Skilled based	Village/Town	Metal supply, marketing assistance, credit
Non-metallic				
(*i*) Pottery/Brick making	Village/Haat/Town	Simple technique	-do-	–
(*ii*) Ceramic	Town/City	Sophisticated processing – skill based	-do-	Process-training, design-research, marketing assistance, credit.
Animal Products				
(*i*) Tanning	Village/Haat	Simple techniques	-do-	–
(*ii*) Leather Products/ Footwear	Town	Simple techniques	-do-	Design-research, marketiing assistance, credit.

CORE COMPETENCE

"Core groups are not inherently bad or good; they are simply part of the nature of organisational systems. Without them, it would be impossible for organisations to exist, simply because the complexity of most organisational environments would be too great to manage effectively."

— Art Kleiner, Organisational Learning Consultant

27

Marketing Assistance

▸▸ Introduction

Laura Parkin
National
Entrepreneurship
Network

Over the years, India has worked on beneficial strategies and incorporated technology resulting in the emergence of efficient marketing organisations and distribution centres, thus seeing a shift from the inadequacy of these firms. However, this is just a beginning of designing the products after a study of customer requirements. Very few, so-called marketing organisations possessed adequate resources to spend on advertising and so stimulate interest of prospective customers. In a developing country, its economy can be greatly expanded, improved and diversified by efficient marketing organisation, manned by expert personnel. Small industries need them more. If their share in domestic, government and foreign markets is to be secured and expanded, the small entrepreneur should develop a new attitude and assist in the process of building up powerful and prosperous marketing organisations.

APPLYING THE MARKETING CONCEPT

The marketing concept is applicable to all business organisations irrespective of size or nature of the goods and services marketed. Difference in the types of goods supplied in the size and characteristics of the consumer or user markets for the various classes of goods, in the purposes for which they are acquired and in the methods by which they are distributed, do not invalidate the universal applicability of the marketing concept to business.

As between large and small firms, and as between producers of consumer goods and producers of industrial goods, there may be differences in the permissible scale of marketing effort and in the specific types of marketing techniques that are appropriate to the particular industry or market. A far more fundamental difference, irrespective of size or type of business, is the attitude of management. The following chart attempts to highlight some of the major differences that might be expected to be reflected in business operations according to whether the management ends to think in terms of production or in terms of marketing.

BASIC DIFFERENCES BETWEEN PRODUCTION-ORIENTED AND MARKETING-ORIENTED ORANISATION

F. F. Mayseer, Modern Marketing

Business Functions or Activity	***Company Perspective***	
	Production	***Marketing***
Top Management	Technological considerations predominate. Production and engineering personnel in highest level executive positions.	Customer considerations paramount. Marketing personnel in highest level executive positions.
Objectives	Internal influences predominate. Business objective is to match total company resources against production on technical efficiency and methods be known for technical or production and know-how.	External market influences predominate. Business objective is to match total company. resources against market requirements and opportunities. More emphasis on market strategy and planning. Want to be regarded as style and market leader.
Manufacturing	Production less flexible. The company sells what can be made.	Flexibility in production so as to match product to sales opportunities. The company manufactures what can be profitably sold.
Marketing	Aims to fulfil existing needs and develop workable products to meet these needs. Company's future bound up with markets already supplied and products already in existence. Marketing function not considered to be as valuable as manufacturing, engineering or finance.	Seeks to create markets and develop saleable products. Company's future bound up with markets yet to be identified and developed, and with products not yet in existence. Marketing considered to be coordination with manufacturing, finance and other major business functions.
Research	Leads in technical and scientific research. Marketing intelligence system relatively undeveloped.	Leads in analytical and marketing research. Market intelligence system well developed.

Product Planning	Based on technical research, suggestion for new or improved products system from functional performance and application are prime considerations. Engineering consideration tends to predominate. Laboratory testing more prominent than sales or market. Packaging viewed as a shipping and protective device. Chief concern in engineering, materials handling and packaging machinery.	Based on market research. Suggestions for new or improved products stem from research into customer needs. Performance and applications are prime considerations regarded to be almost as important. Sales and market testing are an integral part of planning. Packaging viewed as a sales tool in terms of user convenience and advertising and promotional effectiveness.
Sales Organisation	Salesman regarded as an order-getter for the factory. Salesman lacks the professional status of the engineer, chemist, lawyer or accountant. Less likely to be promoted to the top management. He lacks formal training, tends to get left to his own devices as the man 'out there.' Motivation of the salesman minimal.	Salesman regarded as an order-maker who keeps the factory running and provides employment to production workers. He is accorded high status in the company and more likely to be promoted to top management positions. Salesman given formal and continuous internal and on-the-job training. Motivation of sales organisation give high priority. Chief sales executive regarded as part of the management team.
Advertising and promotion	Emphasis on cost rather than on the value of this contribution to the total selling effort. Advertising and promotion regarded as an extra cost, not a basis cost like machines, raw materials, research laboratories etc. Not regarded as one of the skills required to run a modern business successfully. Advertising and promotion not looked upon as an important source of competitive differential advantage.	Advertising and promotion is an integral part of the company's marketing effort and a basic cost. Outstanding advertising and promotion considered to be as equally important to the successful running of a business as outstanding manufacturing technique, technical research ability or financial and legal skills. Advertising and promotion regarded as a potential source of competitive differential advantage particularly when the differences in own and competitive products become less and less distinguishable.

Management: An Integrated Approach, McGraw Hill Book Co. Inc., 1961, pp. 10-11. The data above has been adapted from the author's original.

▸▸ Institutional Support

The success of marketing depends solely on well established institutional set-ups and timely assistance without any hassels. Although the institutional set up for marketing has been broad-based, it is biased towards international marketing in preference to internal markets. Another feature is that a majority of these institutions are in the public sector.

With a view to assisting small-scale industries, the government and other agencies have reserved certain items to be purchased from them. The National Small Industries Corporation and State Small Industries Corporations assist small-scale industries in selling their products to the Government.

The Khadi and Village Industries Commission and the Handicrafts and Handlooms have their own distribution agents and their own marketing arrangements.

Moreover, the government has established trade centres to cater to the marketing needs of the small-scale industries sector. The NSIC and the STC help this sector to export its products.

Let us discuss in detail the methods of the marketing of the products of the small-scale industries sector:

➧ Central Government Stores Purchase Programme

The Central Government Stores Purchase Programme provides an outlet for the products of industrial units in the country. This programme was then operated by the Director-General of Supplies and Disposals, Government of India. Under the programme, the DGS & D is responsible for arranging the purchase and delivery of all the stores required by the Central Government, certain specified items from the scope of this department. It also purchases the stores needed by State Government, public sector organisations and other government and semi-government bodies.

The two major recommendations of the Stores Purchase Committee set up under the chairmanship of the Deputy Minister of Works, Housing and Supply, and accepted by the Government of India relating to the small-scale sector were:

(i) Price preference to products of cottage and small-scale industries, including reservation of certain items of stores for purchase only from this sector; and

(ii) Greater facilities for the registration of cottage and small industries.

The objective was to encourage the production and utilisation of industrial products manufactured by the small-scale sector by State purchases. To achieve this objective, the items of Government purchases have been divided into the following four groups by the DGS & D:

Group I: Items which are of no interest to small-scale units and can be procured only from the large-scale sector.

Group II: Items which, by their very nature, require large-scale firms as prime contractors but permit substantial scope to purchase components and parts from small-scale units.

Group III: Residuary items which both small-scale as well as large-scale firms can supply. Tenders for items falling under the groups are invited from all parties, including small-scale industries.

Group IV: Items which are reserved for exclusive procurement from small-scale units. The present list consists of 379 items.

➧ Special Facility for Small-scale Sector

The present policy offers the following special facilities to small-scale units:

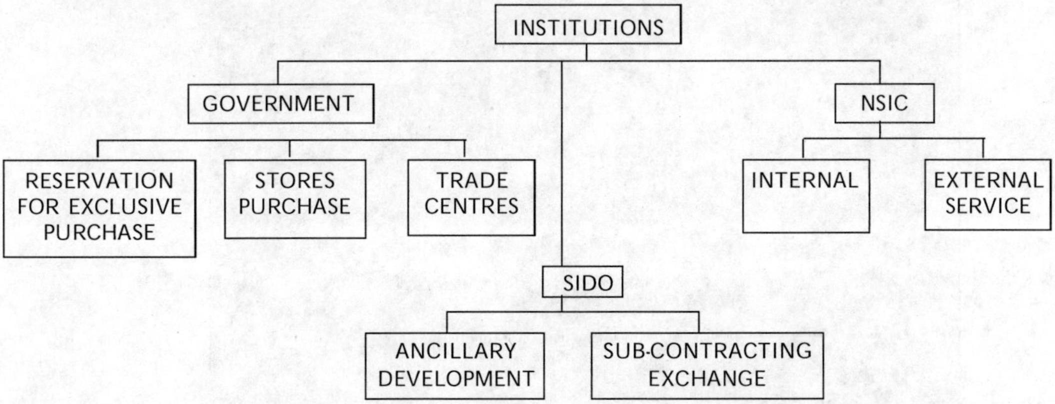

Fig. 1 Institutional Market Support to Small-scale Sector

(i) Application forms for initial registration and renewal are issued free of charge;

(ii) No registration fee is charged;

(iii) Free tender forms are supplied;

(iv) Tenders are accepted without a security deposits from those small-scale units which are registered with the NSIC and whose competency is certified by the Council;

(v) In certain cases, purchase of items in group III is also confined to small-scale industries;

(vi) Where basic considerations like quality and delivery conditions are comparable, or where small-scale industries have an advantage over large-scale industries, or where the former have established themselves as suppliers to the Government on competitive terms, the products of small-scale industries are given preference over products of other manufacturers; and

(vii) In the case of Group III items, which are purchased from both large-scale and small-scale units, the small-scale units are accorded suitable and reasonable price preference up to a maximum of 15%. The actual quantum of price preference is decided in each case on merit.

This price preference is not, however, granted automatically and is subject to certain conditions. The basic consideration is conformity to specification, quality, delivery, capacity, etc.

Price preference is not granted in the following cases:

(a) Where the items are reserved for exclusive purchase from small-scale units;

(b) Where competition against tender enquiries exists amongst the small-scale units alone; and

(c) Where tenders are received from both small-scale units and large-scale units and the lowest offers are from small-scale units and their capacity is more than sufficient to meet the demand.

The offers received from middlemen for the products of small-scale industries are treated as offers from small-scale units for the purpose of price preference. All small-scale units, whether registered with the DGS & D, the NSIC or the Directors of Industries are eligible for price preference.

The sub-committee appointed in 1975 under the chairmanship of the DC (SSI) by the High Power Committee had made recommendations concerning the following aspects:

(i) Categorisation and review of items under groups (referred to above);

(ii) Uniform purchase and price preference to be adopted by all Central and State Government Departments for small-scale units;

(iii) Increased association of DCSSI with decisions affecting small industries;

(iv) Sub-contracting of orders to small-scale units;

(v) Registration procedure;

(vi) Wider circulation of tenders among small-scale units;

(vii) Monitoring of small-scale units' performance by the NSIC;

(viii) Mandatory registration with the NSIC of the small-scale units interested in the Government Purchase Programme;

(ix) Statistics of purchases for small-scale industries; and

(x) Regional imbalance in procurement from this centre.

Marketing Services Offered by SIDO

The organisation provided marketing assistance to small-scale units by providing promoting ancillarisation, marketing intelligence and information, establishing trade centres, encouraging small entrepreneurs to participate in the purchase programmes of the Central and State Governments, setting up sub-contracting exchanges, organising exhibitions, seminars and training programmes in marketing and publishing information booklets etc.

Ancillary Development

One of the important activities undertaken by the SIDO is the promotion of ancillary industries in order to help in the marketing of the products of the small-scale sector in collaboration with Bureau of Public Enterprises (BPE) and other Central Government agencies.

The Small Industries Services Institutes are actively engaged in identifying and promoting new items for ancillarisation, besides rendering technical and managerial assistance to the existing ancillaries. Region-wise seminars, exhibitions and buyer-seller meetings are arranged to promote mutually beneficial relationship between small and large industries through ancillarisation.

Sub-Contracting Exchange

With a view to providing effective support to small-scale units in securing sub-contracting jobs from large and medium undertakings in the country, the SIDO established 16 sub-contracting exchanges at the SISIs. The main functions of these sub-contracting exchanges are:

- To invite small-scale units to register with the exchange their spare capacity on specific machines;
- To approach large industries with a view to listing out items which may be manufactured in small-scale units;
- To render technical assistance to small-scale units in creating new capacity for specific processes or for the manufacture of items/stores which are required by large-scale undertakings; and

– To furnish information on firms from whom enquiries can either secure orders to meet their requirements or on sub-contract their requirements.

The 16 sub-contracting exchange (SCEs) established in the SISIs provide a suitable linkage between large industries and small-scale feeder units to maintain up-to-date information on spare capacities available within the small-scale units and the requirements of large industries.

The Standing Committee on Ancillary Development appointed by the Small-Scale Industries Advisory Board held sittings in all the regions and gathered information from such agencies as the Association of Industries, private institutions (private/public are undertakings), etc., and their recommendations on ancillary development are under preparation. The committee was also furnished with a full techno-economic analysis of all the industries. Suitable recommendations on regular programmes, licensing and direct incentive systems have been made.

MARKETING

Marketing is one of the major stumbling blocks for small-scale industries. The many problems which they face in marketing their products are enumerated below:

(*i*) Lack of standardization;

(*ii*) Poor designing;

(*iii*) Poor quality;

(*iv*) Lack of quality control;

(*v*) Lack of precision;

(*vi*) Poor finish;

(*vii*) Poor bargaining power;

(*viii*) Lack of service after sales;

(*ix*) Scale of production;

(*x*) Brand preferences;

(*xi*) Distribution contacts;

(*xii*) Lack of knowledge of marketing;

(*xiii*) Competition;

(*xiv*) Ignorance and Potential markets;

(*xv*) Unfamiliarity with export activities – procedures and market know-how;

(*xvi*) Financial weakness; Limited resources;

(*xvii*) Limited local market; Heavy dependence on middlemen;

(*xviii*) Lack of advertisement in building, a brand image;

(*xix*) Lack of testing equipment;

(*xx*) Absence of a marketing strategy;

(*xxi*) Ill-equipped marketing organisation;

(*xxii*) Lack of liaison activity;

(*xxiii*) Delayed payments; and

(*xxiv*) Weak bargaining position.

As mentioned earlier, because of his weak financial base, a small industrialist cannot afford to spend as heavily as a large unit does on marketing his products. A rare exception is the pharmaceutical industry, in which the gap between the manufacturing cost and the selling price is very large. This is a special situation, in which marketing techniques are different, and therefore the cost of marketing is very high, particularly the marketing cost of those drugs for which there is stiff competition. The small industrialists in this line have to follow this trend in order to survive.

In the absence of a marketing channel of their own, many small units sell their products to large selling houses. Voltas, for instance, markets a number of products produced by small units. Similarly, the Bata Shoe Company sells the shoes manufactured by the small sector. As a result, small units invariably gets a raw deal. The large companies make handsome profits from marketing the products of small units by charging a much higher price from the consumer. In this respect, there is a need for a large number of marketing consortia, whose primary responsibility will be to assist small units.

Government Purchase Schemes: NSIC

In 1956, the small-scale industry had not grown sufficiently in the technology of manufacturing processes and skills to be able to produce goods according to the rigid specifications of the Government Purchasing Agency. A scheme was, therefore, evolved, according to which the National Small Industries Corporation would take prime contracts from the Purchasing Agencies and get such contracts executed by farming them out to a number of small-scale units scattered all over the country.

This arrangement for the pre-emption of the orders of the corporation was soon stalled by a basic problem. Some small units would quote through the Corporation and others directly; as a result, the Corporation inadvertently became the sponsor of one set of the small units against another when, constitutionally, it was to serve them all equally well. Besides, there were the operational problems of co-ordinating the production of units located in different parts of a vast country. A fresh thinking was, therefore, called for on the issues involved. The scheme was re oriented. The corporation now acts as a liaison agency to enable small-scale units to secure a larger share of government business. The salient features of the scheme are:

(*a*) Instead of purchasing tender sets from the DGS & D, the small units enlisted with the corporation automatically get them, free of cost, from it and its branches;

(*b*) After verifying the technical competence of the small units, the corporation issues certificates of competency. The units, subsequently do not have to pay any security deposits to Government Purchasing Agencies;

(*c*) Provided that the specifications and quality are acceptable, the small units get a price preference up to 15% over the quotations of large-scale units, depending on the merits of each case;

(*d*) Whenever the small units feel that injustice has been done to them, the NSIC takes up their cases with the DGS & D in order to find out the reason for the non-placement of contracts with these units and tries to redress their grievances wherever feasible or possible;

(*e*) As a result of the efforts of the NSIC, another big purchase department, the Ministry of Defence, has come in line with the DGS & D, and has now started exempting small units from the payment of security deposits.

In addition, the following facilities are available to the small scale units registered with NSIC under the Single Point Registration Scheme under the Government Store Purchase Programme.

1. Issue of tender sets free of cost;
2. Exemption from payment of Earnest money;
3. Waiver of Security Deposit into the monetary limit for which the unit is registered;
4. Price preference upto 15% over the large scale unit.

Internal Marketing

In this field, the NSIC had undertaken the marketing of some products – tapioca starch, handmade paper and hosiery items. By organising and co-ordinating the productive efforts of a consortium of hosiery manufacturers, the sale of ISI-marked hosiery products has been encouraged. Under its future programme, the NSIC intends:

(a) To cover domestic appliances, hand tools, malleable castings, light engineering products, soap;

(b) To provide marketing intelligence within the country and abroad for the benefit of the small-scale sector;

(c) To assist small-scale units in their survey of the markets and marketing research;

(d) To provide the necessary technological inputs in developing and standardising products in the small-scale sector;

(e) To establish raw material banks to meet the requirements of the small-scale sector in ferrous and non-ferrous raw materials.

Trade Centres

The Government of India has established trade centres to cater to the marketing needs of units in the small-scale sector.

These trade centres provide an integrated marketing system for small industries; they collect and disseminate information relating to all types of small-scale industries in the region, giving full details of products, capacities and prices. They provide a focal point for buyers and sellers who have the required supplementary service for trade centres and transactions, between small-scale industries and the buyers of their products, including large-scale manufacturers, importers and merchant exporters, export houses, purchasing organisations and consumers in general. A library function as an agency for contracts between small-scale units and prospective buyers in the country and abroad. Moreover, they assist the small units in the maintenance of quality control and the introduction of standardisation. About 50% of the total recurring and non-recurring expenditure on equipment, stores, library and documentation, etc., on these centres was met by the Central Government (excluding the cost of land and buildings), subject to a maximum limit of Rs. 200,000 per year for a period of five years.

The need for setting up trade centers for small-scale industries was keenly felt of their phenomenal growth and because of the fact that they manufactured a wide range of products – from simple consumer goods to capital goods and other sophisticated items, such as machine tools, television sets, scientific equipment, automobile ancillaries, drugs and pharmaceuticals, etc. But if the small-scale sector is very important, it is also very vulnerable, so far as its marketing capacity is concerned. It is essential, therefore, that the products of small units should become competitive and should be able to contribute in a large measure to the national industrial output.

Small-scale industrialists cannot organise sales and market promotion activities on their own; they cannot display their products; they cannot spend much on advertising and publicity, market research etc. because their resources are limited and they are handicapped in their exports know-how and trade contacts. Buyers in India and abroad, on the other hand, are not aware of the quality, specifications and range of the products manufactured by the small-scale industry. The setting-up of trade centres in different parts of the country has therefore considerably filled up the information and communication gap between small manufacturers, consumers and buyers.

Exports

Responding to the widespread belief that the small industrial sector has not been marking a proportional contribution to the overall export earning of the country, the NSIC has set up an Export Department to encourage the export of small industry products. Because of their small size and lack of resources and effort the small industrialists do not have an easy access to world markets. Very often, they are unable to infuse confidence in foreign buyers. The NSIC aims at filling this need by functioning as an export house. Following the latest in marketing concepts, the corporation identifies the demand abroad for labour intensive products. It collects intelligence about specifications, prices etc. It locates small industries in the countries with the required production facilities and helps such units to make dyes and tools, counter samples, small-units, and takes the entire responsibility for the execution of the contract. It helps small industry products such as hand tools, fasteners, casting etc., from some of the most sophisticated markets in the world – from the US, West Germany and Canada.

FUNDAMENTALS FOR TARGETING THE GLOBAL MARKET

Any SME planning to enter the markets abroad must decide upon an executable strategy to gain entry into that market.

Some of the factors that have to be kept in mind include:

- Market Size
- Growth Potential
- Regulatory Framework
- Competitors
- Risks

An SME could also look to create alliances or JVs with existing players in that country for an easier market entry.

Payment Options

Even after considering the above-mentioned factors, there is always the risk of default on payments, both to the buyer as well as the seller in the import/export business. However, there are a few options SMEs can look at to minimise such risks and ensure faster payments. Some of the options are:

- **Advanced Payment**

  The buyer makes the necessary payments before the goods are shipped.

- **Documentary Collections**

  The exporting side sends documents to its bank with instructions to remit them to the importing side under predetermined terms and conditions.

- **Documentary Credit**

  A contractual relationship is established between the buyer and seller and the bank undertakes responsibility of payment.

- **Open Accounts**

  Both parties agree that the buyer will make the required payments at the end of a period that has been agreed upon mutually.

Export Assistance

The government has formulated policies to provide incentives to small-scale exporters allowing them to maximise their earnings from export. Some of these incentives include refund of duties paid on the raw material used in export production by a system of Duty-Draw-Back, Pre and Post Shipment Credit to the exporters at concessional rate of interest, interest subvention etc.

A Market Development Assistance Scheme is currently operated by the Ministry of Commerce with a view to encourage exporters (including MSME exporters) to access and develop overseas markets. The scheme offers funding for participation in international fairs, study tours abroad, trade delegations, publicity, etc.

Marketing Development Assistance (MDA)

To facilitate various measures being undertaken to stimulate and diversify the country's export trade, Marketing Development Assistance (MDA) Scheme is under operation in the Department of Commerce. The Scheme supports the following activities:

- Assist individual exporters for export promotion activities abroad.
- Assist Export Promotion Councils (EPCs) to undertake export promotion activities for their product(s) and commodities.
- Assist approved organisations/trade bodies in undertaking limited exclusive non-recurring innovative activities connected with export promotion efforts for their members.
- Assist Focus Area export promotion programmes in specific regions abroad like Focus LAC, Focus Africa, Focus CIS and ASEAN+2 programmes.
- Promote residual essential activities connected with marketing promotion efforts abroad.

Eligible Agencies

- Recognised Export Promotion Councils (EPCs)
- Exporting companies with an f.o.b. value of exports of upto Rs. 15.00 crore in the preceding year
- Export Promotion Agencies like ITPO, FIEO, KVIC

Details about outlays during 2002-2009 and actual expenditure are given below:

(Rs. Lakh)

Year	***Budget***	***Actual***
2002-03	4500.00	4484.91
2003-04	5200.00	5200.00
2004-05	5500.00	5500.00
2005-06	5500.00	3800.00
2006-07	5225.00	5225.00
2007-08	5225.00	5225.00
2008-09	5225.00	5225.00

Source: Department of Commerce.

➧ Export Incentives

The Government has offered special incentives to encourage export of the products of the small-scale sector. The minimum export performance limits for the grant of export house certificates have been lowered for small-scale manufacturers and their consortiums. The Government has also made arrangements to educate the small-scale units in the export prospects of different products abroad, by collecting information from various sources and disseminating it among them. Some of the important sources of information are the reports prepared by the Trade Development Authority, the Indian Institute of Foreign Trade, the Export Promotion Councils and the Directorate General of Commercial Intelligence Statistics. Periodical reports from Indian missions abroad are consulted for the purpose of identifying export opportunities for small-scale industries or taking note of the developments affecting such opportunities in foreign countries.

➧ Export Promotion Councils (EPCs)

There are at present eleven Export Promotion Councils in India. The EPCs perform both advisory and executive functions.

➧ Indian Institute of Foreign Trade (IIFT)

The IIFT is engaged in the following activities:

(i) Training of personnel in modern techniques of international trade;

(ii) Organisation of research, area surveys, commodity surveys, market surveys; and

(iii) Dissemination of information arising from its activities relating to research and market studies.

➧ Commodity Boards

The five statutory Commodity Boards for Rubber, Coffee, Tea, Tobacco and Spices are responsible for production, development and export.

➧ Export Inspection Council (EIC)

The EIC, a statutory body, is responsible for the enforcement of quality control and Pre-shipment inspection of various exportable commodities.

➧ Indian Institute of Packaging (IIP)

The main aims of the Institute (IIP) are to undertake research into raw materials for the packaging industry, to develop new types of packaging for export products, to organise programmes on packaging technology and to stimulate consciousness of the need for good packaging.

India Trade Promotion Organisation (ITPO). The ITPO has come into effect from January 1, 1992 with the main objective of promoting exports and imports and upgradation of technology, through the medium of fairs to be held in India and abroad, to undertake publicity through the print and electronic media, to assist Indian companies in product development, to organise export development programmes, buyer-seller meets, contact promotion programmes and integrated marketing programmes.

➧ Export Credit Guarantee Corporation of India Ltd.

The Prime objective of ECGC is to support the country's export by providing a range of insurance covers to the Indian exporters against the risk of non-realisation of export proceeds due to political or commercial reasons and guarantees to financial institutions to facilitate grant of credit facilities to exporters on a liberal basis.

⏩ Export Processing Zones

The Export Processing Zones set up as enclaves, separated from the Domestic Tariff area by fiscal barriers, are intended to provide an internationally competitive duty free environment for export production, at low cost. This enables the products of EPZs to be competitive, both quality-wise and price-wise, in the international market. India has seven Export Processing Zones at Kandla (Gujarat), Santacruz (Mumbai), Falta (West Bengal), Noida (UP), Cochin (Kerala), Chennai (Tamil Nadu) and Visakhapatnam (Andhra Pradesh). The one at Visakhapatnam (Andhra Pradesh) has become operational.

The Santacruz Electronics Export Processing Zone (SEEPZ) is meant exclusively for export of electronics and gem and jewellery items whereas the other zones are multiproduct Zones.

⏩ Export Oriented Units

The EOU Scheme introduced in early 1981, is complementary to the EPZ scheme. It adopts the same production regime but offers a wide option in locations with reference to factors like source of raw materials, ports of export, hinterland facilities, availability of technological skills, existence of an industrial base and the need for a larger area of land for the project. As on 31.3.95, there were 2,944 valid approved units out of which 710 were in operation under the EOU Scheme.

At present 502 units are in operation in the Export Processing Zones.

⏩ Export Promotion Industrial Park Scheme (EPIP)

A centrally sponsored "Export Promotion Industrial Park" (EPIP) Scheme has been introduced in August 1994 with a view to involving the State Governments in the creation of infrastructural facilities for export-oriented production. The scheme provides that 75% of the capital expenditure incurred towards creation of such facilities, ordinarily limited to Rs. 10 crores in each case, will be met from a central grant to the State Governments. In addition a maintenance grant equivalent to 2% of export turnover of each unit established therein will also be made available to State Governments for a period of 5 years from the date of commercial production of that unit.

The Central Govt. have so far approved 18 proposals for establishments of EPIPs in the states of Punjab, Haryana, Himachal Pradesh, Rajasthan, Karnataka, Kerala, Maharashtra, Tamil Nadu, Andhra Pradesh, Uttar Pradesh, Gujarat, Bihar, Jammu & Kashmir, Assam, Madhya Pradesh, West Bengal, Orissa and Meghalaya.

⏩ Export Houses, Trading Houses and Star Trading Houses

The objective of the Scheme of Export Houses, Trading Houses and Star Trading Houses is to give recognition to the established exporters and large Export Houses to build up the marketing infrastructure and expertise required for export promotion. The registered exporters having a record of export performance over a number of years are granted the status of Export/Trading Houses/Star Trading Houses/Super star Trading Houses subject to the fulfilment of minimum annual average export performance in terms of FOB value or net foreign exchange earnings on physical exports prescribed in the EXIM Policy.

The Export Houses, Trading Houses, Star Trading Houses and Super Star Trading Houses Scheme allows the Registered Exporters certain additional benefits available to them under the policy.

⏩ Jute Corporation of India

The Jute Corporation was established on 2nd April, 1971 as a wholly owned limited company of the Government of India. The main functions of the corporation are:

(i) Export and import of raw jute;

(ii) Internal marketing of jute; and

(iii) Undertaking measures for the export promotion of jute goods.

The objectives of the JCI are to ensure the minimum prices of raw jute; to conduct commercial operations in a judicious manner; to import and export jute fibre as authorised by the Government; to process raw jute and export jute goods; and to undertake export promotion measures for jute goods. It also aims at maintaining stability of jute production and prices.

State Trading Corporation of India (STC)

The State Trading Corporation of India was set up in May 1956 as an autonomous corporation to implement the Government's policies in regard to the promotion and diversification of foreign trade. The principle objectives of the STC are:

(i) To explore new markets for existing as well as new products;

(ii) To diversify and consequently increase India's export trade; and

(iii) To promote long-term export operations and the sale of "difficult-to-sell items."

The Corporation's major export items are semi-processed leather, castor oil, art silk fabrics, rice, jute goods, etc. With the pace of canalisation of India's foreign trade gathering momentum, the share of the STC in India's trade has increased substantially in recent years.

The STC provides a package of services to this sector with a view to encouraging it to produce more and market its products in foreign countries. These services include the supply of raw materials service, and warehousing, exporting, marketing and shipping facilities.

The Corporation deals in agricultural products, chemicals and fats, leather goods, textiles, imported cars and marketing. It has setup an Industrial Raw Materials Assistance Division to make off-the-shelf deliveries of imported raw materials to manufacturers against import licences.

In addition, the STC has set up four subsidiaries, namely: *(a)* The Projects and Equipment Corporations of India (PEC); *(b)* Handicrafts and Handlooms Exports Corporation of India; *(c)* The Cashew Corporations of India Ltd.; and *(d)* The State Chemicals and Pharmaceuticals Corporation Ltd. The subsidiaries assist the parent Corporation in furthering the main objectives of export promotion.

***(a)* The Projects and Equipment Corporations of India (PEC):** The PEC was formed on 21st April, 1971, and has taken over the Railway Equipment and Engineering Divisions from the STC.

This corporation was formed to promote more intensively the export of non-traditional sophisticated engineering and railway equipment. In addition to this, it specialises in large-scale joint ventures and turnkey projects in the railways, public utilities and in complete industrial plants and projects. In view of the promising turnkey project opportunities in most developing countries, the corporation is expected to play a very important role in developing the exports of Indian engineering goods and technical now-how on a continuing basis.

The PEC plans to concentrate on undertaking turnkey projects and large-scale ventures. These vary from the construction of new railway lines or the putting up of complete industrial plants on an integrated basis, from the initial project report stage to that of final commissioning.

***(b)* Handicrafts and Handloom Exports Corporation of India:** The HHEC came into existence in October 1962 as a subsidiary of the State Trading Corporation, with the merger of the Indian Handicrafts Development Corporation (set up in 1958) and the Handloom Export Organisation, a department of the STC. The main objective of the corporation is to develop new markets and expand traditional ones, thus supplementing and aiding the existing private sector trade in handicrafts and handlooms.

With a view to projecting the image of Indian handicrafts and handlooms in international markets, the corporation has opened showrooms known as "Sona of India" in New York, Tokyo, Paris and Nairobi, and also at the Akbar Hotel in New Delhi. A carpet warehousing depot was set up in Hamburg in July 1965.

The HHEC undertakes the export of handicrafts, handlooms, ready-to-wear garments and canalised export of woolen knit-wear. Product development is one of the main activities of the HHEC. In its attempts to increase overseas sales of its products, it has secured the help of many popular designers in different countries – France, Japan, Italy and the U.K.

The HHEC also conducts consumer preference surveys abroad and introduces new products which project the excellent craftsmanship of India, helps the trade by means of advice and market exposure: participates in trade fairs and exhibitions abroad; and encourages delegates from abroad to visit India, study the products and offer valuable suggestions for improvement.

***(c)* Cashew Corporation of India:** The Government of India set up the Cashew Corporation of India (CCI) on 19th August 1970 as a wholly-owned subsidiary of the STC to stabilise the import trade in raw cashew. The import of raw cashew, handled under the Open General Licence (OGL), was canalised through the Cashew Corporation with effect from 1st September 1970. The CCI has floated a joint stock company to raise cashew plantations.

⏩ The Minerals and Metals Trading Corporations of India (MMTC)

The Minerals and Metals Trading Corporation of India was established by the Government of India on 1st October, 1963. The central aim of the corporation is to broaden and enlarge the scope of exports of Indian minerals and ores and to arrange for the import of essential raw materials for distribution to industrial units in the country. Iron ore, fifth largest foreign exchange earner of the country, is the principal item of the export handled by the MTC. The other items of export handled by it are manganese ore, ferro-manganese, coal, silimanite, ferro-silicon and ferro-chrome.

Besides Japan, which still accounts for more than 65 per cent of MMTC's exports, several other markets have been cultivated. Notable among these are South Korea, Taiwan, Romania, Czechoslovakia, Poland, Hungary, Yugoslavia, West Germany and the Netherlands. It has sought to secure continuous export outlets by entering into long-term contracts with importing countries.

⏩ The Trading Corporation of India Ltd. (TTCI)

Tea Trading Corporation of India was established in 1971 to create a stable export market for Indian tea particularly in the value added forms, which include packet tea, tea bag, instant tea, etc. Other activities of this Corporation include marketing of tea for domestic consumption, management of tea establishment of other facilities beneficial to the tea industry. TTCI has been a subsidiary company of the State Trading Corporation of India since January, 1986, TTCC owns five gardens, namely, Pathini Tea Estate in Assam and Pashok, Looksan, Vah-Tukvar and Potong in West Bengal.

⏩ The Spices Trading Corporation Limited (STCL)

Spices Trading Corporation Limited (formerly known as Cardamom Trading Corporation Limited) was established in October 1982 and commenced its trading activities in September, 1983. The Corporation was set up to carry on domestic and international trade in spices and their products. The Memorandum of Association permits the Corporation to also carry on business as a dealer/exporter of other agricultural commodities and related products. The Corporation diversified its trading to include agricultural inputs such as fertilizers, pesticides and sprayers.

The authorised Share Capital of the Corporation is Rs. 5 crores while the paid up Share Capital is Rs. 1.50 crores. For its commercial activities, the Corporation mainly depends on borrowings from Banks.

Small-scale industries have made a significant contribution not only by increasing industrial production but also to non-traditional exports from the country. Programmes for promoting the export capabilities of small-scale units have been further intensified. Export market training courses and seminars have been held in different parts of the country to create the necessary awareness and motivation among the small-scale units engaged in export business.

Promotional Activities

The Small Industries Development Organisation (SIDO), through its network of Small Industries Service Institutes and Extension Centres, provides techno-managerial assistance and extension services for promotion of the exports of the products of these industries. The SIDO intensified its activities relating to the dissemination of information on foreign markets to export-worthy small-scale units; provided on consultancy services in all matters of export procedure to facilitate the disposal of replenishment, claims, drawbacks and other incentives; on export prices; on the identification of small-scale units already possessing the necessary equipment and skills to undertake the production of items having an export potential; on the organisation of training programmes on export marketing; and on the maintenance of liaison with the concerned agencies. A large number of meetings, seminars and open-house discussions on export promotion were organised in collaboration with the concerned promotional agencies and associations of industries. Training programmes on export packaging, too, were organised by some of the Small Industries Service Institutes in collaboration with the Indian Institute of Packaging.

A quarterly 'Small Industry Export Bulletin', which covers the important areas of interest to exporters, continued to be brought out by the SIDO. It contains useful information on export marketing, Government policy announcements and the procedures relevant to small industry exports, abstracts of market/commodity reports prepared by such professional agencies as the Indian Institute of Foreign Trade and Trade Development Authority, special features on export-oriented industries, markets and facilities, etc. The Export Promotion Division has started another feature in the form of Trade Enquiry Service Bulletin, in which the names and addresses of overseas buyers, importers and importing organisations are provided. As a result of these efforts, the communications are provided. As a result of these efforts, the communication and information gap between the small-scale manufacturers/ exporters and overseas markets will be partially bridged.

SIDO also dealt with the special problems of small-scale exporting units, especially in regard to import entitlement, cash assistance, duty drawback, etc., and took them up with the authorities concerned.

In order to encourage the formation of export consortia of small-scale units, a scheme for financial assistance to them in the initial years of their formation was formulated and submitted to the Ministry of Industry. Under the scheme, the export consortia of small-scale units would be provided financial assistance during 3 or 4 years till they are able to develop themselves into full-fledged export houses.

Co-operation with Other Organisations

The SIDO actively collaborated with other Central and State institutions in their export promotion efforts, especially for small-scale industries. The SISIs prepared techno-managerial reports on export-worthy small-scale units, and collaborated with State Small Industries Corporations, Export Promotion Councils, the National Productivity Council and associations of small industries in organising seminars, training programmes, exhibitions, etc.

Under the scheme of Export Awards of the Ministry of Commerce, the Development Commissioner (Small-Scale Industries) has been designated as a sponsoring authority for small-scale units. The Small Industries Development Organisation, through its network of SISIs, therefore, invited applications from various small-scale units and recommended suitable exporting units for the Award.

One classic instance was when SIDO encouraged small units to participate in buy-seller meets and exhibitions organised by the Trade Development Authority at Rotterdam and Birmingham. Interested units were given detailed information and advice in this regard.

State Small Industries Corporations

Some of the State Small Industries Corporations have, in recent years, shown interest in export promotion activities. These corporations were actively associated with the various programme of export promotion organised by the SISIs.

Export House & Turnkey Projects: The NSIC, a recognised export house, has been pushing up the export of such small industry products as hardwares, industrial fasteners, sanitary fittings, locks and machine tools, etc. Goods worth more than Rs. 2 crore have been exported to such countries as the UK, the USA and countries in the Middle East. The NSIC has supplied complete plant and machinery for 32 turnkey projects for 62 small-scale units in Tanzania against the IDBI credit line of Rs. 20 million. This has evoked interest for similar projects from other countries, *viz.*, Nigeria, Mauritius, Uganda and Yemen. The corporation also considered proposals to assist Tanzania and Indonesia in setting up industrial estates for small-scale units.

Some small industries have good prospects of selling their products in international markets. If they cannot develop a consortium for the export of their products, they should at least associate with and support an export house. If marketing is a war, it is the most fierce in the international field. Well-equipped and highly professionalised export houses are indeed necessary, if the products of small industries are to be established in overseas markets. India has not made any serious inroads in these markets, not because the products do not conform to specification or are not competitively priced, but because exportability – the organised power to export – is somewhat low. There is a distinct need of large, strong, high-voltage and high resources export houses, which have specialised in the promotion of the export of the products of small industries. Individual small units may succeed when entrepreneurs have a high degree of marketing competence. But this is not true of most small units. They should not, therefore, enter the foreign markets on their own.

Exports have their own attractions; but unfortunately, very few entrepreneurs care to equip themselves adequately to export successfully and satisfactorily. The complaints one hears from foreign buyers of Indian goods, particularly, against manufacturers in the small-scale sector, bear testimony to this fact, though it may be conceded that some Indian small entrepreneurs do enjoy a high reputation abroad; but their number is woefully small. In these circumstances, the small entrepreneur should, as far as possible, utilise the services of an export house. In fact he should help build up the right type of export houses which have specialised in the promotion of the production of small industries in foreign markets. All export houses can neither do justice to the products of the small sector, nor all their operations likely to be of real benefit to small exporting units. Hence the need for specialised export houses capable of producing and pushing the products of small industries in overseas markets.

Responsibilities of Management

The major responsibilities of the general management are to establish marketing objectives, to make policy decisions and communicate these decisions to the managers of the operating (or implementing) divisions of the company; to establish standards for measuring and guiding the overall performance of the company. The responsibilities of operational or line management are to plan programmes, methods and procedures and implement the decision necessary to achieve the stated objective; to organise and co-ordinate the activities and resources necessary to carry out the programmes and to see that operating results conform as nearly as possible to agreed plans and standards of performance.

THE BASIC DIFFERENCES BETWEEN PRODUCTION-ORIENTED AND MARKETING-ORIENTED ORGANISATION

Business function or Activity	***Company Perspective***	
	Production	***Marketing***
Top Management	Technological considerations predominate. Production and engineering personnel in highest level executive positions.	Customer considerations paramount. Marketing personnel in highest level executive positions.
Objectives	Internal influences predominate. Business objective is to match total company resources against production on technical efficiency and method. Want to be known for technical or production know-how.	External market influences predominate. Business objective is to match total company resources against market requirements and opportunities. More emphasis on market strategy and planning. Want to be regarded as style and market leader.
Manufacturing	Production less flexible. The company sells what can be made.	Flexibility in production so as to match product to sales opportunities. The company manufactures what can be profitably sold.
Marketing	Aims to fulfil existing needs and develop workable products to meet these needs. Company's future bound up with markets already supplied, and products already in existence. Marketing function not considered to be as valuable as manufacturing engineering as finance.	Seeks to create markets and develop saleable products. Company's future bound up with markets yet to be identified and developed, and with products not yet in existence. Marketing considered to co-ordinate with manufacturing, finance and other major business functions.
Research	Leads in technical and scientific research. Marketing intelligence system relatively undeveloped.	Leads in analytical and marketing research. Market intelligence system well developed.

Product Planning	Based on technical research, suggestions for new or improved products stem from functional performance and applications are prime considerations. Engineering consideration tends to predominate. Laboratory testing more prominent than sales or market. Packaging viewed as a shipping and protective device. Chief concern is engineering, materials handling and packaging machinery.	Based on market research. Suggestions for new or improved products stem from research into customer needs. Performance and applications are prime considerations regarded to be almost as important. Sales and market testing an integral part of planning. Packaging viewed as a sales tool in terms of its user convenience and advertising and promotional effectiveness.
Sale Organisation	Salesman regarded as an order-getting for the factory.	Salesman regarded as an order-maker who keeps the factory running and provides employment to production workers. Salesman accorded high status in the company and more likely to be promoted to top management position.
	Salesman lacks the professional status of the engineer, chemist, lawyer or accountant. Less likely to be promoted to top management. Salesman lacks formal training. Tends to get left to his own devices as the man 'out there.' Motivation of the salesman minimal.	Salesman given formal and continuous internal and on-the-job training. Motivation of sales organisation given high priority. Chief sales executive regarded as part of the management team.
Advertising and Promotion	Emphasis on cost rather than on the value of its contribution to the total selling effort. Advertising and promotion regarded as an extra cost, not a basic cost like machines, raw materials, research laboratories, etc. Not regarded as one of the skills required to run a modern business successfully. Advertising and promotion not looked upon as an important source of competitive differential advantage.	Advertising and promotion is an integral part of the Company's marketing effort and a basic cost. Outstanding advertising and promotion considered to be as equally important to the successful running of a business as outstanding manufacturing technique, technical research ability or financial and legal skills. Advertising and promotion regarded as a potential source of competitive differential advantage, particularly when the differences in own and competitive products become less and less distinguishable.

GLOBAL AND REGIONAL TRADE ARRANGEMENTS

➧ World Trade Organization (WTO)

The WTO, established in January 1, 1995, as the successor to the General Agreement on Tariffs and Trade (GATT), serves as the legal and institutional foundation of the multilateral trading system.

The Uruguay Round Trade Agreement that created the WTO also eliminated tariffs for some manufactured goods and reduced other tariffs; reduced barriers to trade in agriculture; expanded protection for copyrights, patents, and other intellectual property; and provided some reduction in barriers to services and foreign investment. It also reformed the multilateral trade process itself, including the introduction of a stronger dispute-settlement mechanism.

North American Free Trade Agreement (NAFTA)

NAFTA, which built on he 1989 U.S. - Canada Free Trade Agreement, went into force January 1, 1994, phasing out tariffs on trade between the United States, Canada, and Mexico over 15 years. Side agreements require each country to enforce its own labour and environmental laws.

U.S. trade with Canada and Mexico increased 29 per cent in the first two years of NAFTA. Nevertheless, trade disputes between the partners persist, mitigated somewhat by dispute-settlement mechanisms.

Failing for three years to get abroad fast-track authority from Congress to negotiate any trade agreements, the Clinton Administration is grappling with a strategic decision: whether to request fast-track authority solely for negotiating accession to NAFTA by Chile.

Free Trade Area of the Americas (FTAA)

At the December 1994 Summit of the Americas in Miami, Forida, 34 political leaders of the Western Hemisphere adopted a U.S. proposal to construct an FTAA by 2005, with substantial progress expected before 2000. Trade ministers held subsequent meetings in September 1995 in Denver, Colorada, and in March 1996 in Cartagena, Colombia, where they set up working groups; other meetings are planned for Belo Horizonte, Brazil, in 1997 and for Costa Rica in 1998. Cuba alone among hemisphere countries does not participate in the FTAA.

The working groups have begun moving toward the first concrete actions for an FTAA, which are likely to involve procedures dealing with mutual acceptance of product standards and electronic customs filing.

Lack of fast-track negotiating authority has hurt U.S. credibility with other FTAA participants. For the Clinton administration, the strategic issue has become how to rebuild U.S. political consensus for FTAA negotiations while other Western Hemisphere countries continue to make trade agreements with each other – usually accepting lower standards on services, investment and intellectual property protection than the United States is seeking in an FTAA.

Asia-Pacific Economic Cooperation (APEC)

Formed in 1989 as an informal dialogue group with limited participation, APEC has become a forum for negotiations to achieve the goal of freer trade and investment in the Asia-Pacific region – by 2010 for industrialised economies and by 2020 for developing economies.

APEC has 18 members: Australia, Brunei, Canada, Chile, China, Hong Kong, Indonesia, Japan, South Korea, Malaysia, Mexico, New Zealand, Papua New Guinea, Philippines, Singapore, Taiwan, Thailand and the United States.

New Transatlantic Agenda

Part of the New Transatlantic Agenda agreed to at the U.S. European Union (EU) summit in December 1995 in Madrid was an initiative to expand trade between the two sides called the New Transatlantic Market place, assisted by meetings of businessmen called collectively the Transatlantic Business Dialogue.

Among a number of agreed goals were tariff cuts, including elimination of tariffs on information technology products (an information technology agreement), and negotiation of mutual recognition agreements to harmonize product standards and testing. Progress has been slow.

Meanwhile, U.S.-EU relations have been disturbed in 1996 by a number of irritants, especially U.S. imposition of sanctions against third-country investments in Cuba, Iran, and Libya.

▸▸ Ten Golden Rules of Integration

Marketing Strategy

(to be agreed before briefing marketing staff, outside agencies and other suppliers)

1. Set specific objectives for marketing communications to achieve the goals required by your company business plan.
2. Review the decision-making process in your market in order to identify the key target audiences, the best techniques and media to reach them effectively and to help develop the most persuasive selling message.
3. Set out the common elements required for corporate image and house style.

Campaign Tactics

(to develop a campaign most likely to meet the objectives)

4. Single out the lead activity – the one whose success will most influence the outcome of the campaign. Make it a basic principle that all other activities must incorporate and reflect the creative theme of the lead activity.
5. Give all marketing staff, marketing communications agencies and other suppliers the same full briefing – and ideally do it at a single meeting.
6. Within this briefing clearly define the (ideally unique) role to be played by each marketing activity in achieving the overall objectives and specify how each will be evaluated.
7. Set up a campaign development time table, with at least two liaison dates built in, to ensure that all agencies and suppliers are on brief and are playing the same time.

Evaluation and Feedback

8. Set up a monitoring system to evaluate the execution and effectiveness of the whole campaign and of each activity against its specific objectives. Review results with all agencies and suppliers first hand.
9. Be ruthless in bringing back into line any part of the campaign which does not adopt the agreed common direction, message and corporate image.
10. Highlights any weaknesses encountered in the integration of all the individual elements developed for the campaign and identify how it can be made more effective in future.

BEHAVIOURAL SIGNS

Over the years, there is a paradigm shift in customer behaviour. As a natural corollary, Robert Lauterborn thinks that it is time to blow away integrated marketing communication and focus on integrated customer behaviour management.

Integrated marketing communications – IMC, in short – was a label that Don Schultz, Stan Tannenbaum and I stuck on to a process a decade ago in a book titled *Integrated Marketing*

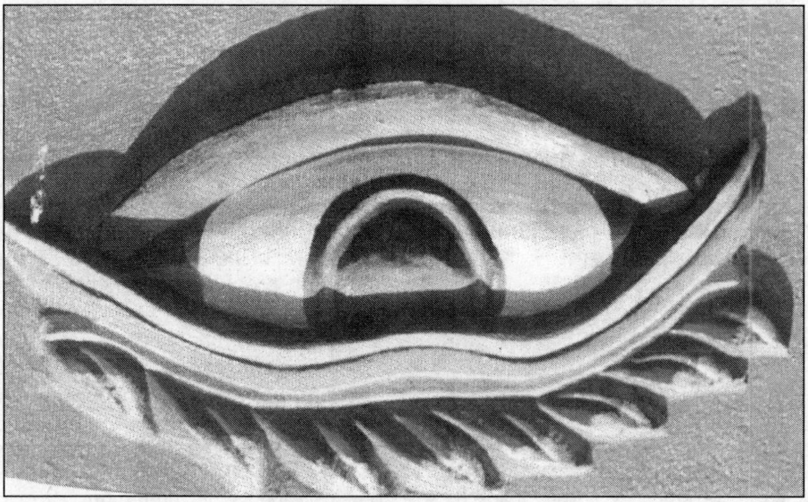

Robert Lauterborn is the James L. Knight Professor of Advertising at the University of North Carolina's School of Journalism, Chapel Hill, USA.

Communications: Pulling It Together and Making It Work. What we thought we were describing, was a strategic problem-solving approach; a new way of thinking and working, a banner under which multiple functions could march together in lockstep to accomplish a business objective accountably.

Instead, what IMC has come to mean to many people is little more than 'two-from-Column A, one-from-Column B' media selection. IMC is too often perceived even by the authors of some subsequent textbooks as simply making sure that PR efforts are in synch with advertising placements.

We've battled to get out of this box for too long. Maybe its time to blow it all away and rebuild. Let's start with a new name: ICBM. Integrated Customer Behaviour Management.

Here's the thinking that fuels the ICBM concept:

- Profitability is a function of customer behaviour.
- Any programme launched without specific, measurable behavioural objectives is doomed to veer off course.
- Marketing and marketing communications are investment functions, and the return on investment is a commutation based on the incremental revenue that results from altered customer behaviour.

Here's how to Launch the ICBM Process

1. What core business objective does the company want to achieve? What is the net value of success to the company?
2. Exactly whose behaviour needs to be changed for these results to happen?
3. Exactly what do we want these people to do, and why should they do it?
4. How do we engage them in a dialogue over time to make it happen?
5. How will we measure success? How will we demonstrate a return on the investment?

Some readers may squint at the fourth point and say, 'Aha, here's where he's talking about IMC.' But of course, that's the problem. IMC has been pigeonholed as an end-of-the-food-chain function that only kicks in at the tactical level and then only deals with communication issues.

STAGES OF DEVELOPMENT IN MARKETING MANAGEMENT

Production Orientation	***Sales Orientation***	***Customer/Market Orientation***
Market is viewed as dependent variable and production capacity as the independent variable. Production Deptt. → Market	Market as dependent variable and sales department capacity as the independent variable. Sales Deptt. → Market	Market and the firm are mutually interdependent; firm is highly dependent on market; it is extension of the market. Market → Firm
Emphasis is on the production process – on technical unit. Focus is on problems of manufacturing/ finance.	Emphasis is on own products of the firm – on sales.	Emphasis is on the customer needs and wants – on demand. Focus is on problems of marketing.
Marketing means: 'Sell what is produced.'	Marketing means: 'A good product does not sell by itself. It has to be pushed. Customers have to be manipulated.'	Marketing means: Targeting on customer needs present or future purchasing patterns of demand.
Prevalent in a situation of absolute scarcity, or during the seller's market.	Prevalent in a situation of surplus production, surplus capacity, or when the market has not been surveyed properly.	Prevalent in a situation of relative affluence during the buyer's market.
Prevalent in the West prior to 1930. Prevalent in areas, *e.g.,* developing nations a production economy stage.	Prevalent in the West during 1930-1950 and when demand is declined in certain industries.	Prevalent in the developed and affluent countries since 1955.
Production was the centre of the universe.	Salesmanship and promotion acted as the focus of marketing universe.	Customer satisfaction is the focus of the marketing universe.
It was summed that the best product could attract buyers automatically. Consumer choice could be based on quality in relation to price.	It is assumed that goods are not bought. They have to be sold at any cost, and profit is through sales volume.	It is assumed that goods are bought and not sold and profit is through customer satisfaction only.
No need of aggressive salesmanship and publicity. Company sells what it can make.	Special selling efforts and promotion to capture and maintain demand.	If demand clicks with supply, no special selling efforts are necessary, problem is only of disribution, *i.e.,* serving of demand. Company makes what it can sell.

Note: Since 1965, under environmental approach, marketing concept has been widened in the West. Government, market and pressure groups influence the firm and its marketing strategy. The firm has to adopt socially responsible marketing strategies. It has to cater to the needs of consumers as well society market needs in a social framework. It has to ensure quality of life, *e.g.,* absence of food, air and water pollution. Consumerism and government should achieve consumer protection and environmental protection. The firm now aims at benefits for both sides, *i.e.,* customer satisfaction and profitability. Societal or social marketing concept appeared in many affluent countries from 1965. It is slowly spreading over also in other developing countries. It is now said that the so-called affluent countries have become really effluent countries. Developing countries should not be effluent countries.

So maybe the vision of IMC is too limited. ICBM integrates everything that impacts customer behaviour. Product development to meet customer needs more precisely packaging that communicates with equal precision. Pricing that reflects the value the customer perceives in the product, compared to other ways to satisfy the need or want. A distribution scheme that makes it convenient for the customer to buy. Channel management, sales management, financing, CRM, TQM, Six Sigma and whatever else needs to be happening to change how the customer thinks and behaves, plus the timing of it all and the dialogue around it, internal and external – all of that is part of ICBM. And, yes, the multidimensional, interactive, continuously measured communication package that connects the brand or product and the customer, because that's what makes the whole process lift off and stay in orbit.

IMC as it was designed, works. But we need to blow away the misconceptions that keep the IMC concept from making the contributions it could to marketers and agencies alike. Integrated Customer Behaviour Management sounds a lot more powerful, doesn't it?

ONLINE MARKETING TIPS FOR SMALL BUSINESSES

1. If you don't have a website, get one. If you have one, invest more in making it better. Perhaps more startups would get online if they realise that a website does not need to be complex to serve its purpose.
2. Make sure people can find you. The web keeps growing. Creating a user-friendly, well-structured website will also help search engines like Google find and index it easily.
3. By being easily 'found' online, startups can win customers outside of their traditional markets. Once you have moved to where your customers are, get inside their heads.
4. Manage your return on investment (RoI). Advertisers can bid to appear only against specific user search queries, so they are sure to be targeting a relevant and interested audience.
5. "Anticipated, personal and relevant advertising always does between better than unsolicited junk," says US-based marketing-guru Seth Godin. This phrase expresses very well the ability of online marketing to connect you with your customers at the right time.
6. Write 'must-click' ads. To attract the right kind of customers to your business, you need to be writing the right kind of ads – those that will compel them to click on your ad to learn more.
7. Work out your goals and market accordingly. You need to know your ultimate goal-be it increased traffic to your website, conversions, or brand awareness – so you can measure success.
8. Good marketers measure. Free tools like Google Analytics allow you to track visitor patterns so you can better understand your customers. You can make sure you are paying for results.
9. Test and adapt. Online advertising is dynamic. You can pause, cancel or resume campaigns quickly. Use this to your advantage and continually review what you have set up, keeping in mind that there's always room for improvement.
10. Embrace the nature of the web. It can be easy to bring an offline mindset to online marketing, and miss out on some of the greatest benefits it has to offer, like its truly global nature.

By Narasimha Jayakumar, Business Head, Google India

Conclusion

Marketing is a system of integraded business activities designed to develop strategies and plans including marketing mixes to the satisfaction of customer wants of selected market segments or targets. It is on process involving a set of multi-directional as well as multidimensional activities. Marketing is a matching process by which a producer provides a marketing mix *(product, price, promotion and physical distribution)* that meets consumer demand of a target market within the limits of society.

Of late, marketing management has been given much importance, especially by the SSI sector and will continue to get this importance with different market situations existing now.

The marketing of products has become difficult for SMEs in an open economy is reflected in the findings of the Third Census of SSIs. The main reason only a few companies make their presence felt in foreign markets, while others having the same potential are left behind, is that they are unable to market themselves abroad. In the increasingly competitive global market, there arises a need to shift the productive base from low-value, price-determined modes of operation to higher-value, knowledge-based patterns of production and products. SMEs also need to reorient their focus on exports. As a result of globalisation, coupled with the WTO regime, SMEs have been passing through a transitional period. "With enhanced competition from China and a few low-cost centres of production from abroad, many units have, of late, been facing a tough time," points out D.K. Nair, Secretary General, Confederation Indian Textile Industry (CITI).

"Marketing takes a day to learn. Unfortunately, it takes a lifetime to master," remarked that uber marketing guru, Philip Kotler. Marketers, both seasoned ones as well as new kids on the block, will relate to that statement. For marketing, unlike say production or finance, is not about cold logic but rather it operates in the grey and uncertain domain of a constantly evolving consumer's thoughts and feelings and an ever changing environment. Take marketing in India for example.

Two decades ago, marketers in India made one product and flogged it for years, commissioned a TV commercial and ran it for years. Buying media was a simple affair – buy spots on Doordarshan and when in doubt buy more spots on Doordarshan. The new product launch calendar was a leisurely affair, planned to give ample amount of breathing space to marketing teams. Response to competitive moves would take an entire quarter, if not the whole year, as marketers carefully recalibrated their strategies.

Fast forward to today when a company like Nokia launches close to 50 products in a single year and a Vodafone creates the Zoozoos for the second edition of IPL. When a Big Bazaar manages to arm twist big consumer product companies into lowering margins and marketers grapple with a 100 TV channels, countless publications to reach the picky consumer. The landscape itself has undergone a radical transformation not to mention the consumer.

And yet there have been marketers who have managed to keep pace with the consumer and build brands that have earned the love and respect of millions. Marketers who have been relentless in their pursuit of raising the bar when it comes to making bold and brave marketing decisions. These are marketers who have won not only the admiration of millions in the marketplace but of their peers as well. They are charting out new territory in the world of marketing and unafraid to go where no marketing men or women have gone before.

LINE OF CONTROL

"In the context of the increasingly global nature of business and capital in the 21st century, there is a clear need for global businesses to be able to operate across borders with consistency of practice."

— James Turley, CEO, Ernst & Young

28

Sickness and Remedial Assistance

Introduction

Partha Parthasarathy
Nu Street Technologies

Rapid industrial growth has brought in its wake incidence of sickness in the industrial sector including small-scale industries.

Sickness in industrial units is a gradual process and does not develop suddenly. In the initial stages, it gets reflected in the form of defects and mistakes in the unit's functional areas like production, finance and management. Later it is observed in the form of symptoms like irregular or unsatisfactory turnover in the account, slow and unsatisfactory movement of stocks, decline in production, sales and profitability, frequent violation of terms and conditions and asking for additional grants.

Definition

The term *industrial sickness* has been defined in a number of ways and its concept lacks uniformity. A sick industrial unit may be defined as one when it fails to generate surplus on a continuous basis and depends on frequent infusion of external funds for its survival. According to the Reserve Bank of India (RBI), a S.I. unit should be considered so if it has "incurred cash loss in the previous accounting year and is likely to continue to incur cash loss in the current accounting year, and has an erosion on account of cumulative cash losses to the extent of 50 per cent of those of its net worth."

A unit is likely to continue to incur cash losses for the current year as well as the following year and which has imbalance in its financial structure such as current ratio of less than 1:1 and worsening debt-equity ratio. According to ICICI "a sick industry is one whose financial viability is threatened by adverse factors present and continuing. The adverse factor might relate to management, market fiscal burden, labour relations or any other. When the impact of factors reaches a point where a company begins to incur cash losses leading to erosion of its funds, there is threat to its financial stability."

The sick industrial companies (special provision) Act 1985 identifies sickness in terms of cash losses for two consecutive financial years and accumulated losses equalling or exceeding the net worth of the company at the end of the second financial year.

The definition of sick SSI units has been modified as under: "A small-scale industrial unit should be considered as sick if it has, at the end of any accounting year, accumulated losses equal to or exceeding 50 per cent of its peak net worth in the immediately preceding five accounting years" (Bihar Chambers of Commerce, Sep. 1989).

An analysis of all the definitions given above indicate that sickness, more or less, has a perfect positive correlation with profitability. Profitability alone can generate cash surpluses for an industrial unit to meet its various obligations to the creditors like financial institutions, the government and others.

Table 1

INDUSTRIAL SICKNESS

End of	*Sick/Weak Units*		
	Large & Medium	*Small* *Number of Units*	*Total*
Dec. 1980	1,401	23,148	24,550
Mar. 1980	2,269	218,828	221,097
Mar. 1995	2,391	268,815	271,206
Mar. 1996	2,374	262,376	264,750
Mar. 1997	2,368	235,032	237,400
Mar. 1998	2,476	221,536	224,012
Mar. 1999	2,792	306,221	309,013
Mar. 2000	3,164	304,235	307,399
Mar. 2001	3,317	249,630	252,947
Mar. 2002	3,261	177,336	180,597
Mar. 2003	3,396	167,980	171,376

OUTSTANDING BANK CREDIT

(Rs. crores)

Dec. 1980	1,502	306	1,809
Mar. 1990	6,926	2,427	9,353
Mar. 1995	10,192	3,547	13,739
Mar. 1996	10,027	3,722	13,749
Mar. 1997	10,178	3,609	13,787
Mar. 1998	11,825	3,857	15,682
Mar. 1999	15,150	4,313	19,463
Mar. 2000	19,047	4,608	23,656
Mar. 2001	21,270	4,506	25,775
Mar. 2002	21,246	4,819	26,065
Mar. 2003	29,110	5,706	34,816

Table 2

VIABILITY OF SICK/WEAK UNITS

(As at end-March 2003)

	Potentially Viable	*Non-viable*	*Violability not decided*	*Total*
No. of Units	**4,011**	**164,727**	**2,638**	**171,376**
SSI sick units	3,626	162,791	1,563	167,980
Non-SSI sick & weak units	385	1,936	1,075	3,396
Outstanding bank credit (Rs. crores)	**8,315**	**14,771**	**11,730**	**34,816**
SSI sick units	625	4,869	213	5,706
Non-SSI sick and weak units	7,690	9,902	11,517	29,110

VARIOUS REASONS FOR SICKNESS/INCIPIENT SICKNESS

Reason for sickness/ incipient sickness	*Proportion of sick/incipient sick units.**		
	Total SSI Sector	*Regd. SSI Scotor*	*Unregd. SSI Sector*
1. Lack of demand	66%	58%	69%
2. Shortage of working capital	46%	57%	43%
3. Non-availability of raw material	12%	12%	12%
4. Power shortage	13%	17%	12%
5. Labour problems	5%	6%	4%
6. Marketing problems	36%	37%	36%
7. Equipment problems	11%	9%	12%
8. Management problems	4%	5%	3%

Extent of Sickness

The number of ailing small-scale units, according to RBI data rose from 24,550 in December 1980 to 3,09,013 in March, 1999 and declined to 1,71,376 in Mar. 2003 of which 3011 units are potentially viable, 1,64,727 non-viable and viability not decided in case of 2,636 units as at end March, 2003..

The number has been increasing year after year, and the malady if not checked, might erode the roots of industrialisation in the country, which is a vital component of the economy of the country. A number of reasons could be attributed for the sickness of small-scale industries in the country, prominent among them being:

(*a*) Management deficiency.

(*b*) Inadequate and timely availability of finance.

(*c*) Outdated technology; and

(*d*) Marketing problems.

Box 1

10 REASONS WHY STARTUPS FAIL

- They run out of money. They are too optismistic about when their product is going to be accepted by the market.
- Founders don't have complete faith in each other. They fight instead of delegating, trusting and verifying.
- CEO hires weak team members. Strong CEOs sometimes try to carry everyone with them.
- They want to do too much. A successful startup finds a narrow niche that they can dominae and then expands.
- They go after too small a market.
- They don't charge enough from their customers to survive. They often think their mentors/ investors are their customers, and think that a nice sale is all they need.
- They hire too many people up front.
- They get unlucky. Competitors, new technologies, *et al.*
- They don't work hard enough or fast enough or smart enough. All those little decisions add up to an outcome.
- They don't take enough risks. Some startups think they should operate like big firms. They can never beat MS or Google at their own game. They should get creative and do things differently, even at the risk of embarrassment.

Tim Draper, MD, Draper Fisher Jurvetson

Causes of Sickness

A. Internal Causes

1. Planning

(a) *Technical feasibility*

Inadequate technical know-how
Locational disadvantage
Outdated production process

(b) *Economic viability*

High cost of inputs
Break-even point too high
Uneconomic size of project
Underestimation of financial requirements
Unduly large investment in fixed assets
Overestimation of demand.

2. Implementation

Cost overruns resulting from delays in getting licences and sanctions etc.
Inadequate mobilisation of finance.

3. Production

(a) Production management

Inappropriate product-mix
Poor quality control
Poor capacity utilisation
High cost of production
Poor inventory management
Inadequate maintenance and replacement
Lack of timely and adequate modernisation etc.
High wastage

(b) Labour management

Excessively high wage structure
Inefficient handling of labour problems
Excessive manpower
Poor labour productivity
Poor labour relations
Lack of trained skilled labour or technically competent personnel

(c) Marketing management

Dependence on a single customer or a limited number of customers/single or a limited number of products
Poor sales realisation
Defective pricing policy
Booking of large orders at fixed prices in an inflationary market
Weak market organisation
Lack of market feedback and market research
Lack of knowledge of marketing techniques
Unscrupulous sales/purchase practices

(d) Financial management

Poor resources management and financial planning
Faulty costing
Liberal dividend policy
General financial indiscipline and application of funds for unauthorised purposes
Deficiency of funds
Over-trading
Unfavourable gearing or keeping adverse debt-equity ratio
Inadequate working capital
Absence of cost consciousness
Lack of effective collection machinery

(e) Administrative management

Over centralisation
Lack of professionalism
Lack of feedback to management (Management Information System)
Lack of controls
Lack of timely diversification
Excessive expenditure on R & D

Dividend loyalties (where the same management has interest in more than one unit, cases are known where promoters of limited companies who also own private ownership firms tend to look after the interests of the latter, often at the cost of the former)

Dissension within the management
Incompetent management
Dishonest management

B. External Causes

(a) Infrastructural bottlenecks
Non-availability of irregular supply of critical raw materials or other inputs
Chronic power shortage
Transport bottlenecks

(b) Financial bottlenecks
Non-availability of adequate finance

(c) Government controls and policies, etc.
Government price controls
Fiscal duties
Abrupt change in Government policies

Procedural delays on the part of the financial/licensing/other controlling or regulating authorities (Banks, Reserve Bank of India, financial institutions, Government departments, licensing authorities, Monopolies and Restrictive Trade Practices Board, etc.)

(d) Market constraints
Market saturation
Revolutionary technological advances rendering one's products obsolete

(e) Extraneous factors
Natural calamities
Political situation (domestic as well as international)
War
Sympathetic strikes
Multiplicity of labour unions.

⏩ Management Deficiency

It could be said that management deficiency is one of the biggest reasons for poor performance and sickness of small-scale units. The new entrants in the fields of small industries in many cases did not have any prior training or background in management of their enterprises and were adverse to innovations and changes. In the beginning of our industrial development era, this problem was not so critical but with growing sophistication and modernisation of market-requirements for the items produced by the small-scale sector, it has become very important for small entrepreneurs to employ modern methods of management, be it in the field of advanced technology or marketing.

Recent experiences have proved that entrepreneurship is not only an inborn gift, but it could also be cultivated through application and training. American Universities and colleges offering courses in starting and managing a small enterprise. The Carnegie Mellon University of USA is one of the prominent universities offering entrepreneurial training courses. In our country, similar entrepreneurship development training programmes are organised by organisations, viz., Centre for Development of Entrepreneurs, Gandhi Nagar (Gujarat), Small Industries Extension Training Institutes, Hyderabad, and other units of the Small Industries Development Organisation. The Centre for Development of Entrepreneurs has trained over 6,000 entrepreneurs till recently, out of which around 3,000 are running their own units successfully. The Small Industries Development Organisation has also been helpful in motivating a good number of entrepreneurs of the first generation. Recently, the Government of India has also established a National Institute for Entrepreneurship and Small Business at New Delhi which would shortly start its own programmes.

Finance

Financial inadequacy is also reported to be one of the most important causes leading to sickness of small-scale units. Undoubtedly, the Government has extended a number of incentives for the growth of small industries and some people feel that these have had negative effect on the small industries. Some others feel that in order to obtain more and more finance and concessions, the small entrepreneur often runs from one agency to another and consequently, cannot concentrate on his industry. There have also been reports that some of these incentives have been misused. However, the discussion here is related to small industries who have genuinely suffered for want of adequate and timely financing facilities. It is well-known that a Committee set-up by the Government of India under the Chairmanship of Prof. A. M. Khusro, Ex-Member, Planning Commission is already looking into the financing/credit problems/needs of small-scale industries and it is hoped that a separate Apex financing Institution for small industries might be recommended. In addition, a separate legislation to protect the genuine interests of small-scale industries, including tiny and ancillary sector, is under consideration of the Government. It could also be expected that the Apex Financing Institution or Bank solely devoted to meet the credit needs of small industries in the country would bring out some hitherto unknown difficulties of the sector and come out with remedial measures to improve health of the weaker small units. The Bank may also provide expertise in guiding small entrepreneurs in their financial management problems and offer preventive assistance to them in case where sickness is anticipated.

Technology

Notable technological innovations and changes are taking place in industrially advanced countries of the world and small-scale industries in those countries are also correspondingly responding by upgrading their technology. For example, use of computers is being made in the design and production of individual components in job shops at costs comparable with costs of mass produced techniques. This has meaningful implications for a country like India, where at present a large number of small and ancillary industries are competing with large industries in a number of common product areas. While fiscal incentives given to small-scale industries are, indeed, of help, the ultimate answer will, of course lie in the small-scale industries upgrading and updating their own technology and skills to meet the stringent within the country and by importers abroad. Small units will have to be technologically modern and price-wise competitive to play a significant role and keep their place in the total industrial structure of the country. In this task, technocrat-entrepreneurs particularly, may have to play a leading role.

There is a misconception in some quarters that modernisation and upgradation of technology necessarily involves costly equipment and labour reduction. While the initial investment cost in modern plant facilities may be somewhat higher, the investment would ultimately result in long-term benefits to economy through higher and consistent quality and higher productivity achievements. Modern technology also need not necessarily mean adopting automation in every case. In case of small industries, the process of modernisation and upgradation of technology could be undertaken in phases depending upon the resources available with the units. Modernisation would, of course need higher and better skills to operate, maintain and run modern plant facilities to get the maximum productivity. While this might mean less demand for uneducated and unskilled personnel, it would on the other hand create opportunities for many skilled and educated operators, technicians and engineers in modern small industries.

Marketing

The last but not the least, the important factor causing sickness is the small industries' inability to market their products in a systematic way. It is well-known that small-scale industries are mostly one man show or a family business and professional marketing is often not practised in such units. However, it may also be stated that during the last decade and a half, some of the progressive small-scale industries have also realised the need for scientific marketing methods and have therefore organised their own marketing networks on regional and national basis. This is true in some cases of manufacturers of domestic electrical appliances where these small-scale industries have a national network and a chain of distributors and retailers. Some of the large marketing organisations have also been helpful in undertaking the field of the products of small-scale industries mostly in the field of domestic electrical appliances. Such contacts have been educative for small industries in learning marketing techniques from their large-scale partners. In this context, it may be admitted that concept of forming consortia of small industries to share the marketing efforts has not been very successful and effective. A view is often expressed that marketing is purely an entrepreneurial function and the Government should only provide necessary training and other facilities with the financing institutions providing necessary financial help in initiating market surveys and other allied marketing activities.

In this context, it may also be stated that the Government has been quite responsive to the marketing needs of small-scale entrepreneurs producing a variety of items and has reserved over 800 items to be procured exclusively from small-scale sector under the Central Government Store Purchase Programme implemented by the DGS & D. In addition, instructions have been issued to the public sector enterprises and purchasing organisations of the Central Government to provide price preference to the products of the small-scale industries, wherever they compete with large scale manufacturers against tenders floated by the purchasing organisations. While the above measures are indeed helpful in providing some sort of marketing assurance to small scale industries, this meets only a small part of small industries production. For a bulk of their production the small industries have necessarily to depend upon their own initiative, drive and innovations. It is here that training programme in modern methods of marketing will be helpful to small industries in upgrading their marketing technology on modern lines.

Constraints in Modernisation

While the need for upgradation of technology and modernisation of production processes and marketing methods is appreciated by small-scale industries, there are certain constraints experienced in bringing about the desired level of modernisation in a definite limited time. These constraints may briefly be stated as follows:

Investment Limits

A view is very often expressed by number of responsible people in various quarters that modernisation cannot be brought out by small-scale industries within the present investment limits of Rs. 3 crore in the case of small-scale industries and Rs. 3 crore in the case of small-scale ancillary units. The investment level of tiny sector has been raised to Rs. 25 lakh with effect from 07.02.97. An opposite view is also expressed that since more than 90% of small units have an investment in the plant and equipment of less than Rs. 5 lakhs any increase in the investment limits would only benefit a very small percentage of small-scale units. Since both points of view have their own merits, the whole question would need to be studied in greater depth to weigh the pros and cons of bringing in an increase in the investment limits of the small-scale industries.

Pace of Change in Technology

Due to increase in R & D activities, undertaken by industries in the advanced countries, technological changes of far reaching importance are taking place rapidly and small-scale industries often find it extremely difficult to keep pace with these changes. Even in case of foreign technical collaboration from abroad into this country, only such technologies are given which have become partly out-moded in the collaborating countries. Many examples of this type are not difficult to seek in the field of electronics, electrical, automobiles, components, etc. This rapidly changing technology in certain industries in developed countries like USA, Japan, UK and West Germany have often forced them to vacate certain areas of production in favour of developing countries where the cost of labour element is still less. The investment dynamics in the field of electronics have resulted in a large number of US and European countries establishing a part of their manufacturing processing facilities in far eastern countries like Malaysia, Taiwan, Korea, Indonesia and Thailand. Even in these countries there has not been any marked transfer of technology or technology upgradation in the small-scale sector. It has also been experienced in these countries that in most cases, the foreign collaborators have not bothered to upgrade the technology of small or medium sector units. The situation in India is perhaps not totally different.

Technology Vs. Employment

One of the biggest constraints felt in upgrading the technology through automation is the fear that it might result in reduction of labour required. Since employment generation is one of the basic objectives for growth of small-scale industries in India, any proposal to induct modern technology, which would ultimately result in loss in employment, is not likely to be received with favour. Here also perhaps such industrial activities could be identified where modernisation would not necessarily mean automation resulting in reduction in overall employment in small-industries.

For example, in the field of electronic industry, the technological upgradation, which is continuously taking place, is also providing lot of scope for horizontal growth of ancillary, as well as assembly based industries in small-scale sector providing thereby increasing scope of employment. It is one of the major industries where small industries are thriving. New technologies are also coming in the field of automobiles an area where the scope of ancillarisation is considered to be of a very high order. Instead of replacing labour from the Small-scale sector, the input of technology will provide more employment in the ancillary and auxiliary sectors in these groups of industries.

Inadequate availability of inputs

Another factor which restricts the pace of modernisation is the non-availability of necessary financial, technical, raw material and other inputs needed by small-scale industries for modernisation. Also many small-scale industries would find it difficult to pay the cost of new technology individually and therefore, it would be necessary to identify and design an effective mechanism for import of modern technology in selected fields and delivering them to the needy small-scale industries. There could be several ways for transfer of technology imported from abroad and the large-scale industries in the private sector have to play a very important role in acting as carriers of technology from foreign countries to the small sector in India. An alternative may be to identify a Government Organisation to negotiate and buy appropriate modern technology in selected areas of development and industrial production.

⏩ Diagnosis

The normal diagnosis to find out the reasons for sickness starts from a series of interviews with people across the organisational structure. The major purpose of the interviews is to have a detailed insight into the working of the organisation, its strengths and weaknesses, the market situation and also the changes expected over a period of time. The following seven steps will enable a proper diagnosis of the orgnanisational sickness:

1. Interview people across the organisational structure (including workers) and the subsidiary structure of unions, suppliers, customers – to have a general feel of the problems that lead to the sickness.
2. Hold fact finding sessions with individuals/groups in the middle/senior management level – to list the known/possible factors contributing to the sickness.
3. Hold discussions with departmental/divisional heads to assess the nature and depth of the departmental problems (production, quality, conduct of business/routine activities in various departments.)
4. Set up feedback/monitoring/audit control systems to periodically assess the performance, deviations and the needed corrections.
5. Implement the use of modern management tools, techniques, information technology (cost control, TQM, JIT, inventory control, budgetary control...), to improve the bottomline.
6. Plug the loopholes and make up the present deficiencies to achieve optimal production, high productivity, improved efficiencies, lower cost of resources, lower consumption factors and finally better realisations.
7. Adopt business process reengineering in an effort to do the "Right Things" effectively and to achieve major breakthroughs in costs, quality and profits. This will help in planning expansions, closing unprofitable units and diversifications.

ORGANISATIONAL STRESS

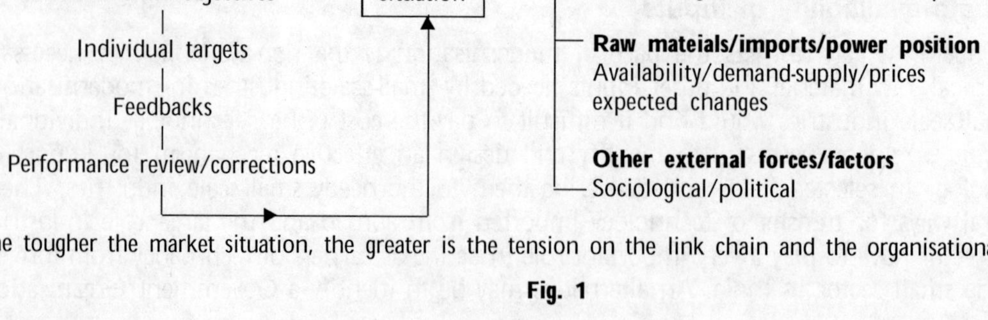

The tougher the market situation, the greater is the tension on the link chain and the organisational factors.

Fig. 1

THE KEY FEATURES OF SICB OF SICB VIS-A-VIS SICA

Features	***New SICB 1997***	***Old SICA 1985***
Definition of sickness	Debt default for four or more quarters in any two successive years to banks, FIs or any other secured creditors	Net worth erosion; i.e., accumulated losses having wiped away paid-up capital plus reserves
Reference of BIFR	Voluntary or optional in case of debt default, but mandatory if net worth has been eroded by 50 per cent from peak networth (in last four years)	Mandatory
Role of BIFR	Of the nature of a mediator or facilitator	Like a court
Decision-makiing	Three well-defined time-bound stages before BIFR, failing which liquidation	No time limits Average time for decision-makiing almost two years
Appellate authority (AAIFR)	To be dissolved. No order or scheme of BIFR shall be appealed against and no Civil Court will have the jurisdiction to grant an injunction or stay.	Appeal against BIFR orders could be made to AAIFR and also high courts
Rights of secured creditors	To vote on scheme, which would deemed to be passed if there is assent from secured creditors representing 75 per cent of the value of secured debt.	*De jure,* to vote a scheme under Section 19(2). *De facto,* had to often acquiesce to BIFR and AAIFR decisions

➧ Revival Plan

In short, the diagnosis will be a SWOT analysis of the organisation describing the Strengths, Weaknesses, Opportunities and Threats. This analysis will lead us to a meaningful revival plan and will also help in determining the right tools, techniques and remedies to be adopted. It may be emphasised that the revival plan has to be time-bound to achieve the expected changes and results.

The method of planning, defining the objectives and setting up of Targets etc. is the subject of a separate chapter, not dealt herewith. However, the seven steps for the Revival Plan are given below:

1. Finalise the goals/objectives/targets for performance at all levels to meet the organisation's mission.
2. Issue policy guidelines on major aspects that affect the image of the company in public and the work culture inside the organisation.
3. Initiate the preparation of detailed systems manuals for the maintenance, budgets, costs, distribution, transportation, purchase, marketing inventory, personnel etc.
4. Analyse past reports on production, quality, costs, performance, accounts receivables etc. and the connected financial and audit reports – to get an overall idea of the present working systems and results.

5. Meet senior executives from marketing/finance/personnel/materials/secretarial/legal departments and (if possible) with competitors – to assess the external situations (Govt. policies, competitor's activities, raw materials position, union-political-social factors.)
6. Brain storm with a select group – to get creative ideas for improvement.
7. Apprise the Board about the diagnosis and request them to spell out a clear "Mission" of the Company.

REVIVAL NETWORK

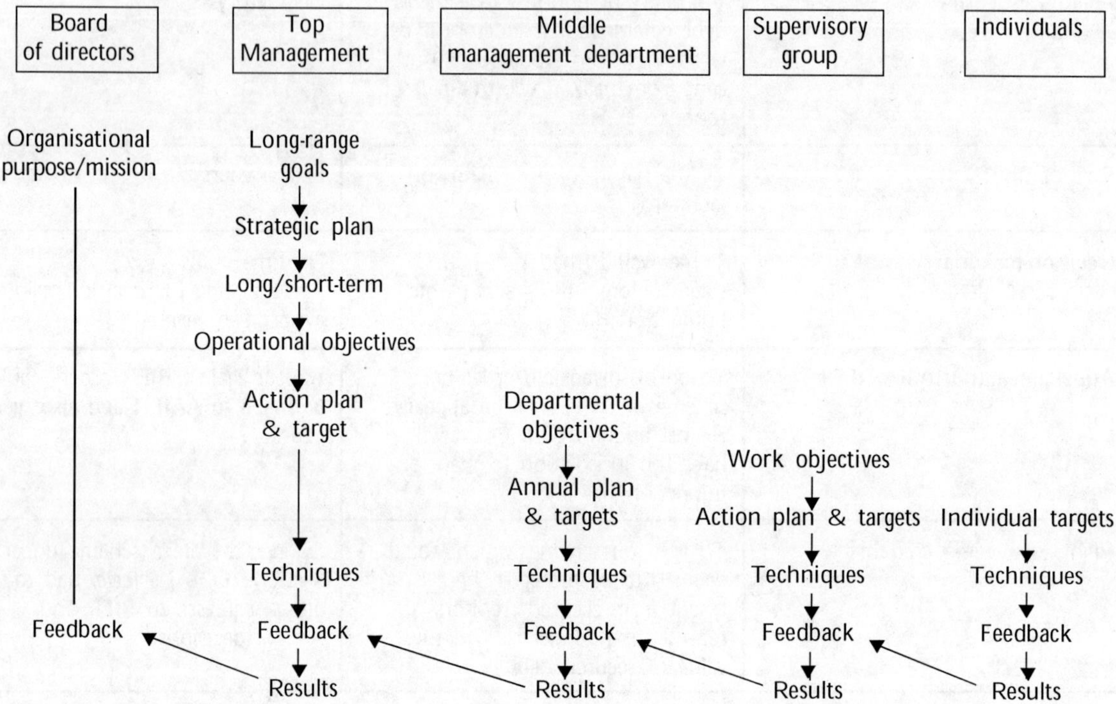

Fig. 2

These measures would bring about cost effective functioning of production units:

Institutional Mechanisms

Pursuant to the enactment of the Sick Industrial Companies (Special Provisions) Act, 1985, a Board for Industrial and Financial Reconstruction (BIFR) was set up in May 1987 under the administrative control of Ministry of Finance.

The BIFR has power to prepare rehabilitation schemes for revival of sick industrial companies in consultation with the agencies concerned. Till March 31, 1998, BIFR has received 3148 references. The Board has sanctioned rehabilitation schemes for 625 units, recommended winding up for 579 units and declared 200 units no longer sick.

A sick industrial company has to report its sickness to the BIFR, once its accumulated losses at the end of financial year exceed 50% of the peak net worth attained during the period of four years immediately preceding the financial year. BIFR provides a forum where the agencies concerned are brought together for analysing, diagnosing and evolving a reasoned decision for revival, or otherwise of the sick industrial unit. The agencies concerned are:

(*i*) Sick Industrial Unit
(*ii*) State Government
(*iii*) Banks and financial institutions
(*iv*) The concerned Departments of the Central Government.

SICA has invested BIFR with the following powers:

(*i*) Potential sickness has to be reported to BIFR.
(*ii*) Mismanagement of industrial units by any person can be looked into by BIFR and the BIFR may direct that person to restore the losses; and
(*iii*) BIFR can initiate changes in management, amalgamation of the sick industrial company with any other healthy company, sale or lease of a part, or whole of the industrial unit, or any other preventive/remedial measures.

Remedial Measures

1. Early detection of sickness, it was generally felt, could go a long way in initiating remedial measures for restoring potential sick units to health. Need was stressed for the establishment of a proper management information system for providing early warning signals from within.
2. Financial institutions and banks should initiate necessary corrective action for sick or prone-to-sickness units based on diagnostic studies. In case of growing sickness, they should also consider assumption of management responsibility where they are confident of restoring a unit to health.
3. Wherever possible, attempts should be made to restore sick units to financial health. However, where the judgement is that a sick unit cannot be retrieved, it should be allowed to be wound up. The divestment of a sick unit, if desired by an industrial group, for handing it over to someone else with the requisite experience of running such a unit should be allowed expeditiously so that it can be restored to health before the situation gets out of control.
4. Excessive concern over unemployment resulting from the closure of a sick unit is unwarranted. This can be taken care of through other measures, such as the setting up of a national fund for the purpose and strengthening of the facilities for retraining of workers.
5. The proposal to set up a special institution – the Board for Financial and Industrial Reconstruction – appears to be a sound one. It should play the role of a single window clearing agency. However, the Board should not be asked to go merely by mechanical indicators to determine sickness in industry. For instance, the criterion of erosion in net worth for determining the seriousness of sickness, although it does indicate that everything is not well with a unit, is not meaningful. Erosion could take place by internal as well as external factors. There is, therefore, no justification for punishing management for erosion in net worth if it is caused by factors beyond its control.
6. Similarly, the proposal visualising that the management of a unit that has lost net worth in entirety will not be allowed to manage that unit any more, needs to be reconsidered. Before branding the management as a bad one, all the aspects of the case ought to be examined.
7. The proposal that managements responsible for mismanagement should not be allowed assistance from financial institutions even for new ventures, too, needs re-thinking.
8. Nothing will do greater damage to the development of the spirit of entrepreneurship in the community than the fear that one is likely to be punished for sickness which is not of one's own market but is the result of lapses committed elsewhere.

9. It is important that in any scheme of reconstruction of a sick unit, all the stakeholders bear sacrifices on equitable and just basis.
10. The important criterion for takeover of a sick unit by another company should be whether the company taking over the sick unit has skill, technology and finance to save it. Considerations on MRTP/FERA accounts should not come in the way.
11. There is need for a fresh look at Section 72-A of Income-tax Act to remove the inhibition caused to companies taking over sick units by insistence on the part of income-tax authorities for prior full implementation of the revival schemes before tax benefits can accrue.
12. Debt-equity ratio ought to be realistic. Fiscal policy, too, requires rationalisation.
13. Incentives should be provided to professional managers helping in reviving sick units.
14. Treatment of capital-intensive units prone to sickness has to be on a different footing than tackling of sickness in industry in general.

Empowering SMEs

Small and medium enterprises (SMEs) have played an important role in the growth of the domestic economy for long. As the process of the globalisation and liberalisation gathers momentum across the globe, SMEs are facing tremendous challenges to survive and sustain. Some of the major challenges faced by SMEs include lack of access to finance, low R&D investment, lack of access to technology, lack of product innovation, inadequate marketing support in an increasingly competitive environment, etc.

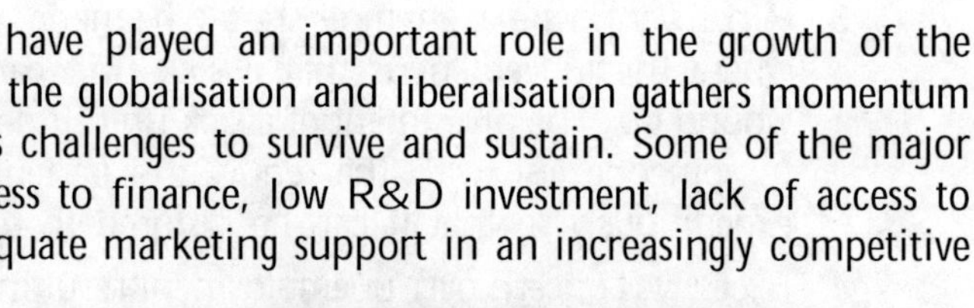

The small and fragmented structure makes these units more vulnerable. Despite their immense contribution, the sector is largely informal. According to the Third Census of Small Scale Industries (SSI), 90 per cent of the units are not registered, and are not covered by annual formal data collection exercise like the Annual Survey of Industries. Around 97 per cent of them are either proprietorship or partnership enterprises. The recent report of the Working Group on Rehabilitation of SMEs has pointed out that close to 95 per cent of units did not have access to any kind of formal institutional credit from banks and other financial institutions.

Moreover, SMEs are also suffering due to variances in policy focus and priorities of different regions in the country. For instance, as much as 16.23 per cent of the country's SME units are in UP, but their share in exports is just 10 per cent. Whereas Tamil Nadu, with just 7 per cent share in enterprises, accounts for 16 per cent of the export earnings, and Haryana, with as little as 2.12 per cent share of enterprises, has got 10.6 per cent share in the total export earnings.

The other problems faced by the sector are laws relating to controls, taxes, red tapism and complicated procedures. These hassles faced by entrepreneurs have made them go slow in their venture.

In its recent recommendation to state governments, the RBI has asked for creation of a Central registry by the states for registration of charges of all banks and other lending institutions in respect of all moveable and immovable properties of borrowers incorporated as proprietorship, partnership, co-operative society, trust, company or in any other form. It has also asked for considering due modification in the provisions of stamp duty. In order to facilitate resources to the sector, state governments have been recommended to form a separate ministry for SMEs.

"The government needs to help them by approving stamp duty exemptions, enhancing their image globally through trade fairs, seminars and development programmes. Entrepreneurs should be provided infrastructure facilities," states B. Datta Gupta, vice president of Kolkata-based FISME.

⏩ Conclusion

Sickness in industry, especially in the small-scale sector in particular is a cause for concern. The banks, financial institution and the Government should address to redressal strategies for these sick units. Revival of sick units should be taken on a priority basis.

Even when detailed project reports are prepared, inexperienced entrepreneurs may 'build' sickness into their units from the conception stage itself. For example, they may opt for an improper location, employ inadequately experienced consultants, choose inappropriate technology, underestimate the fixed and operational costs involved in the manufacture of their products, and embark on a project without a proper market survey.

Given the general spread of sickness in the small-scale sector, it seems that government agencies have not properly scrutinized project proposals. In fact, T. Ragupati, a faculty member of the Industrial Development Department, Small Industries Extension Training Institute, Hyderabad, places the blame squarely on government agencies.

"The sickness among new small-scale units is attributable to their indiscriminate promotion by government agencies in order to achieve employment targets fixed under Plan programmes. During the Fifth Plan, and in later years, there was an increased emphasis on providing job opportunities by developing small-scale and tiny units. It resulted in hastily prepared and implemented programmes for the promotion of these units.

"Campaigns were undertaken by the promotional agencies to select unemployed, educated and technically qualified persons as entrepreneurs in promoting small industries. Financial agencies like banks were subjected to pressures to finance without adequate evaluation of the projects. This appears to be the principal factor for the ever-rising incidence of sickness among newly promoted industries, particularly in backward areas."

In the present context, the only healthy way is to nurse these millions of small units for overall progress. This is easier said than done, due to wide gap in enlightened managers. Our employment scenario does not compel the management graduates to serve these units, at least for some initial period, neither do the owners show an openness for such managerial interaction.

A possible alternative is to counsel these units, without hurting the sentiments of the owner at the very first stage. After some success is achieved, trust is built and confidence is created, one can slowly advance and undertake further reform process, always holding the flag as an external catalyst. This will evidently be time consuming, but expected to be result yielding at slow pace.

While conceptualising and designing the coverage of business consultancy for small and medium scale industries, one essentially needs to consider the totality of its dimension, for understanding, acceptance and application by such clientele. Piecemeal advice may not serve their purpose. The idea is to offer turnkey solutions and induce things to happen. Psychological barrier may hinder the process initially, but once the link is established, demand will cross every hurdle.

Analysing the scope of such total counselling, welcome across three principal areas, for need based steering:

- Technical aspects related to present or proposed activity.
- Managerial functions in isolation and integration.
- Commercial proceedings, with applicable rules and regulations.

Once again, it will require lot of expertise and exposures to plan and extend counselling on all these areas, preferably from a single window. For this, pooling of resources will be necessary. A tall order indeed, but there seems to be no short cut.

The empirical studies show that by adopting better practices, right technology, new work culture and professional management, small-scale industries can improve their health and elevate from smaller status. In the process improve the health of the industry as well as of the economy.

Modern Management, however, has overcome the shortcomings of the old system. It makes a proper and systematic study of the subject. Regular courses are now conducted at university levels. By applying the principles of management learnt in such a course and with on-the-job training available, today's professional managers are at a much better advantage than those who had traditional training alone.

The functions of management lie in collection of relevant material and utilising them to take quick decisions for the attainment of desired goals. Management is a skill which, like any other skill, can be acquired. The success of an industry is largely determined by a satisfactory management of finance, inventory, budgeting, marketing, accounting, and manpower. These areas are deeply studied, and the information collected is utilised to plan and control the activities of a unit. The management of Finance and inventory, by far, is the most important of all. Many units fall sick because of an improper handling of these areas of management. Coordination and Integration.

Purposeful co-ordination and integration of such supporting institutions will go a long way in making these institutions a valuable resource that can go into the small industry, leading to its accelerated growth. Again, such assistance should be easily and constantly made available to the small entrepreneur and this could be possible only if the service institutions are organised regionally, if not locally. Further, the assistance should also be prompt and efficient. Promptness would go a long way in saving time, which amounts to sacking on expenses, and consequently, improving profitability. It should also be equally efficient. The diagnosis should be correct and the remedies should be effective. Efficiency, therefore, means correct diagnosis and effective remedies. The whole object of assistance to small entrepreneurs is to improve the vitality as well as competitive ability of their industrial units. This is important because enterprising service institutions and innovative local entrepreneurship can together change the environment and the horizon of the small industries sector in the developing economies. Infrastructure is thus acquiring a wider connotation and greater significance than ever before. It is essential for the developing countries to realise this and prepare themselves to face the new challenges that await them on the horizon of industrial transformation.

THE OPTIMIST BREAKS THROUGH

I have become my own version of an optimist. If I can't make it through one door, I'll go through another — or I'will make a door. Something terrific will come no matter how dark the present.

— Rabindranath Tagore

29

Preparation of Feasibility Reports

Introduction

Some of the principal lessons that the World Bank has learned in assisting its member countries in managing their investment resources are offered not in the belief that they provide final answers to the formidable problems of development, but in the conviction that better national investment planning, macroeconomic and sector policies, and project work can ease the path of development, bring its benefits to people sooner, and distribute them more equitably.

Saurabh Srivastava
Indian Angel Network

Throughout the several stages of the project cycle, various dimensions of project work are addressed, both separately and in relation to each other, and in varying degrees of detail.

Technical Analysis

Of these dimensions, technical analysis is perhaps the most familiar. Among the issues of technical design are size, location, timing, and choice of a technology package. We have already alluded to the need to select a technology appropriate to the circumstances of the country and the requirements of the project. The point bears repeating in any list of lessons. "Appropriateness" is a relative concept. It generally means that the technology should be determined in relation to the objectives of the project, to the impact on intended beneficiaries, and to local conditions, including the availability and cost of capital, raw materials, and labour, the size of markets, and the present and potential capacity for planning and implementation.

Numerous tradeoffs are implicit in these considerations: for example, the technology may often have to be reduced in complexity to fit the capabilities of local institutions or the socio-cultural traditions of the beneficiaries. The range of choice is very wide, from sophisticated, high technology for long-distance telecommunications even in the least developed countries. Whatever the choice, it is important that it not be unduly biased by government interventions or price distortions of the kind referred to earlier.

Technical analysis also provides an opportunity to consider how a county can best take advantage of its investment plan, policy framework, and development projects to build a capacity to use science and technology effectively throughout the economy. Both trained people and institutions capable of utilizing their skills are required. In the early stages of a country's development, the emphasis should be on building local capacity to import technology from abroad knowledgeably and to adapt it to local conditions. At later stages, the emphasis should shift to the development of local technology and its integration with imported technology, and to the encouragement of local research and innovation.

Economic Analysis

The basic question that economic analysis addresses is how to allocate scarce resources among many competing uses. It seeks to determine not only whether a project can be expected to provide a satisfactory return to the economy, but also whether there is an alternative way of achieving the same objectives that would offer a higher return. The analysis entails a comparison of costs and benefits with and without the project, both discounted to present values, through the use of analytical techniques that by now are highly refined – though no more accurate than the underlying data. Its central concept – that, for purposes of economic analysis, resources should be valued in terms of their opportunity cost to the economy in their best alternative use – is applicable to all economic systems, whether market-oriented, centrally planned, or a combination of the two.

Most lending agencies use cost-benefit analysis to assess the projects they help finance, and many developing countries are applying this analysis in one form or another to projects that they fund from public resources. Private industrial enterprises also use cost-benefit analysis for major investments. If done properly, it can be a powerful tool for guiding investment choices.

Cost-benefit analysis encounters some practical problems, among them: how to define the situation "with" and "without" the project (which should not be confused with the situation "before" and "after" the project); how to handle sunk costs incurred before the analysis (the short answer is to disregard them); how to establish the shadow (that is, opportunity) prices for labour and capital, when market prices are distorted for various reasons; and how to deal with nonquantifiable benefits. For most of these problems of definition or measurement, reasonable approaches can be found that are consistent with the reliability of the available data. The results of the analysis can be presented as a measure of net present value, as an internal rate of return, or as a cost-benefit ratio; each has its particular uses.

Not all types of projects are amenable to cost-benefit analysis; it is not customarily used, for example, in evaluating education or health projects. Nor docs it have the same meaning in different sectors. In power and water, for example, where prices are publicly administered rather than fixed by the marketplace, the economic rate of return is a minimum estimate, more indicative of the appropriateness of the regulated tariffs than of the real return to the economy. Cost-benefit analysis, therefore, is not very useful in comparing the merits or relative ranking of projects in different sectors.

Much depends on the common sense, judgement, and even ingenuity of the analyst. Whim, bias, and intuition will also inevitably play a part. These caveats notwithstanding, economic evaluation can introduce rationality into the decision-making process, identify and measure risks, and avoid some of the more serious mistakes that can occur even in the best laid investment plans.

Financial Analysis

Financial analysis is a scientific tool. It has assumed an increasingly important role as a tool for appraising the real worth of an enterprise, its performance during a period of time and its pitfalls. Financial analysis helps in drawing out the complications of what it contained in the financial statements.

Financial analysis is defined as the process of discovering economic facts about an enterprise and/or a project on the basis of an interpretation of financial data. Financial analysis also seeks to look the capital cost, operations cost and operating revenue. The analysis decisively established a relationship between the various factors of a project and helps in manoeuvring the project's activities. It also serves as a common measure of value for obtaining a clear-cut understanding about the project from the financial point of view.

An analysis of several financial tools provides an important basis for valuing securities and appraising managerial programmes. Financial analysis is a vital apparatus for the interpretation of Financial statements. It can provide an insight into two important areas of management – return on investment and soundness of the company's financial position. David Hawkins observes that the analyst evaluates results against the particular characteristics of the company and its industry. He seldom expects answers from this process; but he hopes that it would provide him with clues as to where he should focus his subsequent analysis.

Internal management accounts provide information which is valuable for the purpose of control. The information is made available in the shape of accounting data, which may be in the form of statements – financial statements and accounting statements. A financial analysis reveals where the company stands with respect to profitability, liquidity, leverage and an efficient use of its assets. Financial reports provide the framework within which business planning takes place. They are the key through which an effective control of a business enterprise is exercised. A financial analysis is the process of determining the significant financial characteristics of a firm. It may be external or internal. The external analysis is performed by creditors, stockholders and investment analysts. The internal analysis is performed by the various departments of a firm.

Significance of Financial Analysis

Financial analysis primarily deals with the interpretation of the data incorporated in the proforma financial statements of a project and the presentation of the data in a form in which it can be utilised for a comparative appraisal of the projects. It is, in effect, concerned with the development of the financial profile of the project. Its purpose is to find out whether the project is attractive enough to secure funds needed for its various constituent activities and once having secured the funds, whether the project will be able to generate enough economic values to achieve the objectives for which it is sought to be implemented. Financial analysis deals not only with the financial aspects of a project but also with its operational aspects. As such it is necessary to undertake such an analysis not only in the case of industrial projects but also in the case of non-industrial projects.

Analysis of financial statements has become very significant due to the widespread interest of various parties in the financial result of a company. In recent years, the ownership of capital of most public companies has become broad-based. A number of parties and bodies, including creditors, potential suppliers, debenture-holders, credit institutions like banks, industrial suppliers, industrial finance corporations, etc., potential investors, employees, trade unions, important customers, economists, investment analysts, taxation authorities and Government have a stake in the financial results of a company. Various people look at the financial statements from various angles. A number of techniques have been developed to undertake analysis of financial statements in order to reach conclusions about the financial health, profitability and efficiency of an enterprise and also to compare an enterprise with other similar undertakings. The technique of ratio analysis is most important tool of financial analysis. It helps in comparing the performance of various companies and judge their financial soundness.

Issue of financial analysis arise in the course of project design in several ways. The first and most universal concern, applicable to all types of projects, is that there be sufficient funds both to complete the project and to operate and maintain it subsequently. This sounds obvious, but far too many development projects have been launched without adequate consideration of the future availability of funds. This is notably true for education projects, in which recurrent costs for teachers' salaries may quickly exceed the capital costs of the facilities; or for projects in irrigation, roads, health, water supply, and other infrastructure, in which facilities once completed may deteriorate rapidly for want of adequate maintenance. This reluctance to provide adequate recurrent expenditures reflects in part the greater political appeal of new investments and in part the unwillingness of most external leaders to finance such expenditures.

A second financial concern is to recover an appropriate portion of the costs from the beneficiaries or users. A cost recovery policy has three separate but related objectives:

- **Economic efficiency:** The resources provided under a project are used most efficiently when, they are priced in accordance with their marginal or opportunity cost. The extent to which efficiency prices can be applied, however, varies widely from sector to sector.
- **Income distribution:** In the interests of equity, the prices or other charges levied to recover costs should take into account differences in income levels (as affected by the project) and in ability to pay.
- **Revenue generation:** Governments in developing countries, being short of resources, need to generate revenue from projects. In addition, revenue-earning enterprises need to be made or kept financially viable. If rural and urban development, water supply, and other projects are to be replicable on the scale necessary to reach the large numbers of potential beneficiaries, a substantial contribution from the initial beneficiaries will often have to be secured.

Difficult tradeoffs may be required among these sometimes conflicting objectives, and the poorer the country the more painful the choices may be. Cost recovery for basic services can be an explosive political issue. This fact, together with administrative considerations, determines what can be accomplished and how quickly. Two important rules to follow are that new or increased levies should be related to benefits as they materalize and imposed in small but regular increments, and that similar situations should be treated similarly to avoid the appearance of discrimination.

The financial viability of revenue-earning enterprises – electric and water utilities, public and private industries, railways, telecommunication entities, and so on – can be translated into three subsidiary objectives or tests of performance:

- Will the enterprise have sufficient revenue to earn a reasonable return on its invested capital? As part of the test of "reasonableness," will it be able to generate enough funds internally from its operations to make a satisfactory contribution to its future capital requirements?

- Will the capital structure of the enterprise enable it to meet all of its capital obligations, including the service of its debt, in a timely manner?
- Will there be adequate liquidity, that is sufficient working capital, to cover all current operational requirements?

Insistence on financial viability is an important means of imposing discipline on an enterprise and encouraging efficient management and use of resources. There is almost always some scope for improving Financial performance by raising operating standards and reducing waste. Achieving financial viability will, however, ultimately throw issues of tariff policy into bold relief. In many cases, increases in prices – often substantial – will be necessary to reach the Financial objectives. To raise the price of a basic product or service that figures prominently in the cost of living is an act of political courage. But not to raise the price may, in the long run, have even more adverse economic, and therefore political, consequences. During an inflationary period, governments are especially reluctant to increase the cost of basic goods and services. This is understandable, but failure to raise prices may also have an inflationary impact if the government must borrow to cover the deficits.

One means of leasing the bureaucratic and political pain of raising the price of public services, as we have noted, is to adjust prices in small increments and at regular intervals. Another is to make price increases automatic or quasi-automatic, as when fuel costs are passed on to users through equivalent increases in electricity prices without the need for government approval cach time.

⏩ Social Analysis

Social analysis deals with the impact of projects on people. Its role is to consider the suitability of the proposed project design for the people it is intended to serve, to make proposals for improving the "fit" between the two, and to fashion strategies for project implementation that can be expected both to win and hold people's support and to achieve project goals by inducing changes in social attitudes and behaviour. Somc projccts – in such fields as rural developments, education, and health – are clearly oriented toward people. Infrastructure projects are less so, but even these may have to deal effectively with people, as workers or consumers, in order to achieve their objectives. A project that puns counter to or ignores the traditions, values, and social organization of the intended beneficiaries, or that is based on objectives which they do not share, has little prospect of success.

Social analysis is a relative newcomer among the dimensions of project analysis. It focuses on four principal areas:

- The socio-cultural and demographic characteristics of the project population.
- The way in which the project population is organized to carry out productive activities.
- The project's cultural acceptability, including its capacity for both adapting to people's behaviour and perceived needs and for bringing about changes in them.
- The strategy necessary to elicit commitment from the project population and to ensure their sustained participation throughout the project cycle.

Predicting social behaviour is even more uncertain than forecasting financial or economic behaviour. Project planners have often made unduly optimistic assumptions about local people's interest in and need for a project, the economic and social incentives for them to participate, and the rate at which change in their social condition can be brought about. Social analysis with professional training and broad cxperience can improve the projections. However, more importantly, they can make a significant contribution to a project's success by helping to design effective organizations and approaches to achieve desirable change in social behaviour.

Social analysis of projects has frequently failed to take adequate account of the particular interests and needs of women. Although they constitute half the world's population, women have reaped far less than their share of the benefits of development. Women tend to have less schooling than men, their mobility is constrained by economic and social considerations, and they often face legal barriers to their ownership of assets or access to credit. Yet women play a key role in the development process, both as producers and consumers; for example, they provide most of the agricultural labour used in production, harvesting, marketing, and storage. Moreover, the central position of women in family life profoundly influences attitudes and decisions on education, nutrition, health, and family size. Thus, even if women never enter the formal labour market, ensuring that they receive an adequate education may be one of the best investments a country can make.

Failure to appreciate the role of women when projects are designed and implemented is not only inequitable but also retards the pace of economic growth. Decisions about which technologies to use and about how to provide a wide range of services must be made with full regard to women's needs and constraints; otherwise, project benefits will be reduced and the position of women made even worse. In many respects, women are the largest underutilized resource for development.

⏩ Institutional Analysis

In recent years, institutional analysis has become one of the important dimensions of project work. The outcome of development projects depends on the quality of the institutions responsible for them. Yet institutions in developing countries typically suffer from an acute shortage of experienced managers and staff, an excess of untrained staff, overstrained services and facilities, low wages and salaries, inadequate data and information system, and an inimical policy environment. There are no standard solutions and few readily transferable institutional models from either developed or other developing countries.

Institutional development must be seen as a lengthy process of experiment and adaptation, subject to many reverses when political or economic fortunes change. Still, when strong institutions have been forged, they have played a key role in development.

The overall policy environment affects the performance not only of projects but also of the institutions responsible for them. If managers of these institutions are compelled to spend time and effort counteracting the impact of government economic policies (such as a critical shortage of foreign exchange for spare parts, owing to an overvalued exchange rate), they cannot build long-term capacity effectively. Institutional problems multiply rapidly when government policies seriously distort the economic environment or when government regulations impose extraneous requirements, such as the employment of extra staff for political or social reasons.

Institutional problems have been compounded as more complex development objectives have been assigned to projects. Executing multicomponent projects or projects focused on alleviating poverty or upgrading social services has placed heavy demands on institutions. Knowledge of the economic, social, and behavioural characteristics of small farmers, urban squatters, or disadvantaged tribal people is still rudimentary. Understanding of the management and institutional techniques for dealing with such projects is also at an early stage.

Institutions in the public sector present a particular challenge, both because of their importance and because of the many problems they characteristically confront. A comprehensive reform of the public administration system – however badly needed – is a very ambitious undertaking. Few countries, developed or developing, have successfully carried out such a reform in the face of the strong resistance that these efforts generate.

While careful diagnosis of the problem of the public service is a necessary first step in establishing an overall strategy for change, implementing the strategy will almost invariably call for a selective approach. The best results have been achieved by concentrating on a few of the more critical problems. The ones to tackle first are those that seriously constrain the performance of the public administration and that are within its capacity to solve; in addition, it should be possible to mobilize and maintain public support for the reform effort.

Parastatals and other forms of state-owned enterprise have proliferated in recent years. Their performance has at best been mixed, and concern has been growing about the need to increase their efficiency, reduce their deficits that burden the public budget, and avoid political interference in their affairs. Given the preponderance of public enterprises in the economies of many developing countries, reforming them has repercussions going far beyond improved project performance. Some governments, in fact, are beginning to devote considerable effort to limiting the spread of public enterprises and to transferring ownership of some of these enterprises to the private sector. The legitimate demands on the public sector are very large, and the capacity for public management is among the scarcest of development resources. This capacity should, therefore, be reserved for use where it is most needed and most likely to be efficacious; governments should exercise caution in deciding which fields are appropriate for public ownership.

For those agricultural and institutional parastarals carrying out processing, manufacturing or marketing operations that private producers and merchants can do efficiently, the simple answer may be to abolish them. For other parastatals, reducing the number of staff, rationalizing their structures, and appointing and promoting staff on the basis of merit are among the measures needed. In several countries, policy reforms are being tried that will improve the "rules of the game" under which the enterprises operate. This reform has two objectives: to give public enterprises greater authority and autonomy to carry out their activities in accordance with broad goals and specific performance targets agreed on with the government; and to hold the enterprises accountable for their results, while improving the flow of information to government about their performance.

A widespread weakness of development institutions, particularly but not exclusively in the public sector, is the shortage of qualified managers at the middle and upper echelons and of experienced specialists such as accountants and engineers. This is a basic characteristic of underdevelopment that can change only gradually. In the long run, the education through universities, vocational schools, and management institutes – must provide the solution. But some steps can be taken immediately. Expatriate managers and consultants can be used to free bottlenecks in the short run – as long as care is taken that this docs not delay the development of local managerial capacity, but rather fosters it through counterpart and on-the-job training. Whatever die source of management, greater attention to organizational questions and improved management, accounting, and information systems and procedures can enhance effectiveness. Continuity of management is also important; frequent changes for political reasons are highly disruptive.

One fruitful approach to strengthening management in the public service is through improved incentives. Salary and other financial incentives for public officials cannot normally match those in the private sector, but disparities can be narrowed. In particular cases, elements of the financial package other than pay can also be improved without disturbing prevailing standards in the public service. Establishing "super-grades" outside the normal system may be a way to meet special needs, while making lateral entry and exit easier can encourage managers to view public service as a natural stage in a career.

Programs for training managers and staff also deserve much more attention. The potential contribution of such programs is very large, yet experience shows that too often they have little effect. Training programs cannot be added on to projects at the last moment, but must be planned carefully in advance and properly executed. Adequate resources, must be provided and skilled trainers recruited. As a general rule, the closer training is to the workplace in which it will be used, the more effective it is likely to be. This argues for on-the-job training when feasible.

⏩ Environmental Analysis

It is now widely recognized that environmental analysis is necessary for a country to ensure the sound management and use of its natural resources as an integral part of its strategy for economic growth. Desertification, deforestation, soil erosion, overexploitation of such renewable resources as fisheries, and air and water pollution are lowering the carrying capacity of the environment. Usually the poor are disproportionately affected by environmental degradation. The objective of environmental management should be to achieve a balance between human demands on the natural resource base and the ability of that resource base to meet these demands on a sustainable basis in the interests of future generations as well as those alive today.

With careful environmental management, the pace of economic and social progress need not be slowed. In environmental work, the "ounce of prevention" is almost always more important and less costly than the "pound of cure." Sometimes remedial action may not be feasible at all. All proposed development projects should be screened to detect those with a potentially harmful impact on the environment. Most environmental problems, if properly anticipated, can be dealt with at relatively small cost – usually less than 5 per cent of total project cost. Analysis of the tradeoffs between different design features and their environmental costs and benefits should be a routine part of project work; the analysis is complicated, however, by the fact that the standard time-discounting methodology, gives insufficient weight to environmental costs and benefits because of their long-term nature.

⏩ Procurement

Managing the procurement process is an important aspect of project implementation. Delays in acquiring the necessary goods and works are likely to be compounded into further delays and increased costs for the project as a whole. Procurement is therefore a process to be carefully planned, organized, and managed, the more so since the number of ways things can go wrong sometimes appears endless.

Procurement must serve three objectives. The first is to help ensure the efficient execution of the project by acquiring goods and works with the optimal combination of quality, price, and delivery time. The second is to promote such national goals as the development of local industry, the balanced regional development of industry, or the support of small-scale enterprises. The third is to comply with the procurement regulations of any external lending institutions helping to finance the project.

There are a wide variety of types and methods of procurement. Which is the most appropriate depends on the size and nature of the project, the particular goods or works to be procured, and the regulations of lending agencies. For large projects, international competitive bidding is generally the best way of ensuring efficient procurement, safeguarding against waste or corruption, and satisfying the interest of lending agencies that all qualified firms be permitted to bid. Local competitive bidding is more appropriate for small-scale procurement of goods and works in which foreign firms will not be interested: changes in procedures may be necessary to ensure effective competition among local firms.

Use of Consultants

Procurement of consulting services raises different issues. There is, first, the question of need. Most of the services for which consultants might be recruited can, in principle, be provided by local staff of the project agency if they are competent, experienced, and available. When such in-house capacity does not exist (as may often be the case) and cannot be put in place by additional training soon enough to meet the demands of the project, the next best choice is the use of local consulting firms. Establishing a local consulting industry is desirable both to provide some competition to stimulate agency staff and to supply more specialized skills or expert services. When local services are not available, firms from other developing countries may offer the dual advantages of better knowledge and understanding of comparable local conditions and relatively low costs. There will, however, remain some assignments – especially for large or complex projects and those requiring highly technical knowledge – for which only expatriate consultants from developed countries are qualified. Joint ventures between foreign and local consulting firms, if entered into voluntarily, are often a good way of developing local capacity.

The consultant-client relationship is a close, personal one; when a satisfactory partnership already exists with a particular firm, it may be eminently sensible to continue it. When no such relationship exists, or when for other reasons it is desirable to invite proposals from a short list of qualified firms, the selection process should ensure that price considerations are subordinated to a concern with quality. The cost of consulting services is usually only a small fraction of total project costs, but the equality of the work performed can have an impact on the final project out of all proportion to the cost.

Conclusion

Feasibility studies are the pro-requisites of a project, and it provides the much needed inputs to the entrepreneur in translating his dreams into a successful venture as per his vision and goals.

A project feasibility analysis includes market analysis, technical analysis, financial analysis and social profitability analysis. Although every feasibility analysis is different and is tailored to suit the product, its goal is to identify the strengths and weaknesses of the project.

The starting point of a project analysis is the establishment of the objectives to be attained. The next stage is the pro-selection stage – the advisability of having an in-depth study. The analysis stage consists mainly of three factors – market, technical and financial analysis. A market analysis is a method of screening project ideas as well as a means of evaluating a project's feasibility in terms of the market.

The technical analysis of a project feasibility study establishes whether the project is technically feasible or not, and whether it offers a basis for the estimation of costs. Moreover, it provides an opportunity for the consideration of the effect of various technical alternatives on employment, ecology, infrastructure demands, capital services, support of other industries, balance of payments, and other factors. Every entrepreneur should focus his attention on this important tool of management.

SPIRIT OF ENQUIRY

"Continuing enquiry is what progress is really about. The core aspects of the current industrial development processs simply cannot continue because they are so illogical at all levels." — ***Peter Senge, Management Guru***

30

Legal Formalities and Documentation

Introduction

Pradeep Gupta
The Indus Entrepreneurs

Regulations are the basis of steady growth. In a society, regulations are the governing factors, ensuring that everything occurs in conformity with the plans and policy adopted, the instructions issued and the principles established. They pinpoint the weaknesses and errors so that they may be rectified and their recurrence may be prevented. They operate on everything – people, objects and actions. Thus, a regulation is a process by which we may check whether or not plans are being adhered to, whether or not a proper progress is being made towards the objectives, whether the environment is saved from pollution, whether law and order is maintained or not, whether the interests of the workers are safeguarded or not, whether the small entrepreneurs are getting the raw materials or not, and whether there are any deviations against which a corrective action needs to be taken.

Objective

The basic objective behind the whole process of regulations is to ensure that the results of operations conform as closely as possible to established standards of goods, specified procedures or instructions. Small-scale industry has to develop as an important segment of society; as such it has to adhere to the rules of the land, *i.e.*, it has to be subject to the various regulations. Regulations governing Small-scale industry are of two types: (*i*) protective and (*ii*) promotional. Protective regulations are by way of various safeguards, while promotional regulations are in the nature of giving a push to the small-scale industry, *i.e.*, they are growth-oriented.

There are various rules and regulations applicable to different group of industries for various purposes. Some of these are described below:

(*i*) Registration/Licensing: Industries with an investment of less than Rs. 75 lakh in plant and machinery are small-scale industries. They may be registered with G.M. District Industries Centres of the district concerned to get benefits.

An ancillary unit (SSI) is defined as one having capital investment in plant and machinery not exceeding Rs. 75 lakh which produces parts, components, subassemblies and makes supplies against known or anticipated demand of one or more large units manufacturing/assembling complete product and which is not a subsidiary or controlled by any large unit in regard to the negotiation of contract for supply of its goods to any large unit. This will not however, preclude an ancillary unit from entering into agreement with a large unit, giving it the first option to take the former's output.

The unit set-up primarily for the replacement market falls within its scope. Manufacture of tools, dies, jigs and fixtures is also recognised as an ancillary industry. These ancillary unit (SSI) can also get themselves registered with G.M. District Industries Centres of the district concerned.

➧ Regulations

Right from the beginning, a small-scale industry is regulated and governed by the following regulations: (*a*) State Industries Acts; (*b*) The Factories Act, 1948; (*c*) The Shops & Establishment Act, 1948; (*d*) The Indian Boiler Act (if applicable); (*e*) The Payment of Wages Act, 1936; (*f*) The Minimum Wages Act, 1948; (*g*) The Workmen's Compensation Act, 1923; (*h*) The Employees Provident Fund Act, 1952; (*i*) The Employees State Insurance Act, 1948; (*j*) The Income Tax Act, 1961; (*k*) The Central Sales Tax Act and State Sales Tax Act; (*l*) The Drugs Control Act; (*m*) The Payment of Bonus Act, 1978; (*n*) The Industrial Employment (Standing Orders) Act, 1926 and (*o*) The Industrial Disputes Act, 1947.

In addition, the small-scale entrepreneur has to be well versed in excise, customs procedures and export and import regulations and procedures. He should always seek assistance from the following professionals: (*a*) Inspecting Staff of Government; (*b*) Labour Consultants; (*c*) Financial Consultants.

The salient features of the regulations governing the small-scale industries are summarised below:

➧ Industrial Development (Regulation) Act (IDRA)

The IDRA is an instrument in the hands of the Government for the control and direction of private sector industrial investment through the mechanism of the industrial licensing system, which enables it to exert pressure on the applicants in a variety of ways. Conceptually, the government ought to direct further industrial investment in such product lines as would better serve the overall national interest and in such geographical areas which need it the most.

It is a complicated, time-consuming and costly exercise to acquire an industrial licence. Sometimes, it takes years before it can be obtained. Obviously, it cannot be the intention of the Government to extend this procedure to the small-scale sector because it would be impossible to work towards implementation. A small unit cannot even prepare an application for an industrial licence, and there is nobody to help it in preparing it. There is no agency which is capable of checking the veracity of what the applicant says in his application, much less comment thereon.

In recent years, there has been quite a clamour from various associations of small-scale industries for their legislative protection. In August 1971, the Small-Scale Industries Board, at its 29th meeting, had recommended to the Government to set up a committee to examine the feasibility of enacting suitable legislations for the development of small-scale industries. Always eager to form committees, the Government speedily acceded to the recommendation of the Board and constituted a committee in January 1972 under the chairmanship of Mr. A. R. Bhat to draft legislation for the small-scale sector. It was, moreover, required to identify specific areas where legislation was considered necessary and to submit drafts for the purpose.

Factories Act, 1948

(i) Definition of a Factory: Section 2 (m) defines a factory as any place wherein ten or more persons are working and in which a manufacturing process is carried on with the aid of motive power supplied by steam, oil or electricity. Premises in which power is not used come under the definition of a factory if twenty or more persons are working in them. This definition brings a greater number of places under the purview of this Act than was the case under the Act of 1934.

(ii) Employment of Children: The Act fixes the minimum age of persons who can enter a factory for work at 14 years. It prohibits the employment of children upto the age of 13.

The Act further lays down that a qualified surgeon must certify that a person has completed the age of 14. Such certificates must be obtained by a factory manager and must be available for inspection by factory inspector.

(iii) Hours of Work for Children: The Act reduces the hours of work for children between the ages of 14-17 from 5 hours a day to 4½ hours a day. It also prohibits work at night for such persons.

(iv) Hours of Work for Adult Female and Male Workers: The Act prohibits employment of women in factories between 6 P.M. and 7 A.M. It reduces the hours of work for adult men and women workers from 54 to 48 per week and from 9 hours to 8 hours a day.

The Act also lays down that the eight hours of work will be spread over a period of not more that 10½ hours. Further it provides that no worker shall work for more than 5 hours before he has had an interval or rest of at least half an hour. Lastly, the Act lays down that those workers who are made to work for more than 8 hours a day or 48 hours a week shall be paid for the extra hours at the rate of twice their ordinary rates of wages.

(v) Cleanliness: The Act lays down that every factory shall be kept clean and free from effluvia arising from any drain, privy or other nuisance. Accumulation of dirt and refuse shall be removed daily from the floor and the benches of work-rooms, from staircases and passages, and disposed of in the suitable manner.

The floor of every work-room in a factory shall be cleaned once a week.

All inside walls, ceilings and partition shall be white-washed at least once in fourteen months; if they are painted or varnished, they shall be re-painted or revarnished once in five years.

Effective arrangements shall be made in every factory for the disposal of wastes arising out of the manufacturing process carried on therein.

(vi) Ventilation and Temperature: Effective and suitable provision shall be made in every factory for securing and maintaining in every work-room adequate ventilation by the circulation of fresh air and the maintenance of such temperature as will secure therein reasonable conditions of comfort for those working there. Where excessively high temperatures are necessary for technical reasons, adequate measures shall be taken by the management to protect the workers from such temperatures.

The State Government may prescribe a standard of adequate ventilation and reasonable temperature for any factory or class of factories and can suggest ways and means for reducing excessively high temperatures.

In any factory, where dust or fumes injurious to the health of workers arise in any manufacturing process, effective measures shall be taken to prevent their inhalation or accumulation in any work-room.

***(vii)* Artificial Humidification:** In factories where humidity is artificially increased, the State Government may make rules:

(*a*) Prescribing standards of humidification;

(*b*) Regulating methods used for humidification;

(*c*) Directing prescribed tests for determining humidity, and directing that such tests are carried out – their results recorded and

(*d*) Prescribing methods to be adopted for securing adequate ventilation and cooling of the air in those rooms where artificial humidity is introduced.

Water used for the purpose of humidification shall be such as has been certified by the municipal authorities as fit for drinking.

***(viii)* Overcrowding :** To prevent overcrowding in a factory, the Act lays down that, in factories built before the passing of this Act, there shall be space of at least 350 cubic feet per worker and in factories built after the Act came into force, it shall be at least 500 cubic feet. To arrive at these figures, a height above 14 feet shall not be taken into consideration. In accordance with this rule, the Chief Inspector of Factories will communicate to each factory manager the maximum number of workers that may be employed on any premises. He has, however, the power to exempt any factory or work-room from this rule, if he is satisfied that its observance of this rule is not necessary in the interest of the workers employed therein.

***(ix)* Lighting:** It is the duty of the management of a factory to maintain sufficient and suitable lighting, natural or artificial or both, in factory and in all the work-rooms.

All glazed windows and sky-lights shall be kept clean on both the inner and outer surfaces, and effective measures shall be taken for the prevention of glare and formation of any shadows which may cause eye-strain or create a risk of accidents.

The State Government may make rules as to what is sufficient and suitable lighting, for a factory or a class of factories.

***(x)* Drinking Water:** In every factory, effective arrangements shall be made to provide, suitable points conveniently situated for all workers employed therein, a sufficient supply of wholesome drinking water.

In every factory, where more than 253 workers are ordinarily employed, provision shall be made for cool drinking water during the hot weather.

***(xi)* Toilets:** In every factory, sufficient toilet facilities of the prescribed types, shall be provided at places which are conveniently situated and are easily accessible to workers at all times while they are at the factory.

The State Government may prescribe the number of public toilet services to be provided in any factory in proportion to the number of male and female workers ordinarily employed therein.

***(xii)* Provision of Spittoons:** In every factory, there shall be a sufficient number of spittoons in convenient places and they shall be maintained in a clean and hygienic condition.

***(xiii)* Safety provisions:** According to the Act of 1934, a factory manager could afford to wait till an Inspector of Factories gave instructions as to what ought to be done to ensure the safety of workers. The Act of 1948 has placed the responsibility for safety matters on the shoulders of the occupier or the manager of a factory. He must comply with all the safety provisions without waiting for the inspector's instructions.

Secondly, the Act places legal responsibility on the management for the maintenance and use of safety guard. It is its duty to supervise the use of these guards by the workers.

The specific provisions for safety are as follows: in every factory all dangerous parts of tall machines, such as the moving parts of prime movers, flywheels, electric generators, motors, rotary converters, etc. shall be securely fenced by safety guards of substantial construction which shall be kept in position while the parts of machinery they fence are in motion.

***(xiv)* Dangerous Fumes:** Adequate provision shall be made in a factory where dangerous fumes are present in any chamber, tank, pipe, etc., for the egress of such fumes.

***(xv)* Explosive Gases, Dust, Fume:** If, in any factory, the manufacturing process raises dust, gas, fume or vapour which is likely to explode on ignition, all measures shall be taken to prevent any such explosion by –

(*a*) Providing an effective enclosure of the plant or machinery used in the process or

(*b*) The removal or prevention of accumulation of such dust, gas or fumes.

***(xvi)* Safety of Factory Building and Machinery:** If it appears to the Inspector that any building or part of factory is in such a condition that it is dangerous to human life or safety, he may serve on the managers of the factory an order in writing specifying the measure that should be adopted and the specific date by which they should be carried out to ensure the safety of the building or factory. He may also serve an order on the manager, prohibiting its use until proper repairs or alterations have been carried out.

(xvii)* Welfare Provisions: *(a) Facilities for Washing: In every factory, adequate and suitable facilities for washing shall be provided and maintained for the workers. Adequately screened facilities for washing shall be provided for male and female workers separately. Such facilities shall be conveniently accessible and shall be kept clean.

(b) Storing and Drying Clothes: The State Government may require any factory or class of factories to make provision therein of suitable places for keeping clothes not worn during working hours and for drying wet clothing.

(c) Facilities for Sitting: In every factory, suitable arrangements for sitting shall be provided and maintained for all workers obliged to working a standing position in order that they may take advantage of any opportunity for rest which may occur in the course of their work.

(d) First-Aid Appliances: First-aid boxes, equipped with the prescribed contents, which will be really accessible during all working hours, shall be provided and maintained in every factory. The number of such boxes shall not be less than one for every one hundred and fifty workers.

(xviii) Penalties for Breach of Provision of the Act: For any contravention of the provisions of the Act, the occupier and the manager of a factory shall each be guilty of an offence and be punishable with imprisonment for a term not exceeding three months or with a fine up to Rs. 500 or with both.

If any person, who has been convicted of any offence punishable under the provisions of this Act, is again found to be guilty of an offence involving contravention of the same provision within a period of two years from the date of conviction with imprisonment upto six months or with a fine up to Rs. 1,000 or with both. This Act, for the time, provides that if any worker contravenes any provision of this Act or any rules or orders, such as the use of safety guards, spitting only in spittoons provided for the purpose, he shall be punishable with fine upto Rs. 20.

India's ratification of International Labour Convention No. 90 prohibiting the employment of young persons in factories at night necessitated an amendment of the relevant sections of the Factories Act, 1948. This was achieved by passing an Amendment Act in April 1954. This Act added a new chapter on "Annual Leave with Wages" to the Factories Act, 1948. It lays down a period of 240 days as the minimum attendance necessary during a calendar year to qualify for leave with wages. It also prohibits employment of young persons on cleaning, lubricating or adjusting any prime mover or transmission machinery while it is in motion, if such work exposes them to a risk of injury.

⏩ Income-Tax Act

The tax concessions provided in the Income-tax Act for small-scale industries are of minor significance. Under Section 80 HHA, which came into effect from the assessment year 1978-79, an assessee is entitled to a deduction in respect of profit and gains derived from new small-scale industrial undertaking set up in any rural area at the rate of 20 per cent for the first ten assessment years. One of the conditions is that the unit should have commenced its manufacturing activity after September 30, 1977. This concession is discriminatory, for there is no justification for denying the benefit to those units which commenced manufacturing activity before September 30, 1977. Moreover, the units in urban areas have been neglected. Unless we have correct statistics of the proportion of small-scale units in rural areas to those in urban areas and the proportion of the tax collected from rural units to the tax collected from urban ones, the significance of such a discriminatory tax concession cannot be evaluated.

Another incentive is the investment allowance under section 32A of the Act, under which a small-scale unit is entailed to a deduction at the rate of 25 per cent of the cost of plant and machinery installed after March 31,1976. This allowance is capital-oriented whereas most of the small-scale units are capital-saving and labour-oriented.

At present, there is no Central Government definition of the term *small-scale industrial undertaking* – a fact which indicates how unimportant these undertakings are in the eyes of the tax department. According to the definitions given under sections 32 A & 80 HHA, the term is used to mean an industrial undertaking whose aggregate value of machinery and plant – other than tools, jigs, dies and moulds – installed on the last day of the previous year for the purpose of the business of the undertaking, does not exceed Rs. 10 lakh. In Section 58 A of the Companies Act, however, the term is defined as any industrial undertaking registered with the Directorate of Industries or the Directorate of Small-Scale Industries.

⏩ SMEs and the Information Technology Act

The Information Technology Act (2000) was formulated in order to regulate online transactions or the exchange of electronic data. It was amended by the Indian Parliament on December 23, 2008.

The Act and its amendments aimed to curb the incidence of cyber or electronic crimes through the imposition of appropriate penalties.

The amendment to the Act added eight offences to the original list, directly-impacting small-scale players, as it deals with cybercafes, which are often small-scale businesses. The amended act also dearly defines cybercafes as 'intermediaries.' Three important sections have been added to the present Act, giving the government the power to intercept, monitor, block and collect traffic data. These sections impose certain responsibilities on the intermediaries and make non-compliance punishable under the Act. Cyber terrorism has been given particular importance as cybercafes have frequently been used to conduct terrorist activities. Accessing a site without proper authorisation and obtaining sensitive data, which can be used to terrorise people and threaten the sovereignty and security of the country, is punishable with a term of imprisonment.

At times, personal information stolen from computers in cybercafes has been used to withdraw money fraudulently. The Act imposes a penalty of a fine or up to three years of imprisonment on the use of stolen hardware or software. Using personal information to defraud people and impersonation with the intent to cheat someone out of money are also punishable by a steep fine or jail term.

The amendment also penalises the dissemination of sexually explicit content or material, in particular, content that involves minors. Anyone who publishes or transmits explicit material or creates, downloads or exchanges such material through electronic means is also liable to punishment.

⏩ The Industrial Employment (Standing Orders) Act, 1946

The absence of standing order clearly defining the rights and obligations of the employer and the workers in respect of recruitment, discharge, disciplinary action, holidays, leave etc. was one of the most frequent causes of friction between management and workers. On the recommendations of the Tripartite labour conferences held in 1943, 1944, 1945, the Government of India passed the Industrial Employment (standing orders) Act in 1946. This Act provides for the framing of standing orders in all establishment employing 100 or more persons. It requires employers to submit, within six months of the enactment of the law, standing orders covering the classification of workmen (permanent, temporary, etc.), the manner of intimating to them their hours of work, holidays, pay days and wage rates, the procedure to be followed while applying for leave and holidays the termination of employment for notice of discharge and for disciplinary action. In pursuance of this Act, the Central Government published the central rules in 1946 which were applicable to the Commissioner's provinces and to the undertaking under the Central Government. Its lead was promptly followed by all State Governments. In Maharashtra state, it has been made applicable to establishments in which fifty or more persons are employed.

⏩ The Warehousing Act, 2007

Implemented for the benefit of small and marginal farmers, the Warehousing (Development and Regulation) Act, 2007, is expected to help the industry by reducing risks related to the extension of credit as the pledging/collateralisation of agriculture produce would have a legal backing in the form of negotiable warehouse receipts.

The Act establishes that no person shall commence or carry on a warehousing business unless he possesses a registration certificate for the warehouse. A warehouse receipt, which may be in writing or electronic form, shall be a document of title to goods. A warehouse registered under this Act shall also be eligible to issue non-negotiable warehouse receipts. Provisions for the negotiation of warehouse receipts and transfer of non-negotiable receipts have also been elucidated.

Listing the duties and liabilities of warehousemen, the Act states that a warehouseman is liable for loss or injury to goods caused by his failure to exercise adequate care and diligence. However, any damage to goods, caused by circumstances such as force majeure, act of war or public enemies would be treated as an exception. A warehouseman is to deliver goods referred to in a negotiable receipt to its holder on his demand, and if refused, the burden of proof shall lie on the warehouseman. Persons aggrieved by an order of an Authority of the Act may appeal to the prescribed Appellate Authority within 60 days from the date of the order.

The Act also calls for the setting up of a Warehousing Development and Regulatory Authority, a corporate body with powers to acquire, hold and dispose of property, both movable and immovable, and to contract and sue or be sued. Detailed further is the body's composition of authority, powers as well as tenure of members, their removal, salaries and allowances, and the powers and functions of a Warehousing Advisory Committee.

The Indian Trade Unions Act, 1926

The experience of the working of the system of free enterprise in the industrial field revealed that, though theoretically both the employers and workers were free to enter into a contract and to agree upon the wages to be paid and received, in point of fact, for various reasons, this freedom did not benefit the workers in any way. Firstly, the commodity that a worker has to sell is highly perishable in the sense that if he refuses to work on a particular day because the wages offered are low, he cannot store up his labour of that day to be used the next day. This compels him to accept work even if the wages offered are unsatisfactory. Secondly, as his income is very low, he is not able to accumulate any savings which he can fall back upon if and when he refuses to work. The only alternative to refusal to work because of low wages is, therefore, starvation. These two factors compel a worker to accept low wages and so the theoretical freedom of contract is not of much use to him. Lastly, the fact that a worker is a small-scale seller and the employer is a large-scale buyer reduces his bargaining power to a very great extent. It is possible for the employer to refuse the wage which a worker demands because it is possible for him to engage somebody else who is willing to work at a lower wage. It is, however, relatively difficult for a worker to find an alternative employer who would pay in the wage he demands. His weak bargaining position thus compels him to accept whatever wages are offered to him.

Rules of a Trade Union: The rules of a union must contain the following provisions: (*a*) the name, (*b*) the objects for which it has been established, (*c*) the purpose for which its general funds will be applicable, (*d*) maintenance of the list of members for inspection by officers and members of the Union, (*e*) the admission of ordinary members who shall be persons engaged in the industry with which the Union is connected and also the admission of honorary members to form the executive of the union, (*f*) the conditions under which members arc entitled to the benefits ensured by the rules and measures which fines or forfeiture may be imposed on them, (*g*) the manner in which any rule shall be amended, altered or rescinded, (*h*) the manner in which the members of the executive and other officers of the Union shall be appointed and removed, (*i*) the safe custody of the funds of the Union, the audit of accounts and inspection of the account books by the officers and members, and lastly (*j*) the manner in which the Union will be dissolved.

Right of Registered Trade Unions: A registered trade union has a right:

(*a*) To collect membership fees on the premises of the factory without interference from the management;

(*b*) To put up notices of the meetings of the union and of other activities of the Union on the premises of the factory;

(*c*) To use the general funds for specific purposes;

(*d*) To raise funds for political purposes at the option of the members;

(*c*) To conduct a strike by peaceful methods;

(*f*) To be exempted from the provisions of Section 120B, subsection (2) of the Indian Penal Code if the members conduct a peaceful strike;

(*g*) To appoint outsiders in a number which is not more than one-half of the total number of office-bearers to the executive of the Union and

(*h*) To send to the Registrar, every year, an audited statement of receipts and expenditure.

The Payment of Wages Act, 1936

The payment of wages to factory workers in a particular form and at regular intervals without any unauthorized deductions is the objective of this Act.

Scope of the Act: The provisions of the Act are applicable to workers engaged in factories as defined by the Factories Act of 1948, and to persons employed on any railway by contractor or sub-contractor. The State Government may, after giving three months' notice of its intention of doing so by a notification in the Official Gazette, extend the provisions of this Act to any class of persons employed in any industrial establishment. The provisions of this Act are applicable to those persons whose wages do not exceed Rs. 400 per month.

The date of payment of wages: The wages of every person employed in a factory, industrial establishment or a railway, where less than 1,000 persons are employed, shall be paid before the expiry of the seventh day after the completion of the wage period, generally a month; the wages for a month, for example, shall be paid before the seventh day of the next month. In the factories in which more than a thousand persons are employed, the wages shall be paid before the expiry of the tenth day of the next month. The wages of a persons whose services have been terminated shall be paid on the next working day after such termination.

The payment of wages shall be made on a working day.

Authorised deductions: The Act authorises an employer to make deductions from wages for the following purposes only: (*a*) fines, (*b*) absence from duty, (*c*) damage to or loss of goods or money, where such damage or loss is due to the negligence or default on the part of the employee, (*d*) housing accommodation supplied by the employer and (*e*) such amenities and services supplied by the employer as the State Government may authorise.

(*i*) Fines shall be imposed for those acts of commission and omission which the employer, with the approval of the State Government, may have specified by notice to his employees.

(*ii*) Fines shall not be imposed on any employee unless he has been given an opportunity to show cause why the fine should not be imposed.

(*iii*) No fine shall be imposed on persons below the age of fifteen.

(*iv*) The fine so imposed shall be recovered in instalments or after the expiry of sixty days from the day on which it was imposed.

(*v*) The fine and the actual amount recovered shall be recorded in a separate register in the prescribed form and all amounts of fines realised shall be utilised only for such purposes as are beneficial to the employees and as are approved by the prescribed authority. Applications for the recovery of fines, or of deductions not authorised under the Act, for delay in payment of wages shall be presented within six months of the date on which such fines were imposed or deductions were made or wages were due.

The Workmen's Compensation Act, 1923

Within the installation of machinery operated by motive power, the number of accidents in factories have increased considerably. Many times, workers lost their fingers, sometimes their hands and feet and in some cases even their lives while working on machines in factories. This meant the loss of earnings for those who were involved in accidents and, in cases where a worker died, his dependents were left to starve. From a purely humanitarian point of view, it would be natural to expect that employers should give some compensation to such workers or their dependents. Further, even on economic grounds, it could be argued that the amount of compensation is a legitimate element of the cost of production under the factory system and, therefore, neither society nor employers should grudge paying it whenever workers were involved in accidents. Some enlightened employers did pay compensation to their employees when they suffered accidents; but a large majority was not willing to accept this responsibility. The workers, however, could not claim compensation as a matter of right; and even when compensation was paid, there was bound to be an honest difference of opinion between an employer and an employee as regards the fairness of the amount paid to the disabled factory worker. Workmen's Compensation Acts have been passed in almost all countries.

The following are the provisions of the Indian Workmen's Compensation Act:

Employer's Liability for Compensation: If a personal injury is caused to a worker by an accident arising out of and in the course of his employment, his employer shall be liable to pay compensation in accordance with the provisions of this Act.

When Employer is not Liable: The employer, however, shall not be liable if (*a*) the injury results in a partial or total disablement of the worker for less than three days; (*b*) if the injury can be directly attributed to the worker having been under the influence of drink or drugs; (*c*) if the injury can be directly attributed to the wilful disobedience by the worker of an order expressly given or (*d*) to the wilful removal or disregard by the worker of any safety guard or other device which he knew has been provided for the purpose of securing his safety.

Occupational Diseases: If a worker engaged in any employment which involves the handling of wool, hair bristles or animal carcasses or loading or unloading of such merchandise, or in processes carried on in compressed air, or in processes which involve the use of lead or tetraethyl or in process involving exposure to nitrous fumes, contracts diseases like anthrax, compressed-air illness, led poisoning by nitrous fumes respectively; or when engaged continuously for not less than six months in any employment specified in Part B of Schedule III, contracts any disease specified in this schedule as an occupational disease, the contacting of such a disease shall be regarded as an injury by accident and shall be deemed to have arisen out of and in employment. The State Governments in the case of employments specified in Part C of the schedule may make additions to the list of employments in Schedule II and specify the corresponding diseases after giving three months' notice in the Gazette.

Types of Injuries: Injuries for the purposes of this act have been classified into the following categories: (*i*) death, (*ii*) permanent total disablement, (*iii*) permanent partial disablement and (*iv*) temporary disablement, partial or total.

Amount of Compensation: The Act provides for Compensation for these categories of injuries in Schedules I to IV.

Medical Examination: A worker who has given notice of an accident shall submit himself to a medical examination, if the employer insists on it, by a qualified medical practitioner and free of charge. Similarly, a worker who is in receipt of half-monthly payments under this Act shall submit himself to such medical examination from time to time.

If a worker refuses to submit himself to such a medical examination without sufficient cause, his right to compensation shall be suspended.

The Employees State Insurance Act, 1948

Experience in the working of the Workmen's Compensate Act of 1923 revealed that the benefits conferred by it upon factory workers in many cases, did not reach them, this was due to various reasons. Firstly, a claim for compensation for injury has to be filed in an ordinary court of law and the lack of finance often made it impossible for a worker to file such a suit and fight it out. Secondly, for an employer armed with expert legal advice, it was often possible to prove that the accident either did not arise out of and in the course of employment, or that it was due to the worker concerned being under the influence of drink or drug at the time of the accident, or that it was due to his negligence or his disobedience of safety rules. In such conditions, workers were generally unwilling to go to a court of law, and preferred to accept whatever compensation employers chose to pay out of a sense of pity or charity. The Employees' State Insurance Act 1948 was framed to prevent such victimization of the worker by the employer.

Contributions: Every person, who is employed for wages in or in connection with the work of a factory or establishment to which this Act applies, shall be insured. All the insured workers, except those who earn wages of less than one rupee per day, shall pay their contribution to the Employees' State Insurance Corporation at the rates specified in the First Schedule to the Act. The employers shall pay their contributions at the rates specified in the above schedule.

Distribution of Benefits under the Act: The insured persons, or as the case may be, their dependants, shall be entitled to the following benefits, namely:

- ***(a)* Sickness Benefits:** Periodical payments, to any insured person in case of his sickness certified by a duly appointed medical practitioner;
- ***(b)* Maternity Benefits:** Periodical payments, in case of confinement, to an insured woman certified to be eligible for such payments, by an authority specified in this behalf by the regulations;
- ***(c)* Disablement Benefits:** Periodical payment to an insured person suffering from disablement as a result of an injury sustained in the course of his employment;
- ***(d)* Dependants' Benefits:** Periodical payments to such dependants of an insured person who dies as a result of an injury sustained in the course of his employment and
- ***(e)* Medical Benefits:** Medical treatment for and attendance on an insured person.

The Corporation may at the request of the government of India, extend medical benefits to the family of the insured person. Accordingly, these benefits have been so extended from 1st January 1962.

A person who is in receipt of sickness or disablement benefit, must observe the following conditions:

- (*a*) He shall remain under medical treatment at dispensary, hospital, clinic or any other institution provided under this Act and shall carry out the instructions of the medical officer or medical attendant in charge thereof;
- (*b*) He shall not, while under treatment, do anything which might retard or prejudice his chances of recovery;

(*c*) He shall not leave the area in which medical treatment provided under this Act is being given without the permission of the medical officer or such other authority as may be specified in this behalf under the rules framed for this purpose and

(*d*) He shall allow himself to be examined by any duly appointed medical officer or any other person authorised by the corporation in this behalf.

Penalties: If a person makes a false statement for the purpose of causing any increase in payment or benefit, or for the purpose of causing any payment or benefit to be made where no payment or benefit is authorised, or for the purpose of avoiding any payment to be made by himself, he shall be punishable with imprisonment for a term upto three months or with fine up to Rs. 500 or with both.

If any person fails to pay any contribution which he is liable to pay, or deducts from the wages of an employee the whole or any part of the employee's contribution or reduce the wages or any privileges or benefits admissible to an employee, dismisses, discharges, reduces or otherwise punishes an employee in contravention of Section 73, or fails or refuses to submit any return required by the regulations or makes a false return, or obstructs any Inspector or the official of the Corporation in the discharge of his duties, or is guilty of contravention of, and non-compliance with any of the requirements of this Act, he shall be punishable with imprisonment upto a period of three months or with fine up to Rs. 500 or with both,

Industrial Disputes Act, 1947

Industrial disputes, strikes and lock-outs were not very common occurrences in India till 1914. It was, however, during the Great War of 1914-18 that the strike came to be regarded as an ordinary weapon of industrial warfare. During the War, while the cost of living went on rising, the wages did not keep pace with it. This gave rise to serious discontent among industrial workers and led to a series of strikes, notably in the textile industry in Mumbai, in the post-war period. In addition to low wages, there were many other causes which were partly responsible for the outbreak of strikes during this period. The more important of these were long hours of work, bad conditions, insanitary housing conditions, absence of any provision rill 1922 for compensation for injuries sustained in the course of employment, absence, till 1925, of the right to form a trade union, ill-treatment of workmen by foremen or other mill officials etc.

The important provisions of the Industrial Disputes Act of 1947 are:

(*i*) If any industrial dispute exists or is apprehended, the appropriate Government now by order in writing, (*a*) refer the dispute to a Board for promoting a settlement thereof; or (*b*) refer any matter appearing to be connected with or relevant to the dispute to a Court of Inquiry or (*c*) refer the dispute to a Tribune for arbitration.

(*ii*) If either of the parties to a dispute or both of them apply to the Government to refer a dispute to a Board, Court or Tribunal, the appropriate Government, if satisfied that the person applying represents the majority of each party, shall make the reference accordingly.

(*iii*) If a dispute has been referred to a Board or a tribunal, the government may prohibit the continuance of any strike or lock-out in connection with such a dispute.

(*iv*) A Settlement arrived at in the course of conciliation proceedings under the Act, or an award which is declared by the Government as binding on all the parties to the dispute for at least six months.

(*v*) An award declared by a Government shall come into operation on such date as may be specified by the government and shall remain in operation for a period of one year, or a shorter period, if so fixed by the Government.

(*vi*) Workers employed in public utility industries shall not go on a strike and the employers in such industries shall not resort to lock-outs –

(*a*) without giving a fourteen days' notice and before the period of notice expires or

(*b*) during the tendency of conciliation proceedings.

(*vii*) Workers employed in any industrial establishment shall not go on strike –

(*a*) during the tendency of conciliation proceeding; or

(*b*) during the tendency of proceeding before a Labour Court, Tribunal or National Tribunal or

(*c*) during a period in which a settlement or award is in operation.

A strike or a lock-out, in contravention of any of these provisions shall be illegal.

No person shall knowingly expend or apply any money in direct furtherance or support of any illegal strike or lock-out.

Penalties: Any worker who commences, continues or acts in furtherance of an illegal strike shall be punishable with imprisonment up to one month or with fine up to Rs. 50 or both.

The Employees Provident Fund Act, 1952

The Act provides for the institution of a contributory provident fund in establishment in which 20 or more persons are employed. The contribution, which shall be paid by the employer to the fund, shall be 8½ per cent of the basic wage and the dearness allowance payable to each employee, while the employee's contribution shall be equal to the contribution payable by the employer.

The Indian Boilers Act, 1923

An owner of a boiler shall not use it or permit to be used,

(*a*) Unless it has been registered in accordance with the provisions of this Act;

(*b*) In the case of a boiler transferred from one state to another, until the transfer has been reported in the prescribed manner;

(*c*) Unless certificate or provisional order authorising the use of the boiler is obtained under this Act;

(*d*) At a pressure higher than the maximum pressure recorded in such certificate or provisional order;

(*e*) Unless the boiler is in charge of a person holding a certificate of competency.

Procedure: The owner of a boiler may apply to the Inspector to have the boiler registered. Every such application shall be accompanied by the prescribed fee. The Inspector shall examine the boiler and submit a report to the Chief Inspector in the prescribed form.

The permit is a 'must' for boilers.

How Labour Laws Still Bite

- Companies of all sizes have laid off a large number of employees in the past three months.
- But the manner and execution of sacking has hurt the interests of employees as well as employers.
- The rigidities in labour laws still affect the quantity – and more so quality – of employment.

- Chapter V(B) of the Industrial Disputes Act (IDA) places administrative and judicial constraints on retrenching workers.
- Too many laws govern a host of practices in the formal sector, relating to service conditions, industrial relations, wages and benefits, social security and insurance.
- For instance, a typical firm in Maharashtra has to deal with 29 different acts pertaining to labour.

The Indian Electricity Act, 1910

The act relates to the supply and use of electricity energy.

Issue of Licence: A State Government may, on an application made in the prescribed form and on the payment of the prescribed fee, grant a licence to supply energy in any specified area and also to lay electric supply lines for the transmission of energy.

Intellectual Property Rights

Intellectual Property (IP) comprises legally protected rights in products of the mind, including useful inventions, novel designs, creative works, symbols of origin or sponsorship, non-public business information, and the like. (Abstract ideas, however, are generally not protected as IP). Intellectual property includes patents, copyrights, trademarks and trade dress, and trade secrets. In the industrial countries and in increasing number of developing nations, owners of IP rights of different kinds receive limited, defined exclusive rights to make, use, sell, copy, distribute, and/or license their inventions or creations.

International Law on Intellectual Property Protection

- *Paris Convention (1883, revised most recently in 1979):* 128 countries are signatories; a landmark agreement on patents, trademarks, and industrial designs.
- *Berne Convention (1886, revised most recently in 1971):* III countries are signatories; an agreement on copyrights encompassing literary and artistic works.
- *Patent Cooperation Treaty (1970, revised most recently in 1985):* 79 countries are signatories; created a union for cooperation in filing, searching, and examining patent applications; facilitates filing of separate applications in member countries.
- *General Agreement of Tariffs and Trade Agreement on Trade-Related Aspects of Intellectual Property Rights (GATT/TRIPS, 1994):* establishes minimum universal standards on patents, copyrights, trademarks, industrial designs, geographical indications, integrated circuits, and trade secrets; includes transitional arrangements.
- *World Intellectual Property Organisation (WIPO, 1967):* A Geneva based agency of the United Nations created to encourage participation of developing countries in the international patent system.
- *Madrid Agreement and Protocol:* provides for international registration of trademarks with WIPO; 35 countries are signatories; the US is not yet a member.
- *Trademark Law-Treaty (1994):* 35 countries are signatories; established maximum formal requirements that may be imposed on trademark applicants and registrants by member countries.
- *Some regional intellectual property agreements:* regional agreements with intellectual-property provisions include European Patent Convention, African Regional Intellectual Property

Organization, Organisation Africaine de la Propriete Intellectually, Pan American Trade Mark Convention, NAFTA, ANCOM, and Caricom.

Four Ways of Going Global

There are four entry level options for Indian players seeking a global market. The first route which is the most basic, and followed by the majority of Indian players, entails a local manufacturer serving as a sourcing agent for local distributors in that country. However, this is at best a short-term strategy susceptible to the whims of distributors.

The second entry option is a collaborative effort wherein local agents provide the distribution and marketing input to the Indian company. This is a route followed by many Indian players including Titan, Balsara, Maruti Udyog and Bajaj Auto.

The Indian company retains control over key marketing and branding issues. Clearly a long-term entry option, the arrangement gives the marketer a controlling interest and an assurance of commonality of product messaging and packaging, irrespective of the country the brand is being sold in. In such an arrangement, the Indian marketer provides development material and business promotion options to local distributors, and media costs are shared jointly by the two parties involved.

Marketers opting to follow the third route make a solo entry through independent distributors, in a manner similar to the route followed in India. However, this route is usually followed only in countries that offer a consumer profile closest to India, since it is a highly expensive route and open to failure.

The fourth more convenient and easily accessible alternative is to start as a private label supplier at the lower price end through the mass merchandising outlets of foreign buyers. Balasara is probably the best example of an Indian company taking the private label route articulately in the North American and European tooth paste markets. Of late, however, market analysts claim that this route is no longer as viable as it once was with private label marketing wars rampant in the US. Moreover, private lable manufacturers can at best be called global suppliers.

The Consumer Protection Act, 1986

Consumer Protection Act, 1986 provides for the establishment of consumer councils and other authorities to settle consumer disputes. It sets out the procedures by which consumers can appeal to the bodies in case of grievances and other matters of consumer interest.

The Act appoints the Central Consumer Protection Council and the State Consumer Protection Council to promote consumer welfare and protect the consumer from unfair trade practices. The Councils regulate the quality, quantity, potency, purity, standard and prices of products; ensure the availability of goods and services at competitive prices and also offer consumers redressal for unfair or restrictive trade practices or exploitation by manufacturers.

A Consumer Disputes Redressal Forum or 'District Forum' will have jurisdiction with regard to complaints where the value of goods or services and the compensation, if any, does not exceed Rs. 20 lakh. In cases where the value of the goods or services and compensation is between Rs. 20 lakh and Rs. 1 crore, the jurisdiction will lie with the State Commission, while cases dealing with amounts exceeding Rs. 1 crore will be handled by the National Commission.

The District Forum has the powers of a civil court. It may request tests for any product thought to be defective. It has the authority to ask manufacturers to replace defective goods with new goods, return to the complainant the price or charges paid and to enforce compensation to the consumer for any loss or injury suffered due to the negligence of the manufacturer. It may also ask the latter to discontinue unfair or restrictive trade practices and to withdraw hazardous goods from the market. If a trader or a person against whom a complaint is made fails to comply with an order made by these authorities, he shall be punishable with imprisonment for a term of 1-3 years, or with fine between Rs. 2,000 and Rs. 10,000, or both.

▸▸ Conclusion

Rules and regulations governing small-scale industries act as a governor ensuring steady growth of the industry as well as the environment (ecosystem) and the labour force. It not only ensured healthy growth but also rapid growth. The basic objective of rules and regulations governing small-scale industries is to ensure that the results of operation confirm as closely as possible to established standards of goods, specified procedures or instructions. Rules and regulations are meant to put small-scale industries, enabling them to move on the successful track.

They are the directions, for excellence, growth and development and regulations is a monitoring mechanism of rules. Since the small-scale enterprise is concerned with land, environment, goods, people and consumers, rules and regulations have been formulated to safeguard these varied interests. If there is greater awareness among the entrepreneurs, these rules and regulations have minimum effect and disturbance. Thus, rules and regulations ensure steady and rapid growth of small-scale industries, develop new products and markets, produce quality goods and promote healthy development of human resources. More importantly, small industries are located nearer to the natural resources and human resources, do not pollute or degrade the ecosystem, intimidate and exploit layout and cheat the consumer on all counts. Rules and regulations are, therefore, the basic component of small-scale industries. They are like the lamp post directing the growth of this sector on a firm ground.

ANNEXURE-1

MSMES ARE STILL ON SHAKY LEGAL GROUNDS

In its current form, there is a yawning gap between the MSMED Act and its implementation

Rohit Kochhar, Managing Partner, Kochhar & Co.

The Indian MSME faces major challenges when it comes to legal issues. Even as constructive steps have been taken towards promotion and development of MSMEs, the Micro, Small and Medium Enterprises Development (MSMED) Act, 2006 requires certain legislative reforms, said Rohit Kochhar, managing partner at law firm Kochhar & Co. while speaking at the ET India MSME Summit. "In its current form, there is a yawning gap between the MSMED Act and its implementation," he added. There are several glaring discrepancies between the provisions of the Act and its implementation. Many states have not established the required councils and those that are set up are barely functioning causing MSMEs to run from pillar to post to realise their unpaid receivables. Though the Facilitation Council envisioned under the Act provides a time limit of 90 days for completion of proceedings, this is seldom adhered to in practice thereby rendering the provisions of the Act meaningless.

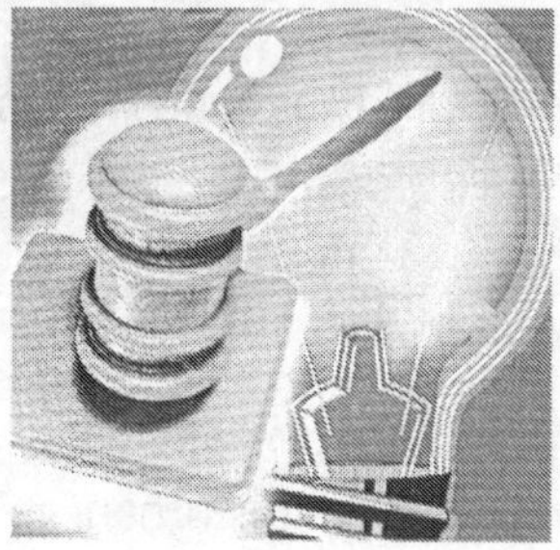

One way is through factoring, which would have been a more effective mechanism but for want of legislative support. "Sadly, the relevant proposed legislation *i.e.,* "Factoring of Debt due to Industrial and Commercial Undertakings Bill 2000" still remains a pending draft. There is a need for enacting a factoring legislation, which would clearly define the legal relationship between the factor and the seller's business unit. Such legislation would also encourage banks and factoring companies to provide factoring services more liberally," said Kochhar.

Another key challenge for SMEs has been getting credit at lower interest rates from banks and financial institutions as compared with their large counterparts. "There is a need for SMEs to be organised in the form of LLPs (Limited Liability Partnership) for them to attract investment and credit facility at a low rate," says Amit Agarwal, Partner, S.N. Gupta & Co. The LLP Bill, 2008, which was passed by the Rajya Sabha last October, is a much awaited legislation that I should provide required breathing space to such SMEs who have till date not been able to avail the benefits of corporate structure. The SME sector has been given special protection under the Industrial Policy of 1948, wherein with RBI guidelines, banks and financial institutions are required to give loans (lesser in amount) to the sector on a priority basis. However, the advent of LLP would give viable option to the existing SMEs in the form of an LLP as the security creation will get easier in case of any loan given as LLP would be a separate entity altogether than the partners who constitute it.

"However, it remains to be seen whether the RBI would still consider SMEs who have acquired the status of an LLP as priority sector to be provided with easy loans. Banks and financial institutions will be able to enforce the securities created while granting the loans specifically as the LLP can be sued being a separate legal entity," says Satwinder Singh, Partner, Vaish Associates. Small retailers, bullion traders, and jewellery retailers will all be benefited by adopting LLP as they now have an option to convert their family owned partnership into a corporate LLP structure. This new Act would also benefit the services sector and professionals like chartered accountants, company secretaries, and lawyers.

Monica Behura

ANNEXURE-2

INSPECTOR RAJ: THE GREAT SURVIVOR

The licence-quota raj may be over but the inspector raj still reigns supreme. Industry may have been delicensed in 1991 bur is still highly regulated. Each industrial unit is visited by between 40 and 60 inspectors in the course of a month. The following is an illustrative, and not an exhaustive, list of inspectors. There maybe several more inspectors depending on the kind of manufacturing activity. As a result, small and medium enterprises are forced to shell out bribes to these officers. Or else face harassment.

Ministry	***No. of Inspectors***	***Work Done***
Industry	5	Check registration, inventories, tax payment, quality control, safety Equipment
Home	2	Check fire protection facilities and compliance with Explosives Act
Planning & Statistics	1	Collect data on production, manpower, man-hours utilised and lost
Finance	12	Five for income tax (three of them checking the same records for three different departments); seven from excise department
Separate Revenue	5	Enforcement, verification and recovery of sales tax enrolment of professional tax, weights and measures
Revenue Department (State government) tax	1	Registration of professional
Labour	8	Checking compliance with different labour laws, checking the same records
Municipal corporations Power & Energy Health & Family Welfare	2 1 2	Municipal byelaws Electricity connections Hygiene and occupational health
Urban Affairs & Employment Environment & Forests Communications Local Self-government Fixed & Drug Administration	1 2 1 2 1	Sanitation Pollution control Telecom facilities Octroi and mass raids Safety standards

ANNEXURE-3

GOODS AND SERVICES TAX (GST)

What is GST?

A dual tax with both central and state GST components levied on the same base. Thus, all goods and services barring a few exceptions will be brought onto the GST base. There will be no distinction between goods and services for the purpose of the tax.

The Benefits

- Taxes will be equitably redistributed between manufacturing and services
- Tax base will broaden, allowing for a reduction in rates
- Distortions will reduce, as will compliance costs
- Investment decisions will be made purely on economic concerns, independent of tax considerations
- Exports will get a leg up; will grow faster than imports
- Will promote employment
- Will spur growth; gains of $15 billion annually have been estimated

Addressing the Concerns

A number of issues remain to be resolved, which are currently under the consideration of the Empowered Committee under the chairmanship of Dr. Asim Dasgupta, Finance Minister of West Bengal. These include:

The Rate Structure and Value

The primary concern of all state governments is protection as well as enhancement of existing revenue services. There are three parameters that need to be balanced: one, the range of taxes being levied, which will be subsumed into the GST. This will determine the tax base of the GST. The other parameters are the number of rates and the numerical value of these rates, which will be applied to this base. All indirect taxes on the supply of goods and services would need to be subsumed into the GST. VAT, stamp duty, vehicle tax, taxes on goods and passengers, taxes and duties on electricity, entertainment tax, entry tax, luxury tax, taxes on

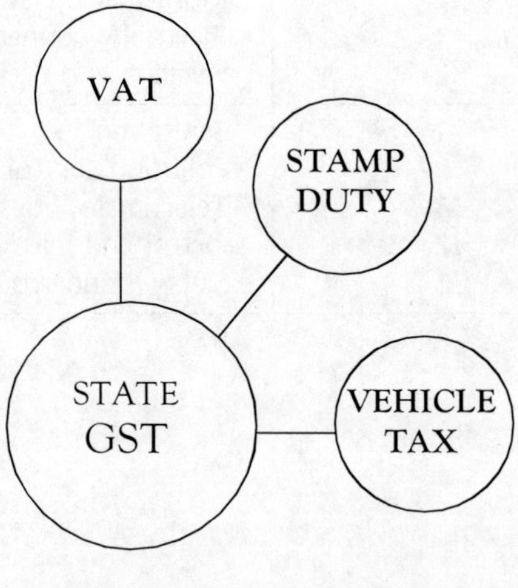

TAXES on goods and passengers and duties on electricity, entertainment tax, entry tax, luxury tax, taxes on lotteries, betting and gambling, purchase tax and all state cesses and surcharges will also be included in the state GST

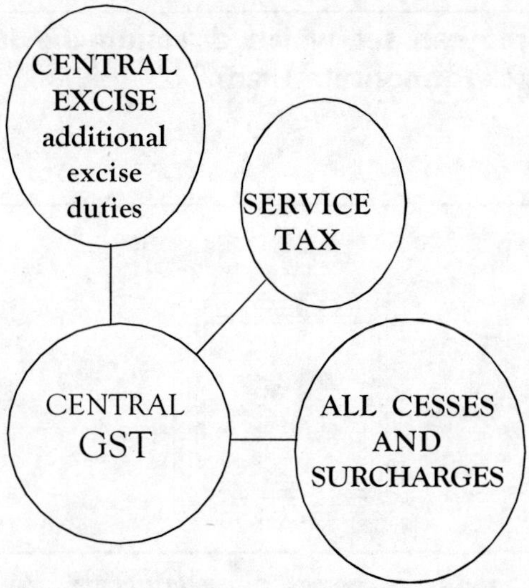

lotteries, betting and gambling, purchase tax as well as all state cesses and surcharges will be subsumed into the state GST. Central sales tax (CST) will stand abolished. From the Centre's side, central excise, additional excise duties, service tax, additional customs duty and all cesses and surcharges (other than educational cess) will be subsumed into the central GST. The best option would be a bare minimum number of rates, at best two, preferably one.

Rules of Supply for Goods and Services

While CST will be abolished in the GST regime, the treatment of inter-state sales will need to be carefully thought through. It would be necessary to guard against tax arbitrage where local sales that will be taxed could be shown as inter-state sales. The CST Act provided for documentation to attest the inter-state nature of the sales. A number of models are being examined by the Empowered Committee which will serve as alternatives.

Putting in place the Rules of Supply for the inter-state provision of services will be demanding. Some services may be supplied from one state, consumed in another and paid for in a third state. A set of rules to determine the taxation jurisdiction and appropriation would need to be worked out.

Operational Issues: Sharing of Information

Recent experience suggests that local sales under the VAT regime are being shown as CST sales (which is a lower tax), leading to revenue loss. Apart from putting in place a comprehensive IT network, sharing of tax-related information and coordination amongst states will be crucial.

IT Infrastructure

The present Tax Information Exchange System (TNXSYS) does not appear to be fully operational across all states.

Edited excerpts from a recent speech by ***Dr. Vijay Kelkar,*** *Chairman, Thirteenth Finance Commission, at* ASSOCHAM

" When people can see which direction the leaders are going in, it becomes easier to motivate them." ***— Lakshmi Mittal***

31

Managing Tomorrow

Introduction

The complex dynamics of liberalisation and globalisation has brought entrepreneurs and managers face to face with the new challenges. This means we have to pay special attention to the development of project managers who are capable of coping with jobs that range from small to mega projects and with life span of several months to ten years. Typically a project manager must not only be able to manage the engineering, procurement and construction aspects of project, he or she must also be able to manage aspects relating to finance, cost engineering, schedule, environmental considerations, regulatory agency requirements, inflation and cost escalations, labour problems, public and client relations, employee relations and changing laws.

Swati Piramal

The New Challenges

- Strong Competition
- Pressures to go global
- Demanding customers
- Deregulated financial markets
- Total quality management in manufacturing

Unfortunately, the sheer pace of change predetermines its usage. Traditional methods of management will get companies nowhere; only a management revolution can produce results.

In any case, for both managers and entrepreneurs, the challenge is to change the way they look at the nine critical areas which constitute a firm's activity: structure, marketing, selling, leadership, people, production, innovation, globalisation and finance. And if they succeed in pulling off this managerial revolution, managers would have played their part in creating India Inc.

Tomorrow's companies will need a radically different set of structures to succeed. Within each company, organisations responsible for a single product on a global basis must be created. Export departments – with regional directorates for groups of countries – will be necessary. There must be companies within companies, each one of them being a global player.

The prime responsibilities of tomorrow's entrepreneur will be to prepare the organisation for the challenge ahead, chalk out long-term strategies proactively, manage their implementation, and provide a vision for the company.

Articulating the corporate mission to your rank and file is not easy. But it will have to be done on a continuous basis, over a period of time, so that the organisation is in tune with the company's broader plans.

⏩ Emphasise Good Teamwork

- Teams of managers chase change best.
- Big companies must break up specialised departments into small, multi-disciplinary teams.
- Fast, innovative and motivated, teams are the only organisational structure capable of taking on the future.

⏩ Get Ideas from the Customer

- Customers should be a firm's obsession tomorrow. Listen to the customer to find out what he needs.
- Deliver more than what he expects. If he wants less, change to match his specs.
- And think less about marketing – just marry the customer.

⏩ Use Innovation Effectively

- Instead of asking the lab what it can deliver, tell the lab what innovations the customer wants.
- Set up labs on the shopfloor, so that production teams too are involved.
- In other words, reverse the management of innovations.

⏩ Trade and go Global

- Trading is the best strategy to go global.
- It exposes an Indian company to the demands of the international market place.
- It also requires far less capital. To leap into tomorrow's global village, take a step into the past.

⏩ Understand Your Market

- As power shifts to the retailer, sales and service teams will be a firm's stars.
- Remember they are close to the trade and they are also closest to the customer.

- Train them pay them – and listen to them. That gives you a sneak preview of the customer's mind.

Learn to Listen and Lead

- If a CEO wants to succeed tomorrow, he must learn to listen to his people.
- Meet them at formal feedback sessions.
- Keep the door to your office open. Chat with people in the corridors.
- Make sure you're in the same company as your people.

Build Pride in Production

- Production managers and workers know their tools – and their products – best.
- Get them to listen to your customers.
- Then, allow the shopfloor to boost quality, cut costs, or change products itself. Put the pride back in production.

Make Managers Entrepreneurs

- Ever heard of an entrepreneur on a wage? If firms of the future are to succeed, their managers must become entrepreneurs.
- To do this, sharing profits with them is essential. Indeed, that's the only way to keep your best managers.

Make Money from Money

- Canny corporation should set up a forex department.
- The moment the rupee is floated, finance managers can start playing the forex markets.
- By buying and selling forward contracts, finance managers can make money from money.

Organisations will have to be designed to produce quality. Flatter companies, with highly decentralised structures, will be essential to combat competition. Elimination of hierarchies will be facilitated by the infotech revolution, which will enable the bypassing of traditional channels of communication.

Temporary task forces will have to supplement formal structures to tackle issues like product launches and cost reduction.

Entrepreneurs should recognise that change is inevitable. Ways will have to be found to cope with competition and overcome the barriers to innovation. Today's competitive realities requires entrepreneurs to do more than just improve a company's financial performance.

External pressure is essential to motivate change. And within companies, a key challenge for the leader will be to create more leaders like himself down the line.

To survive in the era of global competition, organizations need a high level of innovation, speed and flexibility so that they can successfully and continuously innovate and generate new businesses. For this, organizations need to support and manage the process of venture creation. Successful and effective management of the corporate venturing process would require organizations to understand the issues that are instrumental in corporate venturing and entrepreneurship.

In this context, the challenge before established corporations is to revitalize themselves so that they can successfully and continuously innovate and generate new business. To meet this challenge, established firms need to understand how to manage the process of starting a new venture from within. This throws up several complex issues regarding the corporate venturing process, such as:

- How to identify venture opportunities and locate them within the firm?
- How to anticipate and manage collision between firm needs and venture needs?
- How to plan for changing management requirements as venture grows?
- How to transfer know-how from firm to the venture?
- How to evaluate venture performance?

Indian business environment is now no longer sheltered and is being increasingly exposed to global competition rapidly. To survive in the 21st century, Indian business would need to build capabilities for high level of innovation, speed and flexibility. In this context, issues related to effective management of the corporate venturing process would be more relevant.

MANAGING TIME

Managing time is an art and requires specific skills to be incorporated by the entrepreneur. Managing time saves your time and helps you to solve problems effectively.

How to Concentrate on Your Work

Have you ever found yourself simply uninterested in the work that is in front of you? Have you then mentally drifted off to Tahiti for a moment of relief – only to find, suddenly, that the day is over and you have accomplished next to nothing? Here are a few tips to help you regain your concentration – and hold on to it.

Get Focused: Make a list of what needs to be done. Give each task a time-frame. Get out your work tools – including your list. Then go to work, watch your schedule and stick to it. Don't allow yourself out of your chair until the task is completed.

Make your place: When you are interrupted, take a second before you break away to jot down a word or a phrase to help you remember where you were in your work. Taking notes also helps maintain concentration during lengthy conversations or meetings.

Keep track of your thoughts: Whenever you become aware that your thoughts are beginning to wander, yell: "Stop!" (in your mind, of course – not aloud). This will bring your drifting to a halt and redirect your attention towards the job.

Bribe yourself: Promise yourself that as soon as you finish a certain task, you will get a reward: anything from a cup of coffee to the most glamourous prize you can afford. Then, make sure you get it when you complete the job.

The best way to handle uninteresting tasks is to finish them as soon as possible. But grim determination alone isn't always enough to get you through uninspiring chores. These ideas will help you cut through the fog, complete tasks more quickly, and coerce you to pay greater attention to the issues you care about the most.

THE TIME MANAGEMENT AUDIT

Do you prioritise your time during the day? Or do your work at a leisurely pace and delay what is on schedule? Take this audit to evaluate your time management skills.

1.	Do you anticipate stressful, high-pressure periods?	Yes	No
2.	Do you determine, in advance, how you can manage such periods efficiently?	Yes	No
3.	Do you ask employees and colleagues for their ideas to smoothen out work-flows?	Yes	No
4.	Do you free yourself to concentrate on time and energy-saving tasks?	Yes	No
5.	Do you delegate too much work to your staff?	Yes	No
6.	Do you focus on your department's primary goals?	Yes	No
7.	Do you consciously limit the energy you spend on peripheral task?	Yes	No
8.	Do you negotiate realistic deadlines with your boss?	Yes	No
9.	Do you ensure that your staff finishes work before the actual deadlines?	Yes	No
10.	Do you constantly emphasise the value of planned, steady work?	Yes	No
11.	Do you purposefully get rid of last-minute heroics to get the job done?	Yes	No
12.	Do you ever draw up a plan before starting your day?	Yes	No
13.	Do you set certain targets for yourself and your team?	Yes	No
14.	Do you reward yourself and your subordinates after ending a certain task?	Yes	No
15.	Do you intercept interruptions before they disturb your work rhythm?	Yes	No

Total

THE SCORING:

Give yourself 5 point for every YES, and 0 for every NO

THE RATING:

0-25 Points: You don't keep track of your time

30-50 Points: Re-arrange your time schedule quickly

55-75 Points: You have mastered the art of time management

COMPETITIVENESS

Competitiveness is a continuous quest; it is not limited by time or effort. A company has to continuously upgrade itself on several parameters: production efficiency, product development, quality management and marketing skills.

Vision is a dream, and strategy is the breaking down of that dream into small steps.

Whatever product or service a company offers, it must meet the customer's want in the most satisfactory manner. That should be the aim of the company – not profits. Also, one must customise the products to the needs of the market. Cost leadership and customisation are two contrary things. But that is where manufacturing technology counts: even if you are producing slightly different versions for different segments of the market, you can derive economies of scale.

Low-cost manufacturing alone is a sustainable factor of competitiveness. It may initially open the doors to a market, but a company must be truly competitive in other areas as well. Our goal is to make our company truly world-class.

COMPETITIVENESS CANONS

- Use vertical integration to control the market
- Attain global scales in each and every product-line
- Build production capacities ahead of demand
- Leverage technology for process efficiencies
- Manage project engineering to control costs
- Service the customer at his door-step
- Benchmark costs globally to keep them in check
- Focus relentlessly on only some chosen products
- Seek out niches unprofitable for the bigger players
- Use R&D to build unique, unmatched skills
- Seek differentiation in delivery, not product
- Integrate vertically to attain economies of scale
- Focus on only one segment of customers
- Adopt the customer's quality standards to avoid rejection
- Use demanding customers to raise quality levels
- Seek out large customers to operate on a global scale
- Develop a full range of products to meet complete buyers needs
- Build unique skills that are expensive to duplicate
- Create global capacities quickly to attack older players
- Target large commodity buyers for the benefits of scale
- Focus on one basic product, but diversify into new markets
- Use value-addition to provide a basket of related products
- Keep every element of cost below the level of competitors
- Integrate forward to cash in on low-cost in-house supplies
- Control costs to keep the product affordable
- Reengineer processes to improve time utilisation
- Forge relationships with vendors to minimise costs
- Build global capacities if the domestic market is large enough
- Steer clear of diversification even if synergies are available
- Focus on chosen segments without straying into new ones

⏩ Competitiveness Lesson One

THE SCALE STRATEGY

Build manufacturing capacities of global scale, but choose product segments that are either declining in the developed markets, or offer niches that are too small for the big international players to target. Aim at several different markets, representing a cross-section of economies – developing, developed, and high-growth – to ensure demand. Build relationship with at least one major buyer in each market to ensure the off-take of your product.

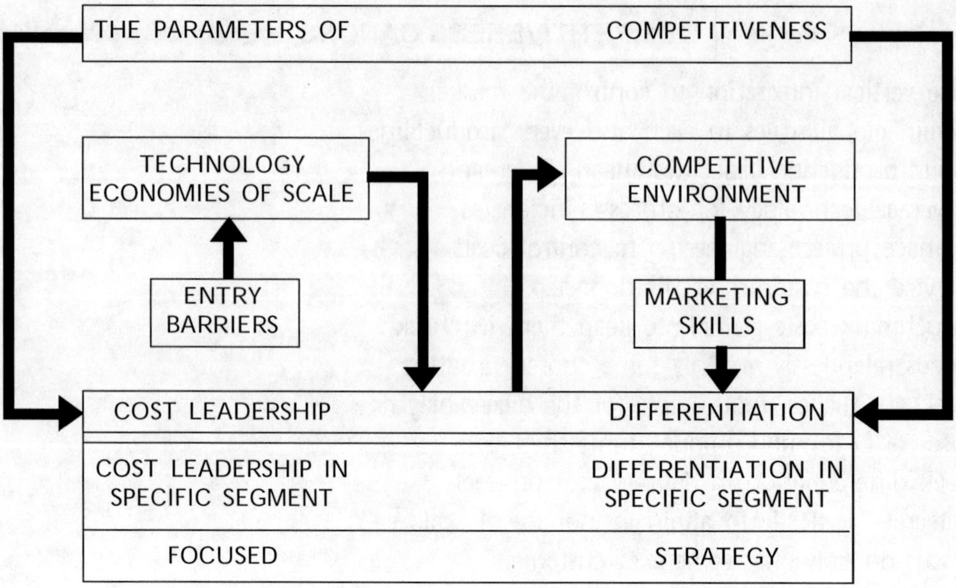

GENERIC COMPETITIVE STRATEGIES

Generic Strategy	Commonly-required Skills and Resources	Commonly-required Organisational Requirements
COST LEADERSHIP	❐ Sustained capital investment and access to capital ❐ Process engineering skills ❐ Intense supervision of labour ❐ Low-cost distribution system	❐ Tight cost-control ❐ Frequent, detailed control reports ❐ Structured organisation ❐ Incentives based on meeting strict quantitative targets
DIFFERENTIATION	❐ Strong marketing abilities ❐ Product engineering ❐ Creative flair ❐ Strong marketiing abilities ❐ Product enginering ❐ Creative flair ❐ Strong capability in basic research ❐ Corporae reputation for quality ❐ Strong co-operation from channels	❐ Strong co-ordinaiton among functions in R&D, product development, and marketing ❐ Subjective measurement and incentives instead quantitative measures and incentives ❐ Amenities to attract highly-skilled labour, scientist, or creative people
FOCUS	❐ Combination of the above qualities directed at one strategic target	❐ Combination of the above qualities directed at one strategic target

⏩ Competitiveness Lesson Two

THE FOCUS STRATEGY

Invest your capital and other resources in just one genre of product so that your company is firmly associated with that product all over the world. Build a level of expertise in it that will be very expensive to duplicate. Be prepared to sacrifice other markets and customers if necessary. And avoid the temptation of making related diversifications even if they hold out the promise of high returns.

⏩ Competitiveness Lesson Three

THE COST STRATEGY

On the global platform, Indian companies already enjoy many natural cost advantages, particularly in terms of labour-costs. However, to attain cost competitiveness on a global scale, start by benchmarking every component of your processes structure against the international leaders. Then, reengineer your process to match their standards. And use TQM as a tool for lowering the cost of poor quality.

THE COMPETITIVENESS AUDIT

The starting point for building a globally-competitive corporation is to create and implement a suitable strategy. Just how strong a strategic infrastructure are you building for your company's competitiveness?

1. Are you analysing your industry in terms of supplier and buyer power, the threat of new entrants and substitutes, and your competitors' actions?	Yes	No
2. Have you crafted a focused strategy aimed at differentiating your company from your competitors on a sustainable, long-term basis?	Yes	No
3. Have you worked out how to reinforce your unique position through every stage, and individual activity, of your business value chain?	Yes	No
4. Do you compare the cost of every activity with those of your competitors' so as to create a long-term cost strategy?	Yes	No
5. Have you analysed the feature, branding, and delivery attributes of your competitors' products to create a differentiated product?	Yes	No
6. Have you scanned the market to decide whether to target all the customers in a broad band? Or just a few of them in a narrow band?	Yes	No
7. Are you developing, acquiring, or licensing technology which can be used to sharpen your strategic focus on cost or differentiation?	Yes	No
8. Are you striving to operate on a global scale, benchmarking against global players, and breaking into at least some international markets?	Yes	No
9. Have you selected which competitors to attack because they are weakening your position, and which ones to protect because they are strengthening it?	Yes	No
10. Are your creating and employing different defensive and offensive strategies for different market conditions?	Yes	No

THE SCORE

Give yourself 10 for every YES, and 0 for every NO.

TOTAL

THE RATING

0-40	The first flush of competition could wipe you out.
50-70	You can become competitive, but you aren't trying.
80-100	Your company is headed for the cutting-edge.

SELF-DEVELOPMENT

To be a successful entrepreneur, you must not only develop cutting edge enterprise strategies, facilitate efficient operations and inspire your people to give their best – thus leading your enterprise to victory in the teeth of competition. Equally important, you must manage yourself – your time, your energy, your career, your learning – same skill.

A vital part of the development process with regard to the influencing skills example is to set up, within the organisation and with process facilitators, a regular feedback-and-review process. Each participant then has a plan to practise influencing skills on the job, get immediate feedback, and review progress regularly with other participants as well as with the process facilitators. Creating a new mindset revolving around developmental processes fits in neatly with the current trend in organisations towards process-thinking generally.

Like personal development, many processes have no end like the process an organisation might initiate for continuous improvement. Processes differ from events in being dynamic rather than static. Processes essentially involve the interplay of various factors and situations over time. A process has a definite structure and purpose, but it is continuously refined as needs change.

A course is a reasonably-good vehicle for knowledge acquisition. Indeed, you could say that knowledge is something you acquire whereas skills can only be developed – and only in the context where they are most frequently used. Courses can teach you the rationale for developing new skills, and provide you with the theory behind them. They can also give you some initial practice, but you can fully develop new skills only on the job, facilitated by effective coaching and feedback.

Inertia is essentially the main reason – combined with the blinding effect which any mindset can have in preventing us from seeing anything wrong with familiar behaviour patterns. Courses and their institutional providers were set up to impart knowledge and, at best indirectly develop skills. It is only recently that influence, for instance, could be seen as a skill at all. Not so long ago, influence amounted to wealth or position.

Similarly, talk of inter-personal skills and leadership skills is relatively recent. While we have begun to develop a fairly sophisticated understanding of what such skills mean to the employees and their organisations, we are still trying to impart them to others using antiquated methods.

THE SELF-DEVELOPMENT AUDIT

Are you learning enough to stand out in your workplace?

That's the question you must ask yourself before you launch your enterprise. Evaluate yourself to determine whether you're ready to nose ahead in life.

1.	Is keeping up with business developments high on your priority list?	Yes	No
2.	Are you constantly apprehensive about the risk of being left behind?	Yes	No
3.	Do you use technology and the Internet as a tool for information gathering?	Yes	No
4.	Do you consciously invest time to hone your skills?	Yes	No
5.	Do you always try to share and pool your learning with your colleagues?	Yes	No
6.	Do you use multiple sources of learning like first-hand experience, courses and feedback?	Yes	No
7.	Do you set targets in terms of what you are going to learn, and by when?	Yes	No
8.	Do you contract with other eager learners to review each other's progress?	Yes	No
9.	Do you consciously look for regular feedback when learning to apply new skills?	Yes	No
10.	Do you use anonymous questionnaires to obtain honest feedback?	Yes	No
11.	Do you feel that the only way to cope with complexity is to specialise?	Yes	No
12.	Are you targeting a few areas at a time to avoid narrowing yourself too much?	Yes	No
13.	Are you watching out for becoming a vague generalist – not knowing much about anything?	Yes	No
14.	If you have opted to be a generalist, are you adding value as an expert generalist?	Yes	No
15.	Do you feel that generalists need to be good at capitalising on the learning of others?	Yes	No

TOTAL

The Scoring:

Give yourself 5 points for every YES, and zero for every NO

The Rating:

0-30	Points: You could be stagnating, and must develop the urge to learn
35-60	Points: You need to speed up your self-development process
65-80	Points: You are on your way to becoming a learning manager.

"CORPORATE MANTRA"

An organisation's ability to learn, and translate that learning into action rapidly, is the ultimate competitive advantage. — ***Jack Welch***

32

Development of Small-Scale Enterprises

⏩ Introduction

Micro, small and medium enterprises (MSMEs), including khadi and village/rural enterprises constitute an important segment of Indian economy in terms of their contribution to country's industrial production, exports, employment and creation of an entrepreneurial base.

Krishna Tanuku
Indian School of Business

To encourage the spread of industrialisation and entrepreneurship in the country, it is essential that the small-scale industries are provided with growth-oriented environment and adequate infrastructure facilities. To ensure this objective, a number of policy initiatives have been taken by the Government and the financial system at large in the last five decades. The framework of policy support for small-scale sector evolved in 1950s has been in existence with required modifications/changes from time to time till initiation of the economic reforms. In 1990-91, the country embarked upon a stabilisation programme whereby various structural reforms were taken up to increase efficiency and achieve a sound economic base. The reform initiatives included abolition of industrial licensing except in the case of some industries of strategic importance, liberal import licensing, easing of restrictions under Monopolies and Restrictive Trade Practices (MRTP) Act, permission for Foreign Direct Investment (FDI), etc. These developments marked a significant shift in the role of Government from a regulator to that of a developer and facilitator.

To analyse the impact of policy initiatives taken by the Government and flow of funds to the sector, including complexities of the system and procedures relating thereto, the Government of India/ RBI have constituted various committees in the decade of nineties. Prominent among these are Nayak Committee (1991), Abid Hussain Committee (1999), S.L. Kapur Committee (1998), and Khan Committee (1998). These committees have given a number of recommendations covering various aspects relating to the SSI sector. A number of recommendations of these committees have been translated into policy prescription by the RBI and the Government of India for players in the financial system and support service institutions engaged in the development of SSI sector.

Micro, Small and Medium Enterprises Development Act, 2006

There was a longstanding demand from entrepreneurs, small industry associations and related stakeholders for a single comprehensive legislation. The "Micro, Small and Medium Enterprises Development (MSMED) Act, 2006" is the first Act for micro, small and medium enterprises which, inter alia, provides for establishment of a statutory National Board for Micro, Small and Medium Enterprises, filing of memoranda, measures for promotion, development and enhancement of competitiveness of micro, small and medium enterprises, credit facilities, procurement preference and provisions related to delayed payments to micro and small enterprises. The medium sector has been defined for the first time in India and Micro enterprises have been defined for the first time in this Act.

The MSMED Act, 2006 classifies enterprises broadly into (*i*) manufacturing enterprises; and (*ii*) service enterprises. These broad categories are further classified into micro enterprises, small enterprises and medium enterprises, depending upon the level of investment in plant and machinery and equipment as the case may be.

(i) Manufacturing Enterprises

(*a*) Micro (manufacturing) Enterprises: Enterprises engaged in the manufacture/production, processing or preservation of goods and whose investment in plant and machinery[1] does not exceed Rs. 25 lakh.

1. Investment in plant and machinery refers to original cost, excluding land and building and the items specified by the Ministry of Small Scale Industries vide its notification No. S.O. 1722(E) dated October 5, 2006.

(*b*) Small (manufacturing) Enterprises: Enterprises engaged in the manufacture/production, processing or preservation of goods and whose investment in plant and machinery is more than Rs. 25 lakh but does not exceed Rs. 5 crore.

(*c*) Medium (manufacturing) Enterprises: Enterprises engaged in the manufacture/production, processing or preservation of goods and whose investment in plant and machinery is more than Rs. 5 crore but does not exceed Rs. 10 crore.

(ii) Service Enterprises

(*a*) Micro (service) Enterprises: Enterprises engaged in providing/rendering of services and whose investment in equipment[2] does not exceed Rs. 10 lakh.

(*b*) Small (service) Enterprises: Enterprises engaged in providing/rendering of services and whose investment in equipment is more than Rs. 10 lakh but does not exceed Rs. 2 crore.

(*c*) Medium (Service Enterprises): Enterprises engaged in providing/rendering of services and whose investment in equipment is more than Rs. 2 crore but does not exceed Rs. 5 crore.

(iii) The small and micro (service) enterprises include small road and water transport operators, small business, professional and self-employed persons, and all other service enterprises. Although medium enterprises are included in the SME sector, credit to medium enterprises is not included under the priority sector.

Role of MSEs

Micro and Small Enterprises constitute an important segment of the industrial and services sectors of India due to their growth potential, employment generation capacity, export generation and their role as seedbed to new entrepreneurship. The contribution of MSEs in the Indian economic development has been immense. The sector currently accounts for about 39 per cent of the manufacturing output and around 33 per cent of the total exports of the country. There are approximately 1.3 crore MSEs which employ nearly 3 crore people. The sector contributes close to 7 per cent of our GDP. Thus, special thrust by the Government to the sector has been consistent with the objectives of employment generation, regional dispersal of industries and fostering of entrepreneurship.

SME — An Overview

Small and medium enterprises (SMEs) have been globally recognised as vital components of a domestic economy and major contributors to employment generation in a country, regardless of geographical barriers. According to a World Bank report, in low-income countries, with Gross National Product (GNP) per capita between \$100 and \$500, SMEs account for over 60 per cent of the GDP.

India has nearly 13.33 million SMEs, which account for almost 50 per cent industrial output and 40 per cent of the country's total exports. However, the biggest problem plaguing small-scale industries is inadequate demand, along with technological, financial and marketing weaknesses, all of which lead to a shortage of working capital. In fact, lack of adequate and timely finance is the root cause of sickness in the small scale sector.

2. Investment in equipment refers to original cost, excluding land and building and furniture, fittings and other items not directly related to the service rendered or as may be notified under the MSMED Act, 2006.

SMEs are contributing heavily to industrial output

Box 1

START YOUR OWN

Entrepreneurship is a creative process. When done successfully, it can give you the highest sense of accomplishment possible

David Thomas will turn 40 on Friday. He is smart, competent and devoted to his organisation. A graduate from one of the Indian Institutes of Technology, he went on to get an MBA from one of the best management schools before starting his career with a leading Indian company. Somewhere during his career, he felt that he should be working for a multinational company, partly because of the lure of higher compensation, but also he was succumbing to the pervasive Indian mindset that working for an MNC is the more prestigious thing to do. Sometimes an aunt or an uncle does not quite know the name of the company you work for, nor can they explain what you do. Yet, just the smug words 'works in an MNC' conveys that you are doing alright. That was then.

Today, as he looks at the next 20 years of his life, David feels deeply troubled. He feels that he has levelled out. The work that he performed so well just a few years ago is no longer as consequential to the organisation. There is something in the air that tells him that his career is festooned with autumn colours. Too many organisational changes confuse him. How can he create a long-term career plan for himself? How will he get that plan nested in the larger landscape of the huge organisation? Something in him tells him to be bitter with the system for his present situation. At the same time, he knows that bitterness is not going to solve anything. He is at crossroads. A simple change of jobs will not magically take him back to the time when he was 23 and his next 20 years looked inviting. What can David Thomas do today?

He has an option. Unfortunately, no one is telling him about it. That option is to start his own, to become an entrepreneur. Here is why:

Entrepreneurs create jobs. Jobs provide people with livelihoods. Without a livelihood, everyone feels lost. Given a good livelihood, we all feel secure and able to raise families; we have the comfort of exploring higher callings; we are able to provide emotional security to people around us.

(Contd.)

(Contd.)

There is an estimated 6.5 billion people on earth. Out of these, a third live right here in India and China. In the Indian sub-continent alone, there are 450 million children below the age of 15 who will need to join the workforce very soon. It is neither for the government, nor for large businesses to create avenues for employment and growth for these people. It can only be done by entrepreneurs.

Entrepreneurs drive innovation. Seldom does innovation come from very large, very established players. The reason is simple. Innovation disrupts the established way of doing things. Large, profitable organisations frown at disruptions of any kind. For innovative people like David Thomas, it is sometimes easier to start something ground-up than trying to change the existing behemoth.

Entrepreneurs create great wealth not just for themselves, but for others as well. They also use the power of wealth, sometimes, to build sustained legacy for society at large. Behind the educational system of the US is a huge amount of personal wealth donated by entrepreneurs. Without their support, some of the greatest initiatives to protect heritage, arts and literature and the environment would be difficult.

Entrepreneurship can be deeply rewarding. The richness of experience and sheer self-confidence you get by starting a small shop is sometimes larger than running a huge department for an established entity. This is because entrepreneurship is the most hands-on thing you will ever do. Nothing about entrepreneurship is a spectator sport. Many things in a well-paid job in a large organisation could well be. Entrepreneurship is a creative process. When done successfully, it can give you the highest sense of accomplishment possible. That sense of accomplishment is next only to delivering and raising your baby.

Finally, the world has become an entrepreneur-friendly place like never before. No government in the world says, "We do not like entrepreneurs." Funding for new ventures is becoming increasingly cross-border. Also, today, more resources are chasing fewer ideas, rather than the other way round.

Well then, David Thomas, probably the time has come to shed your sense of being at crossroads. Consider breaking free to start on your own. It could well bring back the sheer feeling of exhilaration when your first appointment letter was delivered in your youthful hands, a good 17 years back!

(Subroto Bagchi is cofounder & CEO of MindTree Consulting)

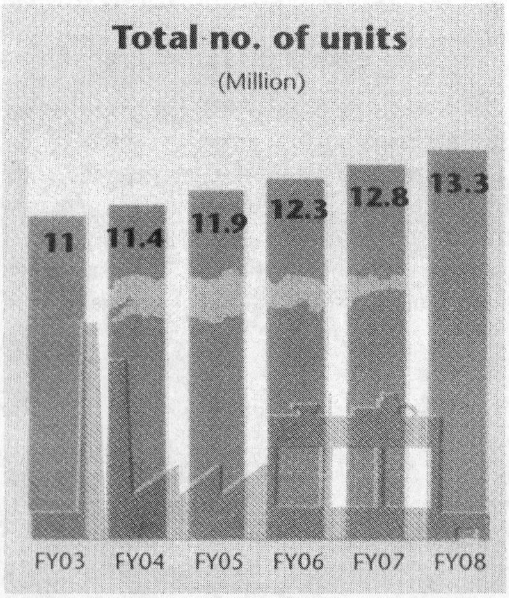

Source: Ministry of MSME

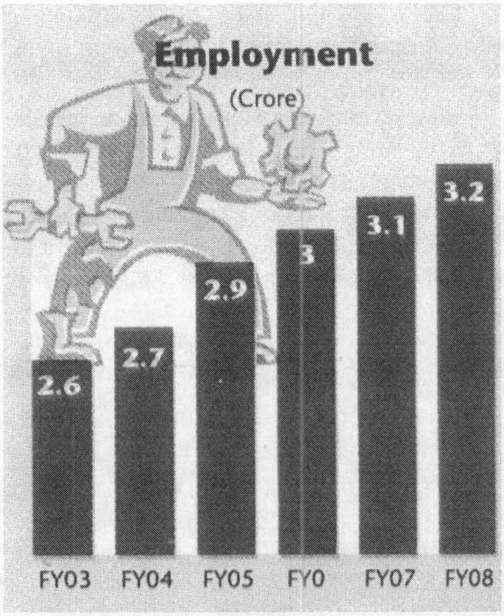

Source: Ministry of MSME

Source: Ministry of MSME

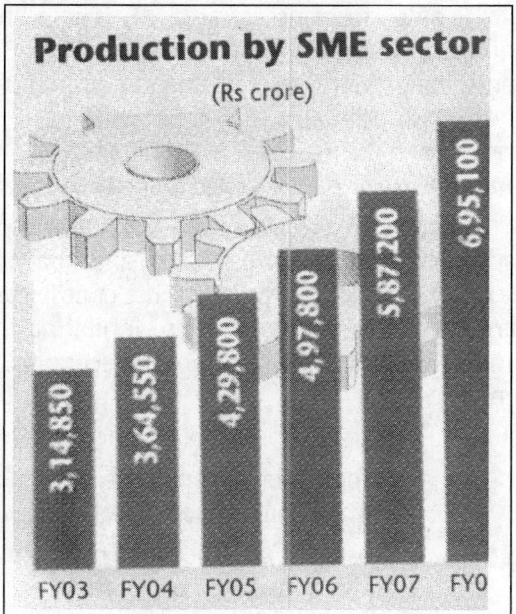

Source: Ministry of MSME

The SME segment plays a major role in developing countries, such as India, to alleviate poverty and propel sustainable growth. Moreover, SMEs lead to an equitable distribution of income due to the nature of business.

"SMEs form the lifeblood of any vibrant economy. In an emerging economy like India, SMEs have a significant socio-economic role as they are estimated to employ more than 42 million people in the country,

"SMEs, particularly in developing countries, are the backbone of the nation's economy. They constitute the bulk of the industrial base and also contribute significantly to their exports and their GDP," states Anil Bhardwaj, secretary general, Federation of Indian Small and Medium Enterprises.

In fact, the SME sector plays a dual role since the output produced by SMEs is not only about final consumption, but also a source of capital goods in the form of inputs to heavy industries. "The significance of SMEs in the Indian economy is growing. The output of SMEs is not only increas-ing, but the productivity in terms of per unit is also growing at a higher rate in the past four years. The relative advantage of SMEs is well-recognised by the resurgence of the manufacturing sector in India during recent months," says Dhananjay Sinha, economist, Centrum Broking.

The SME sector is often credited for granting national economies flexibility, diversity and the strength to weather economic downturns. The highly heterogeneous Indian SME sector, producing 8,000-odd items, contributes 45 per cent of the industrial output, in sharp contrast to other BRIC (Brazil, Russia, India and China) countries, which have a less diversified SME sector, with over 65 per cent of their production catering to export markets. Moreover, factors like low export orientation, high import substitution and diversification of Indian SMEs have contributed to restraining their downward spiral during the current global meltdown.

"The performance of an SME is interlinked to the performance of the economy," says Varun Tuli, group president, business banking, Yes Bank. "As we have seen with large corporates, there has been some pressure on the demand and liquidity fronts. However, SMEs, by virtue of being promoter-driven, have been able to weather this storm due to strong backing by the promoters, scale-down of operations, reducing costs, etc. Though SMEs have been impacted in line with the current economic conditions, they have adapted well to the situation."

Though small-scale sector has shown substantial progress, a number of major problems like inadequate credit flow from banks and financial institutions (FIs), inadequate infrastructure facilities, low quality standards of products, use of obsolete technology, plant, machinery and equipment, inefficient management techniques, etc., are inhibiting the sector. Besides, this sector has to face challenges of competition from opening up of the economy, globalisation, need from increasing exports, and WTO commitments.

The major environmental changes are:

(*i*) opening up of the Indian economy with competition from abroad and the initial impacts related to commitments to WTO;

(*ii*) increasing reliance at home on the market economy with freer competition in prices and for qualities and lowering of several existing support systems like subsidies and other forms of protection; and

(*iii*) the need for an accelerated growth in India, much higher compared to the cost to reduce poverty and unemployment.

It has been found that against these environmental changing circumstances, the SSI sector in India is suffering from certain handicaps to meet the new competitive environment.

There is an immediate need for a suitable policy package to enable SSI sector to enjoy a level playing field in order to be competitive with their trading partners by upgrading their technology, quality of products and improving their marketing organizations in order to maintain the tempo of their past record in growth and generation of employment. In this context, with "capital shortage and abundant labour and skill" and scarce resource base, the comparative advantage enjoyed by SSI for growth, needs no special focus.

The policy support provided so far has acted as a catalyst in promoting this sector. However, the Planning Commission felt an urgent need to review the policy measures so as to make this sector more growth oriented and enable it to withstand the pressures of global competition.

The planning commission constituted a Study Group under the chairmanship of Dr. S. P. Gupta, Member, Planning Commission, to look into the problems of the small-scale enterprises and to suggest policy modifications as well as new policy initiatives in 1999.

The report of the Study Group contains a number of valuable recommendations, taking into account both future challenges to be faced by the SSI Sector and India's present development strategy.

The recommendations of the Study Group would be useful to all agencies in implementing new policy measures for development and growth of small-scale enterprises and in enhancing their contribution to the economy in terms of employment, production, value addition and exports.

Some of the important recommendations of the Study Group are:

(*a*) A three-tier definition of SSEs covering tiny, small and medium sector. Medium sector definition has been brought in for the first time to help SSI units to graduate to medium and then to large scale. Medium scale units (Rs. 1 crore to Rs. 10 crore) would not be provided fiscal and other policy support as available to SSI units. However, these units would be helped by providing credit for technology upgradation and modernisation from a separate fund.

(*b*) Need of bringing awareness in small industries sector about WTO implications and its impact on SSI sector, particularly due to bringing more items under OGL as per WTO obligation. Setting up of a new cell in the office of DC (SSI) for matters relating to WTO and its implications in SSI sector.

(*c*) Need for a single comprehensive law for SSI sector, like Small Business Administration (BBA) Act of United States.

(*d*) This Study Group has recommended that presently reservation should be continued for SSE sector. However, to enhance exports, the Study Group has recommended that non-SSI units can take up production of reserved items with 30 per cent export obligation to be completed over three years.

(*e*) The Study Group has recommended to raise investment ceiling from Rs. 1 crore to Rs. 5 crore for plant and machinery for export-oriented industries like leather products, garments, hosiery, hand tools, toys, packaging materials, auto components, pharmaceuticals, food processing, etc.

(*f*) For infrastructure development, the Study Group has recommended a corpus of Rs. 2,000 crore so that adequate infrastructure facilities are available to the SSI sector.

(*g*) To encourage technocrat entrepreneurs in high-tech industries like electronics, information technology, bio-technology, pharmaceuticals, an Incubation Infrastructure Development Fund with a corpus Rs. 1,000 crore has been recommended by the Study Group for setting up of Incubation Centres (ICs) in the Tenth Plan. These ICs would provide all facilities and Finance, technical consultancy, etc. to encourage technocrats and first generation entrepreneurs to successfully take up production based on recent technologies having potential, but not tried so far. Such incubation centres have given good results in developed countries as well as South East Asian Countries.

(*h*) With a view to encourage large units to make prompt payment to SSI units against deliveries made by SSI units, the Study Group has recommended:

- Lead role of associations as done by CII by issuing a code of ethics on prompt payment to its members.
- Denial of MODVAT credit to defaulters in respect of payment to SSI units for more than 120 days' delay.
- Amendment of Income Tax Act to disallow unpaid SSI bills from business expenditure.
- Strengthening of factoring services, and
- Monitoring of implementation of Interest on Delayed Payments to Small Scale and Ancillary Industrial Undertakings Act, 1993, by DC (SSI).

(*i*) To encourage better linkages between large and medium units, the Study Group has recommended:

- FDI to be encouraged in SSIs for better technology transfer (within the permitted ceiling of equity participation by large-scale units in the equity of SSI units).
- Allowing excise exemption on SSI manufactured goods for large units under brand name in urban areas as is presently allowed for rural areas.

(*j*) The Study Group has recommended enactment of Limited Partnership Act to bring in more risk capital in SSI sector and the concept of limited liability. SAMADHAN scheme for one time settlement of dues of sick SSI units so that assets could be reutilised. Sick units to make one time payment including interest not more than double of the credit/loan amount. This would provide an exit route to entrepreneurs of sick units.

(*k*) To free the SSI sector from rigid and harassing regulatory laws applicable to the SSI sector and to reduce inspectors' visits, the Study Group has recommended a number of measures, like (*i*) need for a single unified Act for small enterprises, (*ii*) replacement of inspection by self-certification, (*iii*) simplification of regulatory laws, etc.

(*l*) To enhance the data base for the SSI sector, the Study Group has recommended (*i*) conduction of fresh census for SSI sector, (*ii*) collection of detailed data on clusters, (*iii*) sample surveys by the office of DC (SSI) to be conducted annually, and (*iv*) involvement of SSI associations in the census and other data collection activities.

(*m*) The Study Group has made a number of recommendations for human resource development of SSI sector which includes inputs like training, skill upgradation, new management practices, etc.

(*n*) The Study Group has also made a number of recommendations on fiscal and financial measures covering:

- Setting up of targets for tiny and SSI units for credit from banks and FIs under priority sector lending.
- Need for reduction of cost of credit for SSI sector.
- Setting up of more specialised bank branches for SSI sector.
- Measures for strengthening resource support to SIDBI and to make available cheaper resources for on-lending at low interest rates to SSI sector.
- Venture capital for SSIs.
- Setting up of a special venture capital type fund of Rs. 500 crore to be named by Laghu Udyog Nirman Nidhi for equity support.
- Standardisation of procedure and simplification of forms by banks.
- Statutory backing to State Level Inter-Institutional Committees (SLIICs).
- Raising of present excise exemption limit from Rs. 50 lakh to Rs. 100 lakh.
- Fiver per cent notional MODVAT credit to large units buying components etc. from SSI units.
- Exception from excise registration and visits of excise inspectors until the turnover reaches a limit of Rs. 50 lakh with a system of self-declaration.
- Extension of Credit Guarantee Fund Scheme with a corpus of Rs. 2,500 crore.
- Allowing additional 10 percentage point abatement over and above the existing rate of abatement under Maximum Retail Price (MRP) based assessment to levy excise duty on SSI products. Presently large and small units are allowed 30 to 50 percentage point abatement on MRP for levying excise duty.
- More effective monitoring of credit flow to SSI sector by the Monitoring Committee of Reserve Bank of India.

- To make available credit to SSI sector at a reasonable cost, *viz.*, PLR plus three per cent.
- Raising the limit of composite loans from Rs. 10 lakh to Rs. 25 lakh to encourage tiny units to get term loan and working capital from same bank/FI.
- Not to cover all future fixed assets of assisted units for securing its advances.
- Need for restructuring of SFCs.
- Measures to enhance resource support to SIDBI.
- Measures for time-bound disposal of loan applications and easy documentation.

(*o*) The Study Group has recommended following measures for technology upgradation and modernisation of SSI units:

- Setting up of a technology Bank for collection and dissemination of information about technology sources.
- A Technology Upgradation and Modernisation Fund of Rs. 5,000 crore with an interest subsidy of five per cent.
- Accelerated depreciation on plant and machinery installed for technology upgradation and modernisation.
- Five per cent customs duty on capital goods with import obligation and five per cent interest subsidy as recommended for technology modernisation.

(*p*) To provide increased marketing support to the SSI sector, the Study Group has recommended that:

- Statutory backing and continuation of the Price Preference (up to 15 per cent to SSI products) under Government Purchase Programme and Purchase Preference Scheme in respect of 358 items on purchases made by government departments.
- Up to 33 per cent of government purchases may be done from SSI sector on the lines of USA.
- Industry status to all types of consortium industries so that they can avail finance from banks and FIs.
- Subsidisation of participation of SSI units up to 50 per cent in air fare for export related buyer-seller meets.
- Timely release of institutional finance for export orders of SSI units.

The recommendations made by the Study Group are far-ranging and important. But it is more important that these are accepted and implemented in letter and spirit, so as to provide maximum possible benefits to the SSI sector. It is also important to get a reciprocal response from the SSI sector.

⏩ Benefits to Micro & Small Enterprises due to MSMED Act

1. Extends the scope of benefits from SSI undertaking and Ancillary Units to Micro, Small & Medium Enterprises (MSMEs).
2. Preference policies in respect of procurement of goods and services produced and provided by Micro and Small enterprises (MSEs).
3. Strengthens the legal provisions to check delayed payments to micro & small enterprises.
4. Time-bound resolution of disputes with buyers through conciliation and arbitration.
5. Timely credit and progressive credit policies and practices.

Government Initiatives

1. Credit Linked Capital Subsidy Scheme for improvement of technology to Micro & Small Enterprises.
2. Incentive Scheme of Reimbursement of expenses for acquiring Quality Management System (QMS), ISO 9000 certification/Environment Management System (EMS) ISO 14001.
3. National Manufacturing Competitiveness Program (NMCP) Schemes to improve competitiveness, build abilities to acquire, develop or assimilate new technology, reduce cost of production, cut down delivery time, practice total quality management (TQM), enhance productivity and improve customer service.
4. Scheme of Fund for Regeneration of Traditional Industries for development of clusters in Khadi, Village & Coir Sector.
5. Product Development, Design Intervention and Packaging (PRODIP) scheme for improving the quality of khadi products and also to diversify into new products.
6. Market Development Assistance Scheme to support representatives of small/micro manufacturing enterprises to participate under MSME India stall at International Trade Fairs/Exhibitions etc.
7. Prime Minister's Employment Generation Programme.
8. Rajiv Gandhi Udyami Mitra Yojna for Entrepreneurship Development.
9. MSME development Institutes & Tool Rooms for Skill Development.

Bank's Initiatives

1. Simplified procedure for extending assistance to MSMEs.
2. Specialised SME branches with dedicated team for fast processing of applications.
3. Priority Credit to Micro Enterprises.
4. Competitive rate of interest.
5. No collateral security for loans upto Rs. 5 Lacs to MSE sector Units.

- To make available credit to SSI sector at a reasonable cost, *viz.*, PLR plus three per cent.
- Raising the limit of composite loans from Rs. 10 lakh to Rs. 25 lakh to encourage tiny units to get term loan and working capital from same bank/FI.
- Not to cover all future fixed assets of assisted units for securing its advances.
- Need for restructuring of SFCs.
- Measures to enhance resource support to SIDBI.
- Measures for time-bound disposal of loan applications and easy documentation.

(*o*) The Study Group has recommended following measures for technology upgradation and modernisation of SSI units:

- Setting up of a technology Bank for collection and dissemination of information about technology sources.
- A Technology Upgradation and Modernisation Fund of Rs. 5,000 crore with an interest subsidy of five per cent.
- Accelerated depreciation on plant and machinery installed for technology upgradation and modernisation.
- Five per cent customs duty on capital goods with import obligation and five per cent interest subsidy as recommended for technology modernisation.

(*p*) To provide increased marketing support to the SSI sector, the Study Group has recommended that:

- Statutory backing and continuation of the Price Preference (up to 15 per cent to SSI products) under Government Purchase Programme and Purchase Preference Scheme in respect of 358 items on purchases made by government departments.
- Up to 33 per cent of government purchases may be done from SSI sector on the lines of USA.
- Industry status to all types of consortium industries so that they can avail finance from banks and FIs.
- Subsidisation of participation of SSI units up to 50 per cent in air fare for export related buyer-seller meets.
- Timely release of institutional finance for export orders of SSI units.

The recommendations made by the Study Group are far-ranging and important. But it is more important that these are accepted and implemented in letter and spirit, so as to provide maximum possible benefits to the SSI sector. It is also important to get a reciprocal response from the SSI sector.

⏩ Benefits to Micro & Small Enterprises due to MSMED Act

1. Extends the scope of benefits from SSI undertaking and Ancillary Units to Micro, Small & Medium Enterprises (MSMEs).
2. Preference policies in respect of procurement of goods and services produced and provided by Micro and Small enterprises (MSEs).
3. Strengthens the legal provisions to check delayed payments to micro & small enterprises.
4. Time-bound resolution of disputes with buyers through conciliation and arbitration.
5. Timely credit and progressive credit policies and practices.

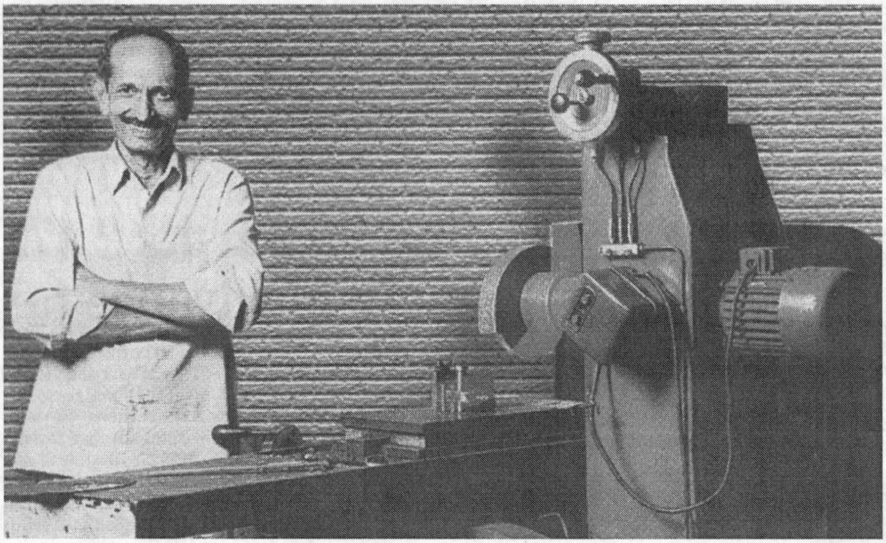

Government Initiatives

1. Credit Linked Capital Subsidy Scheme for improvement of technology to Micro & Small Enterprises.
2. Incentive Scheme of Reimbursement of expenses for acquiring Quality Management System (QMS), ISO 9000 certification/Environment Management System (EMS) ISO 14001.
3. National Manufacturing Competitiveness Program (NMCP) Schemes to improve competitiveness, build abilities to acquire, develop or assimilate new technology, reduce cost of production, cut down delivery time, practice total quality management (TQM), enhance productivity and improve customer service.
4. Scheme of Fund for Regeneration of Traditional Industries for development of clusters in Khadi, Village & Coir Sector.
5. Product Development, Design Intervention and Packaging (PRODIP) scheme for improving the quality of khadi products and also to diversify into new products.
6. Market Development Assistance Scheme to support representatives of small/micro manufacturing enterprises to participate under MSME India stall at International Trade Fairs/Exhibitions etc.
7. Prime Minister's Employment Generation Programme.
8. Rajiv Gandhi Udyami Mitra Yojna for Entrepreneurship Development.
9. MSME development Institutes & Tool Rooms for Skill Development.

Bank's Initiatives

1. Simplified procedure for extending assistance to MSMEs.
2. Specialised SME branches with dedicated team for fast processing of applications.
3. Priority Credit to Micro Enterprises.
4. Competitive rate of interest.
5. No collateral security for loans upto Rs. 5 Lacs to MSE sector Units.

6. Policies for Rehabilitation/Restructuring.
7. Sanction of credit facilities upto Rs. 100 Lacs without any collateral or third party guarantee under Credit Guarantee Scheme for Micro & Small Enterprises.

Entrepreneurs can also avail up to 75% financial assistance for using global standard in Bar Coding that the government now provides to enhance the global competitiveness of Micro & Small Enterprises (MSEs).

Micro, Small & Medium Enterprise-Development Institutes (MSME-DIs)

The Scheme has been in operation since the 6th Five Year Plan. Since 1983-84, 12 new Branch Institutes, mostly in the backward and hilly areas of the country have been sanctioned, making a total of 15 such Institutes under the Scheme.

The main activities of MSME-DIs and their Branches are as follows:

- Assistance/Consultancy to prospective and existing entrepreneurs
- Preparation of State Industrial Profiles and District Industrial Potential Surveys
- Preparation/updation of Project Profiles
- Entrepreneurship Development Programmes
- Motivational Campaigns
- Production Index
- Management Development Programmes
- Energy Conservation
- Pollution Control
- Ancillary Development
- Common Facility Workshop/Lab.
- Preparation of Directory of Specific Industries
- Linkages with State Government Functionaries
- Market Surveys
- Other Action Plan Activities Assigned by the Headquarters.

Package for Promotion of Micro and Small Enterprises (MSEs): The micro and small enterprises (MSEs) have a vital role in the socio-economic development. The resilience of the MSE Sector to adjust to the fast changing economic scenario is reflected in the fact that its growth rate has always been higher. Accordingly, in order to assist the MSEs in fully harnessing their potential by enhancing their competitiveness to face the challenges of stiff competition (both in the domestic and global markets) and in availing opportunities generated by trade liberalization, the Government in its NCMP declared that a "major promotional package" will be announced for this segment to provide full support in the areas of credit, technological upgradation, marketing and infrastructure upgradation in industrial infrastructure. Infulfillment of the assurance in the NCMP, the *'Package for Promotion of Micro and Small Enterprises.'* This promotional package, *inter-alia,* includes measures to address concerns in the areas of credit, fiscal support, cluster-based development, infrastructure, technology and marketing and so on. Capacity building of MSME Associations and support to women entrepreneurs are the other important features of this Package.

Table 1

SMALL AND MEDIUM ENTERPRISES

Year	Total SSI Units (numbers in lakh)	Fixed Investment (Rs. crore)	Production (Rs. crore) Current Prices	Production (Rs. crore) Constant Prices (1993-94)	Employment (lakh persons)	Exports (Rs. crore)
1990-91	67-87	93555	63518	68295	158.34	9664
1991-92	70.63 (4.07)	100351 (7.26)	73072 (15.04)	79180 (15.94)	165.99 (4.83)	13883 (43.66)
1992-93	73.51 (4.07)	109623 (9.24)	85581 (17.12)	93523 (18.11)	174.84 (5.33)	17784 (28.10)
1993-94	76.49 (4.07)	115795 (5.63)	98804 (15.45)	98804 (5.65)	182.64 (4.46)	25307 (42.30)
1994-95	79.60 (4.07)	123790 (6.9)	122210 (23.69)	109116 (10.44)	191.40 (4.79)	29068 (14.86)
1995-96	82.84 (4.07)	125750 (1.58)	148290 (21.34)	121649 (11.49)	197.93 (3.42)	36470 (25.46)
1996-97	86.21 (4.07)	130560 (3.82)	168413 (13.57)	135380 (11.29)	205.86 (4.00)	39248 (7.62)
1997-98	89.71 (4.07)	133242 (2.05)	189178 (12.33)	147824 (9.19)	213.16 (3.55)	44442 (13.23)
1998-99	93.36 (4.07)	135482 (1.68)	212901 (12.54)	159407 (7.84)	220.55 (3.46)	48979 (10.21)
1999-2000	97.15 (4.07)	139982 (3.32)	234255 (10.03)	170709 (7.09)	229.10 (3.88)	54200 (10.66)
2000-01	101.1 (4.07)	147348 (3.32)	261289 (11.54)	184428 (8.04)	239.09 (4.36)	69797 (10.66)
2001-02	105.21 (4.07)	154349 (4.75)	282270 (8.03)	195613 (6.06)	249.09 (4.18)	71244 (2.07)
2002-03	109.49 (4.07)	162317 (5.30)	314850 (11.84)	306771 (8.68)	260.21 (4.36)	86013 (20.73)
2003-04	113.95 (4.07)	170219 (4.87)	364547 (15.78)	336344 (9.64)	271.42 (4.31)	97644 (13.52)
2004-05	118.59 (4.07)	17869 (4.98)	429796 (17.90)	372938 (10.88)	282.57 (4.1)	124417 (27.42)
2005-06	123.42 (4.07)	188113 (5.27)	497842 (15.83)	418884 (12.32)	294.91 (4.37)	150242 (20.76)
2006-07	128,44 (4.07)	207307 (4.67)	585112 (17.53)	471663 (12.60)	31252 (4.23)	1,77,600 (24.54)
2007-08	133.68 (4.08)	238975 (12.08)	695126 (18.80)	532979 (13.00)	322.28 (3.12)	213500 (20.82)

Note: (1) Figures in brackets show the percentage growth over the previous year.

(2) The production, at constant prices for the year 2003-04, is based on the growth rate achieved in the first three quarters of 2003-04 (*i.e.,* April-December, 2003).

(3) The production at current prices is compiled on the basis of average Wholesale Price Index (April-December, 2003) of manufactured products.

Training and Entrepreneurship Development

Entrepreneurship has been considered the backbone of economic development. It has been well established that the level of economic growth of a region to a large extent, depends on the level of entrepreneurial activities in the region. The myth that entrepreneurs are born, no more holds good, rather it is well recognised now that the entrepreneurs can be created and nurtured through appropriate interventions in the form of entrepreneurship development programmes.

In the era of liberalisation, privatisation and globalisation along with ongoing IT revolution, capable entrepreneurs are making use of the opportunities emerging from the evolving scenario. However, a large segment of the population, particularly in the industrially backward regions/rural areas generally lags behind in taking advantage of these opportunities. Therefore, there is a need to provide skill development and entrepreneurship development training to such people in order to mainstream them in the ongoing process of economic growth.

Entrepreneurship development and training is, thus, one of the key elements for development of micro and small enterprises (MSEs), particularly, the first generation entrepreneurs. To undertake this task on regular basis, the Ministry has set up three national-level Entrepreneurship Development Institutes (EDIs). These are, the National Institute for Micro, Small and Medium Enterprises (NI-MSME), Hyderabad; the Indian Institute of Entrepreneurship (IIE), Guwahati and the National Institute for Entrepreneurship and Small Business Development (NIESBUD), NOIDA. Further, the Ministry has been implementing (in addition to the schemes of MSME-DO) an important scheme, namely, **Scheme for Assistance for Strengthening of Training Infrastructure of Existing and New Entrepreneurship Development Institutes (EDIs)**. The main objectives of the scheme are (*i*) promoting entrepreneurship for creating self-employment through enterprise creation; (*ii*) facilitating creation of training infrastructure; and (*iii*) supporting research on entrepreneurship related issues.

PREMJI'S TEN GOLDEN RULES

1. Dare to dream: People wonder if having unrealistic dreams is foolish.
   My reply: dreams can never be realistic or safe. If they were, they would not be dreams. But one must have strategies to execute dreams and slog to transform them into reality.
2. Define what you stand for as early as possible and do not compromise for any reason. You can't enjoy the fruits of success if you have to argue with your own conscience.
3. Never lose your zest and curiosity for learning. I personally spend at least ten hours a week on reading, or I find myself quickly outdated.
4. Always strive for excellence. In the world of tomorrow, and with globalisation, just being good is not good enough.
5. Build self-confidence. Remember, no one can make you feel inferior without your consent.
6. Learn to work in teams. The challenges ahead are so complex that no individual will be able to face them alone.
7. Take care of yourself. The stress a young person faces today while beginning his career is the same as what the last generation faced at the time of retirement. Along with alternates, physical fitness is important. 1 jog daily.
8. Persevere. It can make miracles happen.
9. Have a broader social vision. While earning is important, we must use for the larger good of our society.

10. Never let success go to your head, for whatever you achieve is with the help of other factors and people outside us. The moment we become arrogant, we become vulnerable to making bad judgements.

    (Extracts from a convocation address by Azim at IIT, Chennai, on July 27, 2001).

Delayed Payment to Micro and Small Enterprises

The existing provisions of the Interest on Delayed Payment Act. 1998 to small scale and ancillary industrial undertakings have been strengthened under the MSMED Act as follows:

(*a*) The buyer to make payment on or before the date agreed upon between him and the supplier in writing or, where there is no agreement in this behalf, before the appointed day. The agreement between seller and buyer shall not exceed 45 days.

(*b*) If the buyer fails to make payment of the amount to the supplier, he shall be liable to pay compound interest with monthly rests to the supplier on the amount from the appointed day or, from the date agreed upon, at three times of the Bank Rate notified by the Reserve Bank.

(*c*) For any goods supplied or services rendered by the supplier, the buyer shall be liable to pay the amount with interest thereon as indicated at (b) above.

(*d*) In the case of dispute with regard to any amount due, a reference shall be made to the Micro and Small Enterprises Facilitation Council, constituted by the respective State Government.

National Board for Micro. Small and Medium Enterprises (MSME)

The Act also provides for constitution of a National Board for Micro, Small and Medium Enterprises under the chairmanship of the Union Minister for MSME, with wide representation of stakeholders, to (*i*) examine the factors affecting the promotion and development of micro, small and medium enterprises; and (*ii*) review the policies and programmes of the Central Government in regard to facilitating the promotion and development and enhancing the competitiveness of such enterprises and the impact thereof on such enterprises, and make recommendations on matter relating thereto.

The Act also provides for the constitution of an Advisory Committee under the chairmanship of Secretary (MSME). Government of India to examine matters referred to it by the National Board and give recommendations thereto, and also provide advice to the Central Government and the State Governments on matters relating to micro, small and medium enterprises.

Memorandum of Micro, Small and Medium Enterprises: The Act has also laid down the procedure for filing of memoranda by persons intending to establish micro or small enterprises or medium enterprise engaged in manufacture or production of goods or engaged in providing or rendering of services.

Conclusion

The enactment of the Micro, Small and Medium Enterprises Development (MSMED) Act, 2006 was a landmark initiative taken by the government of India to enable the SMEs' competitive strength to address the issues and challenges and reap the benefits of the global market. SME policy initiatives at the national and state level are aimed at strengthening the role of SMEs at the base, as well as at the higher level.

The latest policy to redraw the contours of the cluster development programme by developing model clusters across the country is set to integrate efforts across the value chain to achieve optimum results at the industry level. To cater to the need of SMEs to face globalisation, the Small Industry Development Organisation (SIDO) has launched Small Industry Cluster Development Programmes.

The basic problem that SMEs face is their working in isolation and inadequate linkage with marketing channels, support institutions and service providers.

D. K. Nair
Competition is tough

SMEs can significantly increase their competitive advantage through mutual co-operation with emerging business development service providers for cost reduction, capacity building, technological upgradation and common facility creation through cluster approach. Under the same platform, National Resource Centre for Cluster Development was also constituted with the principal charter of helping the SMEs by implementing the cluster development approach.

With globalisation, all forms of production of goods and services are getting increasingly fragmented across countries and enterprises. With large players adopting different models of business that include involvement of their traditional partners, suppliers or distributors at a different level, SMEs are now experiencing a new model of functioning in the value chain. The past few years have seen the role of the SME segment evolve from a traditional manufacturer in the domestic market to that of an international partner.

The restructuring of production at the international level through increased outsourcing is having significant effects on small and medium entrepreneurs in a positive, as well as negative manner. Demand in terms of niche products and services is providing more opportunities for SMEs that are in a better position to take advantage of their flexible nature of operations. At the same time, they have realised their drawback in terms of inadequate availability of managerial and financial resources, lack of working capital, personnel training and inability to innovate at a fast pace.

NEW PACKAGE FOR SSI SECTOR

MAJOR ANNOUNCEMENTS BY THE PRIME MINISTER AT THE NATIONAL CONFERENCE OF SSI UNITS HELD IN NEW DELHI ON 30TH AUGUST 2000 AND OTHER DECISIONS ANNOUNCED BY THE MINISTRY OF SSI, A&RI*

Policy Support

- The investment limit for the micro sector will continue to be Rs. 25 lakh and for the SSI sector it will be more than Rs. 25 lakh but does not exceed Rs. 5 crore.
- The Ministry of SSI, A & RI will bring out a specific list of high-tech and export oriented industries which would require the investment limit to be raised up to Rs. 5 crore to admit suitable technology upgradation and to enable them to maintain their competitive edge.
- The Limited Partnership Act will be drafted quickly and got enacted.

Fiscal Support

- To improve the competitiveness of Small Scale Sector the exemption on excise duty limit raised from Rs. 50 lakh to Rs. 1 crore.

Credit Support

- Composite loans limit raised from Rs. 10 lakh to Rs. 25 lakh.
- The Small Scale Service and Business (Industry Related) Enterprises (SSSBEs) with a maximum investment of Rs. 10 lakh will qualify for priority lending.
- In the National Equity Fund Scheme, the project cost limit will be revised from Rs. 25 lakh to Rs. 50 lakh. The soft loan limit will be retained at 25 per cent of the project cost subject to a maximum of Rs. 10 lakh per project. Assistance under the NEF will be provided at a service change of 5 per cent per annum.
- The eligibility limit for coverage under the Credit Guarantee Scheme has been revised to Rs. 25 lakh from the present limit of Rs. 10 lakh.
- The Department of Economic Affairs will appoint a Task Force to suggest revitalisation/ restructuring of the State Finance Corporations.
- The Nayak Committee's recommendations regarding provision of 20 per cent of the projected turnover as working capital is being recommended to the financial institutions and banks.

Infrastructural Support

- The Integrated Infrastructure Development Centre (IIDC) Scheme will progressively cover all areas in the country with 50 per cent reservation for rural areas.
- Regarding upgrading the industrial estates, which are languishing, SSI Ministry will draw up a detailed scheme for consideration of the Planning Commission.
- A plan scheme for cluster development will be drawn up.
- The funds available under the non-lapsable pool for the North East will be made use of for industrial infrastructure development, setting up of incubation centres, for cluster development and for setting up of IIDCs in the North East including Sikkim.

---

* These announcement and decisions are based on the recommendations of the Group of Ministers, which had examined in depth the recommendations made in the Interim Report of the Study Group.

Technological Support and Quality Improvement

- Capital Subsidy of 12 per cent for investment in modernisation and upgradation technology in selected sectors. An inter-ministerial committee of experts will be set up to define the scope of technology upgradation and sectoral priorities.
- To encourage total quality management, the scheme of granting Rs. 75,000 to each unit forgetting ISO 9000 certification will continue for the next six years, i.e., till the end of the 10th plan.
- Setting up of incubation centres in sunrise industries will be supported.
- The Technology Bank for Small Enterprises (TBSE) set up by SIDBI will be strengthened so that it functions effectively as a Technology Bank. It will be networked with NSIC and SIDO. SIDO's Small Enterprises for Information Resource Centre Network (SENET) Programme and Asia Pacific for Technology Transfer (APCIT) in association with NSIC would be utilised for this.
- SIDO, SIDBI and NSIC will jointly prepare a compendium of available technologies from R & D institutions in India and abroad and circulate among the industry associations for dissemination of the latest technology related information.
- Commercial banks are being requested to develop schemes to encourage investment in technology upgradation and harmonise the same with SIDBI.
- One time capital grant of 50 per cent will be given to small scale associations who wish to develop and operate testing laboratories, provided they are of international standards.

Marketing Support

- SIDO will have a Market Development Assistance (MDA) programme, similar to the one obtaining in the Ministry of Commerce. It will be a Plan Scheme.
- The vendor development programme, buyer-seller meets and exhibitions would be organised more often and in dispersed locations.

Streamlining Inspections/Rules and Regulations

- To minimise harassment to small scale sector a Group will be set up to recommend within three months, means of streamlining inspections. This will include repeal of laws and regulations applicable to the sector that have since become redundant.
- Self-certification will be progressively encouraged in lieu of inspections, which should be prescribed under the following three conditions: (*i*) On receipt of a specific complaint, (*ii*) Selection of unit for sample check (say, 10 per cent of total units), and (*iii*) For audit and safety purposes.

Entrepreneurship Development

- Capacity building in the SSI sector, both for entrepreneurs as well as workers will be given top priority. SSI Ministry and Labour Ministry will jointly work out a strategy.

Facilitating Prompt Payment

- The Reserve Bank of India is being requested to appoint a Task Force to go into the question of how to strengthen and popularise factoring services and how to encourage bills culture, without recourse to the SSI suppliers. The Task Force shall give its report within six months of its constitution.

- RBI is being requested to take up with the banks the question of suballocating overall limits to large borrowers specifically for meeting the payment obligations in respect of purchases from the SSIs, either on cash basis or on bills basis.

Rehabilitation of Sick Units

- RBI is being requested to draw up revised guidelines for rehabilitation of currently sick but potentially viable SSI units. Such guidelines should be detailed, transparent and non-discretionary.

Promoting Rural Industries

- To support the Handloom Sector "Deendayal Hathkargha Protsahan Yojana" has been announced. The scheme has a total financial implications of Rs. 447 crores and will provide comprehensive financial and infrastructural support to the weavers.
- The Government is working out a new comprehensive package to strengthen Khadi and Village Industry that will further upgrade the skills of khadi workers.

Improving Data Base

- A fresh census of small scale industries will be conducted covering, *inter-alia*, the incidence of sickness and its causes.

Policy Package for Tiny Sector

- The investment limit for the tiny sector will continue to be Rs. 25 lakh.
- Under the Prime Minister's Rozgar Yojana, which finances setting up of micro enterprises and generate employment for educated unemployed youths, the family income eligibility limit has been revised from Rs. 24,000 to Rs. 40,000 per annum.

Credit Support

- The Nayak Committee's recommendations regarding provision of 20 per cent of the projected turnover as working capital is being recommended to the financial institutions and banks. In respect of tiny units also twenty per cent of the projected annual turnover of the tiny units would qualify for working capital loan, as indicated for SSI units.
- The National Small Industries Corporation will continue to give composite loans upto Rs. 25 lakh to the tiny sector and continue to change one per cent concessional interest rate.
- SIDBI will continue to give concessional rate of refinance to the tiny sector which is now at 10.5 per cent, as compared to 12 per cent for the SSI sector. This policy will continue.
- In the National Equity Fund (NEF) scheme, the project cost limit will be raised from Rs. 25 lakh to Rs. 50 lakh. The soft loan limit will be retained at 25 per cent of the project cost, subject to a maximum of Rs. 10 lakh per project. Assistance under the NEF will be provided at a service charge of 5 per cent per annum and 30 per cent of the investment will be earmarked for the tiny sector.

Infrastructural Support

- The IID scheme will progressively cover all areas in the country with 50 per cent reservation for rural areas. Under this scheme, 50 per cent of the plots will be earmarked for the tiny sector (as against 40 per cent at present).

- Under the National Programme for Rural Industrialisation (NPRI), cluster development is being taken up by KVIC, SIDO, SIDBI and NABARD. The major beneficiaries of cluster development programme will be tiny sector units. The sponsoring organisation for each cluster will provide for design development capacity building, technology intervention and consortium marketing. A cluster development fund will be created under the plan.

Technological Support

- Capital Subsidy of 12 per cent for investment in technology in select sectors, preference will be given to the tiny sector for loans for technology upgradation.

Marketing Support

- Preference will be given to the tiny sector while organising buyer-seller meets, vendor development programmes and exhibitions.

POLICY PACKAGE FOR STEPPING UP CREDIT TO SMALL AND MEDIUM ENTERPRISES

Major policy measures announced by the Reserve Bank of India are set out below:

- Units with investment in plant and machinery in excess of SSI limit and up to Rs. 10 crore may be treated as medium enterprises (ME). Only SSI financing will be included in the priority sector.
- Banks may fix self-targets for financing the SME sector so as to reflect a higher disbursement over the immediately preceding year, while the sub-targets for financing tiny units and smaller units to the extent of 40 per cent and 20 per cent, respectively, may continue. Banks may arrange to compile data on outstanding credit to the SME sector as on March 31, 2005 as per new definition and also show the break-up separately for tiny, small and medium enterprises.
- Banks may initiate necessary steps to rationalise the cost of loans to the SME sector by adopting a transparent rating system with cost of credit being linked to the credit rating of an enterprise.
- Banks may consider taking advantage of the Credit Appraisal and Rating Tool (CART) as well as a Risk Assessment Model (RAM) developed by SIDBI for risk assessment of proposals for SMEs.
- Banks may consider the ratings developed by National Small Industries Corporation as per availability and wherever appropriate structure their rates of interest depending on the ratings assigned to the borrowing SME units.
- In order to increase the outreach of formal credit to the SME sector, all banks, including Regional Rural Banks may make concerted efforts to provide credit cover on an average to at least 5 new small/medium enterprises at each of their semi-urban/urban branches per year.
- Based on the guidelines earlier issued by the Reserve Bank in July 2005, the Boards of banks may formulate comprehensive and more liberal policies than the existing policies in respect of loans to the SME sector. Till such time the banks formulate such a policy, the current instructions of the Reserve Bank will be applicable to advances granted/to be granted by banks to SME units.

- In view of the benefits accruing on account of cluster-based approach for financing the SME sector, banks may treat it as a thrust area and increasingly adopt the same for SME financing.
- A debt restructuring mechanism for nursing of sick units in the SME sector and a One-Time Settlement (OTS) scheme for SME accounts in the books of the banks as on March 31, 2004 were formulated and advised to all commercial banks and public sector banks respectively, for implementation.
- The existing institutional arrangements for review of credit to the SSI sector such as the Standing Advisory Committee in the Reserve Bank and cells at the commercial bank's head office level as also at important regional centres to review periodically the flow of credit to the SME sector, including tiny sector as a whole.
- Banks may ensure specialised SME branches in identified clusters/centres with preponderance of medium enterprises to inhabit. The SME entrepreneurs to have easy access to the bank credit and to equip bank personnel to develop requisite expertise. The existing specialised SSI branches may also be redesignated as SME branches.
- For wider dissemination and easy accessibility, the policy guidelines formulated by Boards of banks as well as instructions/guidelines issued by the Reserve Bank may be displayed on the respective websites of banks as well as website of SIDBI. The banks may also prominently display all the facilities/schemes offered by them to small entrepreneurs at each of their branches.

ANNEXURE

NUGGETS FOR ENTREPRENEURS

Some good nuggets for the benefit of the starry-eyed entrepreneurs hoping to create successful ventures are given below.

1. Be very clear and precise about the product or service, the target market, the pain point you plan to address, is it a "must-have" or just "nice to have" *et al.*
2. Do ensure that the market for your offering is large and rapidly growing, as this will allow your venture to grow to a significant size quickly. This also minimises risk.
3. Make sure you understand what and who your competition is, how defensible your proposition is and remember that to succeed you must do something "different" or "differently."
4. It is not necessary for a CEO to know everything but, before you seek investment, make sure that the top team collectively has the skills/experience that is required.
5. All businesses are not appropriate for venture capital. One example: Life style businesses – which generate healthy profits but have "flattish" growth trajectories – are not suitable for VCS, who invest in high growth businesses that can go public or get acquired and give them a high return on their investment. Getting a VC into a flat business can only lead to strife between the founders and the VC.
6. Bankers look at your record, VCS at the future, VCS share the risk with the founders, so you should be willing and keen to involve them in your business as they want to add great value. If you cannot treat the VC as a partner, do not raise venture capital.
7. A VC Fund will need to exit its investment in an agreed time frame. You need to be prepared for what this entails, *viz.*, taking the company public, agreeing to have it acquired, etc. Be transparent. VCS invest in hundreds of businesses and are very realistic in their expectations. They neither demand nor expect perfection and understand that things can go wrong. But they are very fixated on a high level of integrity and want the business run fairly and ethically even if they hold a minority stake. So on no account be opaque or hide anything as VCS will discover this anyway and, once a trust is broken, the whole relationship sours.
8. Some of the world's most successful and iconic businesses have been made possible by VC investments so, go ahead take the risk and, if you do not succeed, try again. Remember you have not failed till you decide to give up!